犬夜叉

INUYASHA

ANI-MANGA   Vol. 26

CREATED BY
RUMIKO TAKAHASHI

Inuyasha Ani-Manga
Vol. #26

Created by
Rumiko Takahashi

Translation based on the VIZ Media anime TV series
Translation Assistance/Katy Bridges
Lettering & Editorial Assistance/John Clark
Cover Design & Graphics/Hidemi Sahara
Editor/Ian Robertson

Editor in Chief, Books/Alvin Lu
Editor in Chief, Magazines/Marc Weidenbaum
VP of Publishing Licensing/Rika Inouye
VP of Sales/Gonzalo Ferreyra
Sr. VP of Marketing/Liza Coppola
Publisher/Hyoe Narita

First published by Shogakukan Inc. in Japan as "TV Anime-ban Inuyasha."

Printed in the U.S.A.

Published by VIZ Media, LLC
P.O. Box 77010
San Francisco, CA 94107

10 9 8 7 6 5 4 3 2 1
First printing, April 2008

www.viz.com
store.viz.com

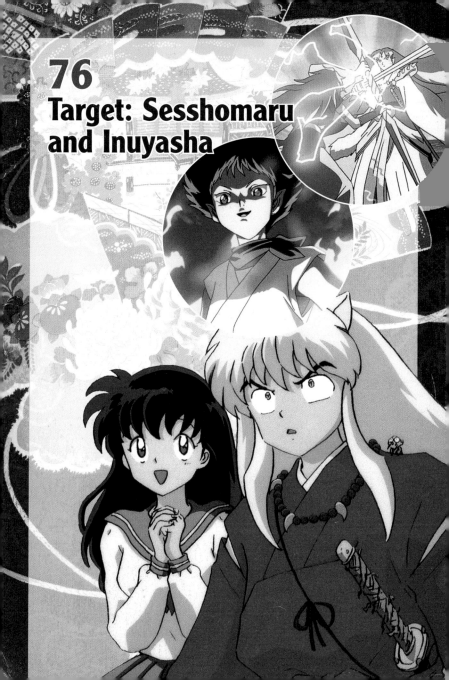

76
Target: Sesshomaru and Inuyasha

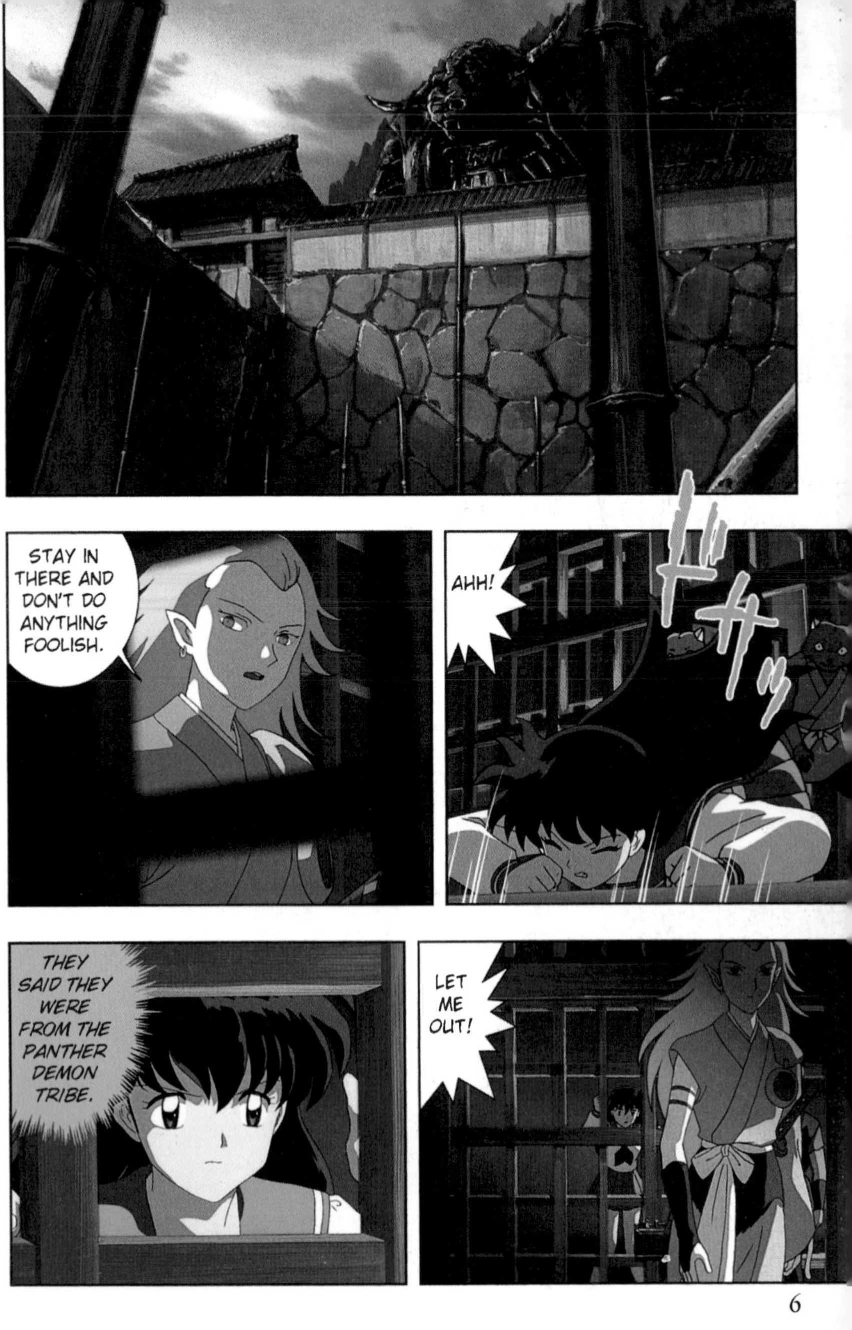
ドサッ
AHH!
STAY IN THERE AND DON'T DO ANYTHING FOOLISH.
LET ME OUT!
THEY SAID THEY WERE FROM THE PANTHER DEMON TRIBE.

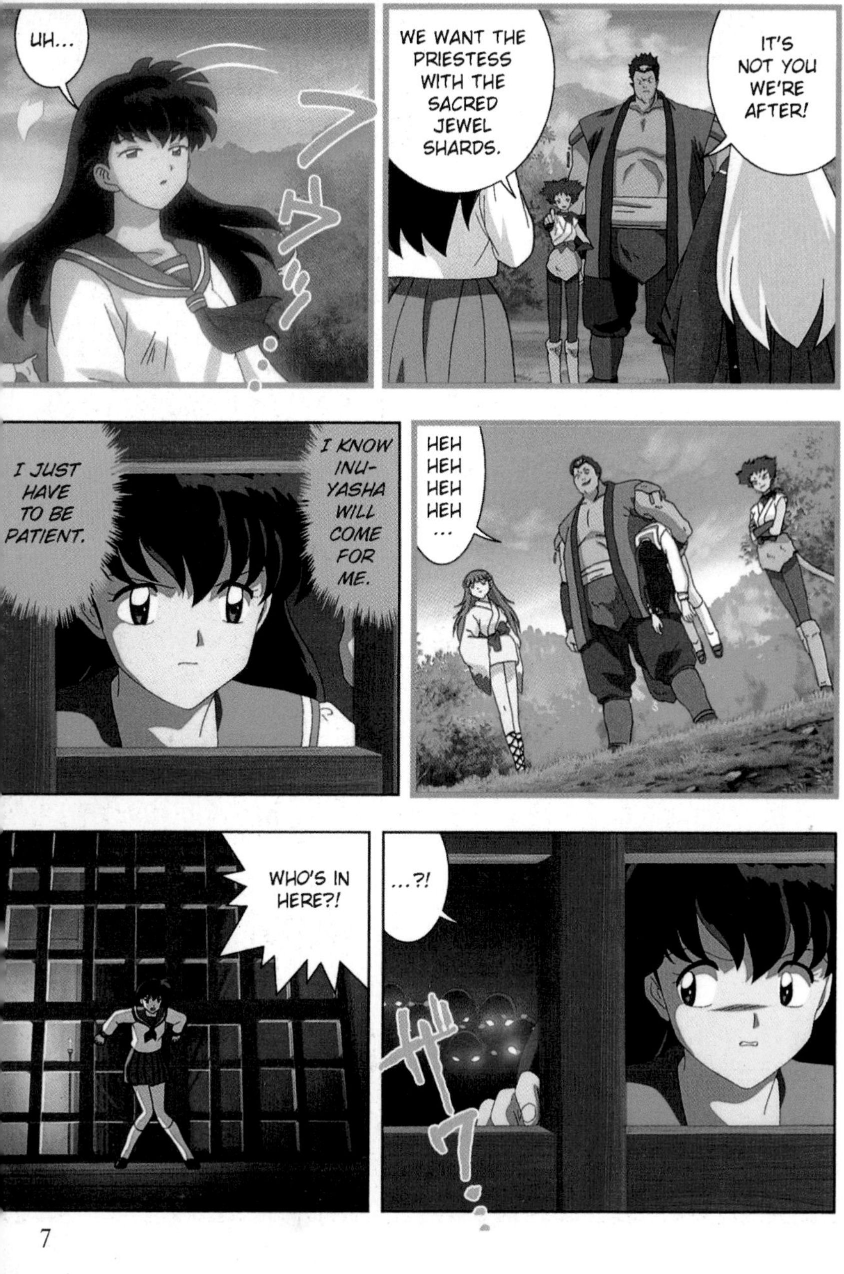
IT'S NOT YOU WE'RE AFTER!
WE WANT THE PRIESTESS WITH THE SACRED JEWEL SHARDS.
UH...
HEH HEH HEH HEH ...
I KNOW INU-YASHA WILL COME FOR ME.
I JUST HAVE TO BE PATIENT.
...?!
WHO'S IN HERE?!

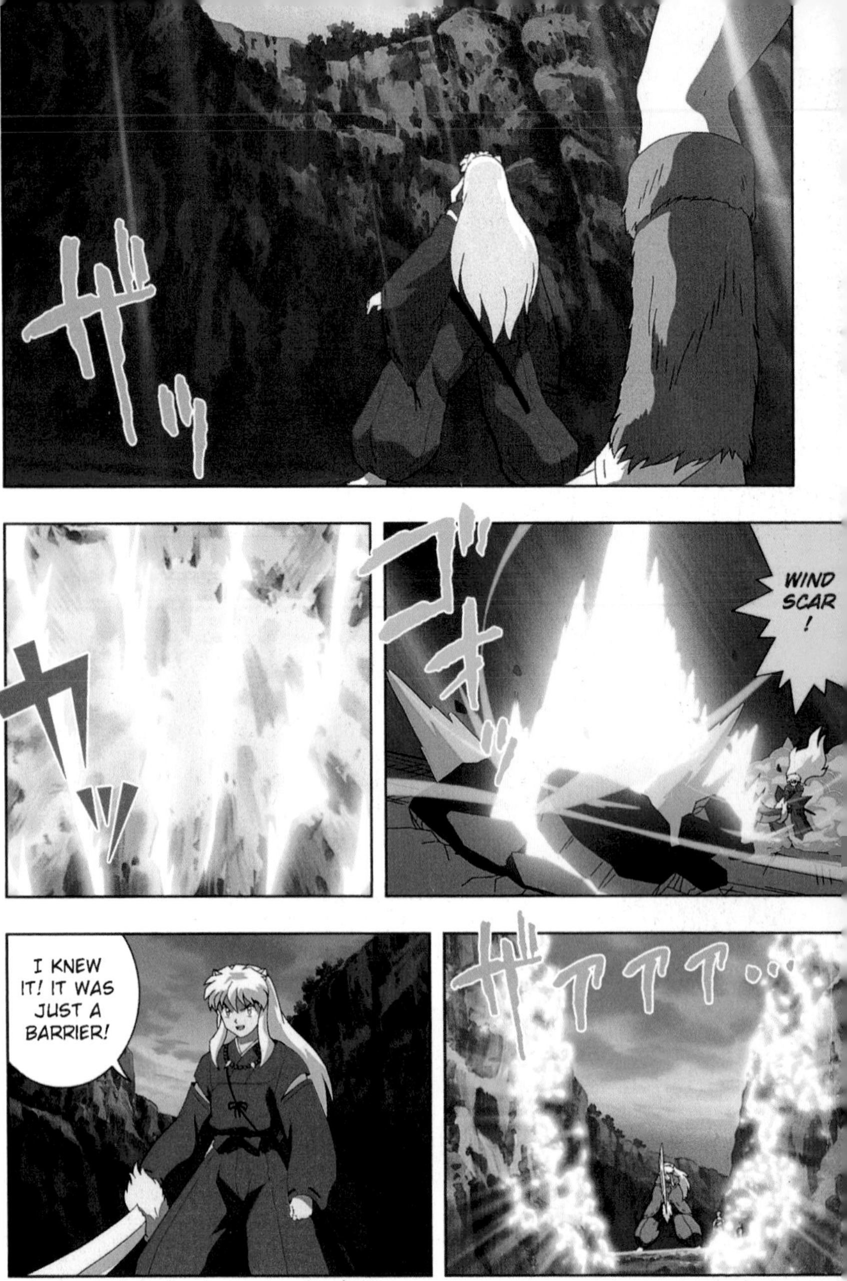
ザッ
ゴォッ
WIND SCAR!
ヤッ
ザァァァ…
I KNEW IT! IT WAS JUST A BARRIER!

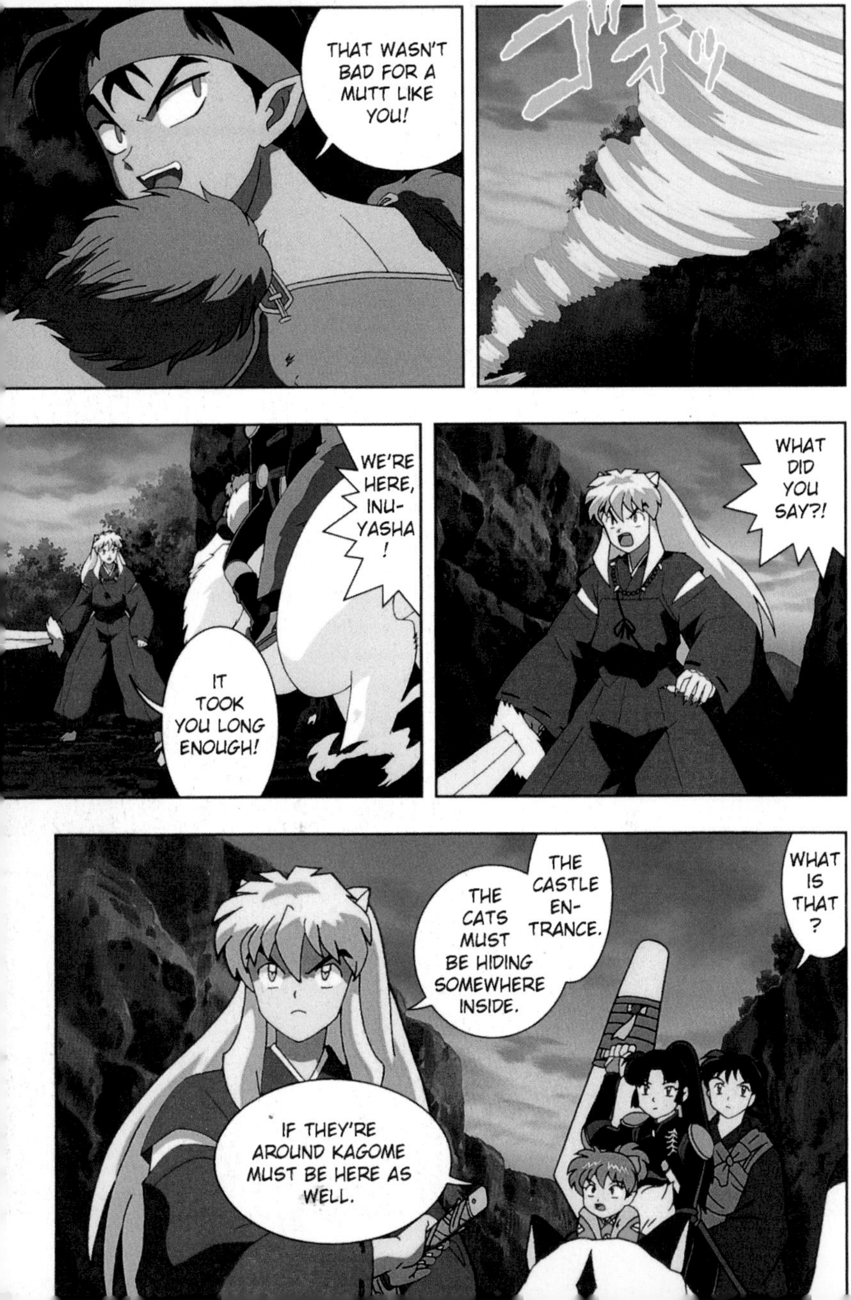
ゴオッ
THAT WASN'T BAD FOR A MUTT LIKE YOU!
WHAT DID YOU SAY?!
WE'RE HERE, INU-YASHA!
IT TOOK YOU LONG ENOUGH!
WHAT IS THAT?
THE CASTLE EN-TRANCE.
THE CATS MUST BE HIDING SOMEWHERE INSIDE.
IF THEY'RE AROUND KAGOME MUST BE HERE AS WELL.

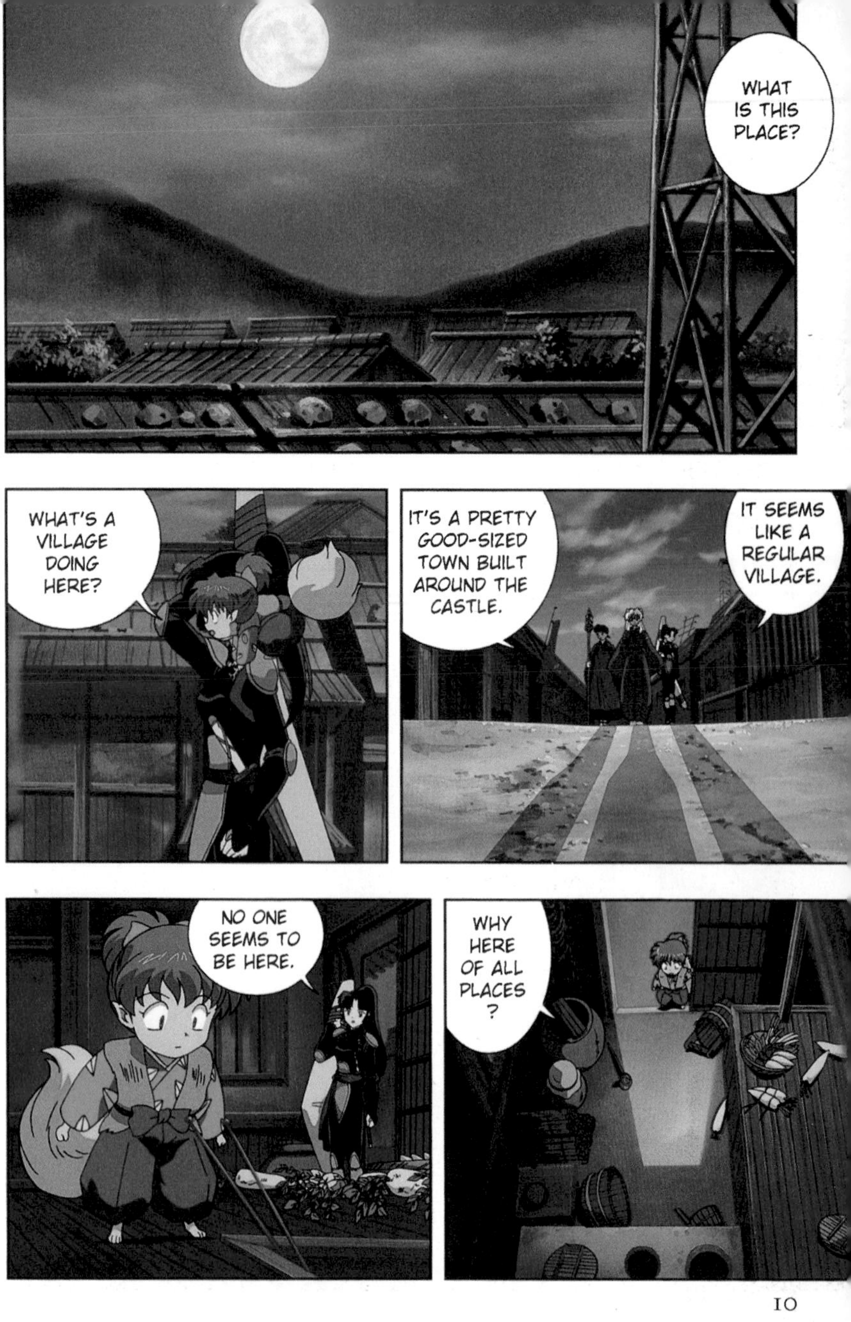
WHAT IS THIS PLACE?
IT SEEMS LIKE A REGULAR VILLAGE.
IT'S A PRETTY GOOD-SIZED TOWN BUILT AROUND THE CASTLE.
WHAT'S A VILLAGE DOING HERE?
WHY HERE OF ALL PLACES?
NO ONE SEEMS TO BE HERE.

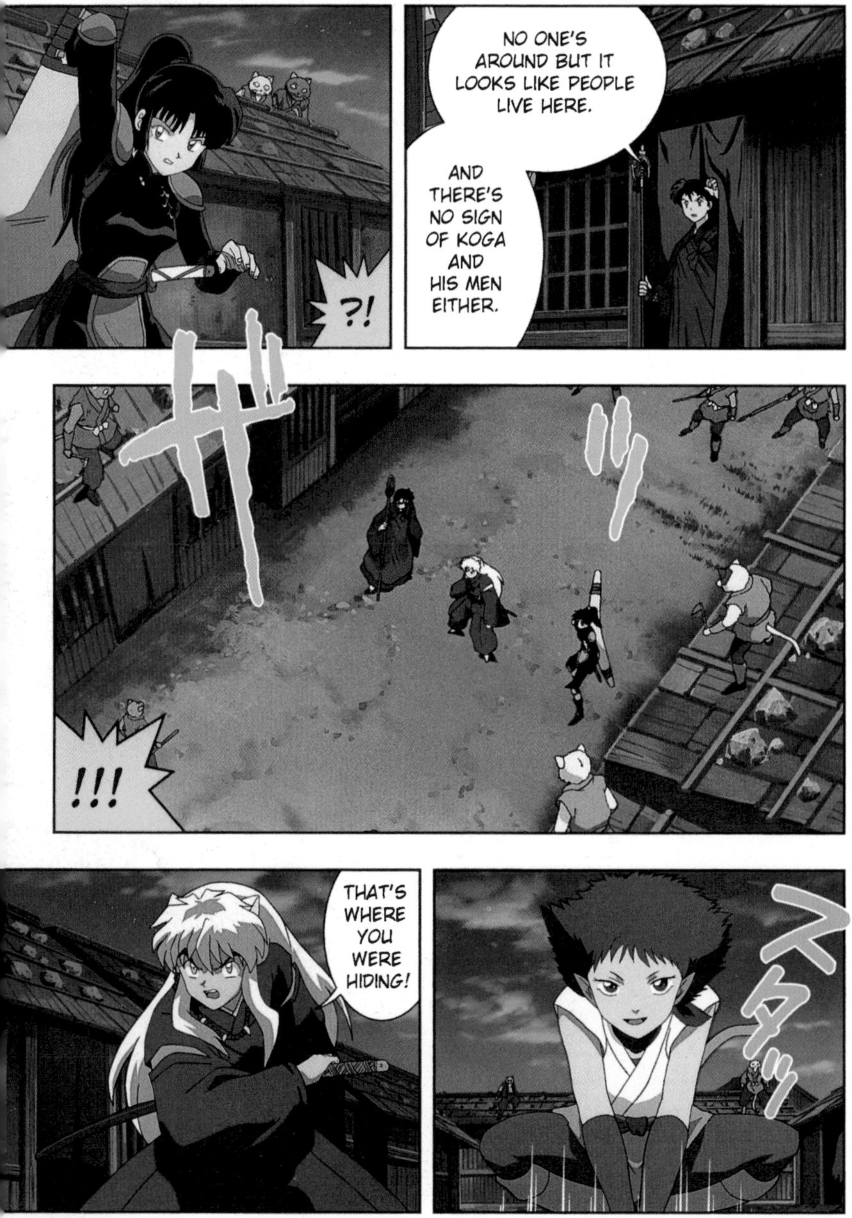
NO ONE'S AROUND BUT IT LOOKS LIKE PEOPLE LIVE HERE.
AND THERE'S NO SIGN OF KOGA AND HIS MEN EITHER.
?!
ザッ
!!!
スタッ
THAT'S WHERE YOU WERE HIDING!

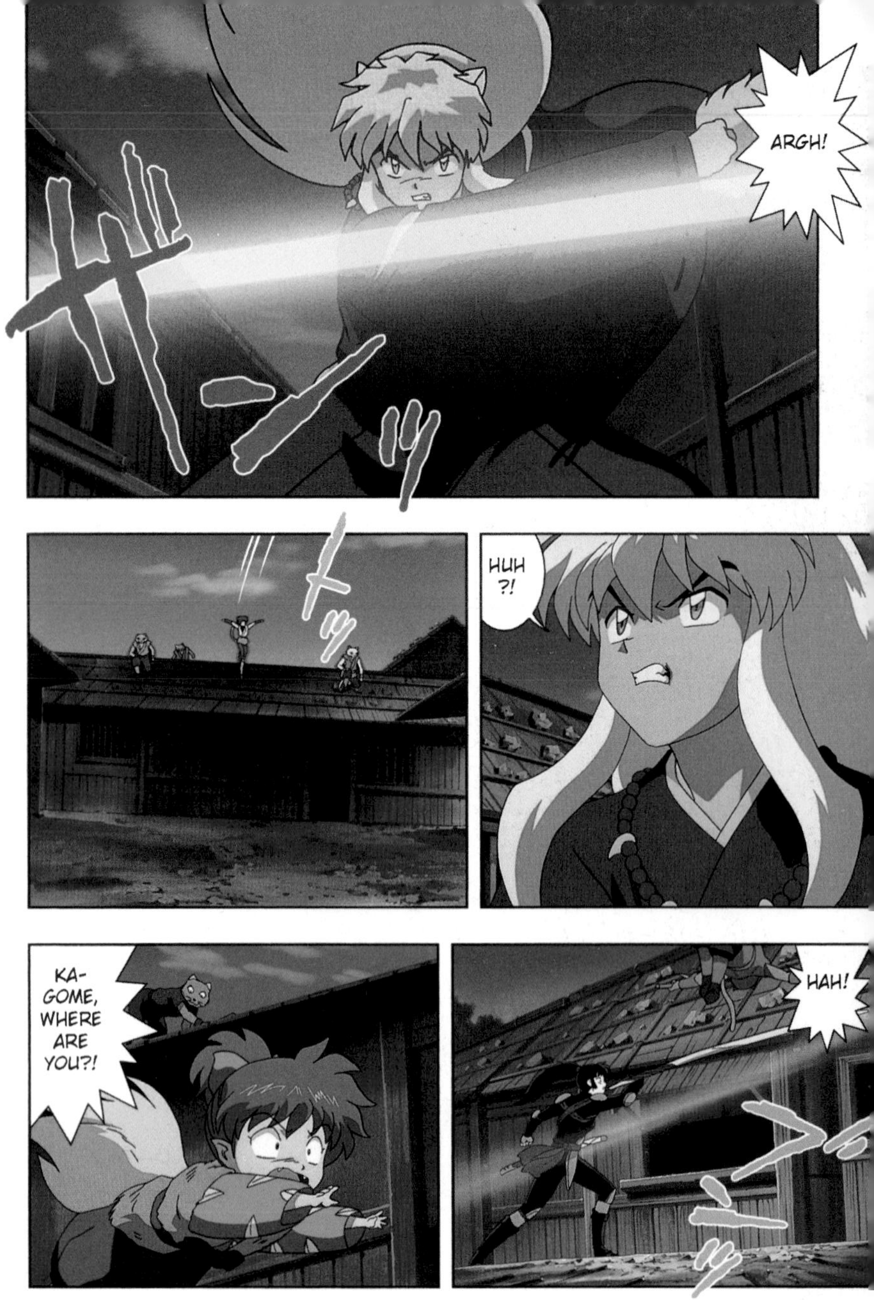
ARGH!
HUH ?!
HAH!
KA-GOME, WHERE ARE YOU?!

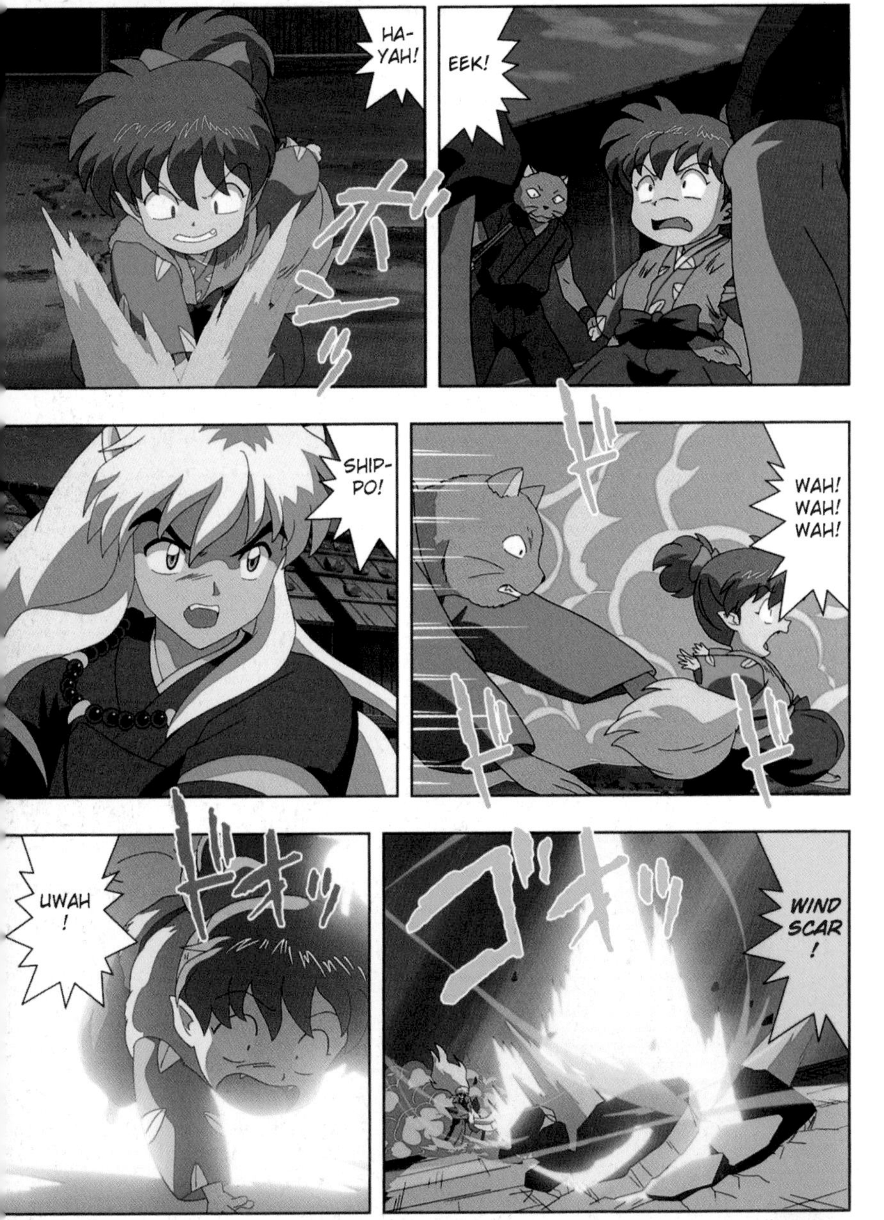
EEK!
HA-YAH!
ボンッ
WAH! WAH! WAH!
ドドド
SHIP-PO!
WIND SCAR!
ゴオッ
ドオッ
UWAH!

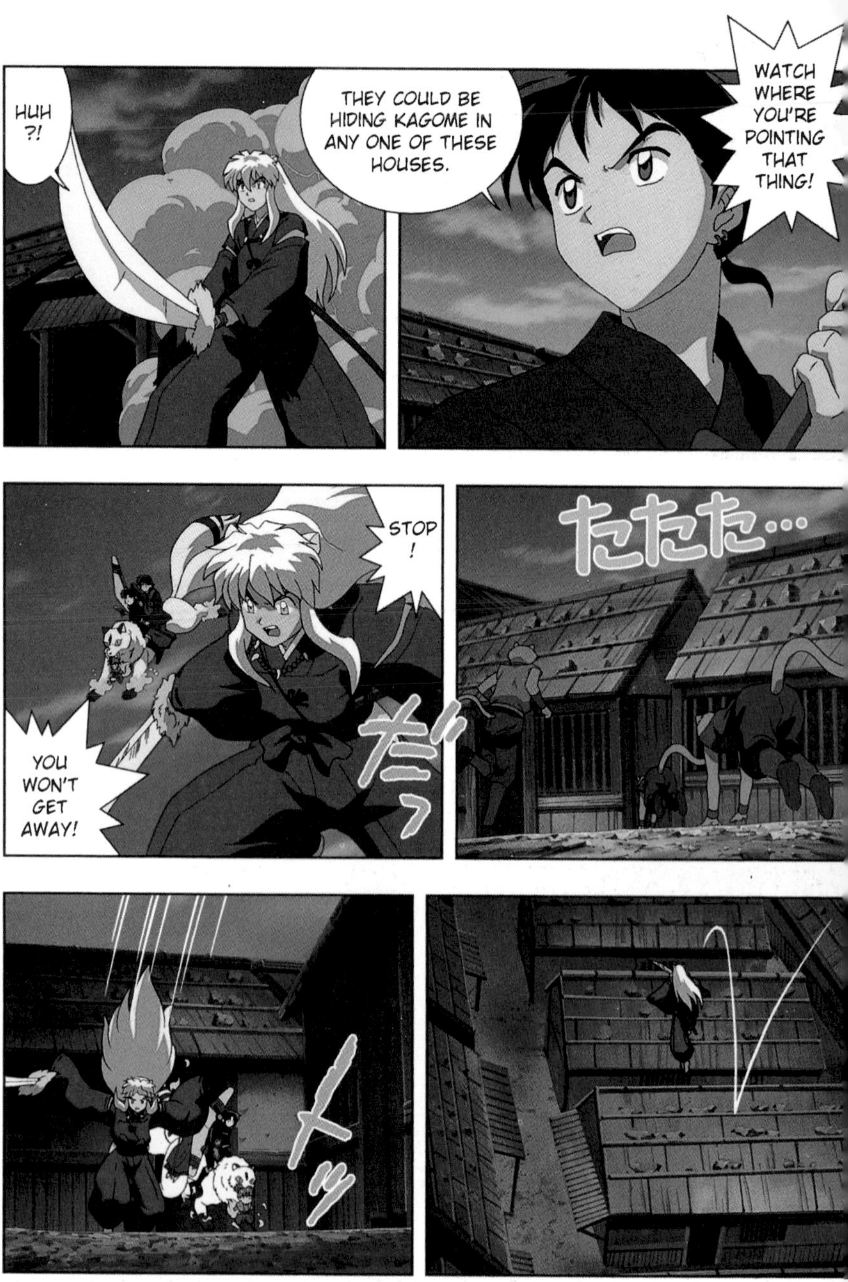
WATCH WHERE YOU'RE POINTING THAT THING!
THEY COULD BE HIDING KAGOME IN ANY ONE OF THESE HOUSES.
HUH ?!
たたた…
STOP !
だっ
YOU WON'T GET AWAY!
トッ

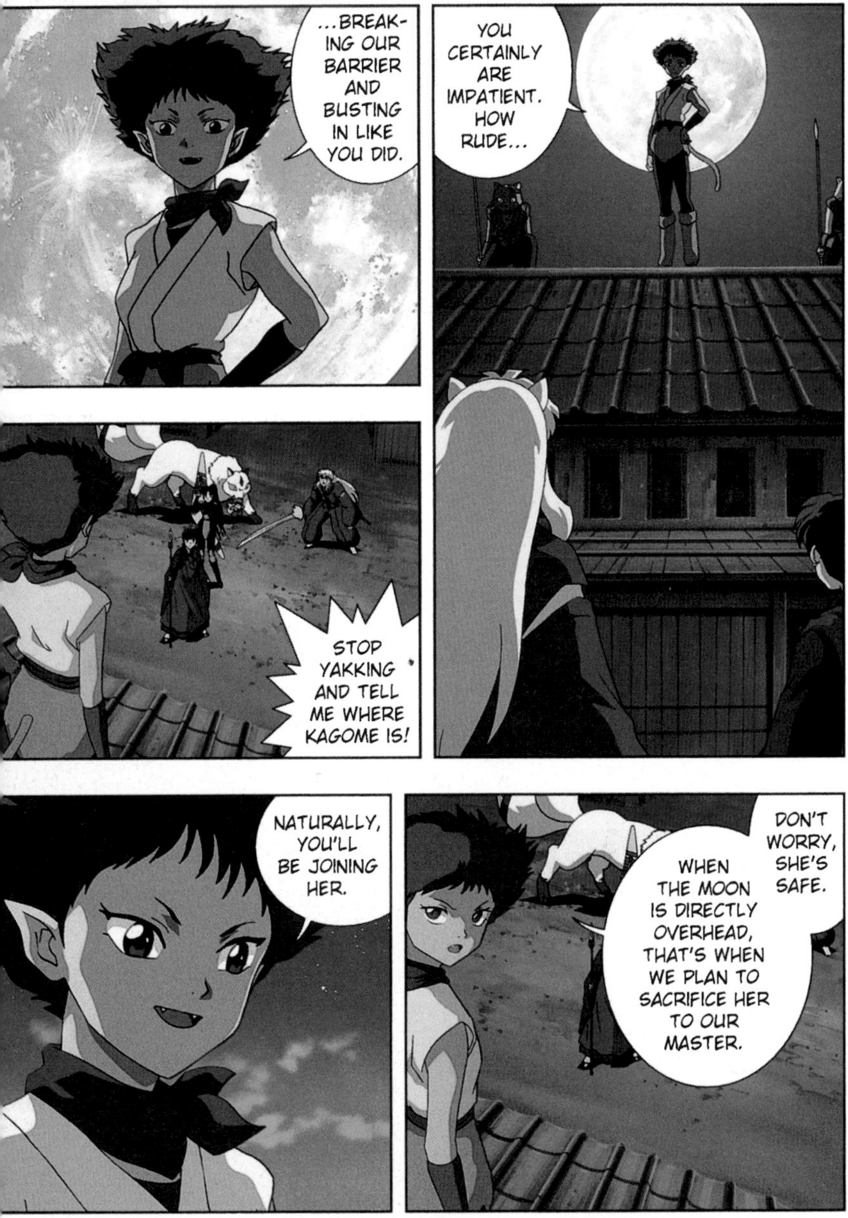
YOU CERTAINLY ARE IMPATIENT. HOW RUDE...
...BREAK-ING OUR BARRIER AND BUSTING IN LIKE YOU DID.
STOP YAKKING AND TELL ME WHERE KAGOME IS!
DON'T WORRY, SHE'S SAFE.
WHEN THE MOON IS DIRECTLY OVERHEAD, THAT'S WHEN WE PLAN TO SACRIFICE HER TO OUR MASTER.
NATURALLY, YOU'LL BE JOINING HER.

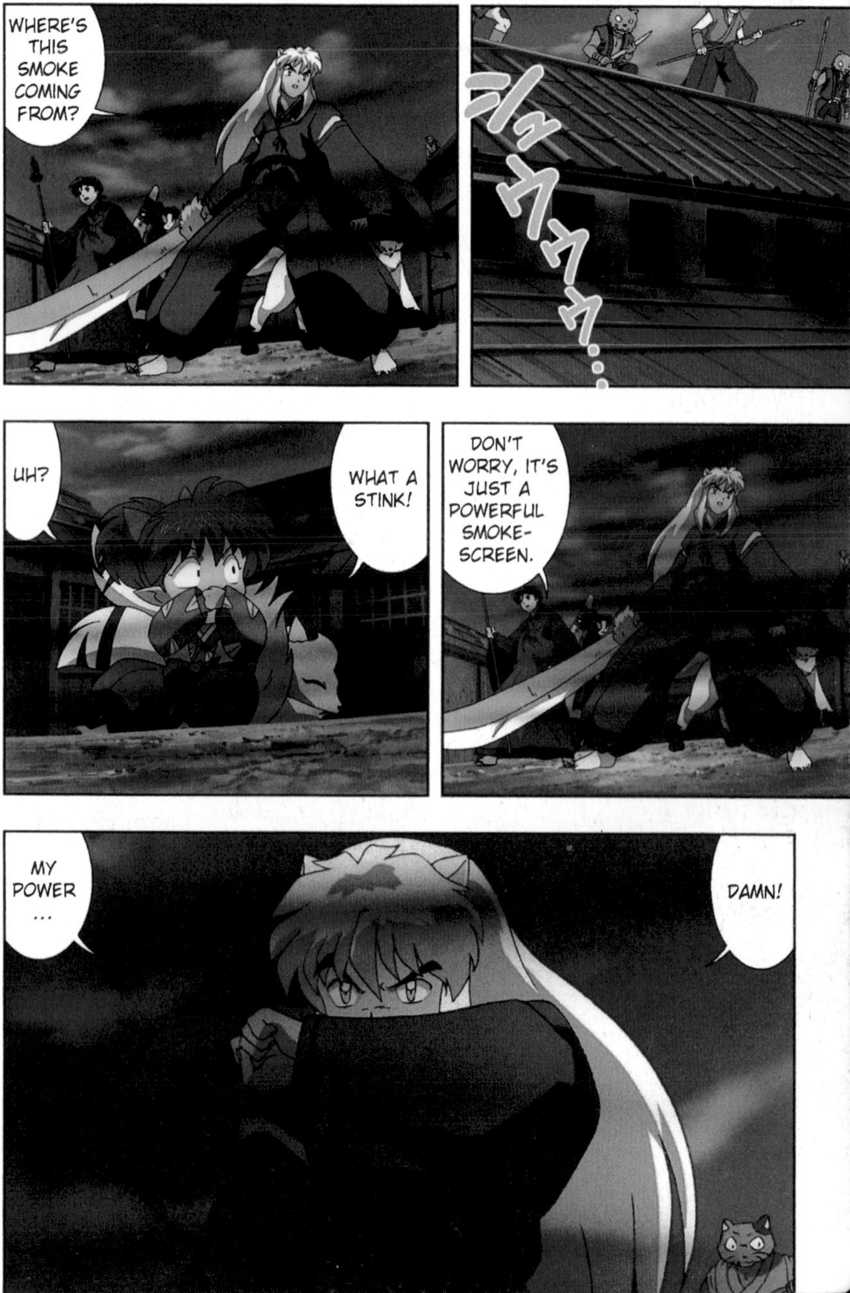
シュウウウ...
WHERE'S THIS SMOKE COMING FROM?
DON'T WORRY, IT'S JUST A POWERFUL SMOKE-SCREEN.
WHAT A STINK!
UH?
DAMN!
MY POWER ...

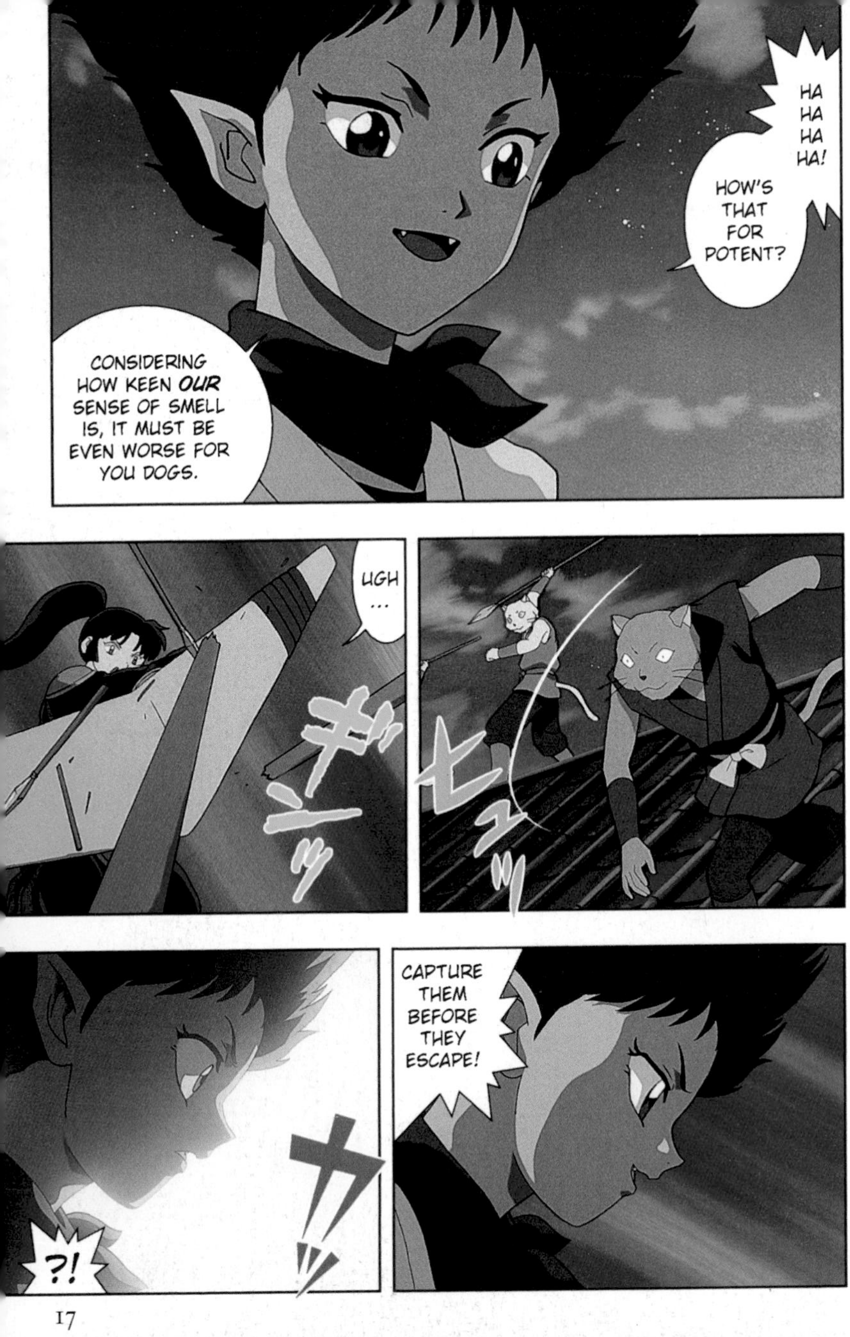
HA HA HA HA!
HOW'S THAT FOR POTENT?
CONSIDERING HOW KEEN ***OUR*** SENSE OF SMELL IS, IT MUST BE EVEN WORSE FOR YOU DOGS.
ヒュッ
UGH ...
ギンッ
CAPTURE THEM BEFORE THEY ESCAPE!
カッ
?!

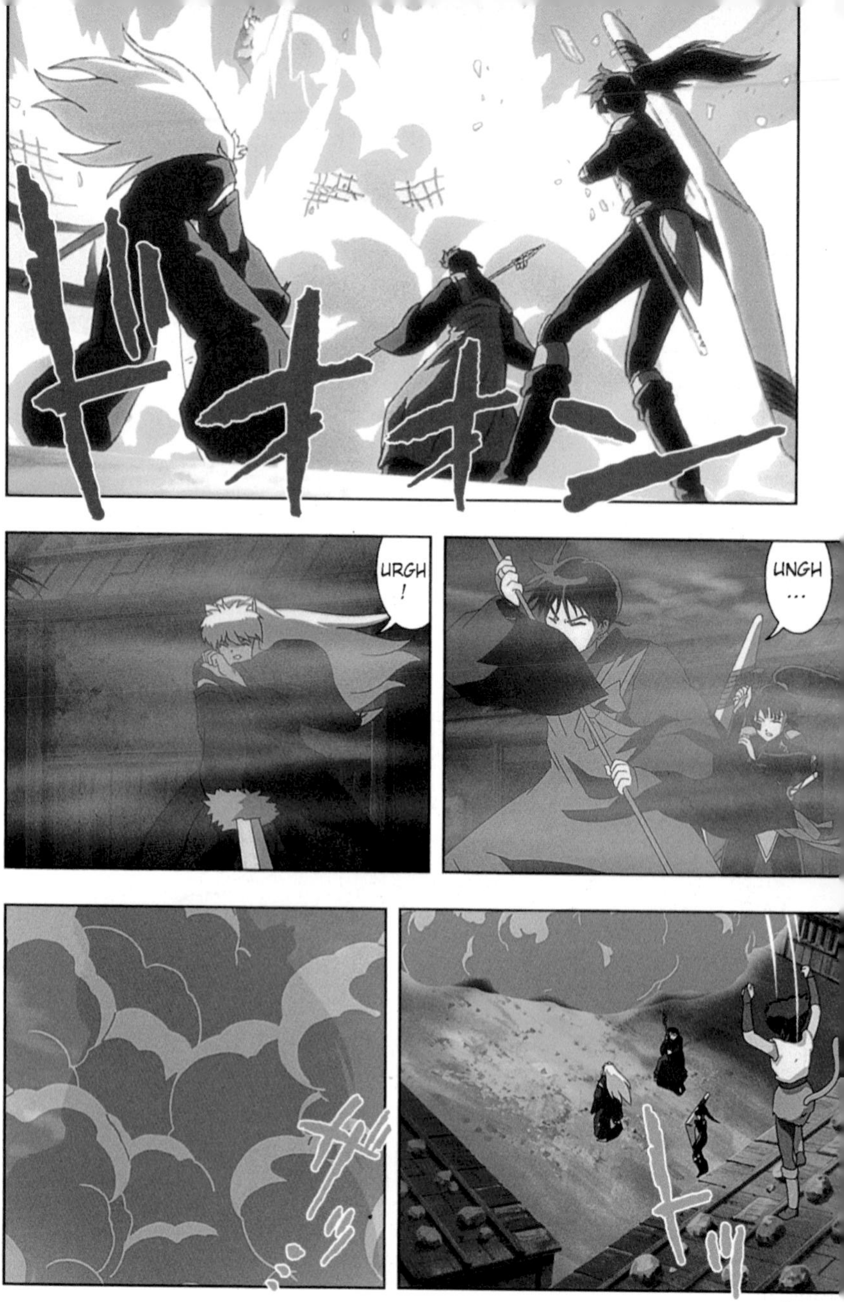
UNGH ...
URGH !

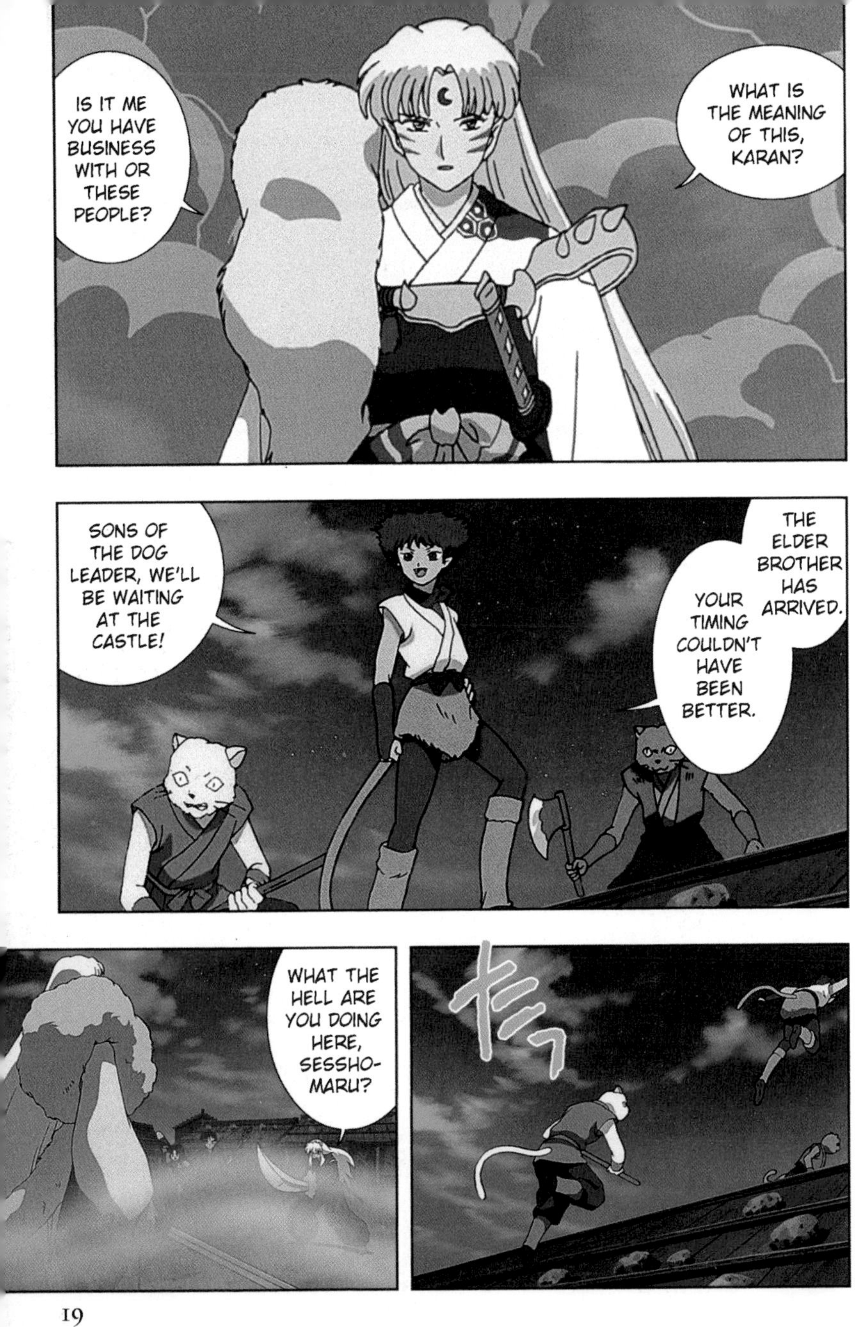
WHAT IS THE MEANING OF THIS, KARAN?
IS IT ME YOU HAVE BUSINESS WITH OR THESE PEOPLE?
THE ELDER BROTHER HAS ARRIVED.
YOUR TIMING COULDN'T HAVE BEEN BETTER.
SONS OF THE DOG LEADER, WE'LL BE WAITING AT THE CASTLE!
WHAT THE HELL ARE YOU DOING HERE, SESSHO-MARU?

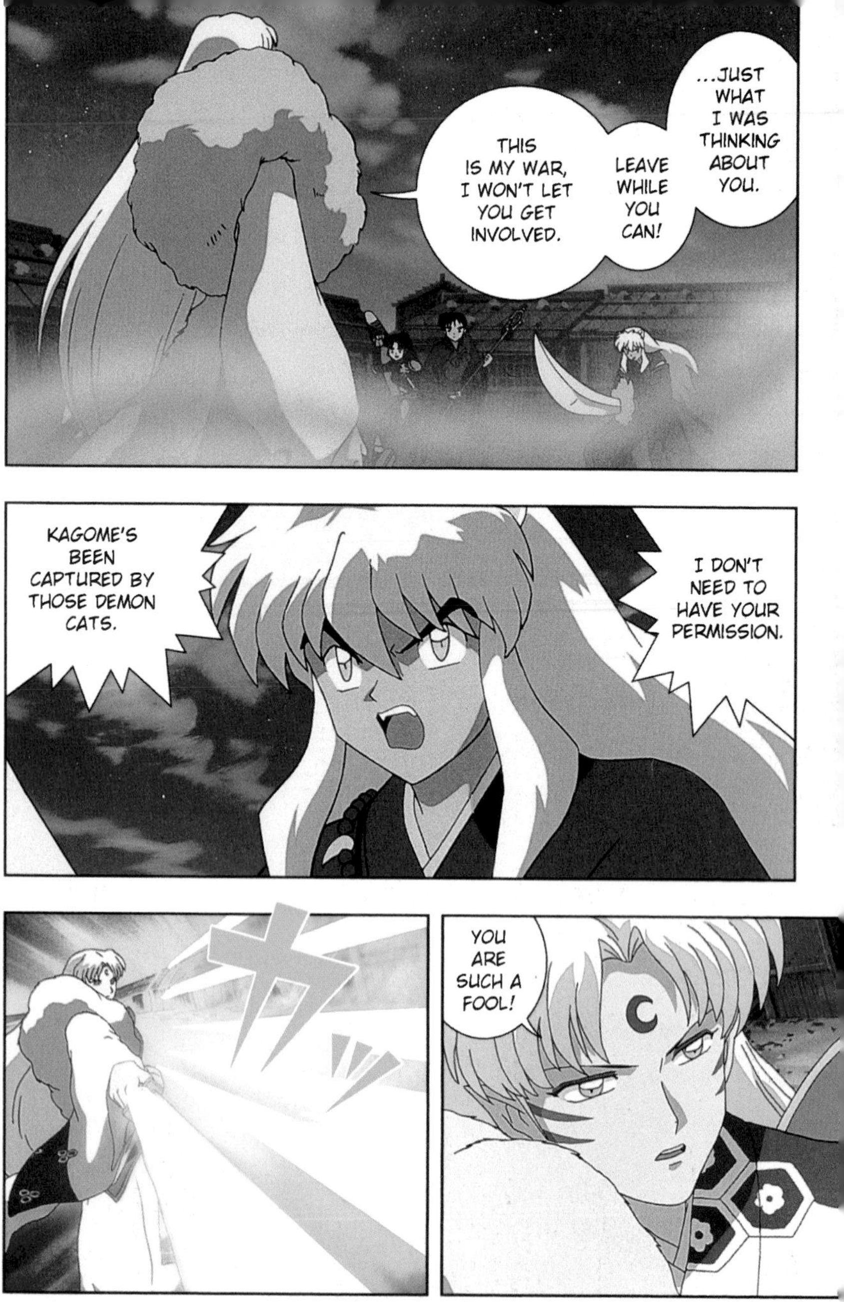
...JUST WHAT I WAS THINKING ABOUT YOU.
LEAVE WHILE YOU CAN!
THIS IS MY WAR, I WON'T LET YOU GET INVOLVED.
I DON'T NEED TO HAVE YOUR PERMISSION.
KAGOME'S BEEN CAPTURED BY THOSE DEMON CATS.
YOU ARE SUCH A FOOL!

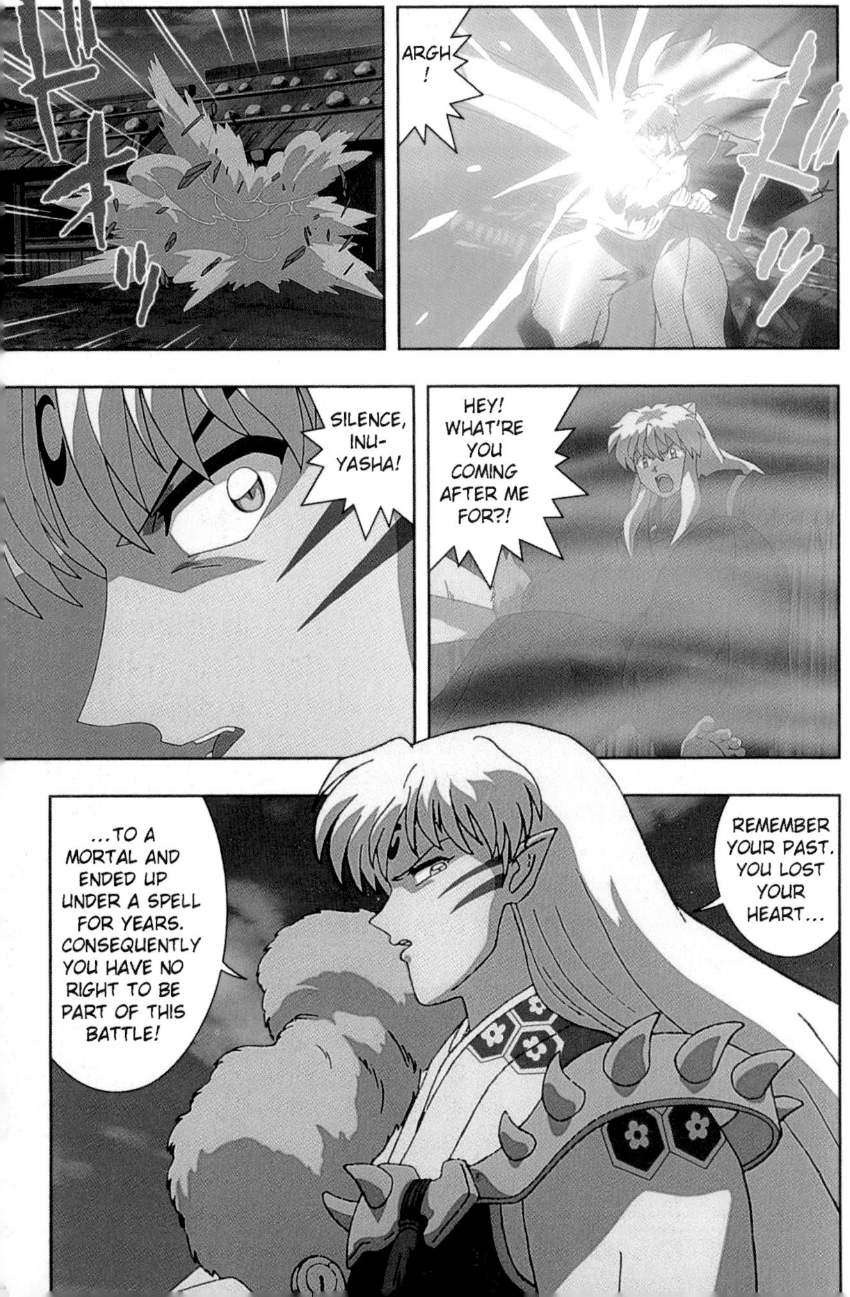
ARGH!
HEY! WHAT'RE YOU COMING AFTER ME FOR?!
SILENCE, INU-YASHA!
REMEMBER YOUR PAST. YOU LOST YOUR HEART...
...TO A MORTAL AND ENDED UP UNDER A SPELL FOR YEARS. CONSEQUENTLY YOU HAVE NO RIGHT TO BE PART OF THIS BATTLE!

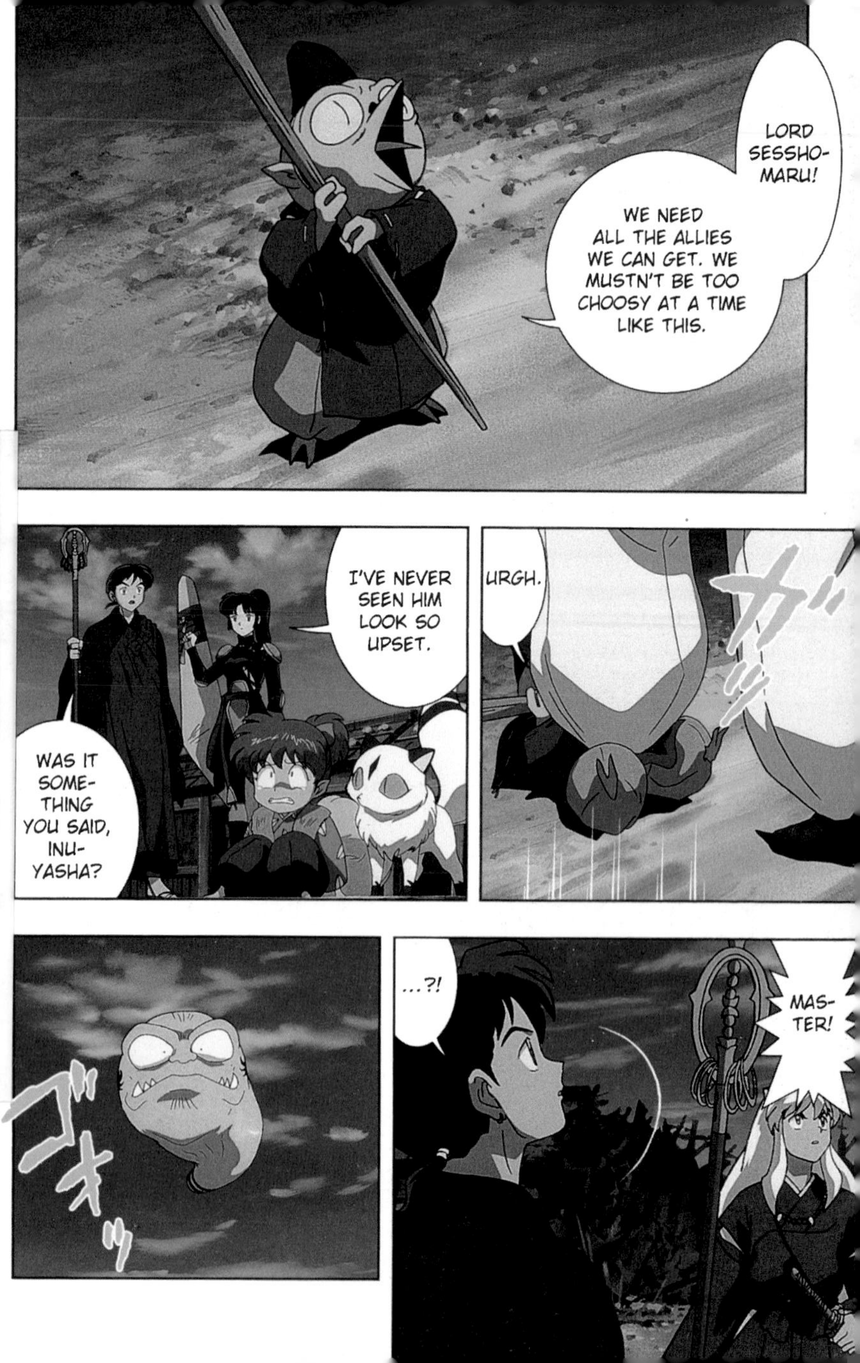
LORD SESSHO- MARU!
WE NEED ALL THE ALLIES WE CAN GET. WE MUSTN'T BE TOO CHOOSY AT A TIME LIKE THIS.
URGH.
ガッ
I'VE NEVER SEEN HIM LOOK SO UPSET.
WAS IT SOME- THING YOU SAID, INU- YASHA?
MAS- TER!
...?!

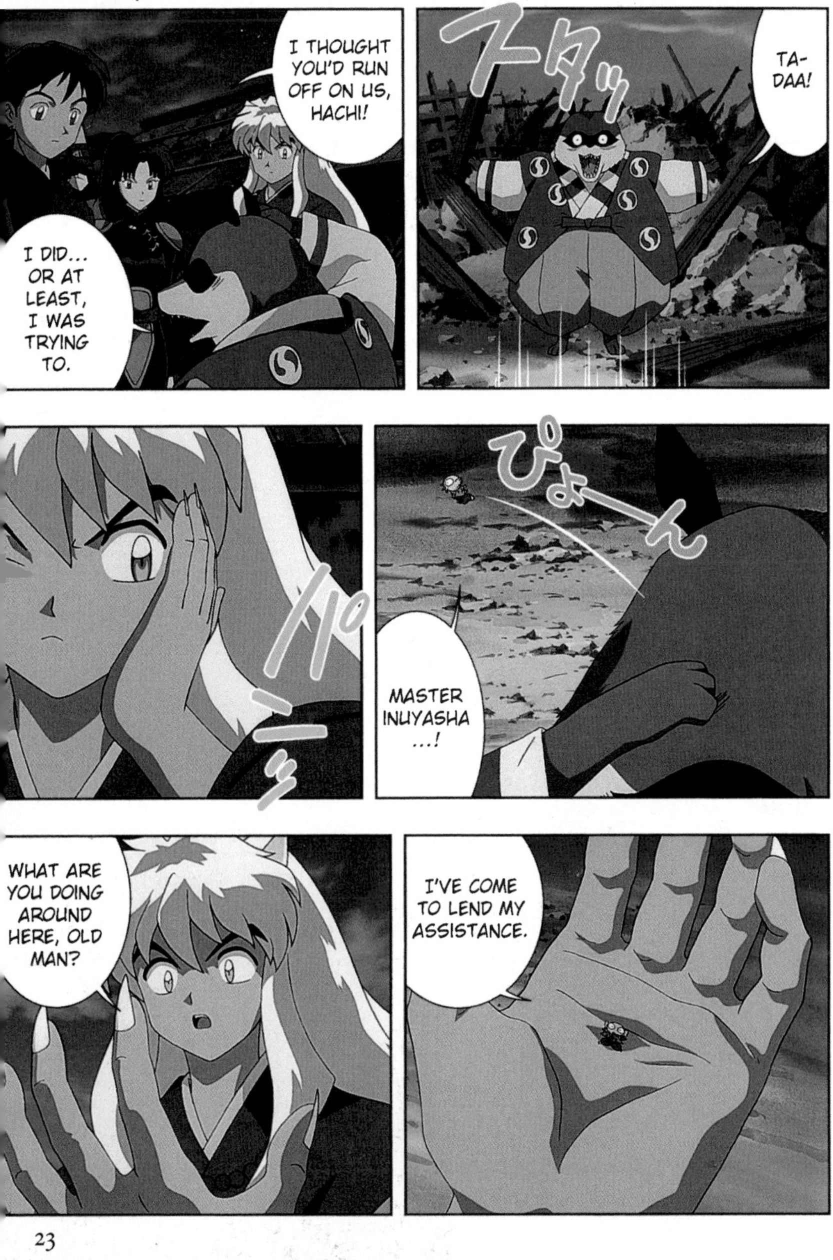
スタッ
TA-DAA!
I THOUGHT YOU'D RUN OFF ON US, HACHI!
I DID... OR AT LEAST, I WAS TRYING TO.
ぴょーん
MASTER INUYASHA ...!
I'VE COME TO LEND MY ASSISTANCE.
WHAT ARE YOU DOING AROUND HERE, OLD MAN?

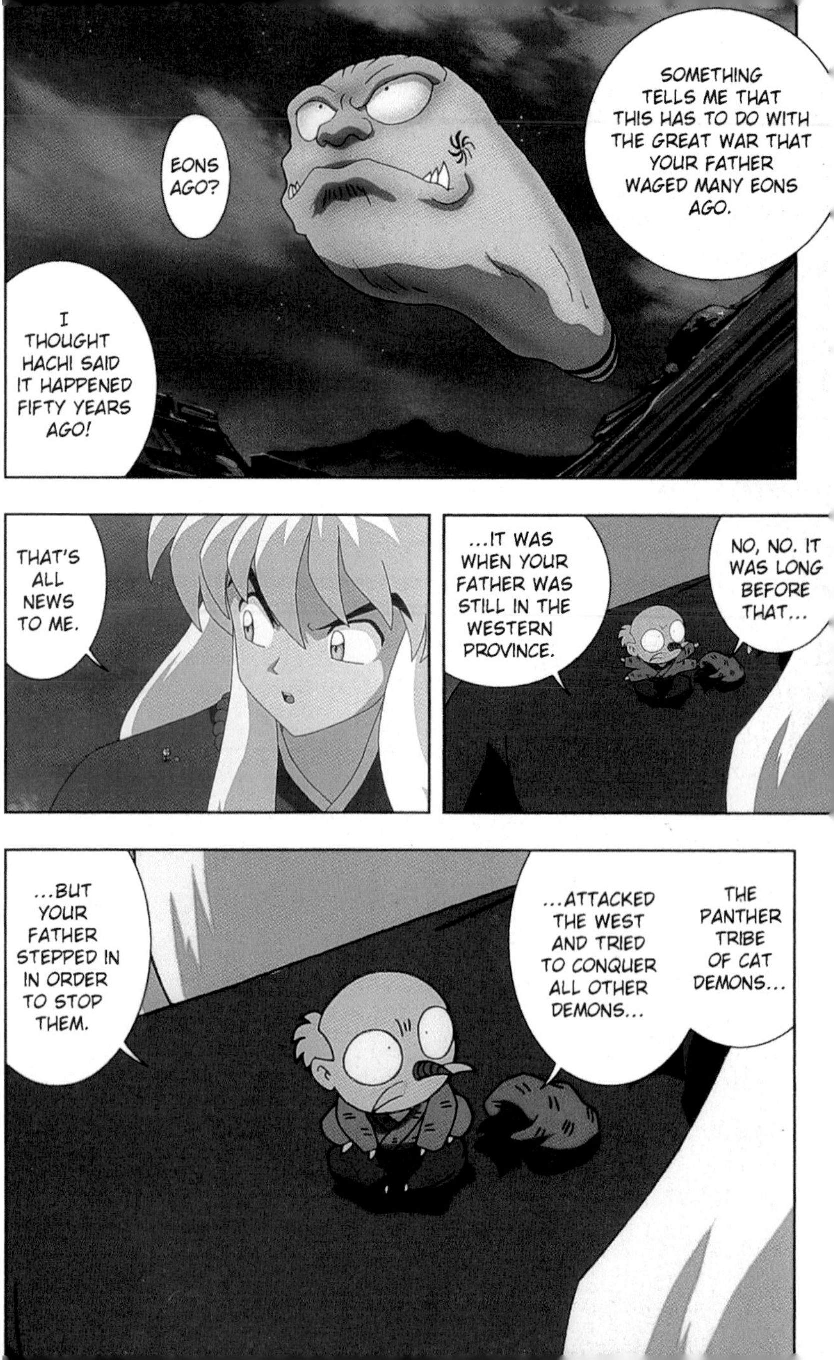
SOMETHING TELLS ME THAT THIS HAS TO DO WITH THE GREAT WAR THAT YOUR FATHER WAGED MANY EONS AGO.
EONS AGO?
I THOUGHT HACHI SAID IT HAPPENED FIFTY YEARS AGO!
NO, NO. IT WAS LONG BEFORE THAT...
...IT WAS WHEN YOUR FATHER WAS STILL IN THE WESTERN PROVINCE.
THAT'S ALL NEWS TO ME.
THE PANTHER TRIBE OF CAT DEMONS...
...ATTACKED THE WEST AND TRIED TO CONQUER ALL OTHER DEMONS...
...BUT YOUR FATHER STEPPED IN IN ORDER TO STOP THEM.

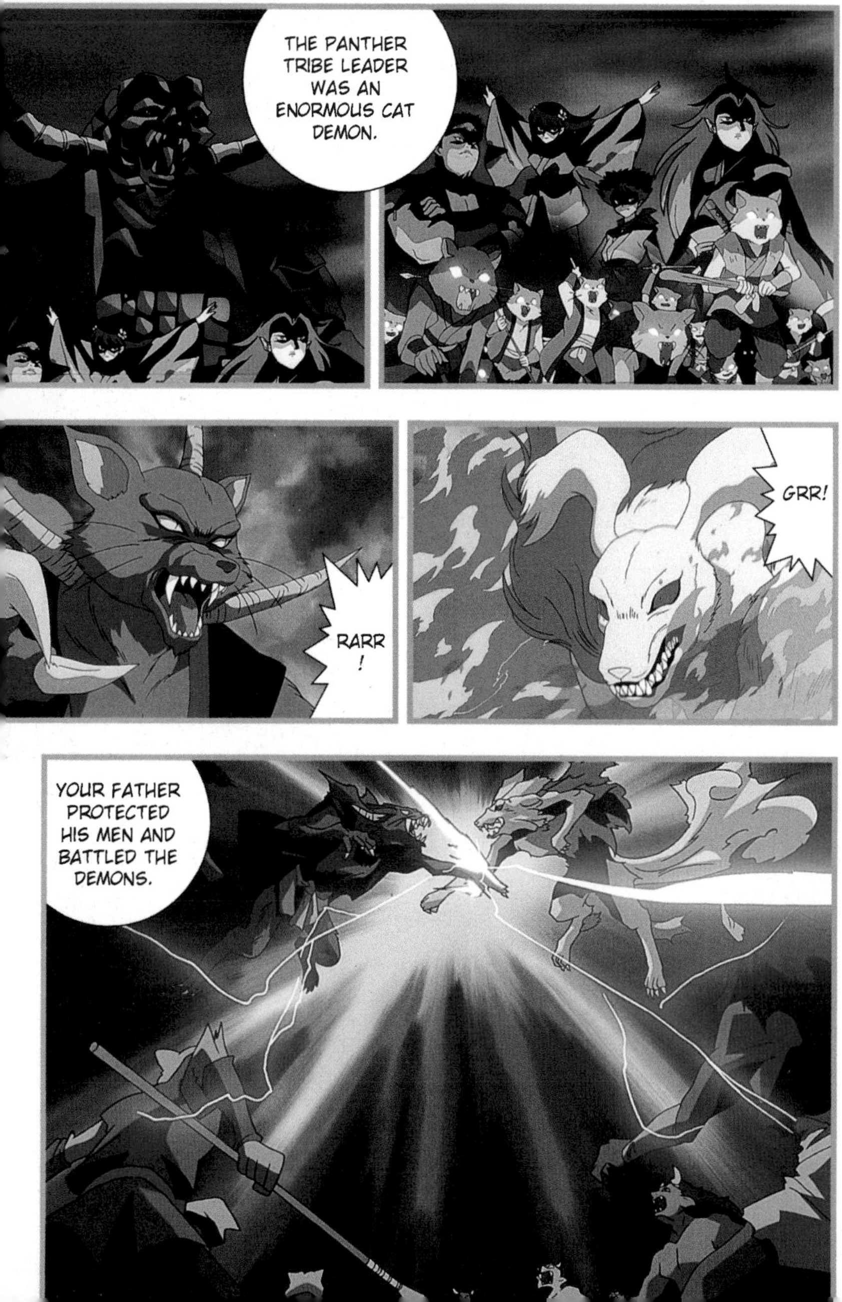
THE PANTHER TRIBE LEADER WAS AN ENORMOUS CAT DEMON.
GRR!
RARR!
YOUR FATHER PROTECTED HIS MEN AND BATTLED THE DEMONS.

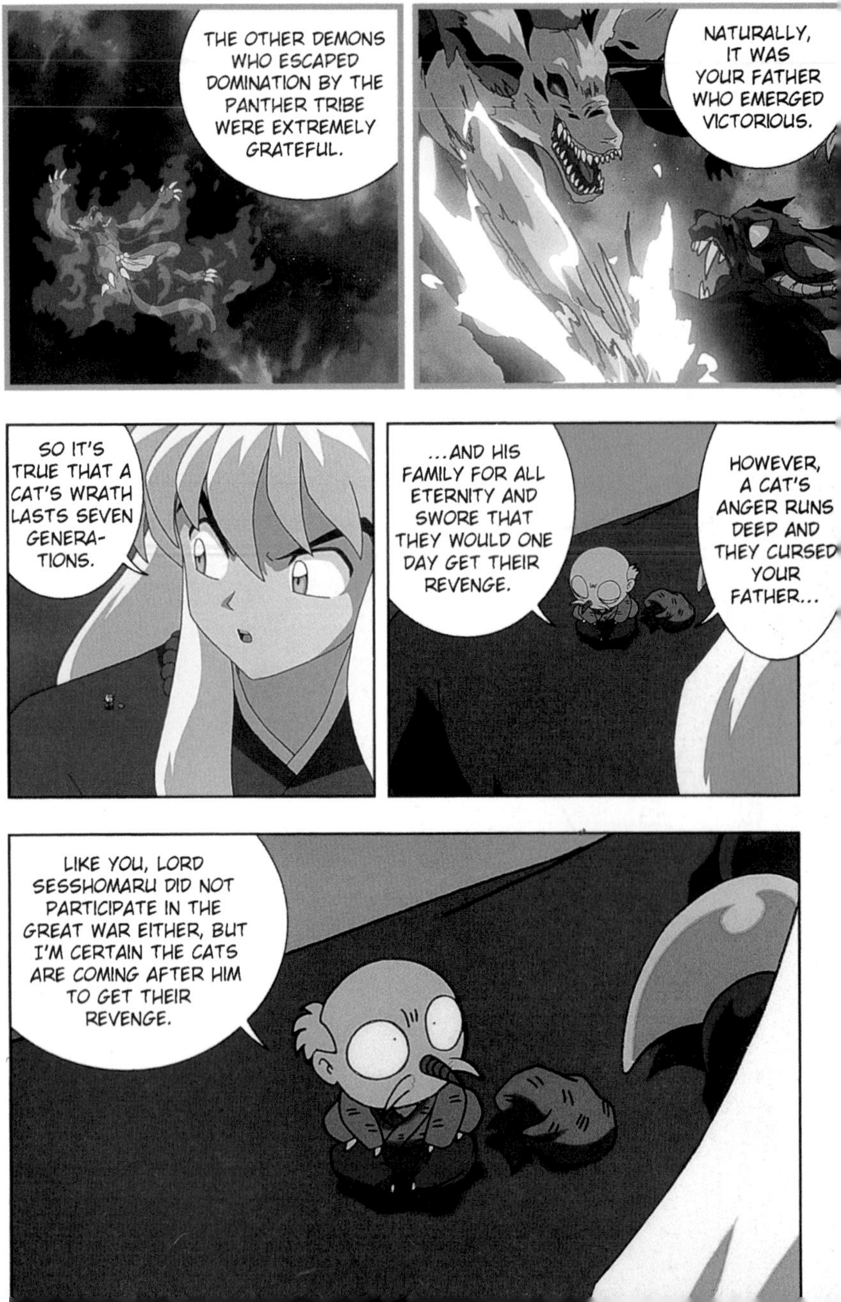
NATURALLY, IT WAS YOUR FATHER WHO EMERGED VICTORIOUS.
THE OTHER DEMONS WHO ESCAPED DOMINATION BY THE PANTHER TRIBE WERE EXTREMELY GRATEFUL.
HOWEVER, A CAT'S ANGER RUNS DEEP AND THEY CURSED YOUR FATHER...
...AND HIS FAMILY FOR ALL ETERNITY AND SWORE THAT THEY WOULD ONE DAY GET THEIR REVENGE.
SO IT'S TRUE THAT A CAT'S WRATH LASTS SEVEN GENERA-TIONS.
LIKE YOU, LORD SESSHOMARU DID NOT PARTICIPATE IN THE GREAT WAR EITHER, BUT I'M CERTAIN THE CATS ARE COMING AFTER HIM TO GET THEIR REVENGE.

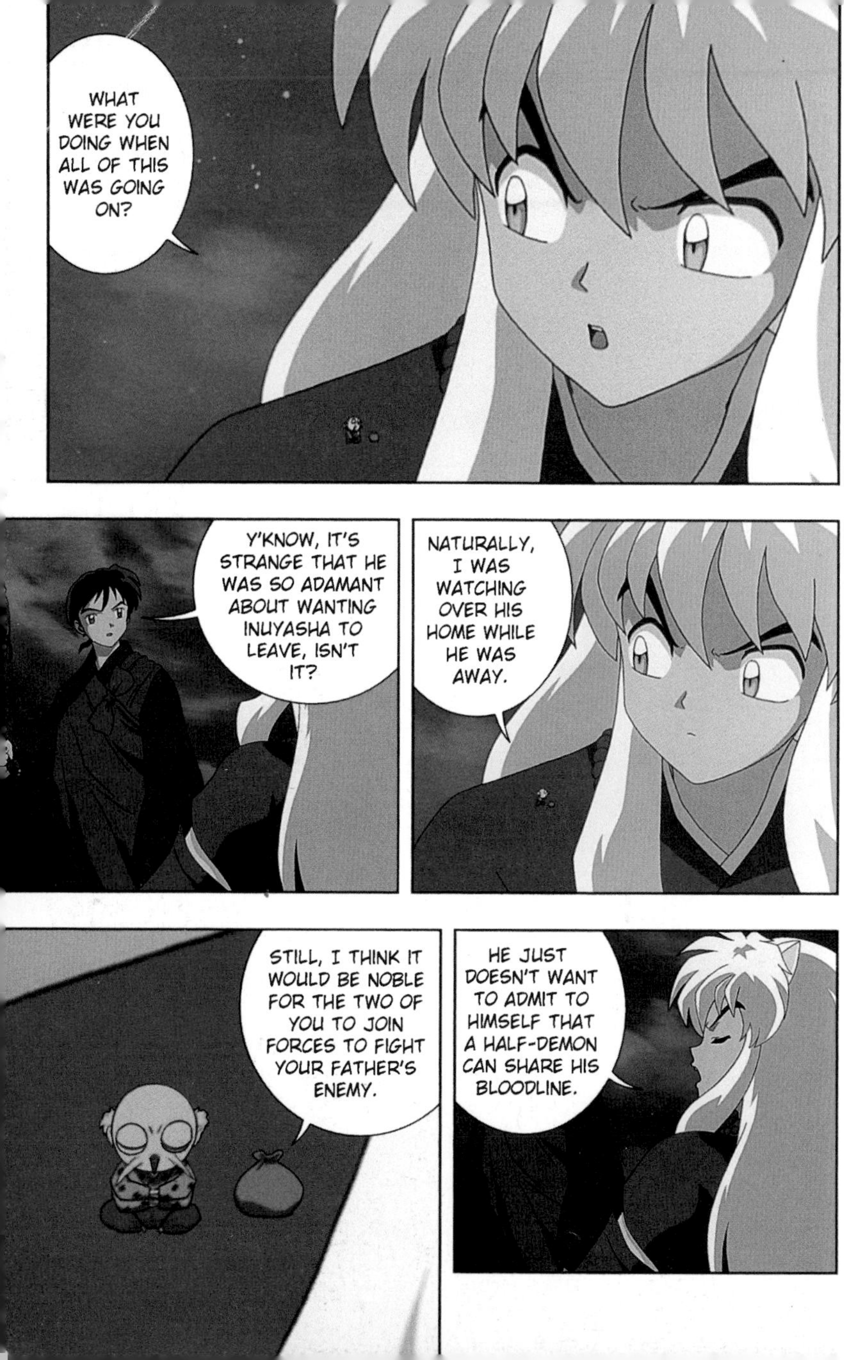
WHAT WERE YOU DOING WHEN ALL OF THIS WAS GOING ON?
NATURALLY, I WAS WATCHING OVER HIS HOME WHILE HE WAS AWAY.
Y'KNOW, IT'S STRANGE THAT HE WAS SO ADAMANT ABOUT WANTING INUYASHA TO LEAVE, ISN'T IT?
HE JUST DOESN'T WANT TO ADMIT TO HIMSELF THAT A HALF-DEMON CAN SHARE HIS BLOODLINE.
STILL, I THINK IT WOULD BE NOBLE FOR THE TWO OF YOU TO JOIN FORCES TO FIGHT YOUR FATHER'S ENEMY.

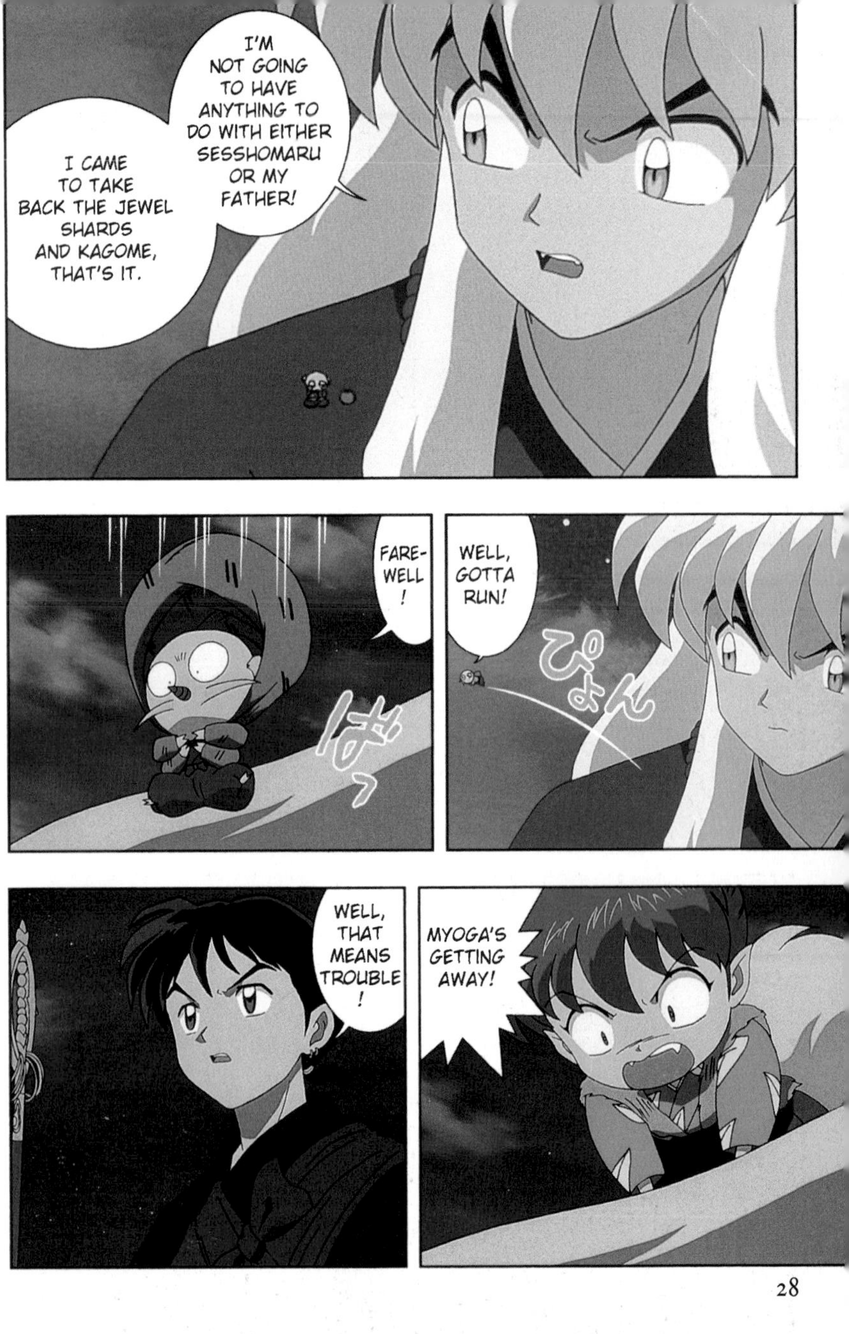
I'M NOT GOING TO HAVE ANYTHING TO DO WITH EITHER SESSHOMARU OR MY FATHER!
I CAME TO TAKE BACK THE JEWEL SHARDS AND KAGOME, THAT'S IT.
WELL, GOTTA RUN!
ぴょん
FARE-WELL!
ぱっ
MYOGA'S GETTING AWAY!
WELL, THAT MEANS TROUBLE!

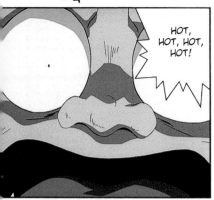

HOT, HOT, HOT, HOT!

UWAH!

ARE YOU GOING TO ASK YOUR BROTHER FOR HELP?

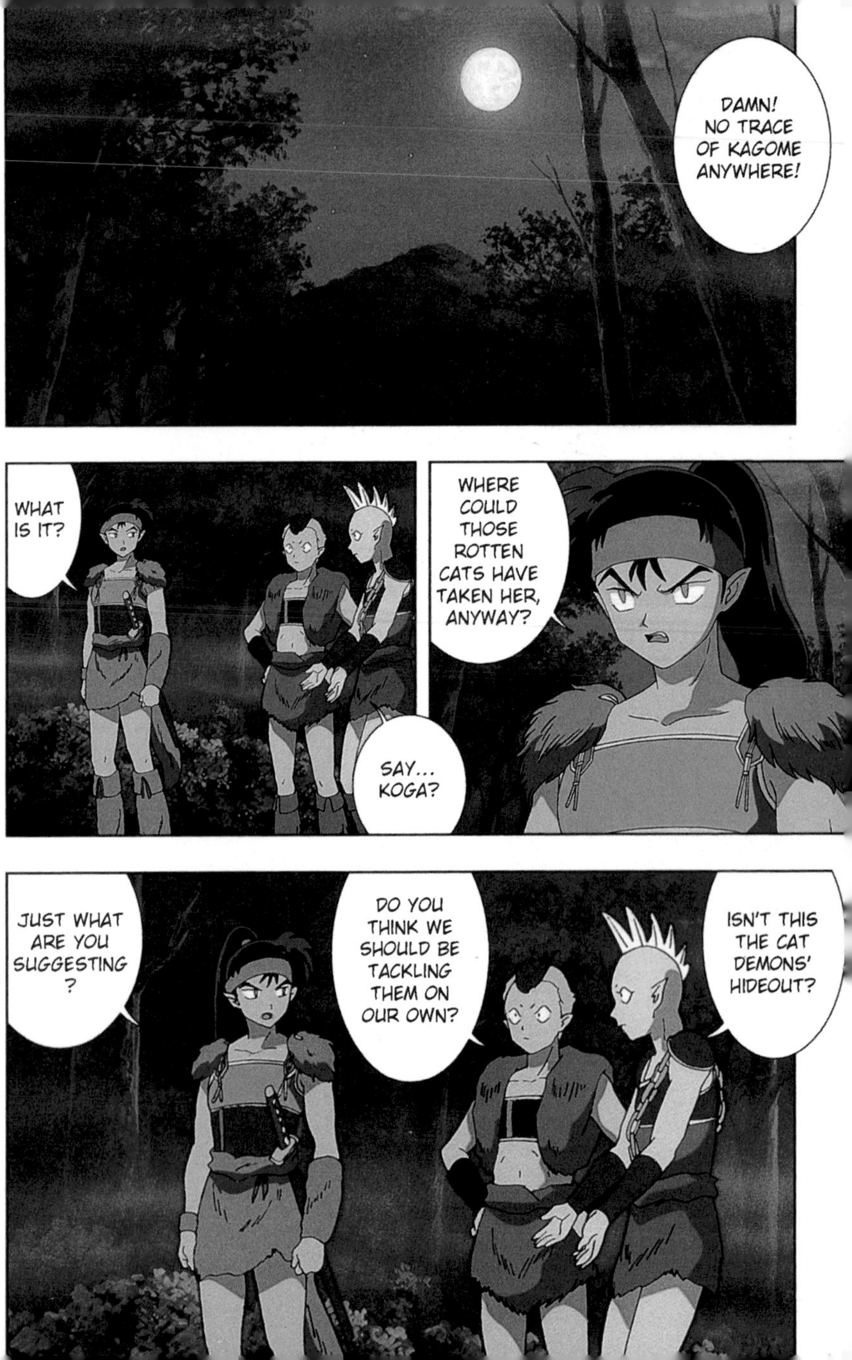
DAMN! NO TRACE OF KAGOME ANYWHERE!
WHERE COULD THOSE ROTTEN CATS HAVE TAKEN HER, ANYWAY?
SAY... KOGA?
WHAT IS IT?
ISN'T THIS THE CAT DEMONS' HIDEOUT?
DO YOU THINK WE SHOULD BE TACKLING THEM ON OUR OWN?
JUST WHAT ARE YOU SUGGESTING?

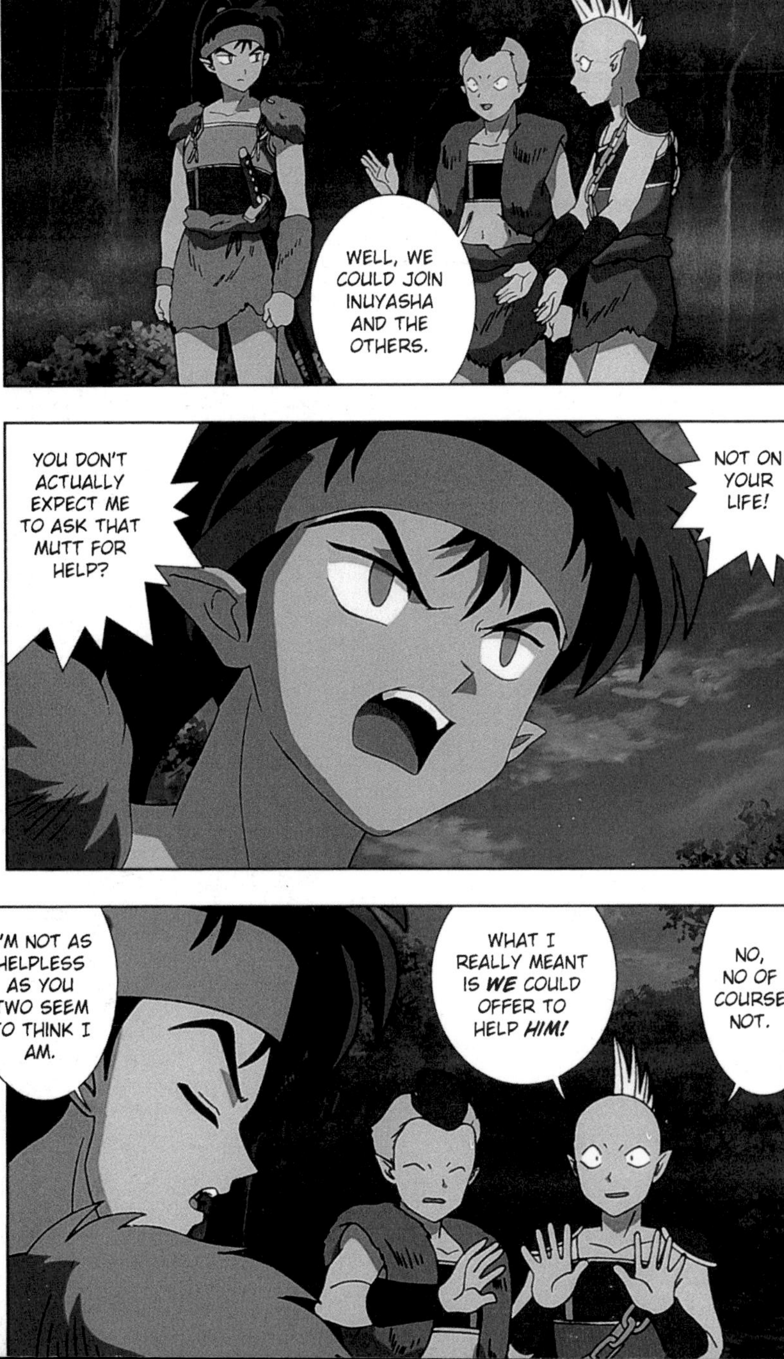
WELL, WE COULD JOIN INUYASHA AND THE OTHERS.
NOT ON YOUR LIFE!
YOU DON'T ACTUALLY EXPECT ME TO ASK THAT MUTT FOR HELP?
NO, NO OF COURSE NOT.
WHAT I REALLY MEANT IS ***WE*** COULD OFFER TO HELP ***HIM!***
I'M NOT AS HELPLESS AS YOU TWO SEEM TO THINK I AM.

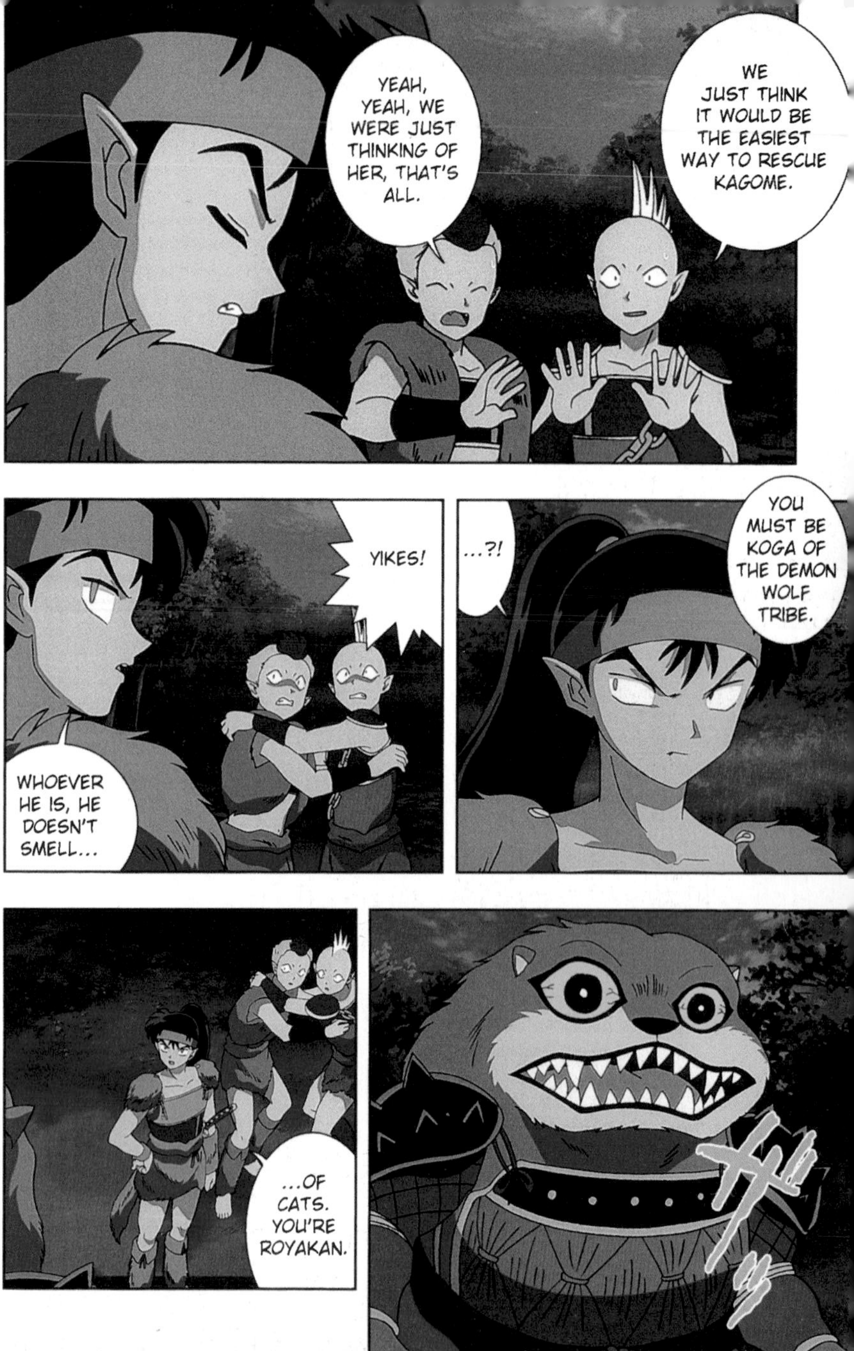
WE JUST THINK IT WOULD BE THE EASIEST WAY TO RESCUE KAGOME.
YEAH, YEAH, WE WERE JUST THINKING OF HER, THAT'S ALL.
YOU MUST BE KOGA OF THE DEMON WOLF TRIBE.
...?!
YIKES!
WHOEVER HE IS, HE DOESN'T SMELL...
...OF CATS. YOU'RE ROYAKAN.

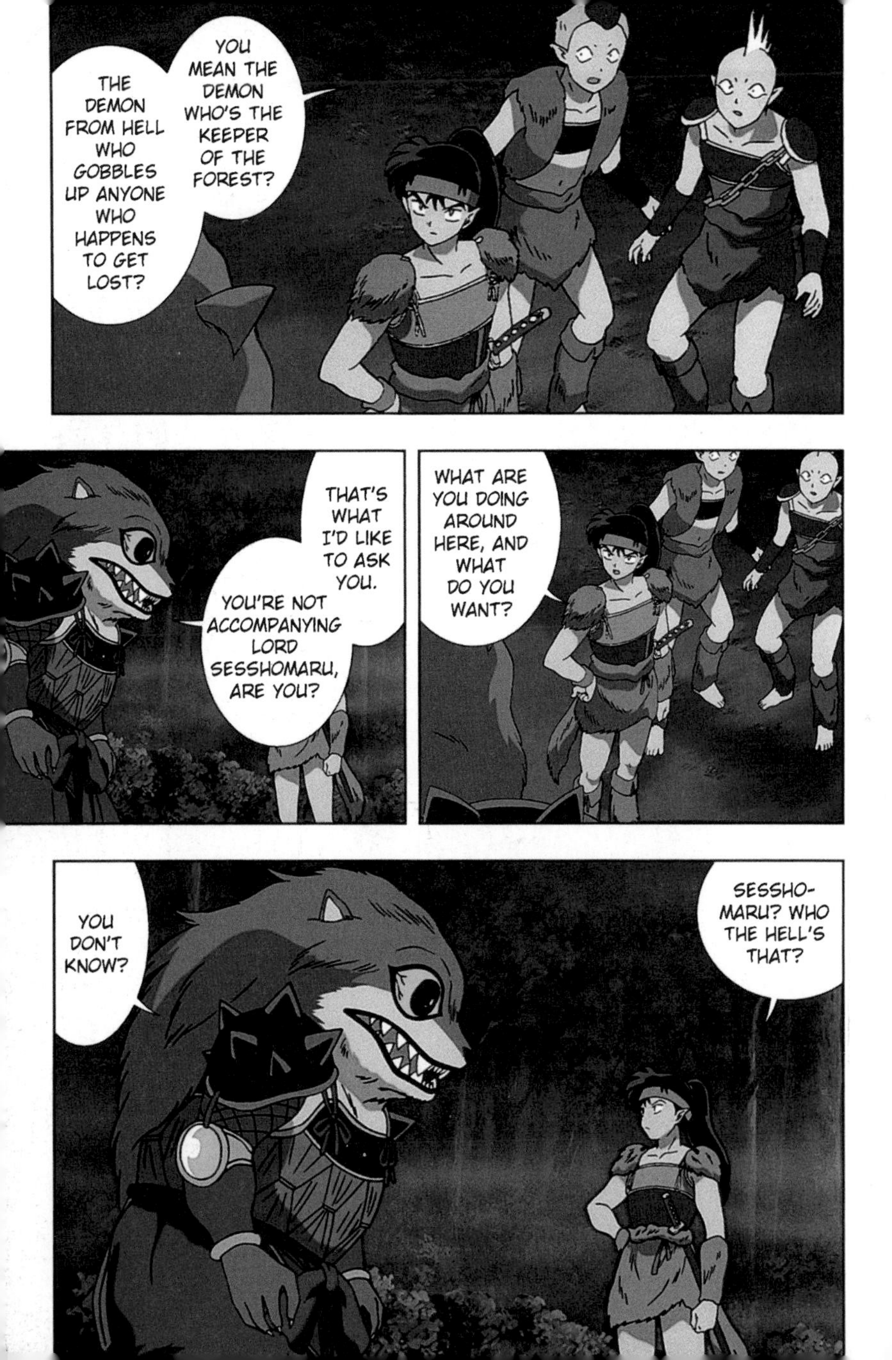
YOU MEAN THE DEMON WHO'S THE KEEPER OF THE FOREST?
THE DEMON FROM HELL WHO GOBBLES UP ANYONE WHO HAPPENS TO GET LOST?
WHAT ARE YOU DOING AROUND HERE, AND WHAT DO YOU WANT?
THAT'S WHAT I'D LIKE TO ASK YOU.
YOU'RE NOT ACCOMPANYING LORD SESSHOMARU, ARE YOU?
SESSHO-MARU? WHO THE HELL'S THAT?
YOU DON'T KNOW?

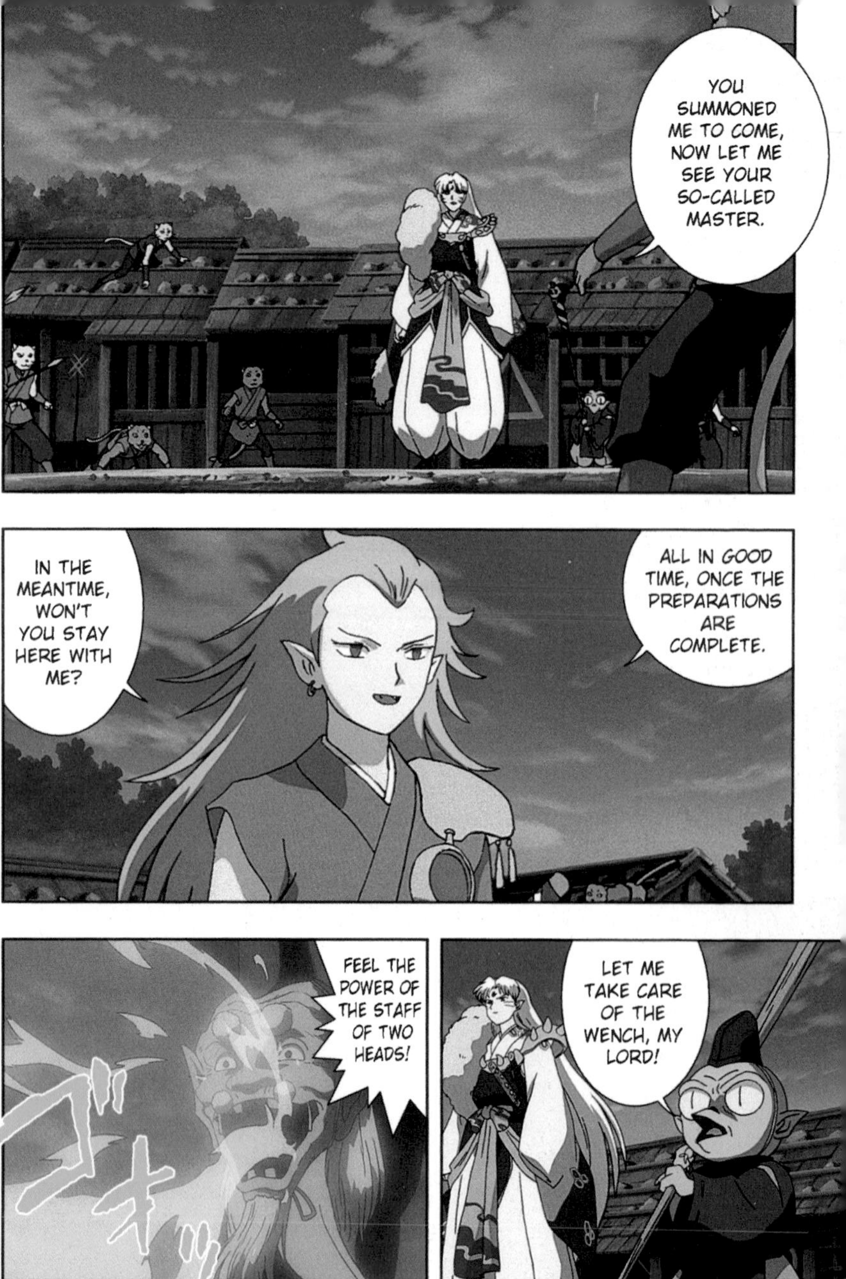
YOU SUMMONED ME TO COME, NOW LET ME SEE YOUR SO-CALLED MASTER.
ALL IN GOOD TIME, ONCE THE PREPARATIONS ARE COMPLETE.
IN THE MEANTIME, WON'T YOU STAY HERE WITH ME?
LET ME TAKE CARE OF THE WENCH, MY LORD!
FEEL THE POWER OF THE STAFF OF TWO HEADS!

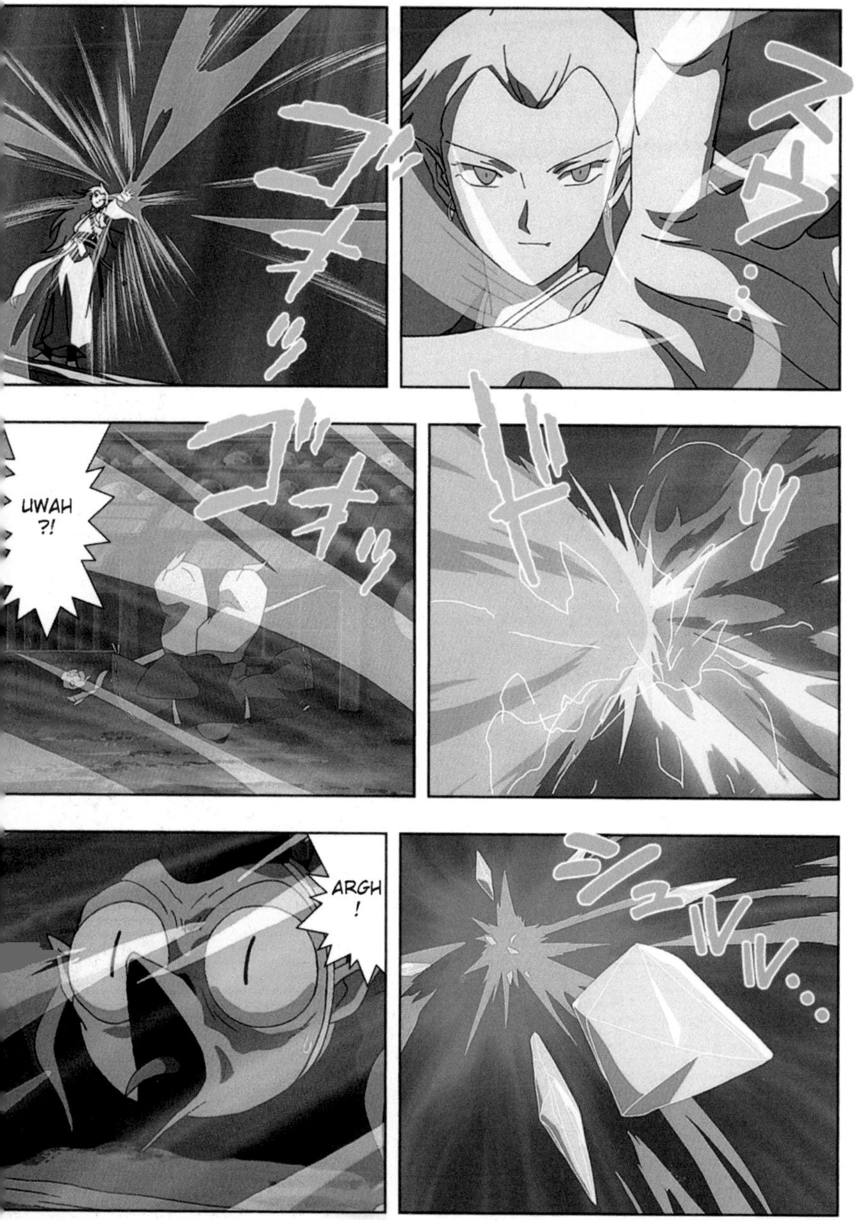
スゥ…
ドッ
ゴキッ
UWAH ?!
シュルル…
ARGH !

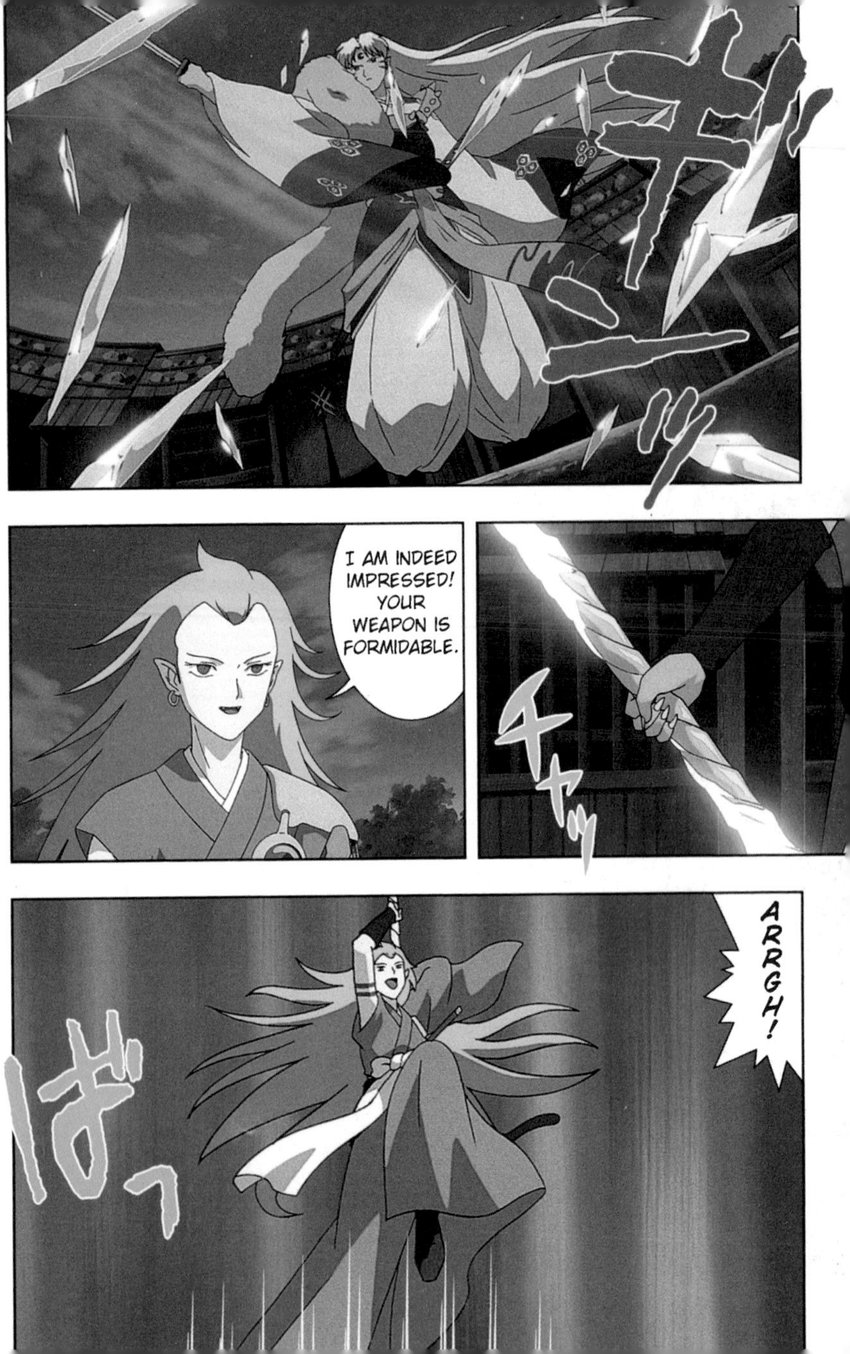
チャッ
I AM INDEED IMPRESSED! YOUR WEAPON IS FORMIDABLE.
ARRGH!
ばっ

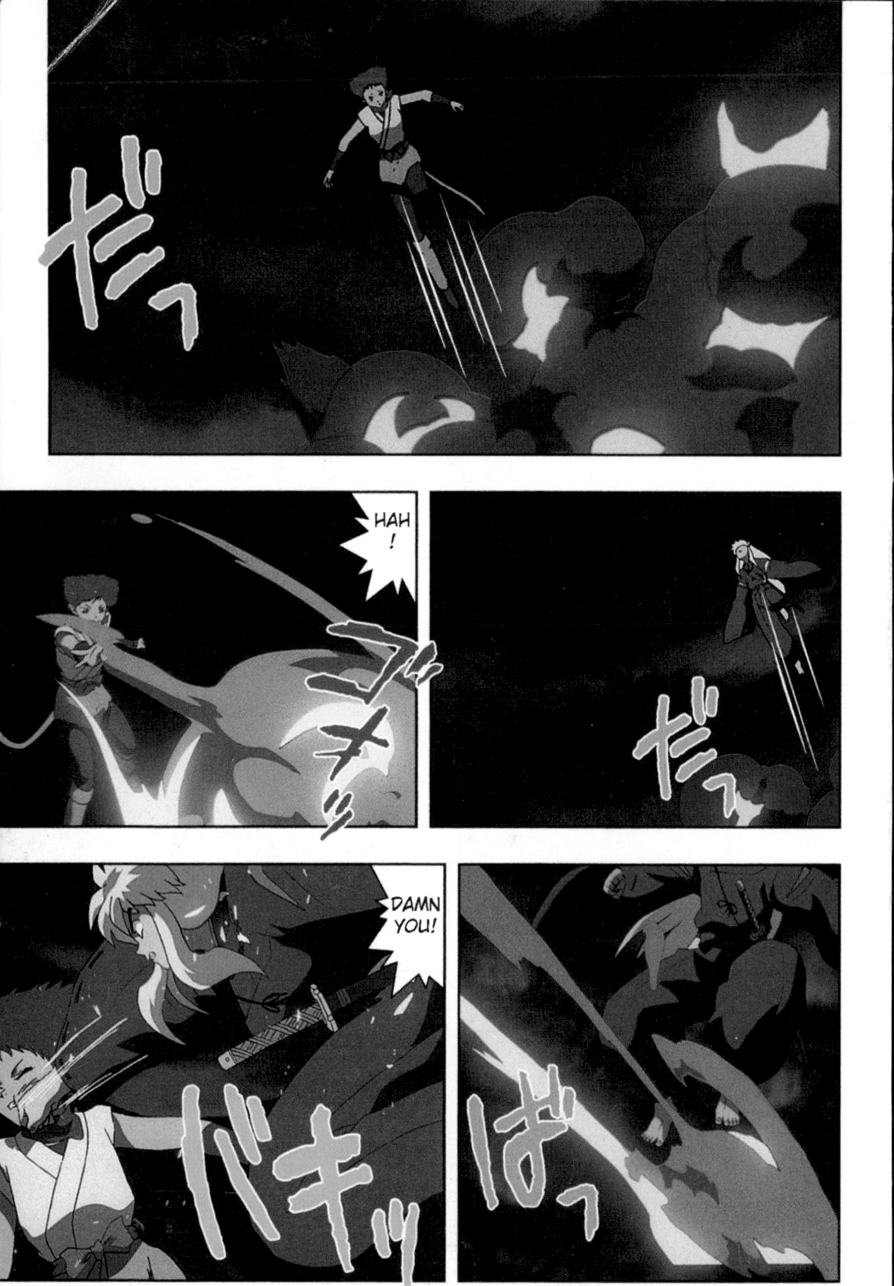
だっ
だっ
HAH!
ぱっ
DAMN YOU!
バキッ

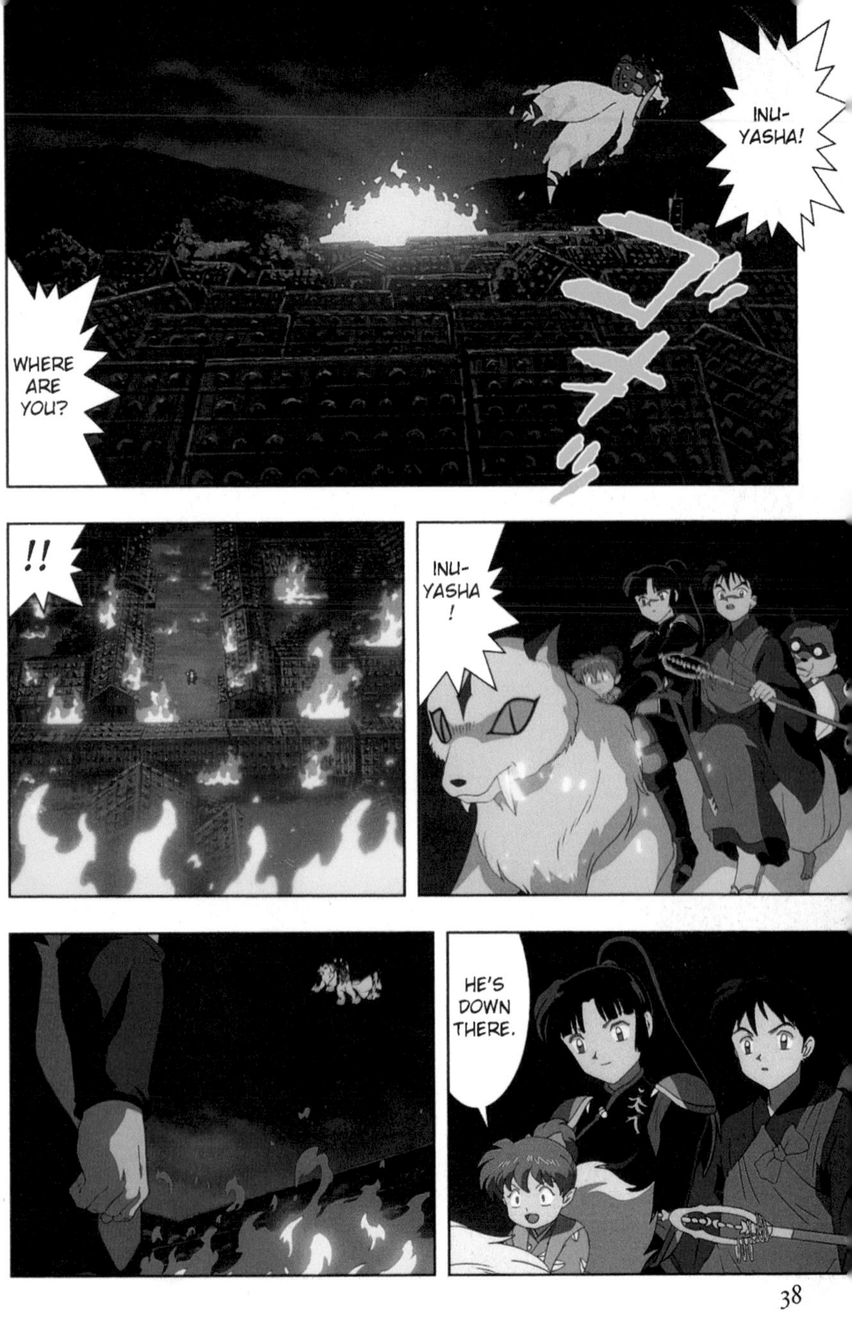
INU-YASHA!
WHERE ARE YOU?
INU-YASHA!
!!
HE'S DOWN THERE.

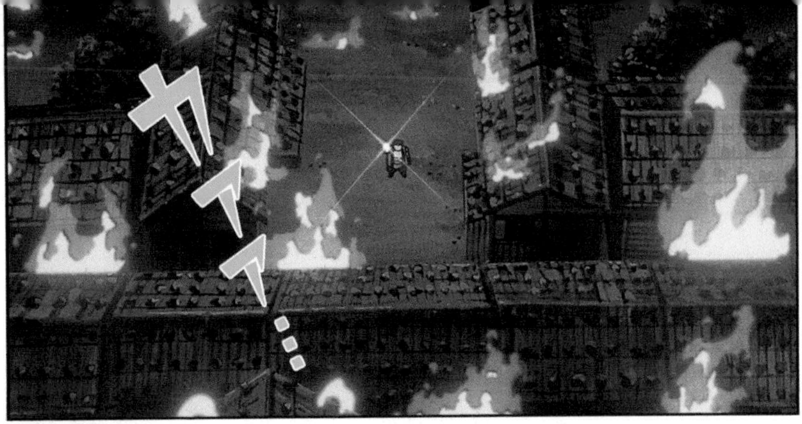
カァァ…

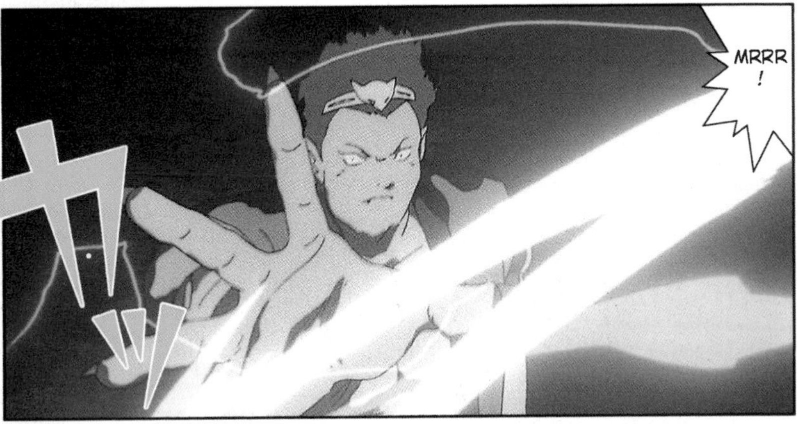
MRRR!
カッ

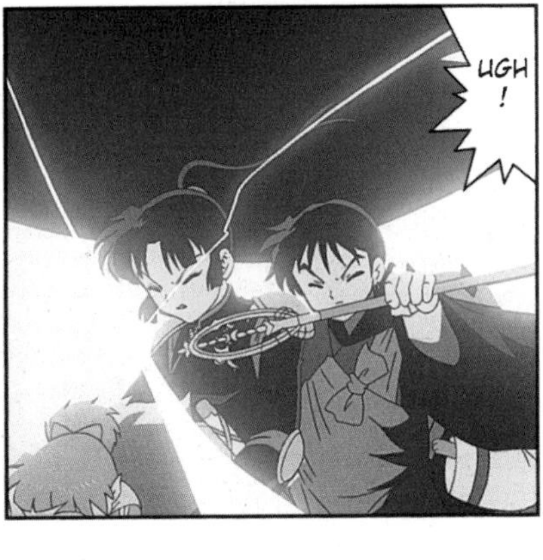
UGH!

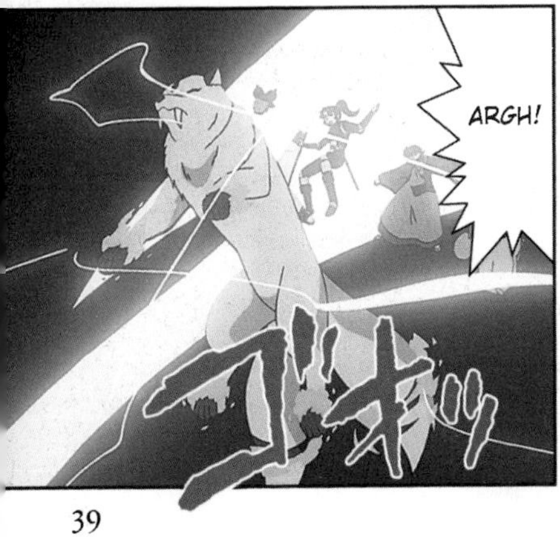
ARGH!
ゴオッ

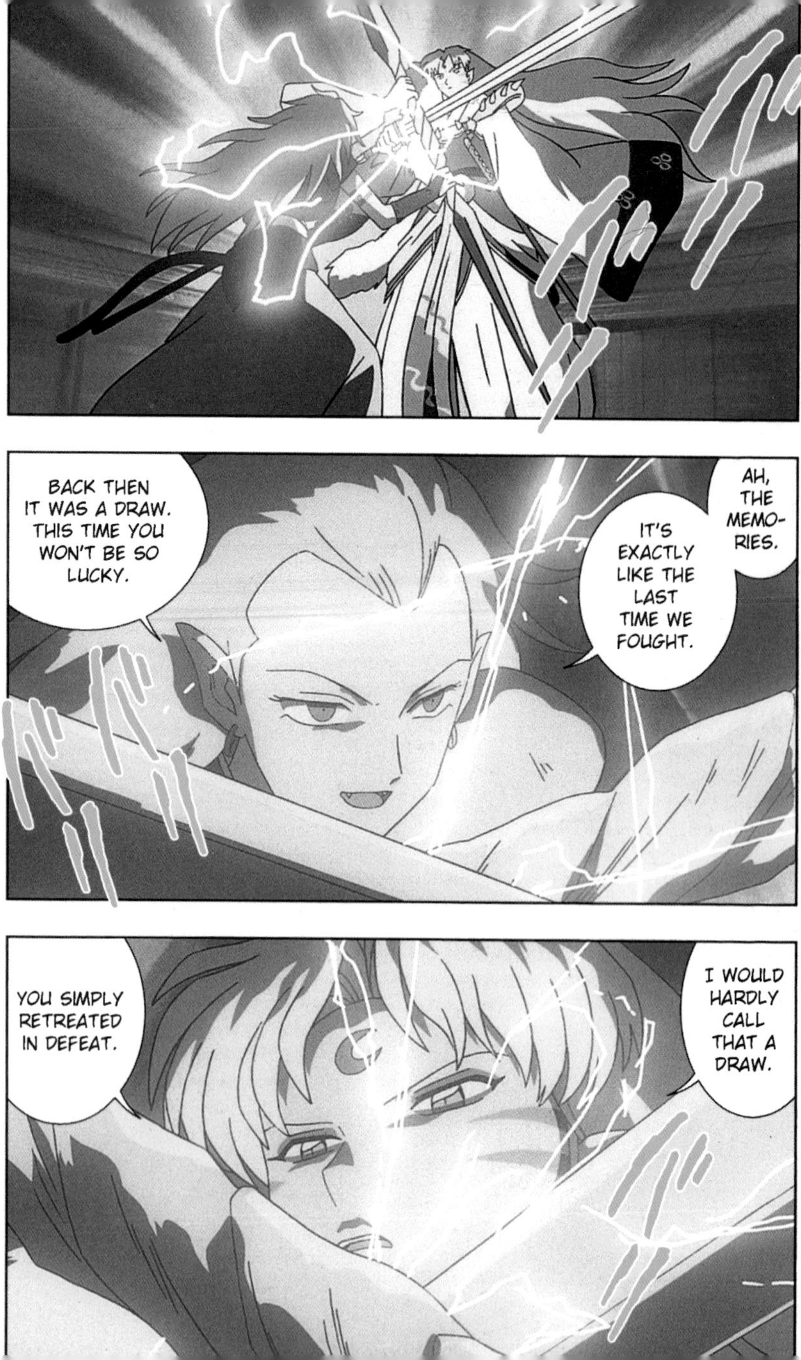
AH, THE MEMORIES.
IT'S EXACTLY LIKE THE LAST TIME WE FOUGHT.
BACK THEN IT WAS A DRAW. THIS TIME YOU WON'T BE SO LUCKY.
I WOULD HARDLY CALL THAT A DRAW.
YOU SIMPLY RETREATED IN DEFEAT.

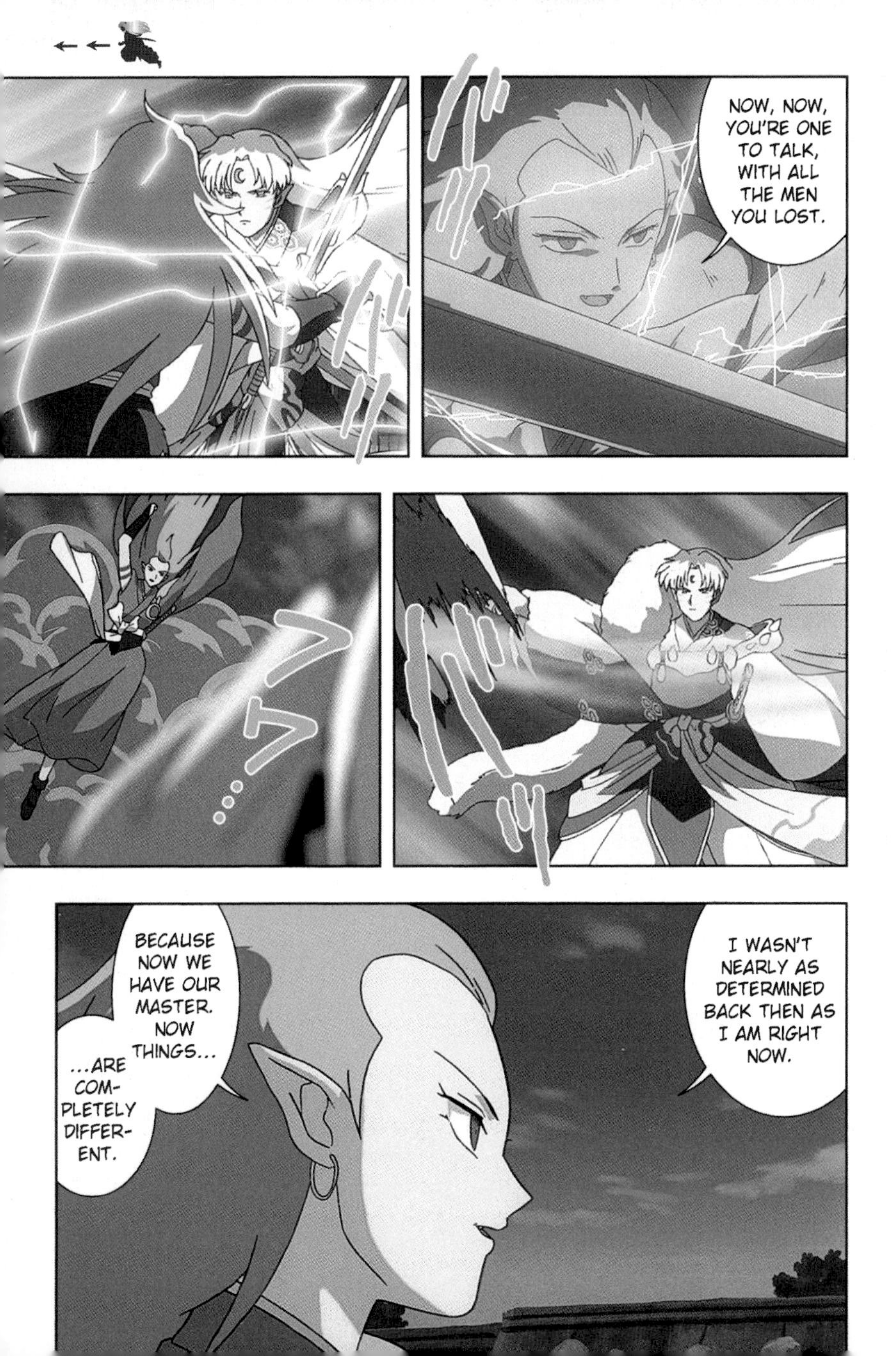
NOW, NOW, YOU'RE ONE TO TALK, WITH ALL THE MEN YOU LOST.
I WASN'T NEARLY AS DETERMINED BACK THEN AS I AM RIGHT NOW.
BECAUSE NOW WE HAVE OUR MASTER. NOW THINGS...
...ARE COM-PLETELY DIFFER-ENT.

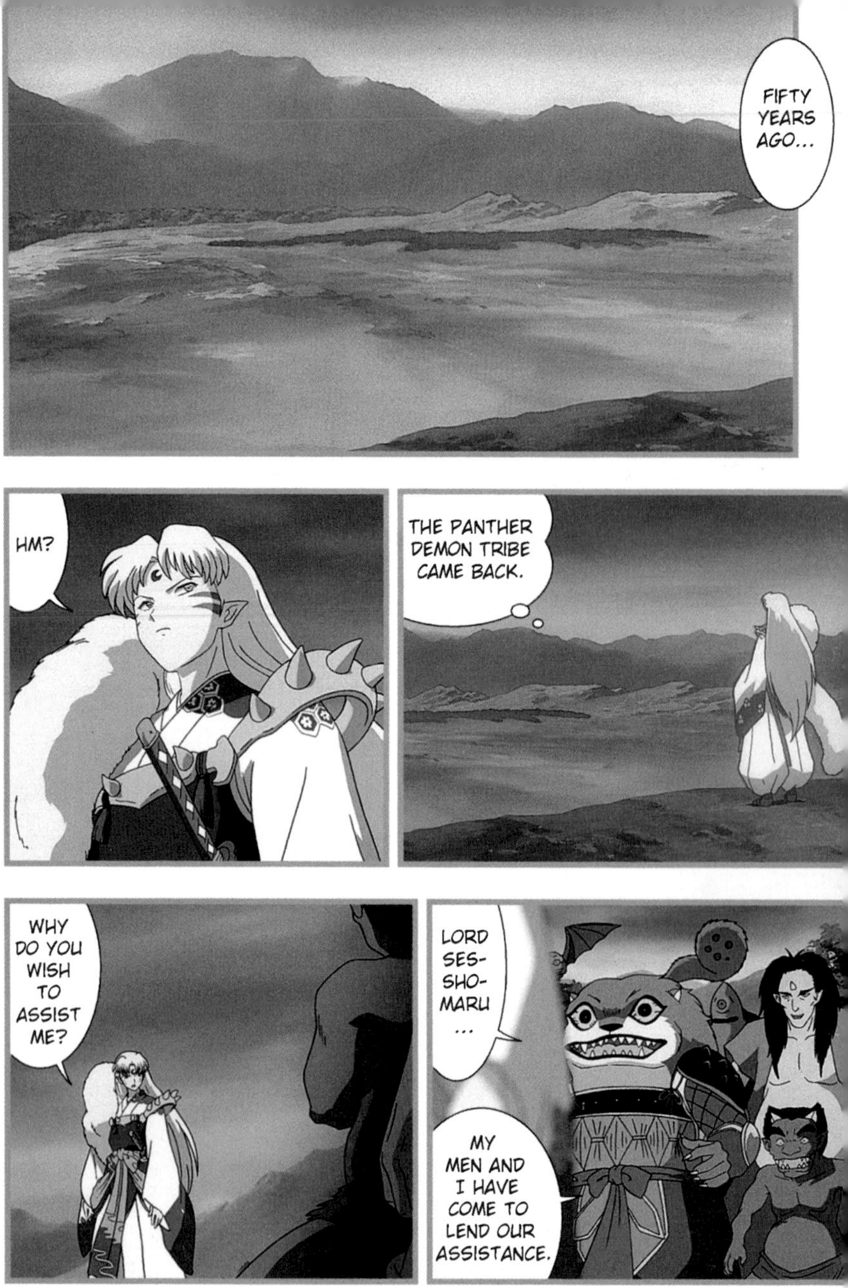
FIFTY YEARS AGO...
THE PANTHER DEMON TRIBE CAME BACK.
HM?
LORD SES-SHO-MARU...
MY MEN AND I HAVE COME TO LEND OUR ASSISTANCE.
WHY DO YOU WISH TO ASSIST ME?

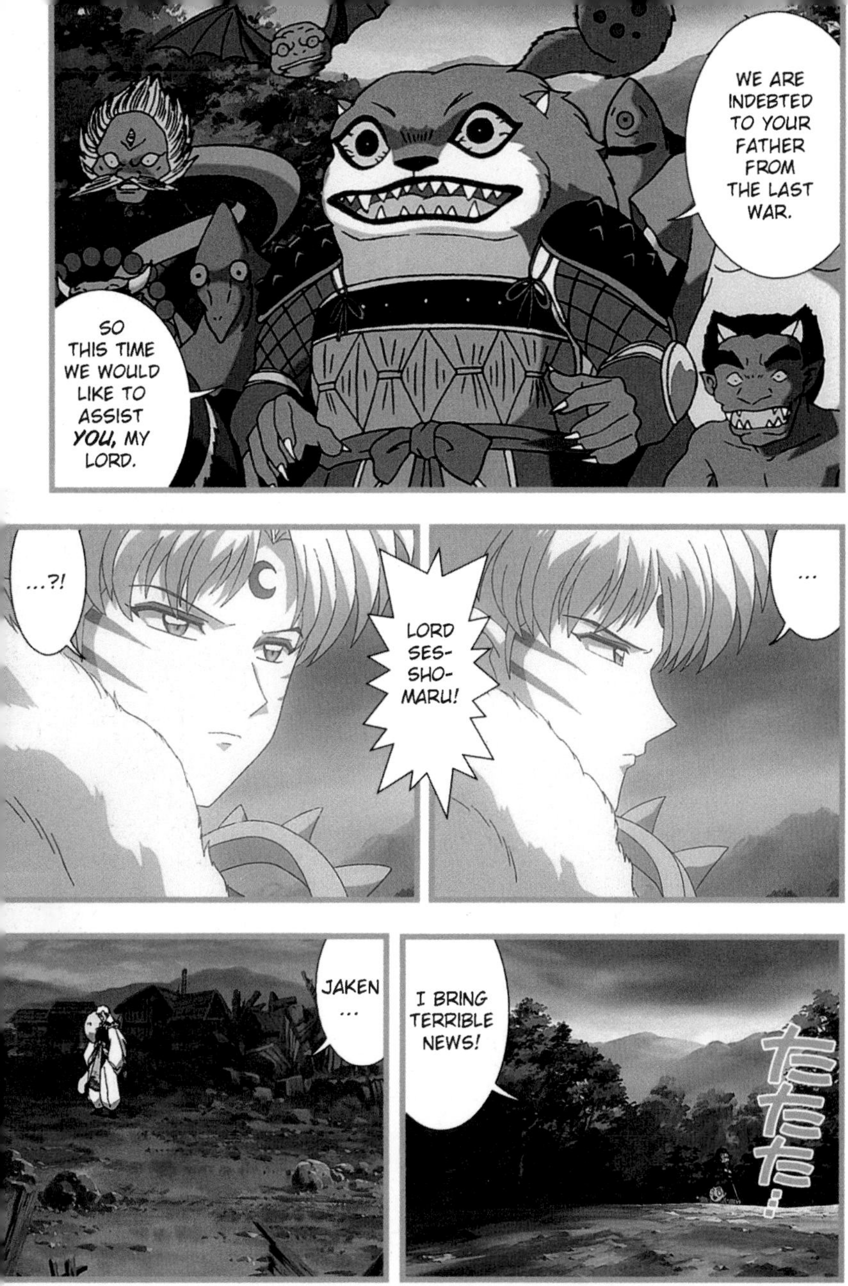
WE ARE INDEBTED TO YOUR FATHER FROM THE LAST WAR.
SO THIS TIME WE WOULD LIKE TO ASSIST *YOU,* MY LORD.
...
LORD SES-SHO-MARU!
...?!
I BRING TERRIBLE NEWS!
たたた…
JAKEN ...

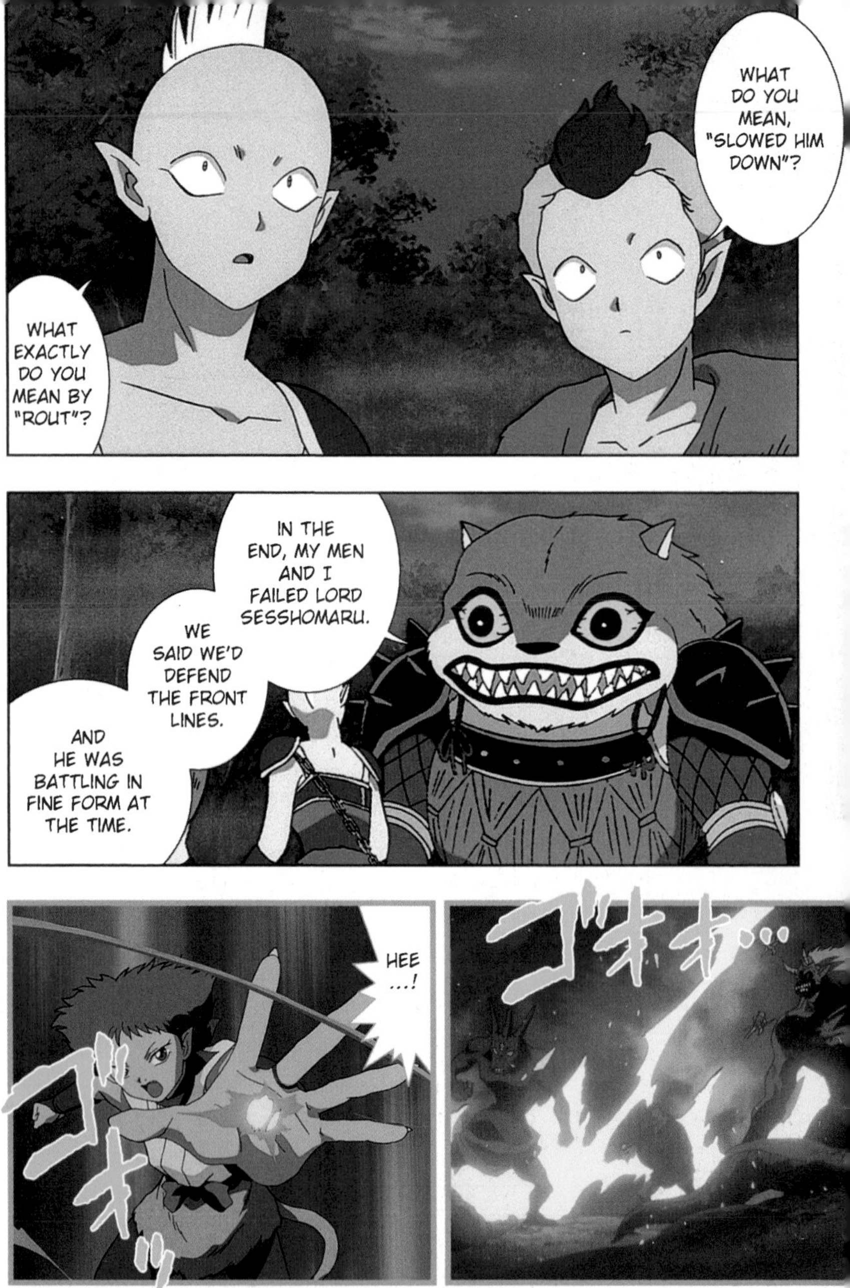
WHAT DO YOU MEAN, "SLOWED HIM DOWN"?
WHAT EXACTLY DO YOU MEAN BY "ROUT"?
IN THE END, MY MEN AND I FAILED LORD SESSHOMARU.
WE SAID WE'D DEFEND THE FRONT LINES.
AND HE WAS BATTLING IN FINE FORM AT THE TIME.
ゴオオ…
HEE ...!
ゴオッ

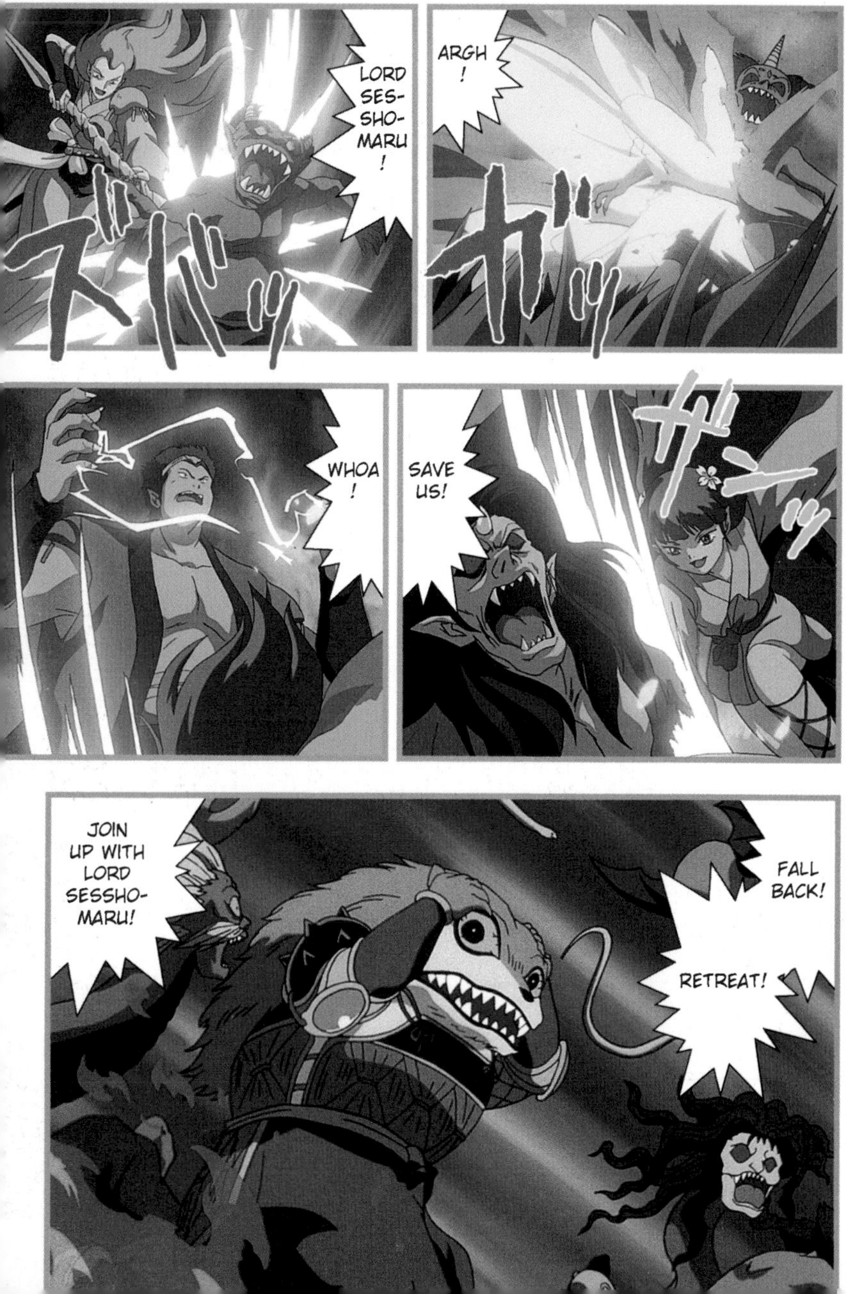
ARGH!
ガッ
LORD SESSHOMARU!
ズバッ
SAVE US!
ザンッ
WHOA!
FALL BACK!
RETREAT!
JOIN UP WITH LORD SESSHOMARU!

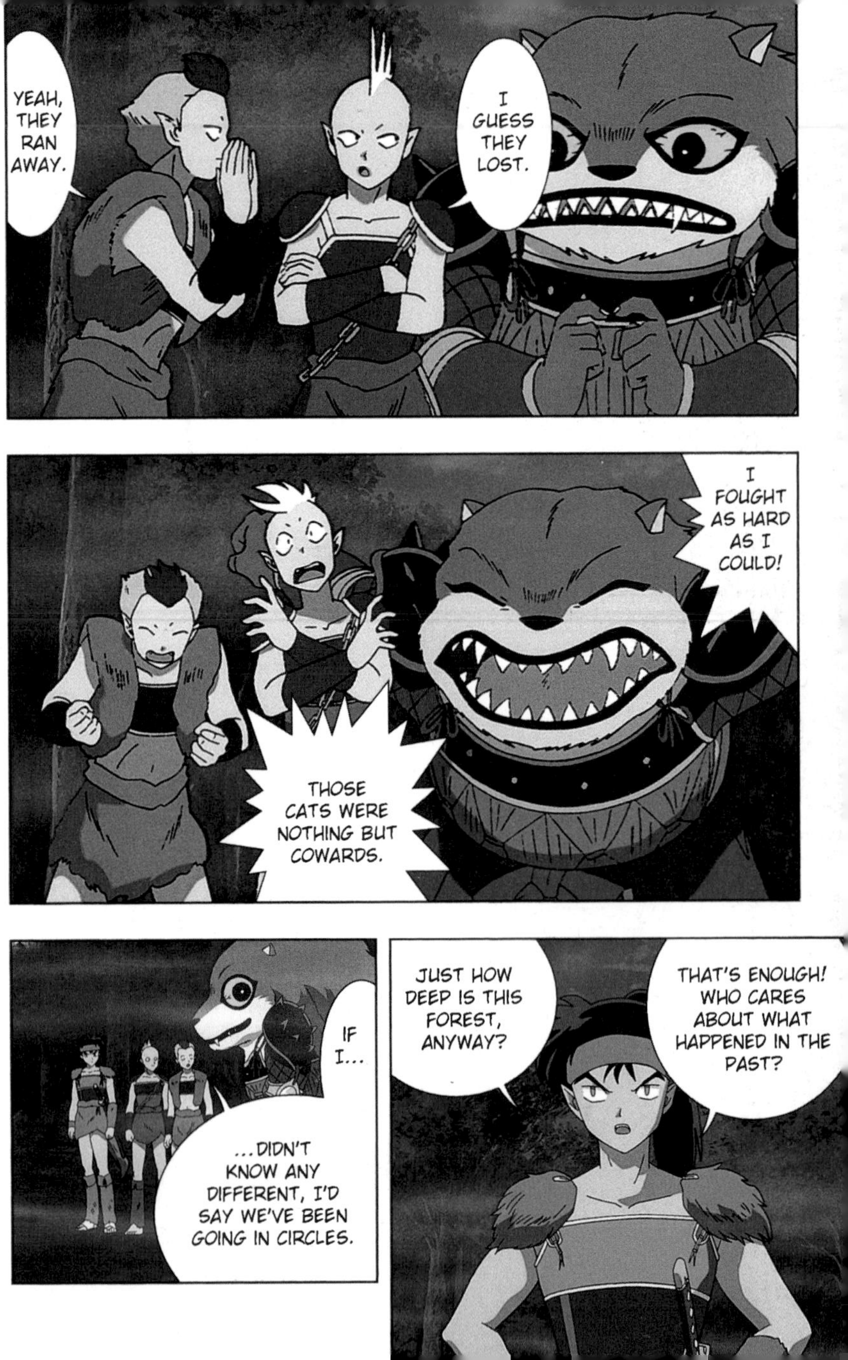
I GUESS THEY LOST.
YEAH, THEY RAN AWAY.
I FOUGHT AS HARD AS I COULD!
THOSE CATS WERE NOTHING BUT COWARDS.
THAT'S ENOUGH! WHO CARES ABOUT WHAT HAPPENED IN THE PAST?
JUST HOW DEEP IS THIS FOREST, ANYWAY?
IF I...
...DIDN'T KNOW ANY DIFFERENT, I'D SAY WE'VE BEEN GOING IN CIRCLES.

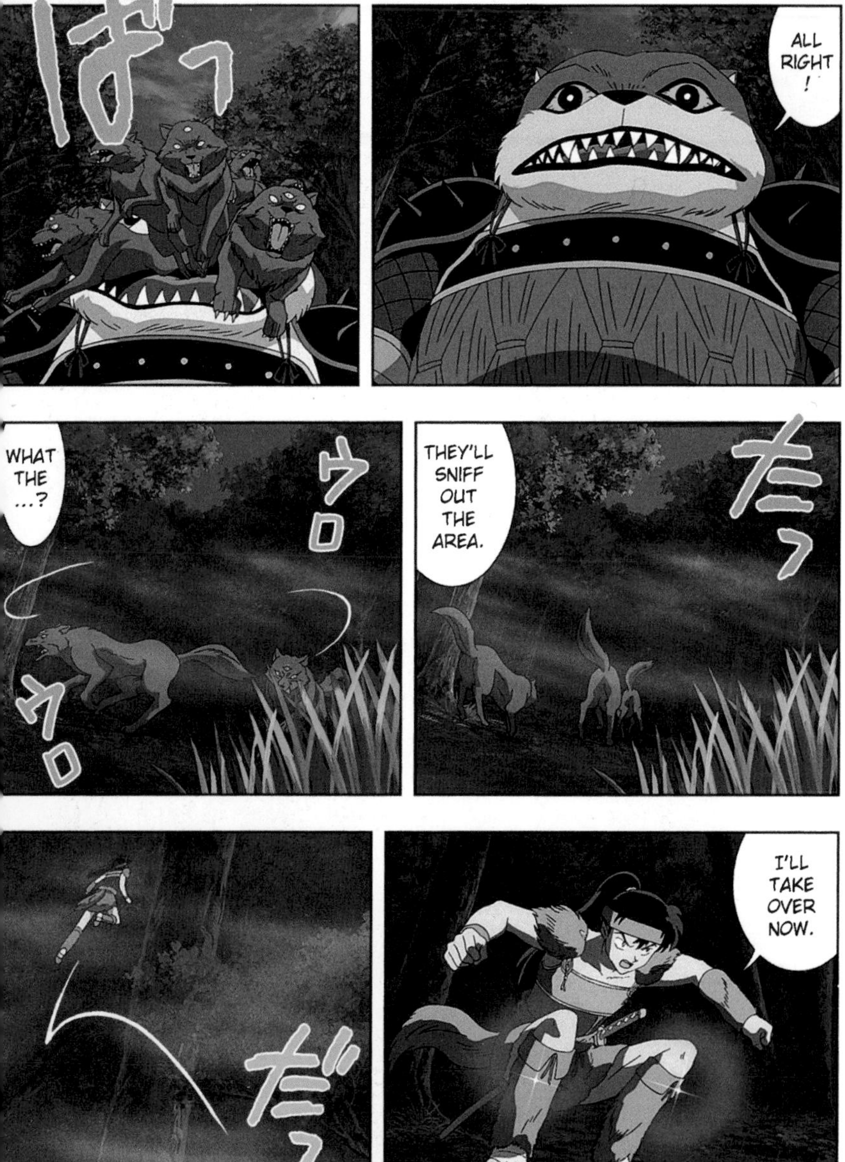
ALL RIGHT!
ばっ
THEY'LL SNIFF OUT THE AREA.
たっ
WHAT THE ...?
ウロ
ウロ
I'LL TAKE OVER NOW.
だっ

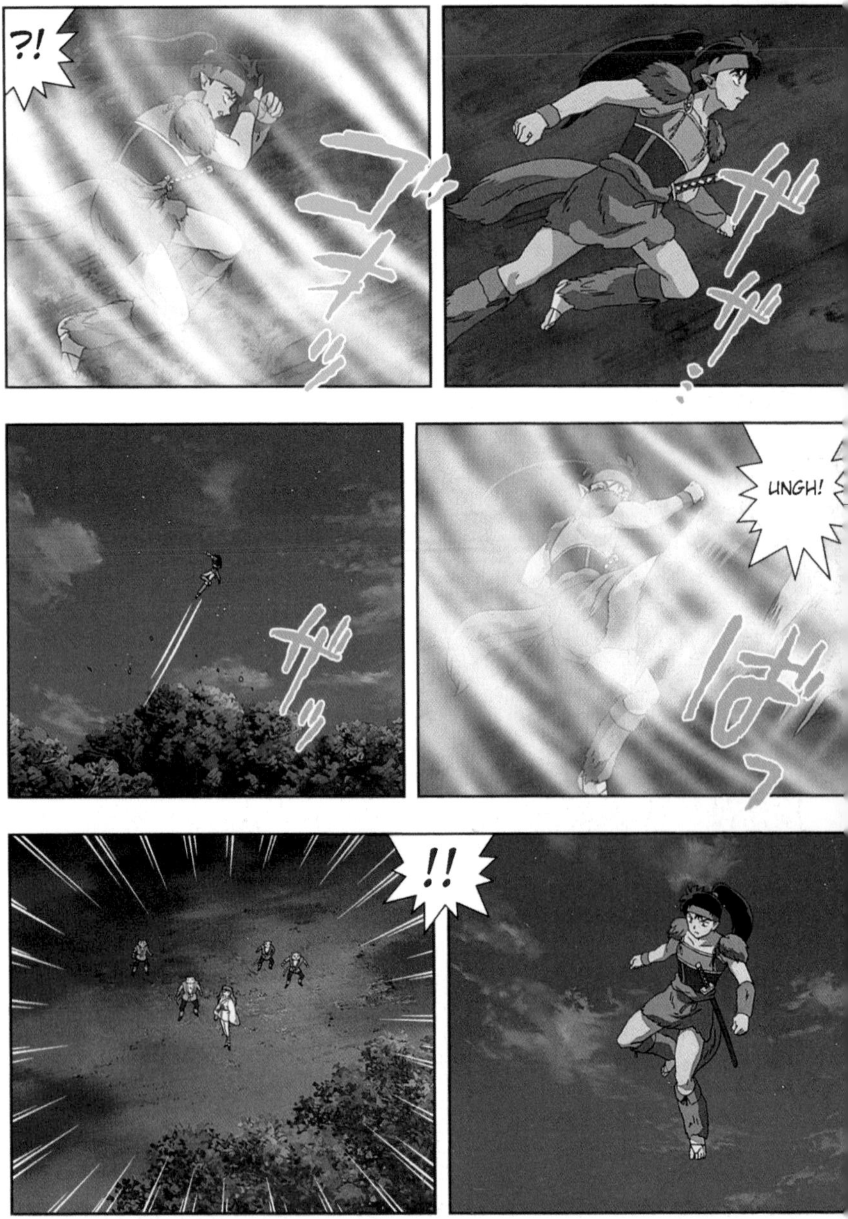
ザザ…
?!
ゴキッ
UNGH!
ばっ
ザッ
!!

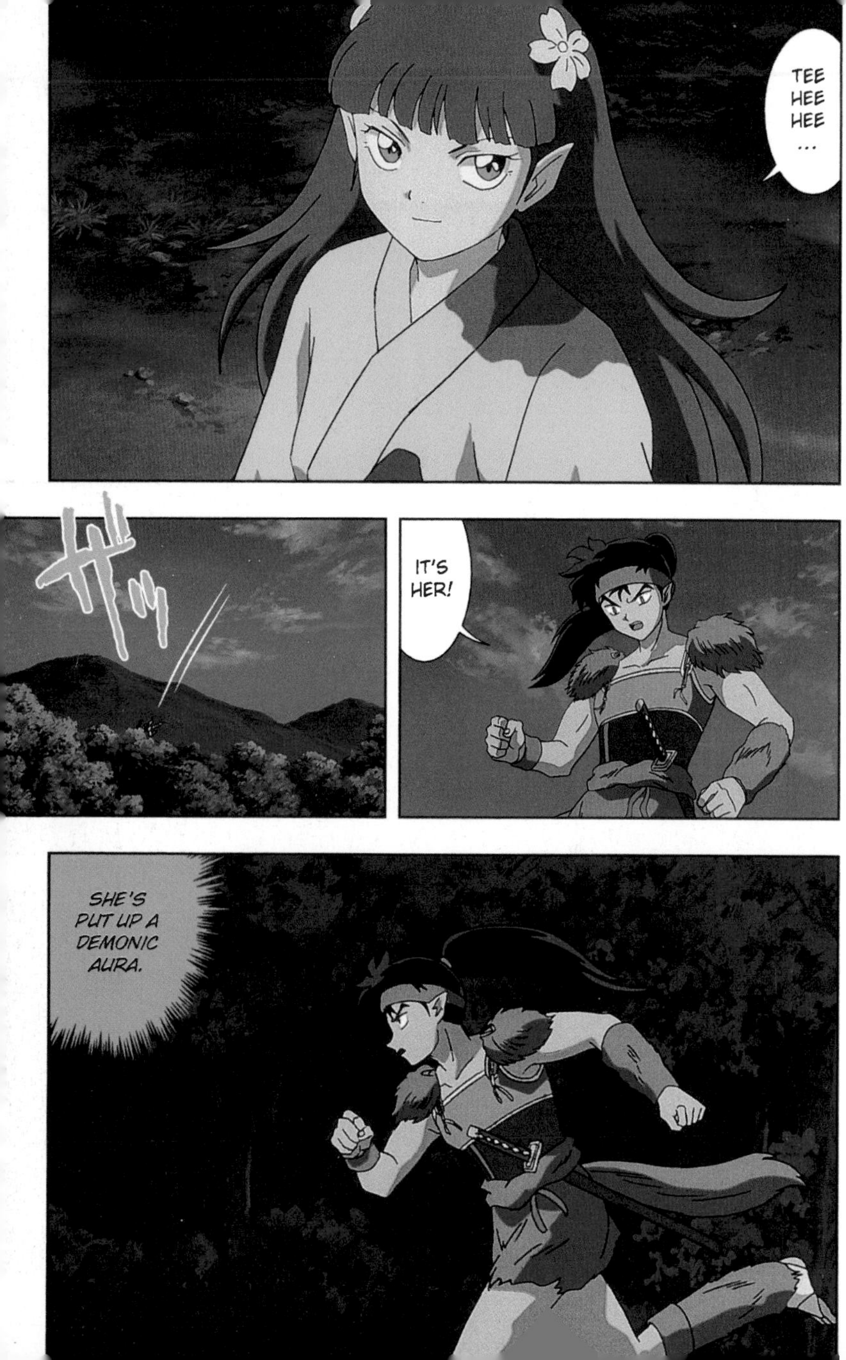
TEE HEE HEE ...
IT'S HER!
SHE'S PUT UP A DEMONIC AURA.

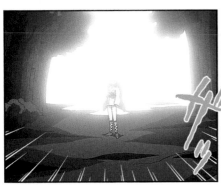

I SEE YOU HAVE A COUPLE OF JEWEL SHARDS.

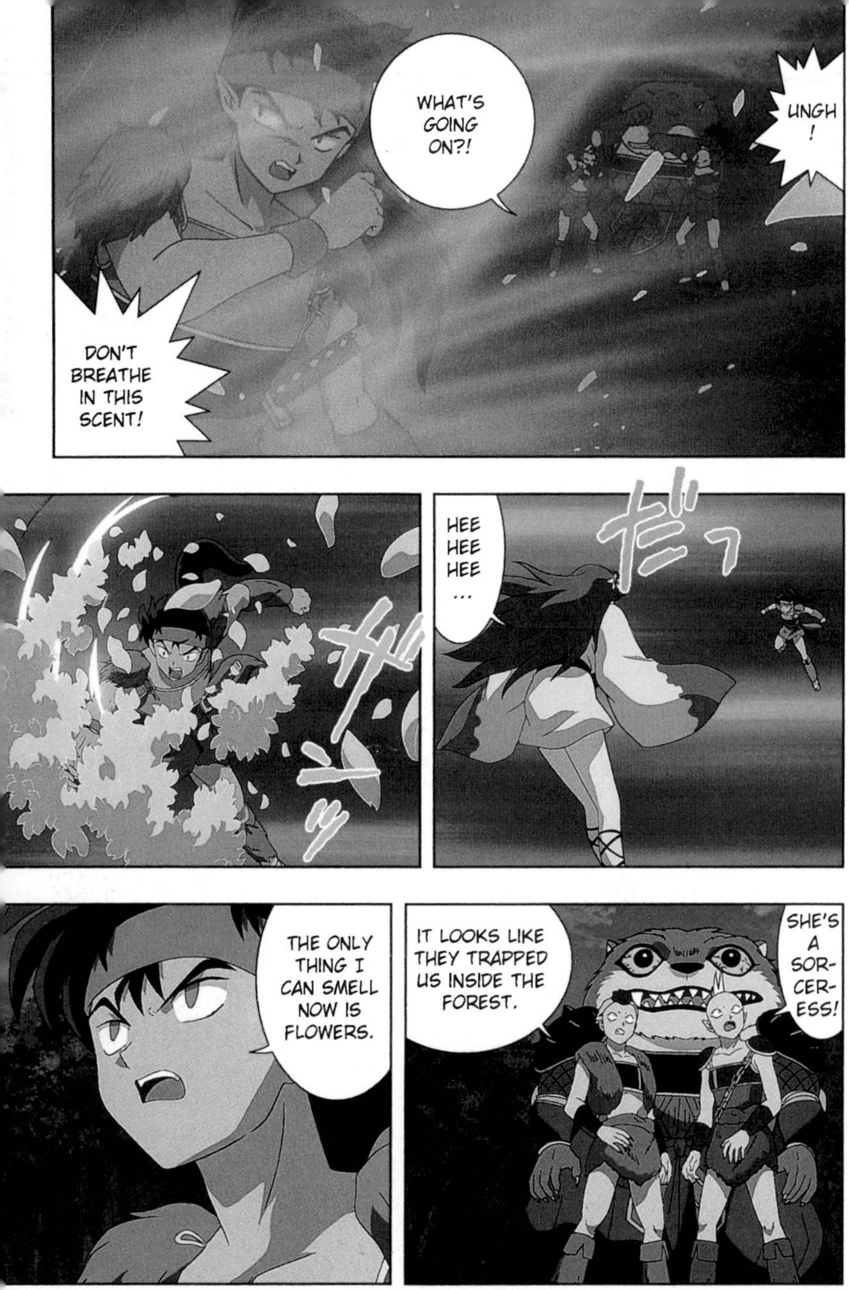
UNGH!
WHAT'S GOING ON?!
DON'T BREATHE IN THIS SCENT!
だッ
HEE HEE HEE ...
ザーッ
SHE'S A SORCERESS!
IT LOOKS LIKE THEY TRAPPED US INSIDE THE FOREST.
THE ONLY THING I CAN SMELL NOW IS FLOWERS.

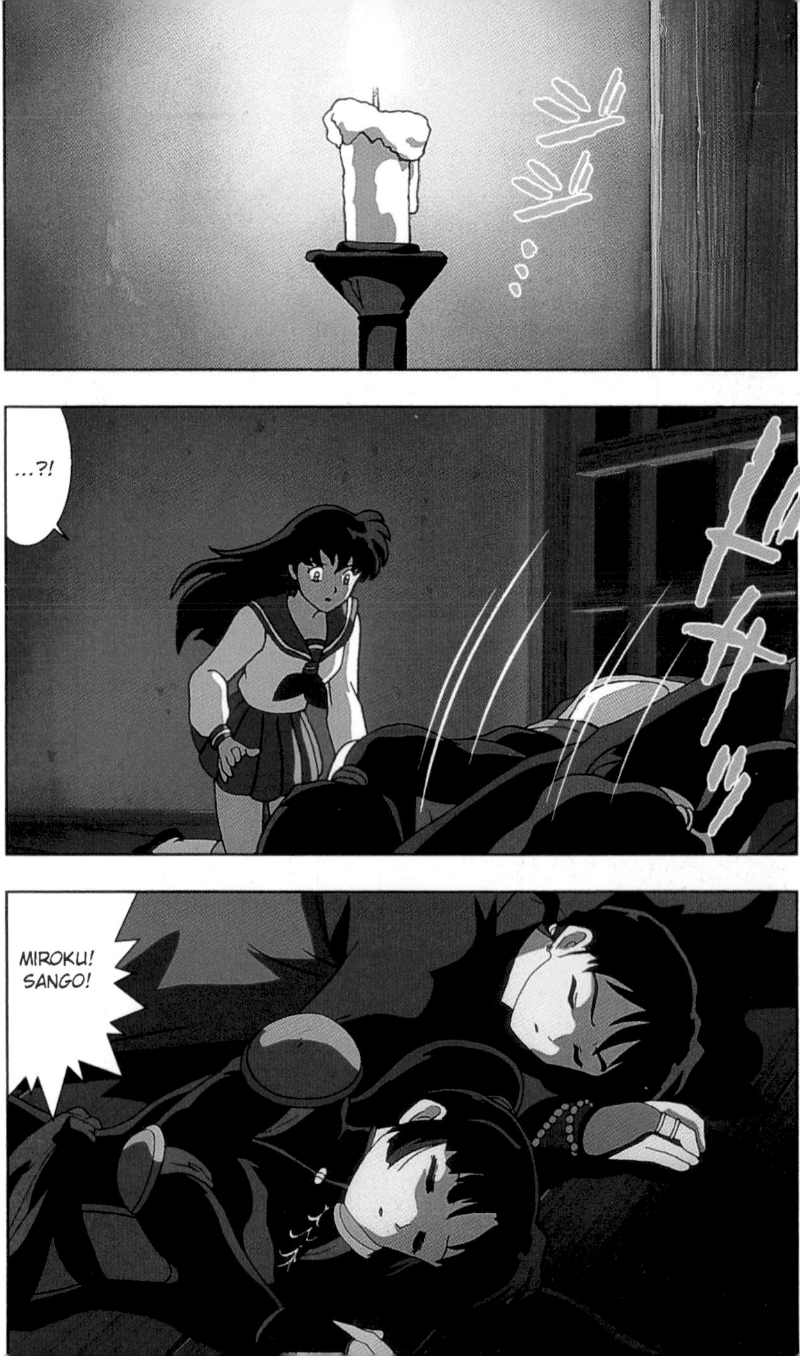
...?!
MIROKU! SANGO!

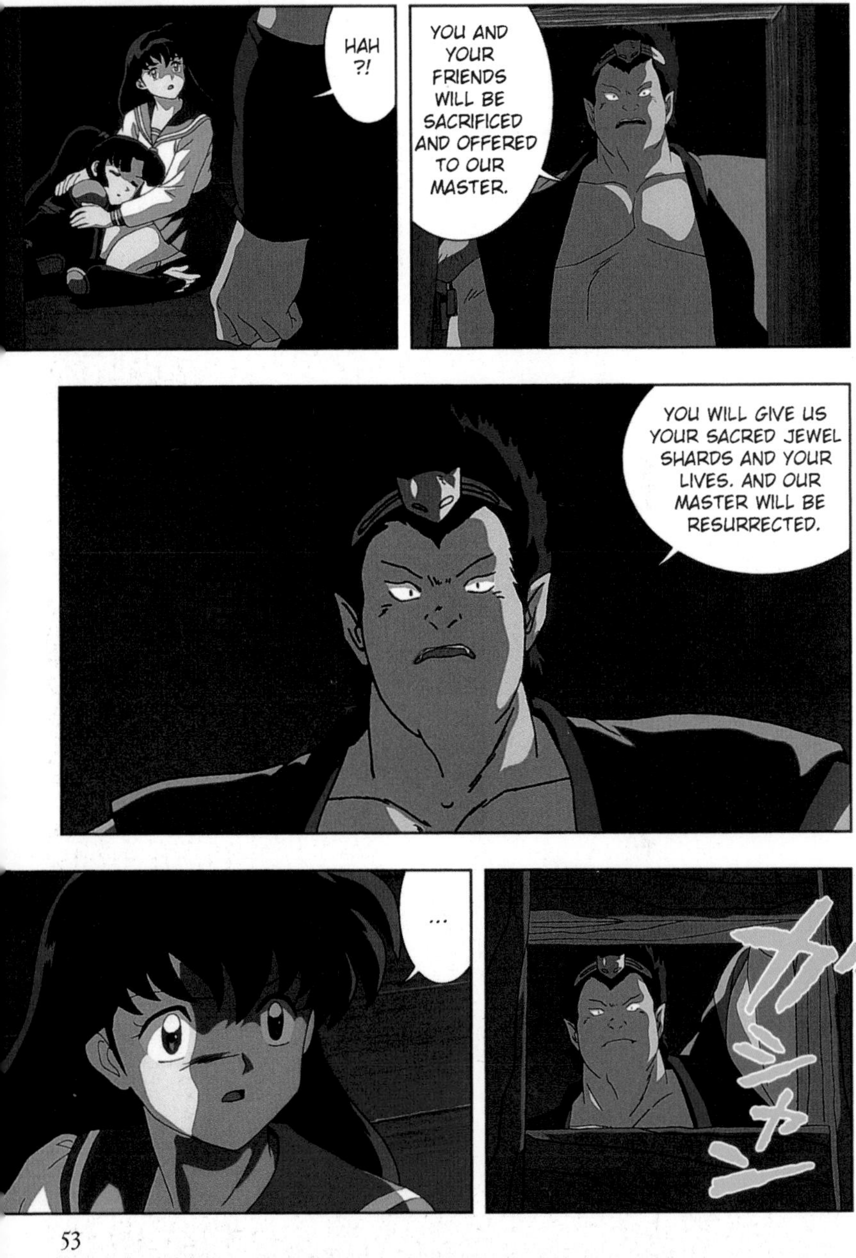
YOU AND YOUR FRIENDS WILL BE SACRIFICED AND OFFERED TO OUR MASTER.
HAH ?!
YOU WILL GIVE US YOUR SACRED JEWEL SHARDS AND YOUR LIVES. AND OUR MASTER WILL BE RESURRECTED.
ガシャン
...

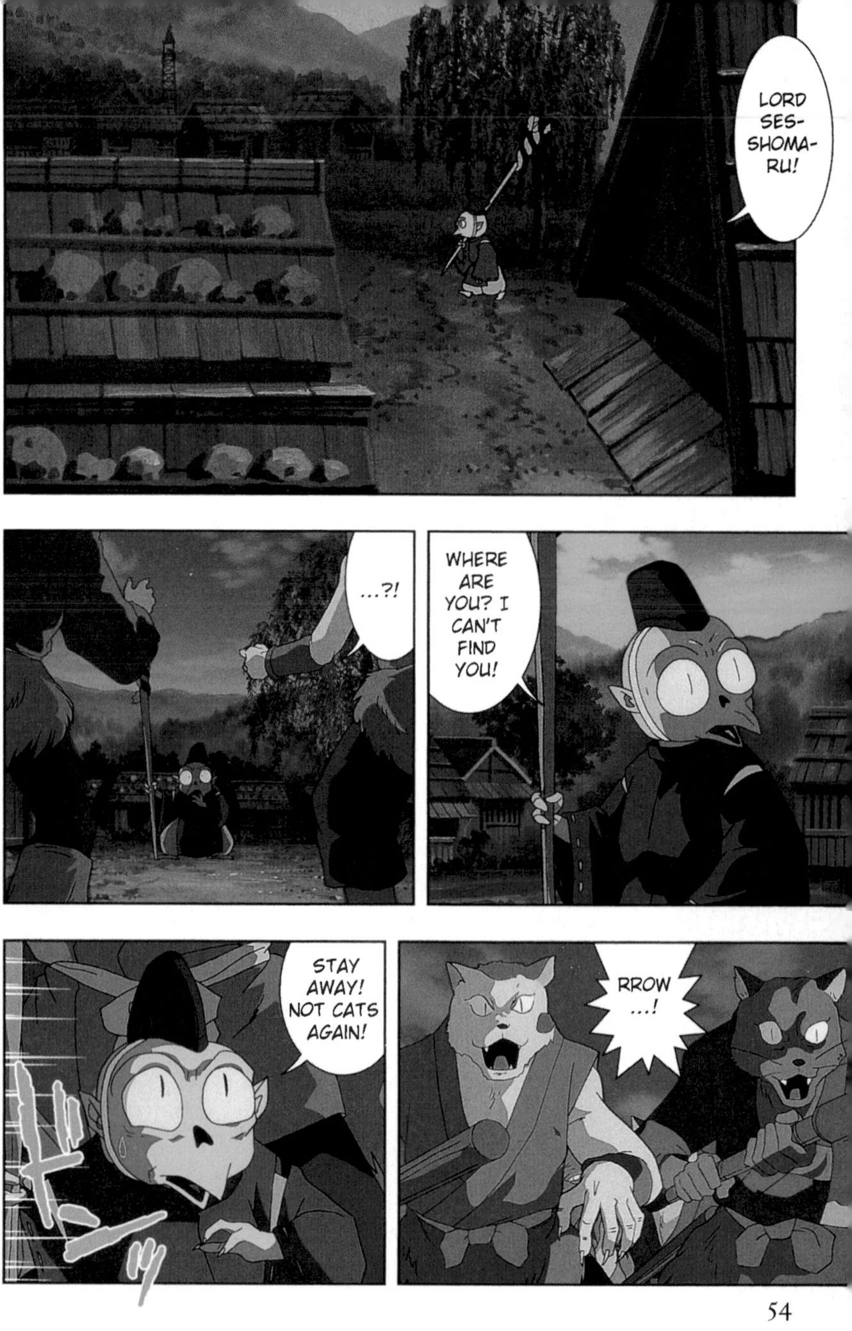
LORD SES-SHOMA-RU!
WHERE ARE YOU? I CAN'T FIND YOU!
...?!
RROW ...!
STAY AWAY! NOT CATS AGAIN!

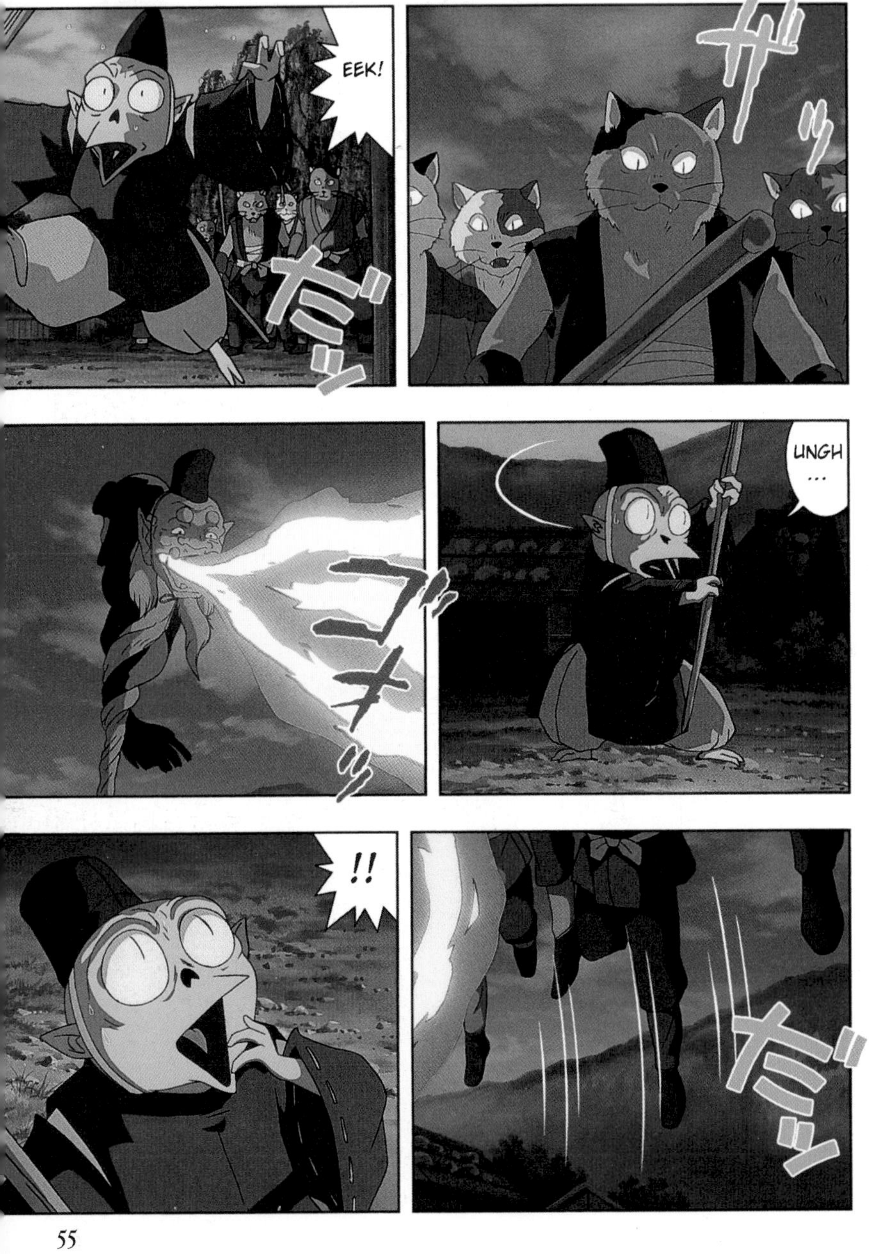
ザッ
EEK!
ダッ
UNGH ...
ゴオッ
ダッ
!!

IRON REAVER SOUL STEALER!

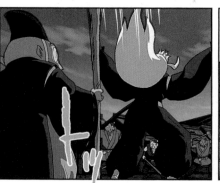

AH WAH WAH...

56

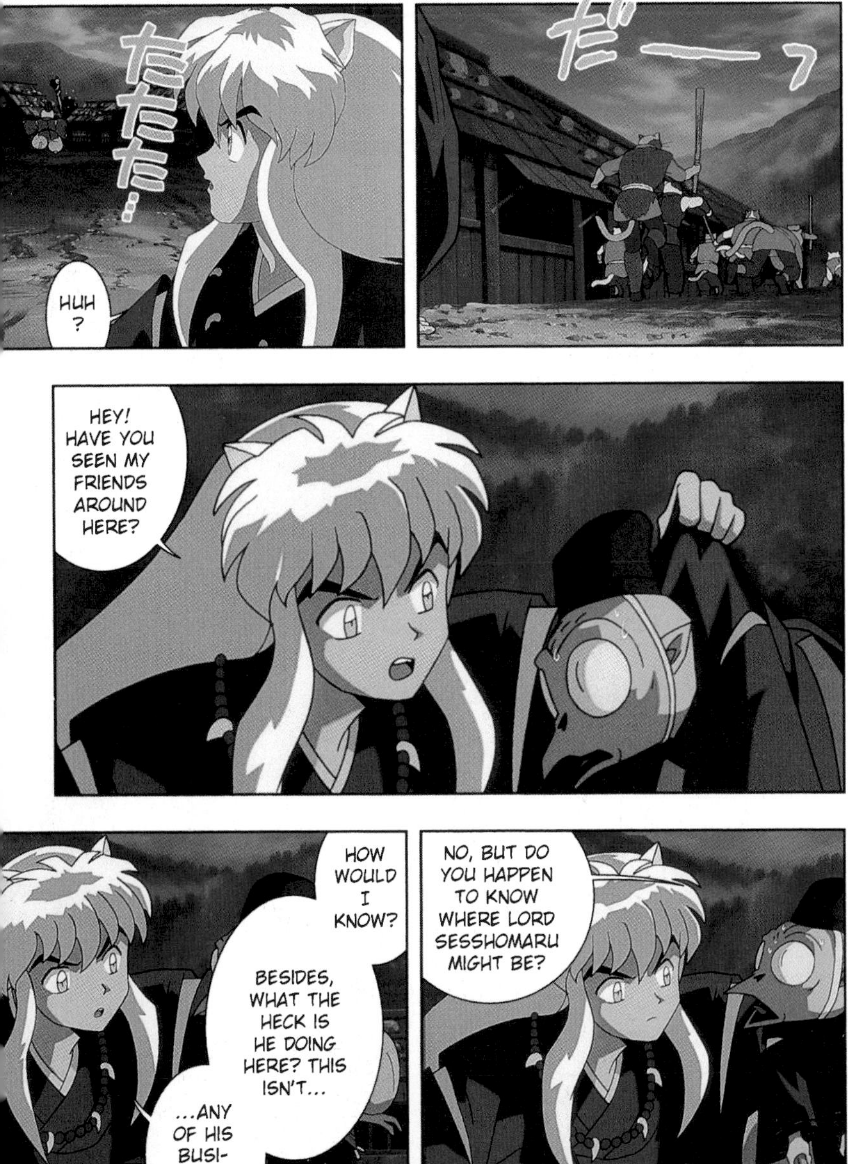
だーーっ
たたた…
HUH?
HEY! HAVE YOU SEEN MY FRIENDS AROUND HERE?
NO, BUT DO YOU HAPPEN TO KNOW WHERE LORD SESSHOMARU MIGHT BE?
HOW WOULD I KNOW?
BESIDES, WHAT THE HECK IS HE DOING HERE? THIS ISN'T...
...ANY OF HIS BUSI-NESS.

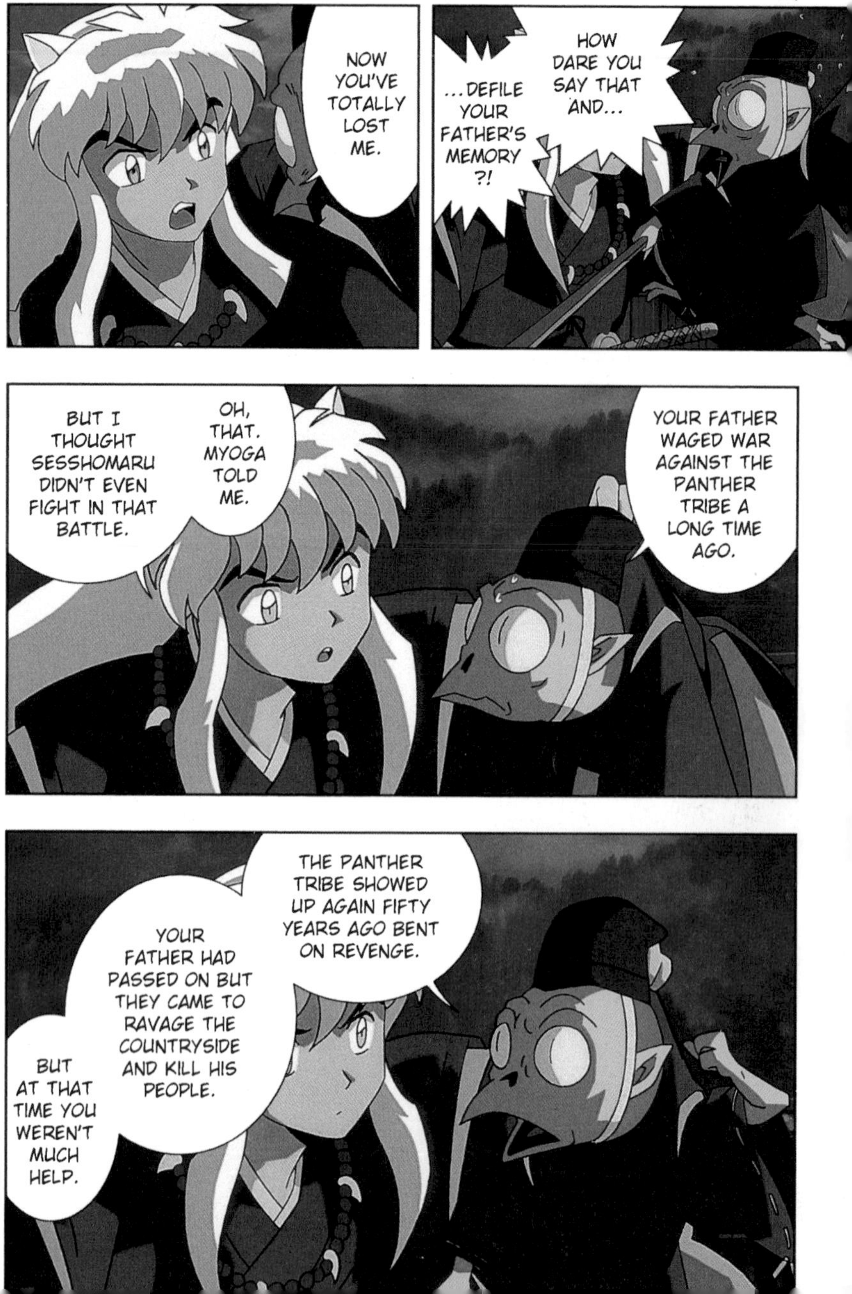
HOW DARE YOU SAY THAT AND...
...DEFILE YOUR FATHER'S MEMORY ?!
NOW YOU'VE TOTALLY LOST ME.
YOUR FATHER WAGED WAR AGAINST THE PANTHER TRIBE A LONG TIME AGO.
OH, THAT. MYOGA TOLD ME.
BUT I THOUGHT SESSHOMARU DIDN'T EVEN FIGHT IN THAT BATTLE.
THE PANTHER TRIBE SHOWED UP AGAIN FIFTY YEARS AGO BENT ON REVENGE.
YOUR FATHER HAD PASSED ON BUT THEY CAME TO RAVAGE THE COUNTRYSIDE AND KILL HIS PEOPLE.
BUT AT THAT TIME YOU WEREN'T MUCH HELP.

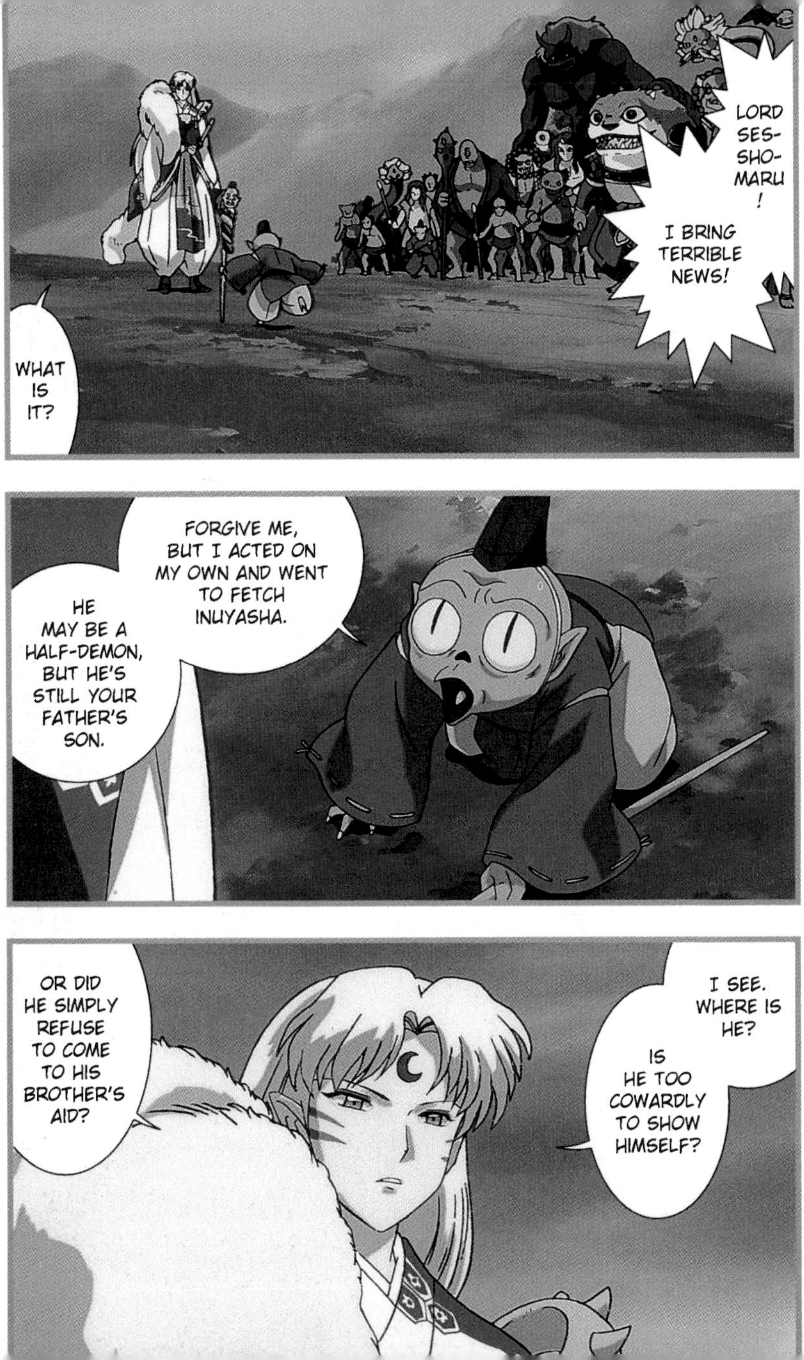
LORD SESSHOMARU!
I BRING TERRIBLE NEWS!
WHAT IS IT?
FORGIVE ME, BUT I ACTED ON MY OWN AND WENT TO FETCH INUYASHA.
HE MAY BE A HALF-DEMON, BUT HE'S STILL YOUR FATHER'S SON.
I SEE. WHERE IS HE?
IS HE TOO COWARDLY TO SHOW HIMSELF?
OR DID HE SIMPLY REFUSE TO COME TO HIS BROTHER'S AID?

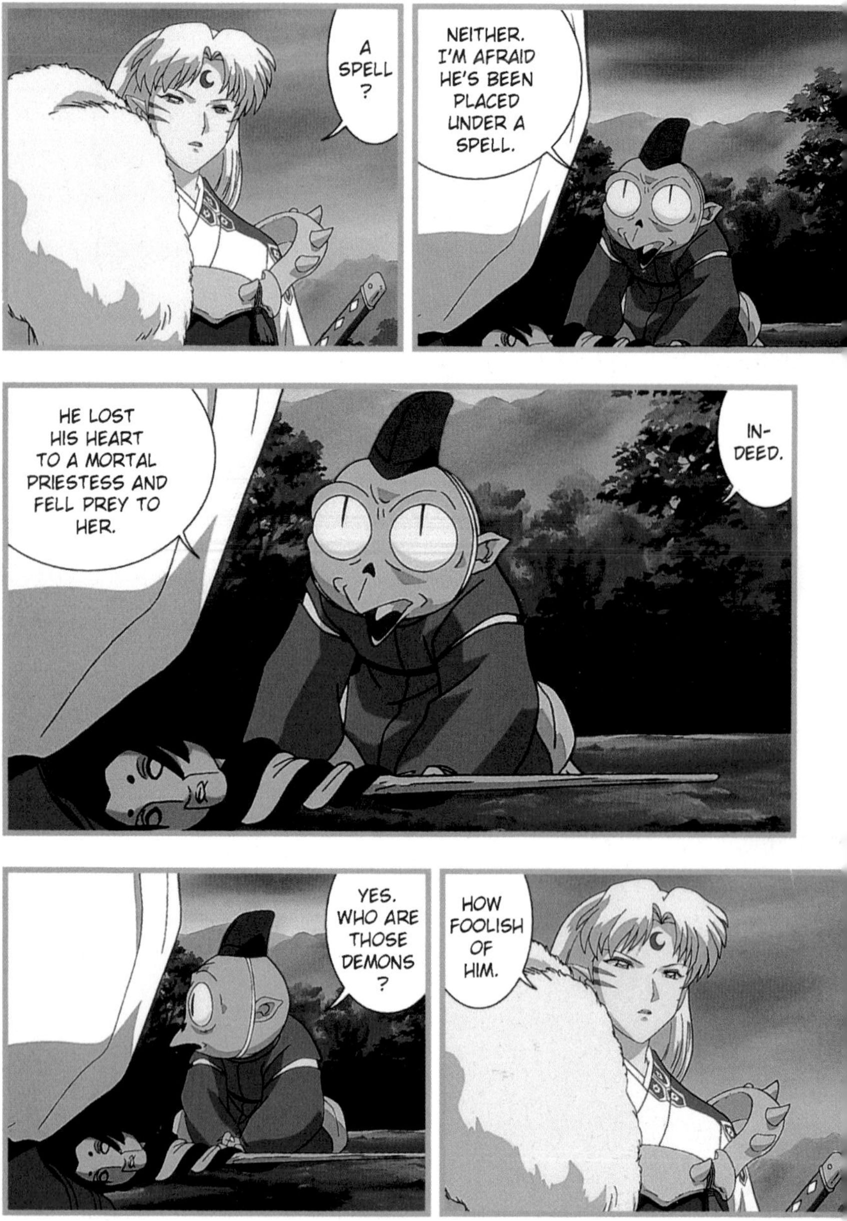
NEITHER. I'M AFRAID HE'S BEEN PLACED UNDER A SPELL.
A SPELL?
IN-DEED.
HE LOST HIS HEART TO A MORTAL PRIESTESS AND FELL PREY TO HER.
HOW FOOLISH OF HIM.
YES. WHO ARE THOSE DEMONS?

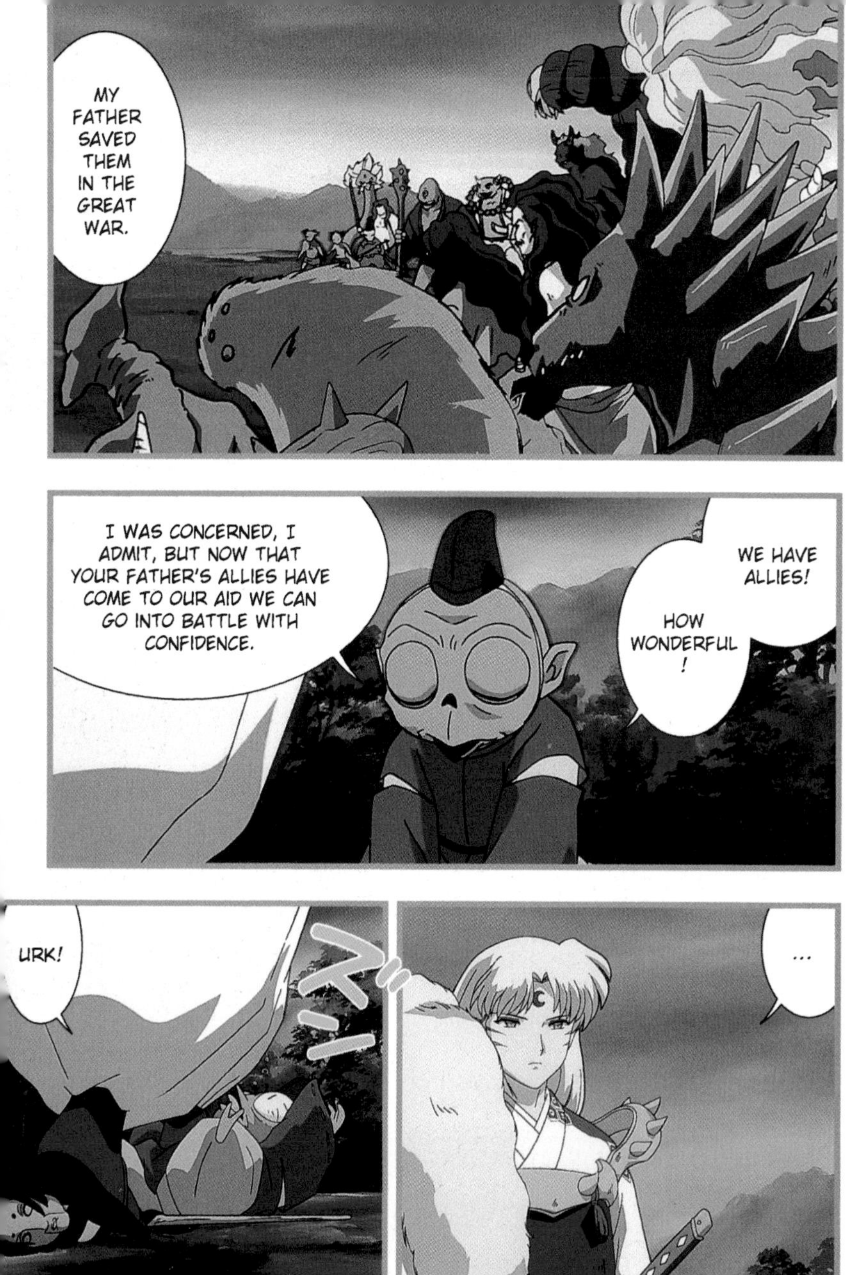
MY FATHER SAVED THEM IN THE GREAT WAR.
WE HAVE ALLIES!
HOW WONDERFUL!
I WAS CONCERNED, I ADMIT, BUT NOW THAT YOUR FATHER'S ALLIES HAVE COME TO OUR AID WE CAN GO INTO BATTLE WITH CONFIDENCE.
...
URK!

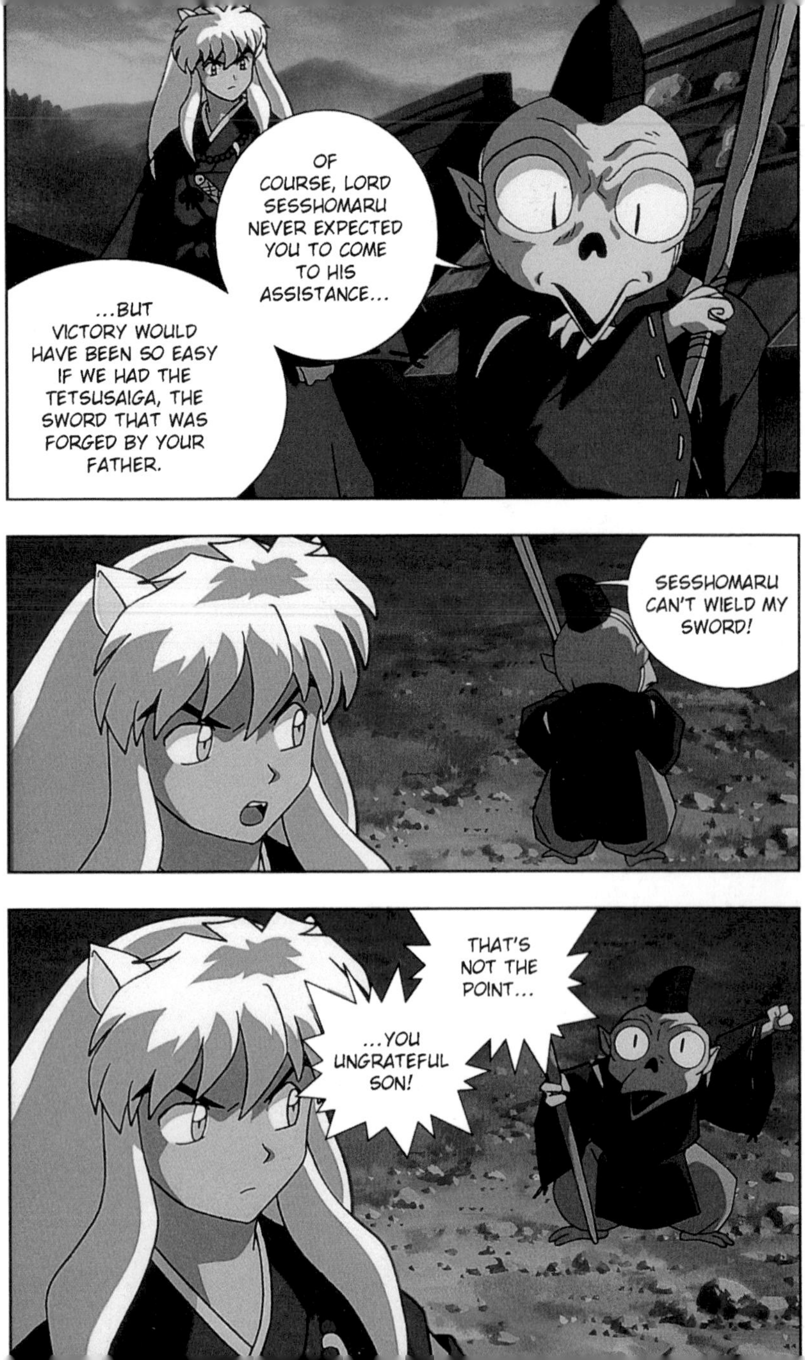
OF COURSE, LORD SESSHOMARU NEVER EXPECTED YOU TO COME TO HIS ASSISTANCE...
...BUT VICTORY WOULD HAVE BEEN SO EASY IF WE HAD THE TETSUSAIGA, THE SWORD THAT WAS FORGED BY YOUR FATHER.
SESSHOMARU CAN'T WIELD MY SWORD!
THAT'S NOT THE POINT...
...YOU UNGRATEFUL SON!

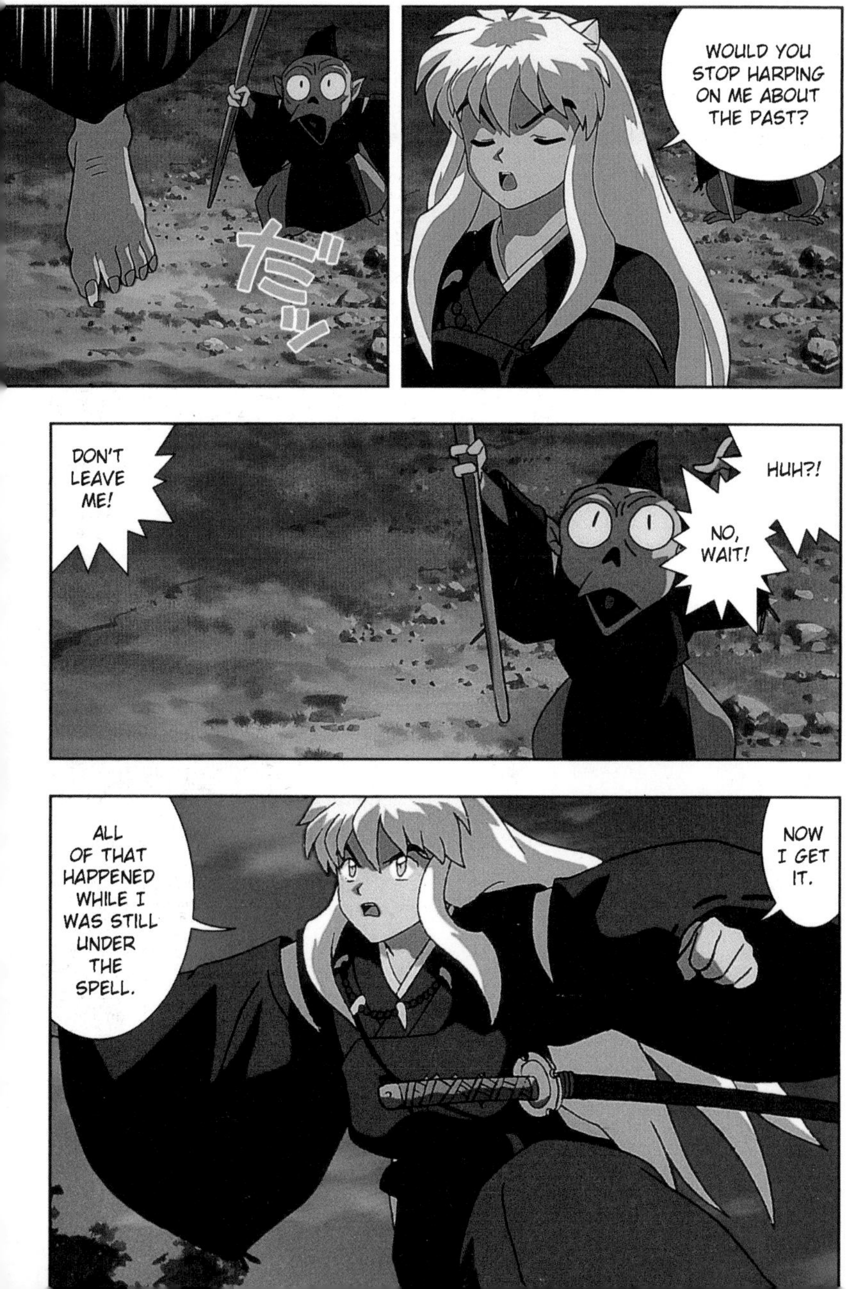
WOULD YOU STOP HARPING ON ME ABOUT THE PAST?
ダッ
HUH?!
NO, WAIT!
DON'T LEAVE ME!
NOW I GET IT.
ALL OF THAT HAPPENED WHILE I WAS STILL UNDER THE SPELL.

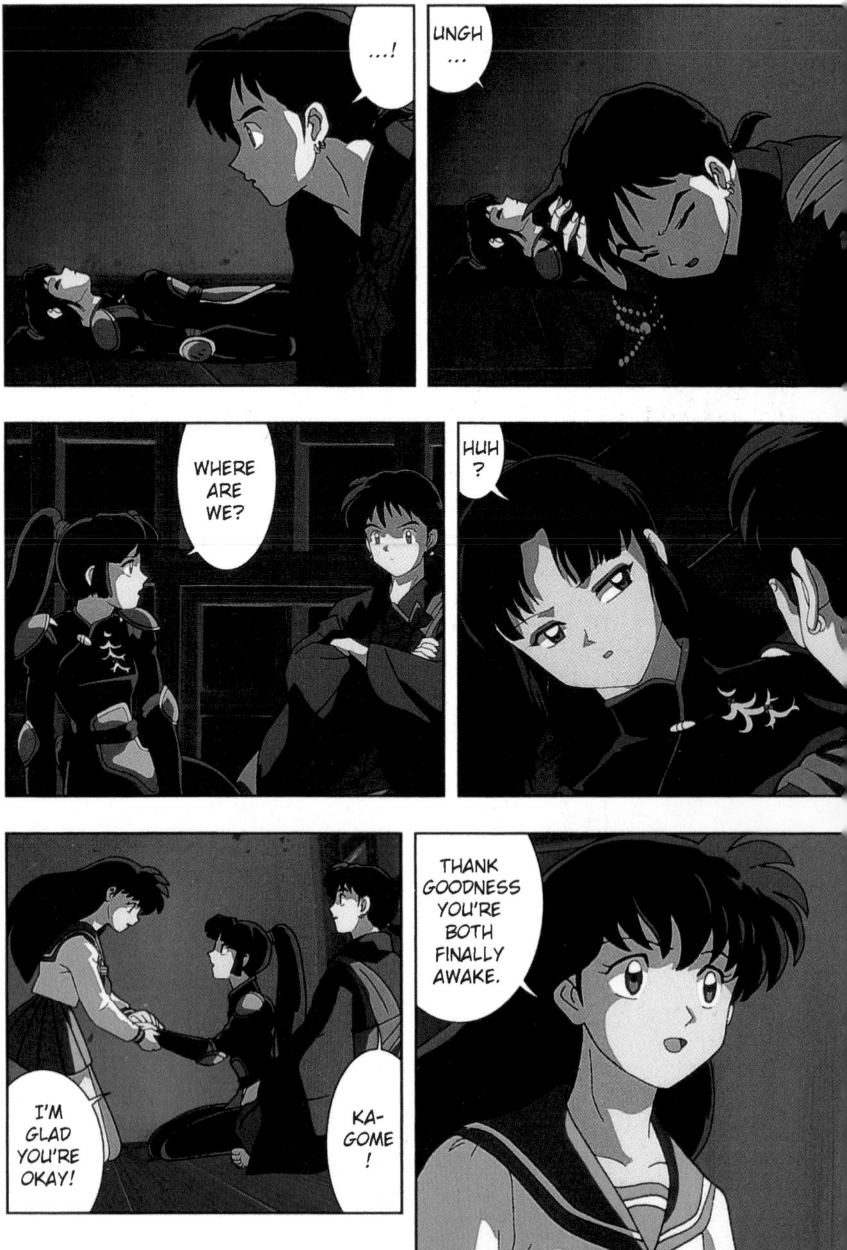
UNGH ...
...!
HUH ?
WHERE ARE WE?
THANK GOODNESS YOU'RE BOTH FINALLY AWAKE.
KA-GOME !
I'M GLAD YOU'RE OKAY!

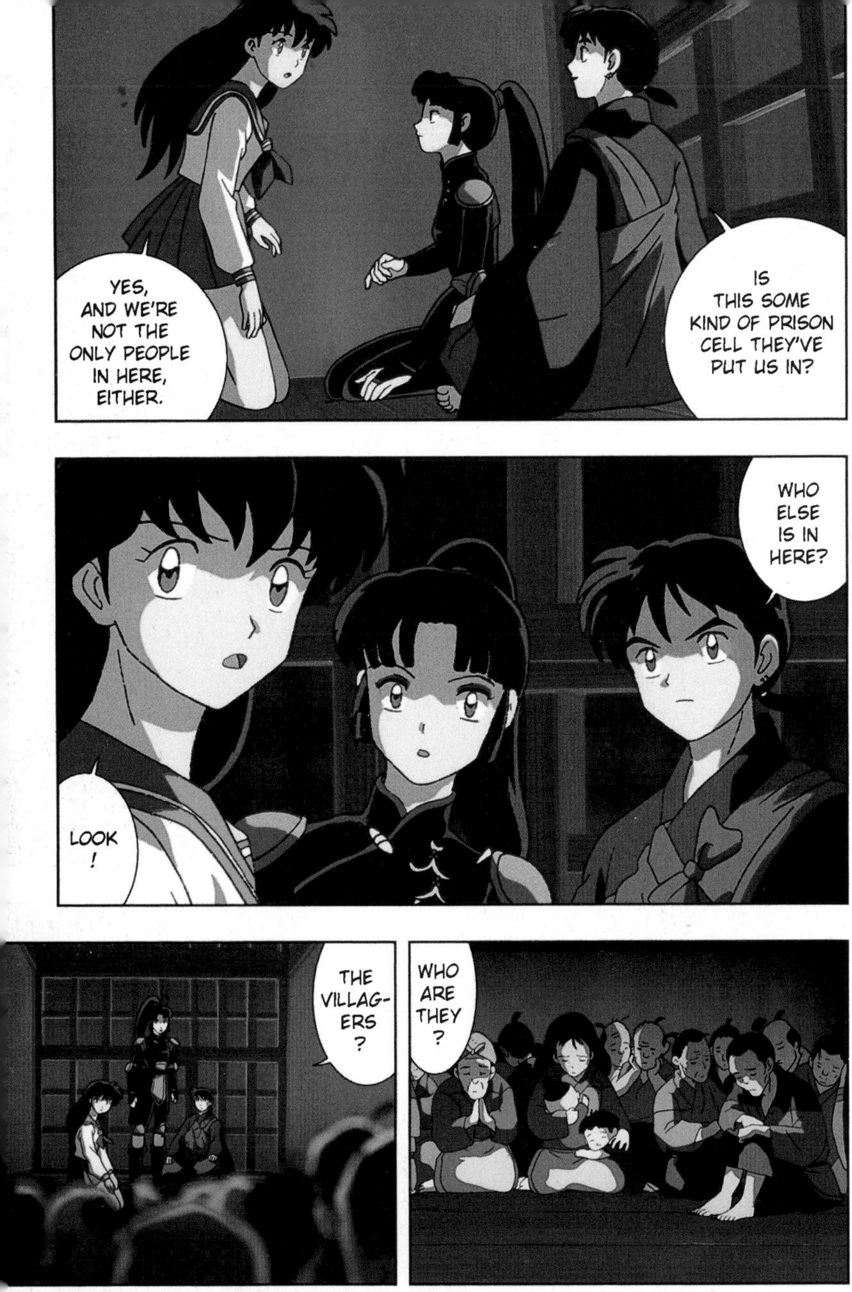
IS THIS SOME KIND OF PRISON CELL THEY'VE PUT US IN?
YES, AND WE'RE NOT THE ONLY PEOPLE IN HERE, EITHER.
WHO ELSE IS IN HERE?
LOOK!
WHO ARE THEY?
THE VILLAGERS?

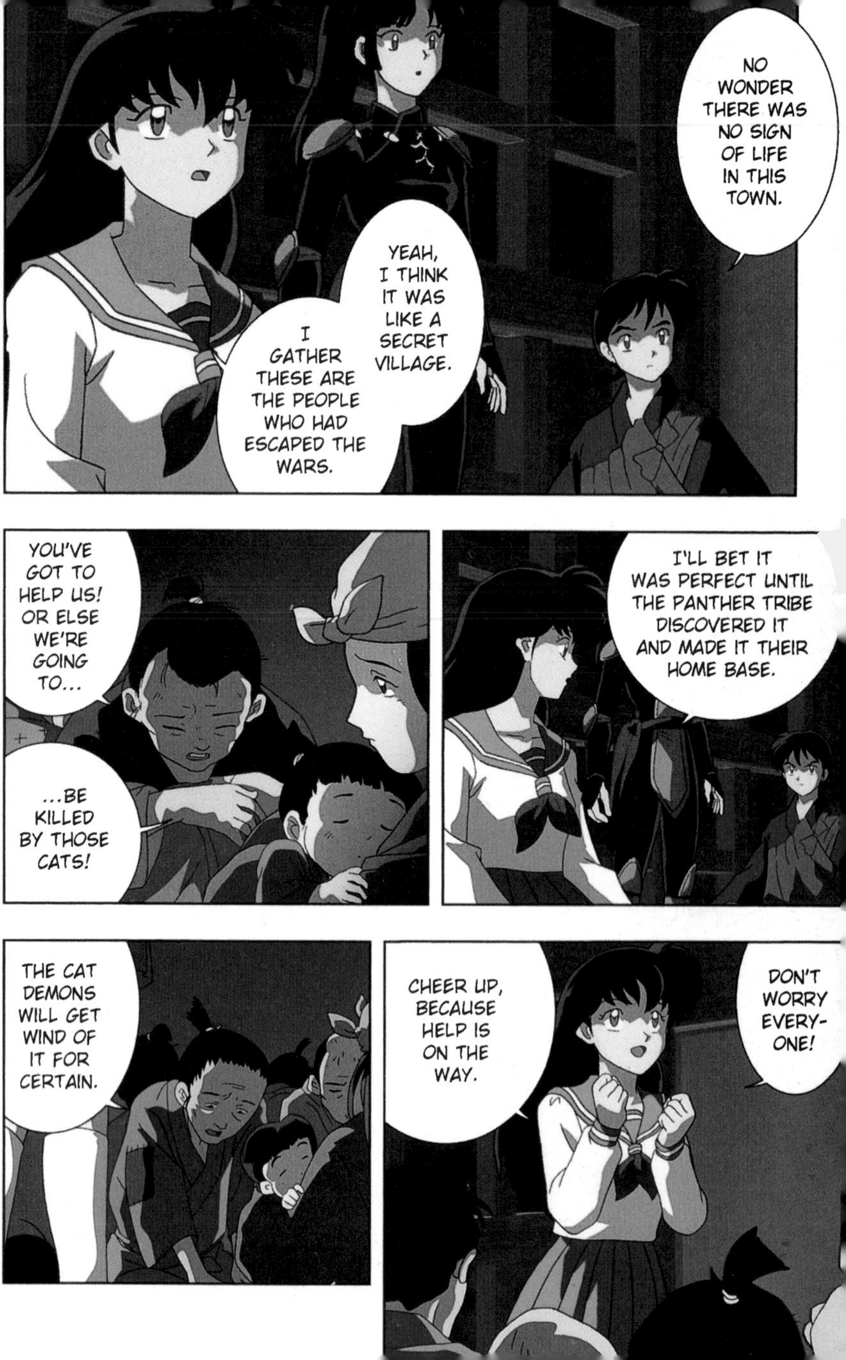
NO WONDER THERE WAS NO SIGN OF LIFE IN THIS TOWN.
YEAH, I THINK IT WAS LIKE A SECRET VILLAGE.
I GATHER THESE ARE THE PEOPLE WHO HAD ESCAPED THE WARS.
I'LL BET IT WAS PERFECT UNTIL THE PANTHER TRIBE DISCOVERED IT AND MADE IT THEIR HOME BASE.
YOU'VE GOT TO HELP US! OR ELSE WE'RE GOING TO...
...BE KILLED BY THOSE CATS!
DON'T WORRY EVERY-ONE!
CHEER UP, BECAUSE HELP IS ON THE WAY.
THE CAT DEMONS WILL GET WIND OF IT FOR CERTAIN.

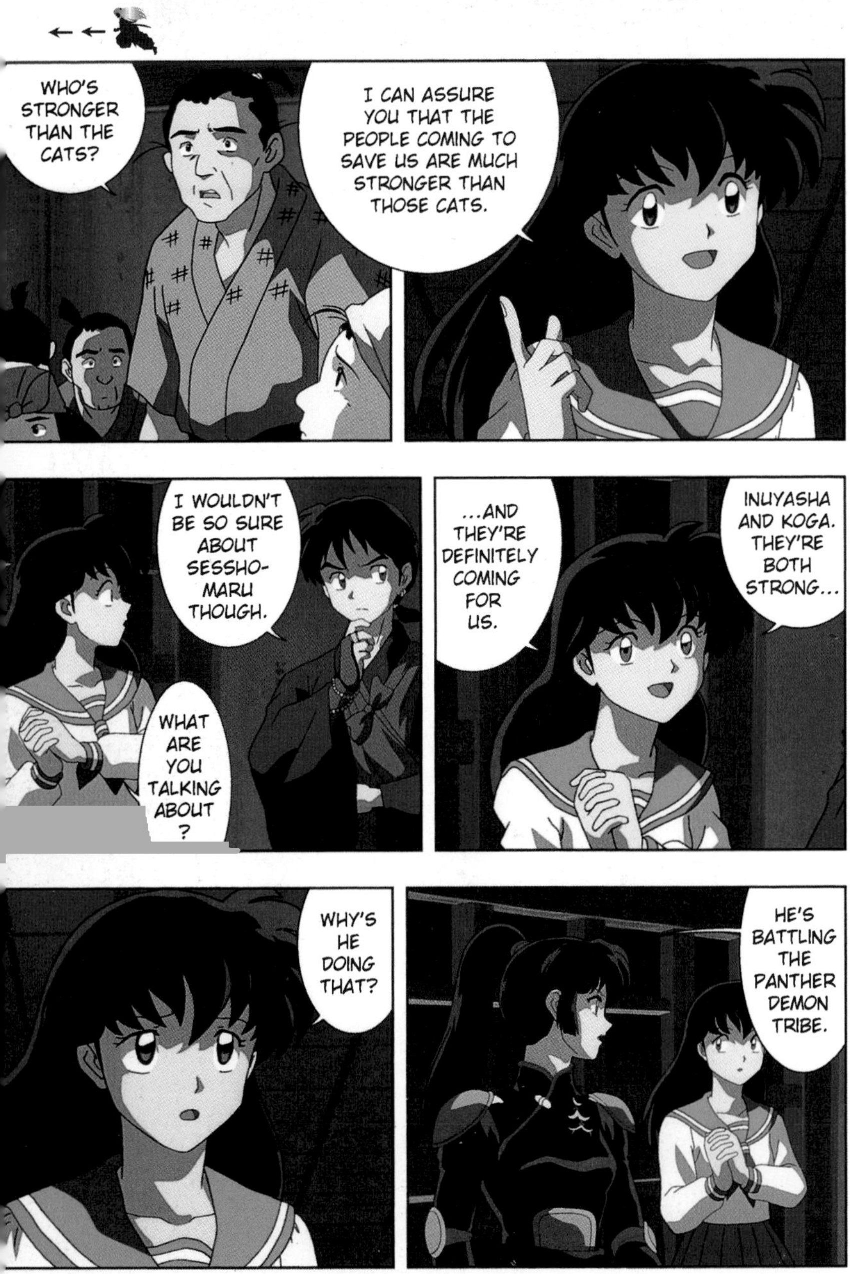
I CAN ASSURE YOU THAT THE PEOPLE COMING TO SAVE US ARE MUCH STRONGER THAN THOSE CATS.
WHO'S STRONGER THAN THE CATS?
INUYASHA AND KOGA. THEY'RE BOTH STRONG...
...AND THEY'RE DEFINITELY COMING FOR US.
I WOULDN'T BE SO SURE ABOUT SESSHO-MARU THOUGH.
WHAT ARE YOU TALKING ABOUT?
HE'S BATTLING THE PANTHER DEMON TRIBE.
WHY'S HE DOING THAT?

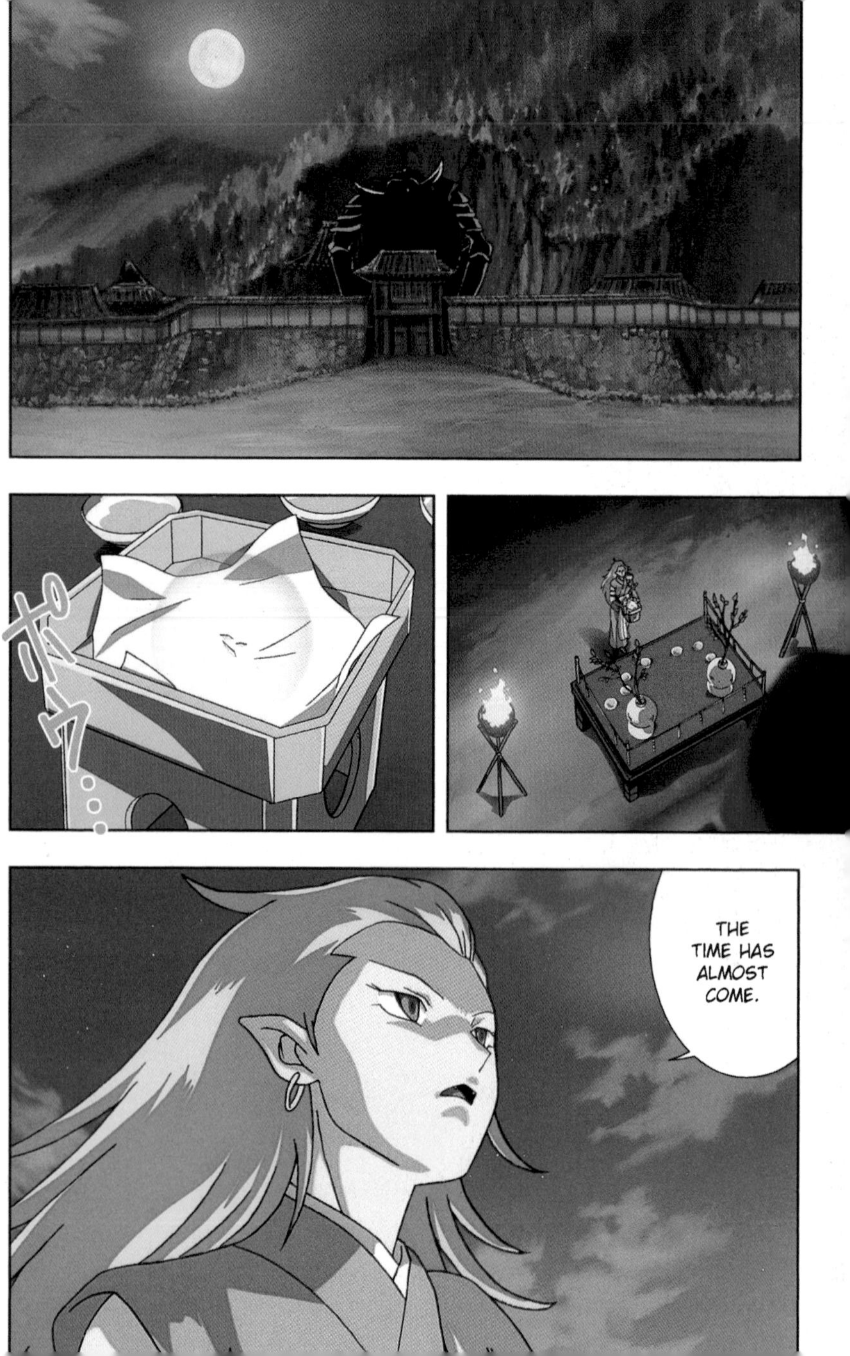
ポウ...
THE TIME HAS ALMOST COME.

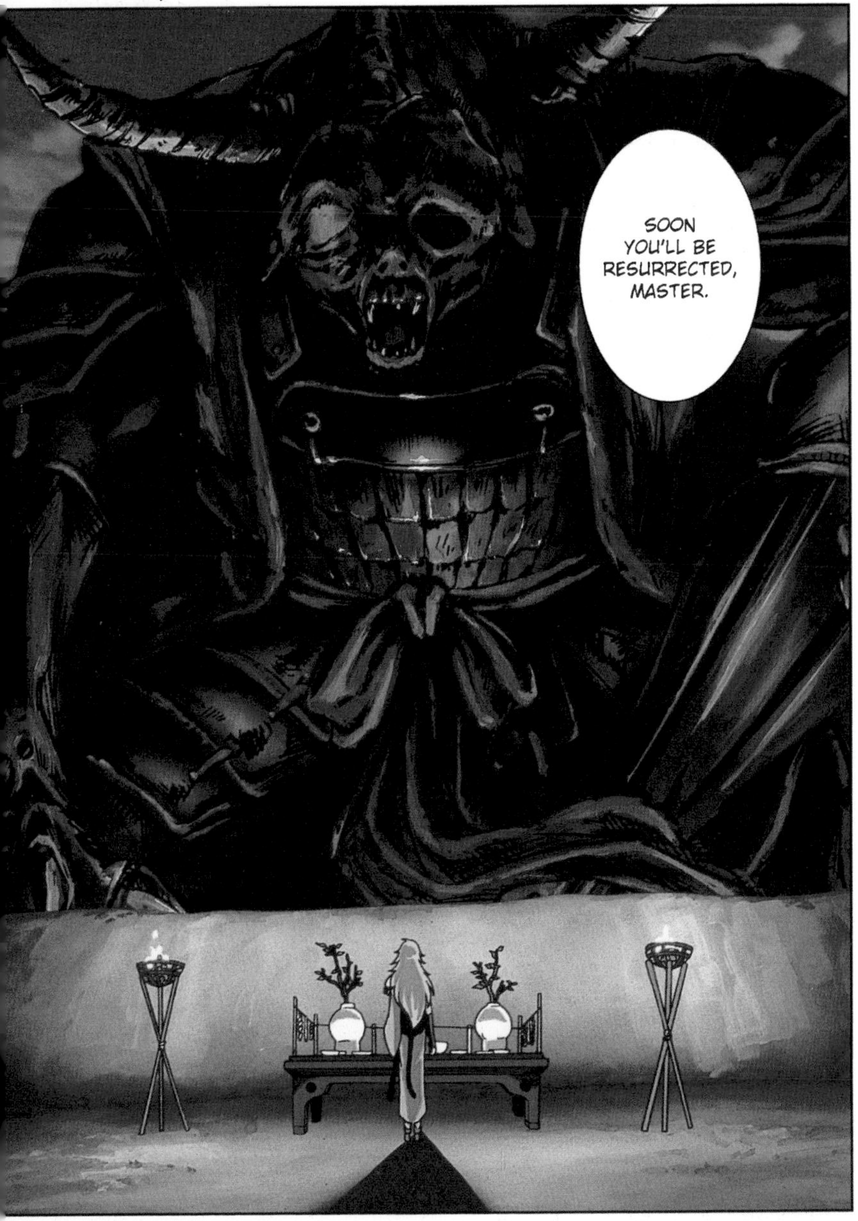
SOON YOU'LL BE RESURRECTED, MASTER.

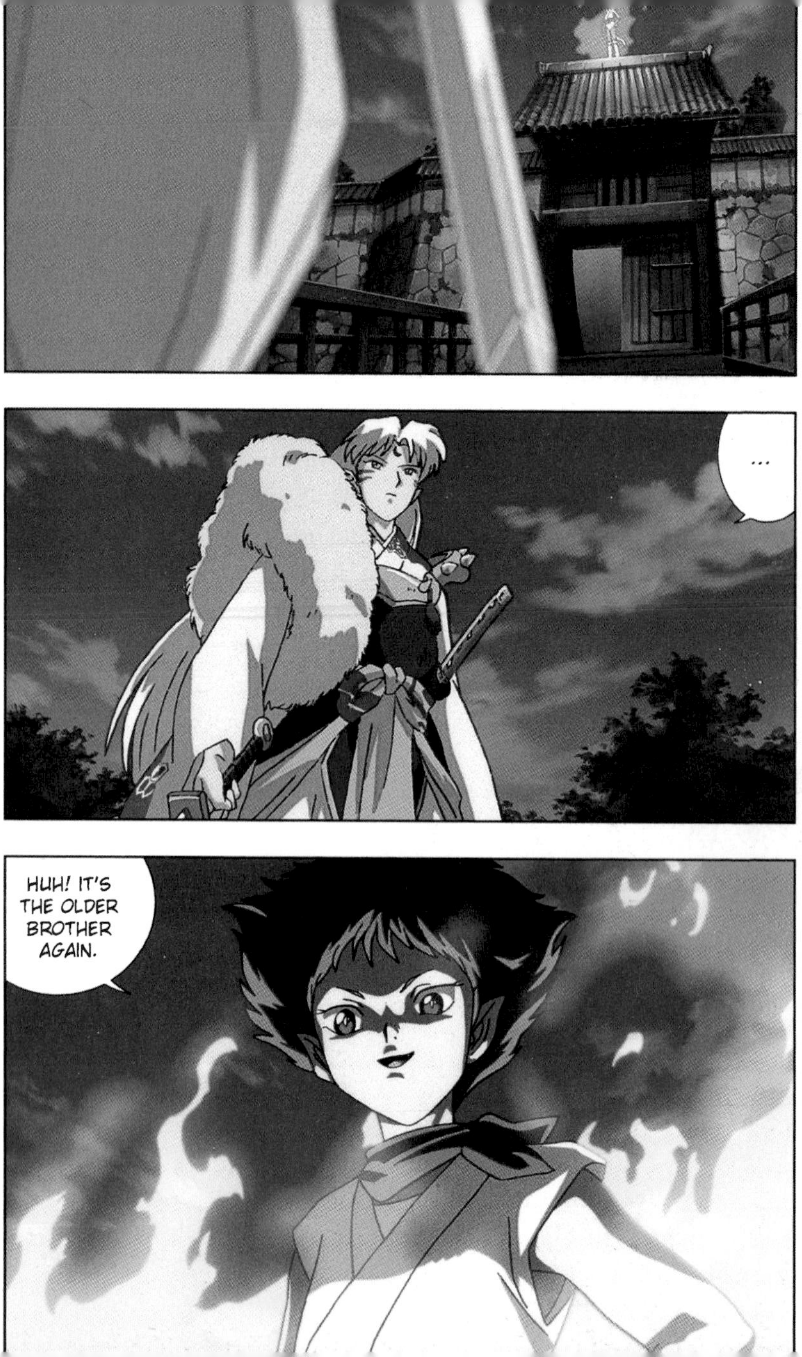
...
HUH! IT'S THE OLDER BROTHER AGAIN.

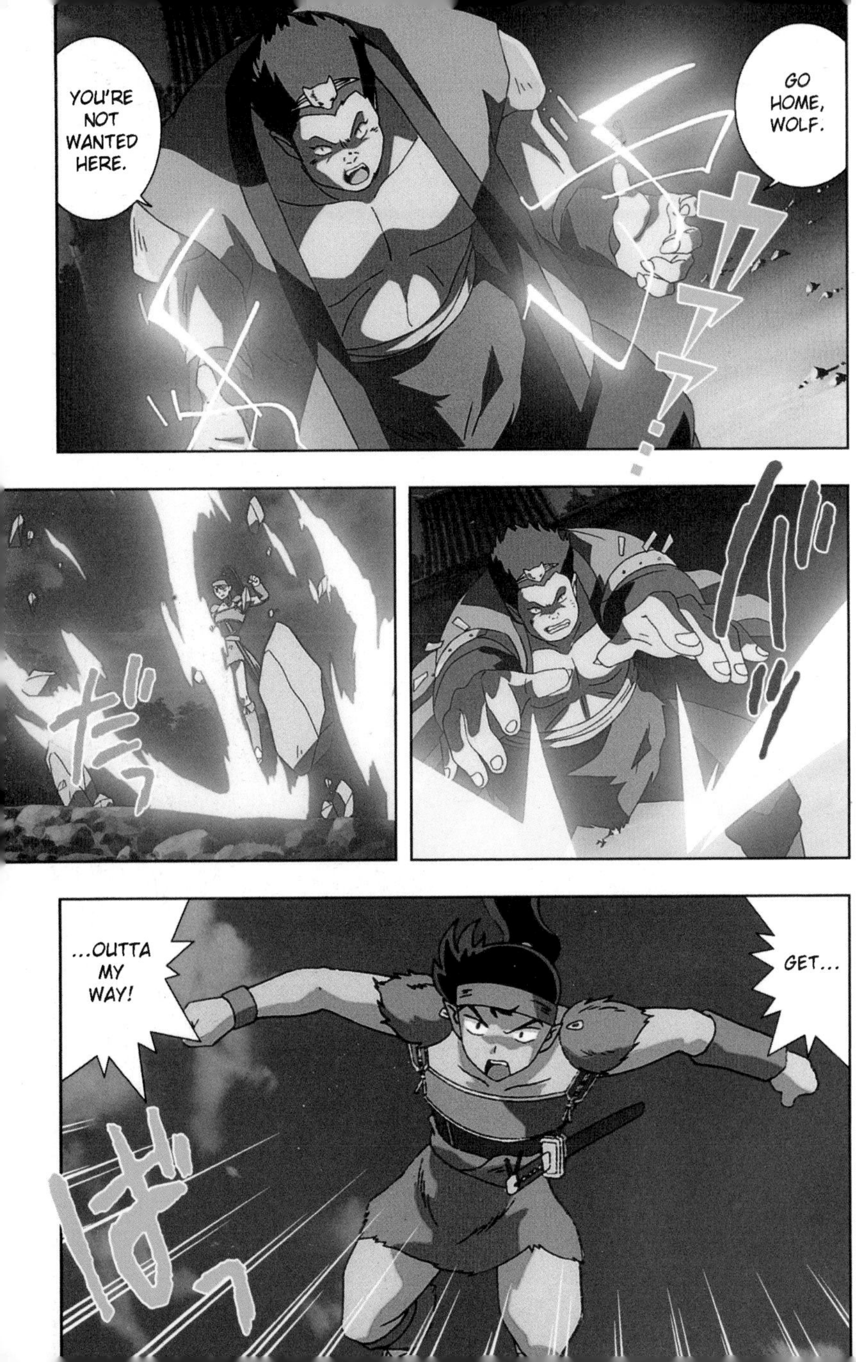
GO HOME, WOLF.
YOU'RE NOT WANTED HERE.
GET...
...OUTTA MY WAY!

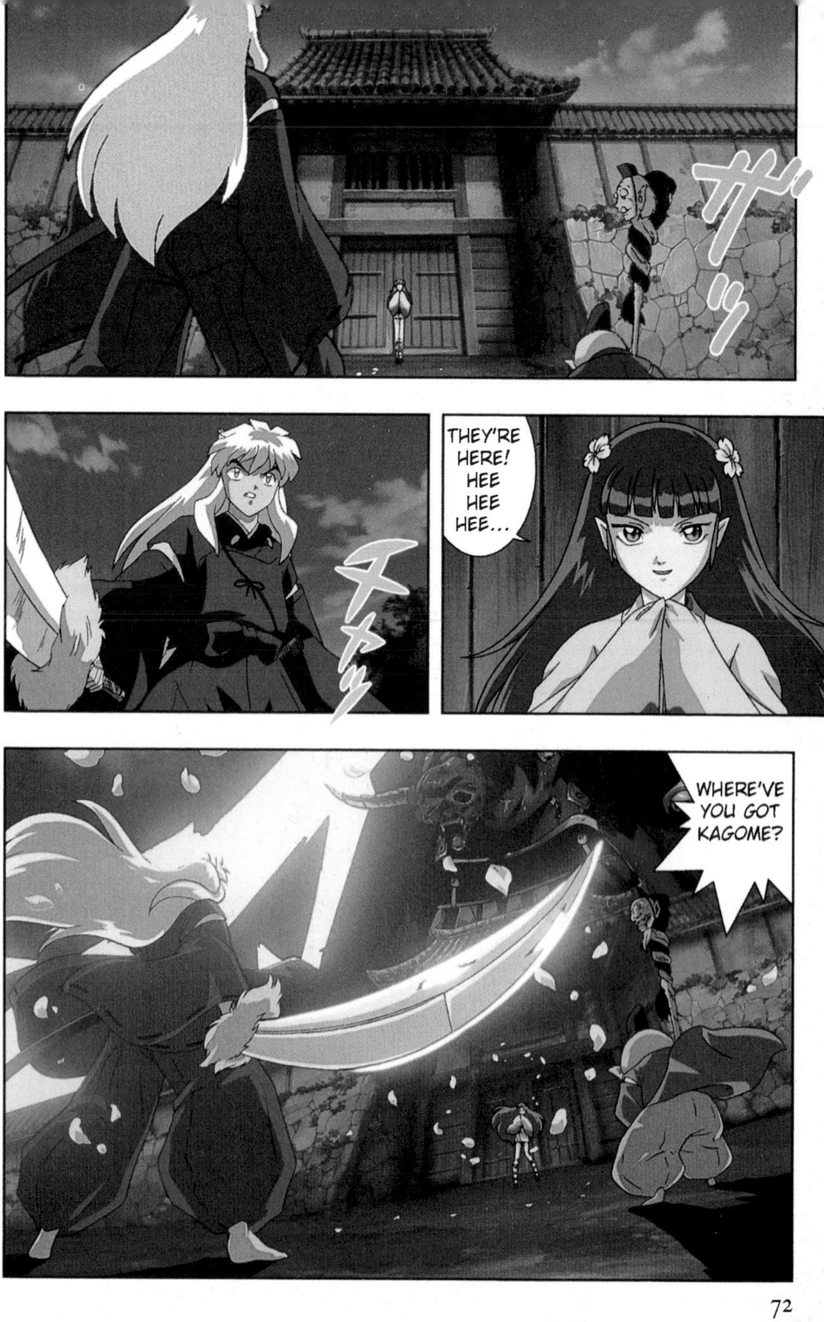
ザッ
THEY'RE HERE! HEE HEE HEE...
チャッ
WHERE'VE YOU GOT KAGOME?

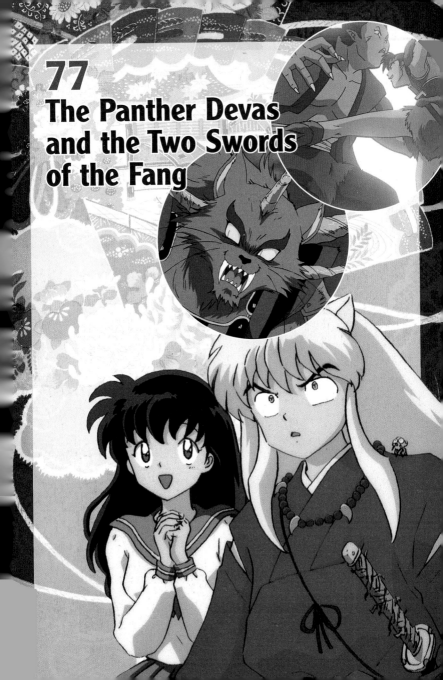

77
The Panther Devas and the Two Swords of the Fang

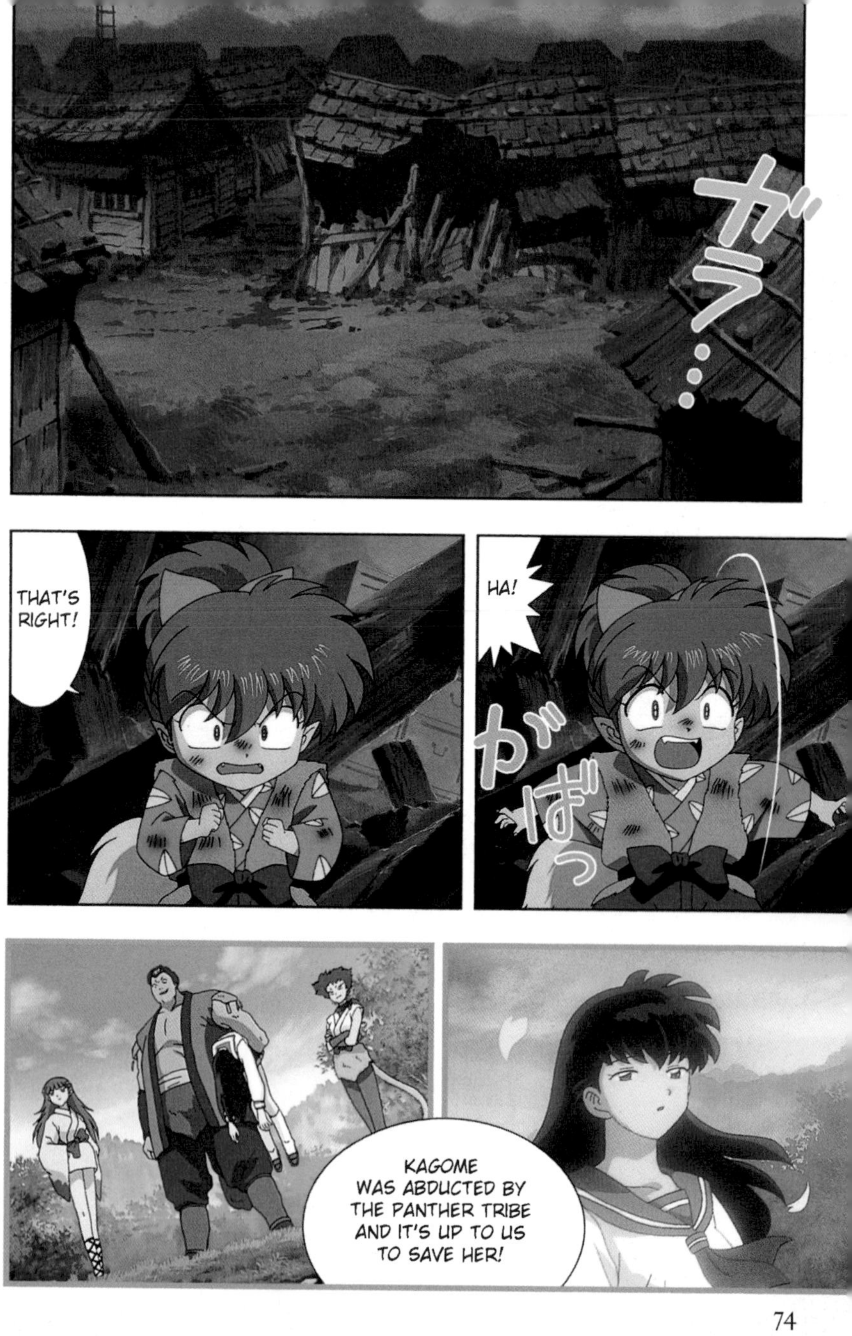
ガラ…
HA!
がばっ
THAT'S RIGHT!
KAGOME WAS ABDUCTED BY THE PANTHER TRIBE AND IT'S UP TO US TO SAVE HER!

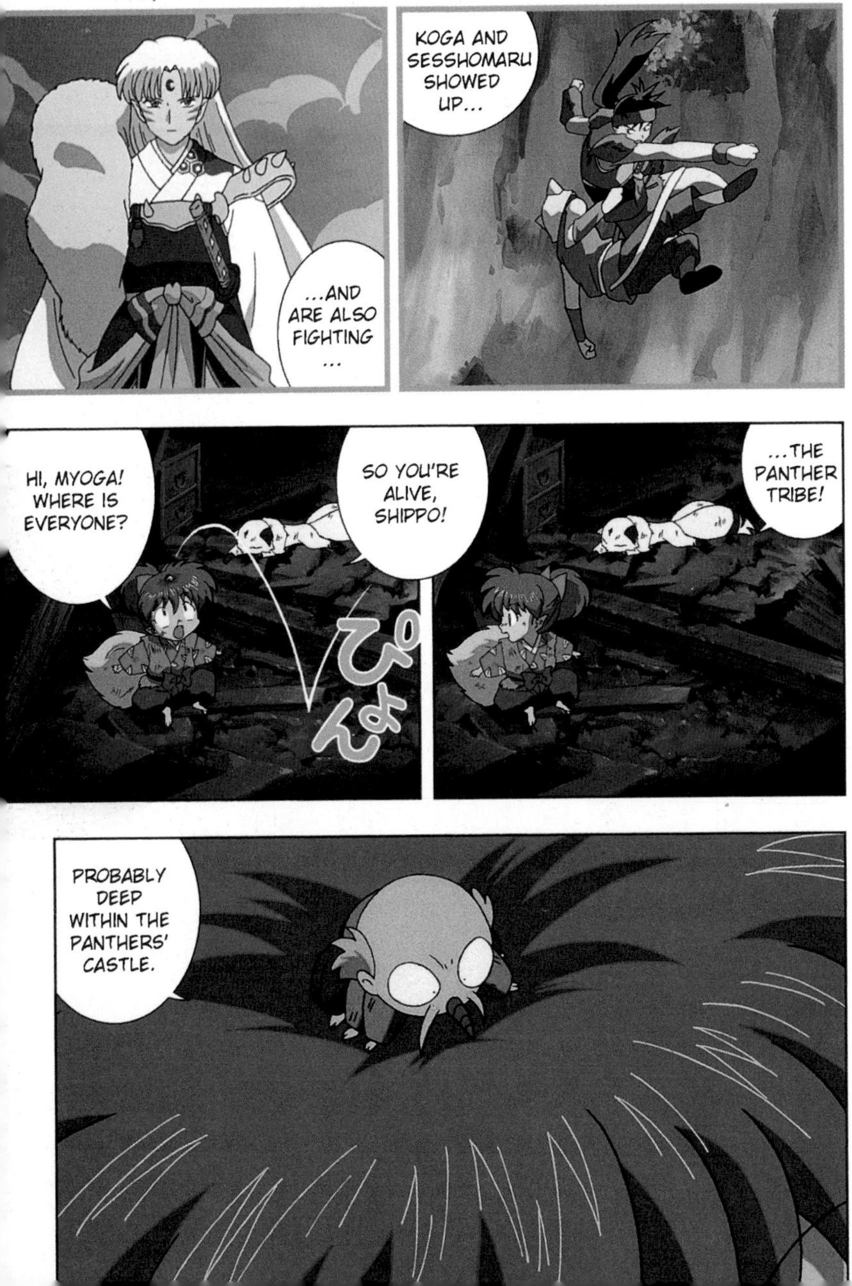
KOGA AND SESSHOMARU SHOWED UP...
...AND ARE ALSO FIGHTING ...
...THE PANTHER TRIBE!
SO YOU'RE ALIVE, SHIPPO!
HI, MYOGA! WHERE IS EVERYONE?
ぴょん
PROBABLY DEEP WITHIN THE PANTHERS' CASTLE.

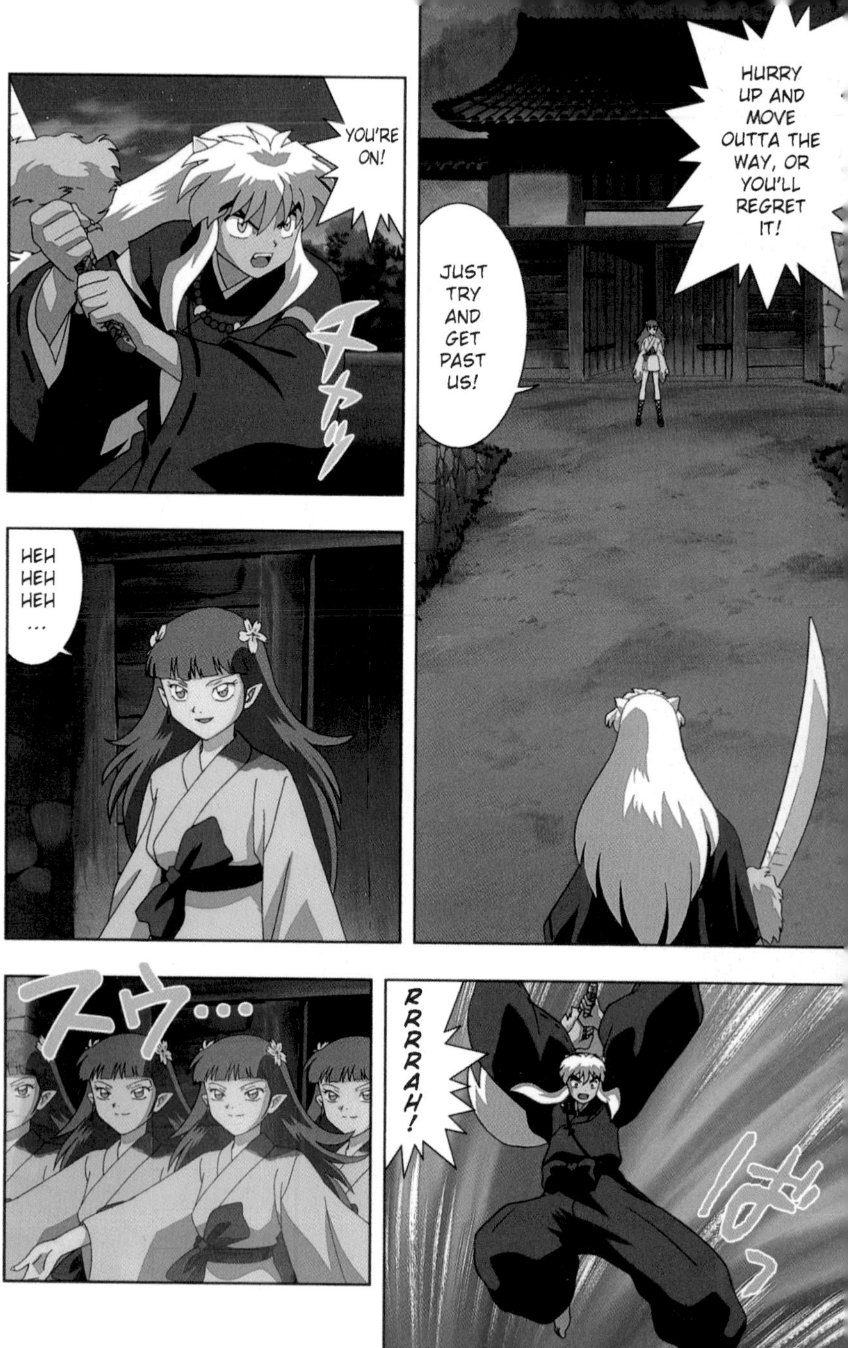
HURRY UP AND MOVE OUTTA THE WAY, OR YOU'LL REGRET IT!
JUST TRY AND GET PAST US!
YOU'RE ON!
チャッ
HEH HEH HEH ...
RRRRAH!
はっ
スウ...

...?!

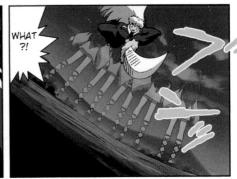

WHAT ?!

HEH HEH HEH ...

HA HA HA ...

WHAT IS THIS ?!

OVER HERE!

DAMN IT!

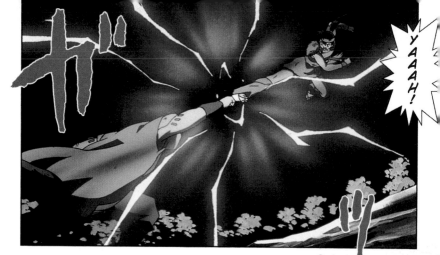

YAAAH!

NO CHANCE!

GET OUTTA THE WAY!

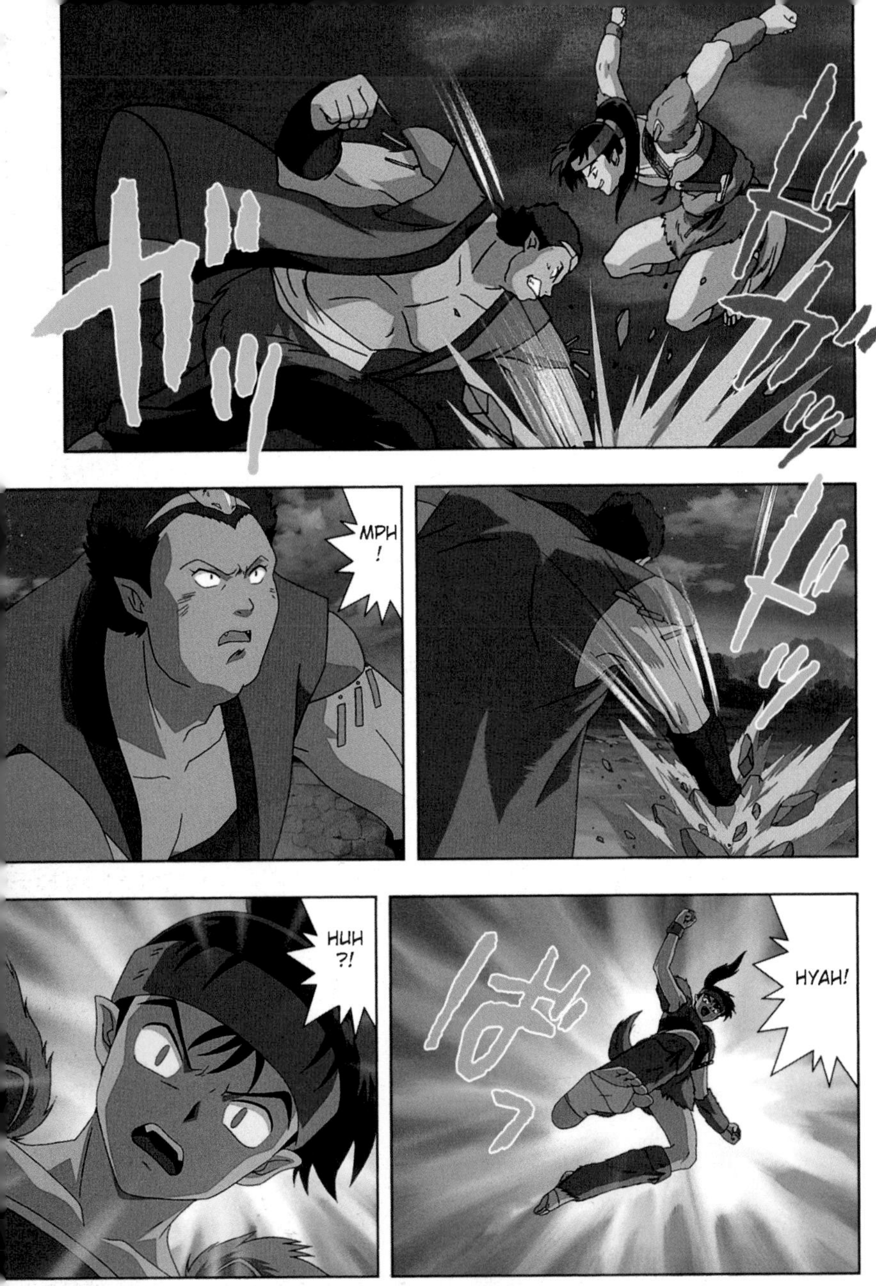
ガッ
ドッ
MPH!
HYAH!
ばっ
HUH?!

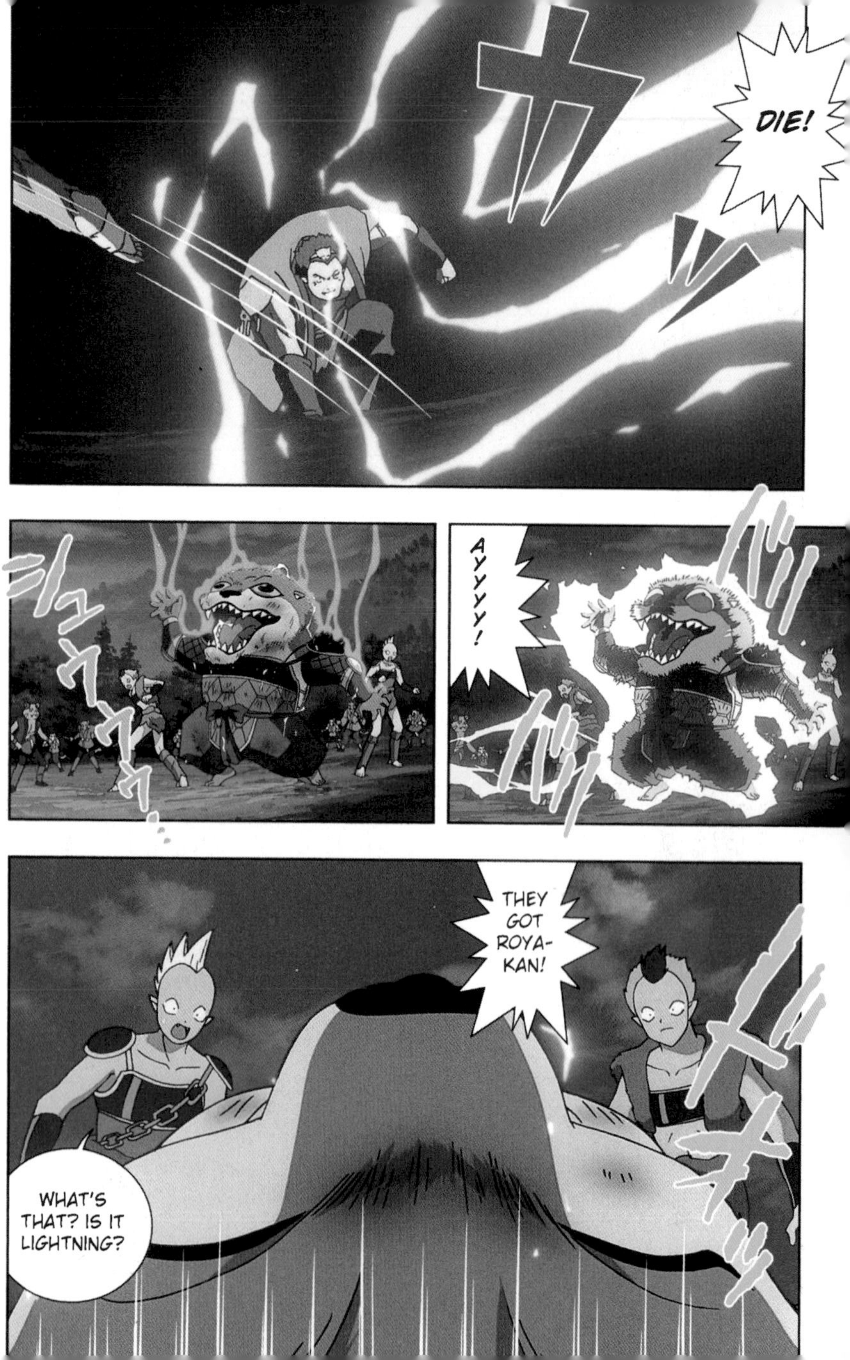
DIE!
AYYYY!
THEY GOT ROYA-KAN!
WHAT'S THAT? IS IT LIGHTNING?

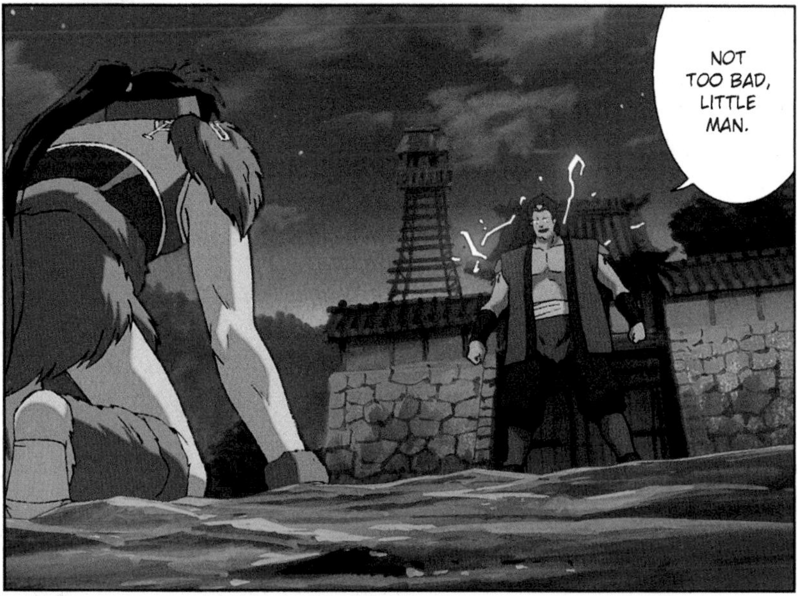
NOT TOO BAD, LITTLE MAN.

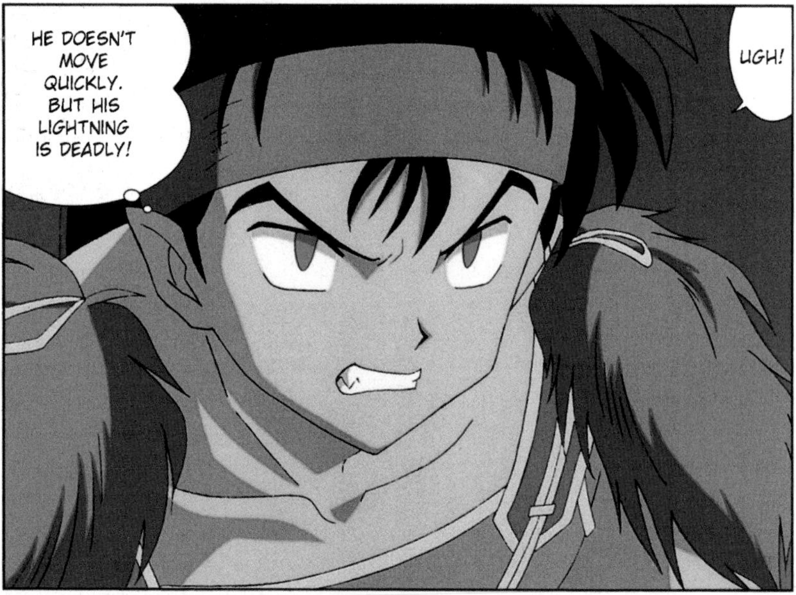
UGH!
HE DOESN'T MOVE QUICKLY. BUT HIS LIGHTNING IS DEADLY!

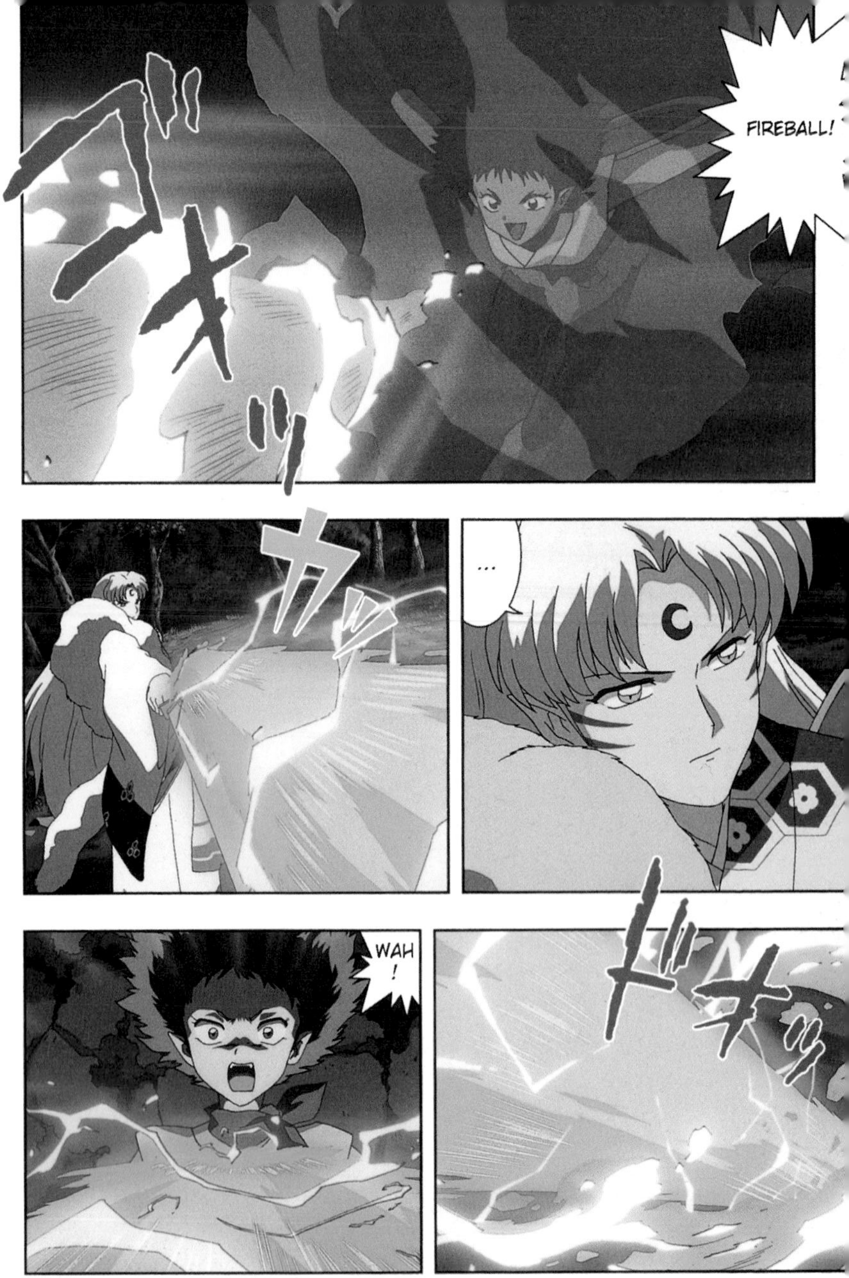
FIREBALL!
...
WAH!

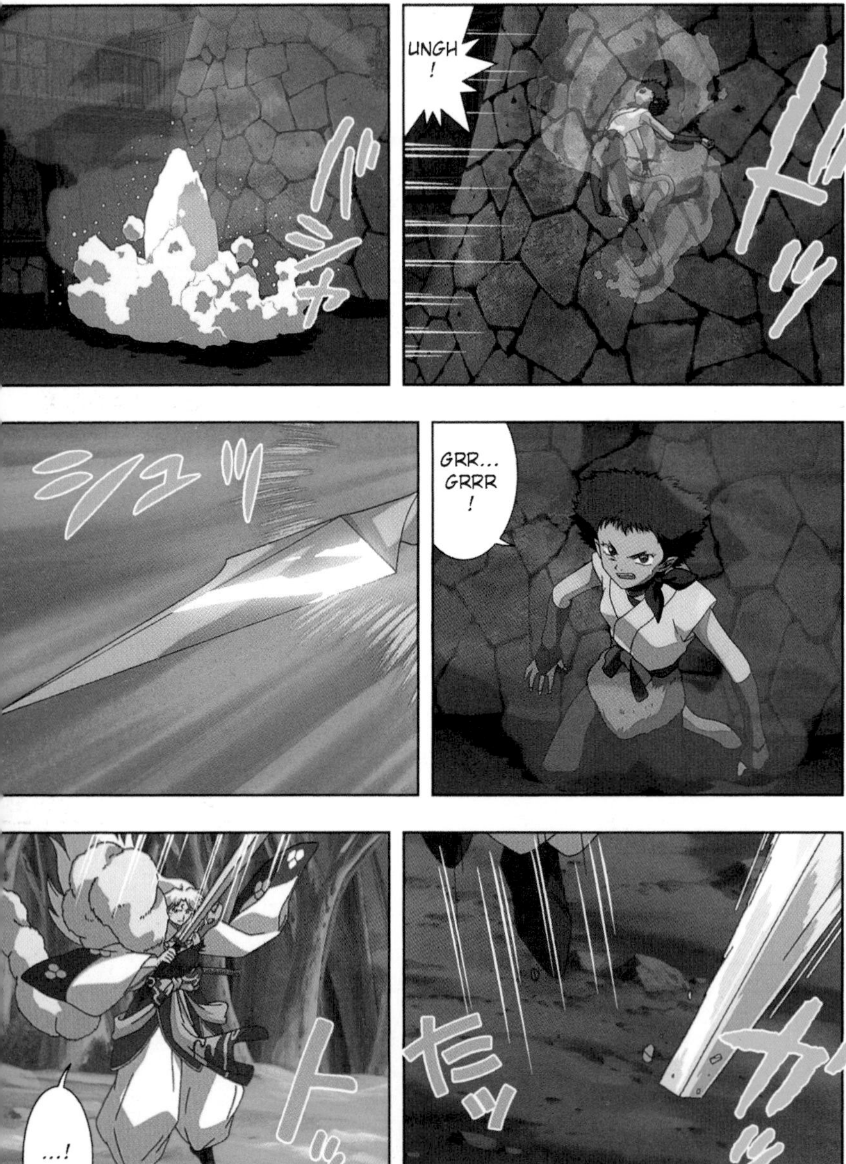
ドッ
UNGH !
GRR... GRRR !
シュッ
ガッ
トッ
...!

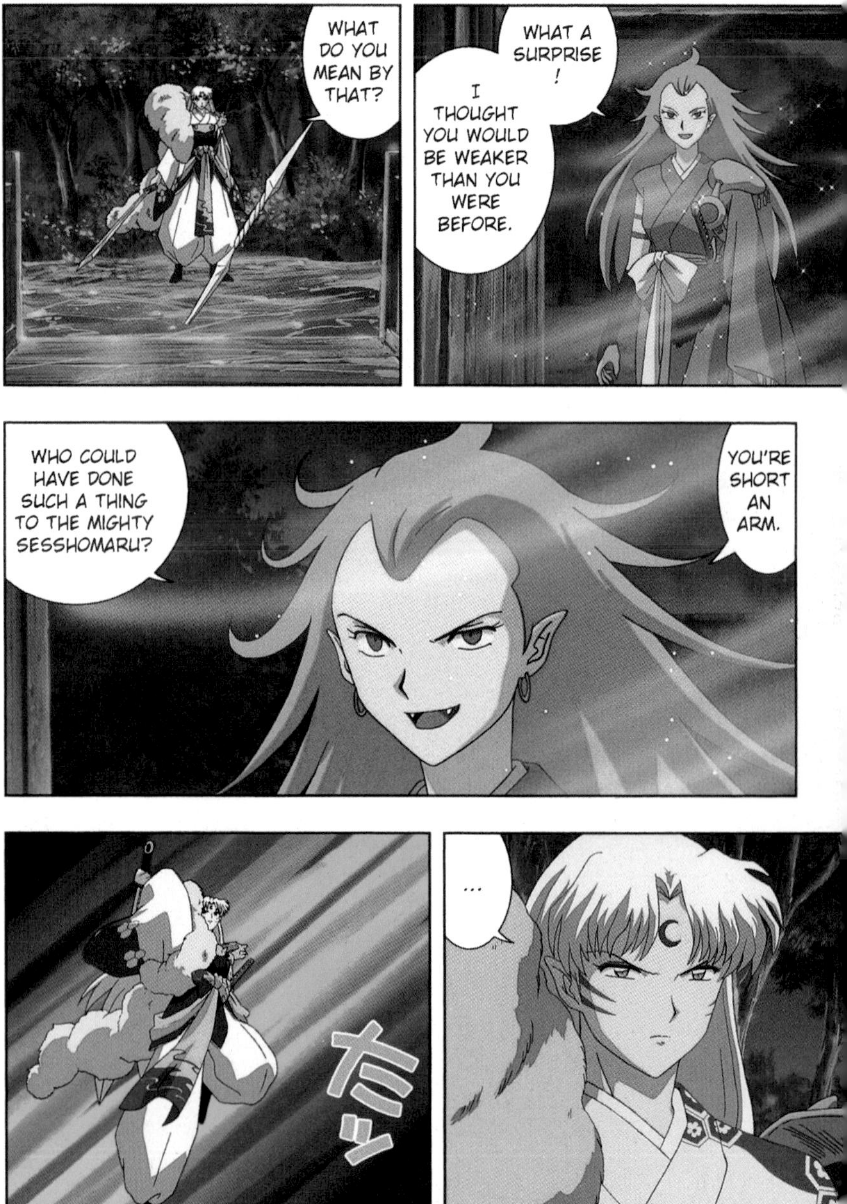
WHAT A SURPRISE!
I THOUGHT YOU WOULD BE WEAKER THAN YOU WERE BEFORE.
WHAT DO YOU MEAN BY THAT?
YOU'RE SHORT AN ARM.
WHO COULD HAVE DONE SUCH A THING TO THE MIGHTY SESSHOMARU?
...
たッ

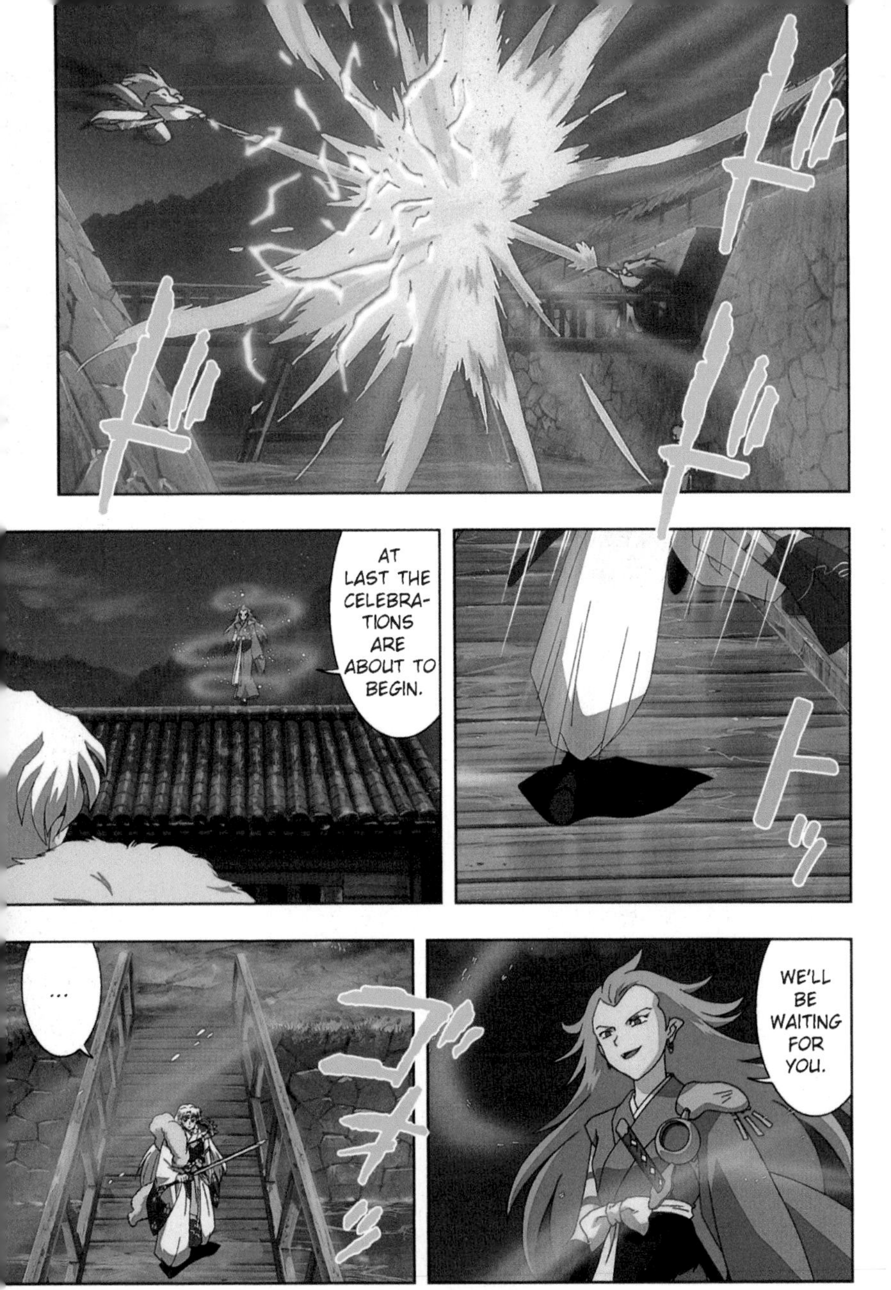
AT LAST THE CELEBRA-TIONS ARE ABOUT TO BEGIN.
WE'LL BE WAITING FOR YOU.
...

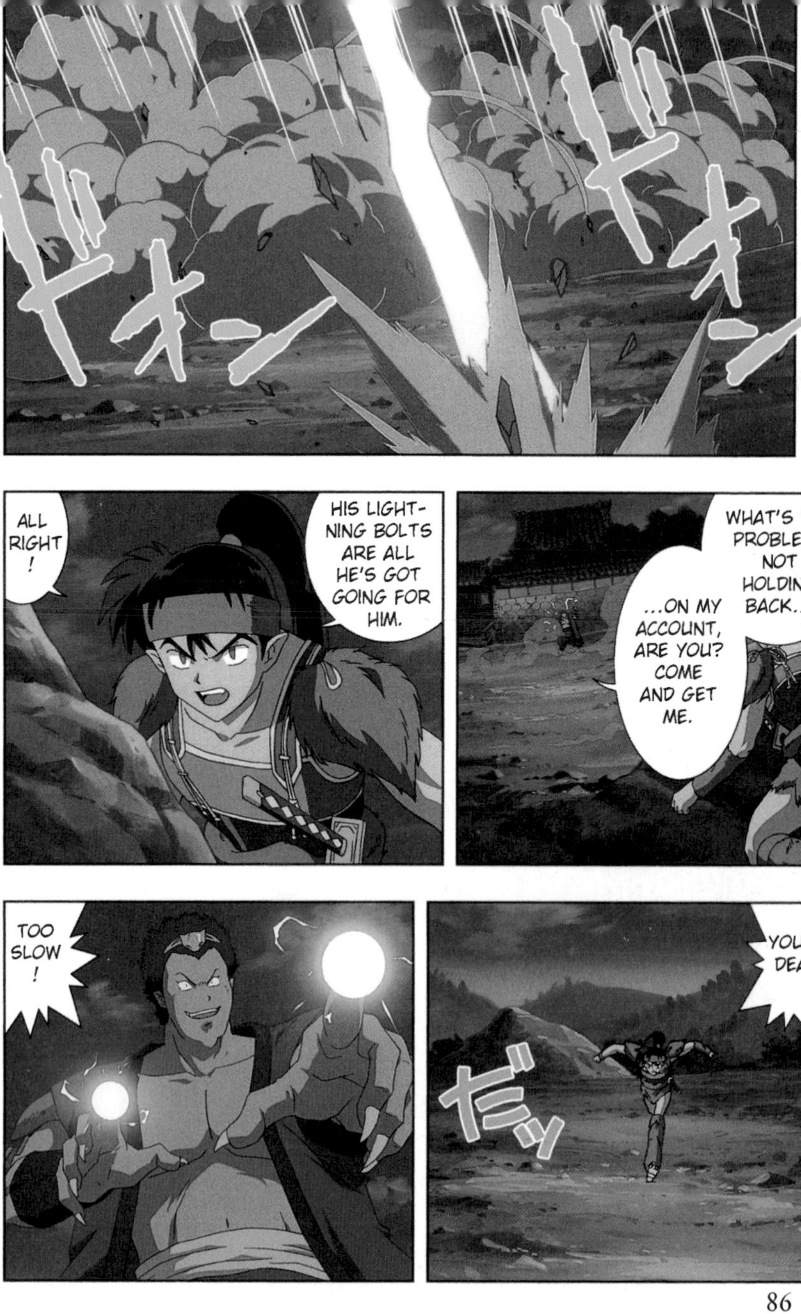
ドォーン
ドォーン
WHAT'S THE PROBLEM? NOT HOLDING BACK...
...ON MY ACCOUNT, ARE YOU? COME AND GET ME.
HIS LIGHTNING BOLTS ARE ALL HE'S GOT GOING FOR HIM.
ALL RIGHT!
YOU'RE DEAD!
ダッ
TOO SLOW!

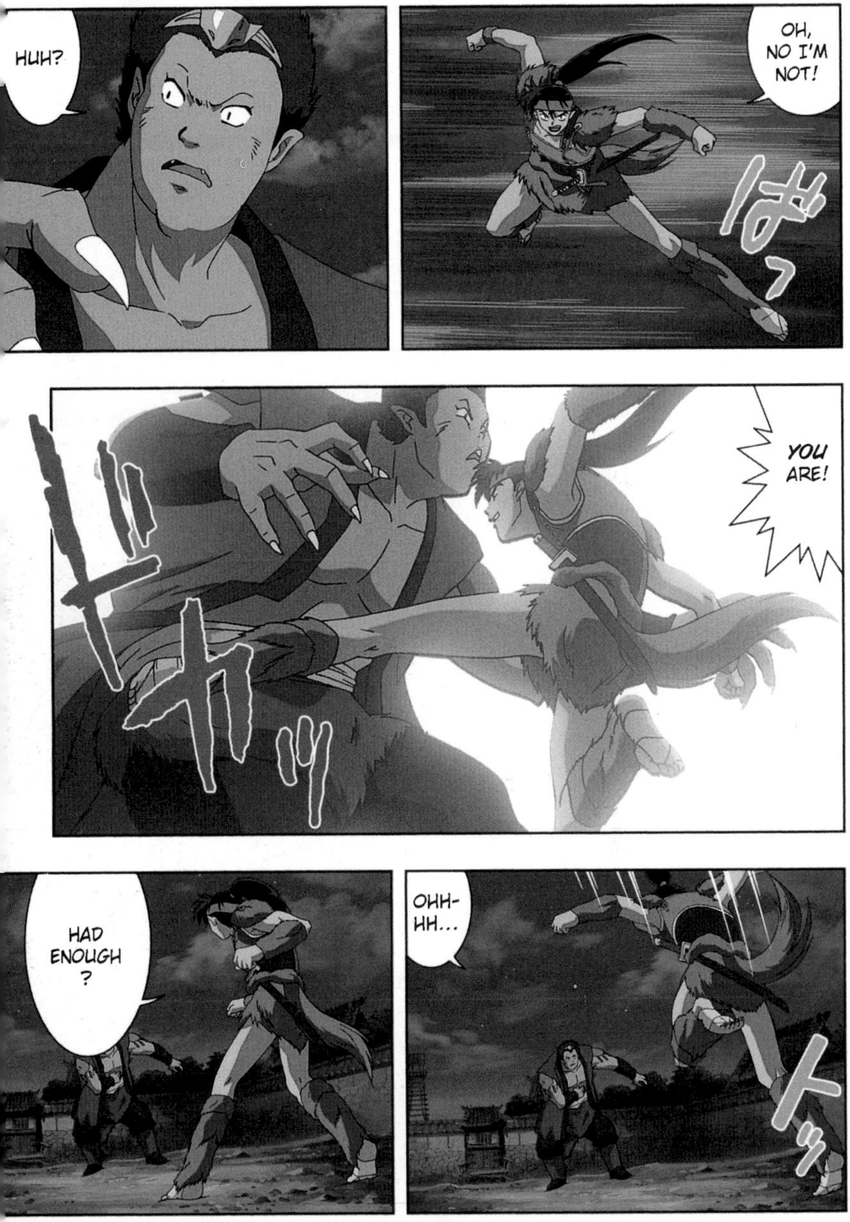

OH, NO I'M NOT!
ばっ
HUH?
YOU ARE!
ドカッ
OHH-HH...
トッ
HAD ENOUGH ?

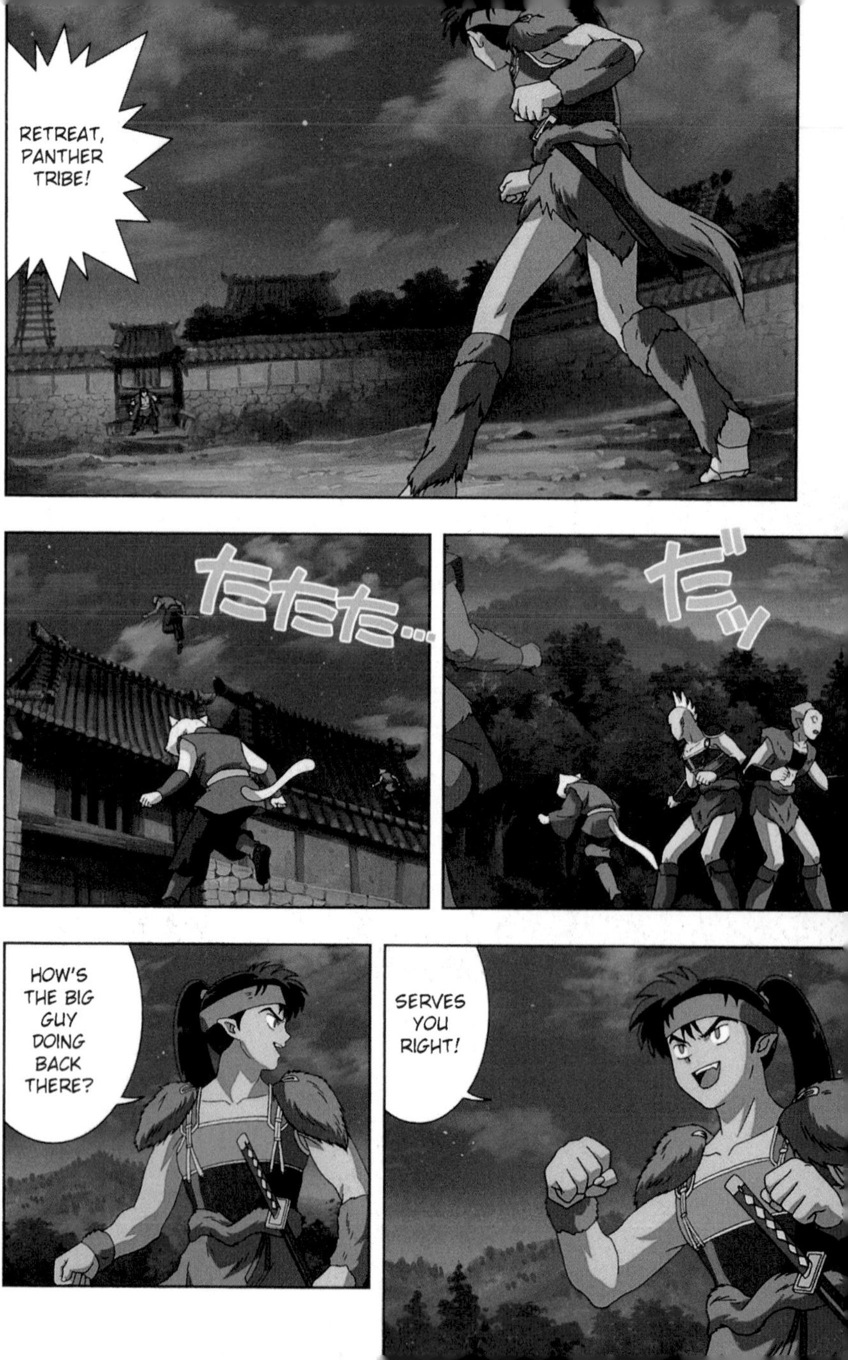
RETREAT, PANTHER TRIBE!
だッ
たたた…
SERVES YOU RIGHT!
HOW'S THE BIG GUY DOING BACK THERE?

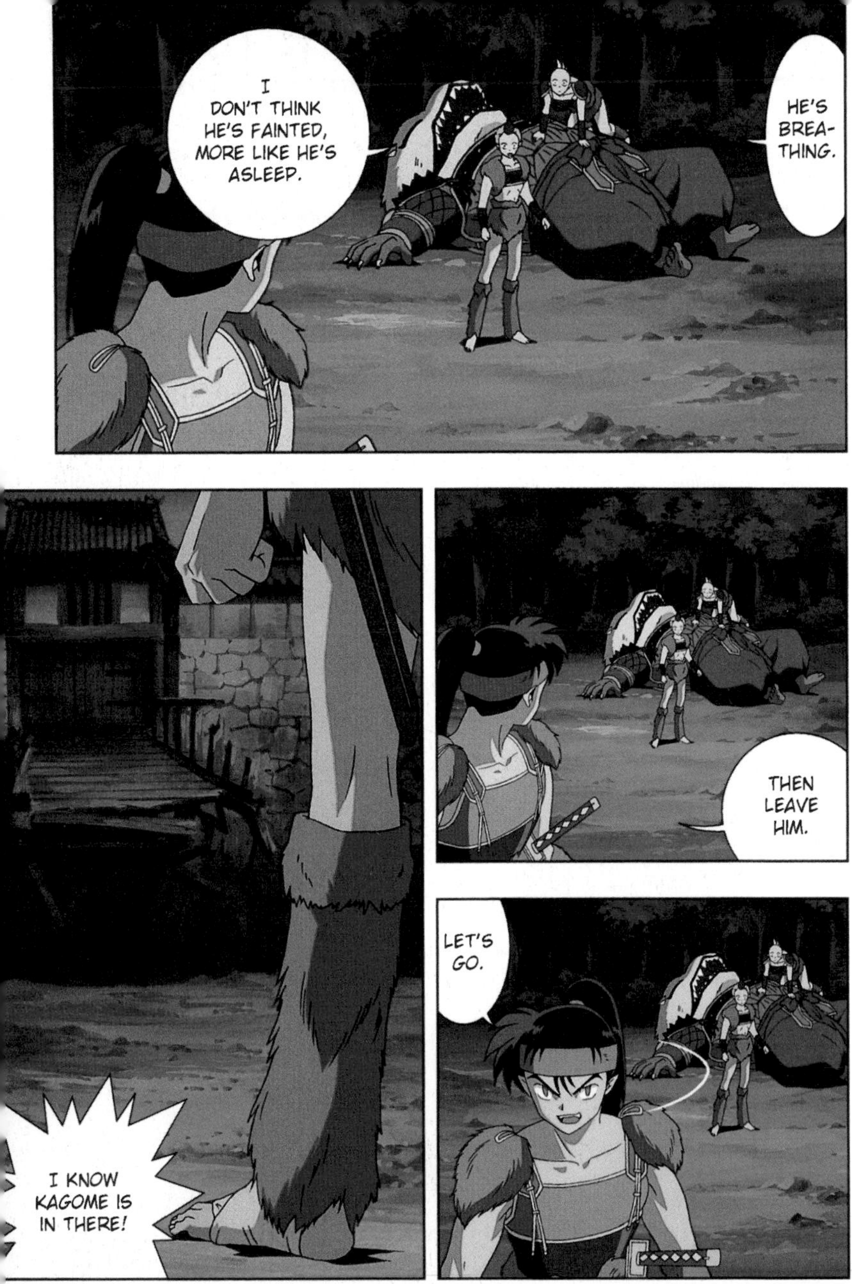
HE'S BREA-THING.
I DON'T THINK HE'S FAINTED, MORE LIKE HE'S ASLEEP.
THEN LEAVE HIM.
LET'S GO.
I KNOW KAGOME IS IN THERE!

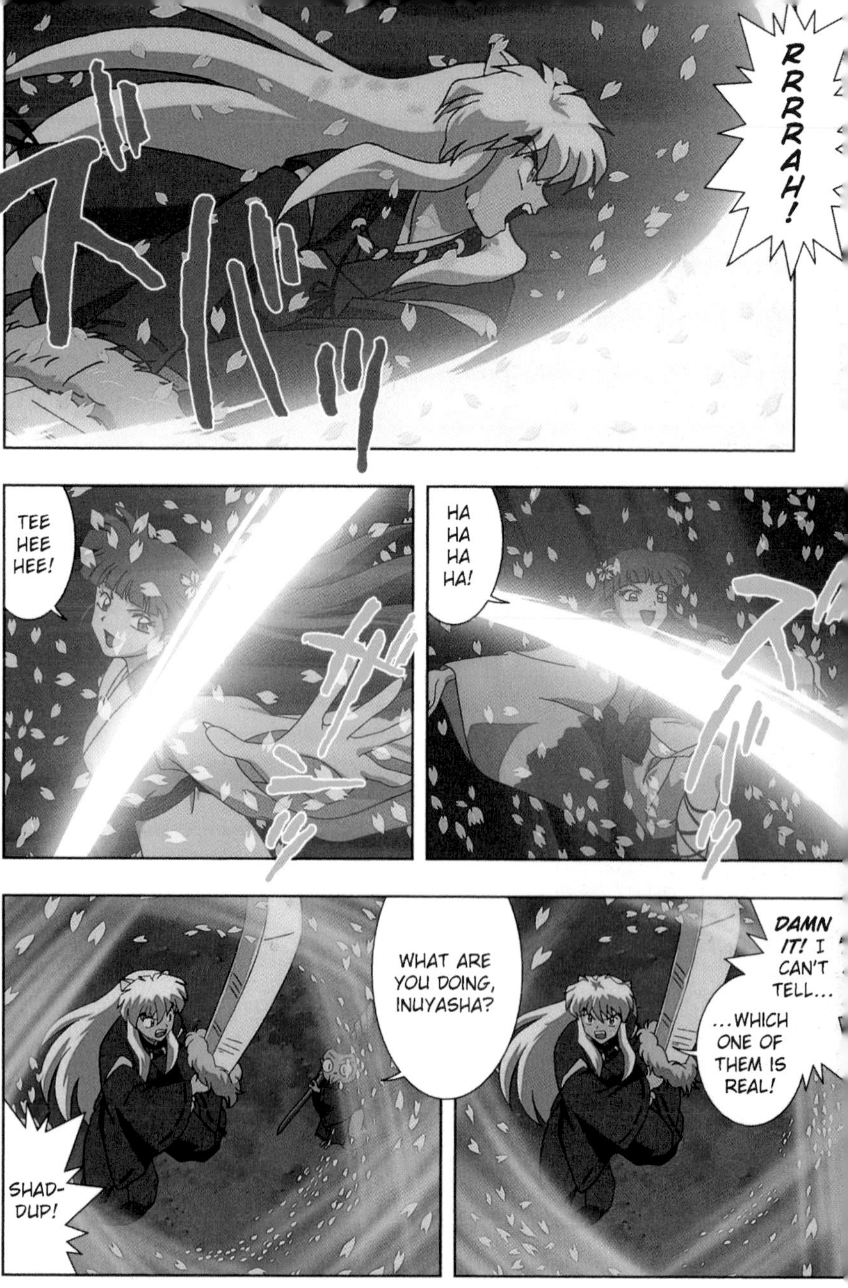
RRRRAH!
HA HA HA HA!
TEE HEE HEE!
DAMN IT! I CAN'T TELL...
...WHICH ONE OF THEM IS REAL!
WHAT ARE YOU DOING, INUYASHA?
SHAD-DUP!

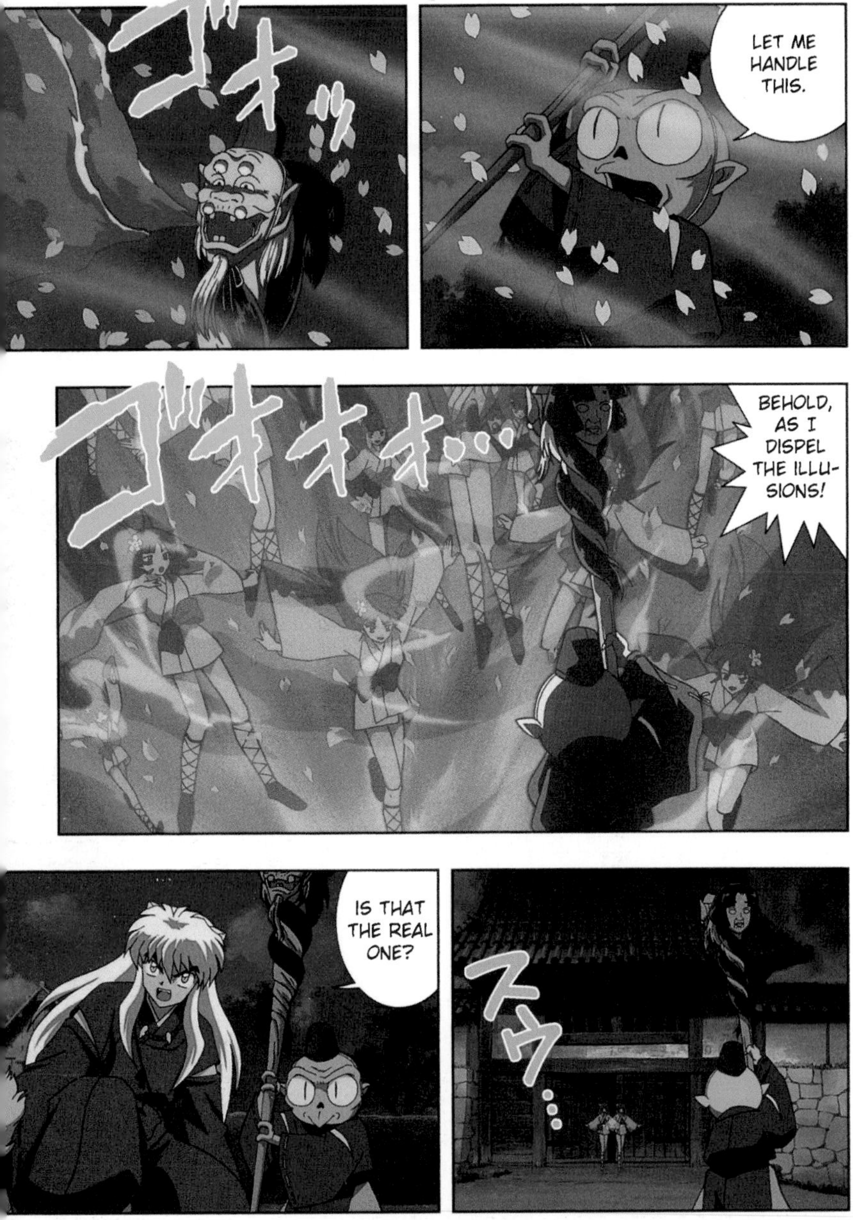
LET ME HANDLE THIS.
ゴォッ
BEHOLD, AS I DISPEL THE ILLUSIONS!
ゴォォォ…
スゥ…
IS THAT THE REAL ONE?

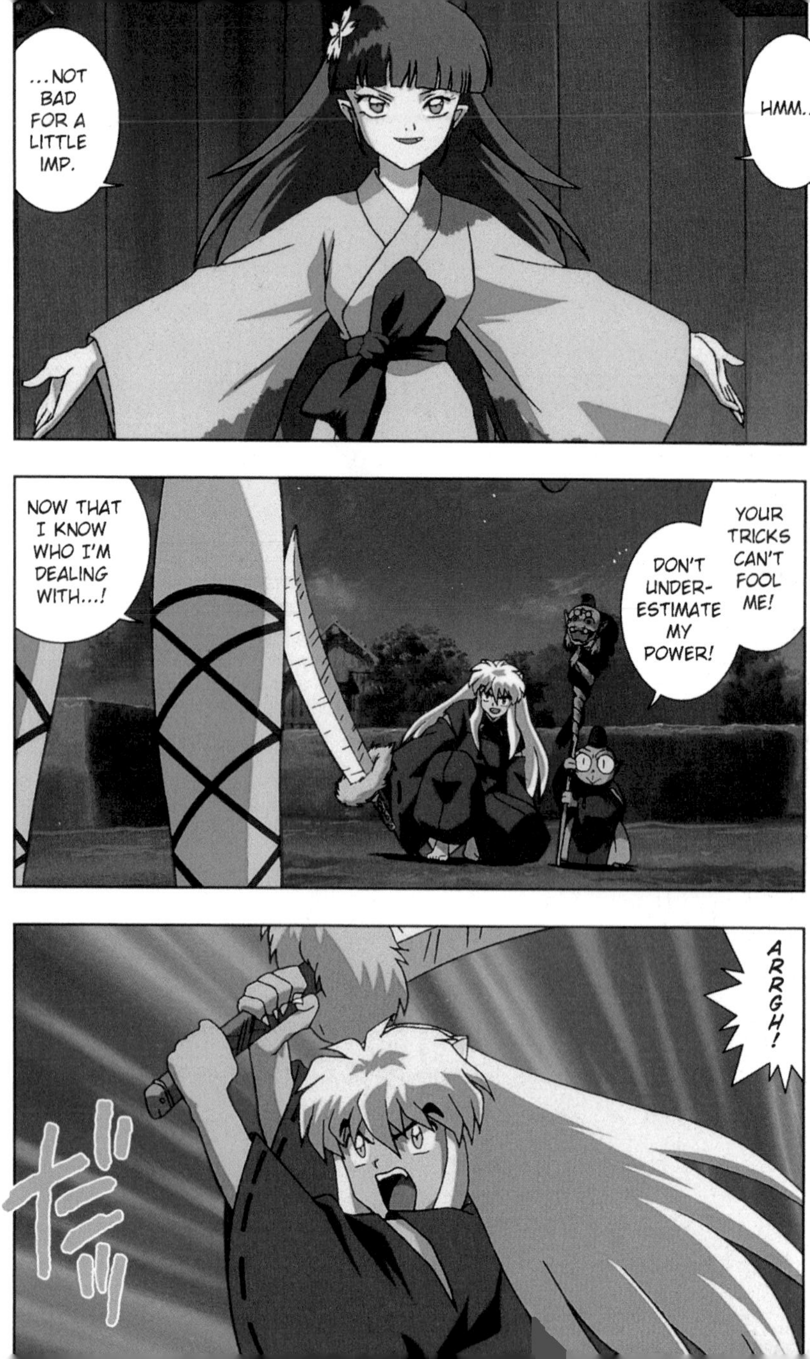
HMM...
...NOT BAD FOR A LITTLE IMP.
YOUR TRICKS CAN'T FOOL ME!
DON'T UNDER-ESTIMATE MY POWER!
NOW THAT I KNOW WHO I'M DEALING WITH...!
ARRGH!

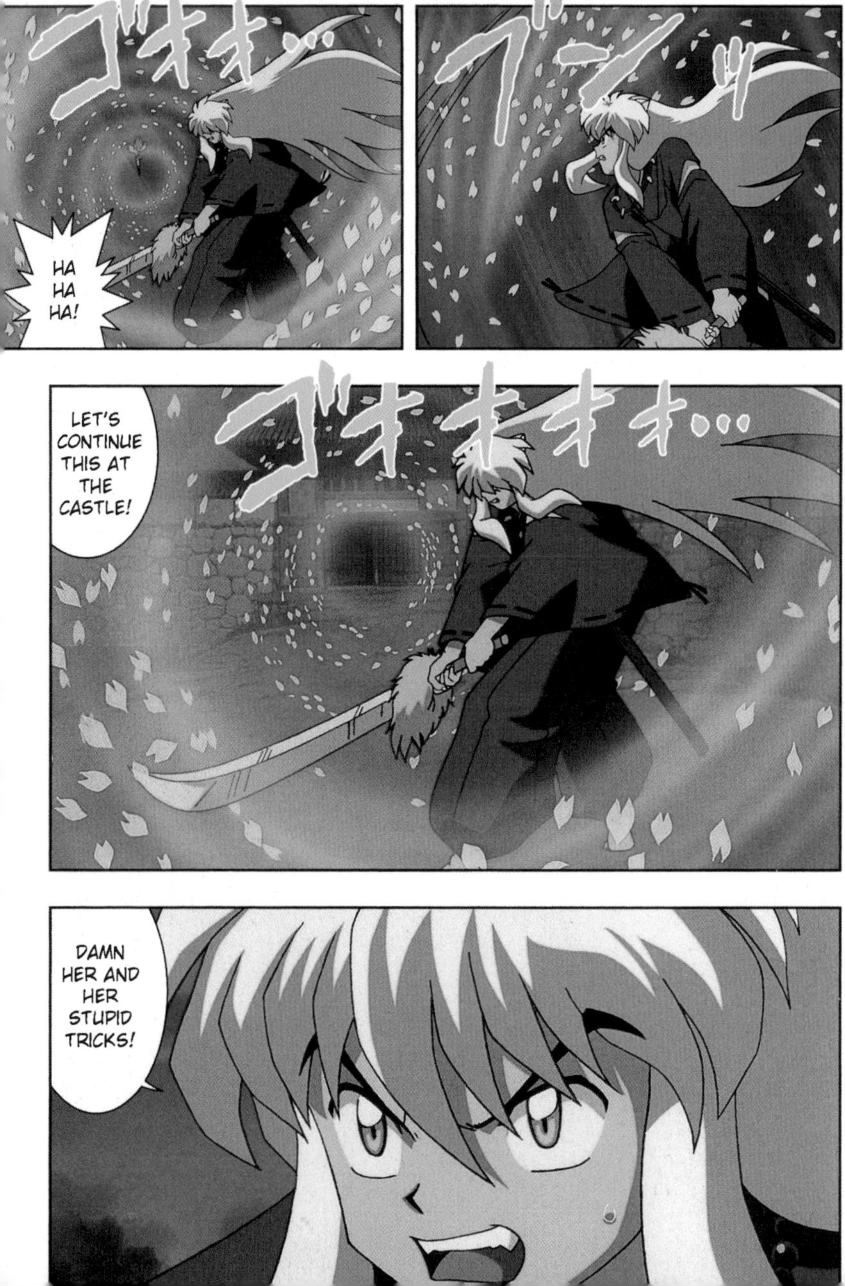
ブーンッ
ゴオオッ
HA HA HA!
ゴオオオオ…
LET'S CONTINUE THIS AT THE CASTLE!
DAMN HER AND HER STUPID TRICKS!

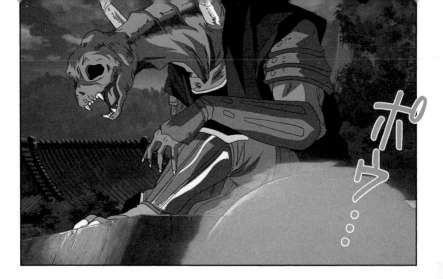

...NOW UPON US!

MASTER! THE TIME IS...

THE MOON IS ALMOST DIRECTLY OVER-HEAD.

94

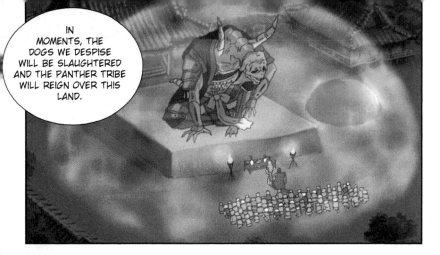

IN MOMENTS, THE DOGS WE DESPISE WILL BE SLAUGHTERED AND THE PANTHER TRIBE WILL REIGN OVER THIS LAND.

...

A BAR- RIER !

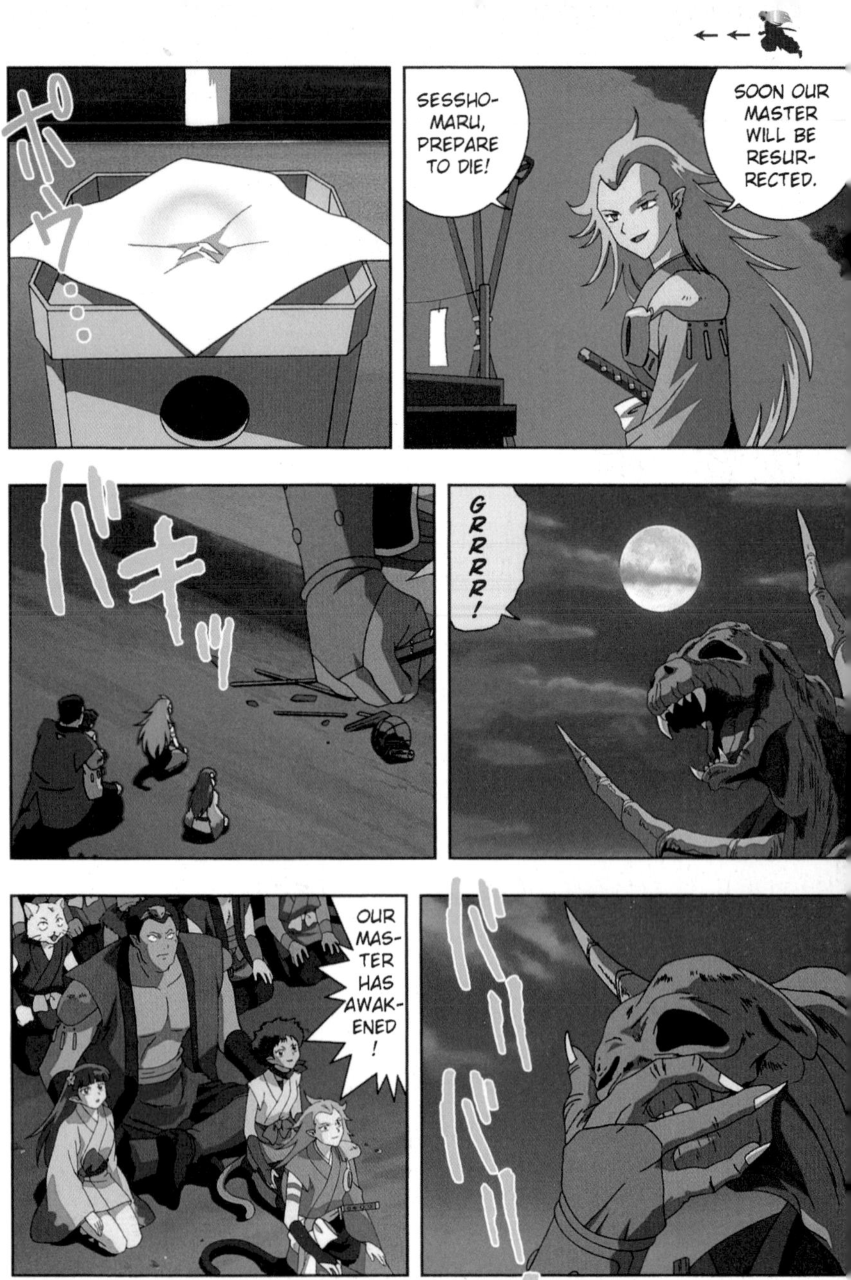
SOON OUR MASTER WILL BE RESURRECTED.
SESSHOMARU, PREPARE TO DIE!
ポウ・・・
GRRRR!
バキッ
バリバリ
OUR MASTER HAS AWAKENED!

GIVE ME BLOOD... FLESH... AND A SOUL!

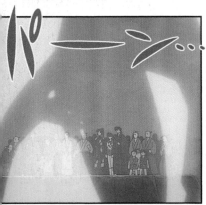

?!

THE PAN-THER TRIBE...!

WHAT'S THIS?!

KA-GOME!

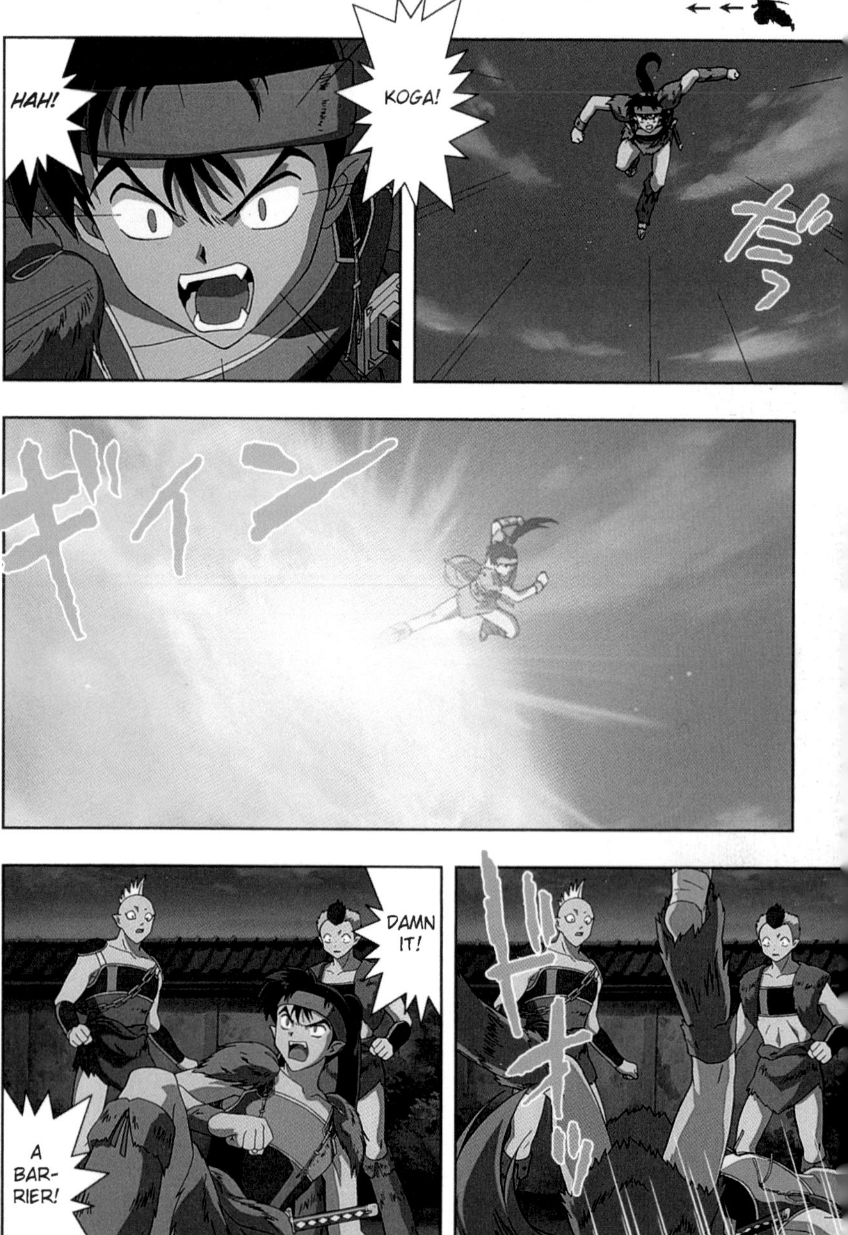
だッ
KOGA!
HAH!
ギィン
ドォッ
DAMN IT!
A BAR-RIER!

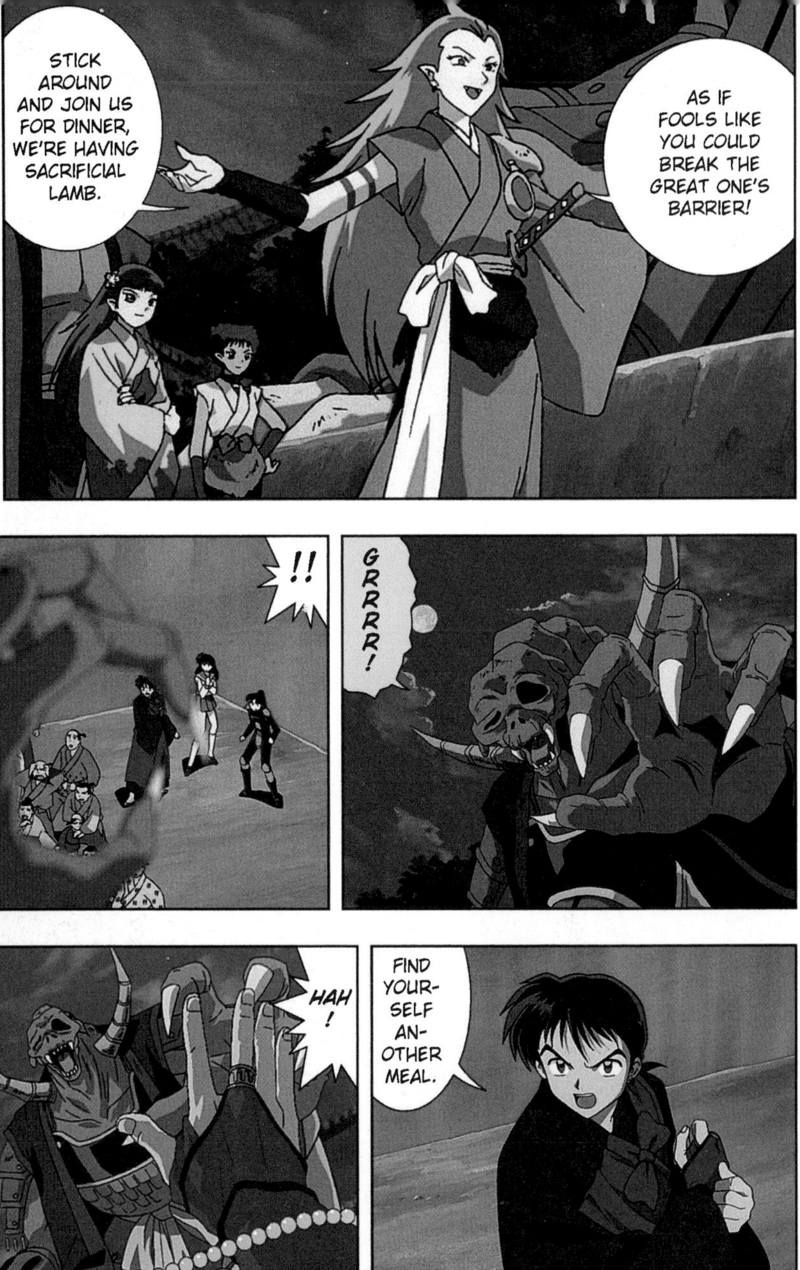
AS IF FOOLS LIKE YOU COULD BREAK THE GREAT ONE'S BARRIER!
STICK AROUND AND JOIN US FOR DINNER, WE'RE HAVING SACRIFICIAL LAMB.
GRRRR!
!!
FIND YOUR-SELF AN-OTHER MEAL.
HAH!

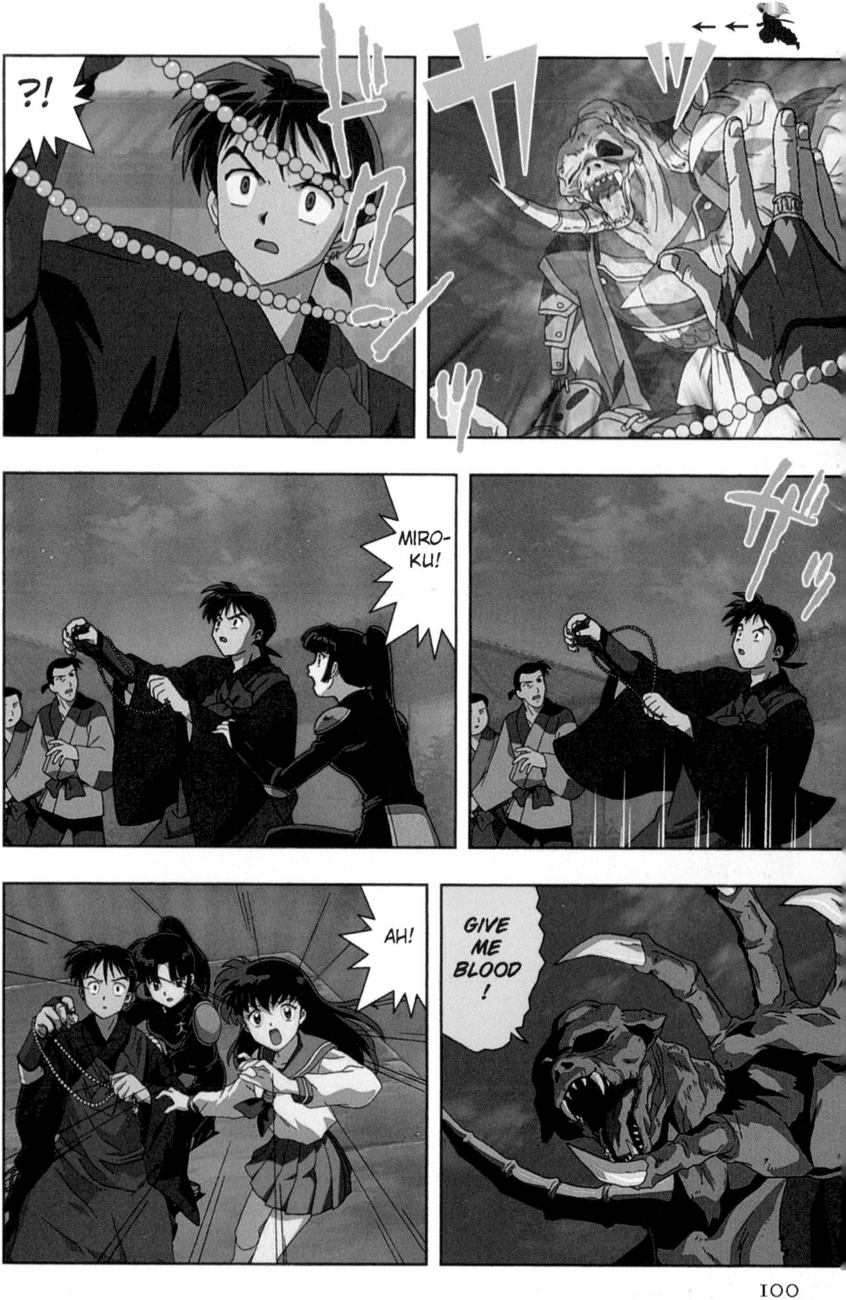
?!
MIRO-KU!
GIVE ME BLOOD!
AH!

...?!

KA-GOME!

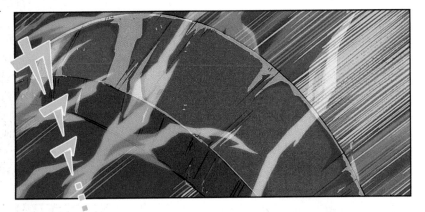

THE TETSUSAIGA IS RED!

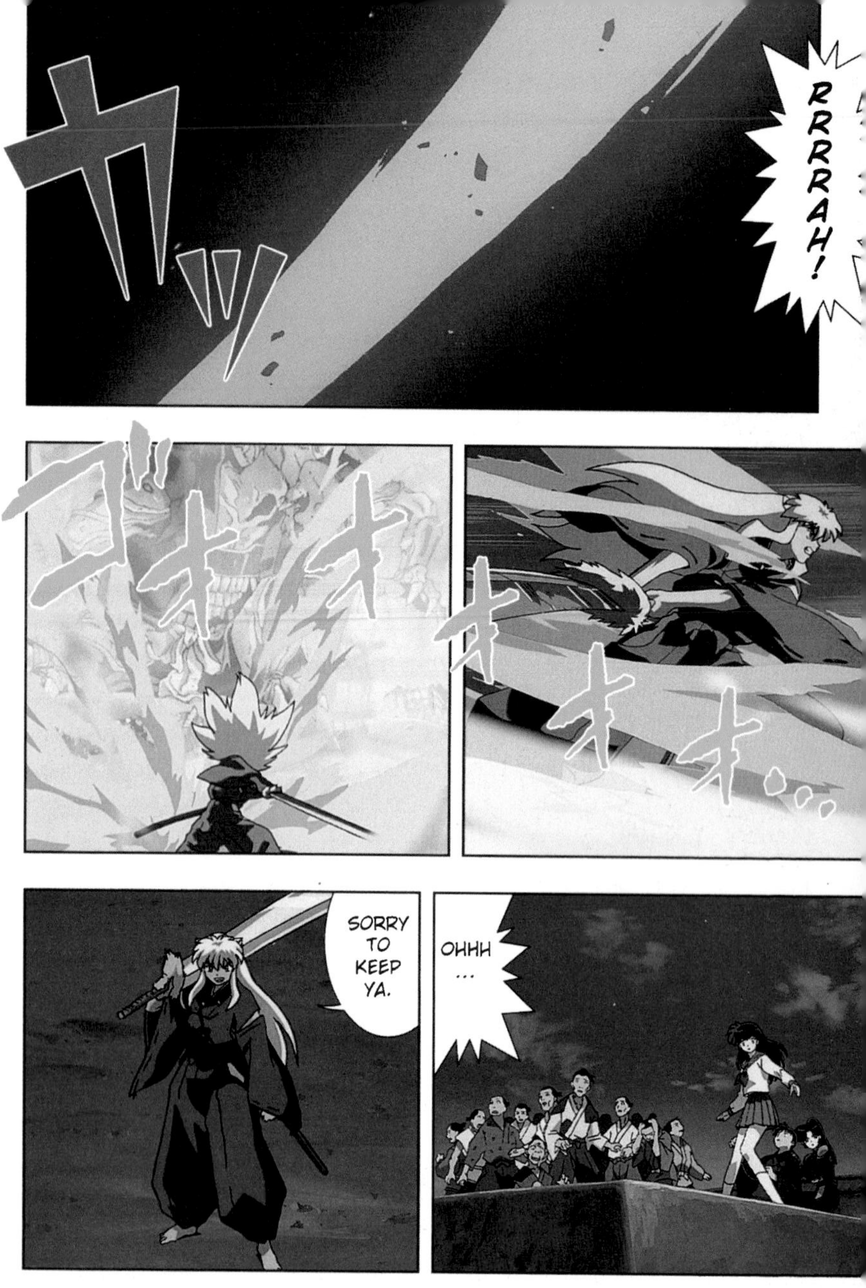
RRRRAH!
ガッ
ゴオオオオ…
OHHH ...
SORRY TO KEEP YA.

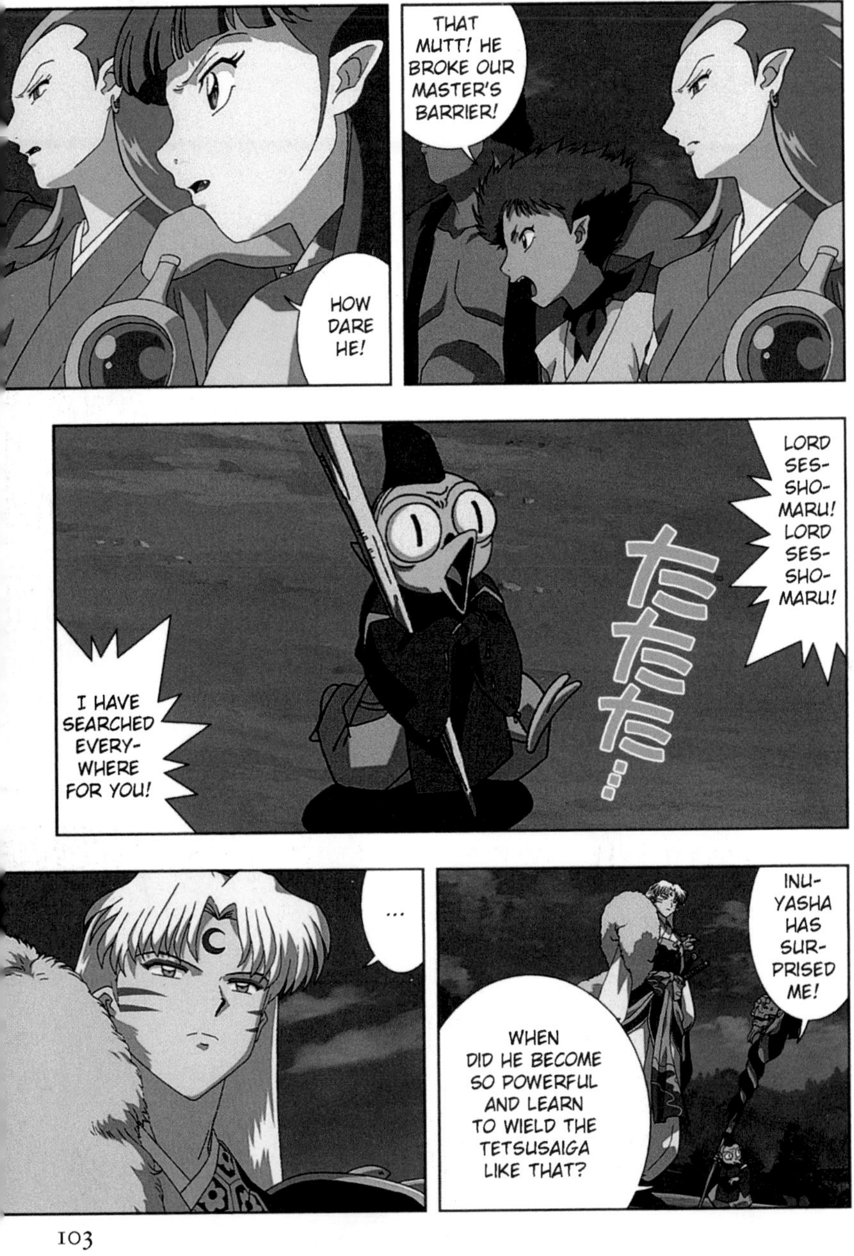
THAT MUTT! HE BROKE OUR MASTER'S BARRIER!
HOW DARE HE!
LORD SESSHOMARU! LORD SESSHOMARU!
たたた…
I HAVE SEARCHED EVERYWHERE FOR YOU!
INUYASHA HAS SURPRISED ME!
WHEN DID HE BECOME SO POWERFUL AND LEARN TO WIELD THE TETSUSAIGA LIKE THAT?
…

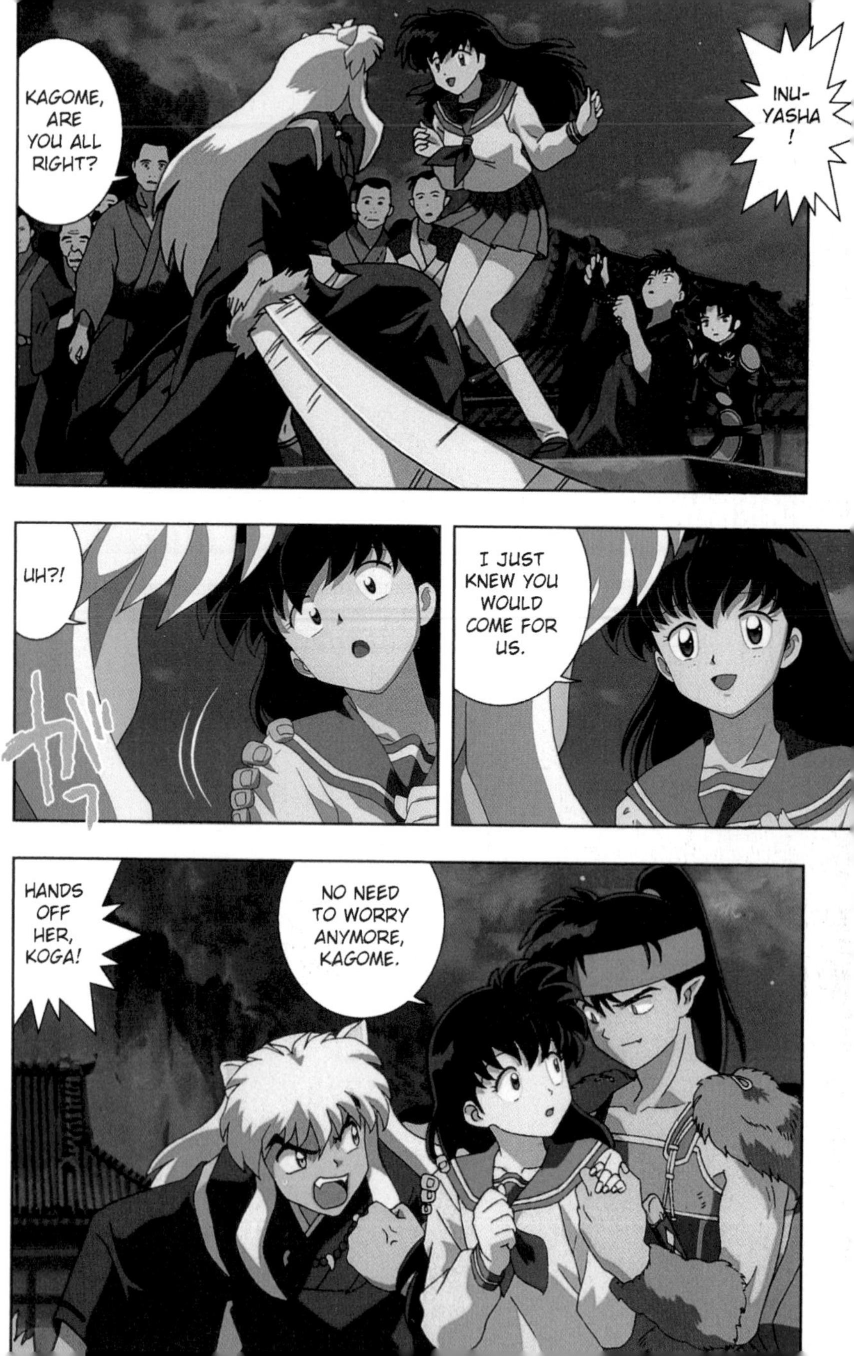
INU-YASHA!
KAGOME, ARE YOU ALL RIGHT?
I JUST KNEW YOU WOULD COME FOR US.
UH?!
NO NEED TO WORRY ANYMORE, KAGOME.
HANDS OFF HER, KOGA!

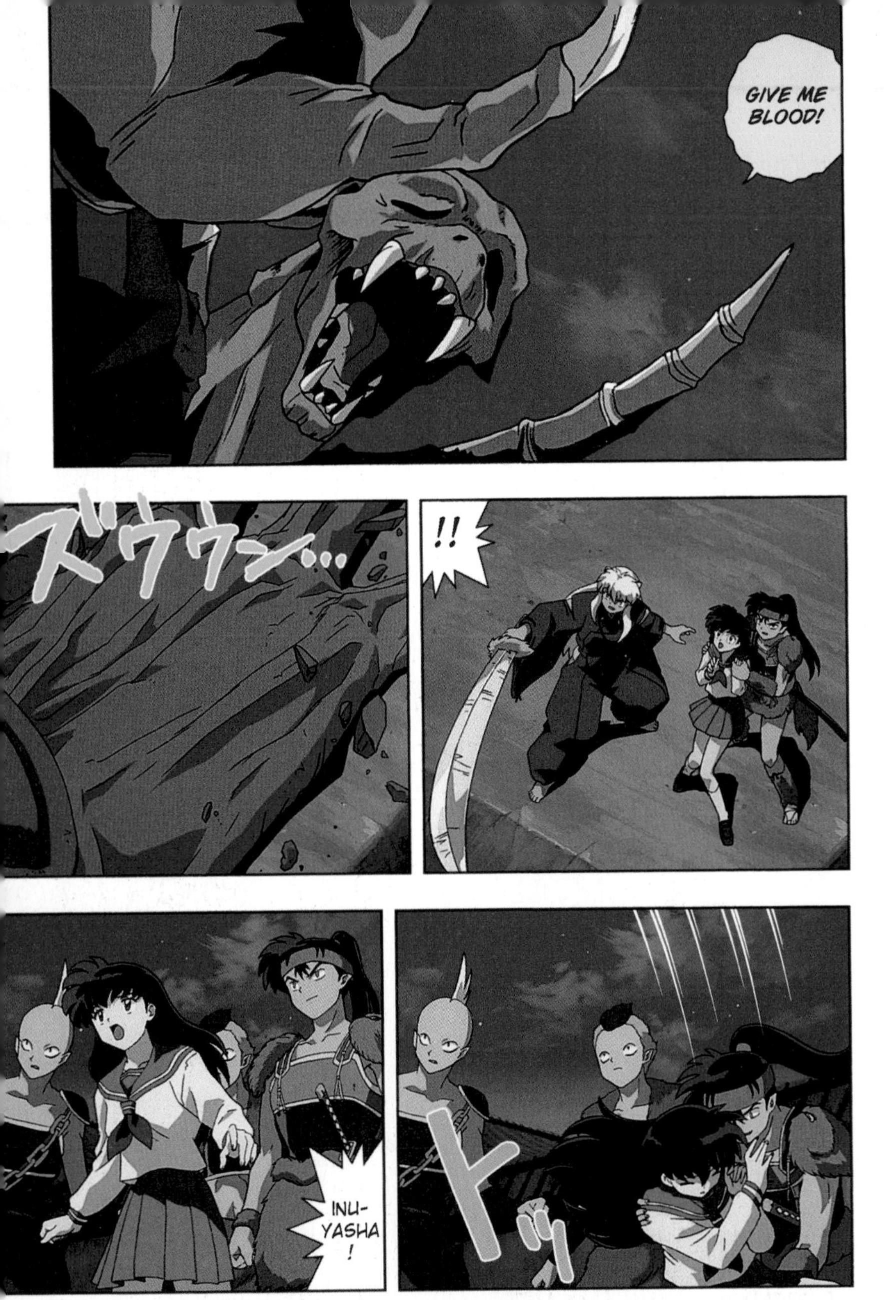
GIVE ME BLOOD!
!!
ズウウン…
ドッ
INU-YASHA!

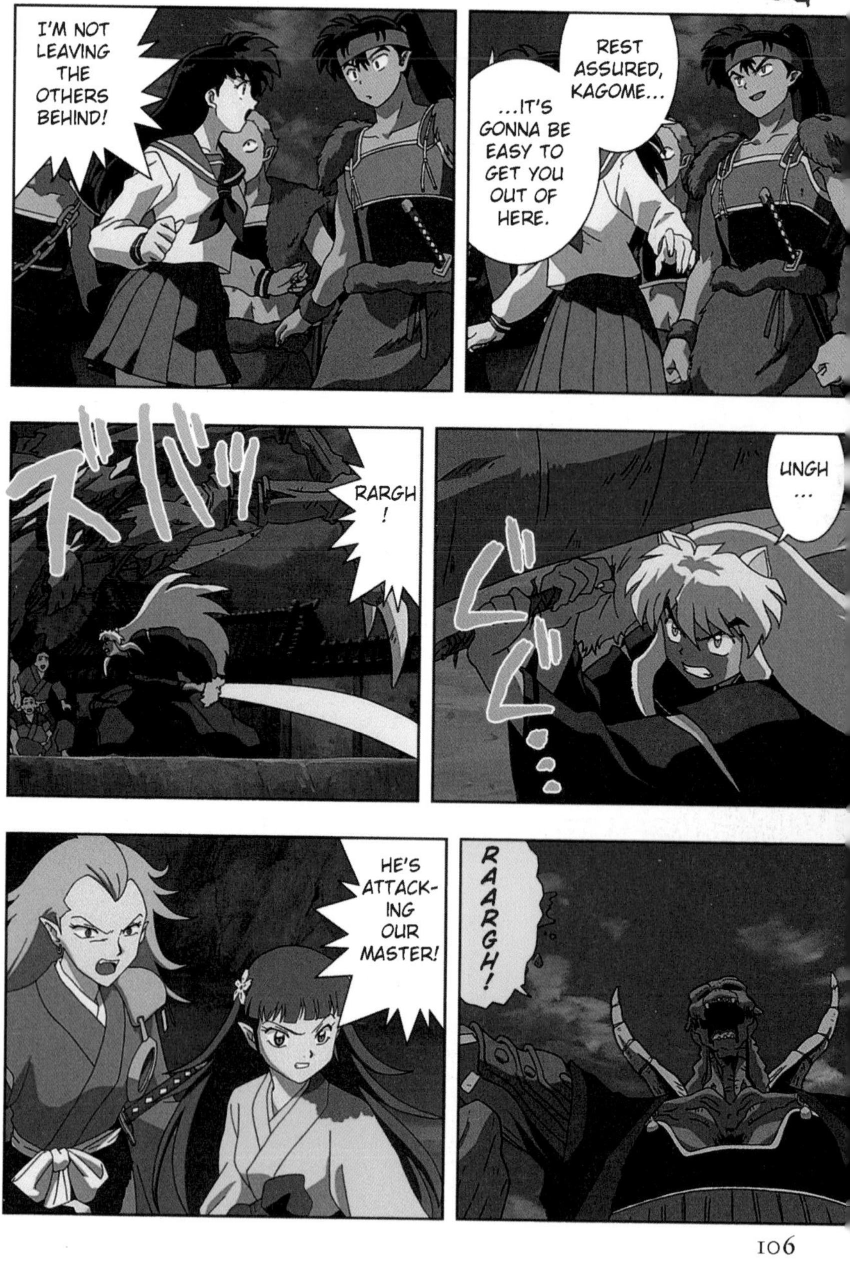
REST ASSURED, KAGOME...
...IT'S GONNA BE EASY TO GET YOU OUT OF HERE.
I'M NOT LEAVING THE OTHERS BEHIND!
UNGH ...
ぐぐ…
ズバッ
RARGH!
RAARGH!
HE'S ATTACK-ING OUR MASTER!

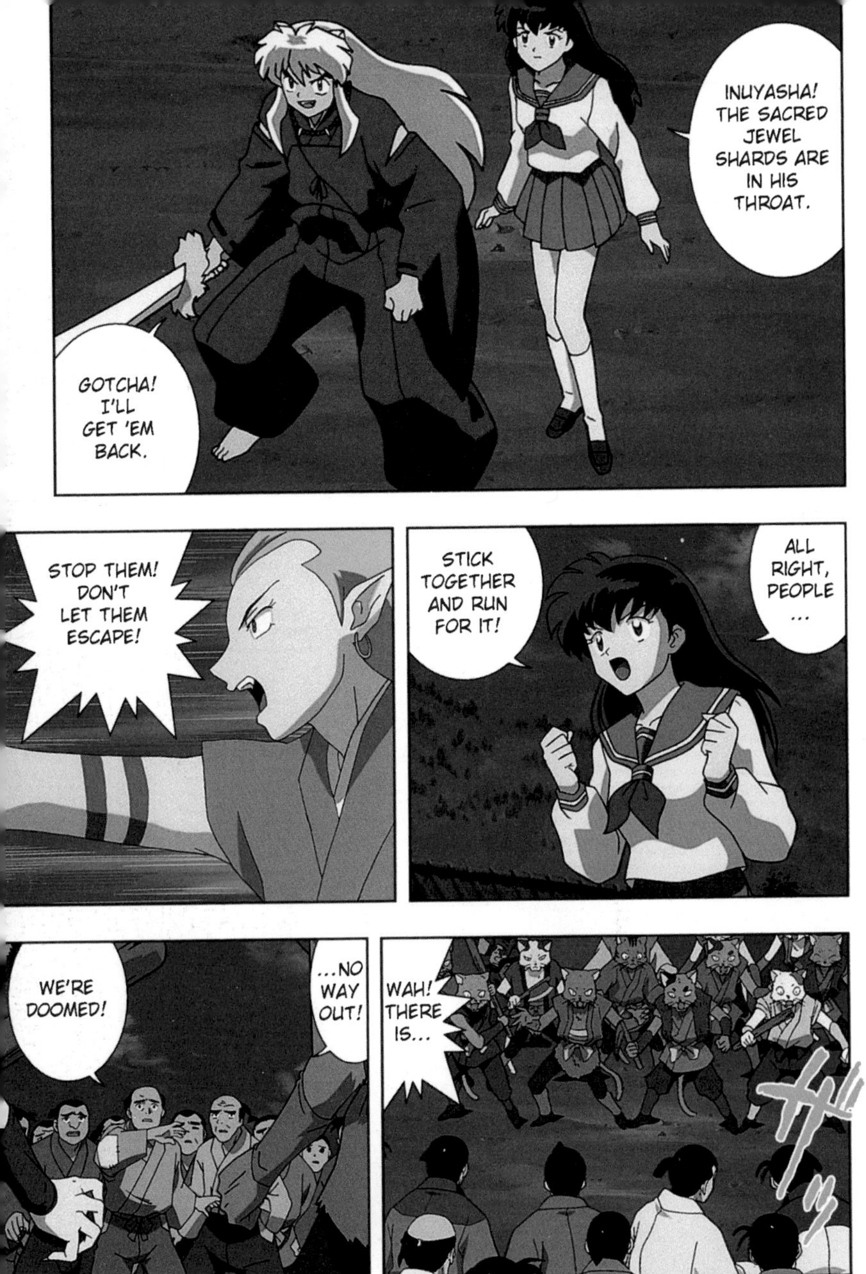
INUYASHA! THE SACRED JEWEL SHARDS ARE IN HIS THROAT.
GOTCHA! I'LL GET 'EM BACK.
ALL RIGHT, PEOPLE ...
STICK TOGETHER AND RUN FOR IT!
STOP THEM! DON'T LET THEM ESCAPE!
WAH! THERE IS...
...NO WAY OUT!
WE'RE DOOMED!

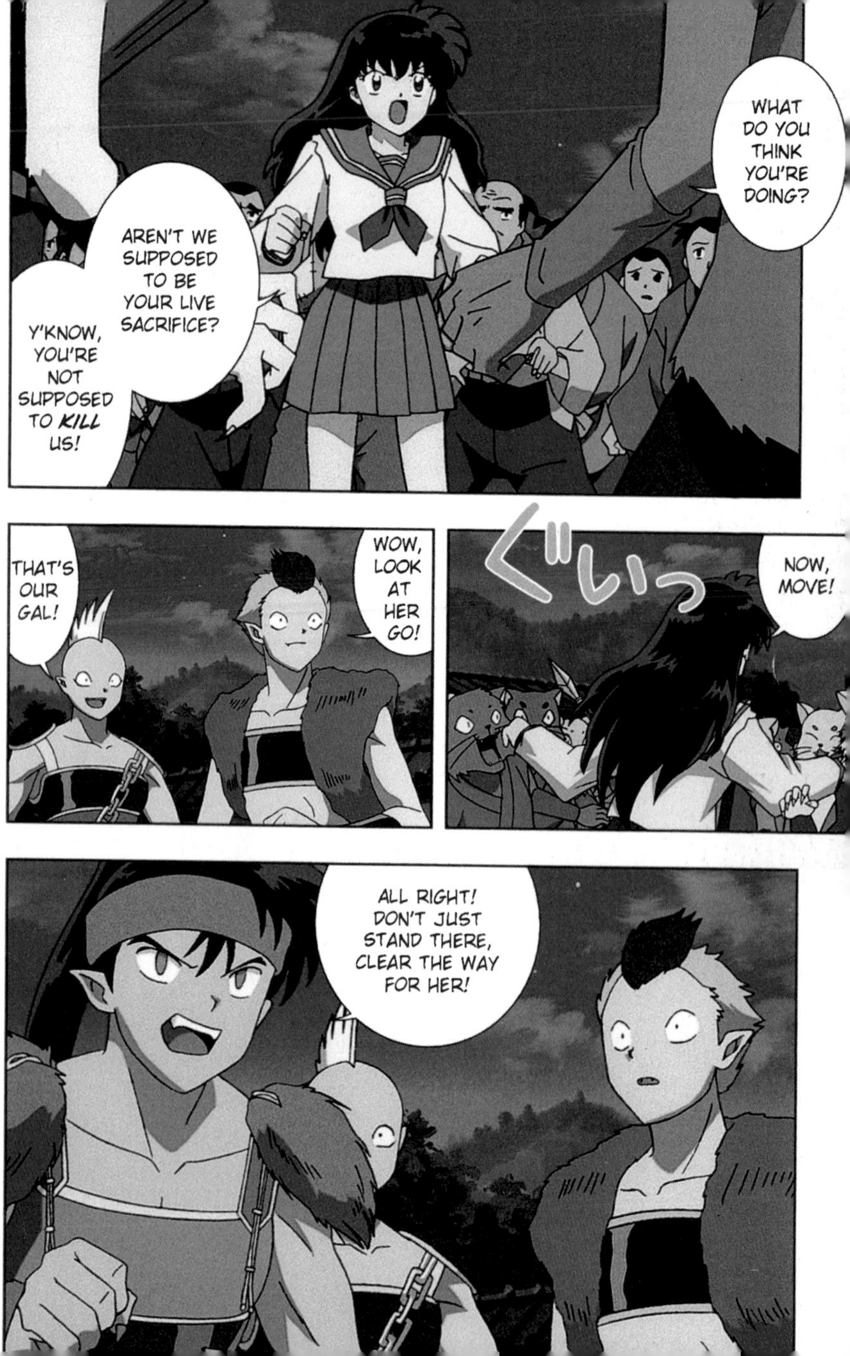
WHAT DO YOU THINK YOU'RE DOING?
AREN'T WE SUPPOSED TO BE YOUR LIVE SACRIFICE?
Y'KNOW, YOU'RE NOT SUPPOSED TO *KILL* US!
ぐいっ
NOW, MOVE!
WOW, LOOK AT HER GO!
THAT'S OUR GAL!
ALL RIGHT! DON'T JUST STAND THERE, CLEAR THE WAY FOR HER!

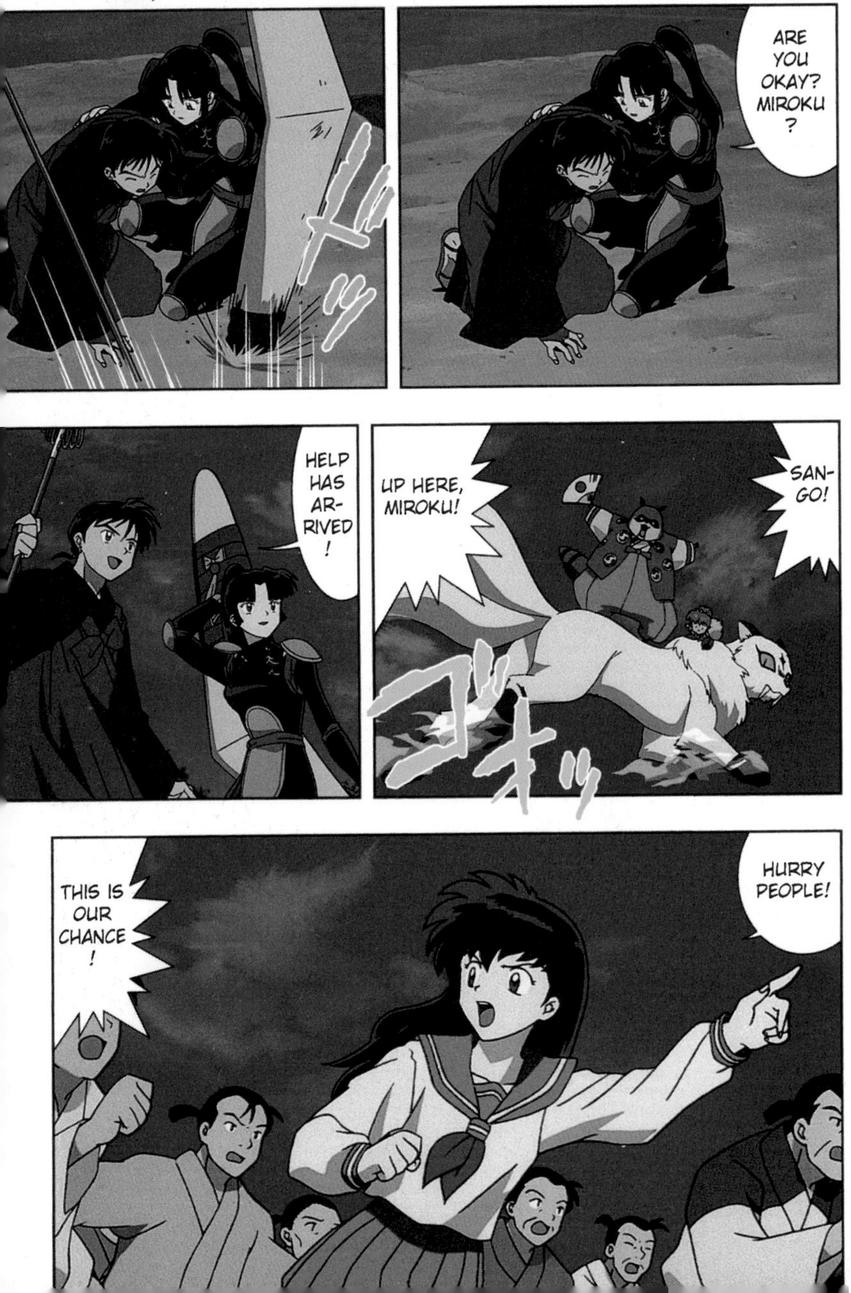
ARE YOU OKAY? MIROKU?
ドッ
SANGO!
UP HERE, MIROKU!
ゴオッ
HELP HAS ARRIVED!
HURRY PEOPLE!
THIS IS OUR CHANCE!

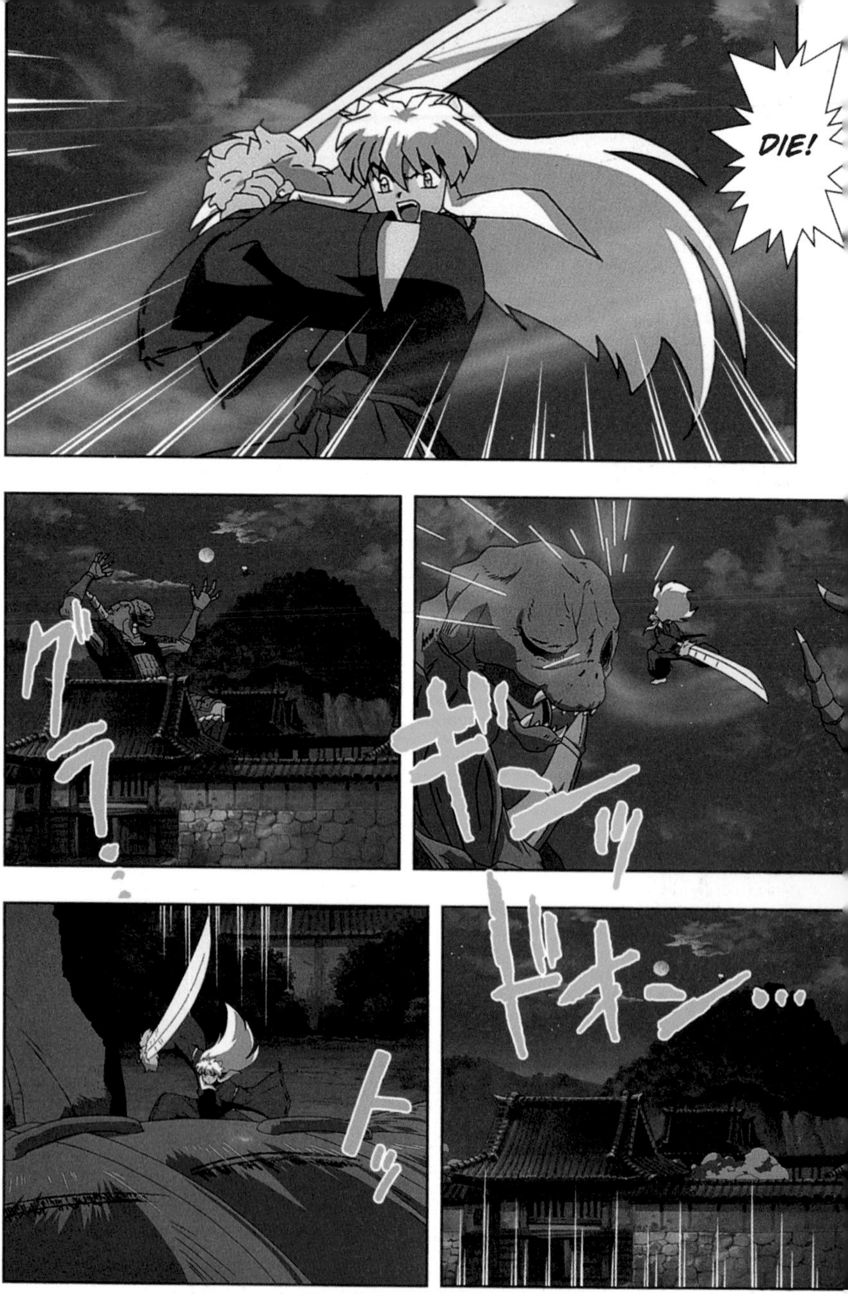
DIE!
ギンッ
グラ
ドオン…
トッ

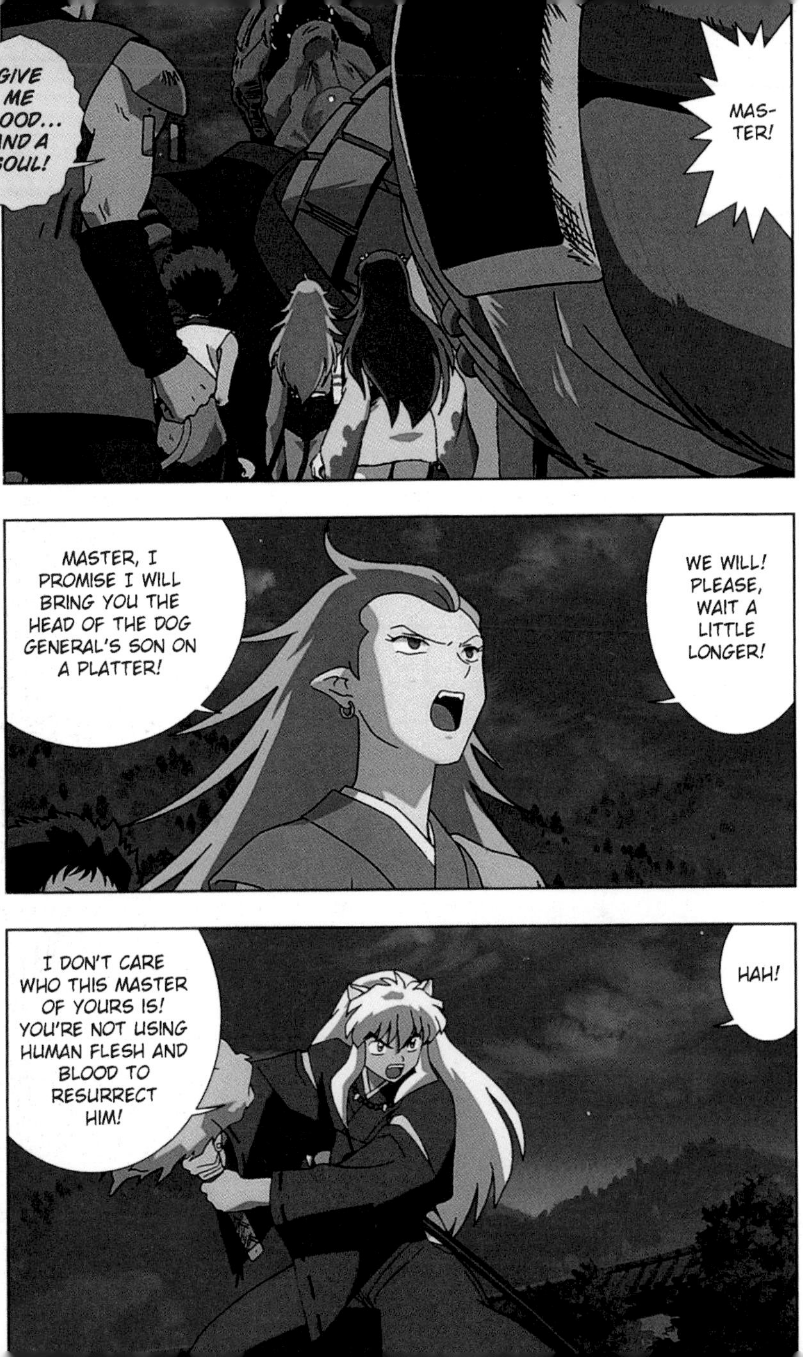
MAS-TER!
GIVE ME BLOOD... AND A SOUL!
WE WILL! PLEASE, WAIT A LITTLE LONGER!
MASTER, I PROMISE I WILL BRING YOU THE HEAD OF THE DOG GENERAL'S SON ON A PLATTER!
HAH!
I DON'T CARE WHO THIS MASTER OF YOURS IS! YOU'RE NOT USING HUMAN FLESH AND BLOOD TO RESURRECT HIM!

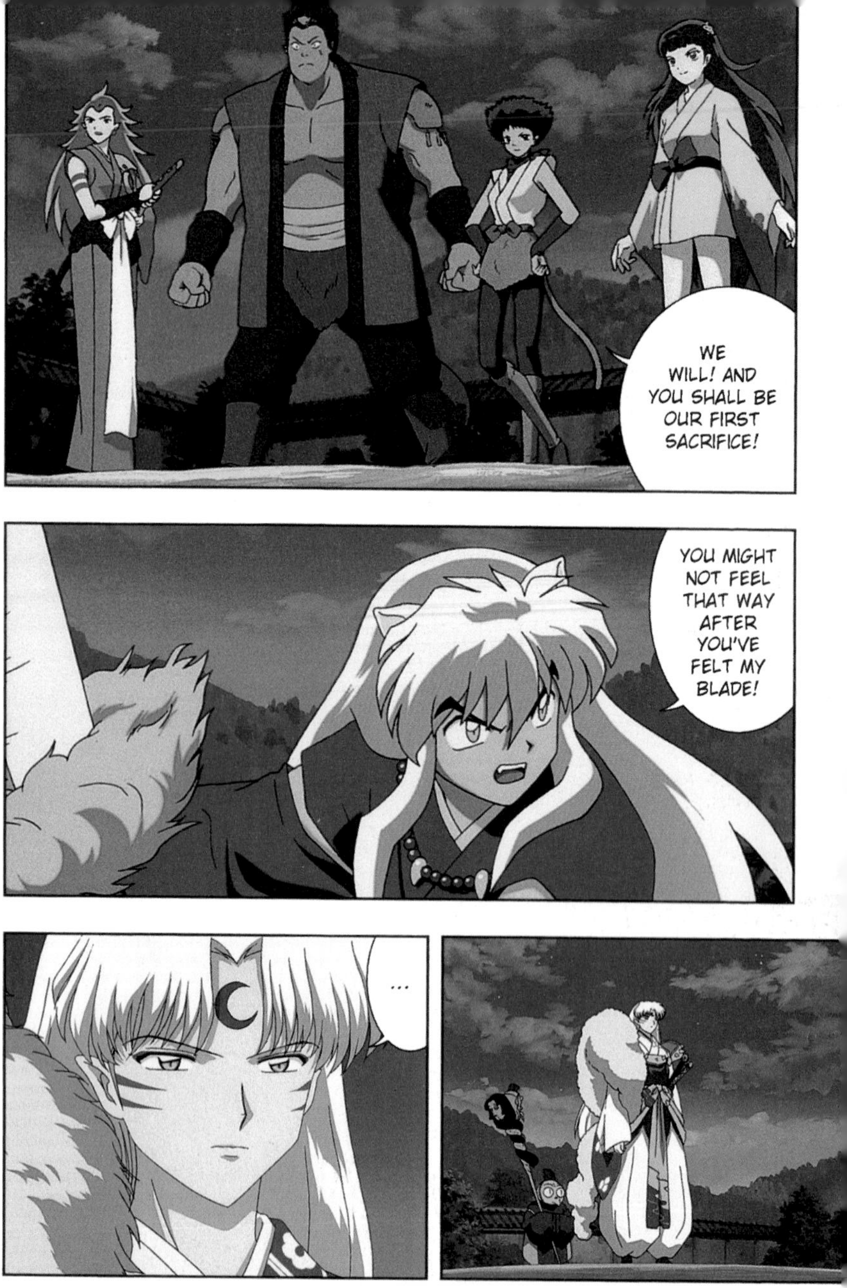
WE WILL! AND YOU SHALL BE OUR FIRST SACRIFICE!
YOU MIGHT NOT FEEL THAT WAY AFTER YOU'VE FELT MY BLADE!
...

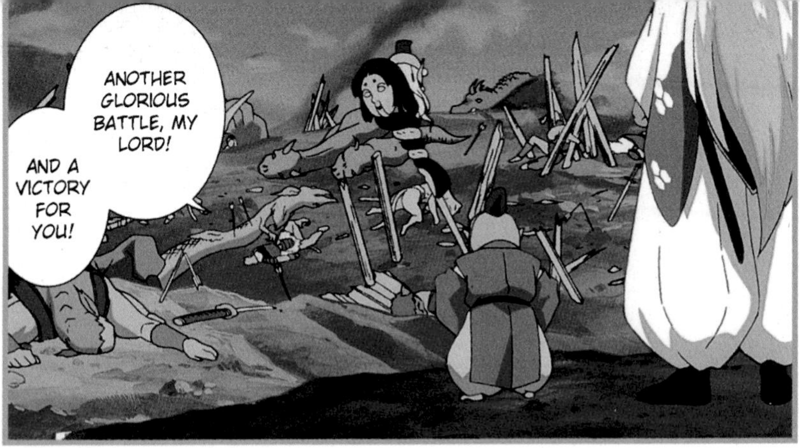
ANOTHER GLORIOUS BATTLE, MY LORD!
AND A VICTORY FOR YOU!

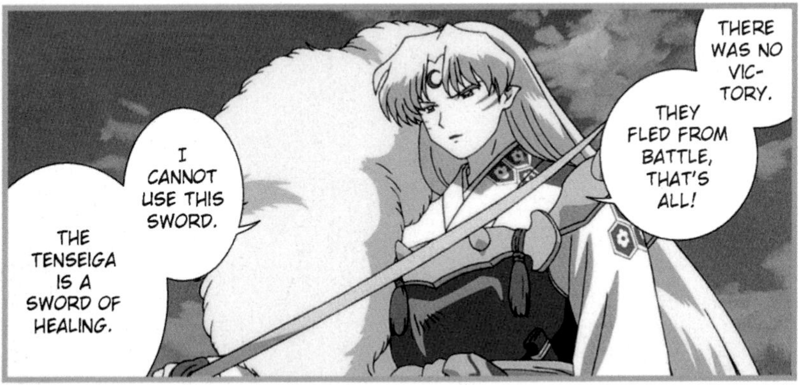
THERE WAS NO VIC-TORY.
THEY FLED FROM BATTLE, THAT'S ALL!
I CANNOT USE THIS SWORD.
THE TENSEIGA IS A SWORD OF HEALING.

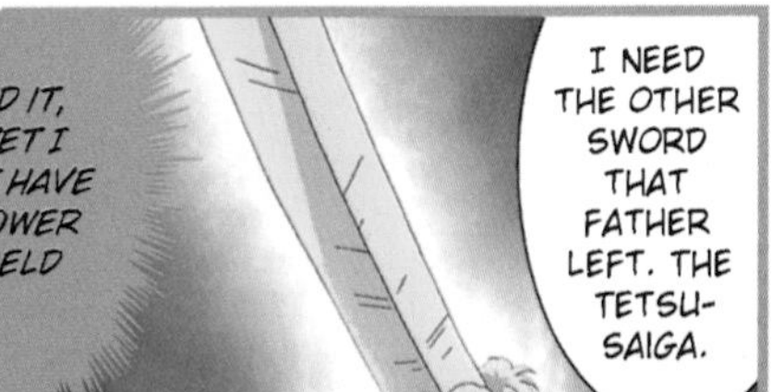
I NEED THE OTHER SWORD THAT FATHER LEFT. THE TETSU-SAIGA.

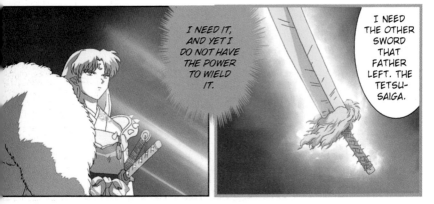

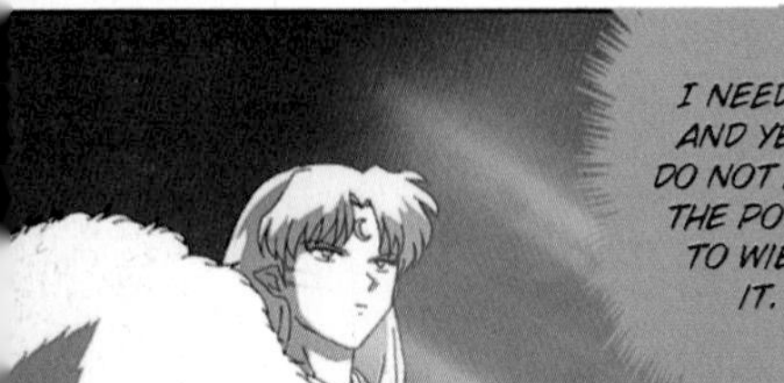
I NEED IT, AND YET I DO NOT HAVE THE POWER TO WIELD IT.

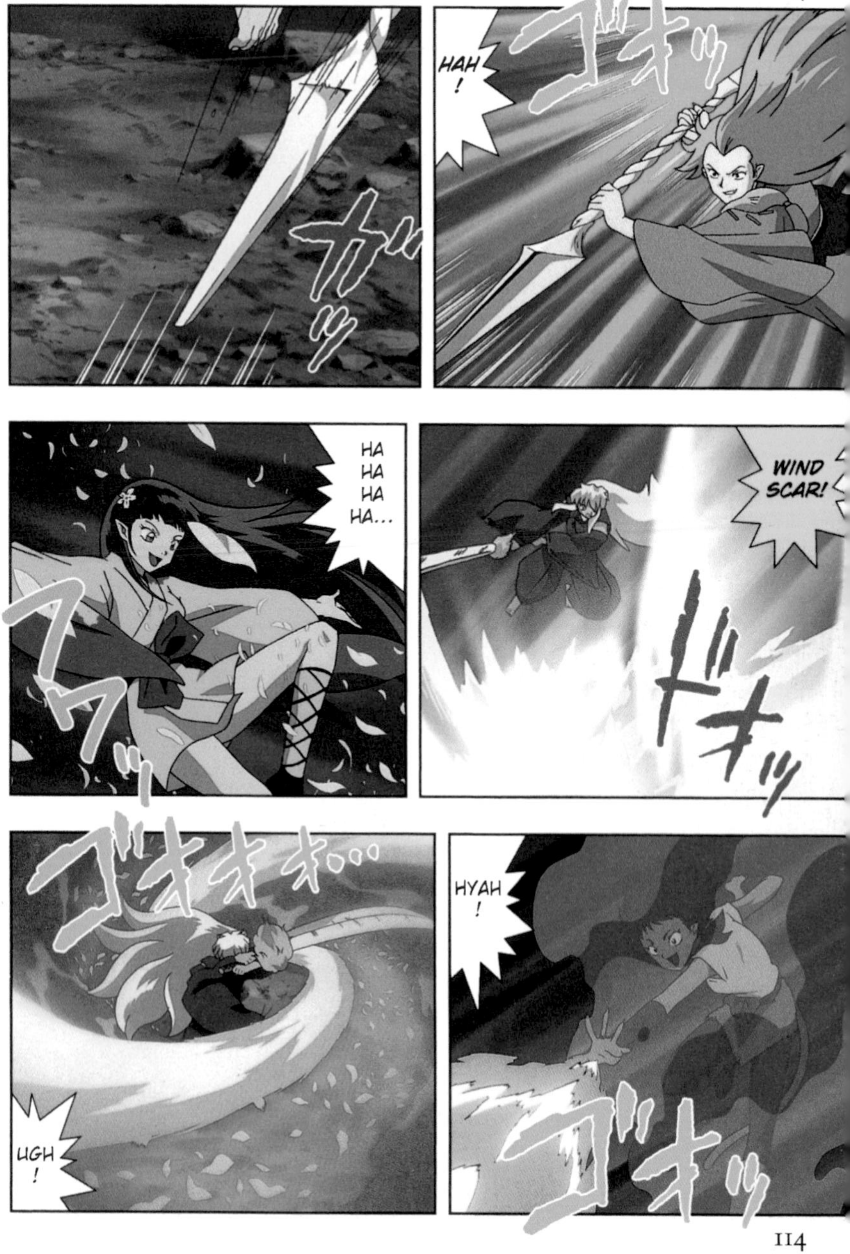
ゴオッ
HAH!
ガッ
WIND SCAR!
HA HA HA HA...
フワッ
HYAH!
ゴオッ
ゴオオオ…
UGH!

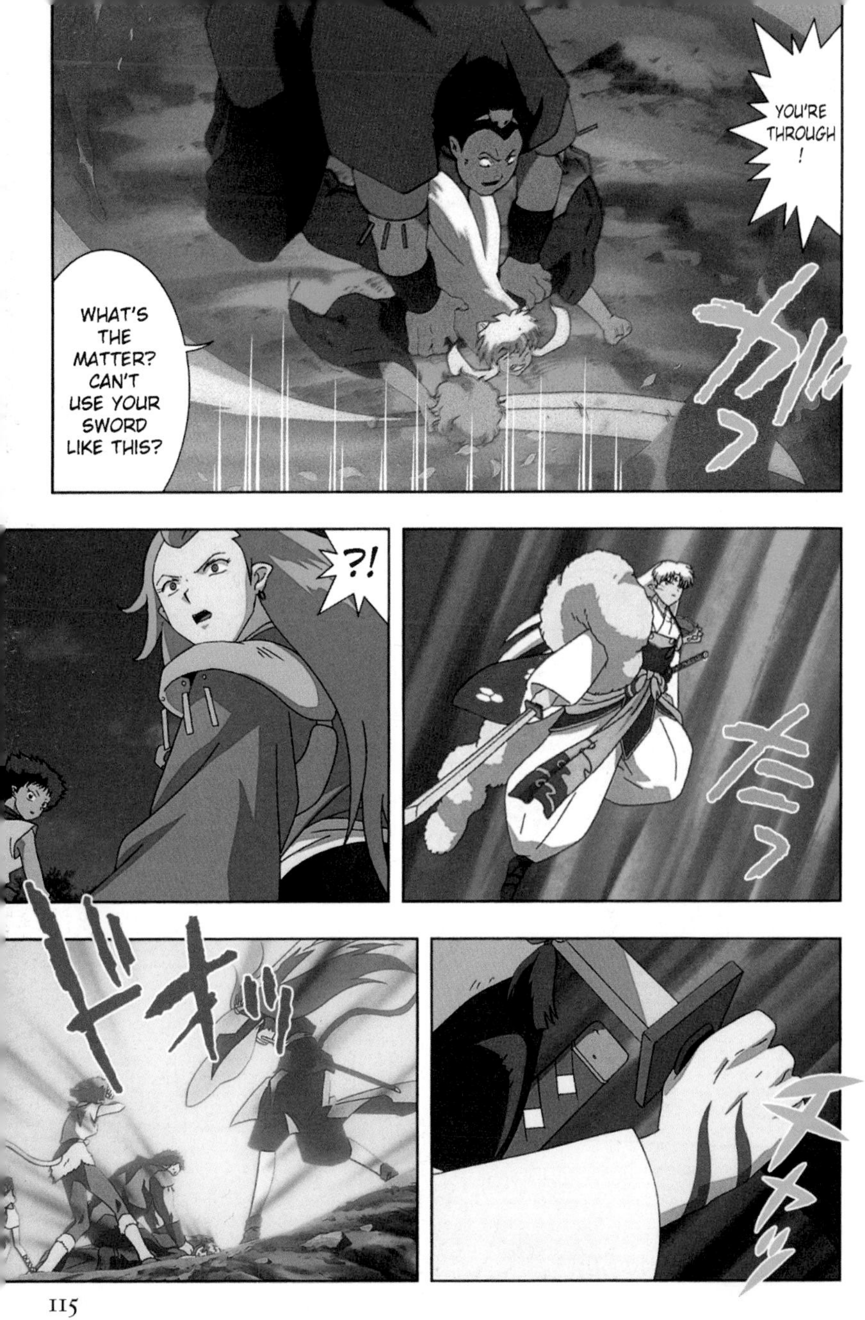
YOU'RE THROUGH!
WHAT'S THE MATTER? CAN'T USE YOUR SWORD LIKE THIS?
?!

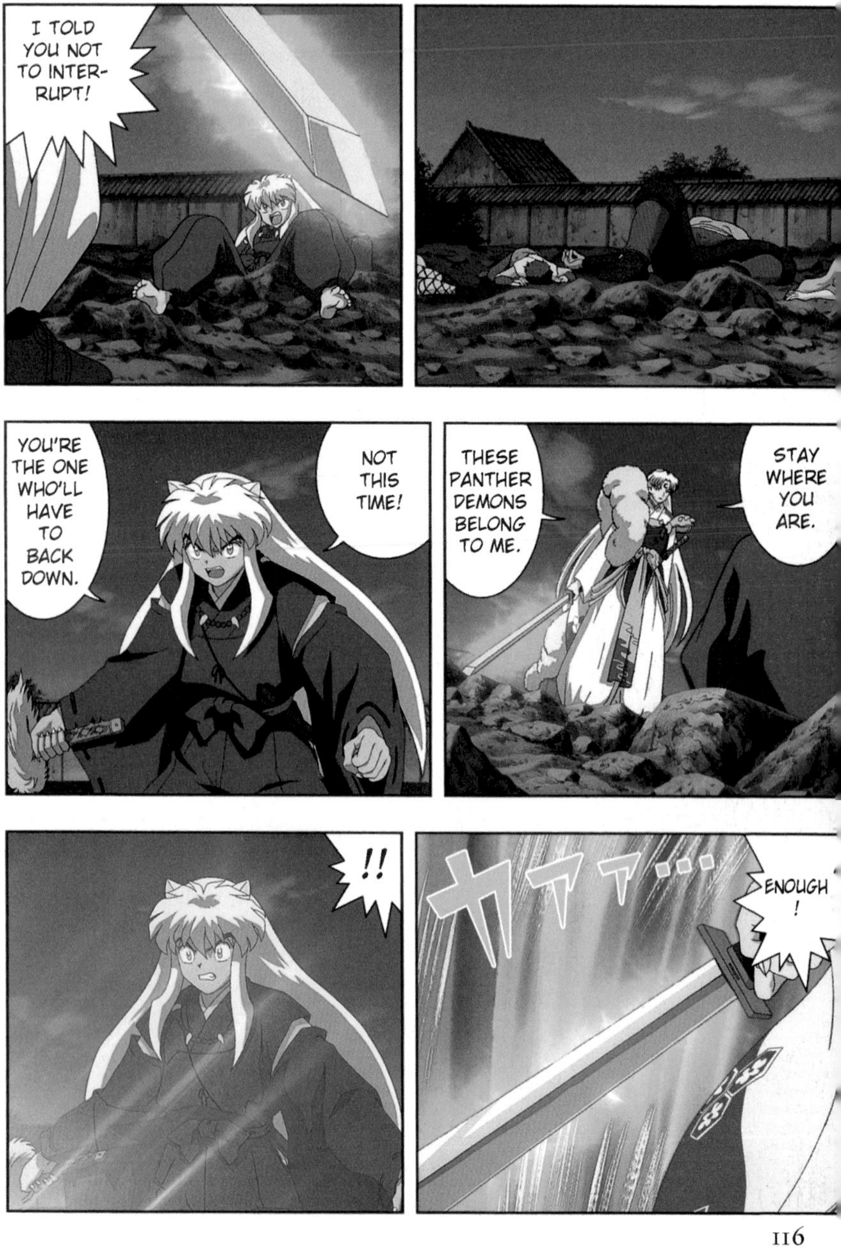
I TOLD YOU NOT TO INTER-RUPT!
STAY WHERE YOU ARE.
THESE PANTHER DEMONS BELONG TO ME.
NOT THIS TIME!
YOU'RE THE ONE WHO'LL HAVE TO BACK DOWN.
カァァ...
ENOUGH!
!!

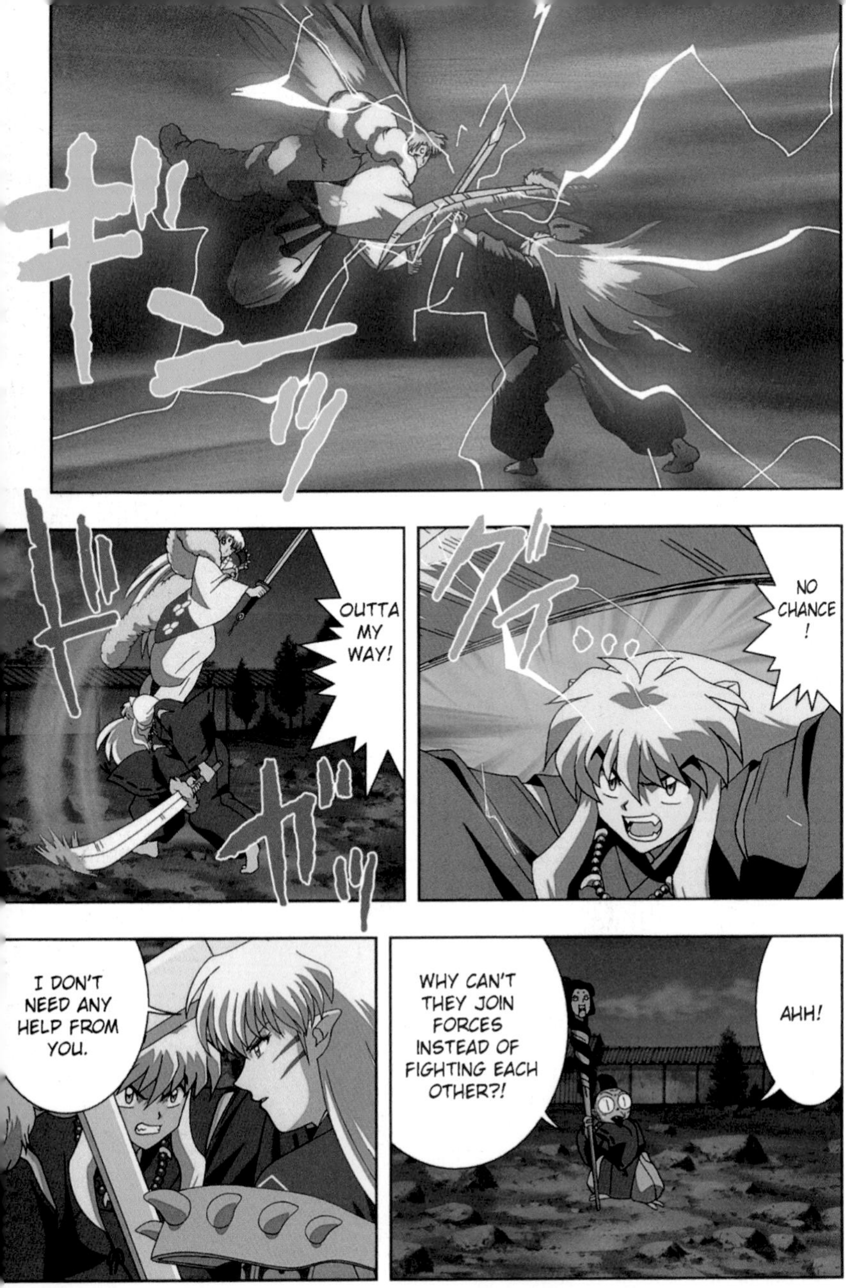
ギンッ
NO CHANCE!
OUTTA MY WAY!
ドッ
ガッ
AHH!
WHY CAN'T THEY JOIN FORCES INSTEAD OF FIGHTING EACH OTHER?!
I DON'T NEED ANY HELP FROM YOU.

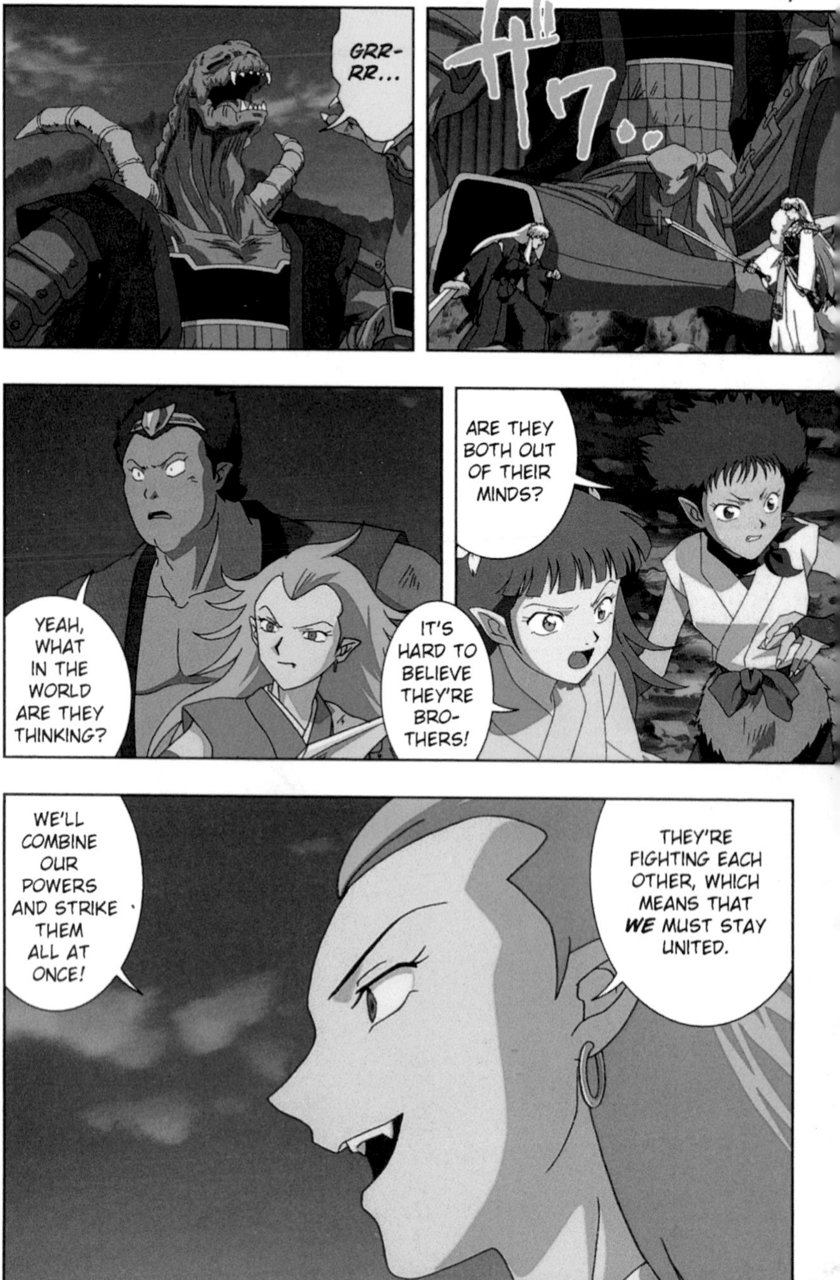
ザワ..
GRR- RR...
ARE THEY BOTH OUT OF THEIR MINDS?
IT'S HARD TO BELIEVE THEY'RE BRO- THERS!
YEAH, WHAT IN THE WORLD ARE THEY THINKING?
THEY'RE FIGHTING EACH OTHER, WHICH MEANS THAT ***WE*** MUST STAY UNITED.
WE'LL COMBINE OUR POWERS AND STRIKE THEM ALL AT ONCE!

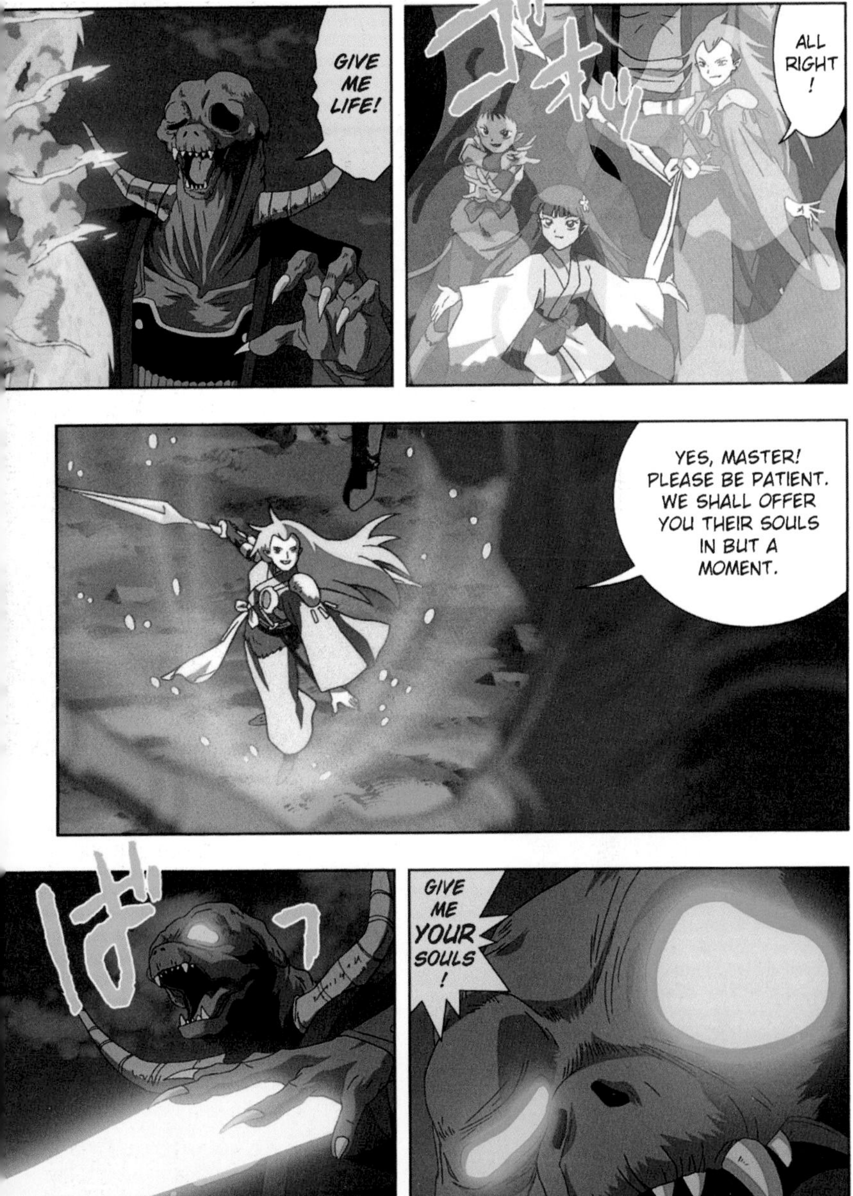
ゴォッ
ALL RIGHT!
GIVE ME LIFE!
YES, MASTER! PLEASE BE PATIENT. WE SHALL OFFER YOU THEIR SOULS IN BUT A MOMENT.
GIVE ME YOUR SOULS!
ばっ

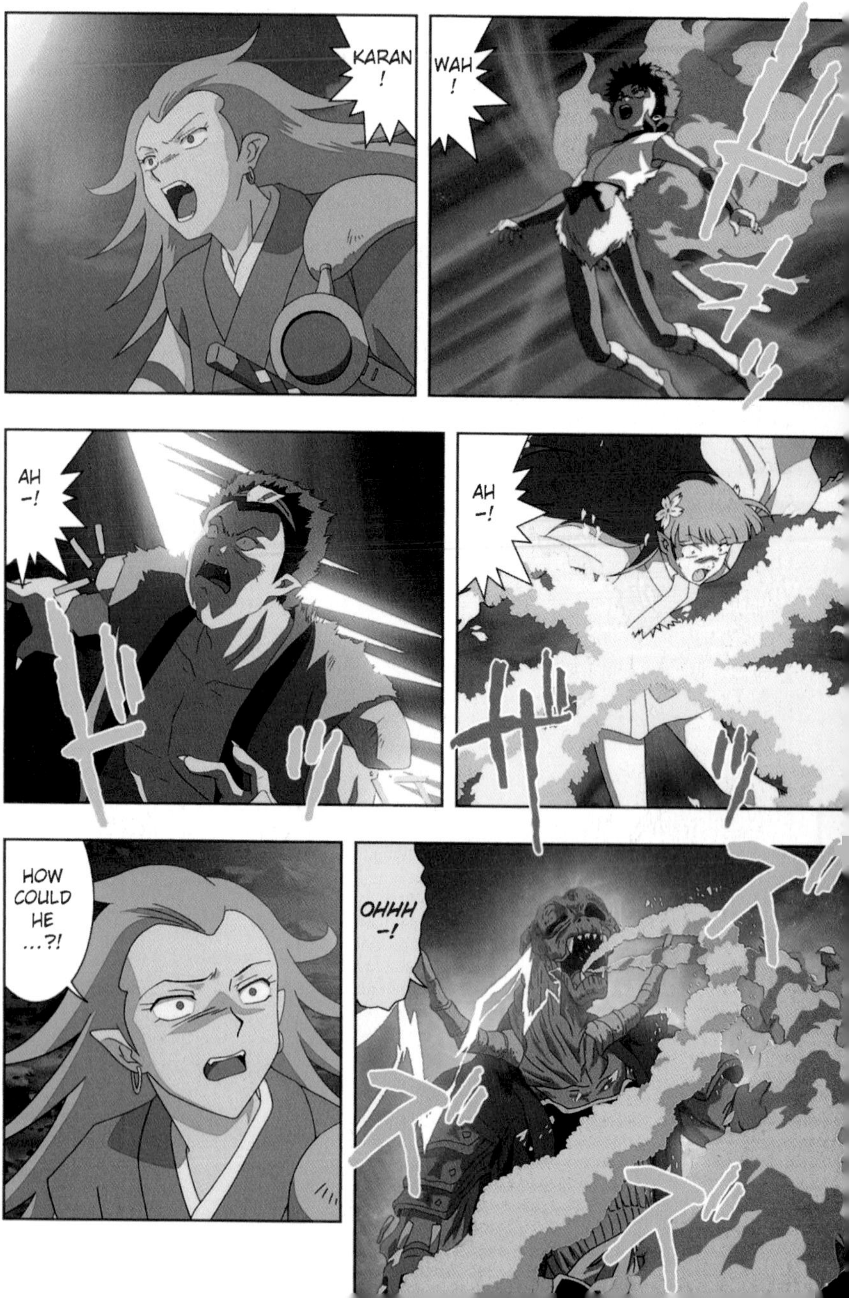
WAH!
KARAN!
AH-!
AH-!
OHHH-!
HOW COULD HE ...?!

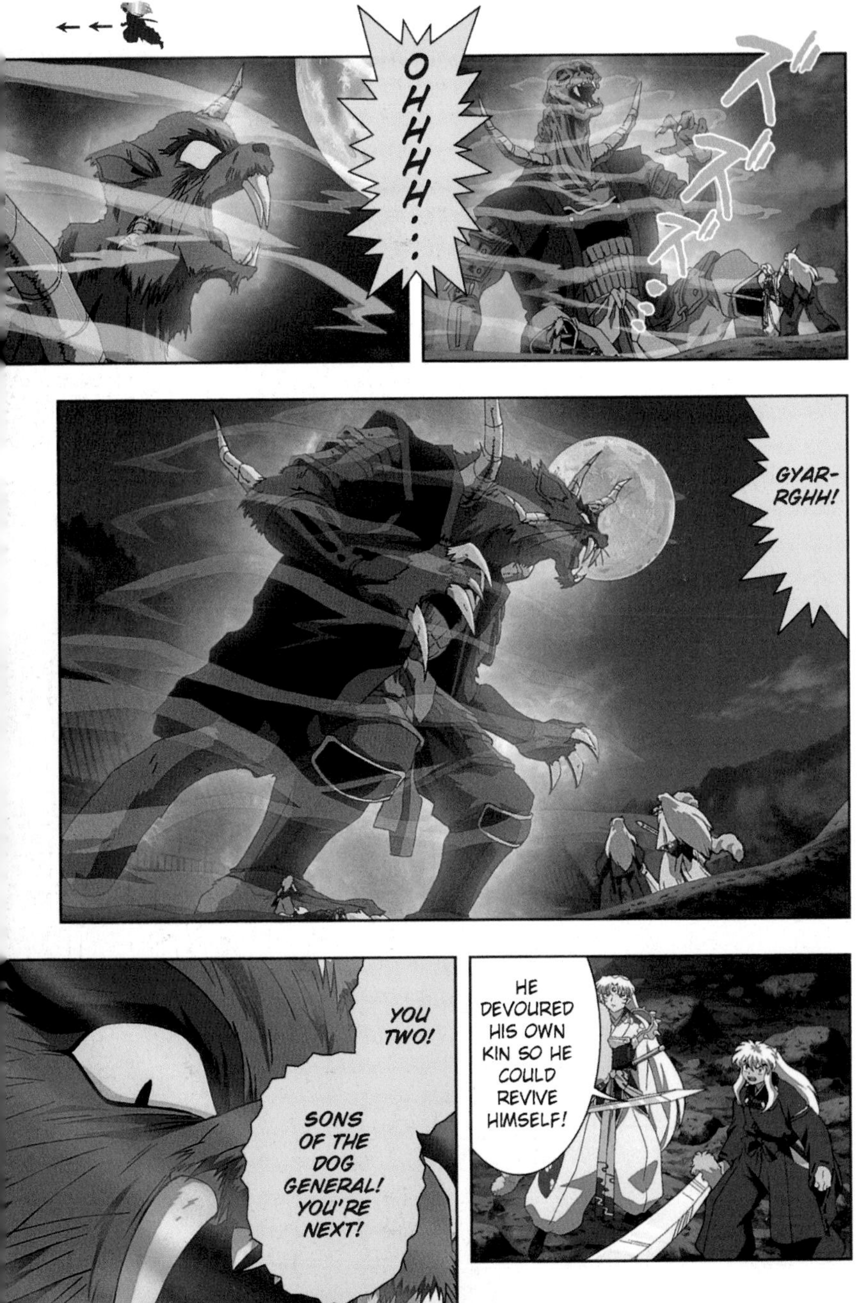
OHHHH...
GYAR-RGHH!
HE DEVOURED HIS OWN KIN SO HE COULD REVIVE HIMSELF!
YOU TWO!
SONS OF THE DOG GENERAL! YOU'RE NEXT!

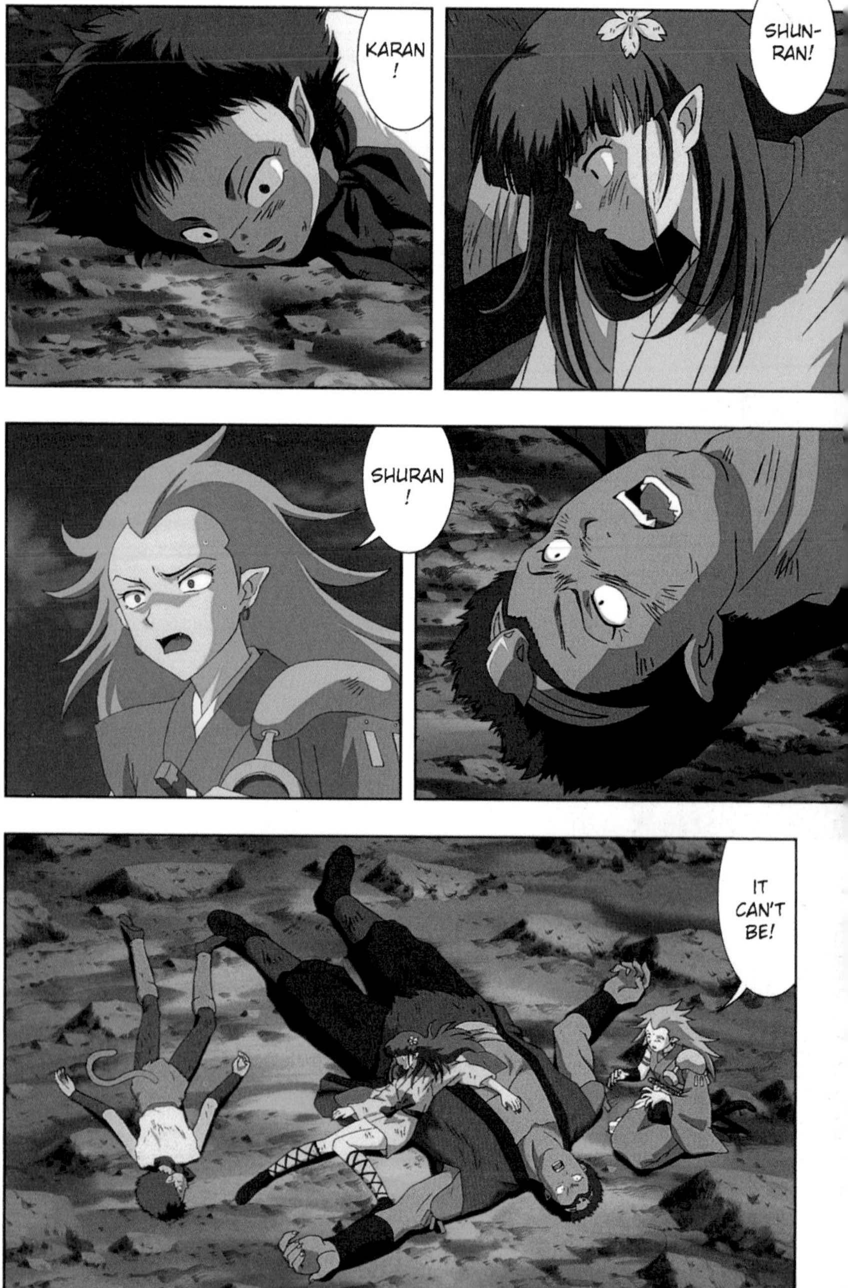
SHUN-RAN!
KARAN!
SHURAN!
IT CAN'T BE!

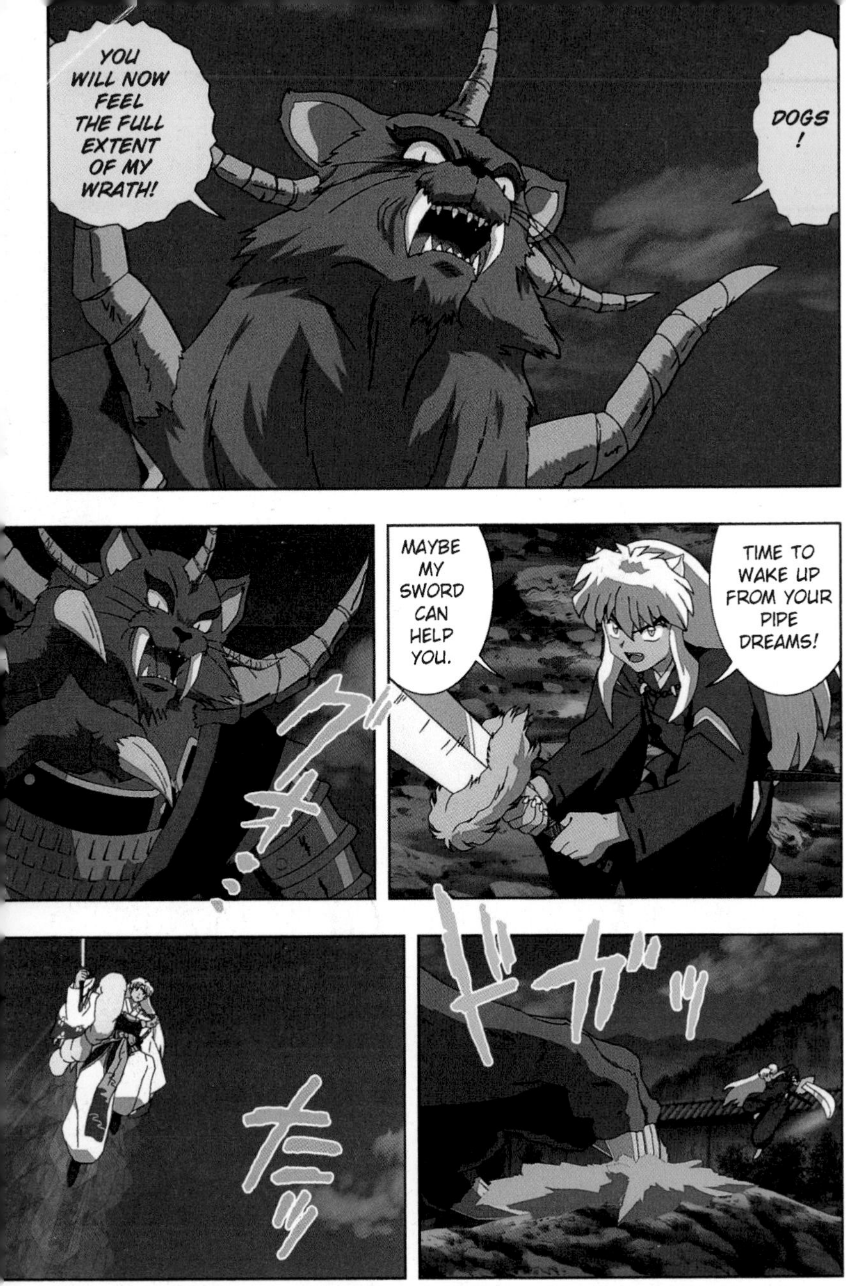
DOGS!
YOU WILL NOW FEEL THE FULL EXTENT OF MY WRATH!
TIME TO WAKE UP FROM YOUR PIPE DREAMS!
MAYBE MY SWORD CAN HELP YOU.
ドガッ
たッ

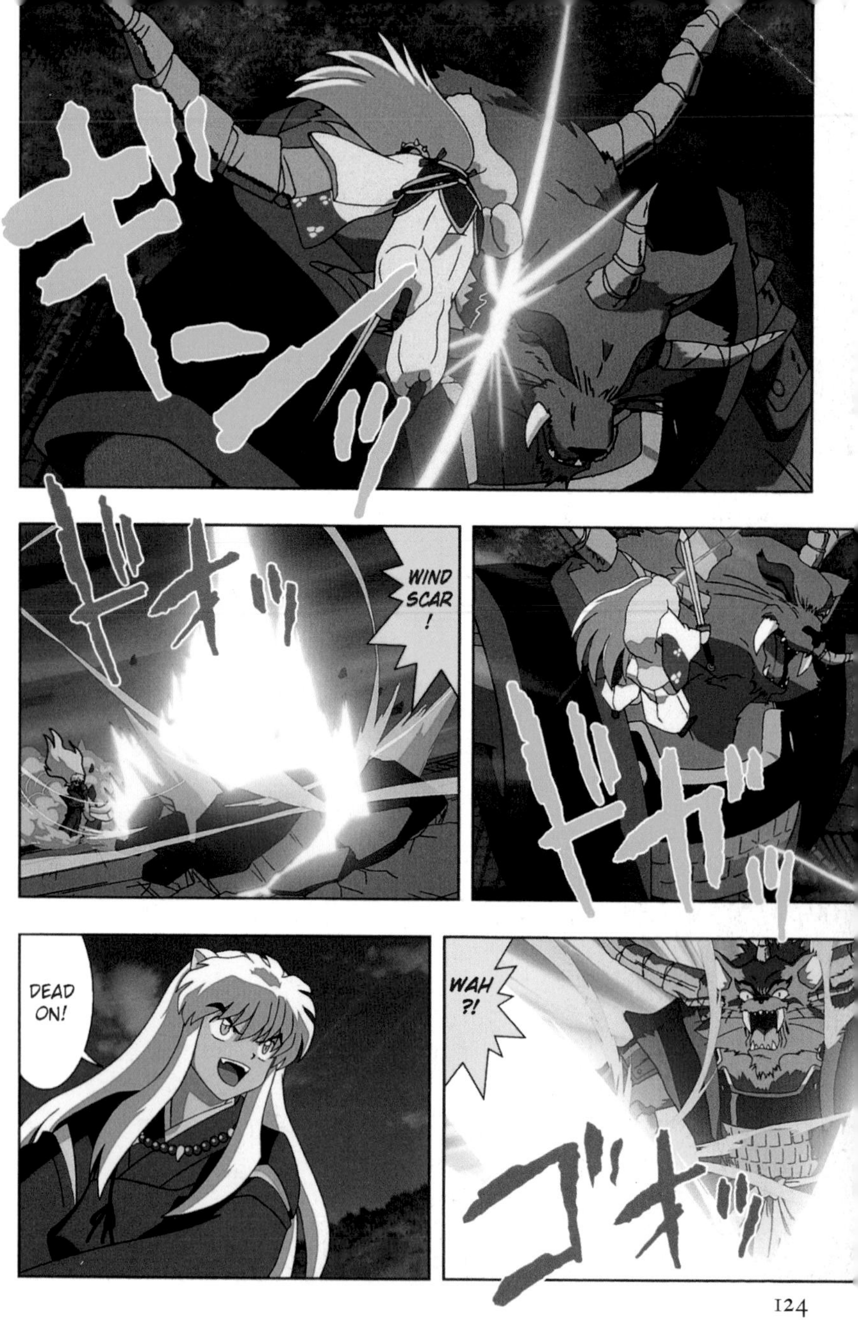
ギーッ
ドガッ
WIND SCAR!
ドオッ
WAH?!
ゴオッ
DEAD ON!

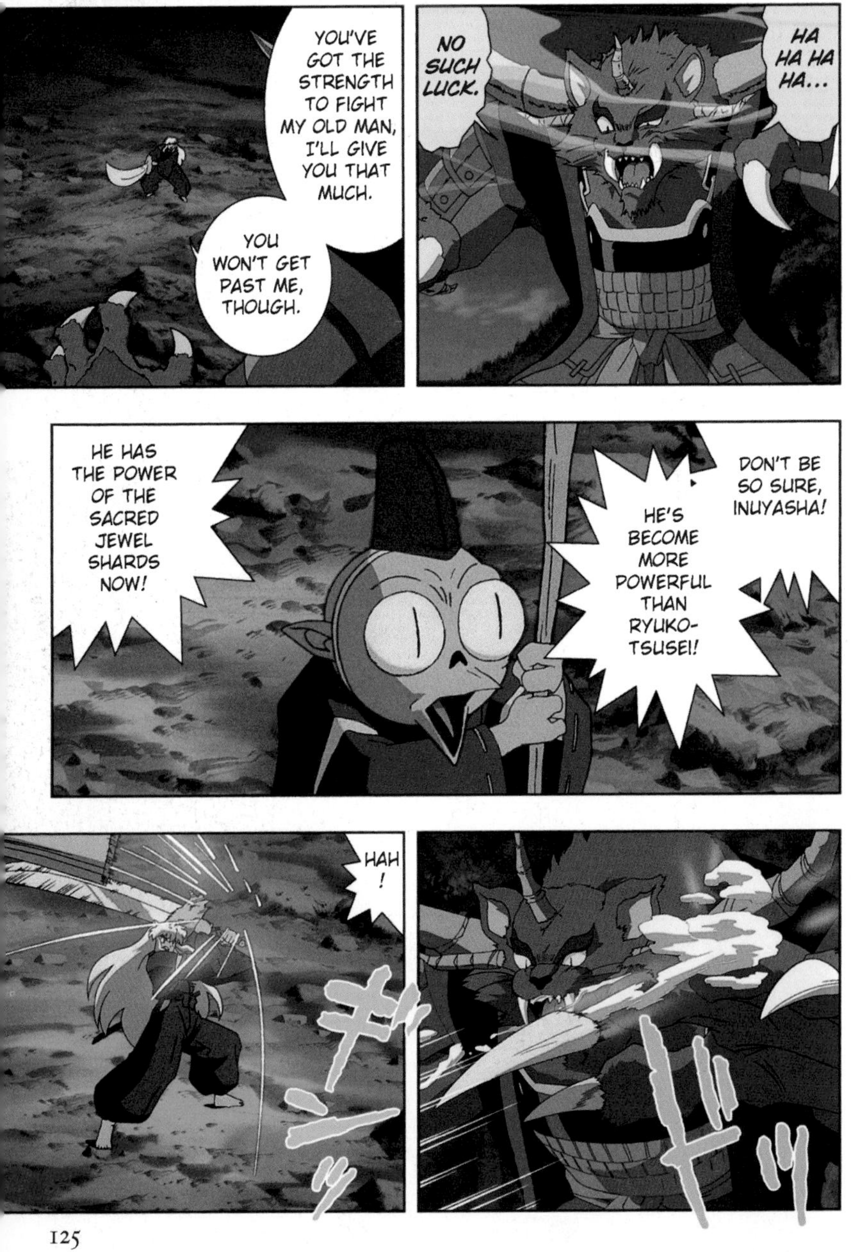
HA HA HA HA...
NO SUCH LUCK.
YOU'VE GOT THE STRENGTH TO FIGHT MY OLD MAN, I'LL GIVE YOU THAT MUCH.
YOU WON'T GET PAST ME, THOUGH.
DON'T BE SO SURE, INUYASHA!
HE'S BECOME MORE POWERFUL THAN RYUKOTSUSEI!
HE HAS THE POWER OF THE SACRED JEWEL SHARDS NOW!
ドッ
HAH!
ギンッ

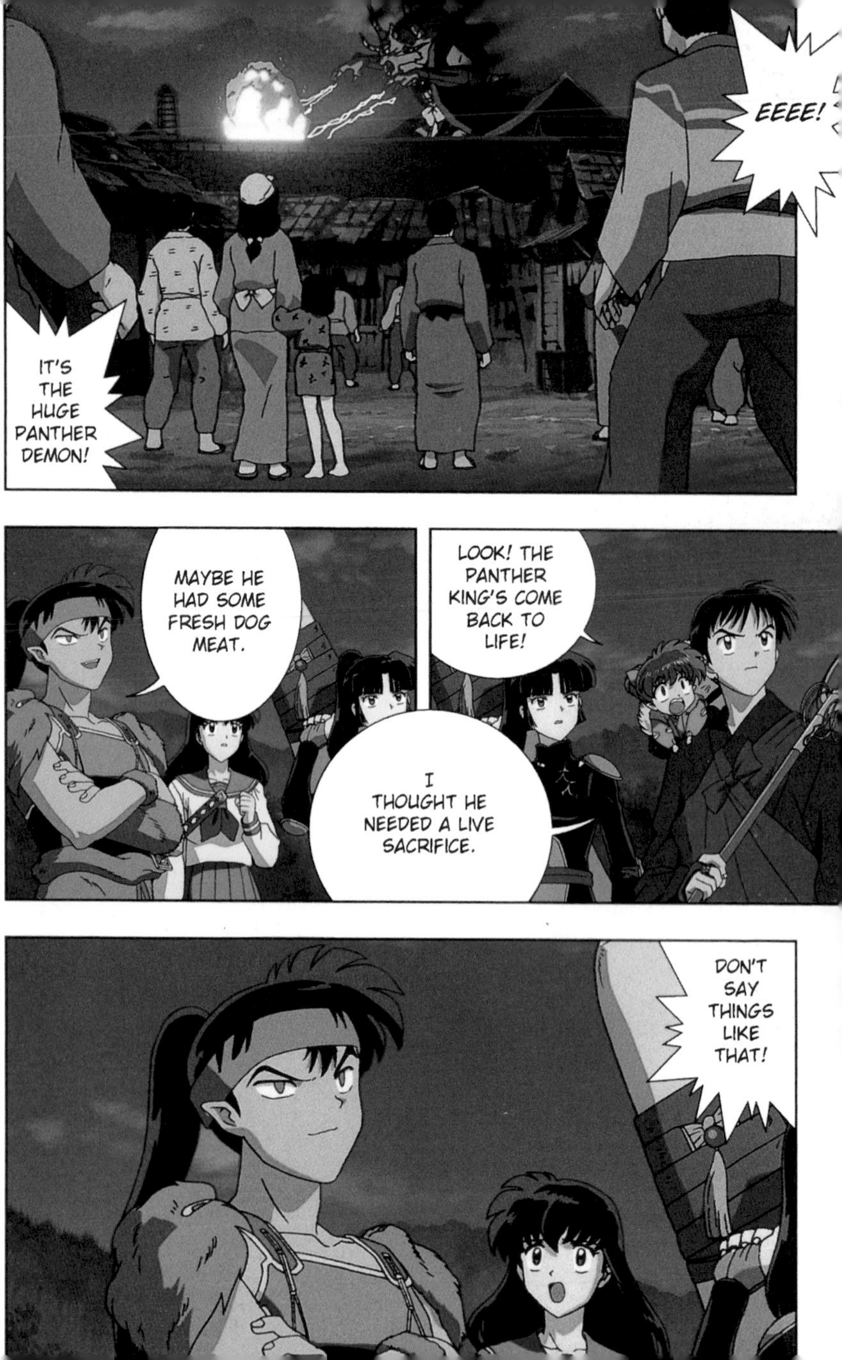
EEEE!
IT'S THE HUGE PANTHER DEMON!
LOOK! THE PANTHER KING'S COME BACK TO LIFE!
I THOUGHT HE NEEDED A LIVE SACRIFICE.
MAYBE HE HAD SOME FRESH DOG MEAT.
DON'T SAY THINGS LIKE THAT!

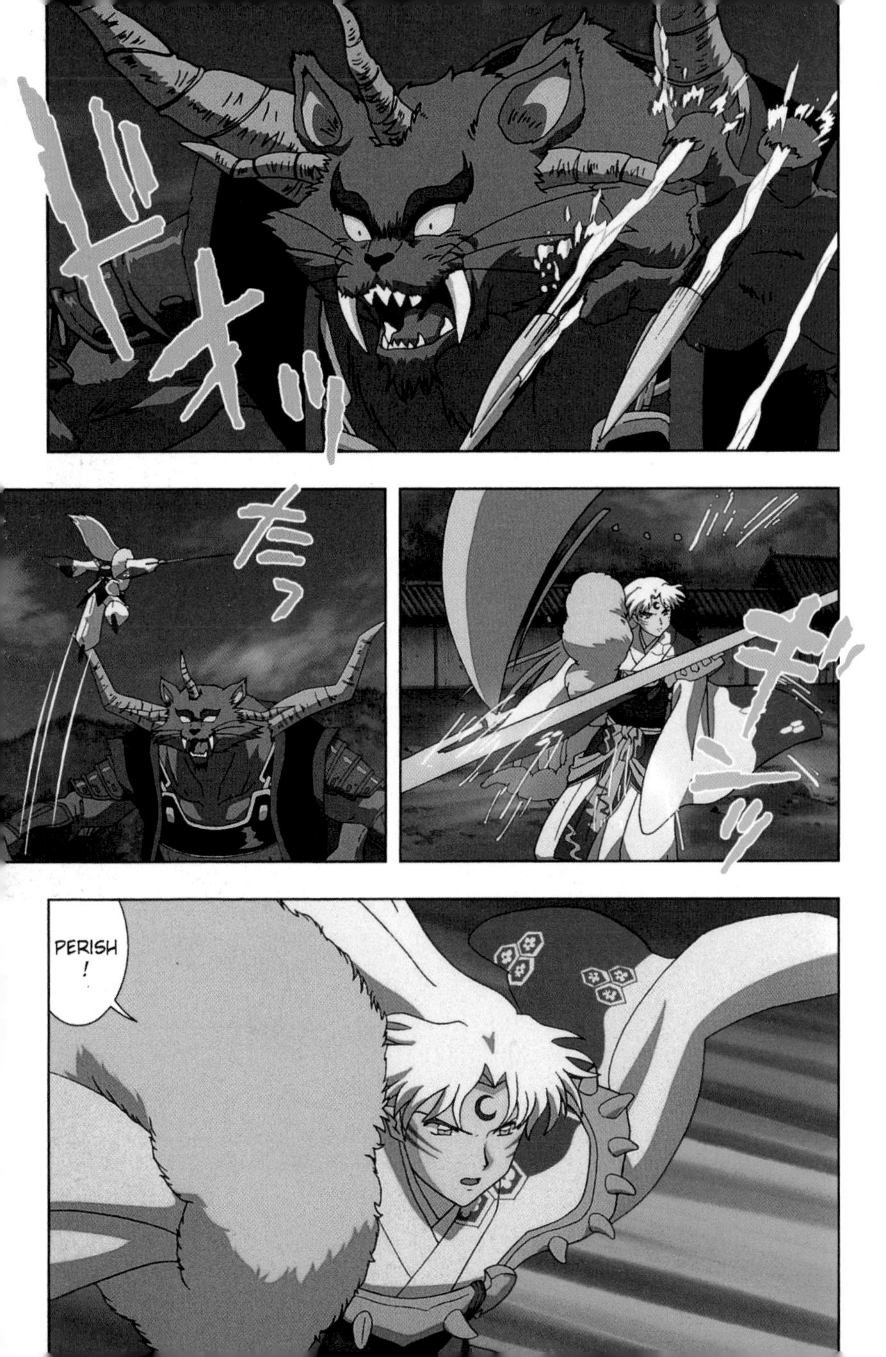
ドオッ
ギンッ
たっ
PERISH!

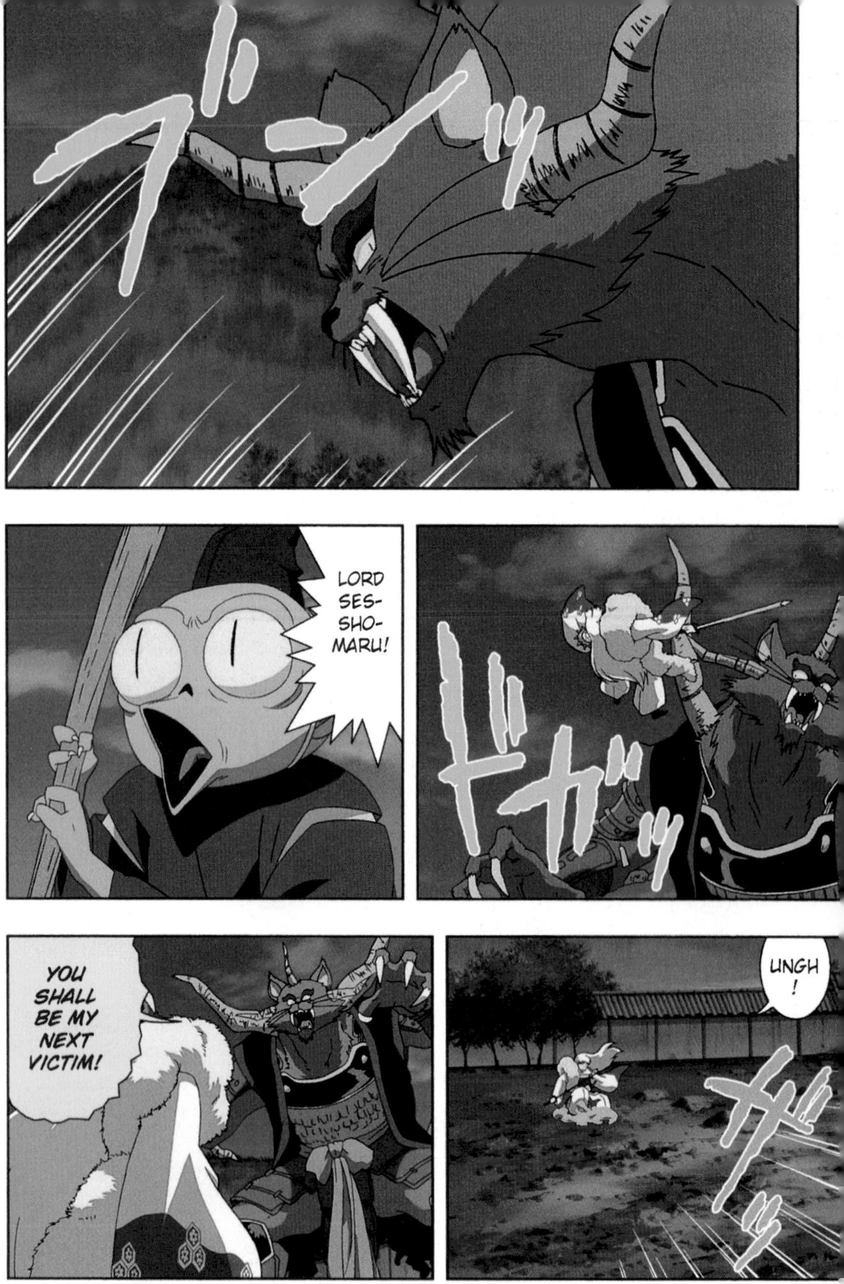
ブーンッ
ドガッ
LORD SES-SHO-MARU!
UNGH!
ザッ
YOU SHALL BE MY NEXT VICTIM!

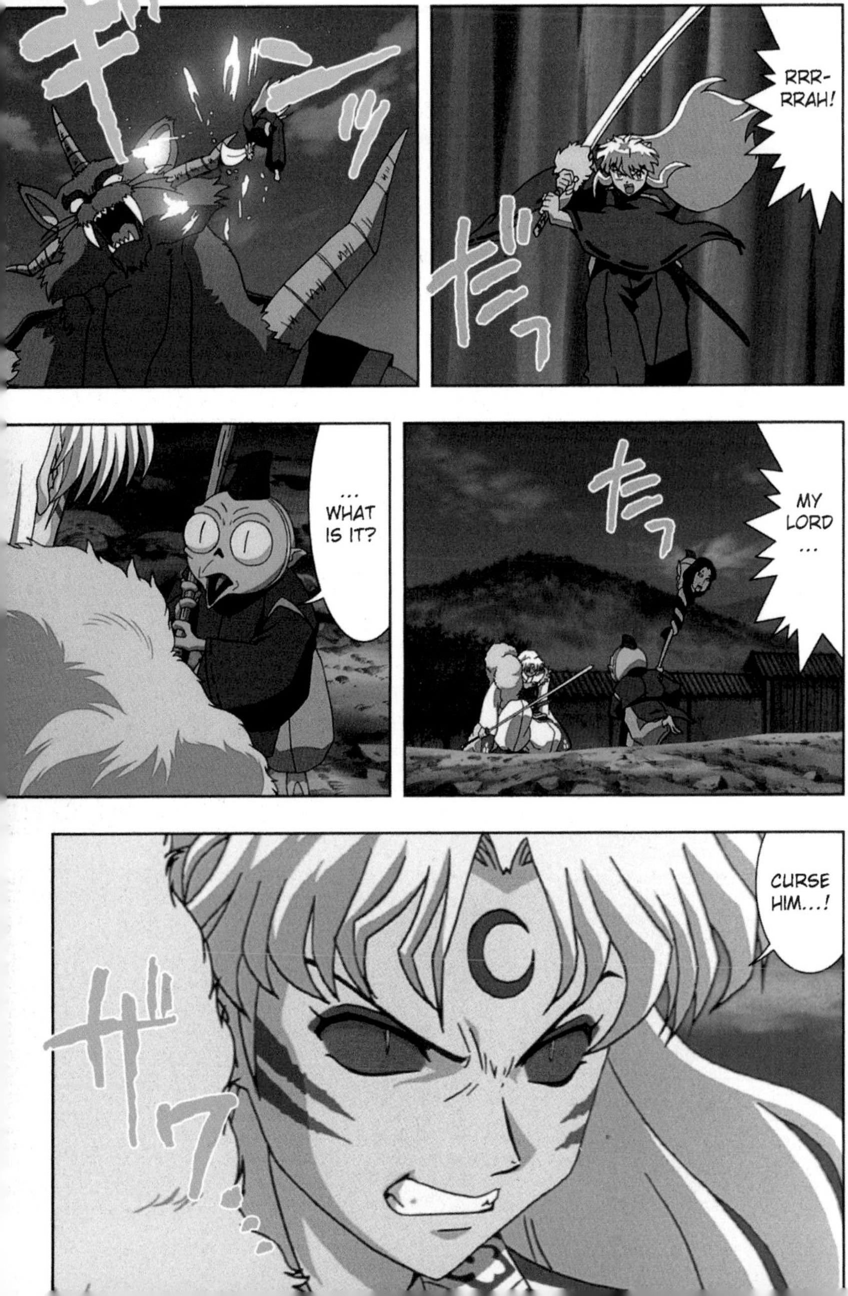
RRR-RRAH!
だっ
ギーンッ
たっ
MY LORD ...
... WHAT IS IT?
CURSE HIM...!

THE TEN-SEIGA ...!

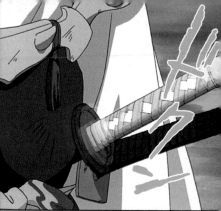

YOU WISH TO BE DRAWN?

HOW-EVER ...

FATHER, WHY DID YOU LEAVE ME THE TENSEIGA? I STILL DON'T UNDERSTAND.

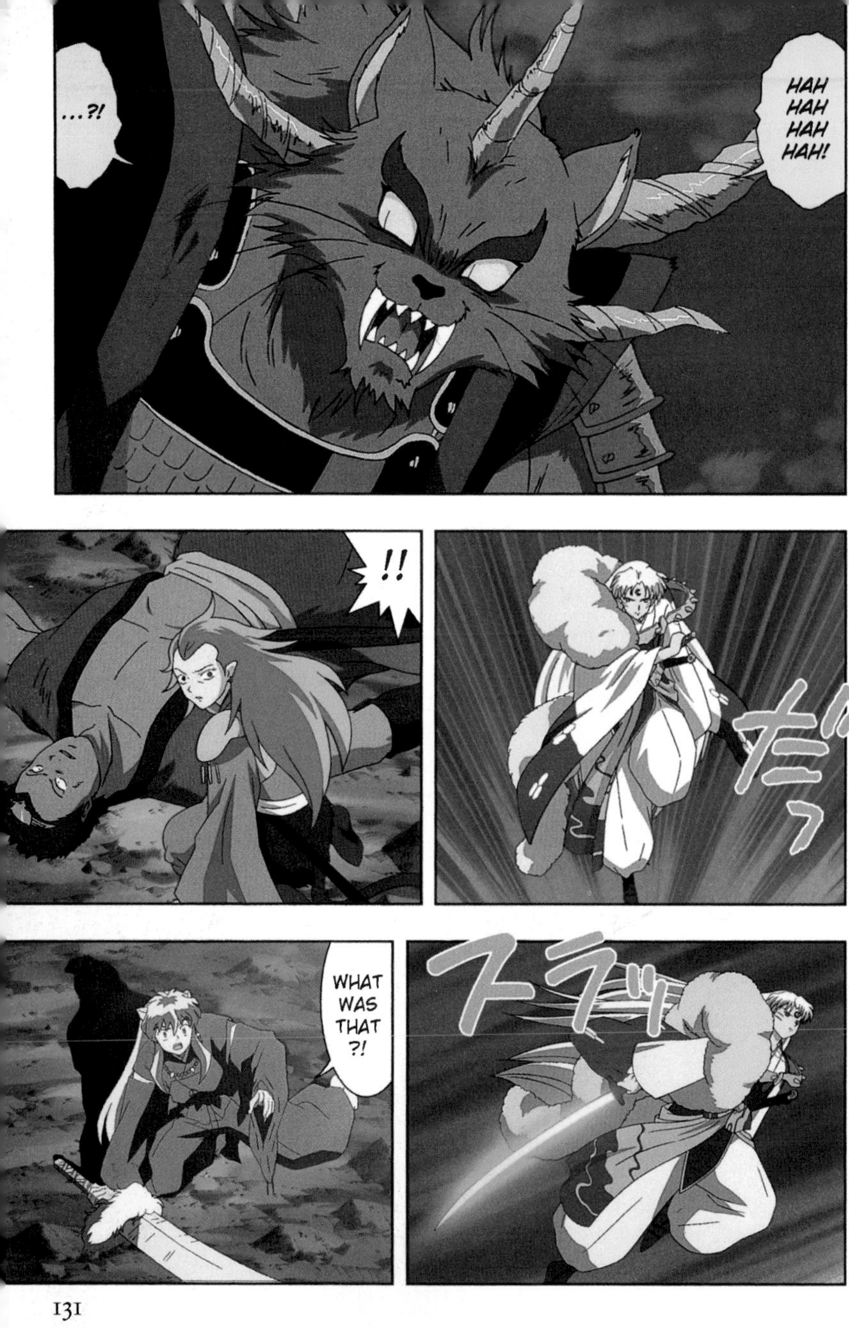
HAH HAH HAH HAH!
...?!
だっ
!!
スラッ
WHAT WAS THAT ?!

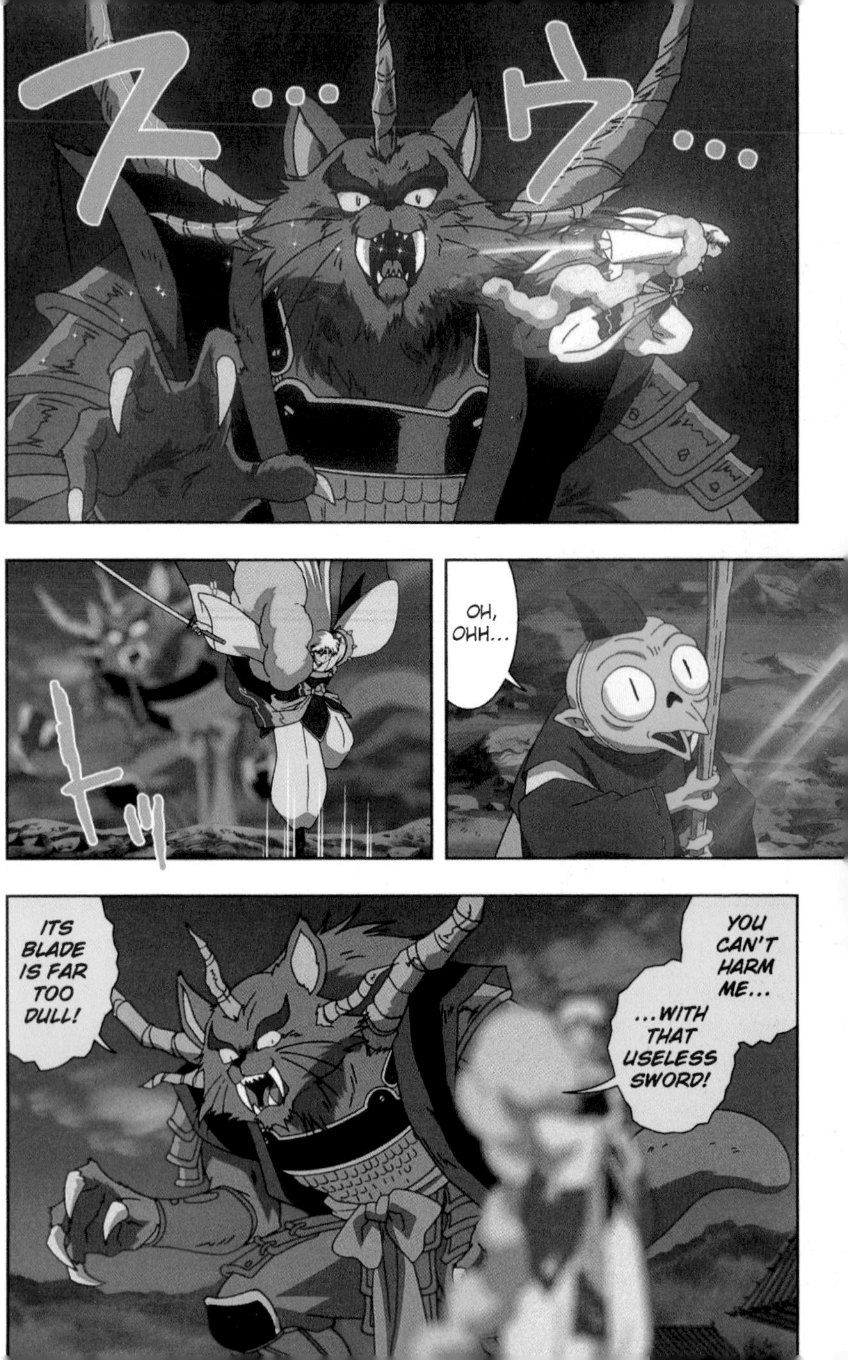

ス…ウ…
OH, OHH...
トッ
YOU CAN'T HARM ME...
...WITH THAT USELESS SWORD!
ITS BLADE IS FAR TOO DULL!

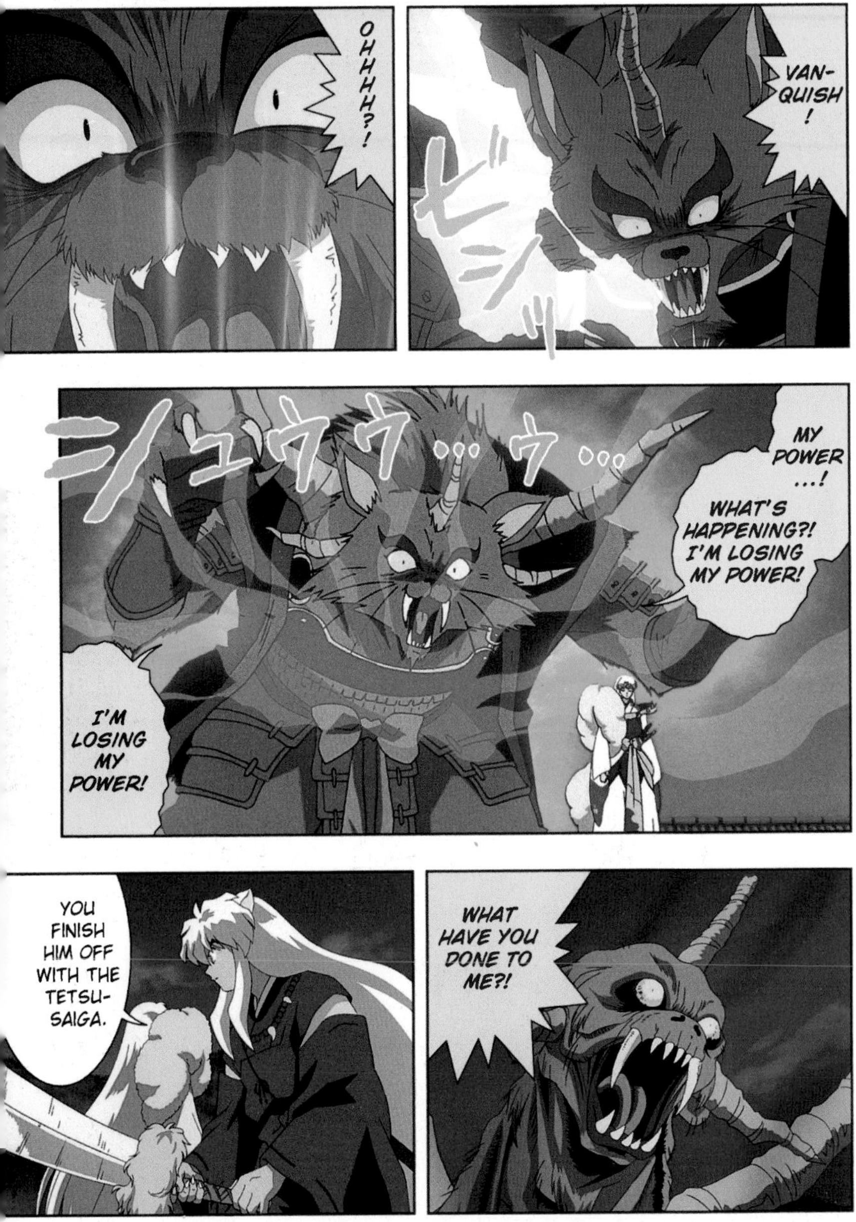
VAN-QUISH!
OHHHH?!
MY POWER...!
WHAT'S HAPPENING?! I'M LOSING MY POWER!
シュウウ…ウ…
I'M LOSING MY POWER!
WHAT HAVE YOU DONE TO ME?!
YOU FINISH HIM OFF WITH THE TETSU-SAIGA.

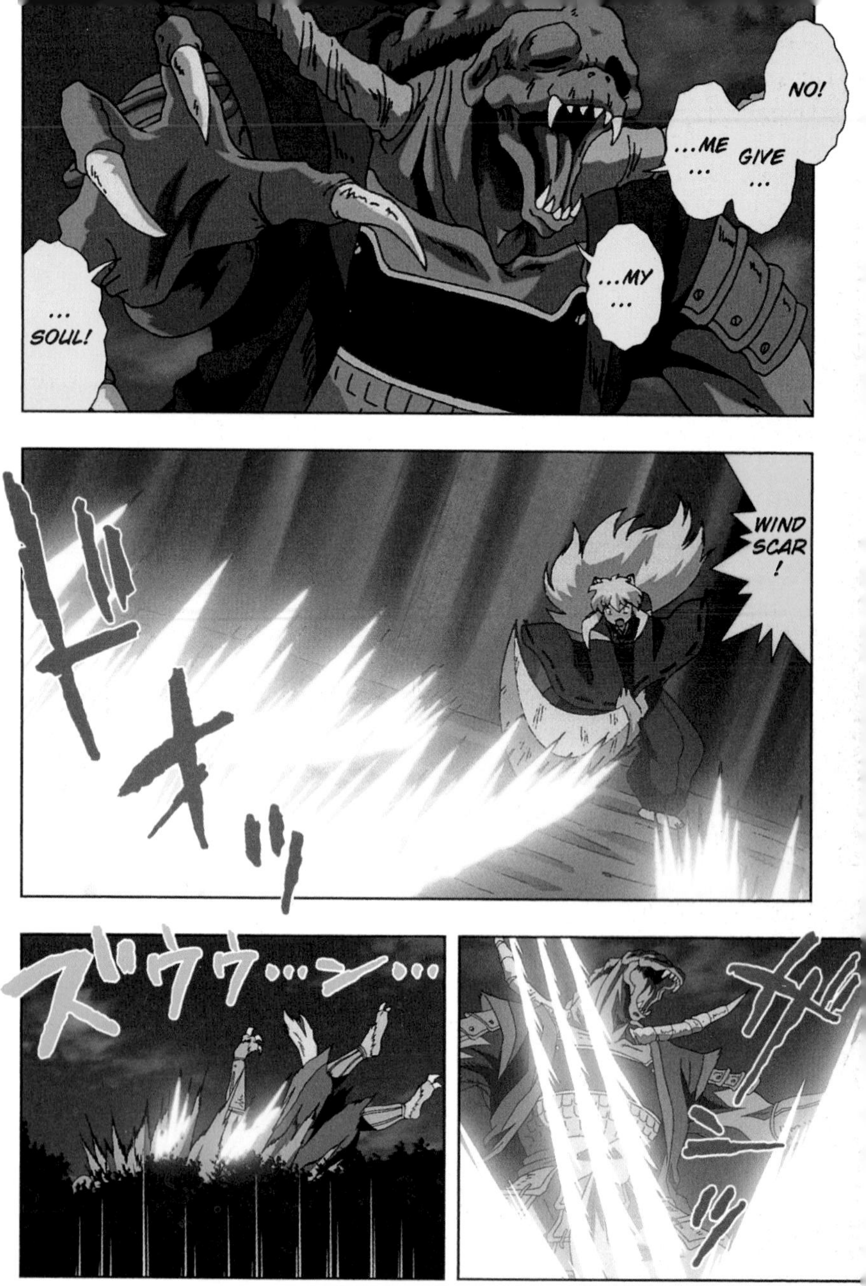
NO!
GIVE ...
...ME ...
...MY ...
... SOUL!
WIND SCAR !
ドオッ
ズウウ...ン...

MY LIFE!

...

I'M TAKING THESE BACK, THANKS!

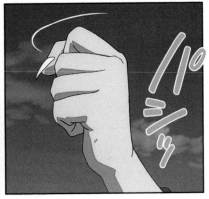

135

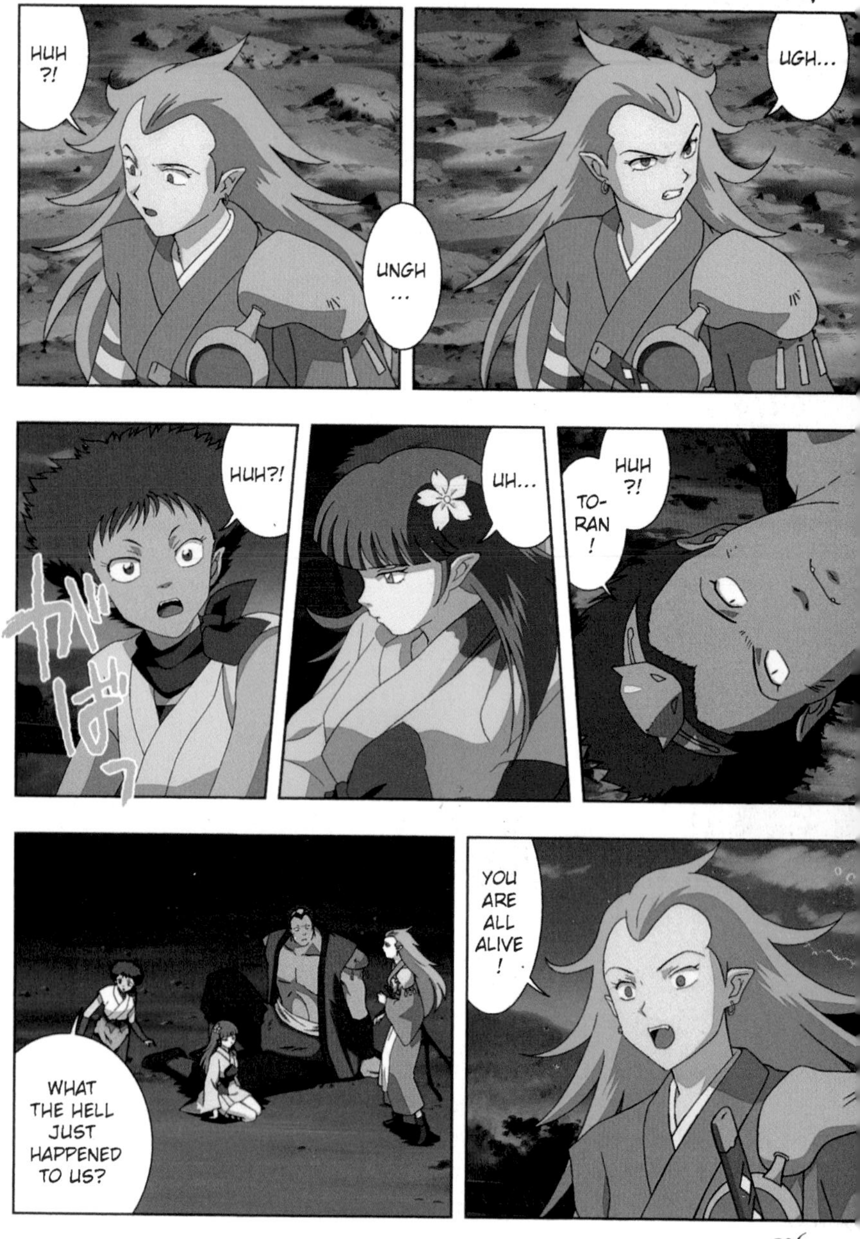
UGH...
UNGH ...
HUH ?!
HUH ?!
TO-RAN !
UH...
HUH?!
がばっ
YOU ARE ALL ALIVE !
WHAT THE HELL JUST HAPPENED TO US?

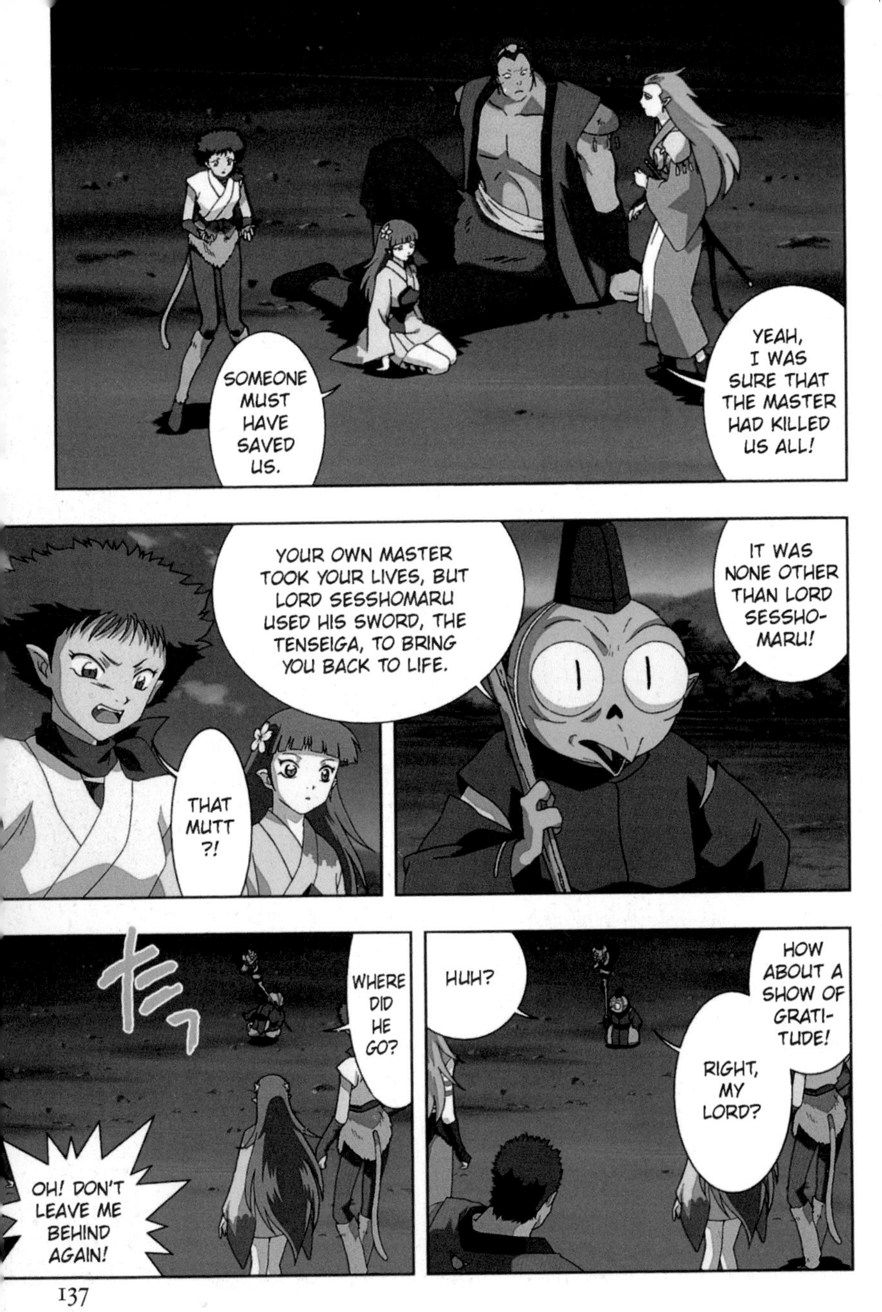
YEAH, I WAS SURE THAT THE MASTER HAD KILLED US ALL!
SOMEONE MUST HAVE SAVED US.
IT WAS NONE OTHER THAN LORD SESSHO-MARU!
YOUR OWN MASTER TOOK YOUR LIVES, BUT LORD SESSHOMARU USED HIS SWORD, THE TENSEIGA, TO BRING YOU BACK TO LIFE.
THAT MUTT ?!
HOW ABOUT A SHOW OF GRATI-TUDE!
RIGHT, MY LORD?
HUH?
WHERE DID HE GO?
OH! DON'T LEAVE ME BEHIND AGAIN!

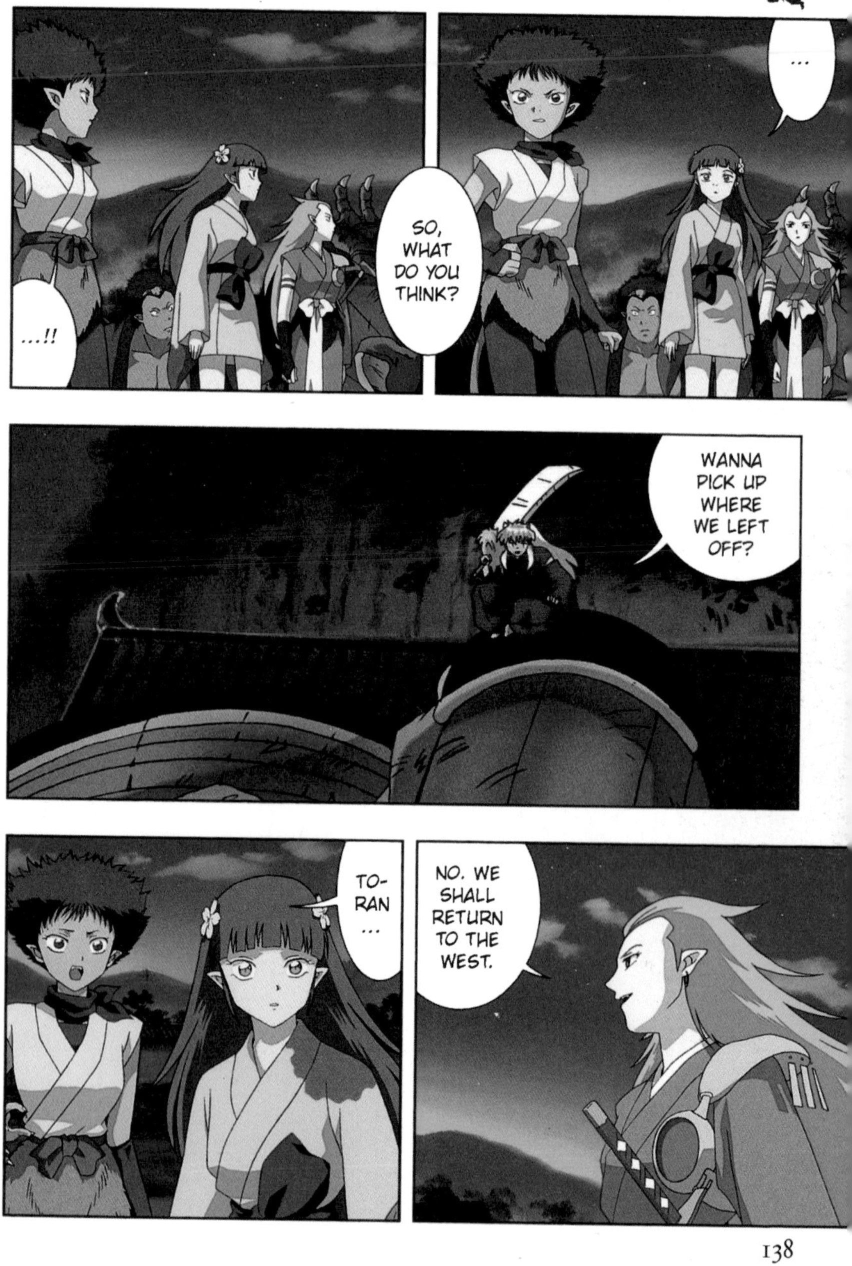
...
SO, WHAT DO YOU THINK?
...!!
WANNA PICK UP WHERE WE LEFT OFF?
NO. WE SHALL RETURN TO THE WEST.
TO-RAN ...

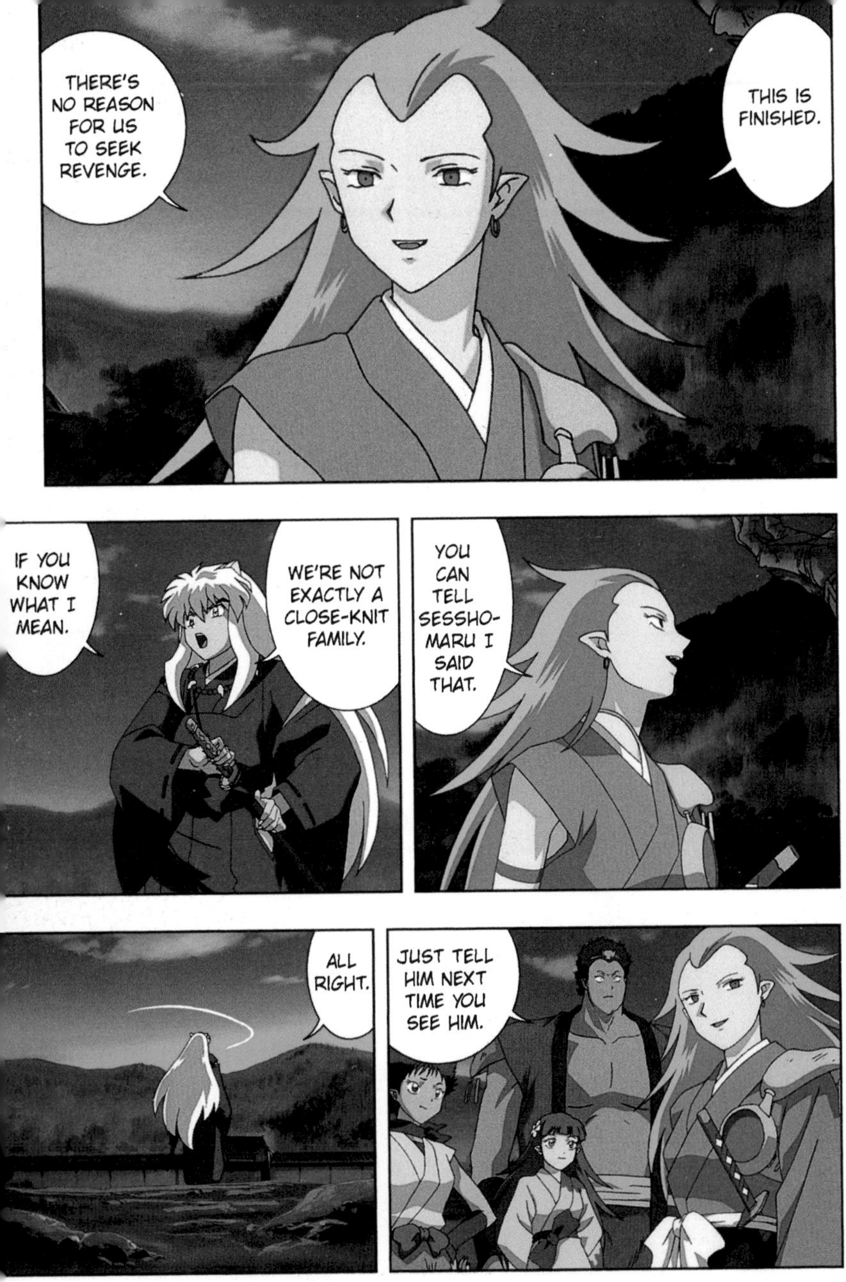
THIS IS FINISHED.
THERE'S NO REASON FOR US TO SEEK REVENGE.
YOU CAN TELL SESSHO-MARU I SAID THAT.
WE'RE NOT EXACTLY A CLOSE-KNIT FAMILY.
IF YOU KNOW WHAT I MEAN.
JUST TELL HIM NEXT TIME YOU SEE HIM.
ALL RIGHT.

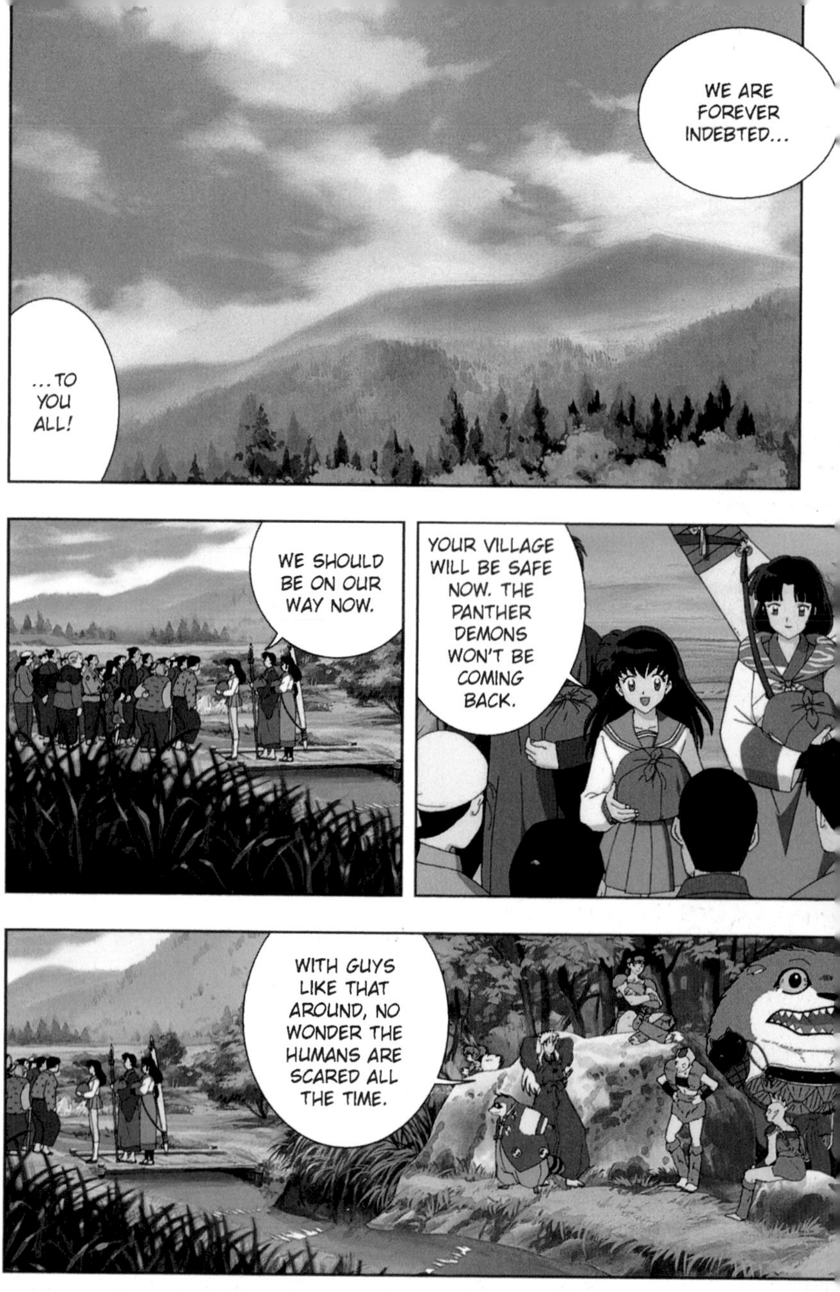
WE ARE FOREVER INDEBTED...
...TO YOU ALL!
WE SHOULD BE ON OUR WAY NOW.
YOUR VILLAGE WILL BE SAFE NOW. THE PANTHER DEMONS WON'T BE COMING BACK.
WITH GUYS LIKE THAT AROUND, NO WONDER THE HUMANS ARE SCARED ALL THE TIME.

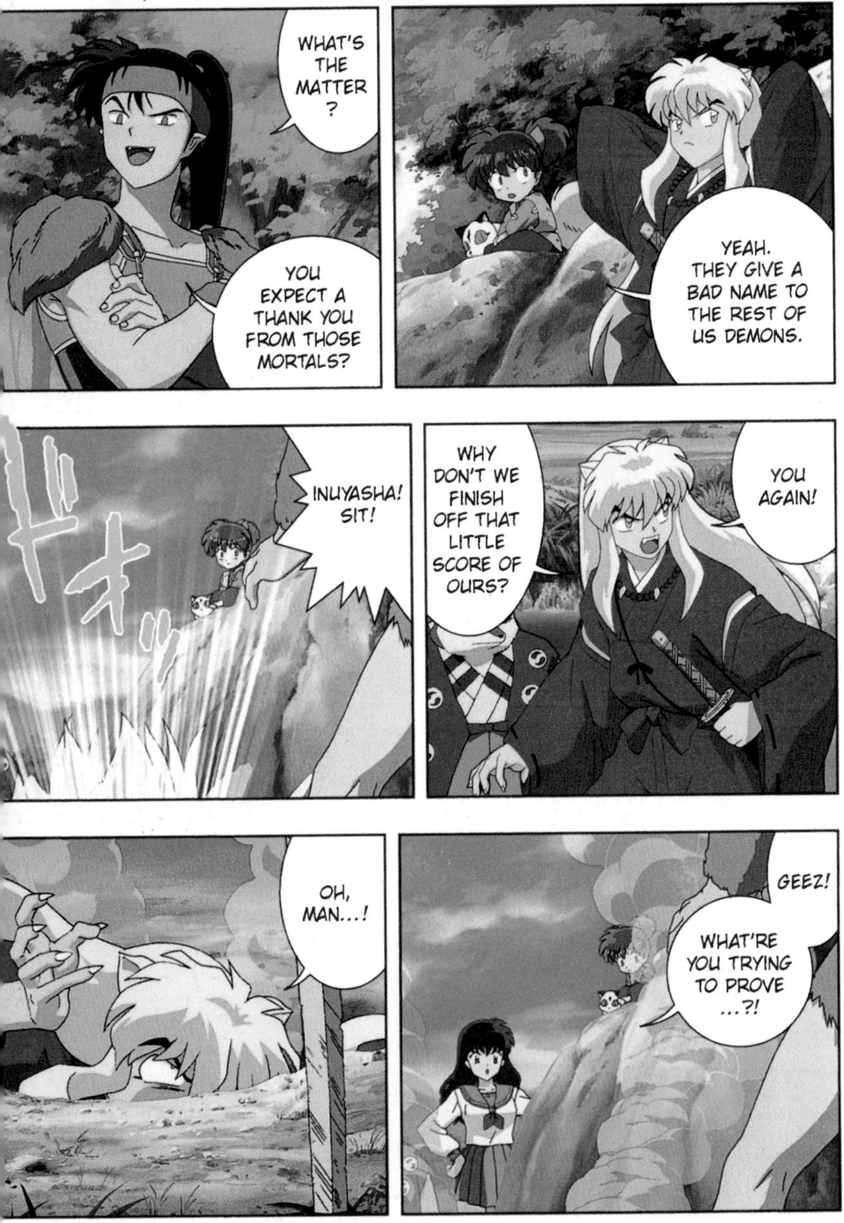
YEAH. THEY GIVE A BAD NAME TO THE REST OF US DEMONS.
WHAT'S THE MATTER?
YOU EXPECT A THANK YOU FROM THOSE MORTALS?
YOU AGAIN!
WHY DON'T WE FINISH OFF THAT LITTLE SCORE OF OURS?
INUYASHA! SIT!
GEEZ!
WHAT'RE YOU TRYING TO PROVE...?!
OH, MAN...!

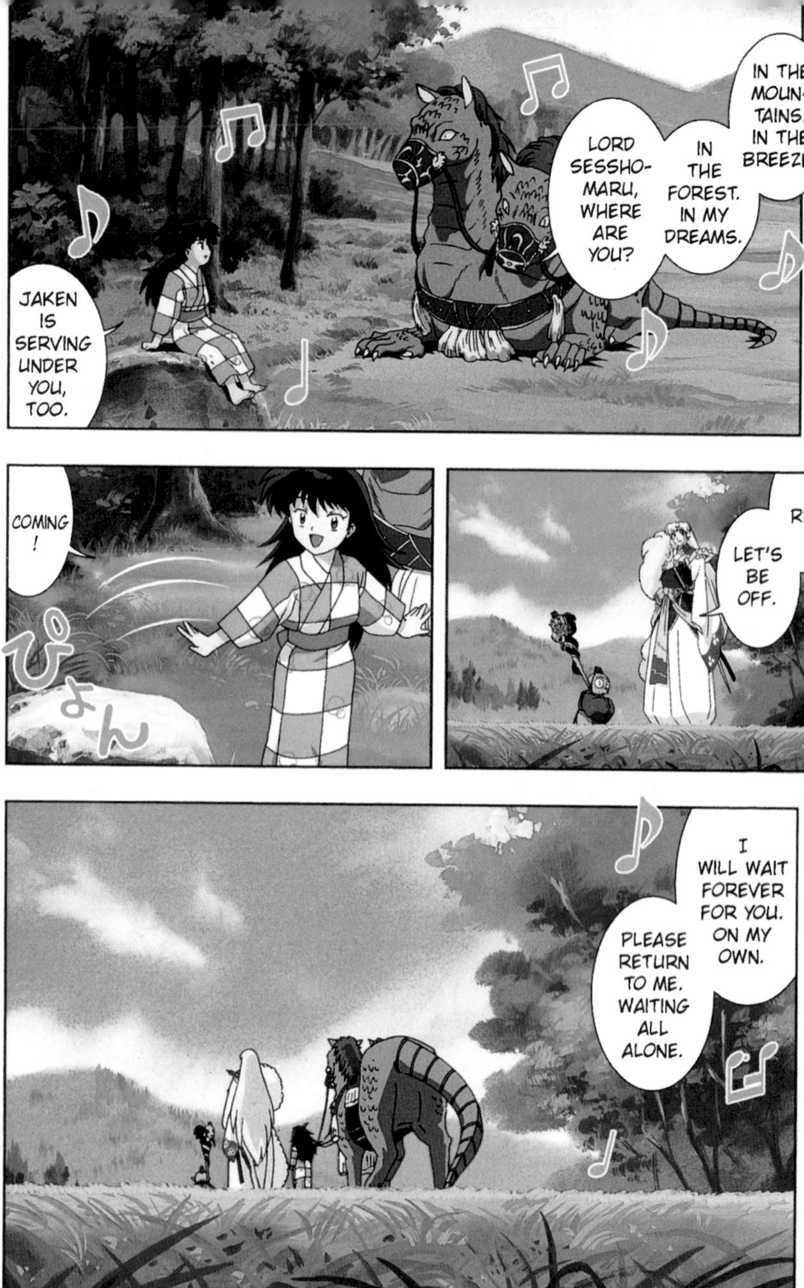
IN THE MOUNTAINS. IN THE BREEZE.
IN THE FOREST. IN MY DREAMS.
LORD SESSHOMARU, WHERE ARE YOU?
JAKEN IS SERVING UNDER YOU, TOO.
RIN.
LET'S BE OFF.
COMING!
ぴょん
I WILL WAIT FOREVER FOR YOU. ON MY OWN.
PLEASE RETURN TO ME. WAITING ALL ALONE.

78
Only You, Sango

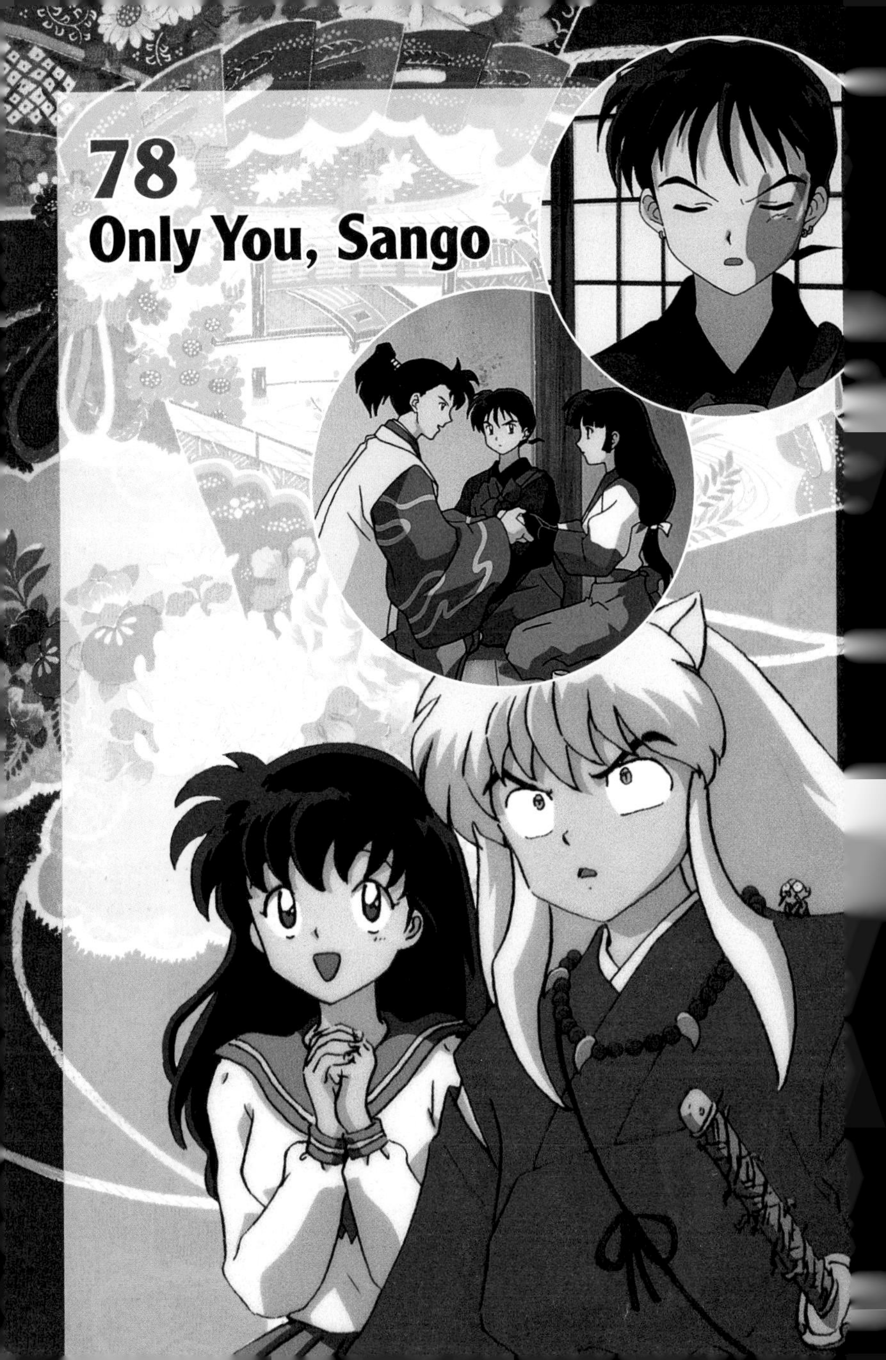

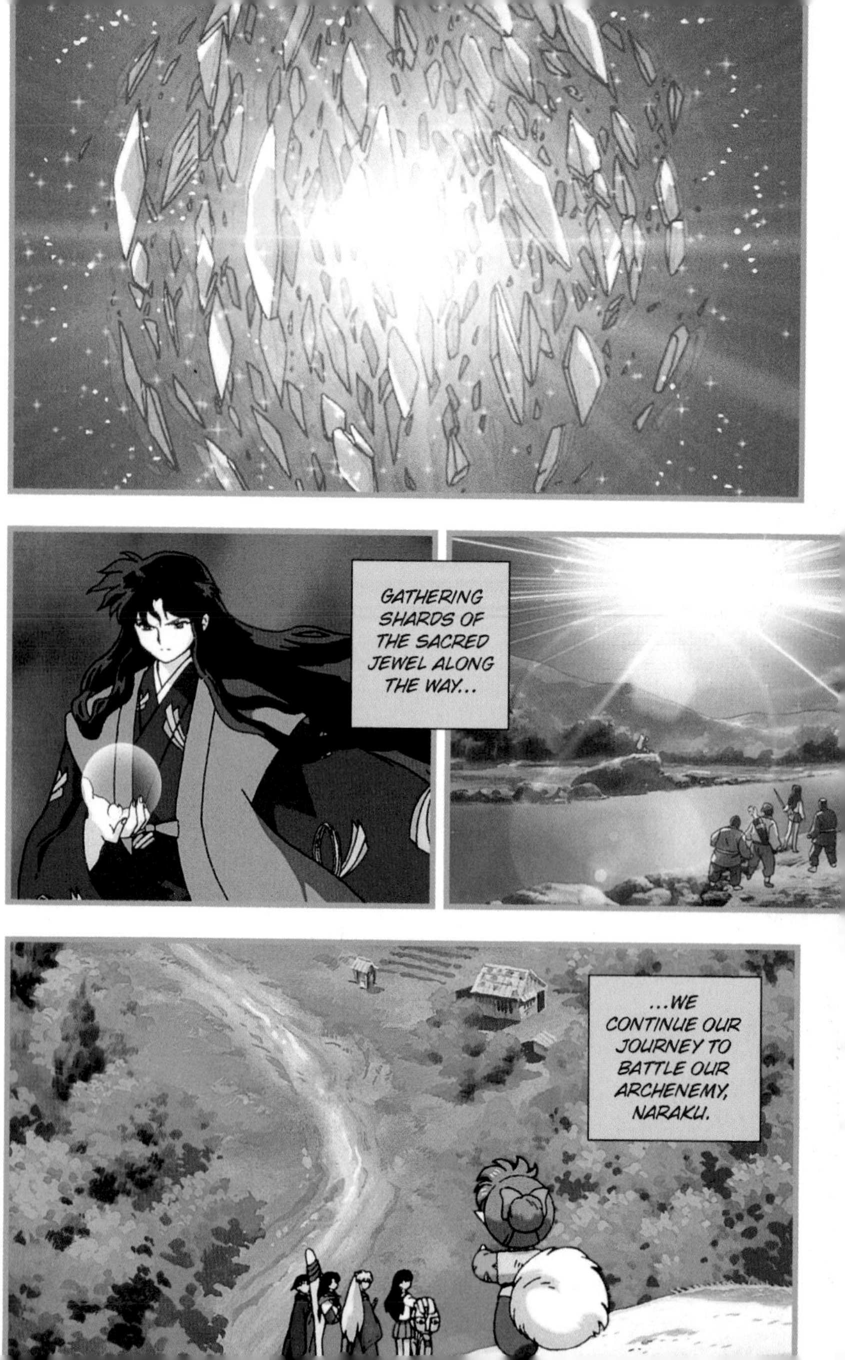
GATHERING SHARDS OF THE SACRED JEWEL ALONG THE WAY...
...WE CONTINUE OUR JOURNEY TO BATTLE OUR ARCHENEMY, NARAKU.

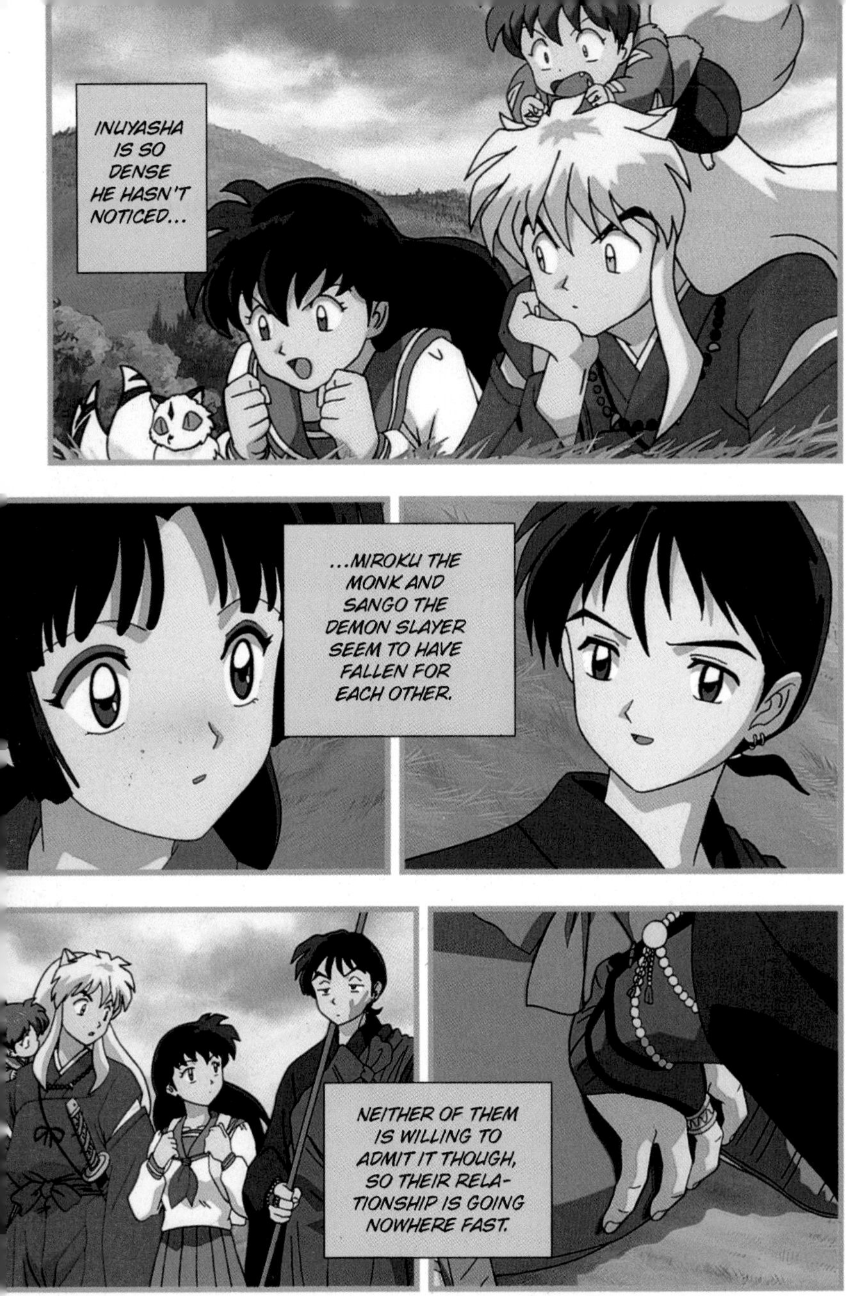
INUYASHA IS SO DENSE HE HASN'T NOTICED...
...MIROKU THE MONK AND SANGO THE DEMON SLAYER SEEM TO HAVE FALLEN FOR EACH OTHER.
NEITHER OF THEM IS WILLING TO ADMIT IT THOUGH, SO THEIR RELA-TIONSHIP IS GOING NOWHERE FAST.

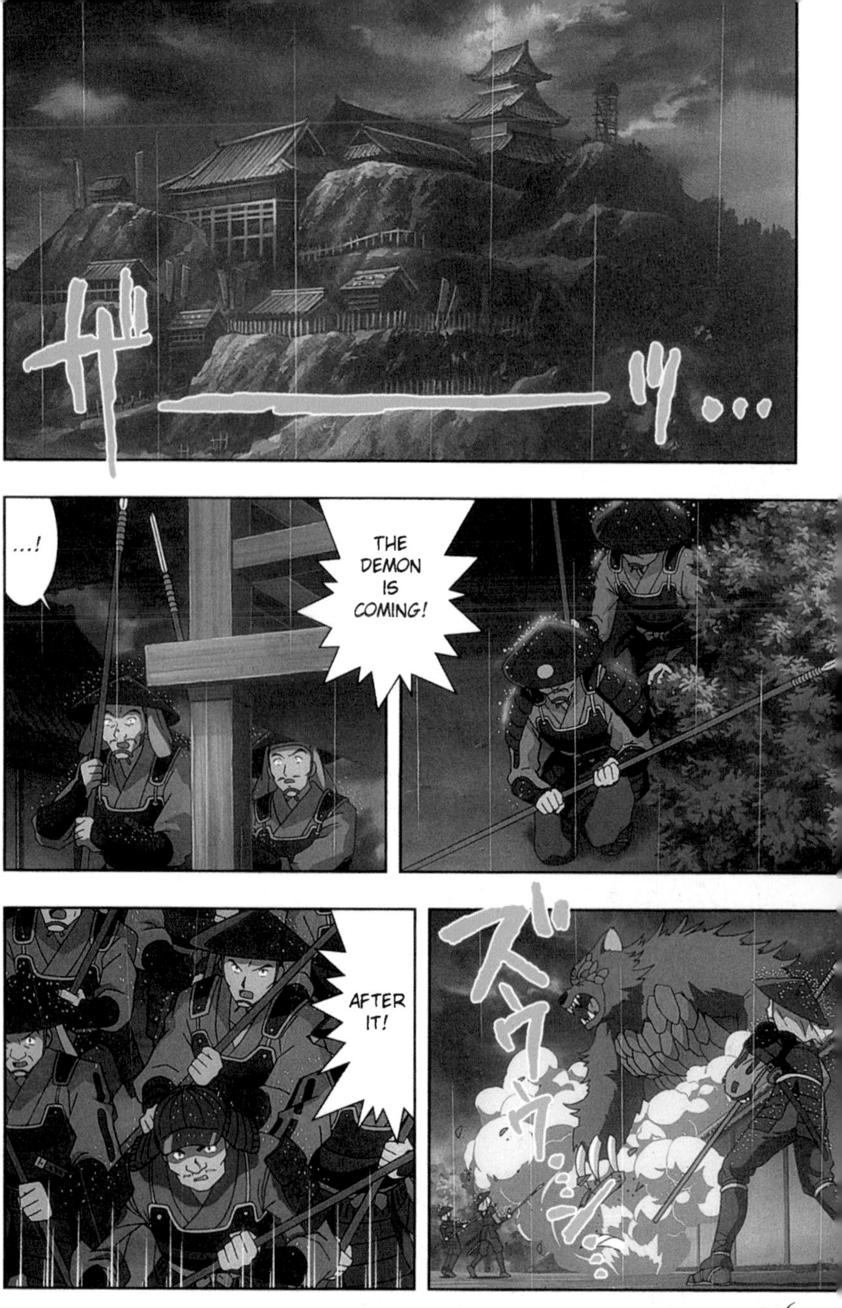
ザーーッ…
THE DEMON IS COMING!
...!
AFTER IT!

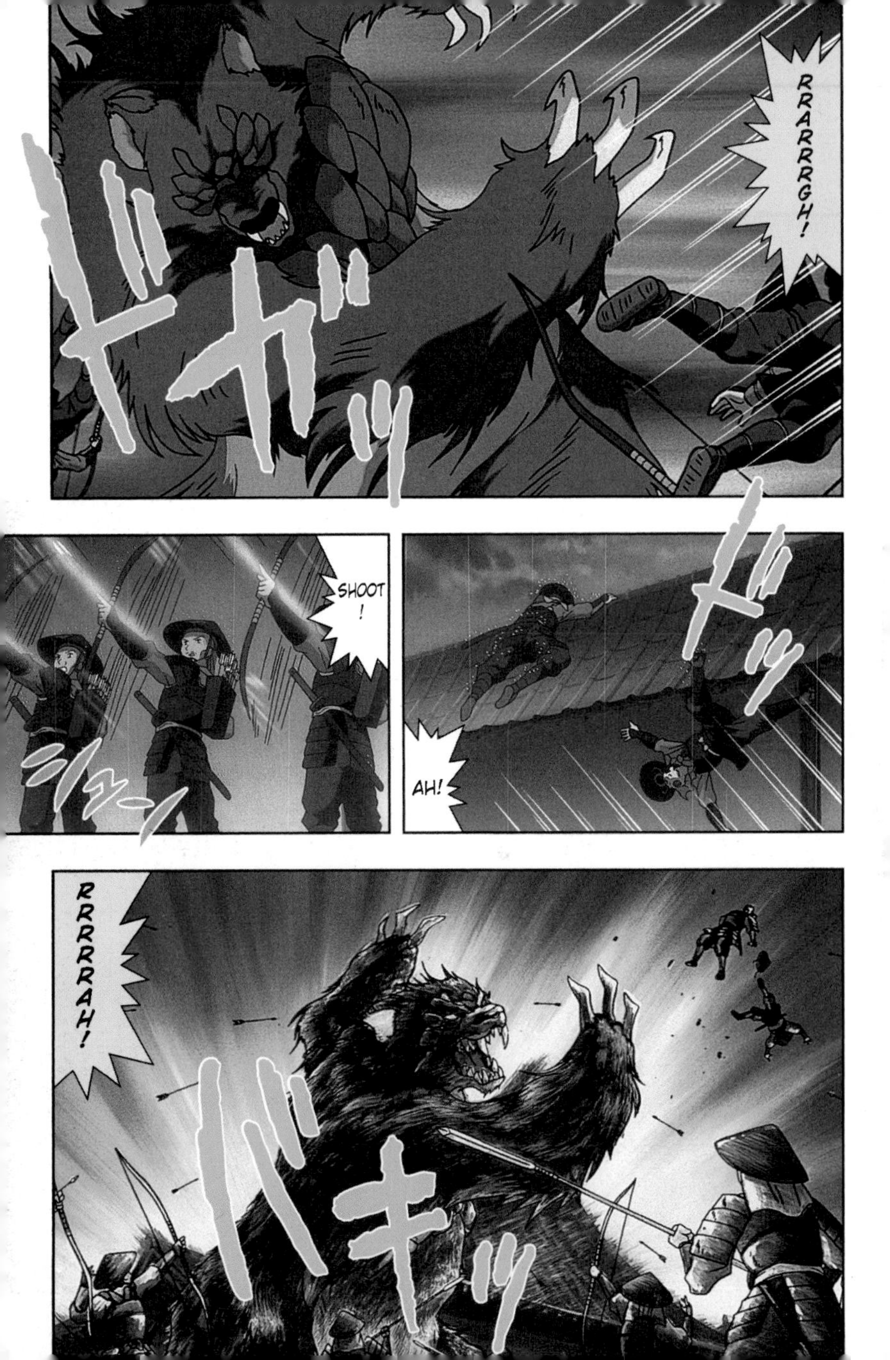
RRARRRGH!
ドガッ
ドッ
AH!
SHOOT!
RRRRRAH!
バキッ

ザーーーッ…
ザァァ…

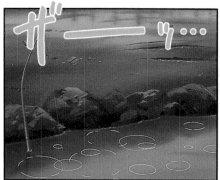

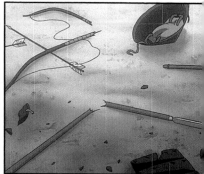

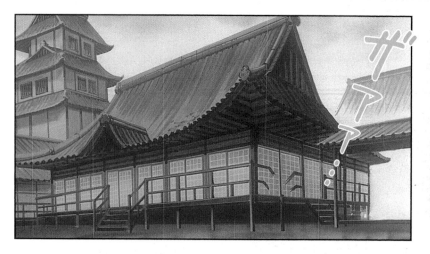

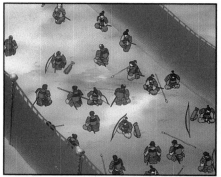

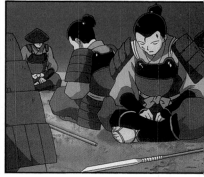

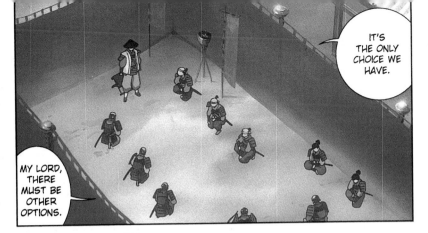

IT'S THE ONLY CHOICE WE HAVE.
MY LORD, THERE MUST BE OTHER OPTIONS.
STOP WASTING MY VALUABLE TIME!
FIND HER! AND LEAVE NO STONE UNTURNED!
MM HM!
HUH HM...

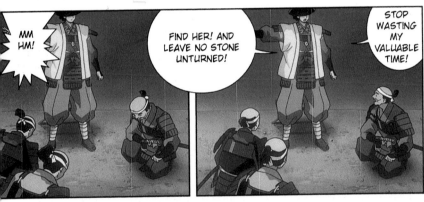

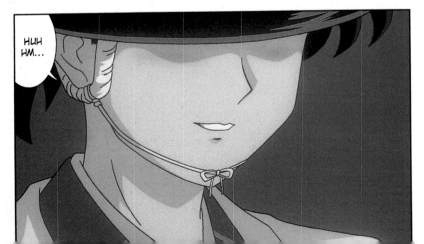

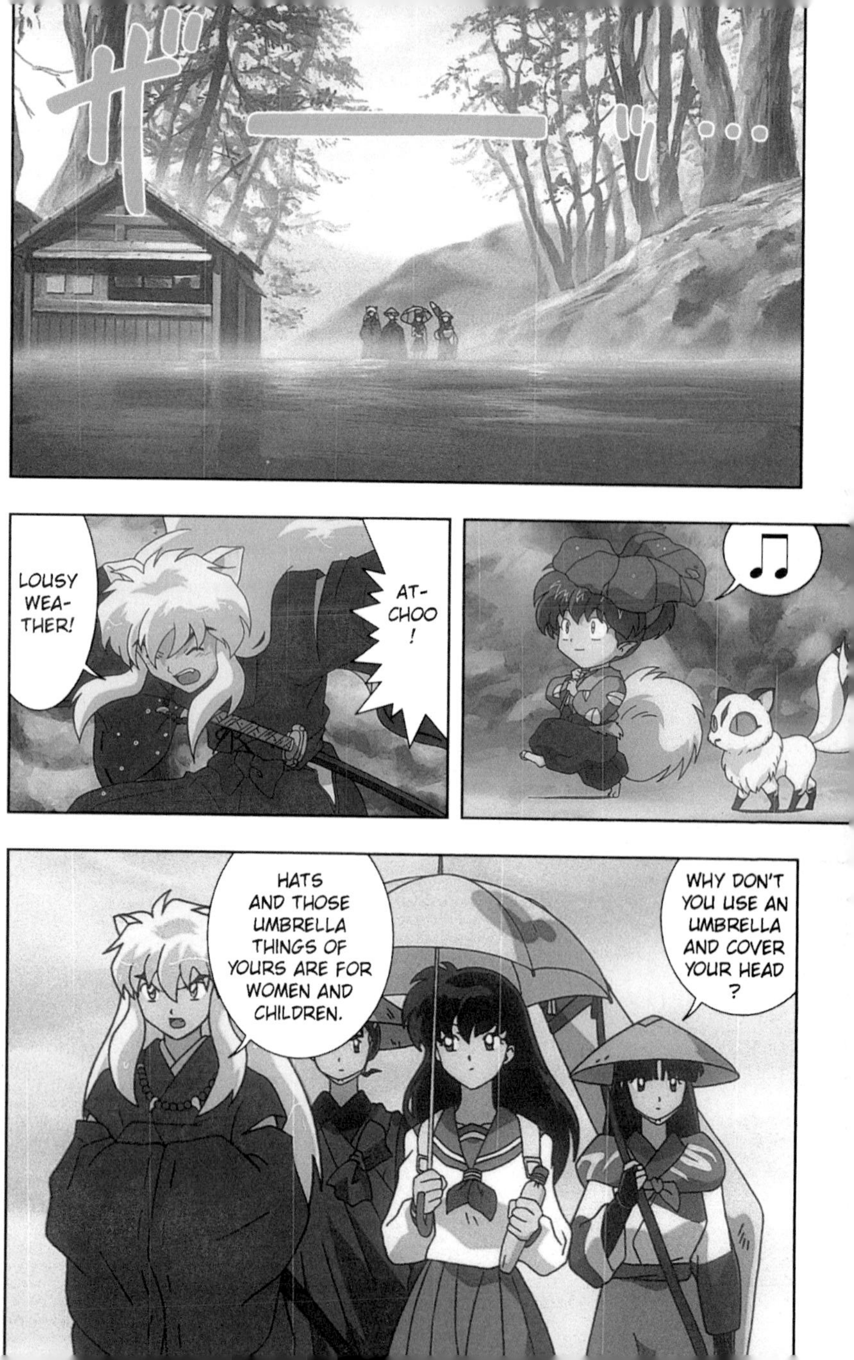
ザーッ...
AT-CHOO!
LOUSY WEA-THER!
WHY DON'T YOU USE AN UMBRELLA AND COVER YOUR HEAD?
HATS AND THOSE UMBRELLA THINGS OF YOURS ARE FOR WOMEN AND CHILDREN.

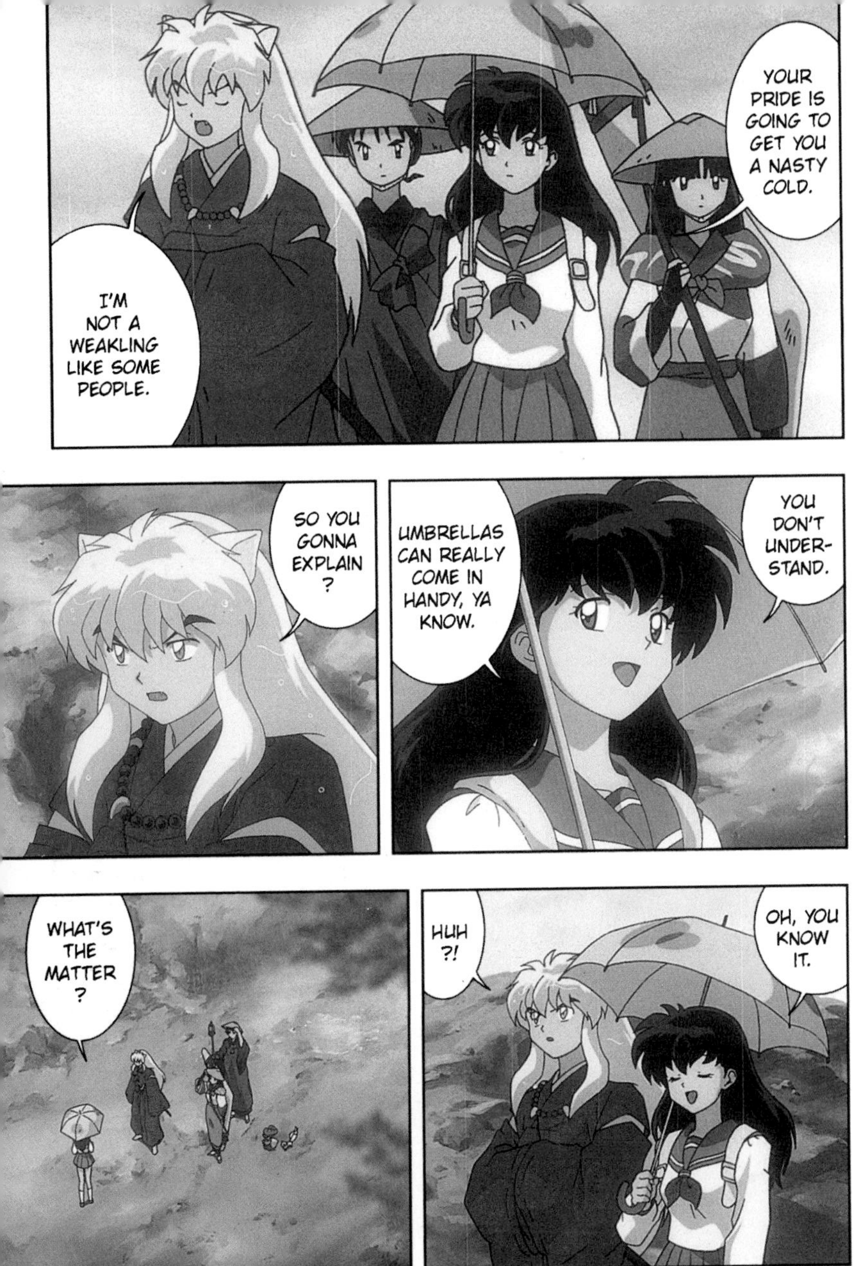
YOUR PRIDE IS GOING TO GET YOU A NASTY COLD.
I'M NOT A WEAKLING LIKE SOME PEOPLE.
YOU DON'T UNDER-STAND.
UMBRELLAS CAN REALLY COME IN HANDY, YA KNOW.
SO YOU GONNA EXPLAIN?
OH, YOU KNOW IT.
HUH?!
WHAT'S THE MATTER?

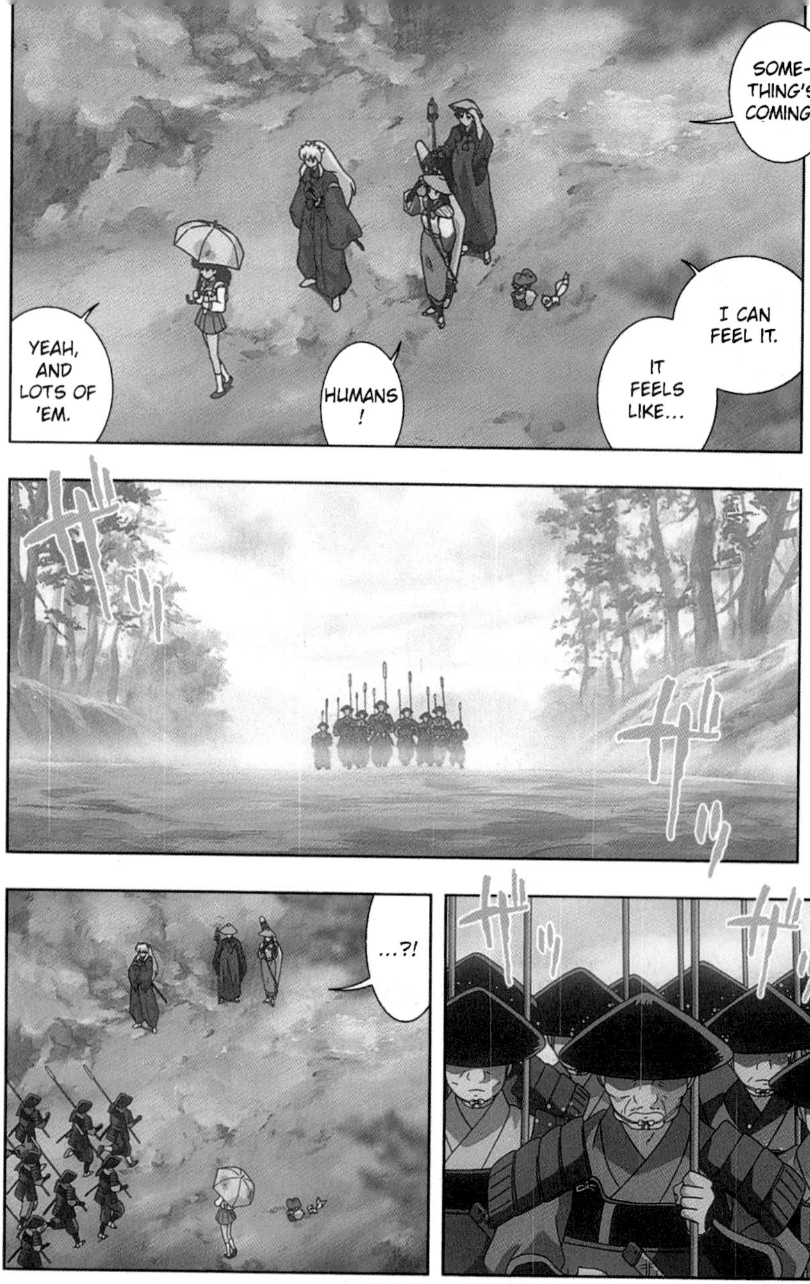
SOME-
THING'S
COMING.
I CAN
FEEL IT.
IT
FEELS
LIKE...
HUMANS
!
YEAH,
AND
LOTS OF
'EM.
ザッ
ザッ
ザッ
ザッ
...?!

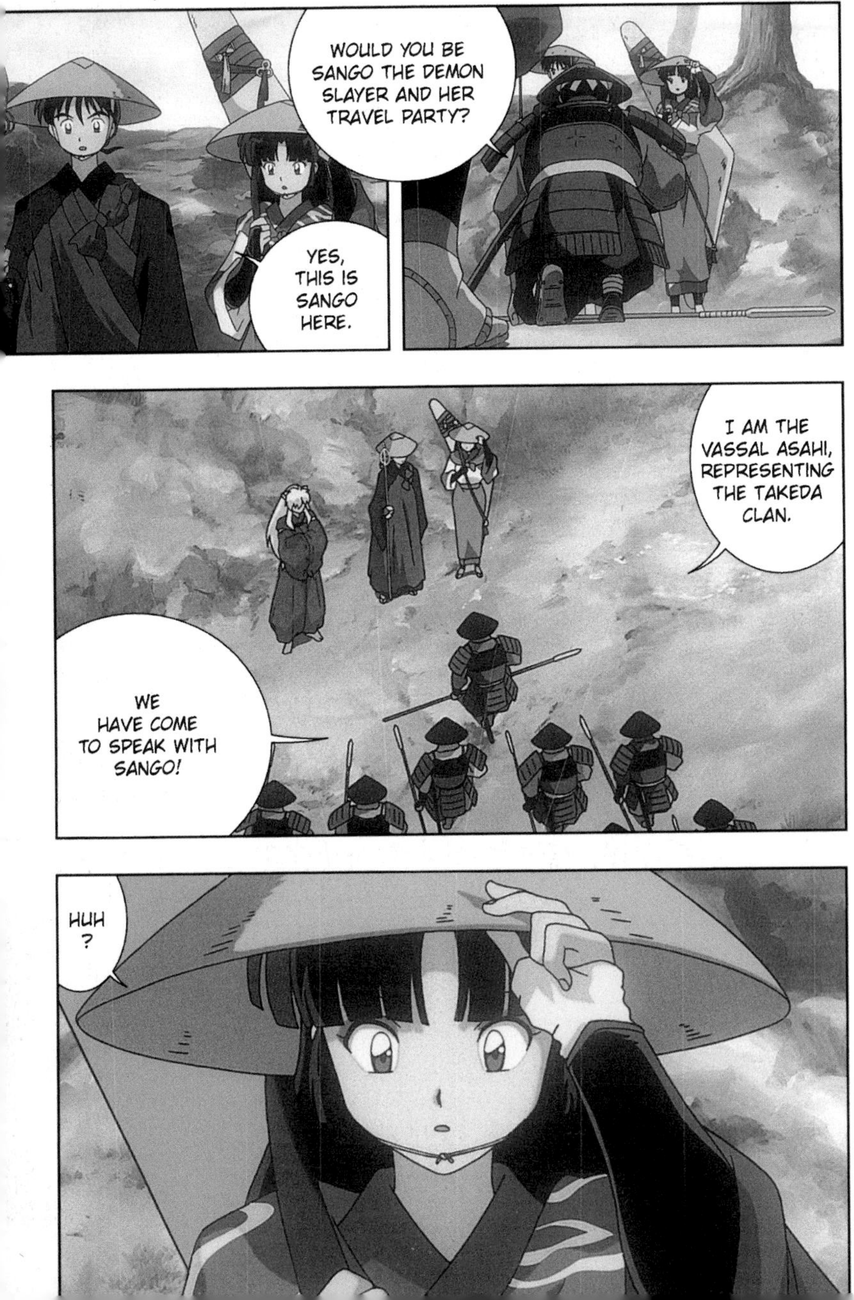
WOULD YOU BE SANGO THE DEMON SLAYER AND HER TRAVEL PARTY?
YES, THIS IS SANGO HERE.
I AM THE VASSAL ASAHI, REPRESENTING THE TAKEDA CLAN.
WE HAVE COME TO SPEAK WITH SANGO!
HUH ?

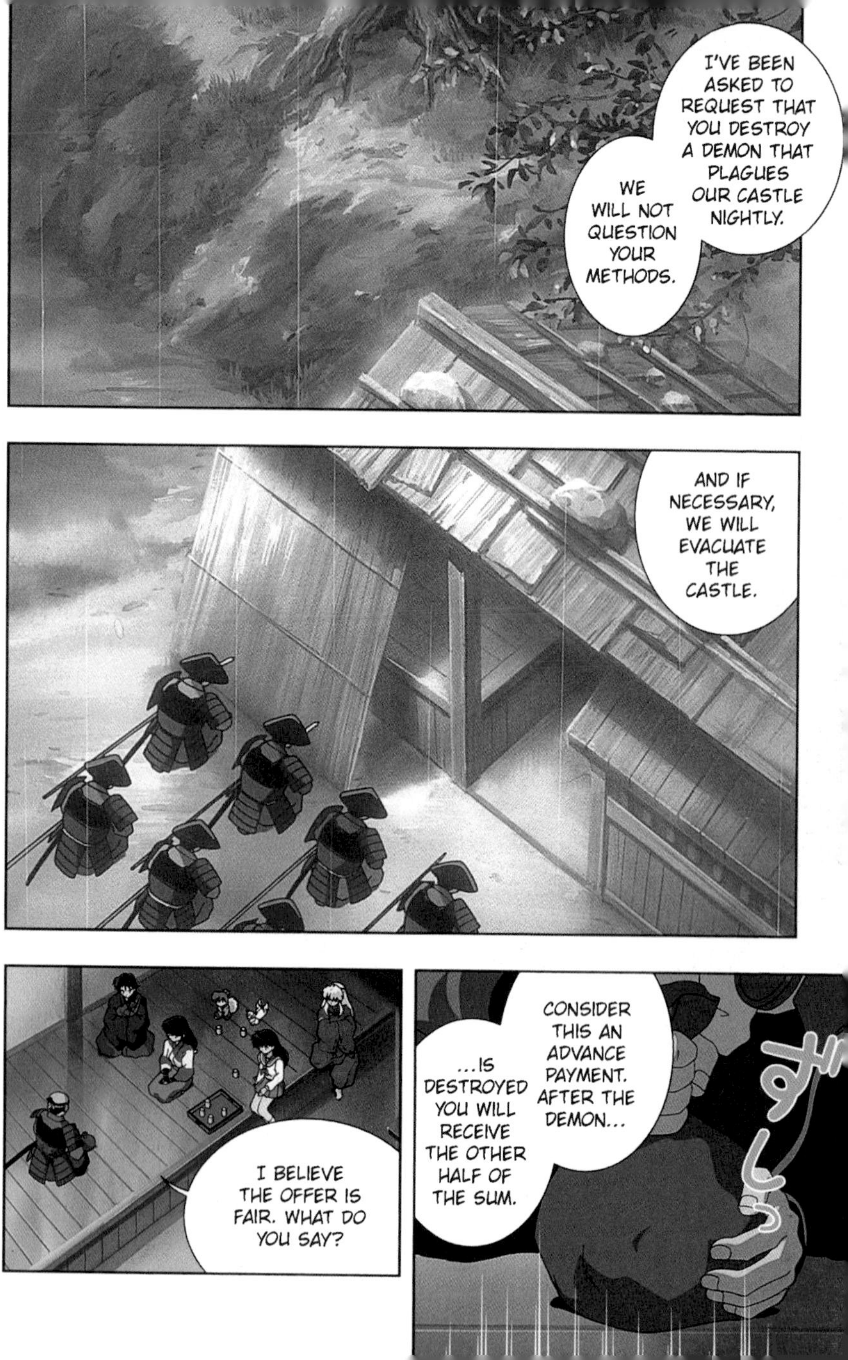
I'VE BEEN ASKED TO REQUEST THAT YOU DESTROY A DEMON THAT PLAGUES OUR CASTLE NIGHTLY.
WE WILL NOT QUESTION YOUR METHODS.
AND IF NECESSARY, WE WILL EVACUATE THE CASTLE.
ずしっ
CONSIDER THIS AN ADVANCE PAYMENT. AFTER THE DEMON...
...IS DESTROYED YOU WILL RECEIVE THE OTHER HALF OF THE SUM.
I BELIEVE THE OFFER IS FAIR. WHAT DO YOU SAY?

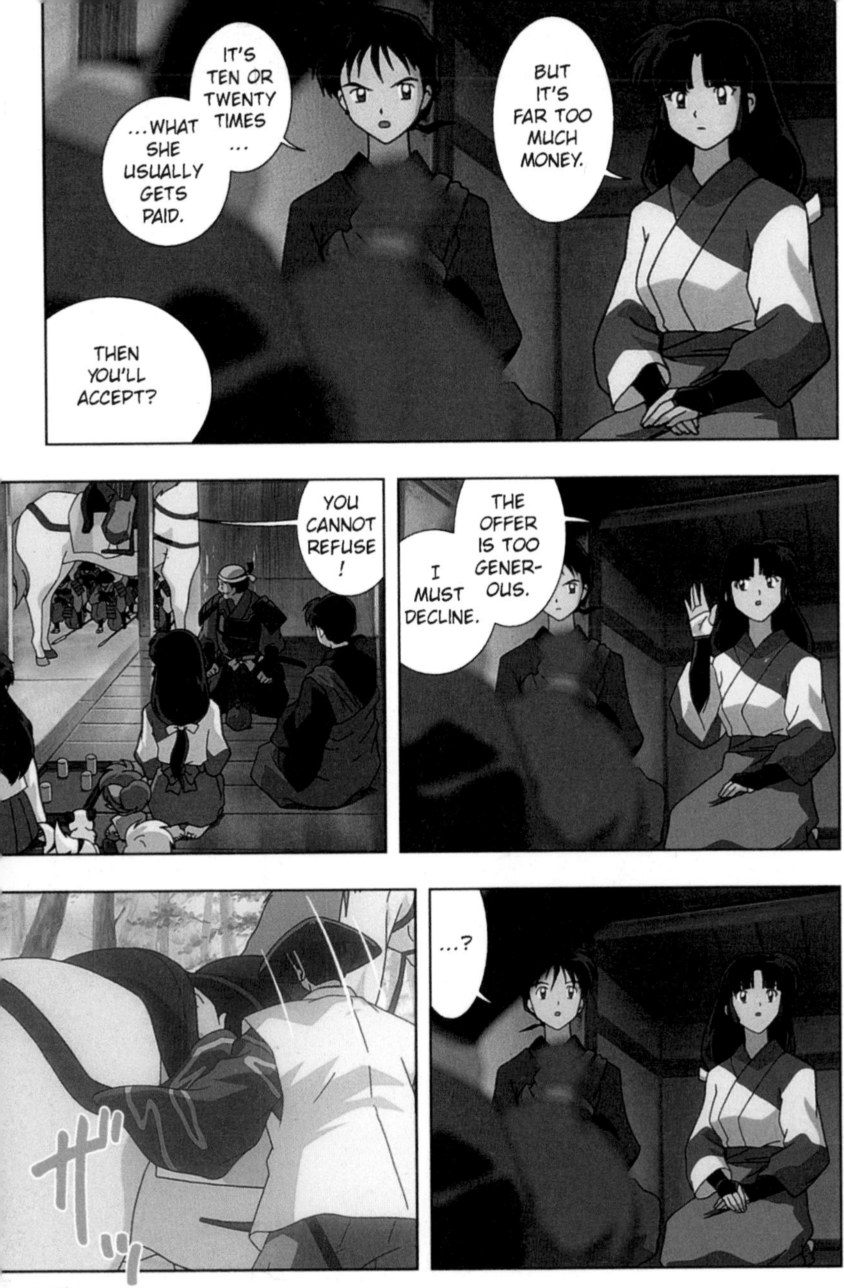
BUT IT'S FAR TOO MUCH MONEY.
IT'S TEN OR TWENTY TIMES ...
...WHAT SHE USUALLY GETS PAID.
THEN YOU'LL ACCEPT?
THE OFFER IS TOO GENEROUS.
I MUST DECLINE.
YOU CANNOT REFUSE!
...?
ザッ

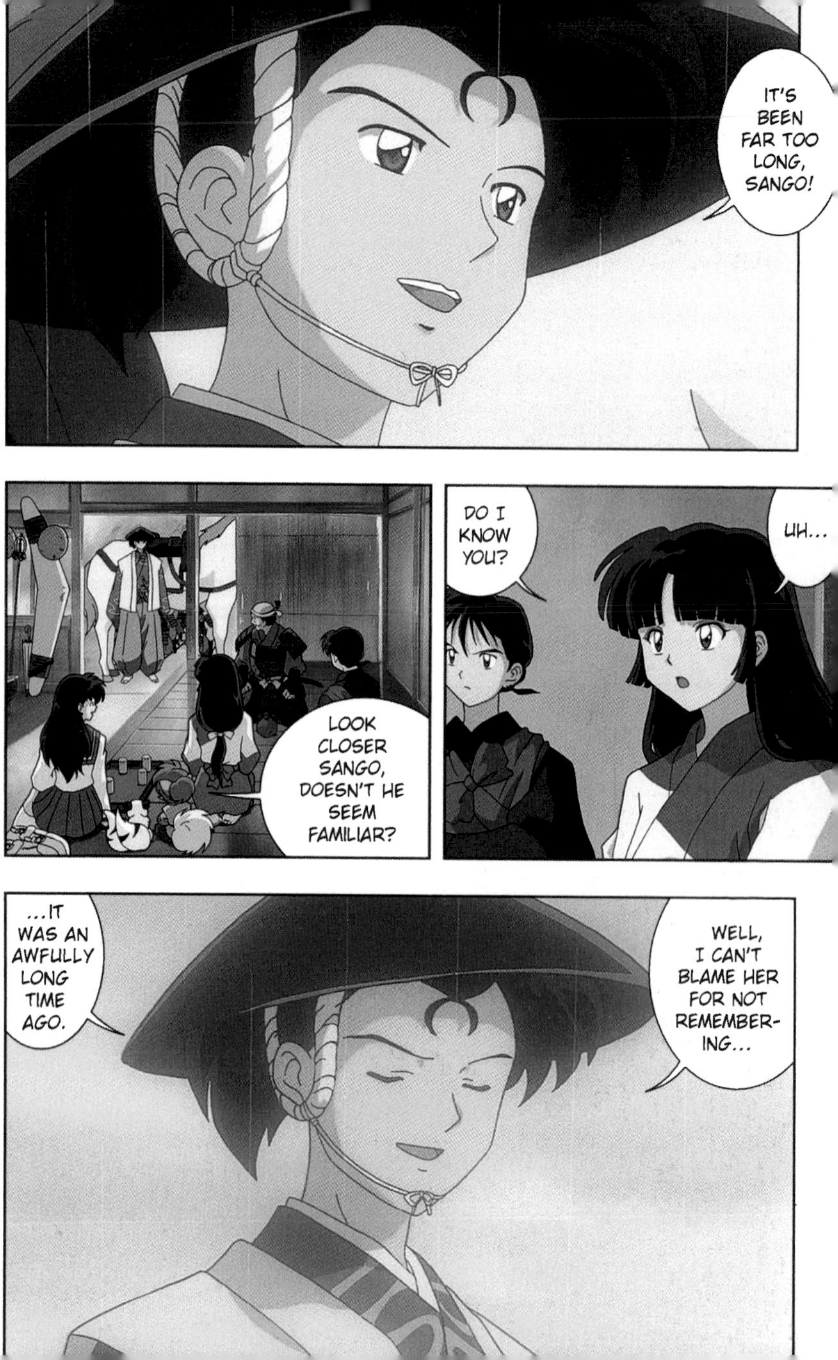

IT'S BEEN FAR TOO LONG, SANGO!
UH...
DO I KNOW YOU?
LOOK CLOSER SANGO, DOESN'T HE SEEM FAMILIAR?
WELL, I CAN'T BLAME HER FOR NOT REMEMBERING...
...IT WAS AN AWFULLY LONG TIME AGO.

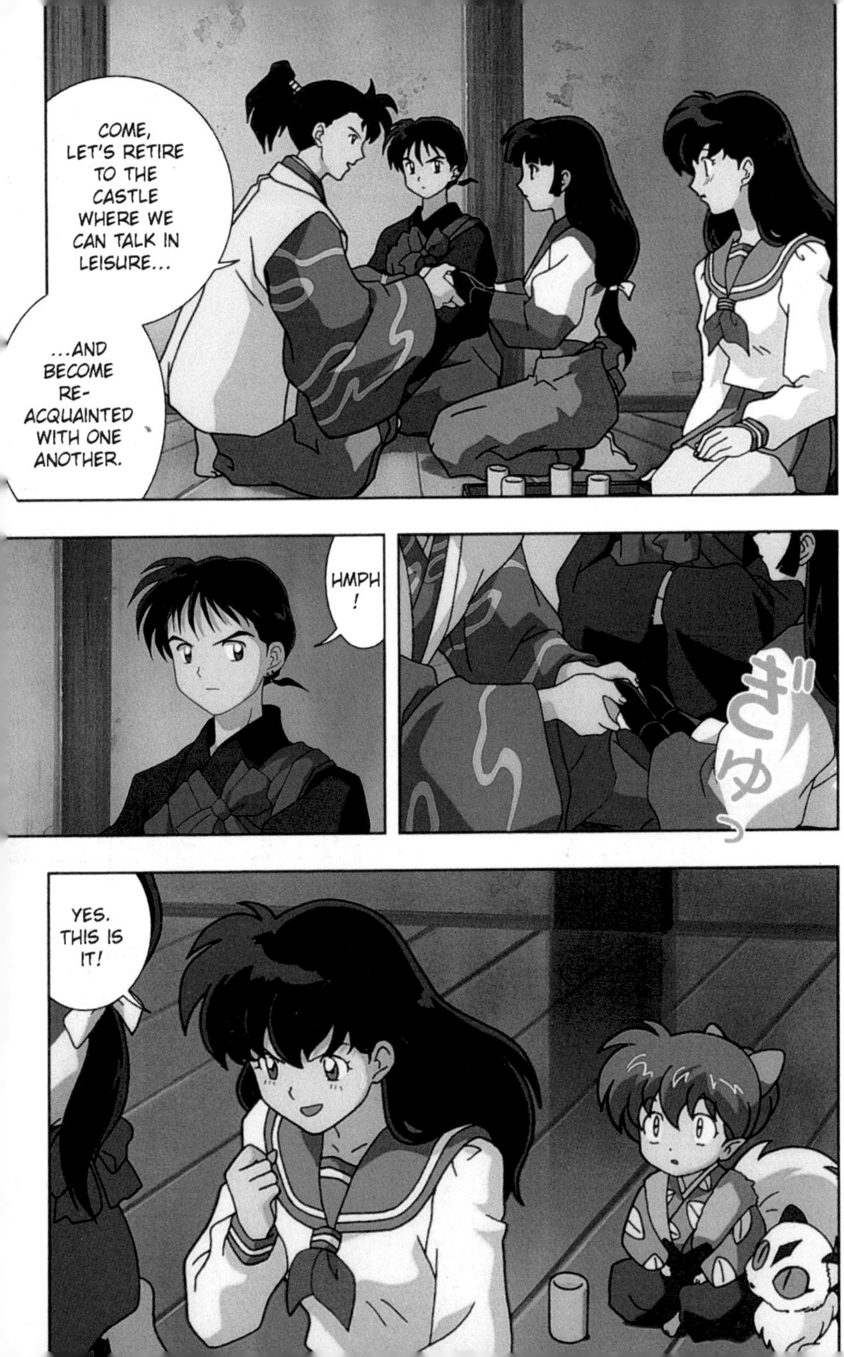
COME, LET'S RETIRE TO THE CASTLE WHERE WE CAN TALK IN LEISURE...
...AND BECOME RE-ACQUAINTED WITH ONE ANOTHER.
ぎゅっ
HMPH!
YES. THIS IS IT!

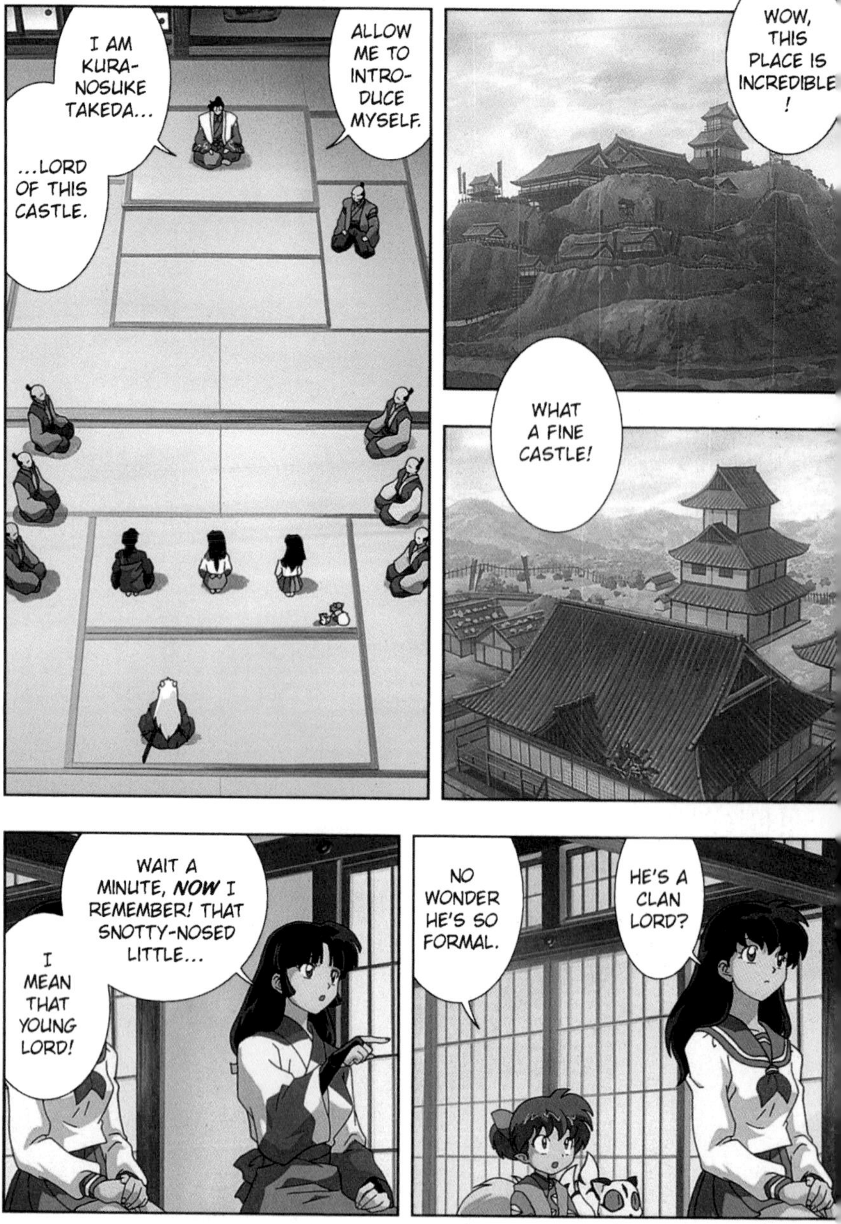
WOW, THIS PLACE IS INCREDIBLE!
WHAT A FINE CASTLE!
ALLOW ME TO INTRODUCE MYSELF.
I AM KURANOSUKE TAKEDA...
...LORD OF THIS CASTLE.
HE'S A CLAN LORD?
NO WONDER HE'S SO FORMAL.
WAIT A MINUTE, *NOW* I REMEMBER! THAT SNOTTY-NOSED LITTLE...
I MEAN THAT YOUNG LORD!

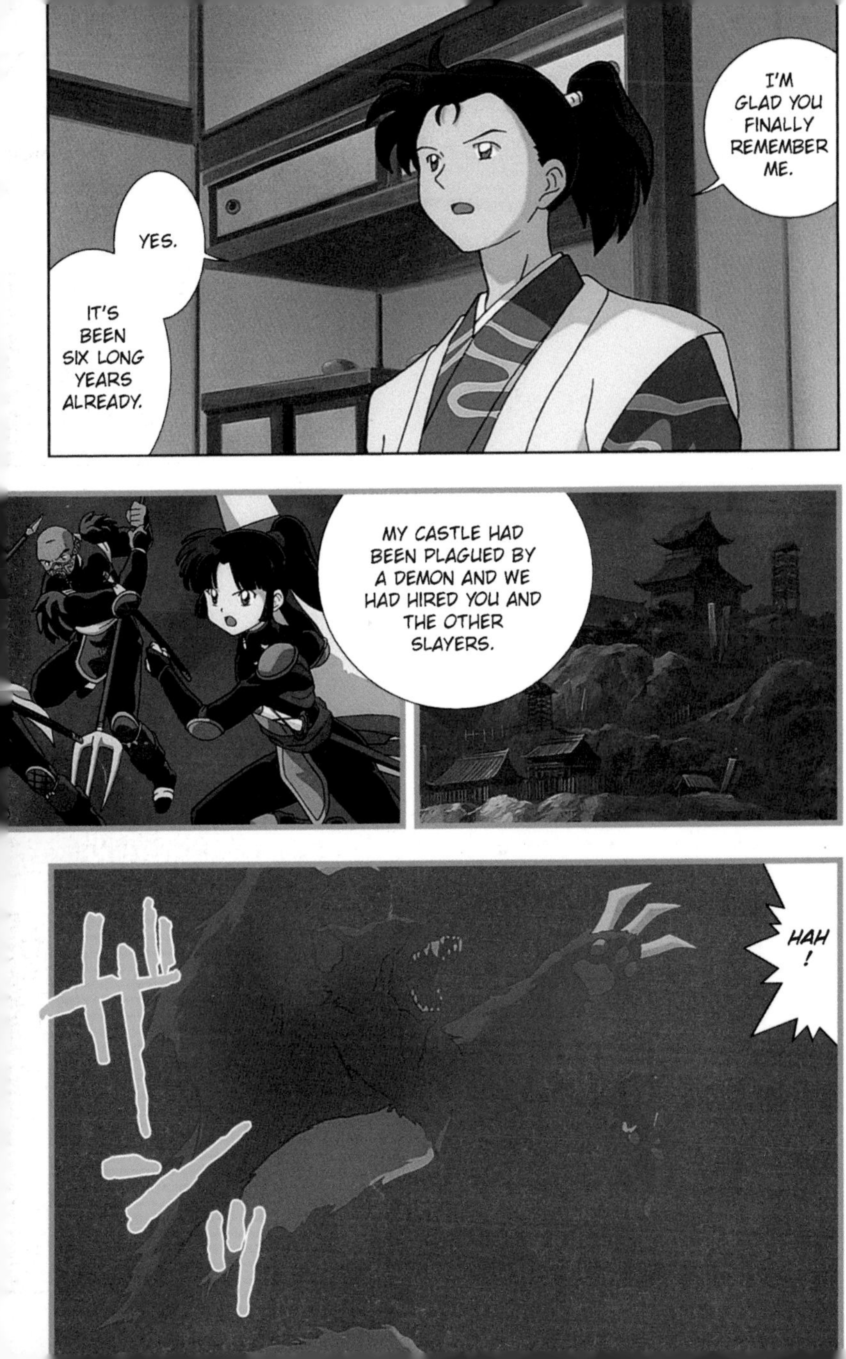
I'M GLAD YOU FINALLY REMEMBER ME.
YES.
IT'S BEEN SIX LONG YEARS ALREADY.
MY CASTLE HAD BEEN PLAGUED BY A DEMON AND WE HAD HIRED YOU AND THE OTHER SLAYERS.
HAH!

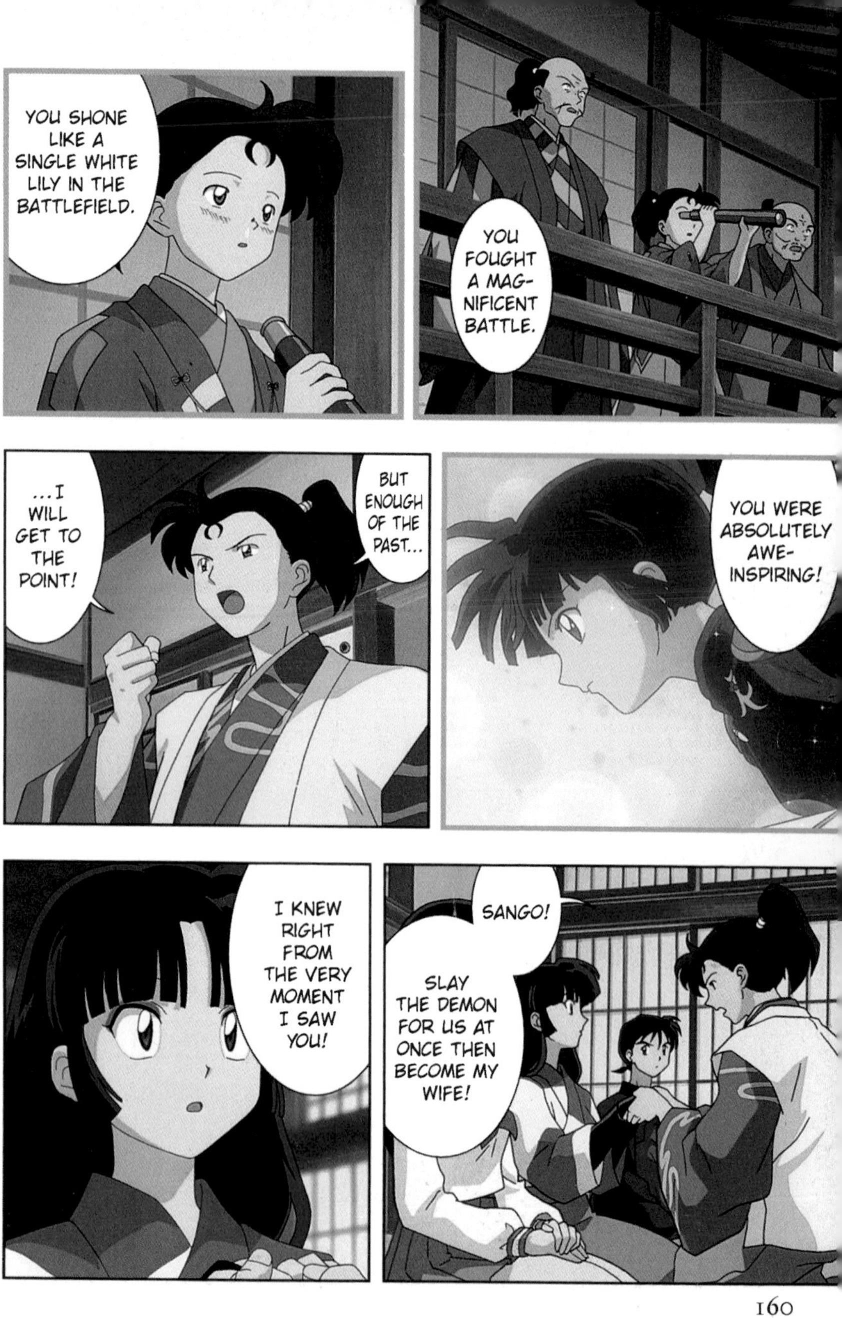
YOU FOUGHT A MAG-NIFICENT BATTLE.
YOU SHONE LIKE A SINGLE WHITE LILY IN THE BATTLEFIELD.
YOU WERE ABSOLUTELY AWE-INSPIRING!
BUT ENOUGH OF THE PAST...
...I WILL GET TO THE POINT!
SANGO!
SLAY THE DEMON FOR US AT ONCE THEN BECOME MY WIFE!
I KNEW RIGHT FROM THE VERY MOMENT I SAW YOU!

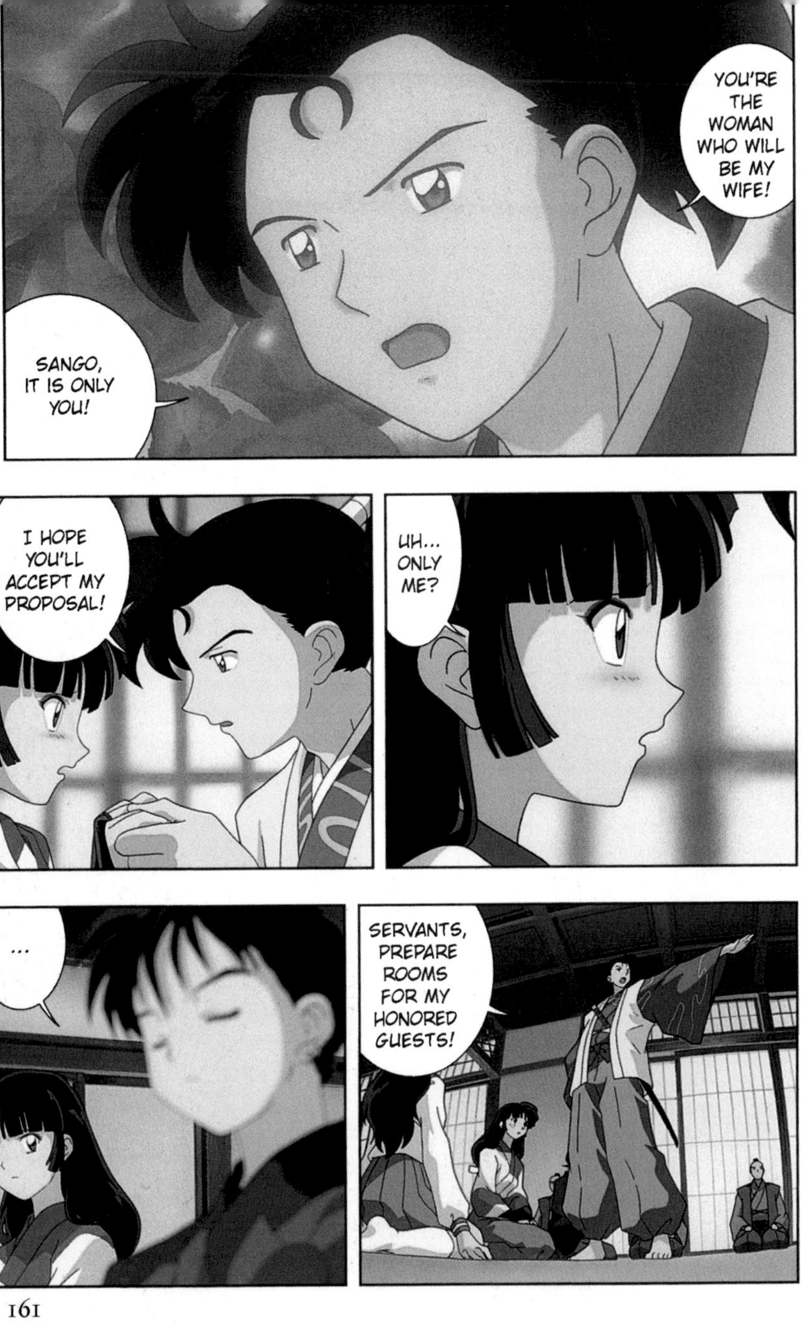
YOU'RE THE WOMAN WHO WILL BE MY WIFE!
SANGO, IT IS ONLY YOU!
UH... ONLY ME?
I HOPE YOU'LL ACCEPT MY PROPOSAL!
SERVANTS, PREPARE ROOMS FOR MY HONORED GUESTS!
...

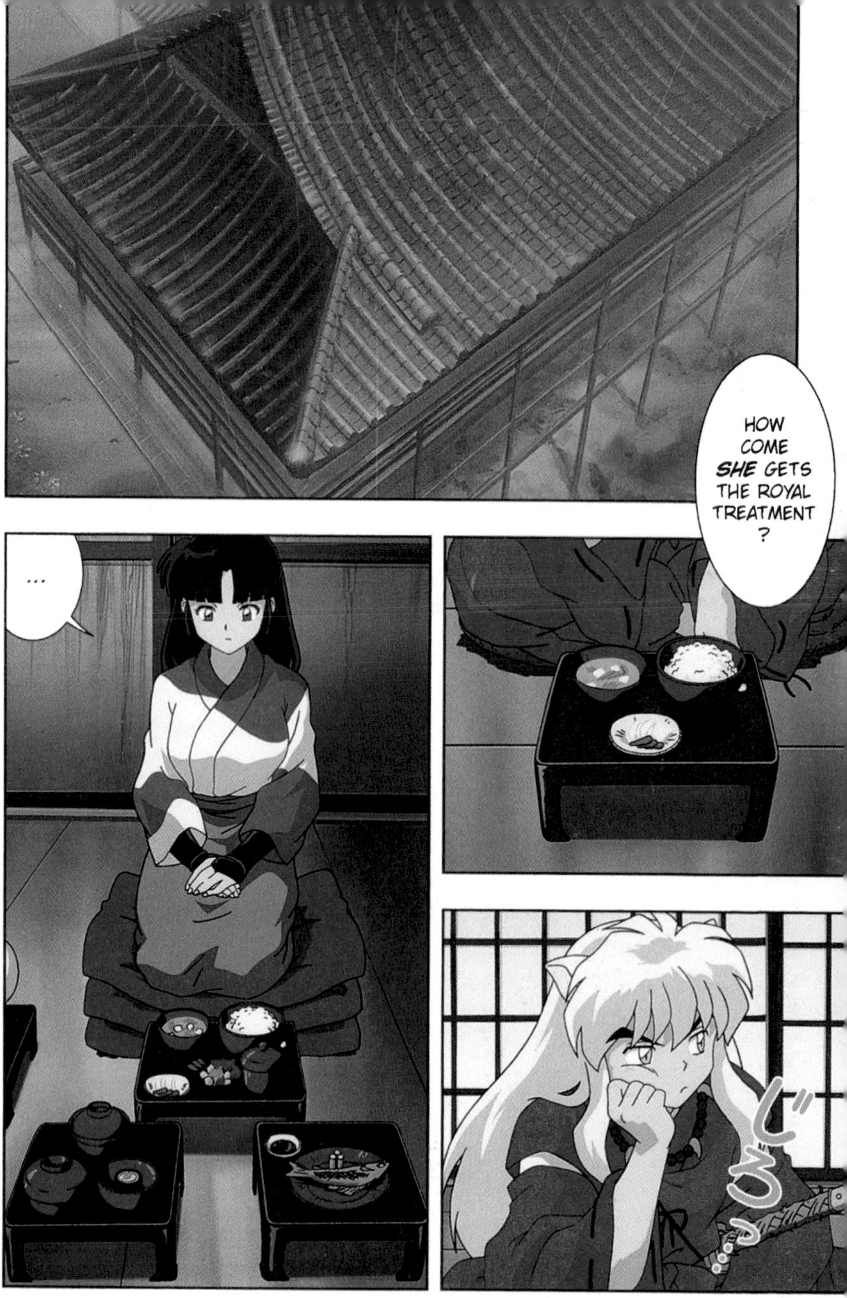
HOW COME SHE GETS THE ROYAL TREATMENT?
じろ…
...

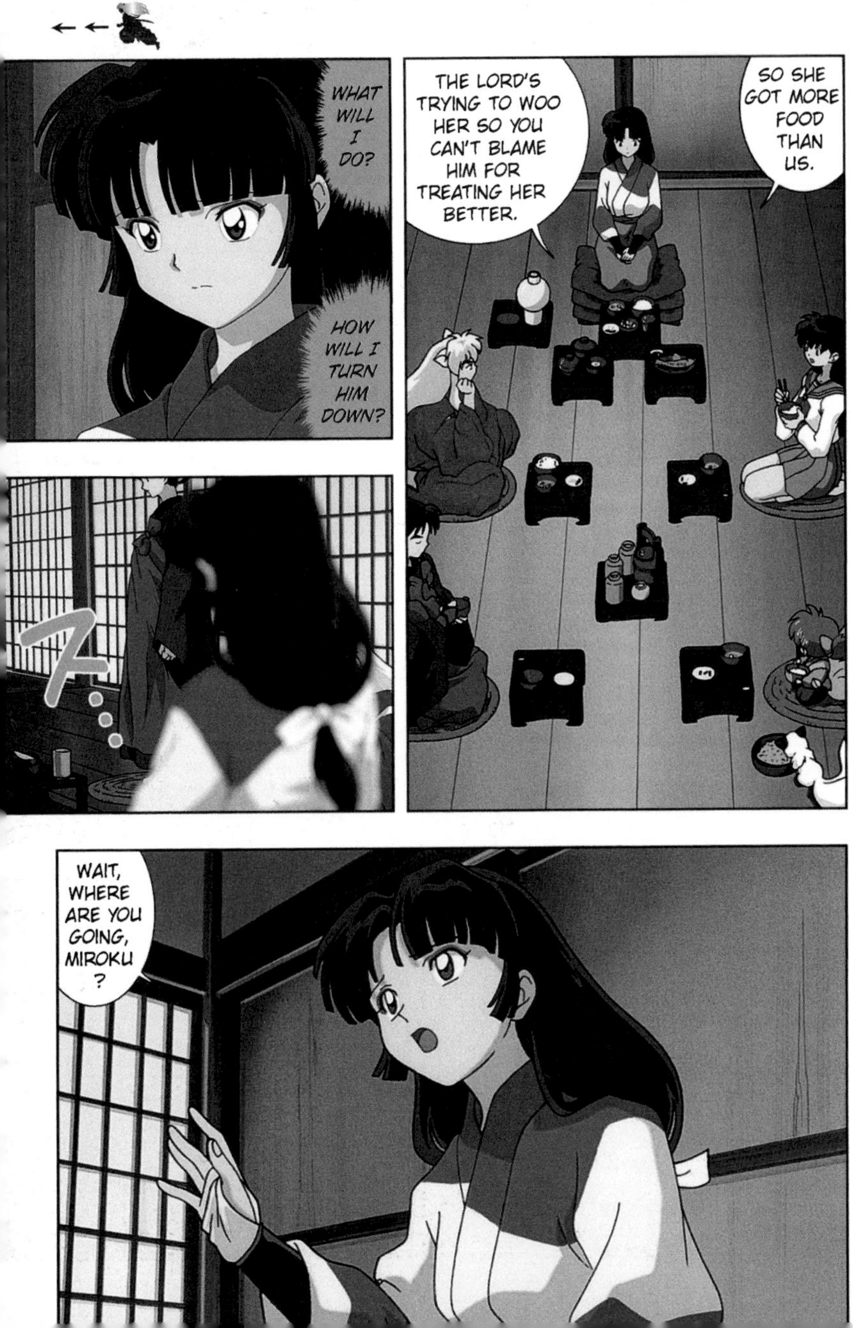
SO SHE GOT MORE FOOD THAN US.
THE LORD'S TRYING TO WOO HER SO YOU CAN'T BLAME HIM FOR TREATING HER BETTER.
WHAT WILL I DO?
HOW WILL I TURN HIM DOWN?
WAIT, WHERE ARE YOU GOING, MIROKU?

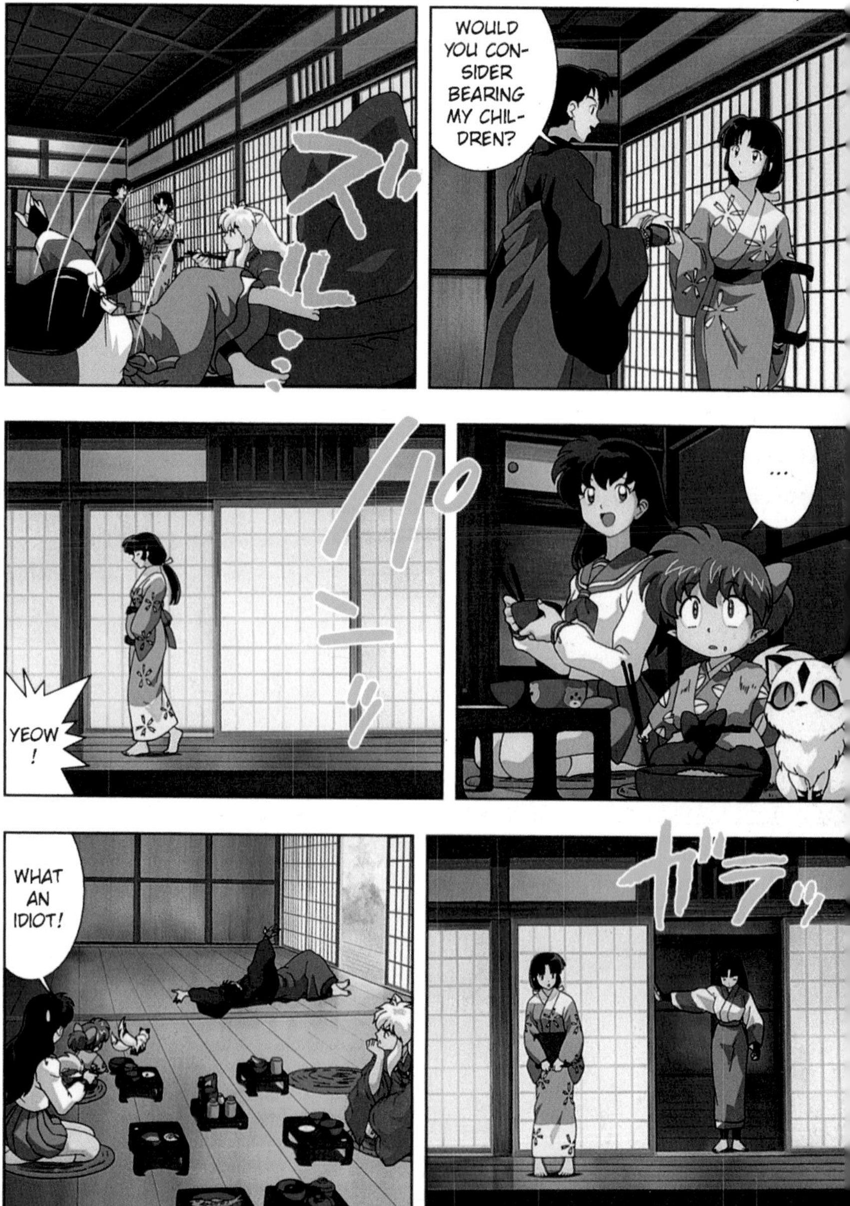
WOULD YOU CONSIDER BEARING MY CHILDREN?
...
YEOW!
WHAT AN IDIOT!

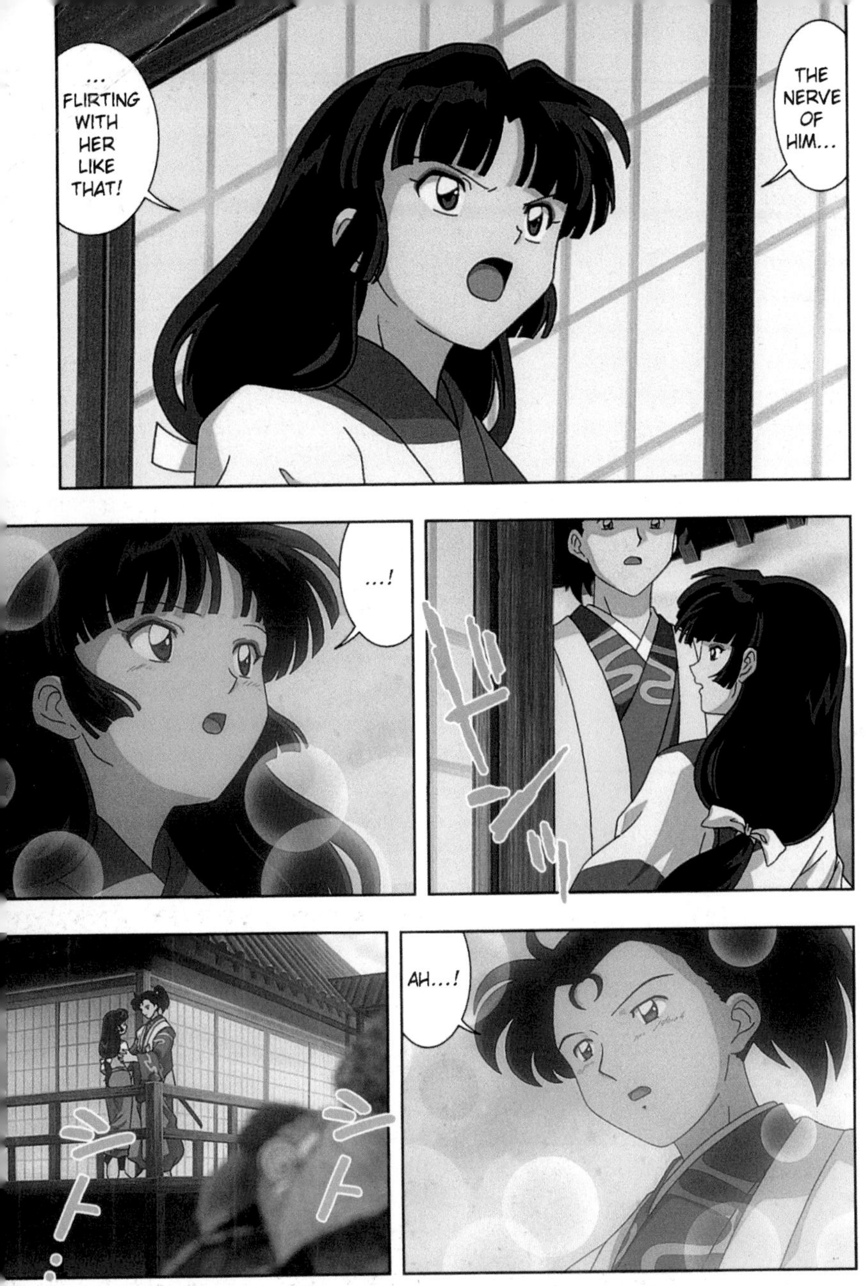
THE NERVE OF HIM...
...FLIRTING WITH HER LIKE THAT!
...!
AH...!
シト
シト...

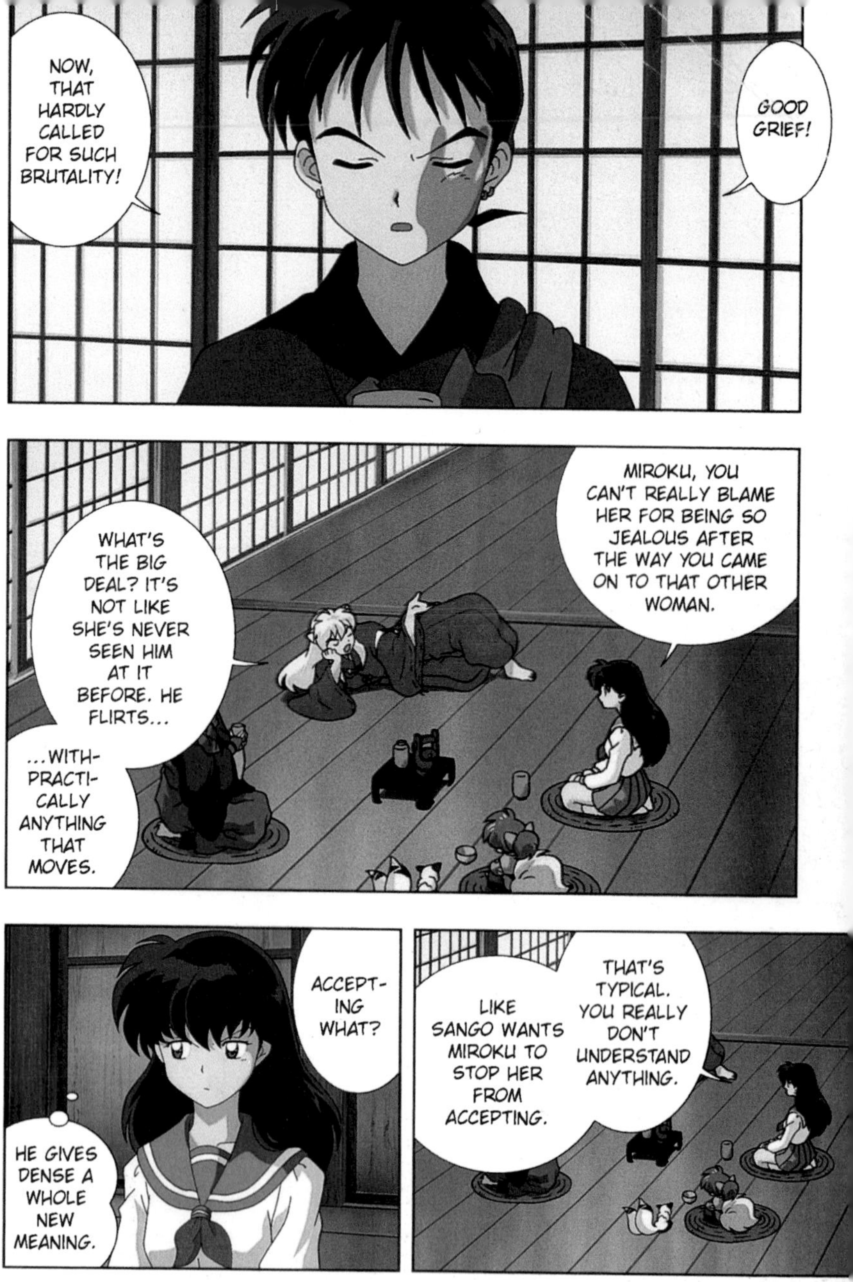
GOOD GRIEF!
NOW, THAT HARDLY CALLED FOR SUCH BRUTALITY!
MIROKU, YOU CAN'T REALLY BLAME HER FOR BEING SO JEALOUS AFTER THE WAY YOU CAME ON TO THAT OTHER WOMAN.
WHAT'S THE BIG DEAL? IT'S NOT LIKE SHE'S NEVER SEEN HIM AT IT BEFORE. HE FLIRTS...
...WITH-PRACTI-CALLY ANYTHING THAT MOVES.
THAT'S TYPICAL. YOU REALLY DON'T UNDERSTAND ANYTHING.
LIKE SANGO WANTS MIROKU TO STOP HER FROM ACCEPTING.
ACCEPT-ING WHAT?
HE GIVES DENSE A WHOLE NEW MEANING.

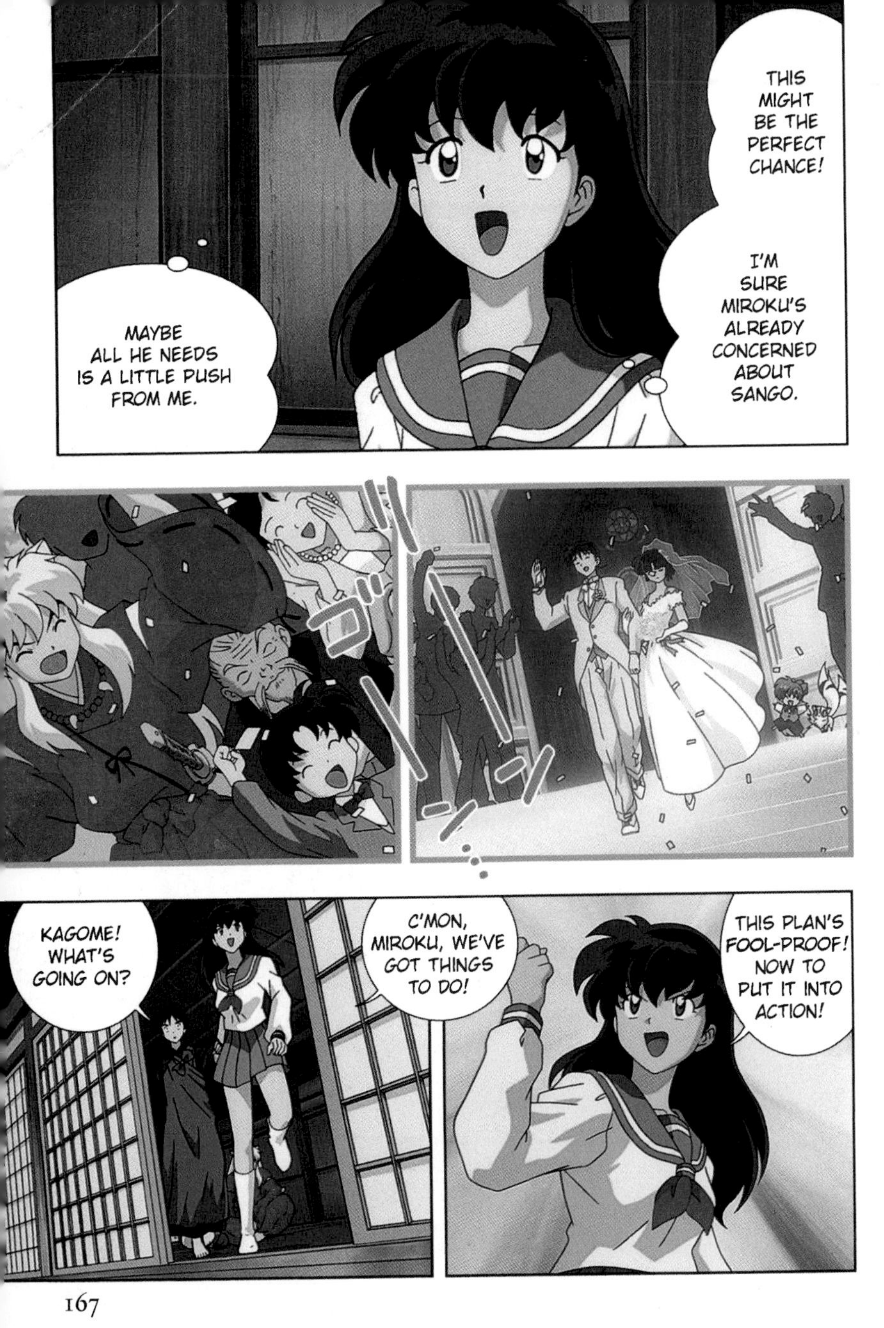
THIS MIGHT BE THE PERFECT CHANCE!
I'M SURE MIROKU'S ALREADY CONCERNED ABOUT SANGO.
MAYBE ALL HE NEEDS IS A LITTLE PUSH FROM ME.
THIS PLAN'S FOOL-PROOF! NOW TO PUT IT INTO ACTION!
C'MON, MIROKU, WE'VE GOT THINGS TO DO!
KAGOME! WHAT'S GOING ON?

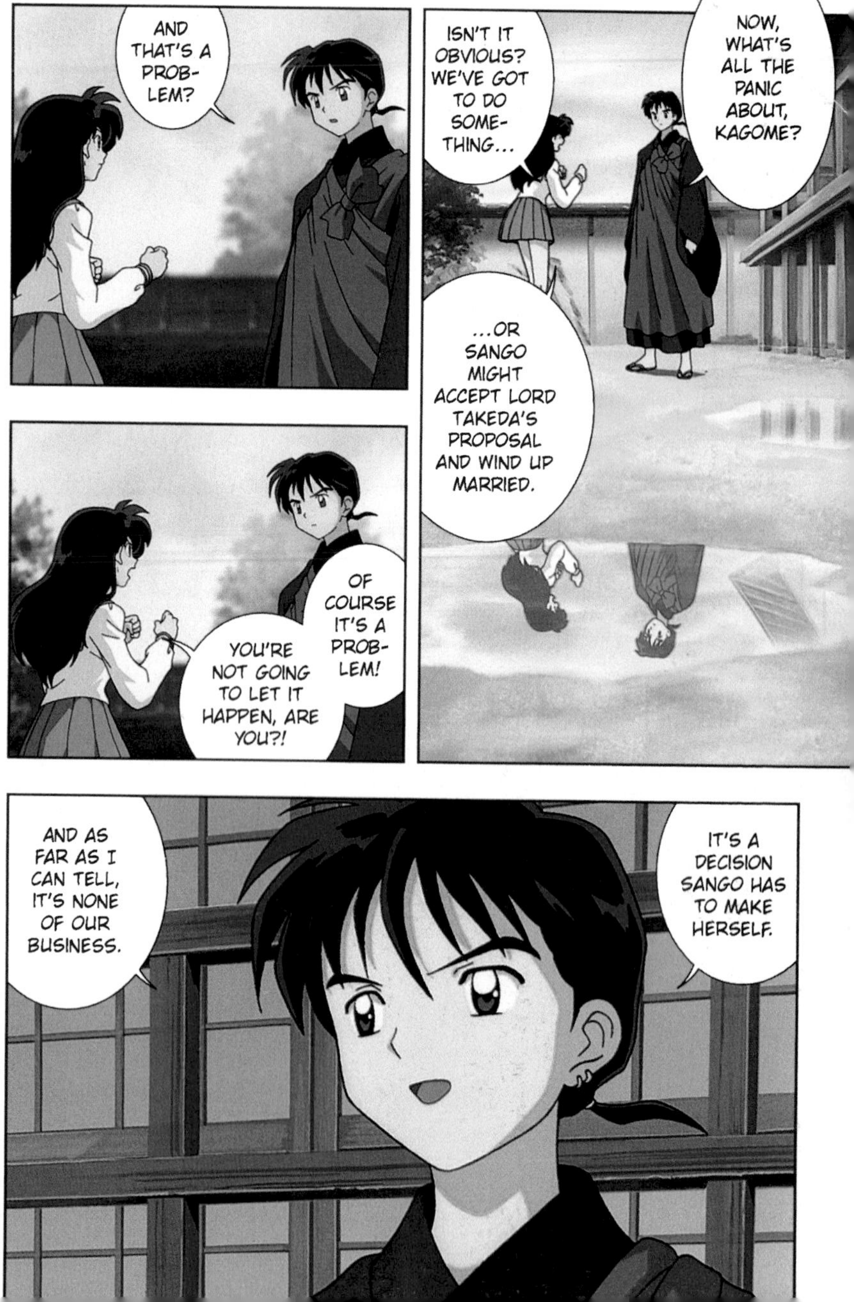
NOW, WHAT'S ALL THE PANIC ABOUT, KAGOME?
ISN'T IT OBVIOUS? WE'VE GOT TO DO SOME-THING...
...OR SANGO MIGHT ACCEPT LORD TAKEDA'S PROPOSAL AND WIND UP MARRIED.
AND THAT'S A PROB-LEM?
OF COURSE IT'S A PROB-LEM!
YOU'RE NOT GOING TO LET IT HAPPEN, ARE YOU?!
IT'S A DECISION SANGO HAS TO MAKE HERSELF.
AND AS FAR AS I CAN TELL, IT'S NONE OF OUR BUSINESS.

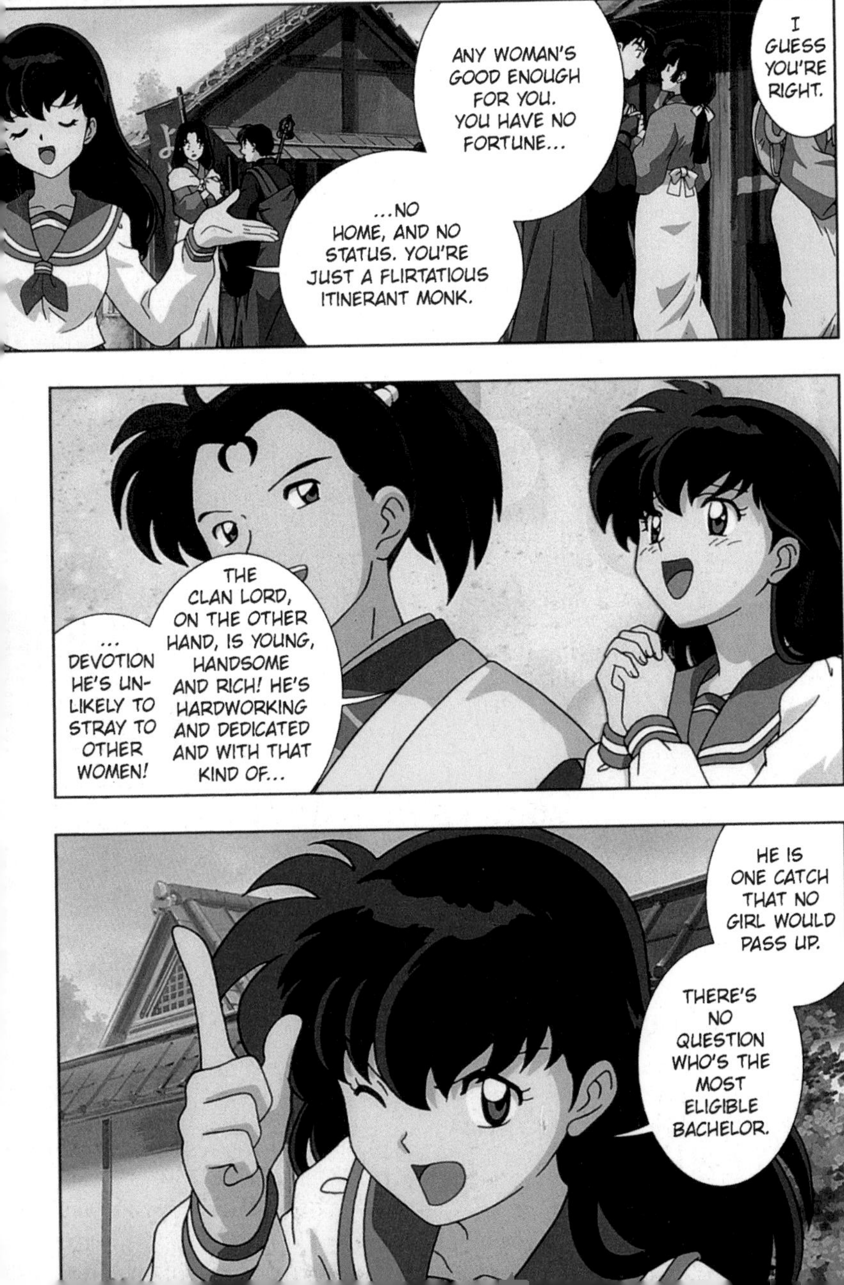

I GUESS YOU'RE RIGHT.
ANY WOMAN'S GOOD ENOUGH FOR YOU. YOU HAVE NO FORTUNE...
...NO HOME, AND NO STATUS. YOU'RE JUST A FLIRTATIOUS ITINERANT MONK.
THE CLAN LORD, ON THE OTHER HAND, IS YOUNG, HANDSOME AND RICH! HE'S HARDWORKING AND DEDICATED AND WITH THAT KIND OF...
...DEVOTION HE'S UNLIKELY TO STRAY TO OTHER WOMEN!
HE IS ONE CATCH THAT NO GIRL WOULD PASS UP.
THERE'S NO QUESTION WHO'S THE MOST ELIGIBLE BACHELOR.

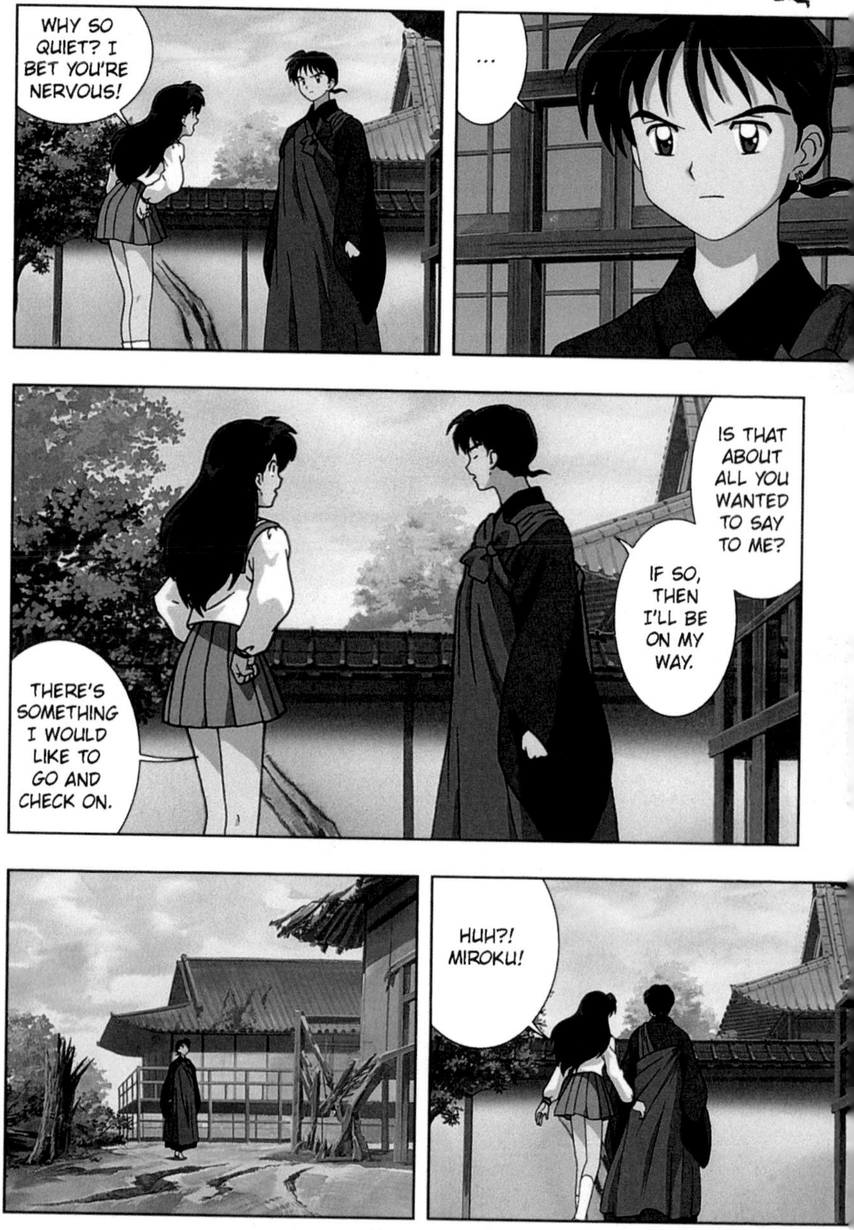
...
WHY SO QUIET? I BET YOU'RE NERVOUS!
IS THAT ABOUT ALL YOU WANTED TO SAY TO ME?
IF SO, THEN I'LL BE ON MY WAY.
THERE'S SOMETHING I WOULD LIKE TO GO AND CHECK ON.
HUH?! MIROKU!

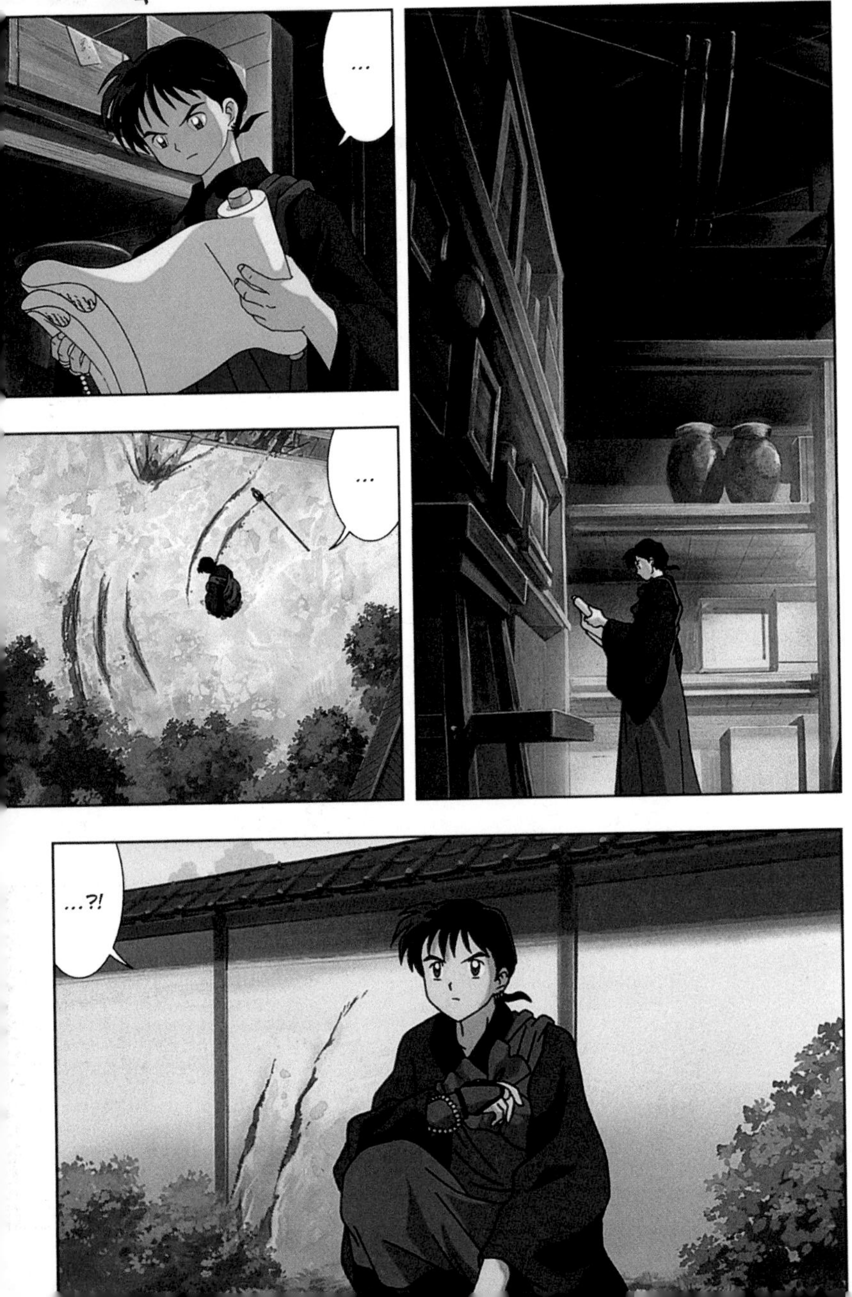
...
...
...?!

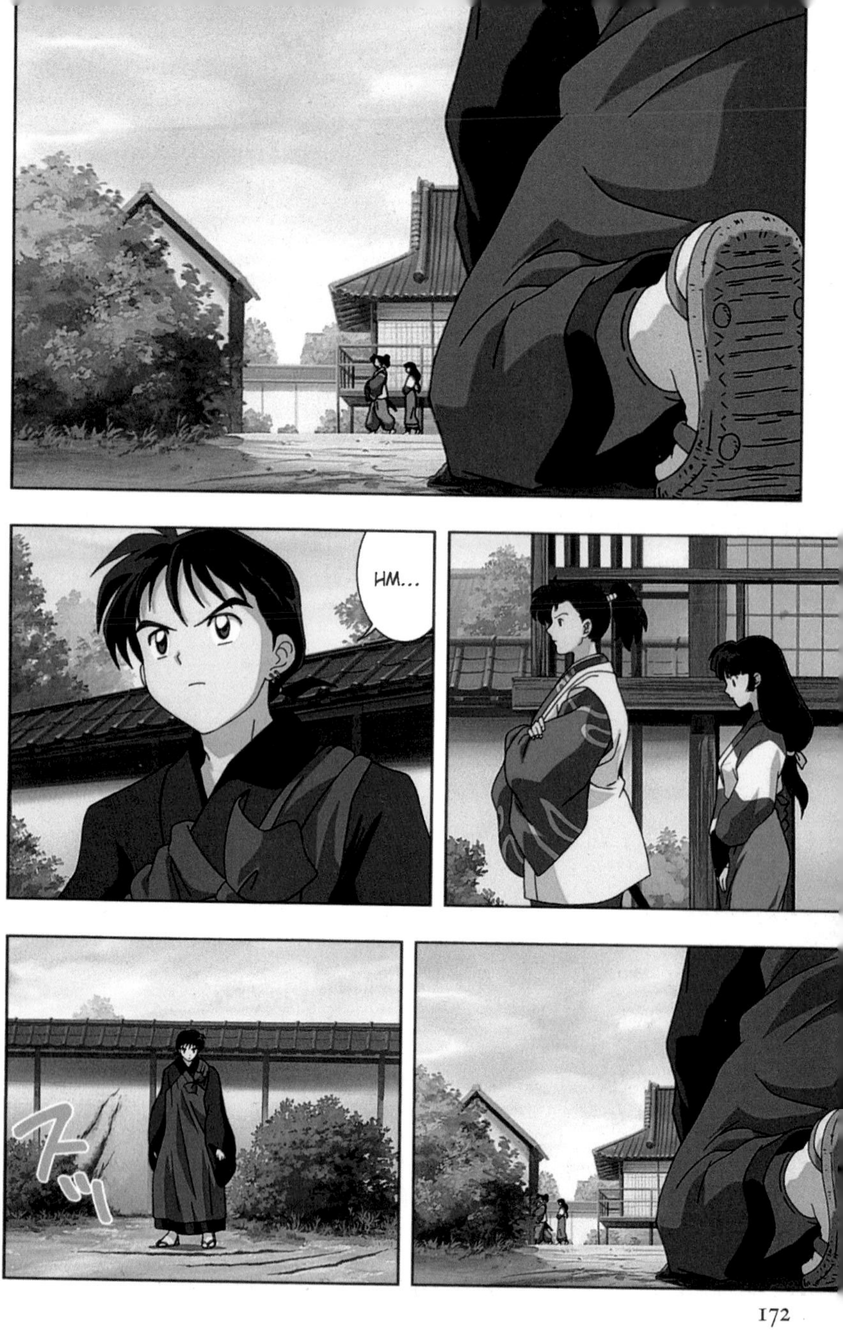
HM...
スッ

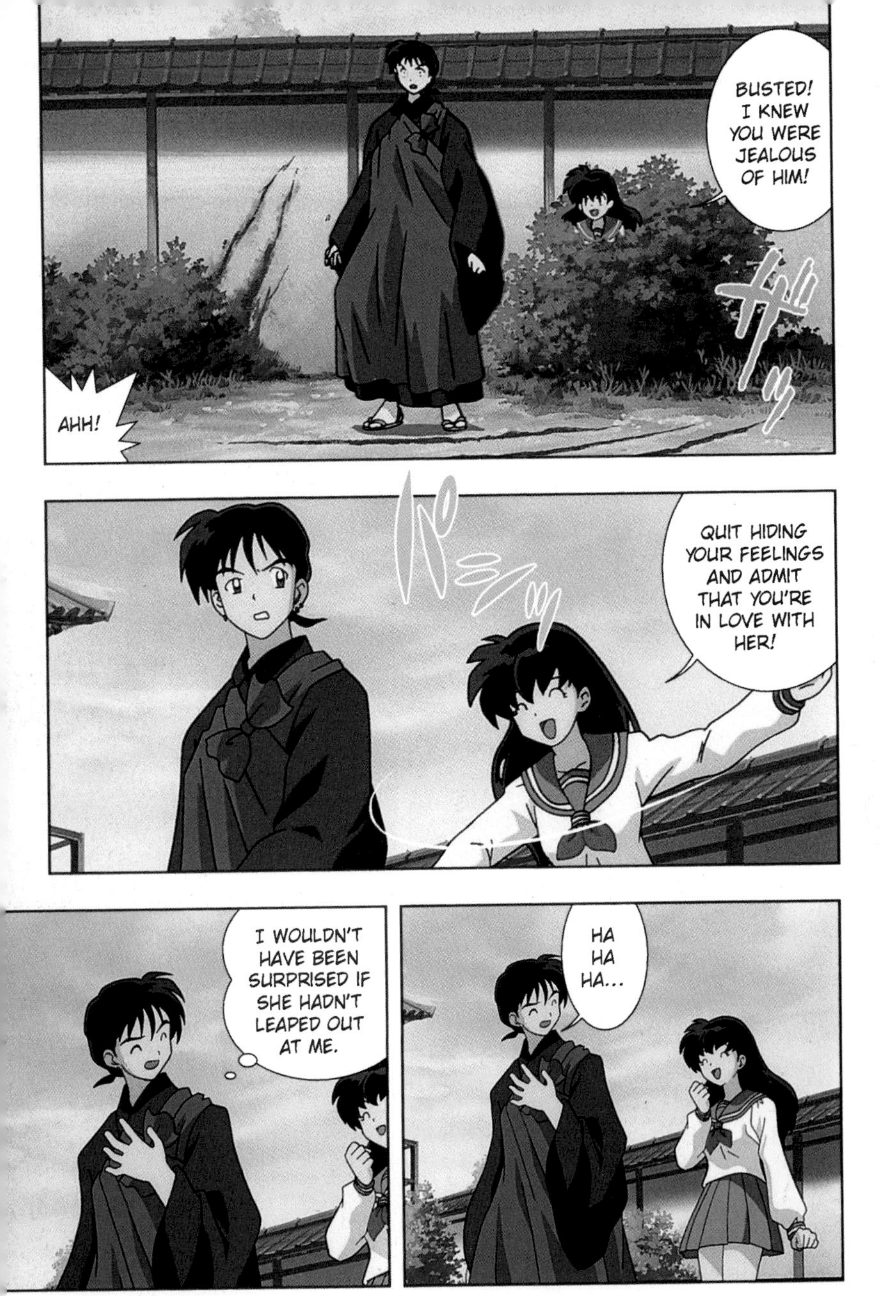
BUSTED! I KNEW YOU WERE JEALOUS OF HIM!
ザッ
AHH!
QUIT HIDING YOUR FEELINGS AND ADMIT THAT YOU'RE IN LOVE WITH HER!
パシッ
HA HA HA...
I WOULDN'T HAVE BEEN SURPRISED IF SHE HADN'T LEAPED OUT AT ME.

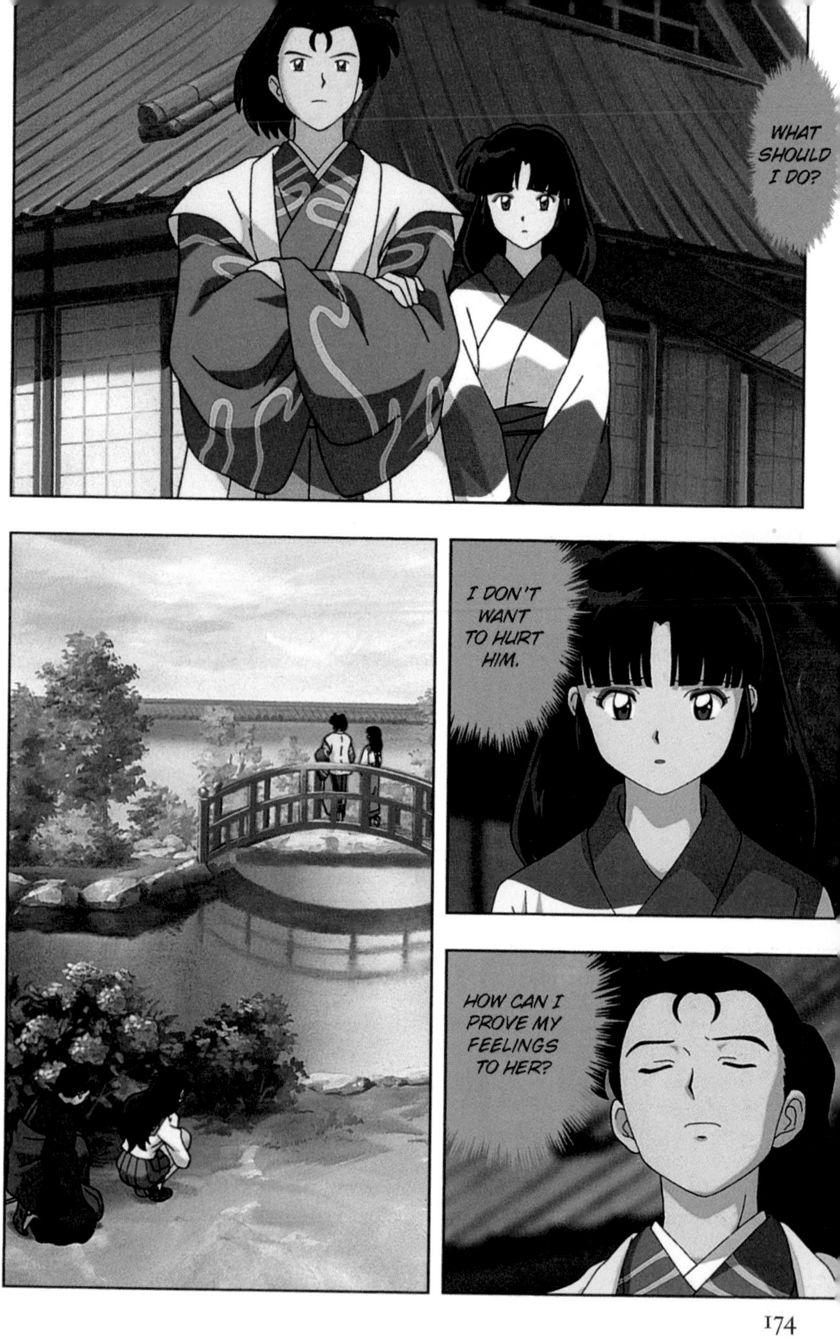
WHAT SHOULD I DO?
I DON'T WANT TO HURT HIM.
HOW CAN I PROVE MY FEELINGS TO HER?

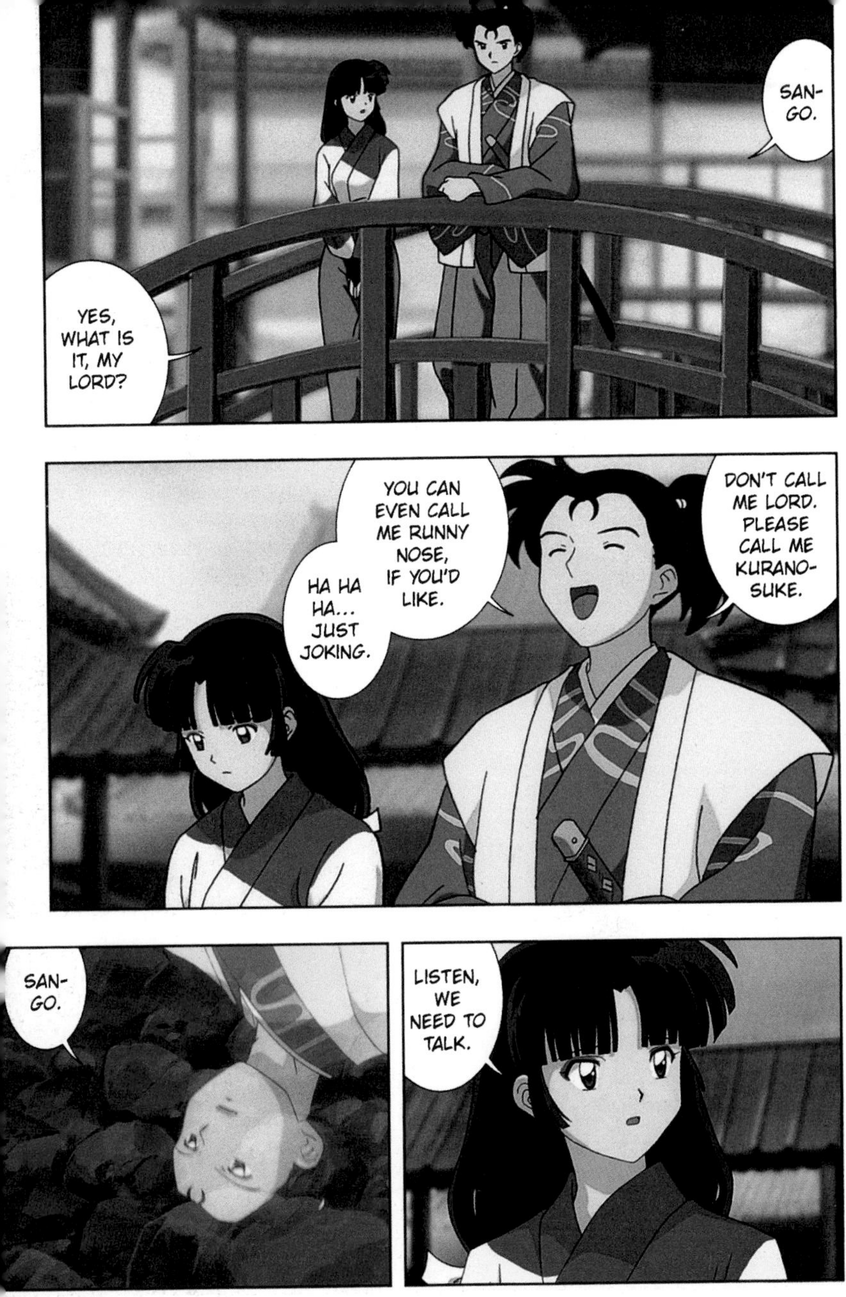
SAN-GO.
YES, WHAT IS IT, MY LORD?
DON'T CALL ME LORD. PLEASE CALL ME KURANO-SUKE.
YOU CAN EVEN CALL ME RUNNY NOSE, IF YOU'D LIKE.
HA HA HA... JUST JOKING.
LISTEN, WE NEED TO TALK.
SAN-GO.

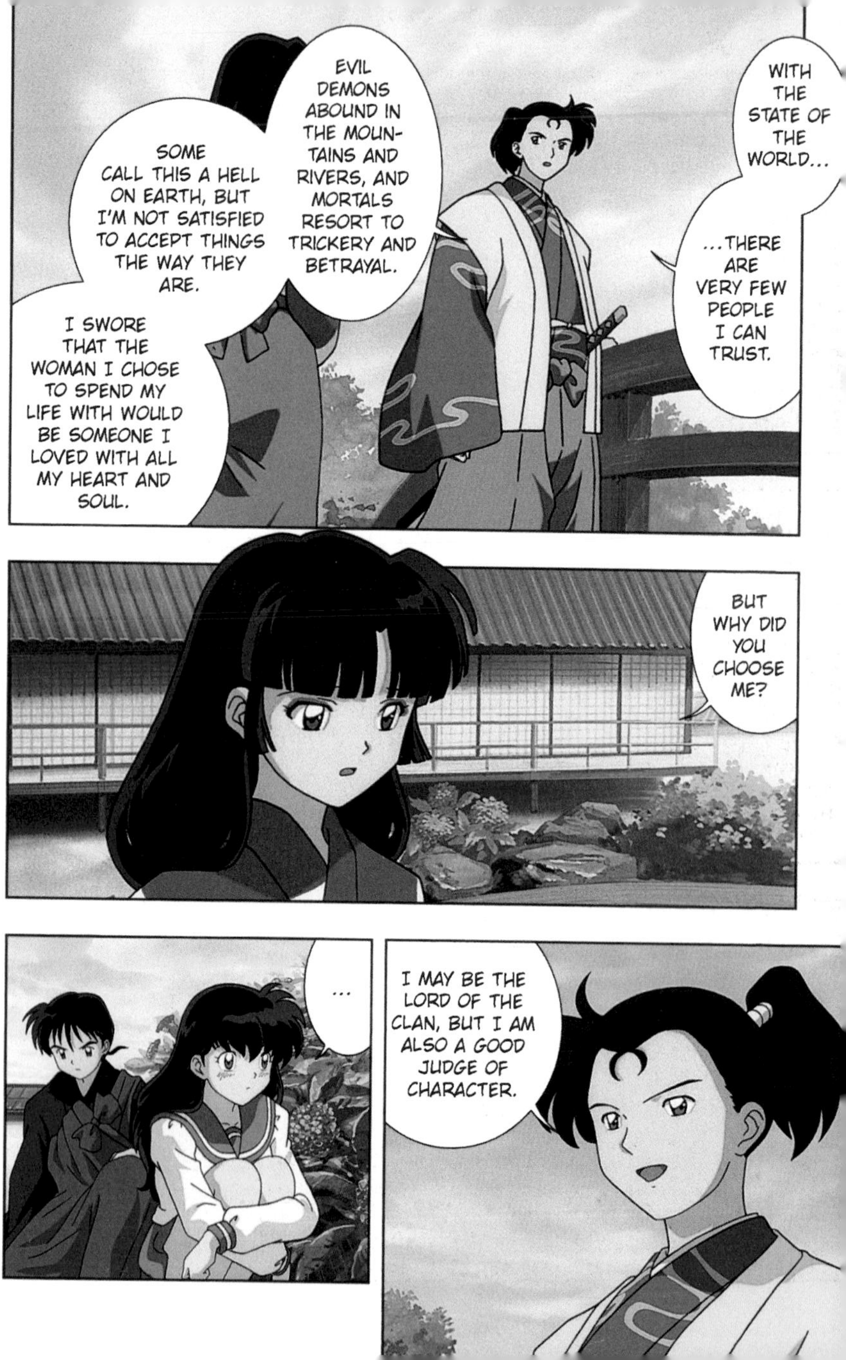
WITH THE STATE OF THE WORLD...
...THERE ARE VERY FEW PEOPLE I CAN TRUST.
EVIL DEMONS ABOUND IN THE MOUNTAINS AND RIVERS, AND MORTALS RESORT TO TRICKERY AND BETRAYAL.
SOME CALL THIS A HELL ON EARTH, BUT I'M NOT SATISFIED TO ACCEPT THINGS THE WAY THEY ARE.
I SWORE THAT THE WOMAN I CHOSE TO SPEND MY LIFE WITH WOULD BE SOMEONE I LOVED WITH ALL MY HEART AND SOUL.
BUT WHY DID YOU CHOOSE ME?
I MAY BE THE LORD OF THE CLAN, BUT I AM ALSO A GOOD JUDGE OF CHARACTER.
...

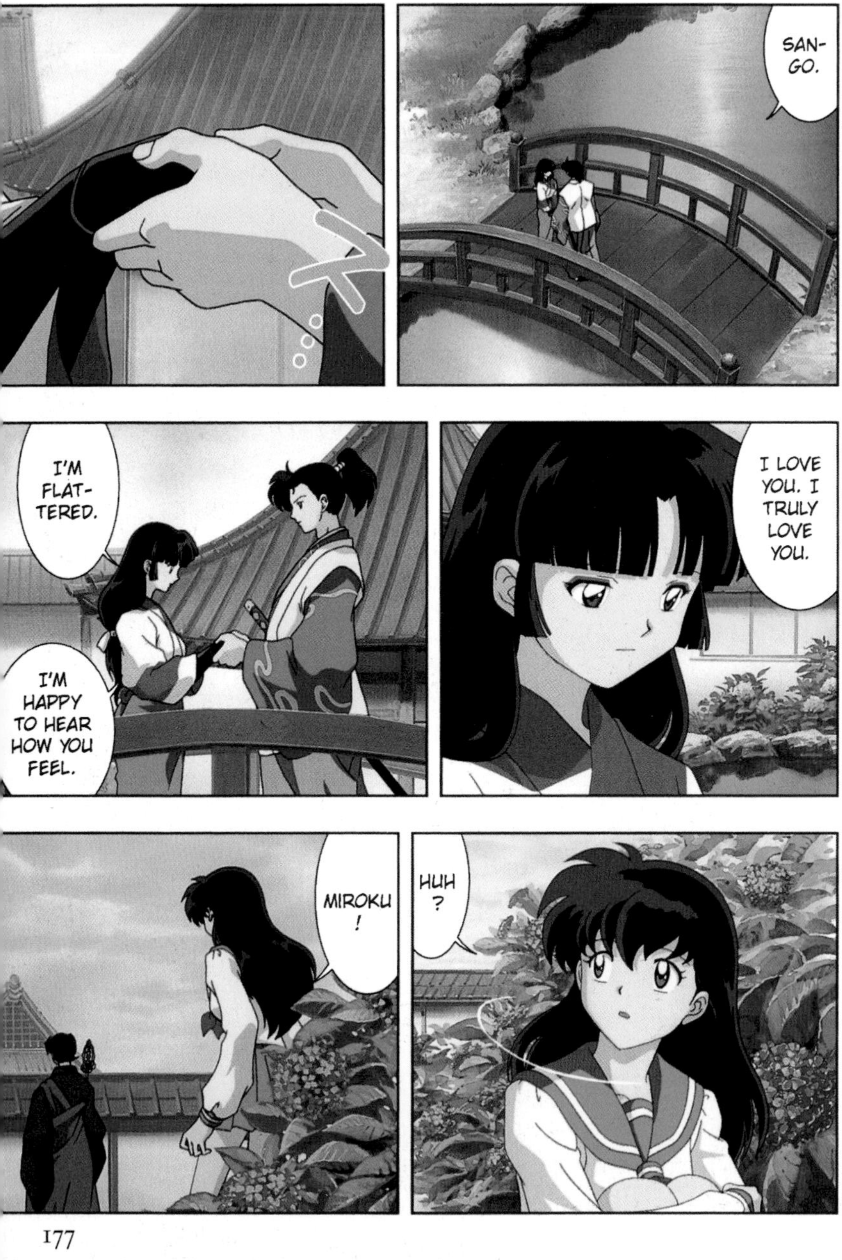
SAN-GO.
I LOVE YOU. I TRULY LOVE YOU.
I'M FLATTERED.
I'M HAPPY TO HEAR HOW YOU FEEL.
HUH?
MIROKU!

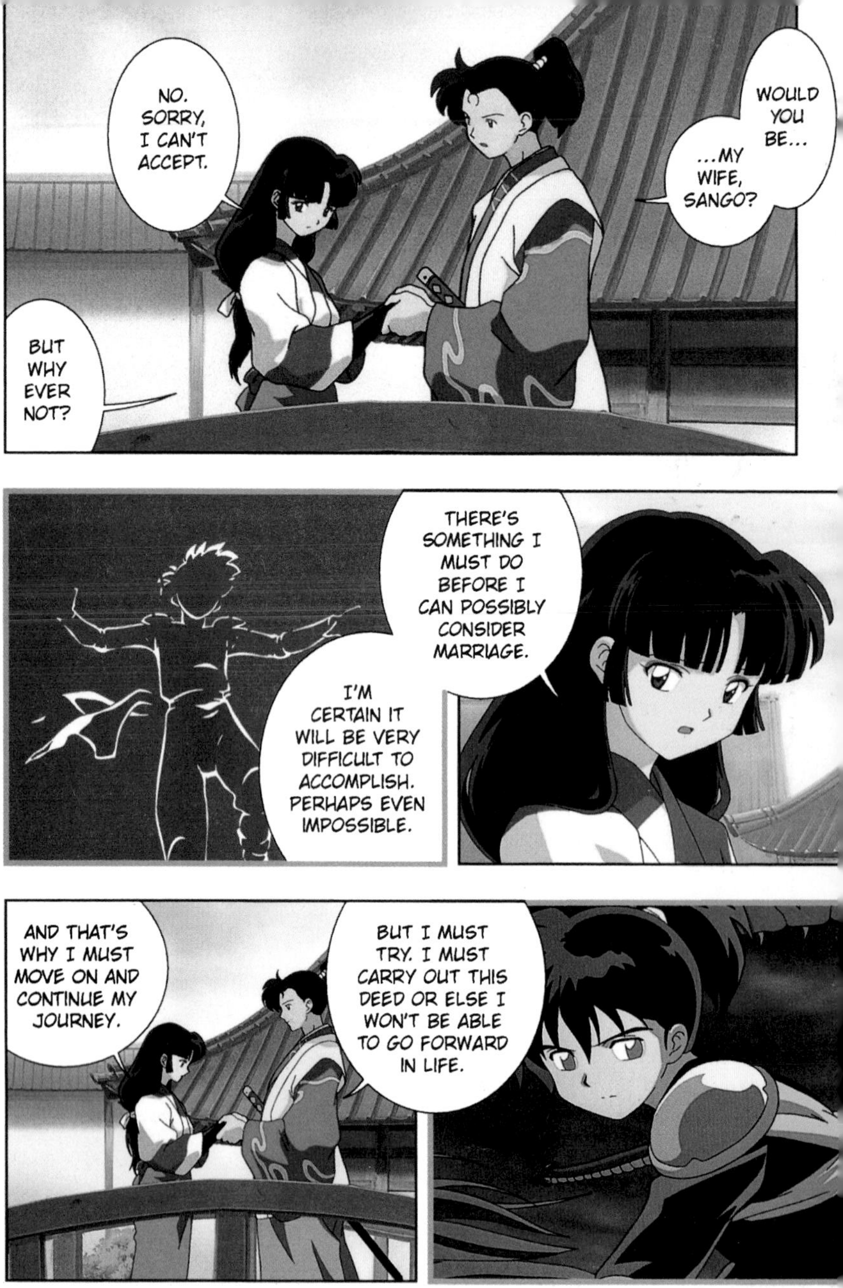
WOULD YOU BE...
...MY WIFE, SANGO?
NO. SORRY, I CAN'T ACCEPT.
BUT WHY EVER NOT?
THERE'S SOMETHING I MUST DO BEFORE I CAN POSSIBLY CONSIDER MARRIAGE.
I'M CERTAIN IT WILL BE VERY DIFFICULT TO ACCOMPLISH. PERHAPS EVEN IMPOSSIBLE.
BUT I MUST TRY. I MUST CARRY OUT THIS DEED OR ELSE I WON'T BE ABLE TO GO FORWARD IN LIFE.
AND THAT'S WHY I MUST MOVE ON AND CONTINUE MY JOURNEY.

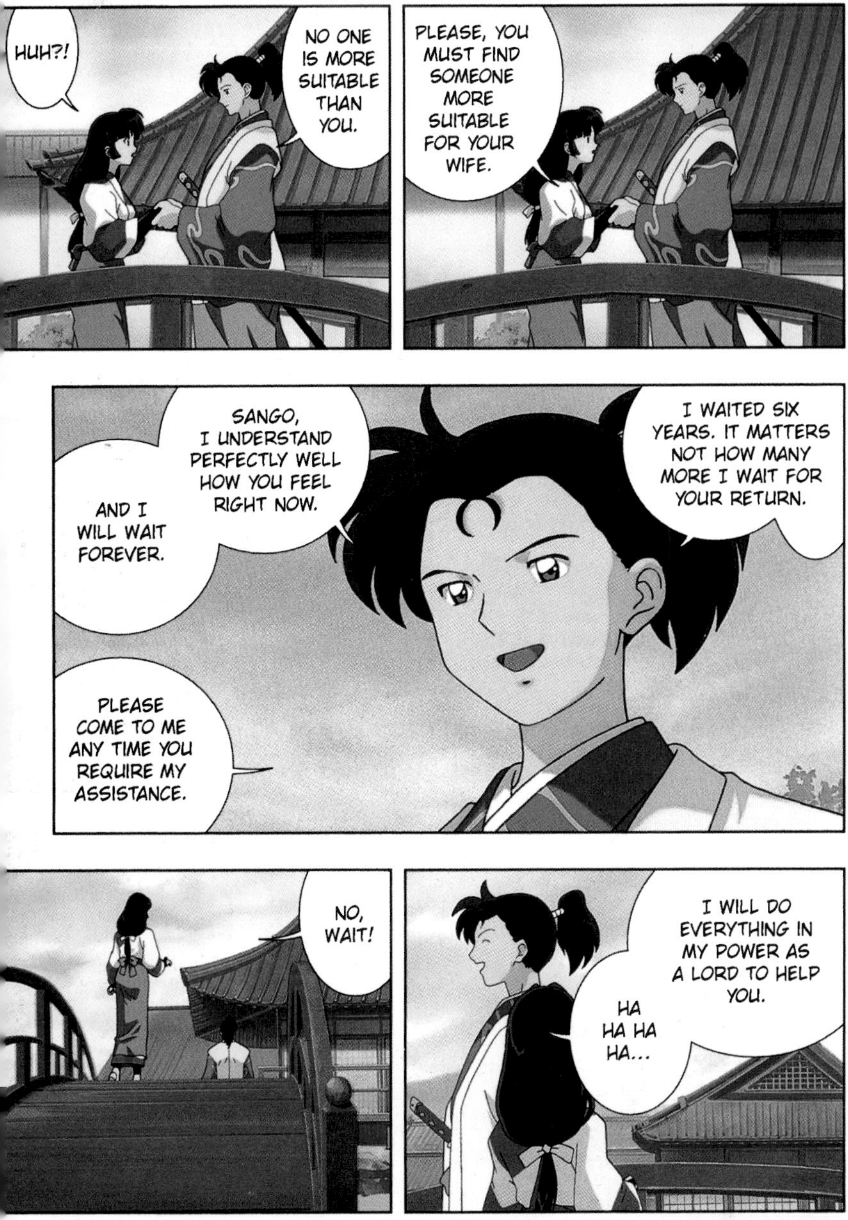
PLEASE, YOU MUST FIND SOMEONE MORE SUITABLE FOR YOUR WIFE.
NO ONE IS MORE SUITABLE THAN YOU.
HUH?!
I WAITED SIX YEARS. IT MATTERS NOT HOW MANY MORE I WAIT FOR YOUR RETURN.
SANGO, I UNDERSTAND PERFECTLY WELL HOW YOU FEEL RIGHT NOW.
AND I WILL WAIT FOREVER.
PLEASE COME TO ME ANY TIME YOU REQUIRE MY ASSISTANCE.
I WILL DO EVERYTHING IN MY POWER AS A LORD TO HELP YOU.
HA HA HA HA...
NO, WAIT!

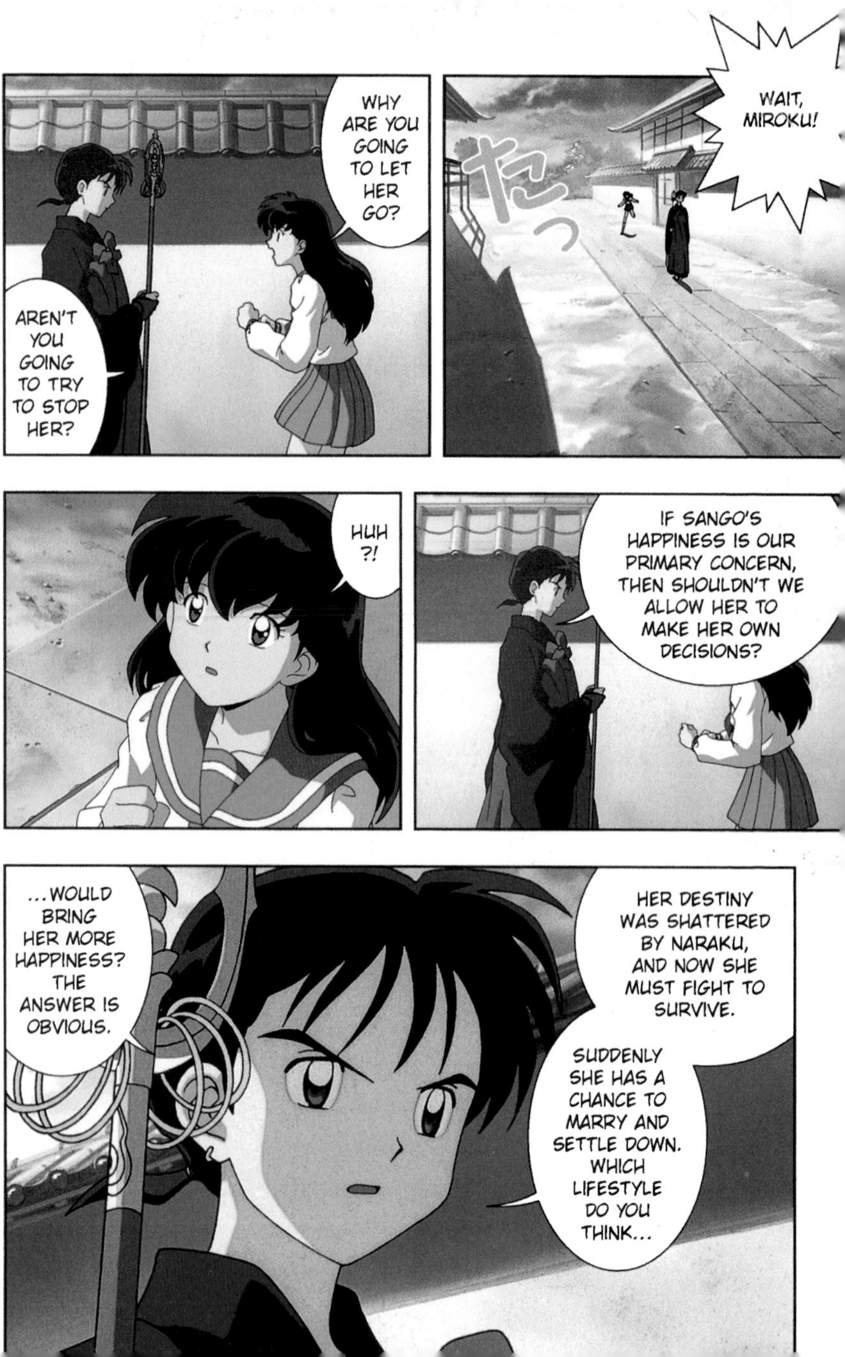
WAIT, MIROKU!
たっ
WHY ARE YOU GOING TO LET HER GO?
AREN'T YOU GOING TO TRY TO STOP HER?
IF SANGO'S HAPPINESS IS OUR PRIMARY CONCERN, THEN SHOULDN'T WE ALLOW HER TO MAKE HER OWN DECISIONS?
HUH ?!
HER DESTINY WAS SHATTERED BY NARAKU, AND NOW SHE MUST FIGHT TO SURVIVE.
SUDDENLY SHE HAS A CHANCE TO MARRY AND SETTLE DOWN. WHICH LIFESTYLE DO YOU THINK...
...WOULD BRING HER MORE HAPPINESS? THE ANSWER IS OBVIOUS.

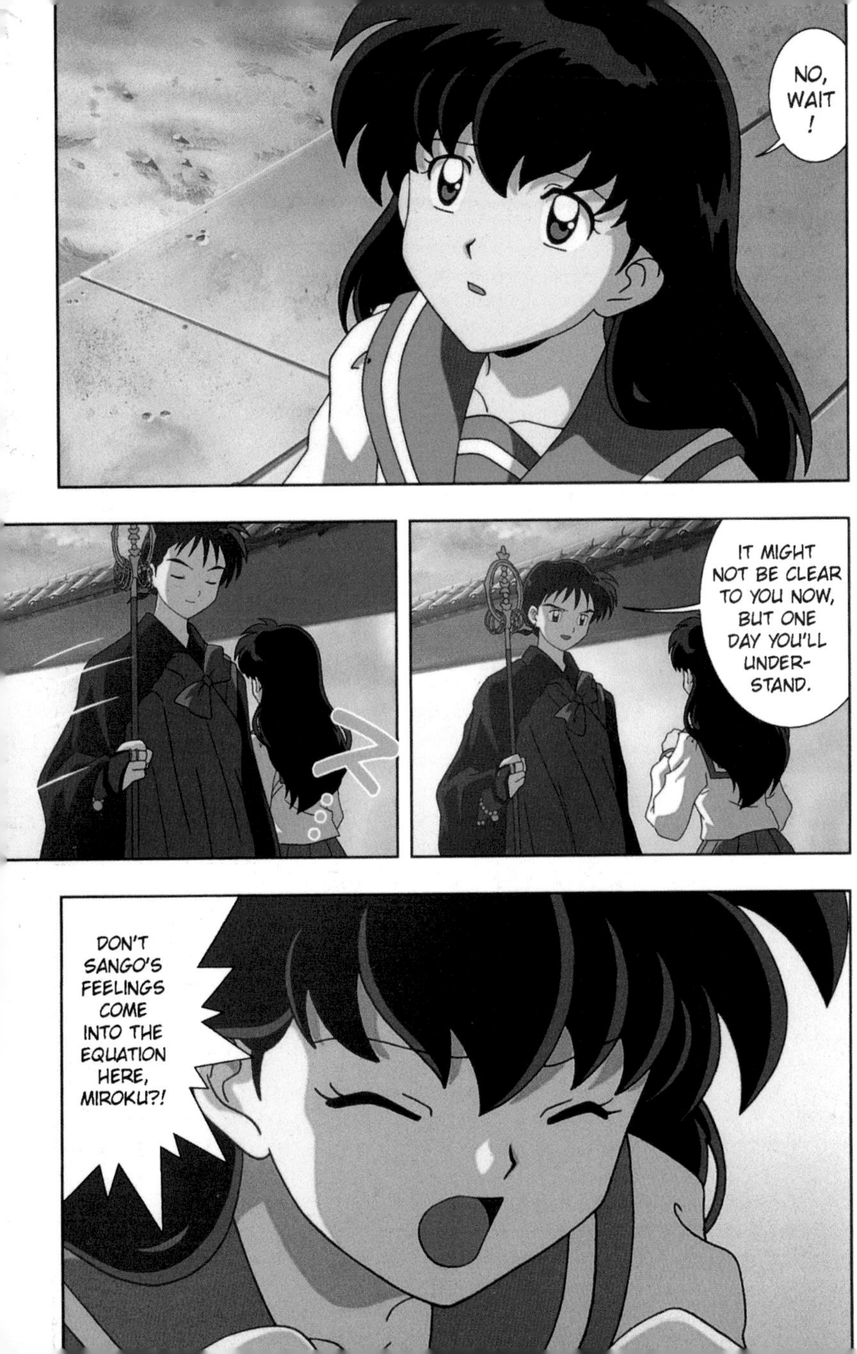
NO, WAIT!
IT MIGHT NOT BE CLEAR TO YOU NOW, BUT ONE DAY YOU'LL UNDER-STAND.
DON'T SANGO'S FEELINGS COME INTO THE EQUATION HERE, MIROKU?!

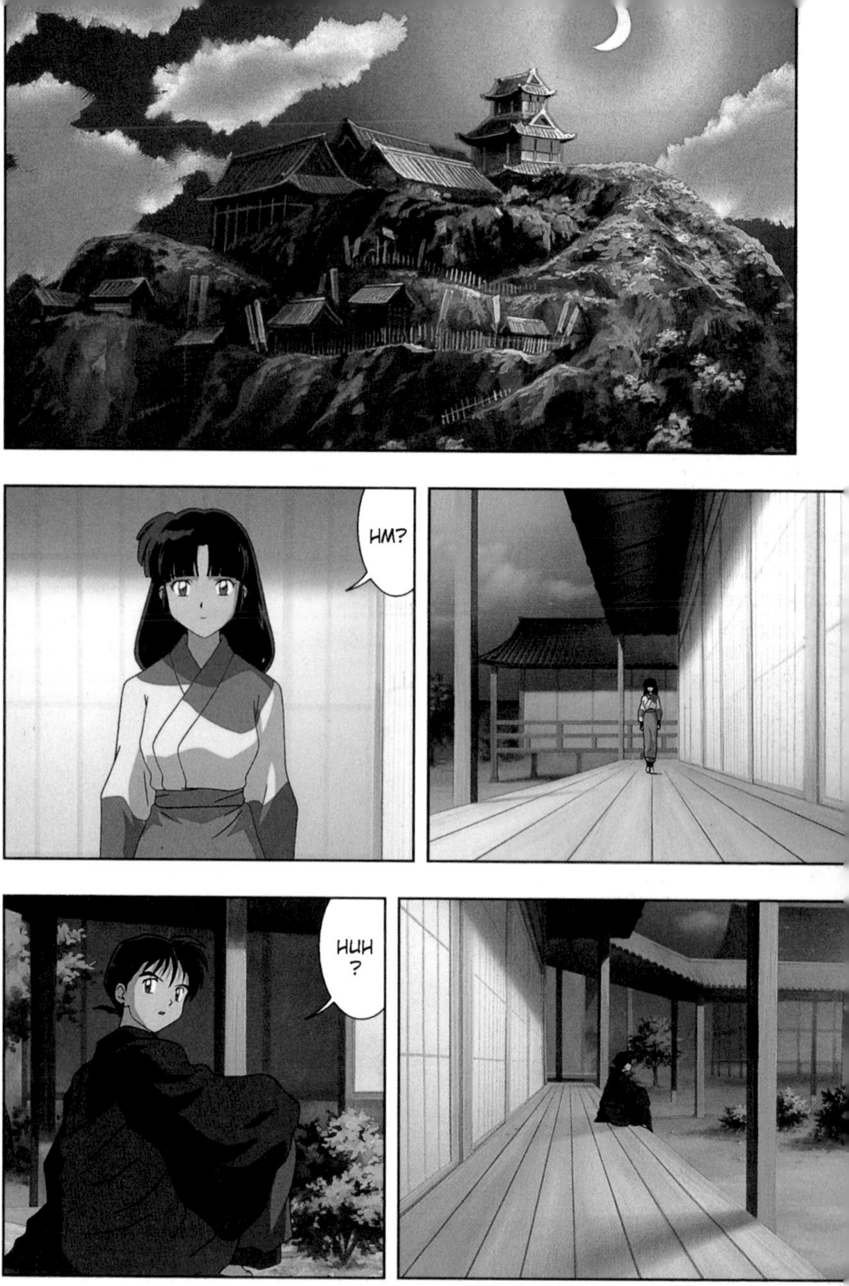
HM?
HUH ?

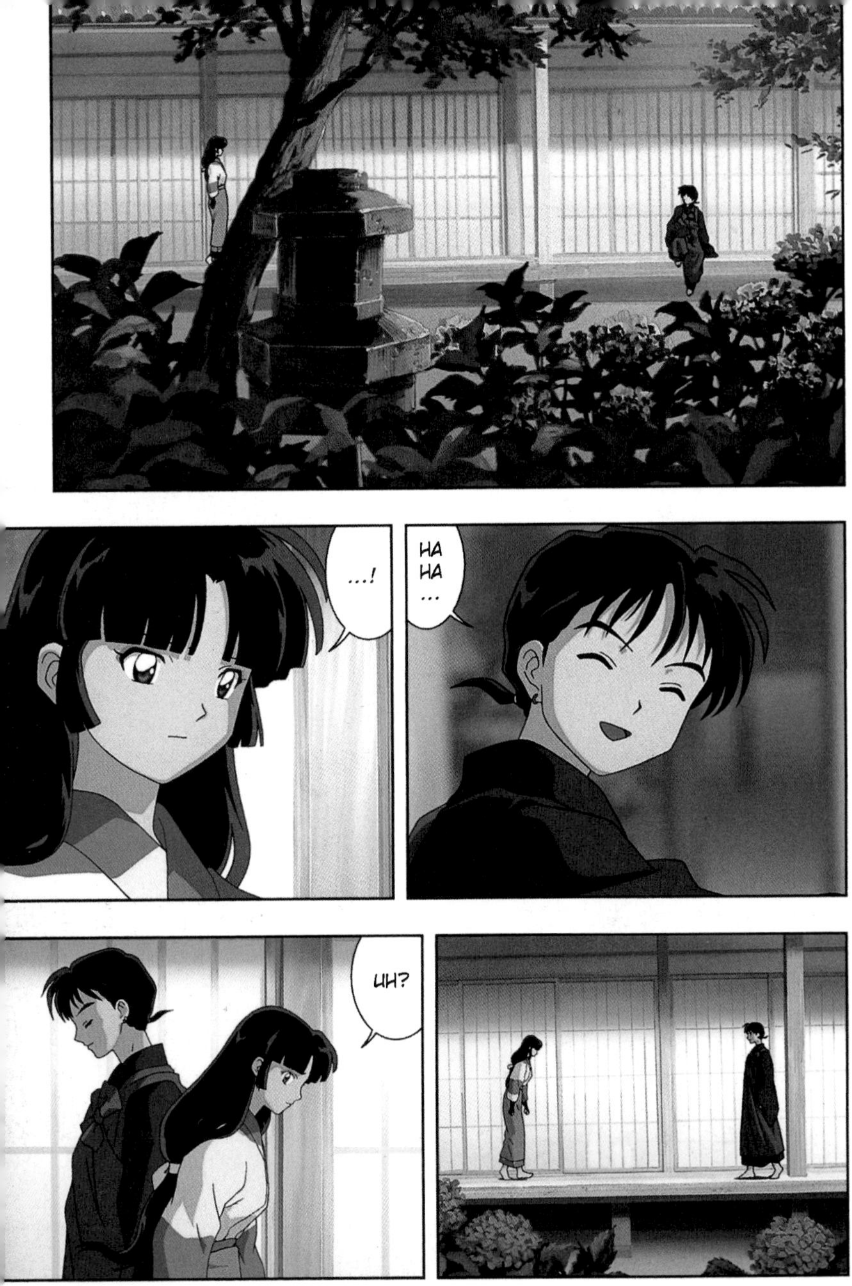
HA HA ...
...!
UH?

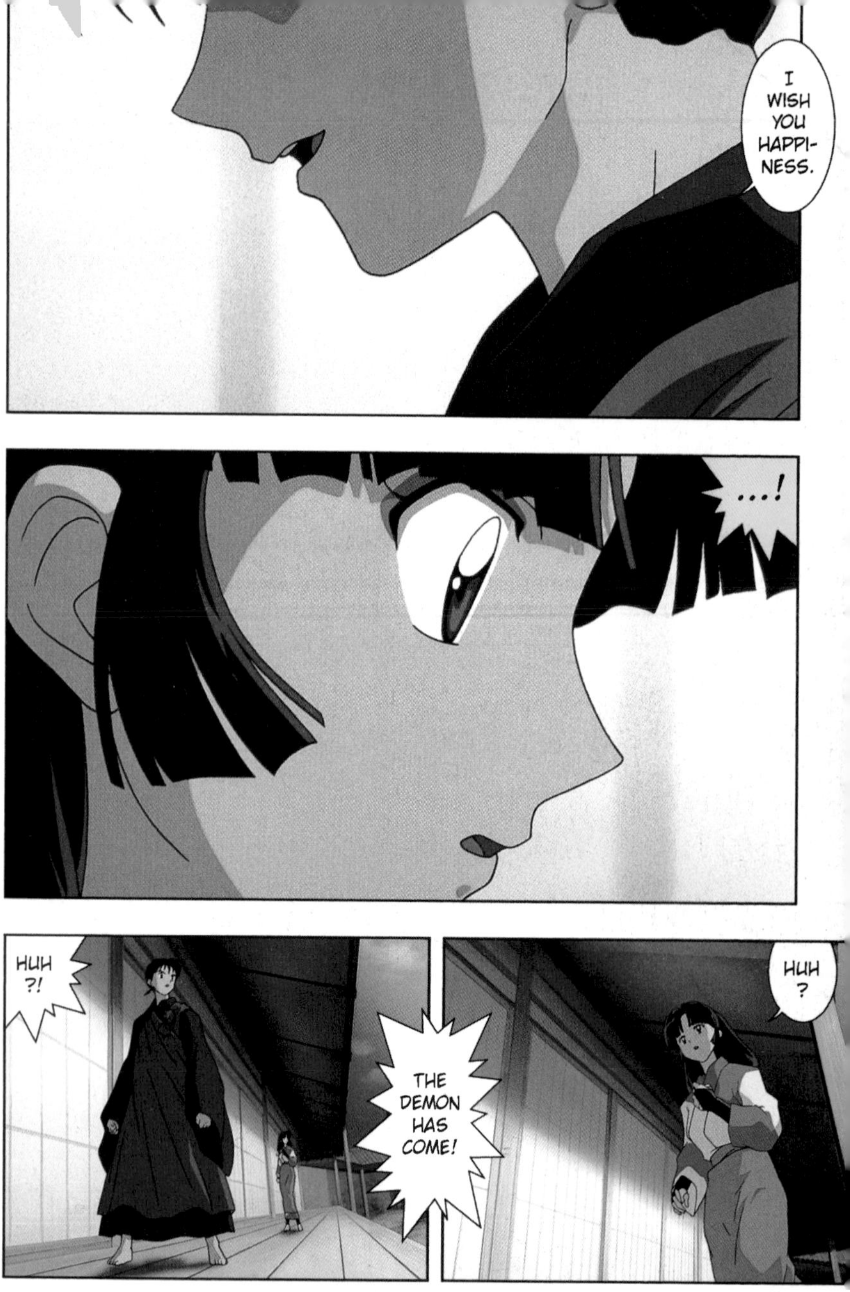
I WISH YOU HAPPI-NESS.
...!
HUH ?
THE DEMON HAS COME!
HUH ?!

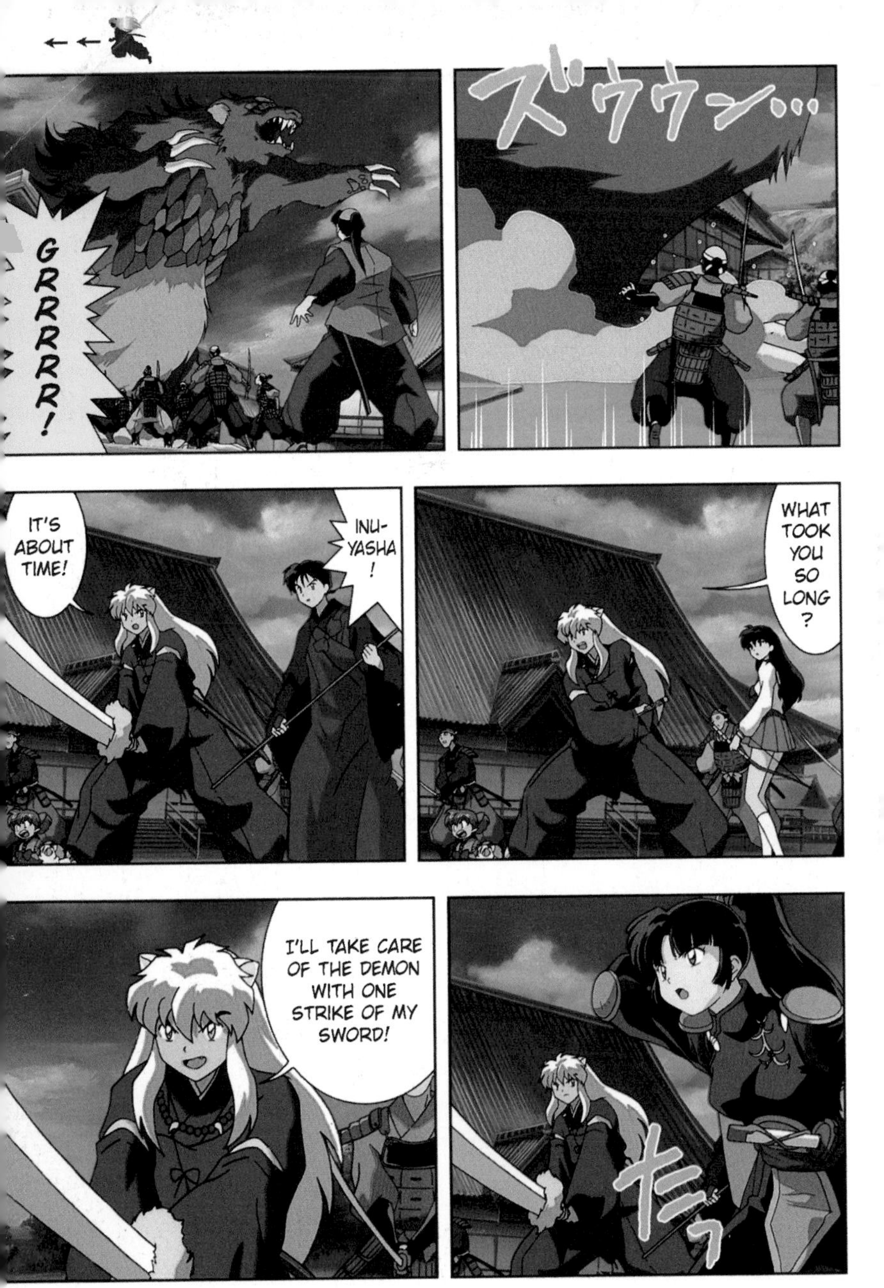
ズウウン…
GRRRRR!
WHAT TOOK YOU SO LONG?
INU-YASHA!
IT'S ABOUT TIME!
たっ
I'LL TAKE CARE OF THE DEMON WITH ONE STRIKE OF MY SWORD!

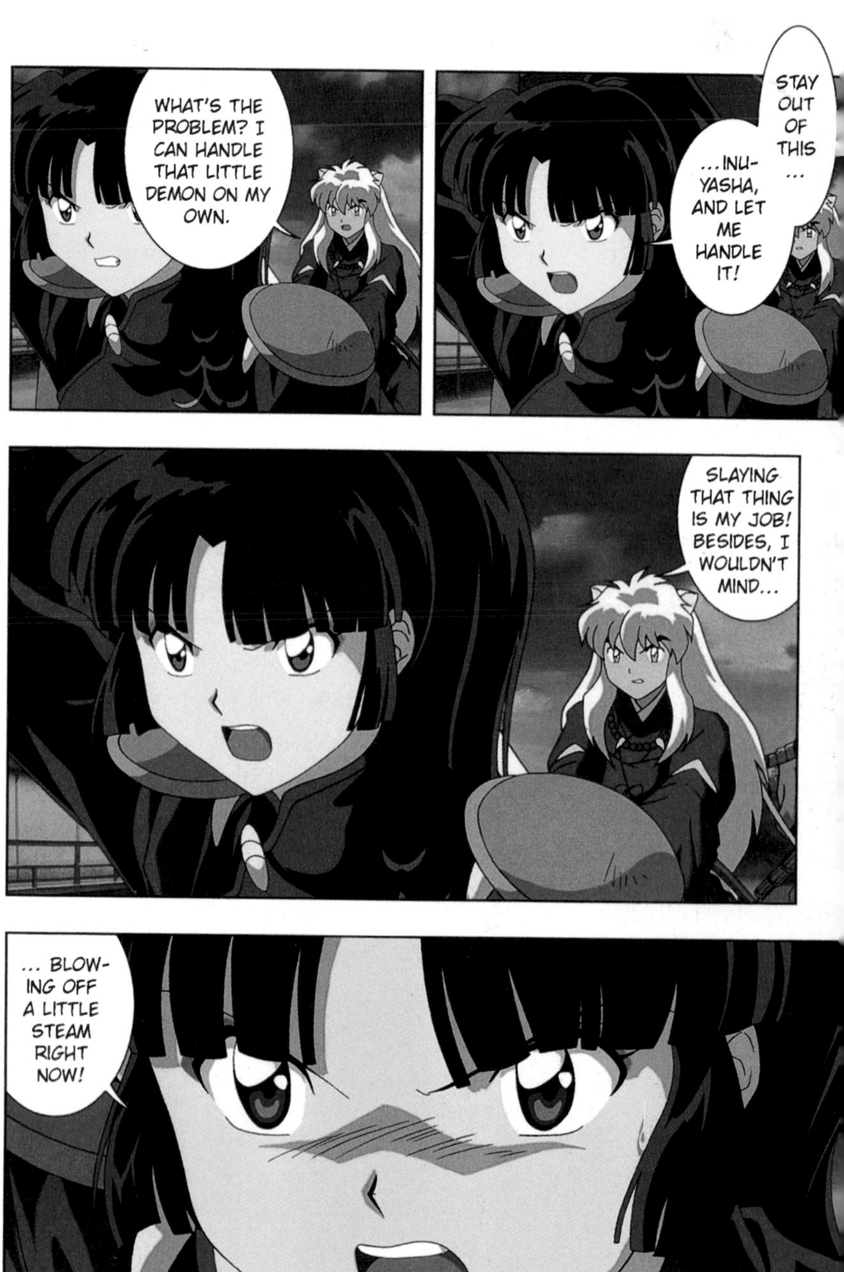
STAY OUT OF THIS...
...INU-YASHA, AND LET ME HANDLE IT!
WHAT'S THE PROBLEM? I CAN HANDLE THAT LITTLE DEMON ON MY OWN.
SLAYING THAT THING IS MY JOB! BESIDES, I WOULDN'T MIND...
... BLOWING OFF A LITTLE STEAM RIGHT NOW!

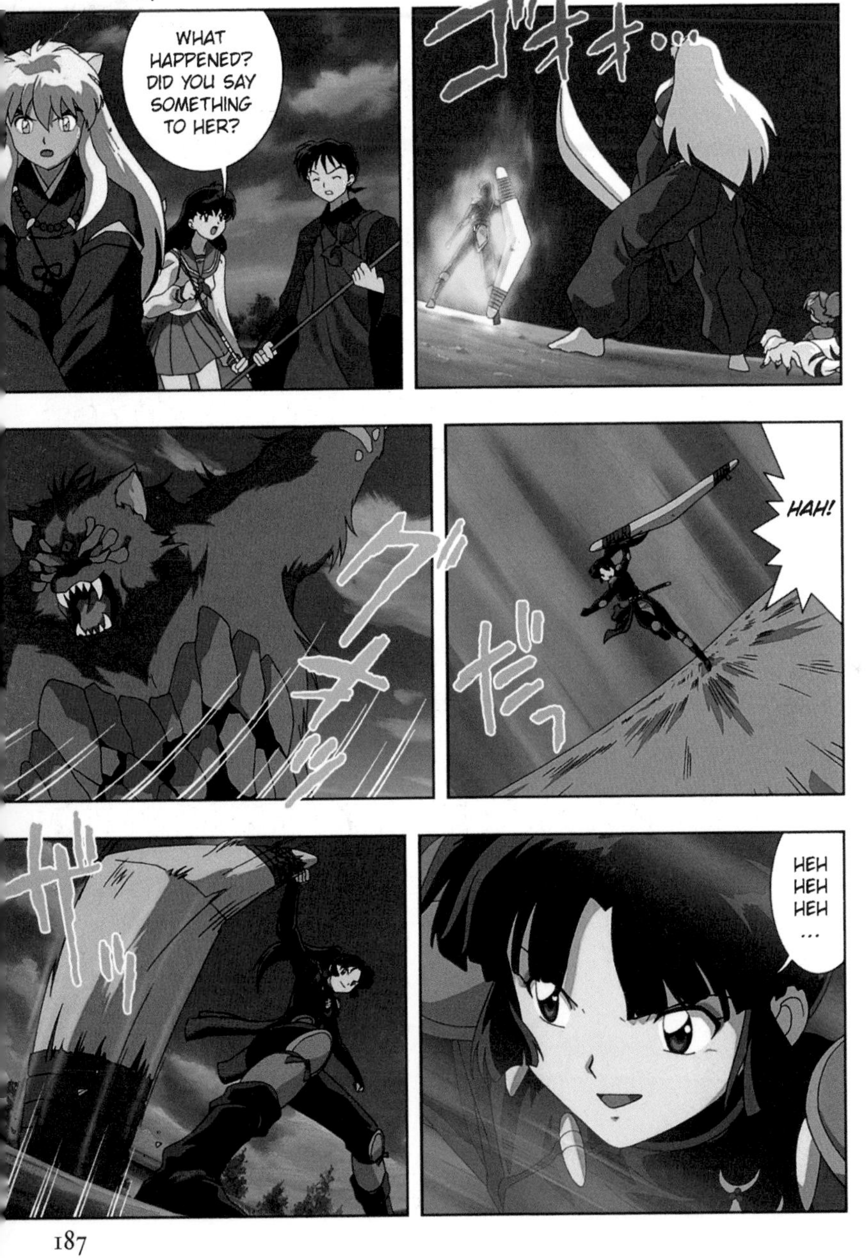
WHAT HAPPENED? DID YOU SAY SOMETHING TO HER?
HAH!
HEH HEH HEH ...

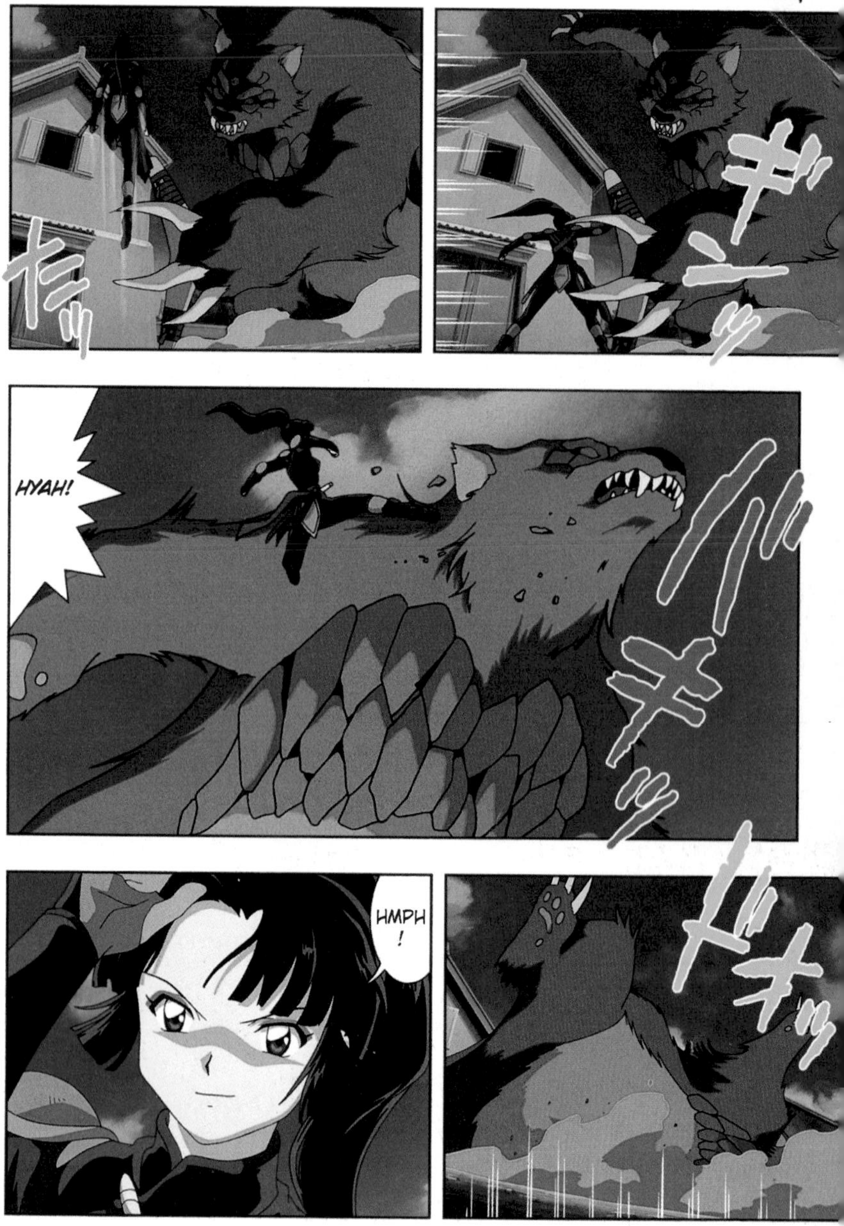
ギンッ
ガッ
HYAH!
バキッ
HMPH!

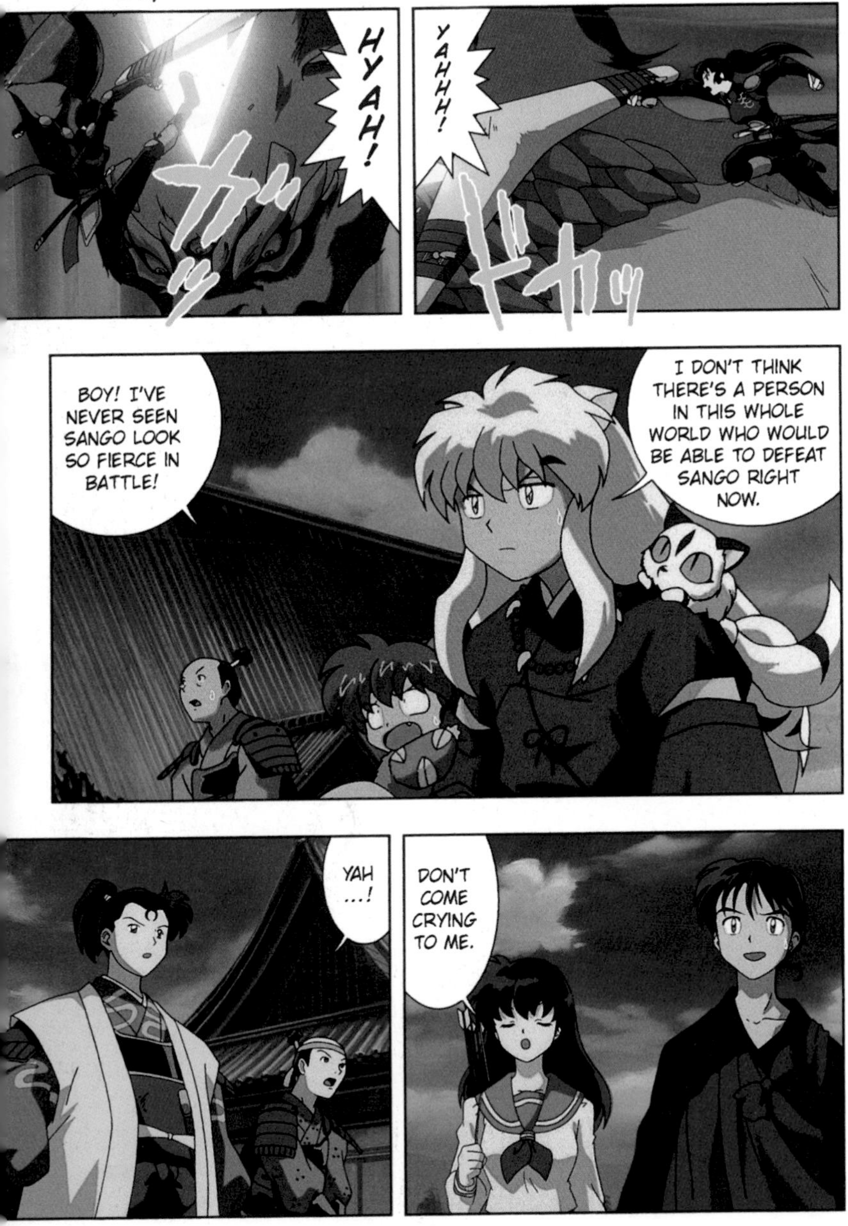
YAHHH!
ドカッ
HYAH!
ガッ
I DON'T THINK THERE'S A PERSON IN THIS WHOLE WORLD WHO WOULD BE ABLE TO DEFEAT SANGO RIGHT NOW.
BOY! I'VE NEVER SEEN SANGO LOOK SO FIERCE IN BATTLE!
DON'T COME CRYING TO ME.
YAH ...!

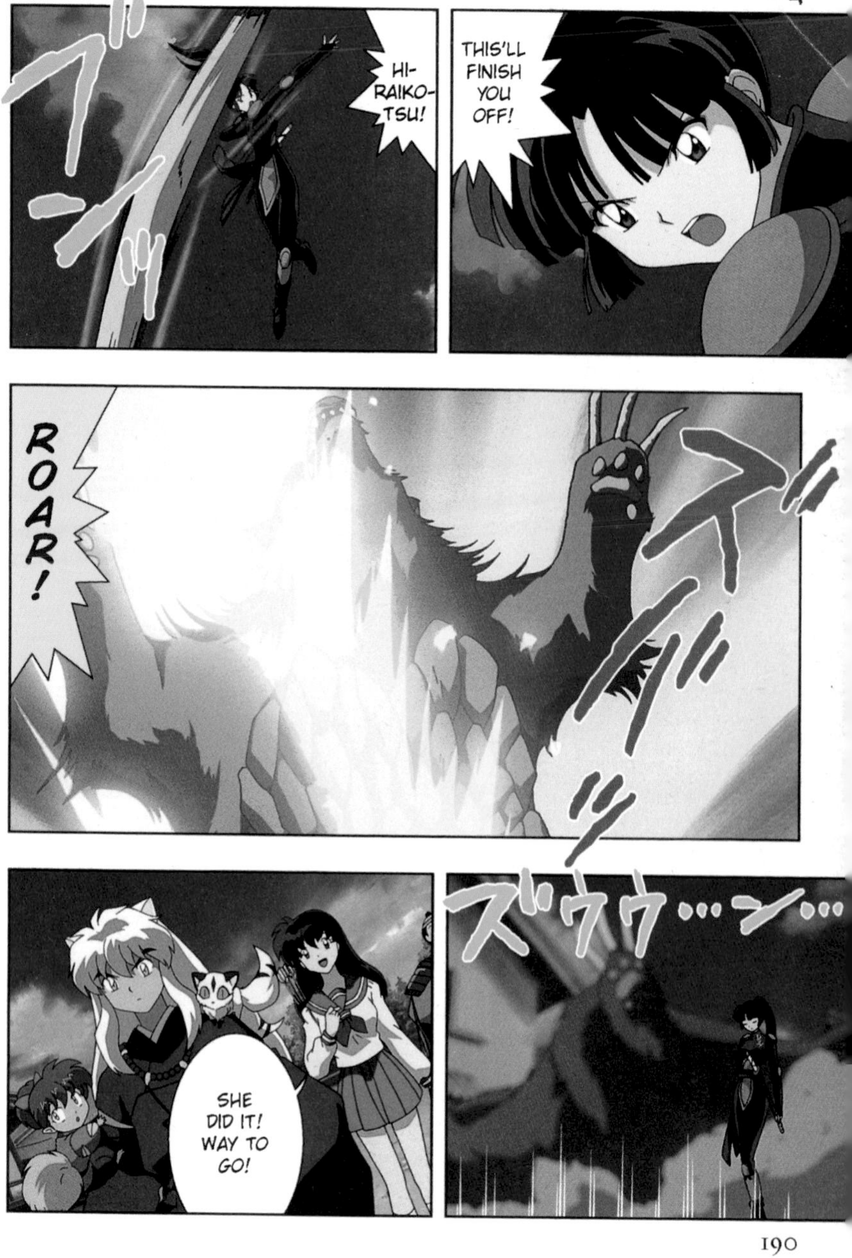
THIS'LL FINISH YOU OFF!
HI-RAIKOTSU!
ブンッ
ROAR!
ズウウ…ン…
SHE DID IT! WAY TO GO!

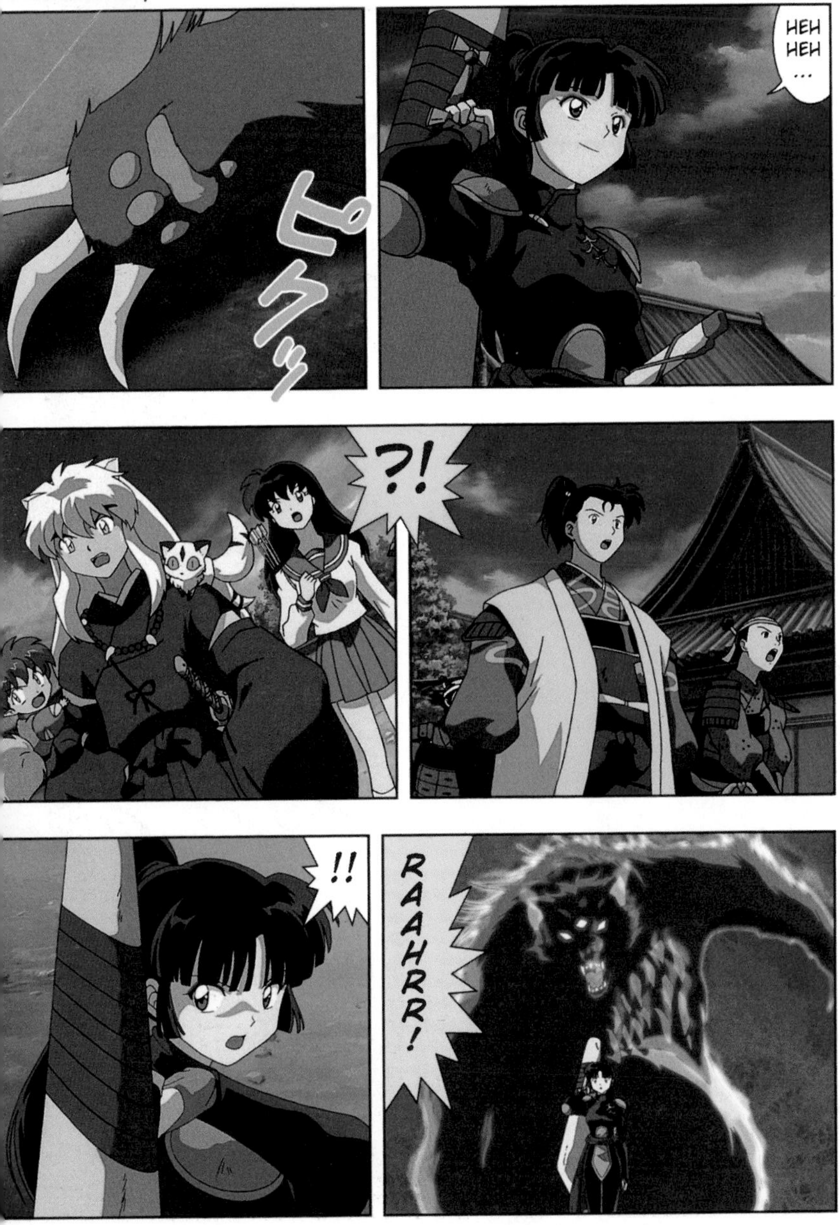
HEH HEH ...
ピクッ
?!
RAAHRR!
!!

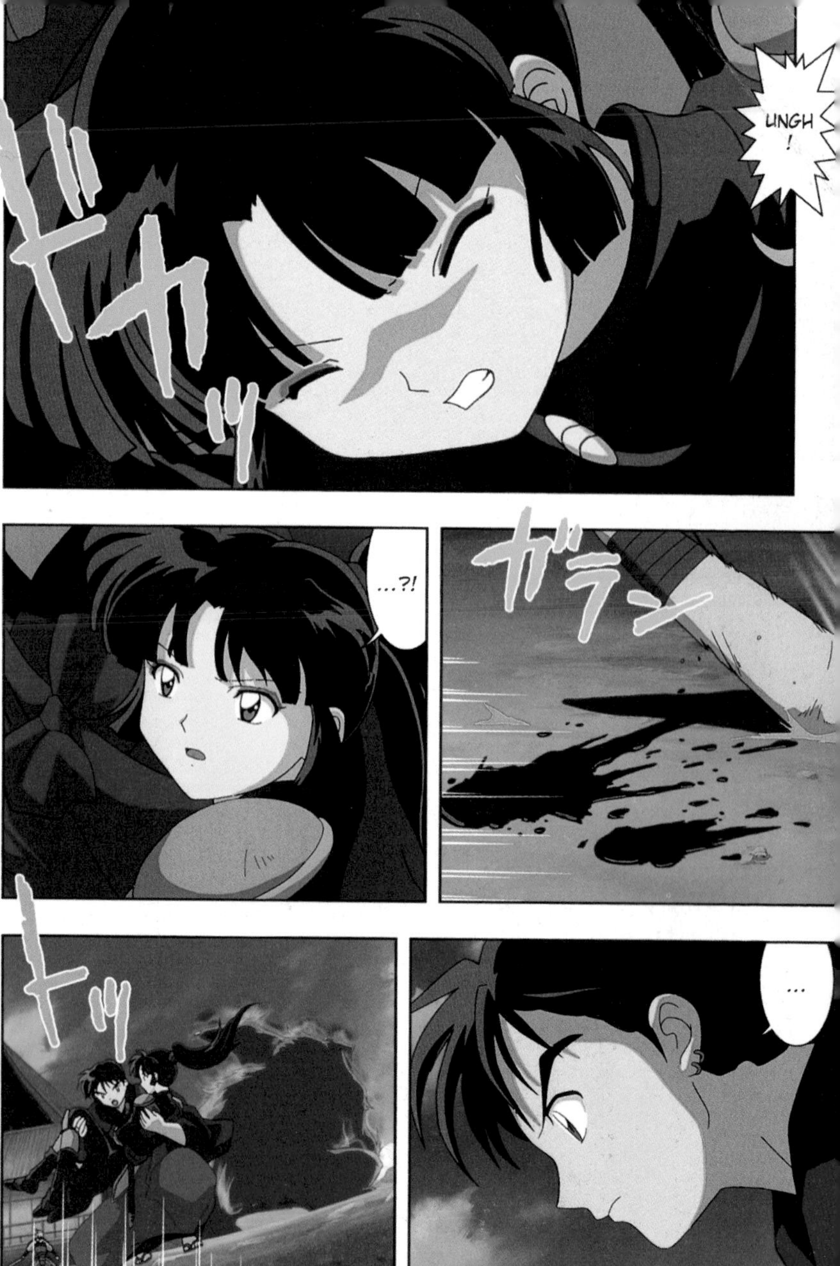
UNGH!
ドカッ
ガラン
...?!
...
トッ

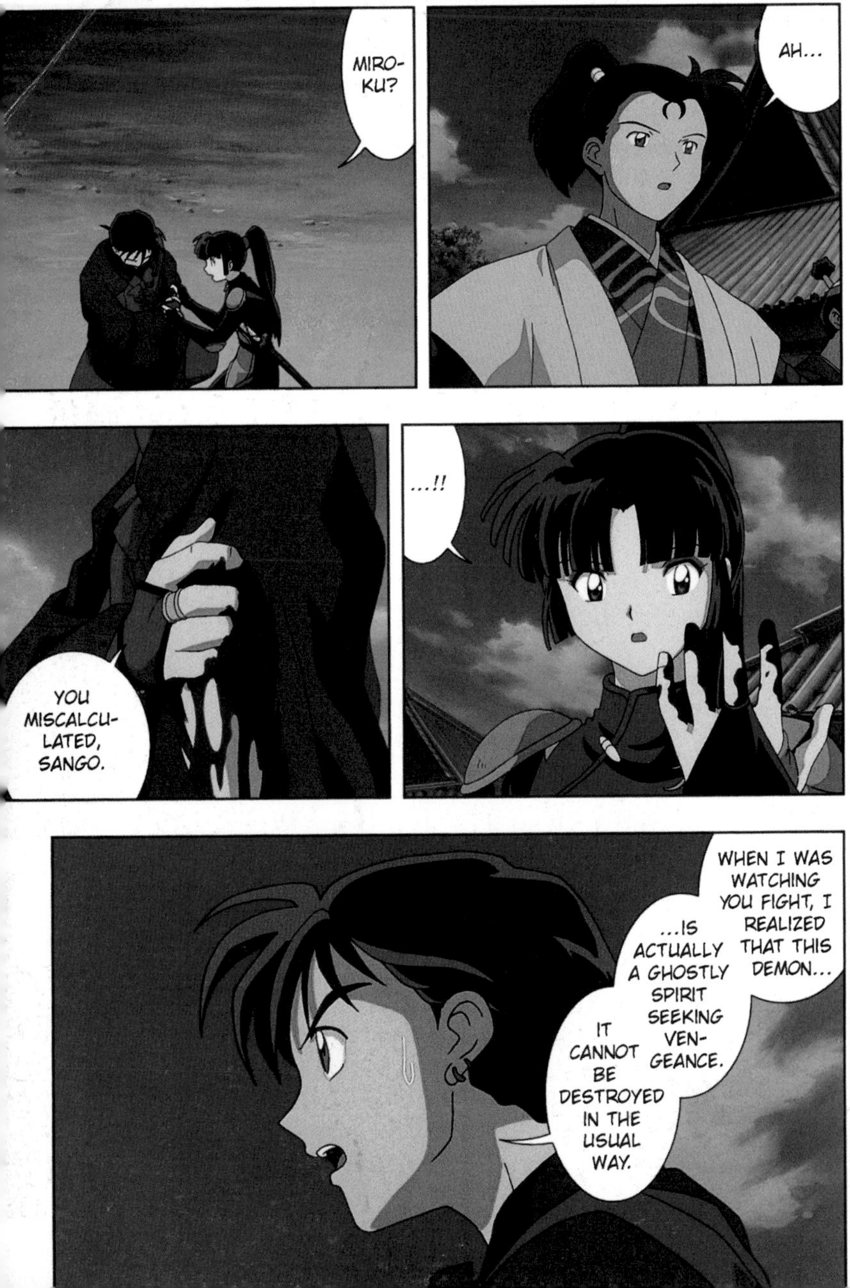
AH...
MIROKU?
...!!
YOU MISCALCULATED, SANGO.
WHEN I WAS WATCHING YOU FIGHT, I REALIZED THAT THIS DEMON...
...IS ACTUALLY A GHOSTLY SPIRIT SEEKING VENGEANCE.
IT CANNOT BE DESTROYED IN THE USUAL WAY.

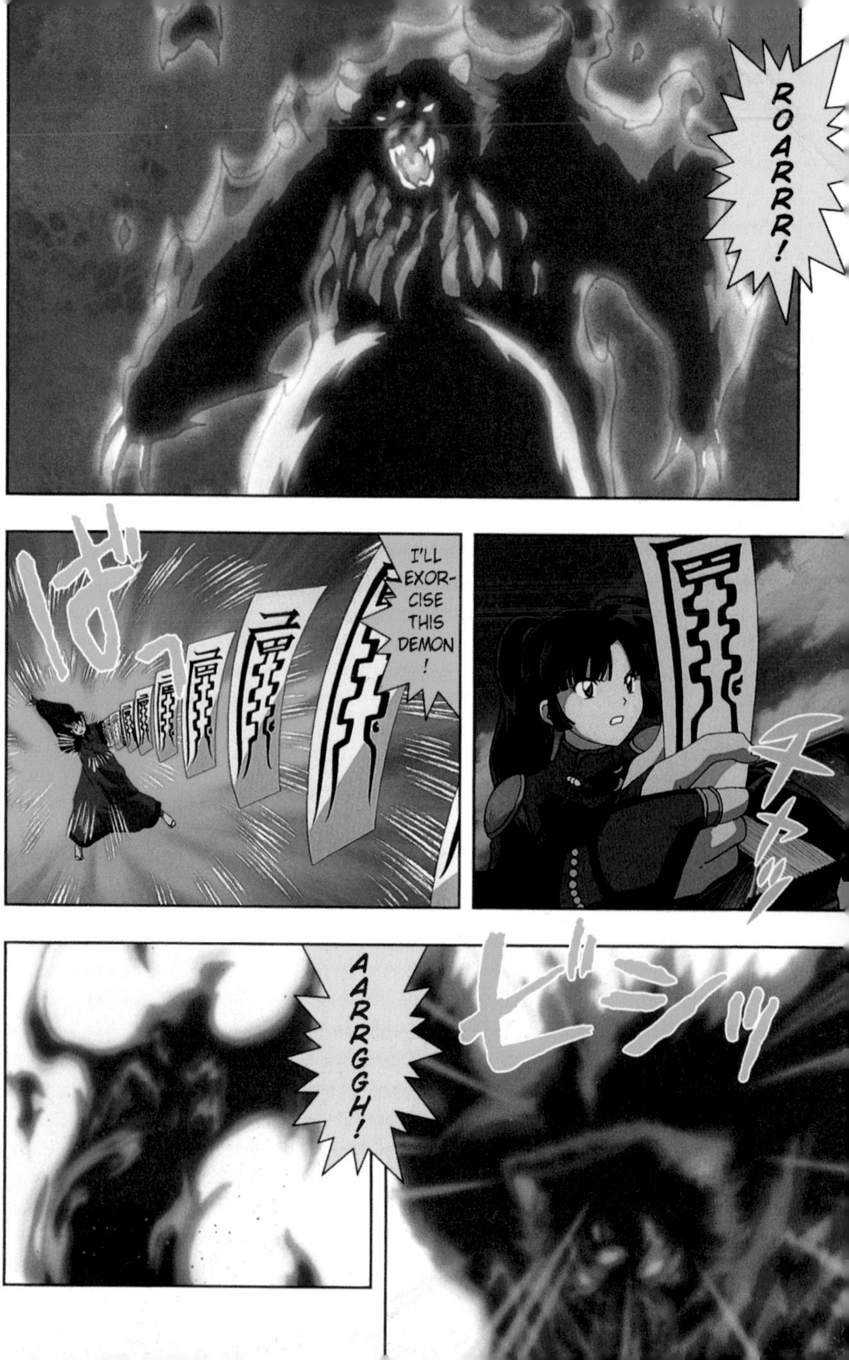
ROARRR!
チャッ!
ぱっ
I'LL EXORCISE THIS DEMON!
ビシッ
AARRGGH!

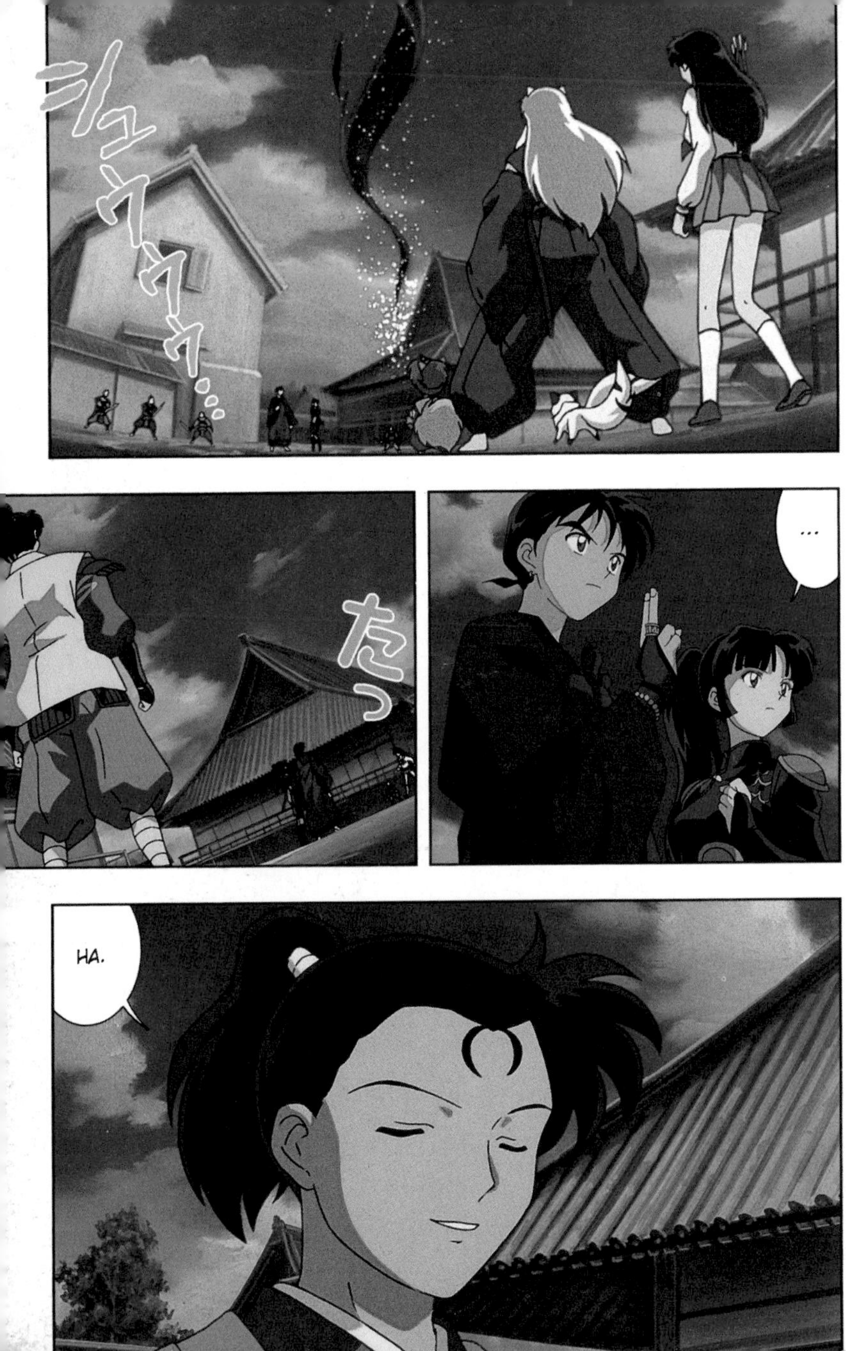
シュウウウ…
…
たっ
HA.

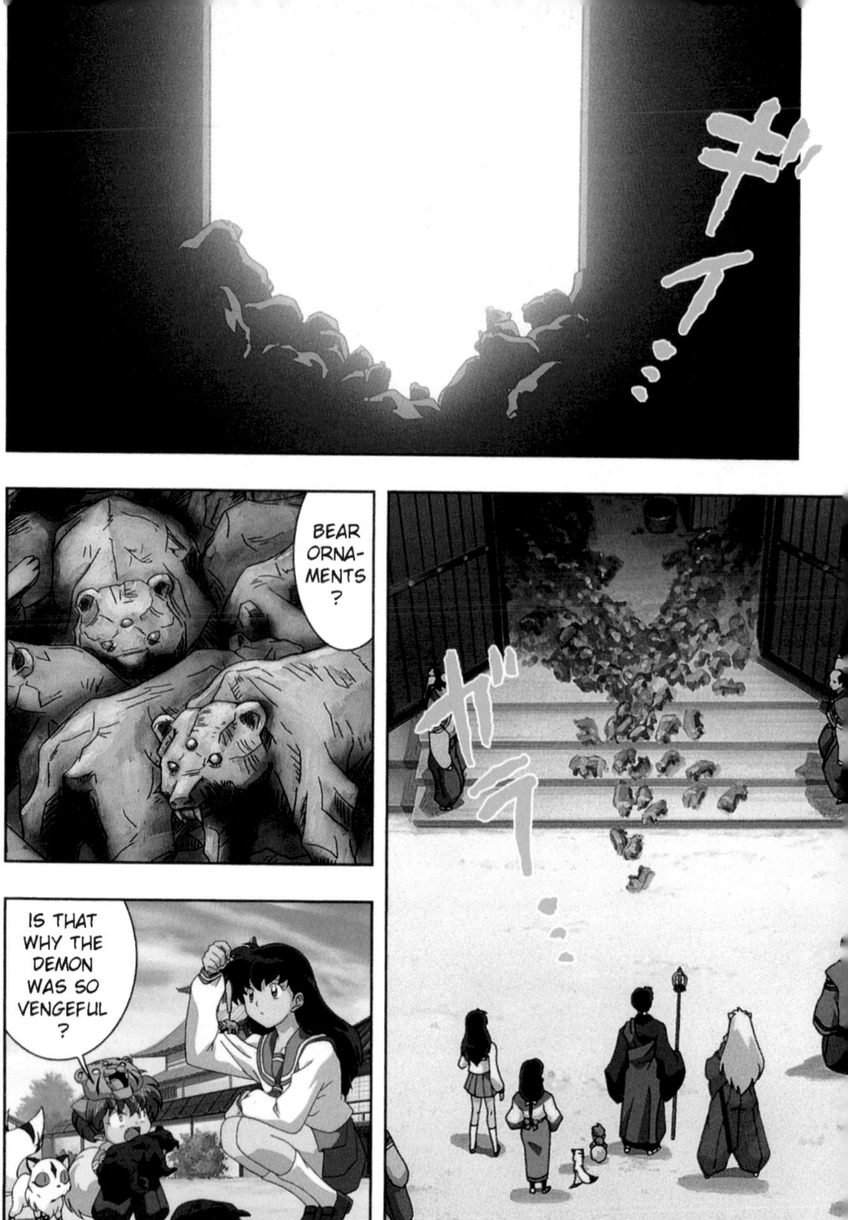
ギィ…
ガラ…
BEAR ORNAMENTS?
IS THAT WHY THE DEMON WAS SO VENGEFUL?

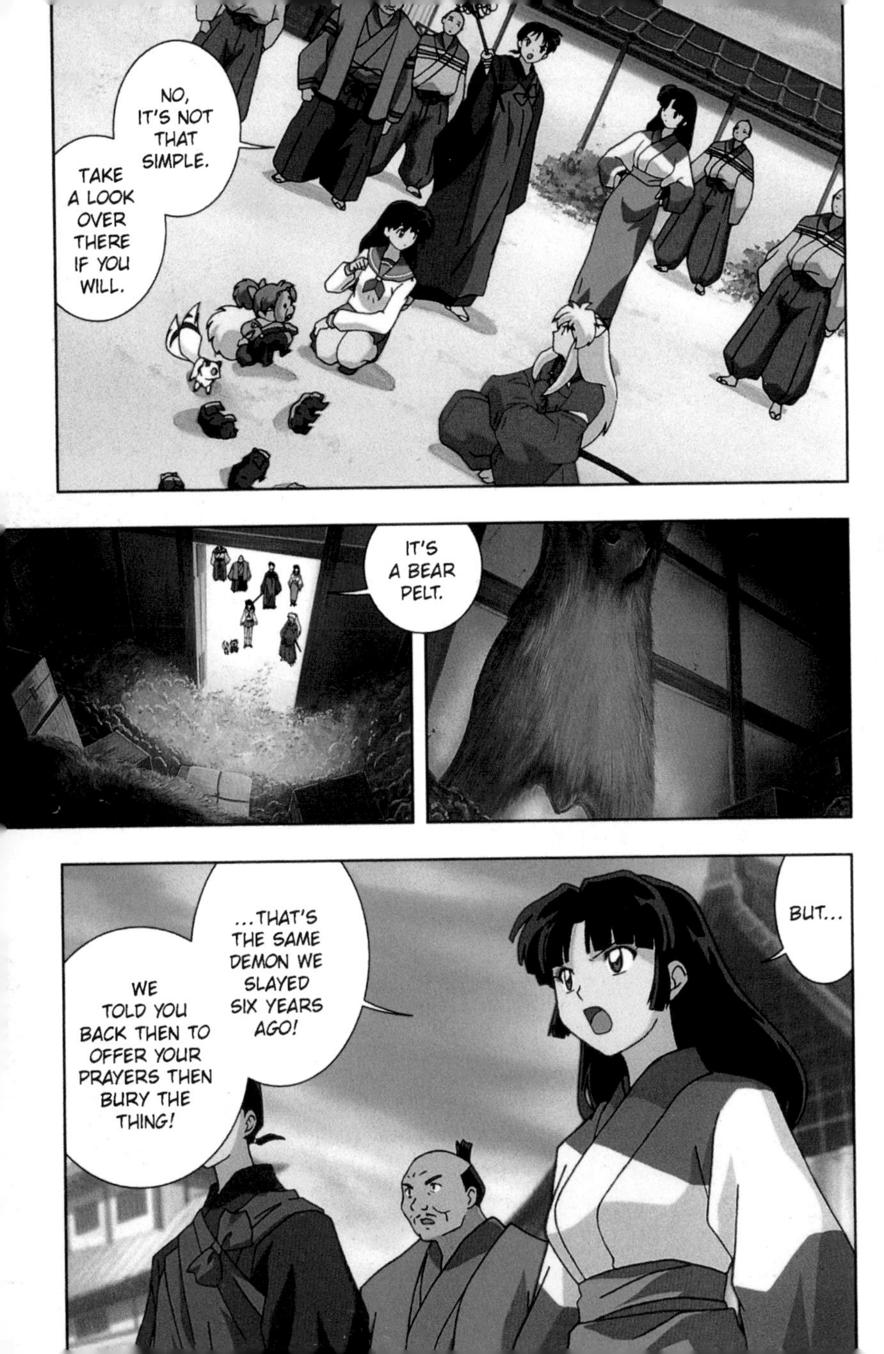
NO, IT'S NOT THAT SIMPLE. TAKE A LOOK OVER THERE IF YOU WILL.
IT'S A BEAR PELT.
BUT...
...THAT'S THE SAME DEMON WE SLAYED SIX YEARS AGO!
WE TOLD YOU BACK THEN TO OFFER YOUR PRAYERS THEN BURY THE THING!

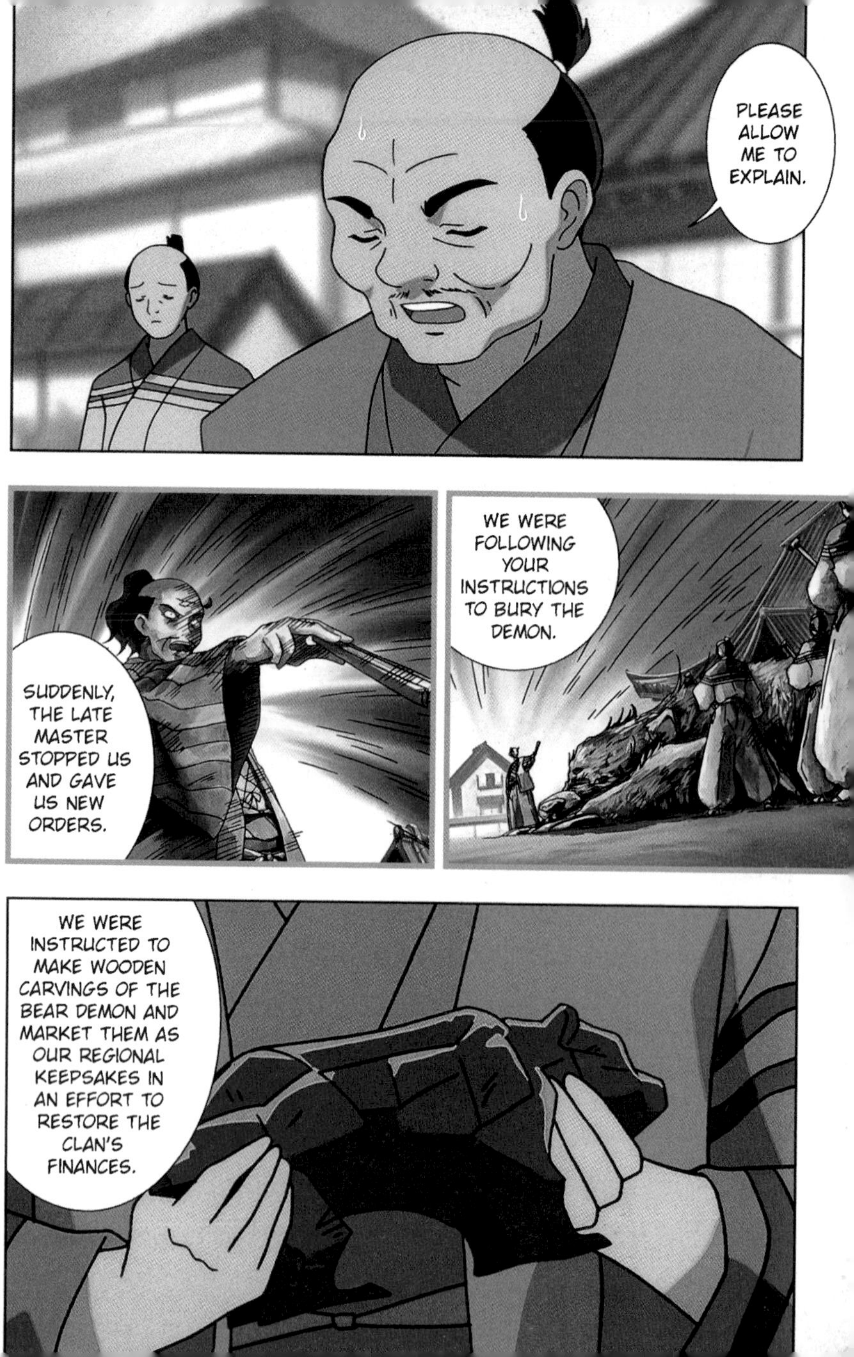
PLEASE ALLOW ME TO EXPLAIN.
WE WERE FOLLOWING YOUR INSTRUCTIONS TO BURY THE DEMON.
SUDDENLY, THE LATE MASTER STOPPED US AND GAVE US NEW ORDERS.
WE WERE INSTRUCTED TO MAKE WOODEN CARVINGS OF THE BEAR DEMON AND MARKET THEM AS OUR REGIONAL KEEPSAKES IN AN EFFORT TO RESTORE THE CLAN'S FINANCES.

THE WOODEN CARVINGS WERE SOON FOLLOWED BY THE BIG-BEAR BEAN JAM CAKES, THE BIG-BEAR TOWELS AND THE BIG-BEAR WOODEN COINS.

DON'T TELL ME. THEY DIDN'T SELL.

NO.

NOT A ONE.

ゴオオオ

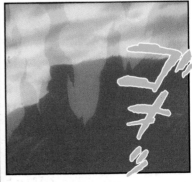

ゴオオ

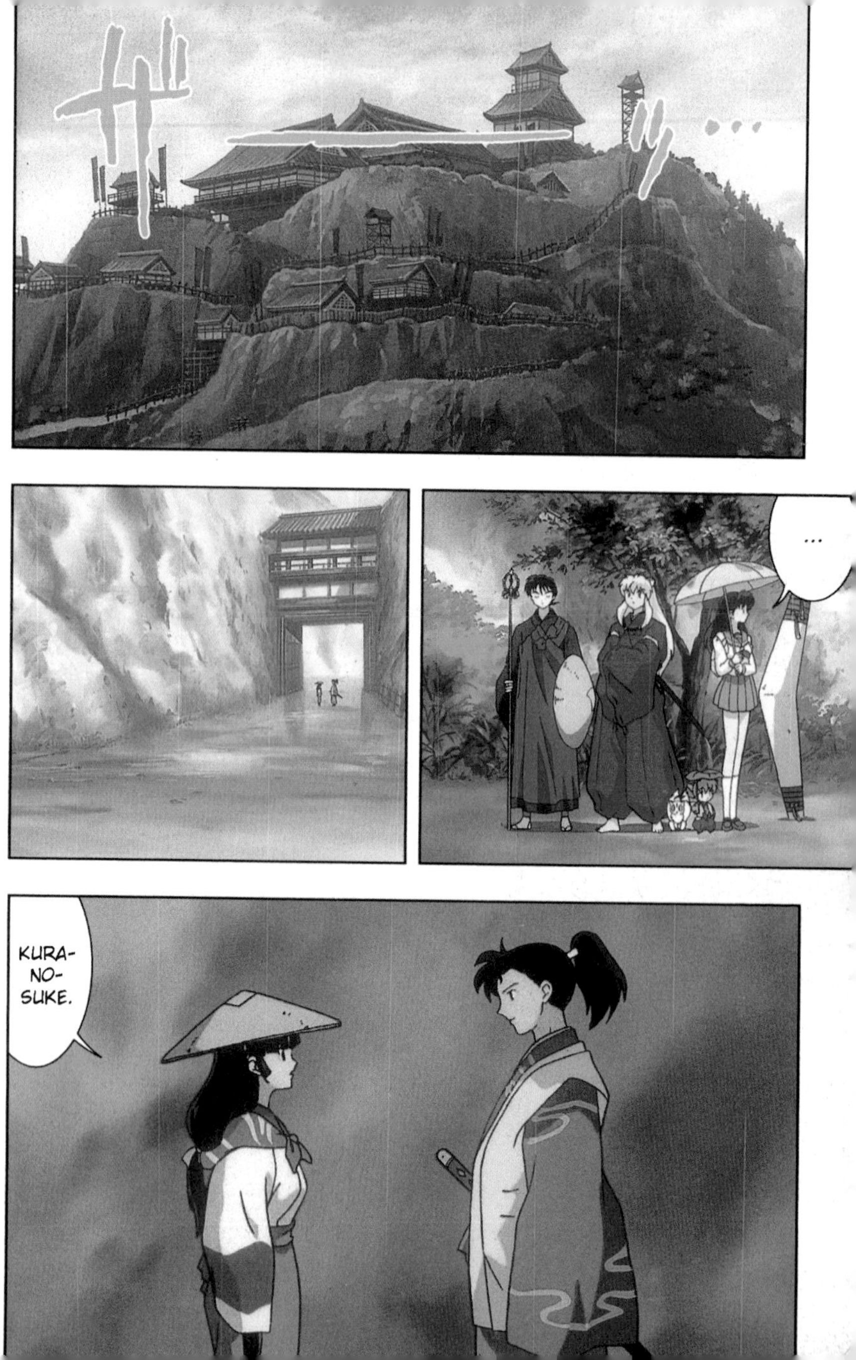
ザーッ…
...
KURA-NO-SUKE.

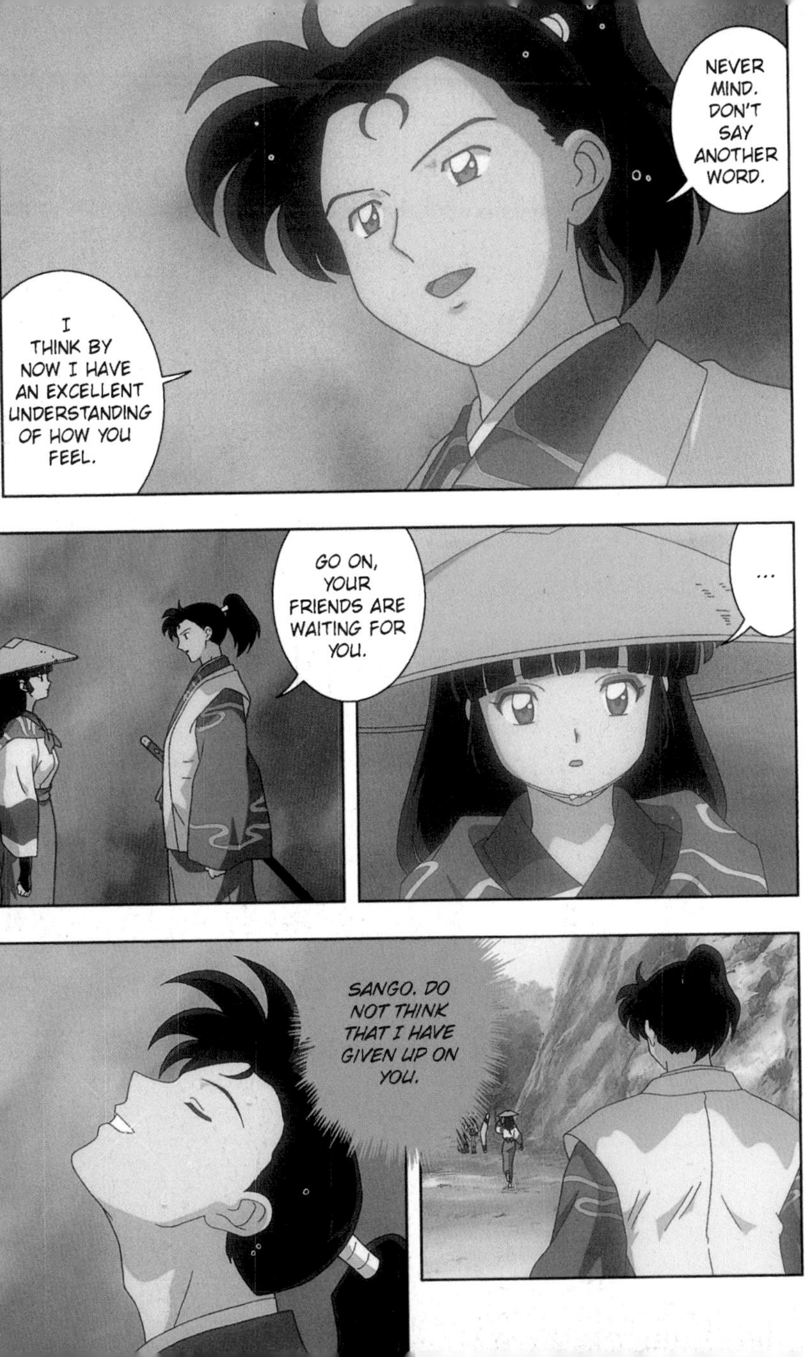
NEVER MIND. DON'T SAY ANOTHER WORD.
I THINK BY NOW I HAVE AN EXCELLENT UNDERSTANDING OF HOW YOU FEEL.
...
GO ON, YOUR FRIENDS ARE WAITING FOR YOU.
SANGO. DO NOT THINK THAT I HAVE GIVEN UP ON YOU.

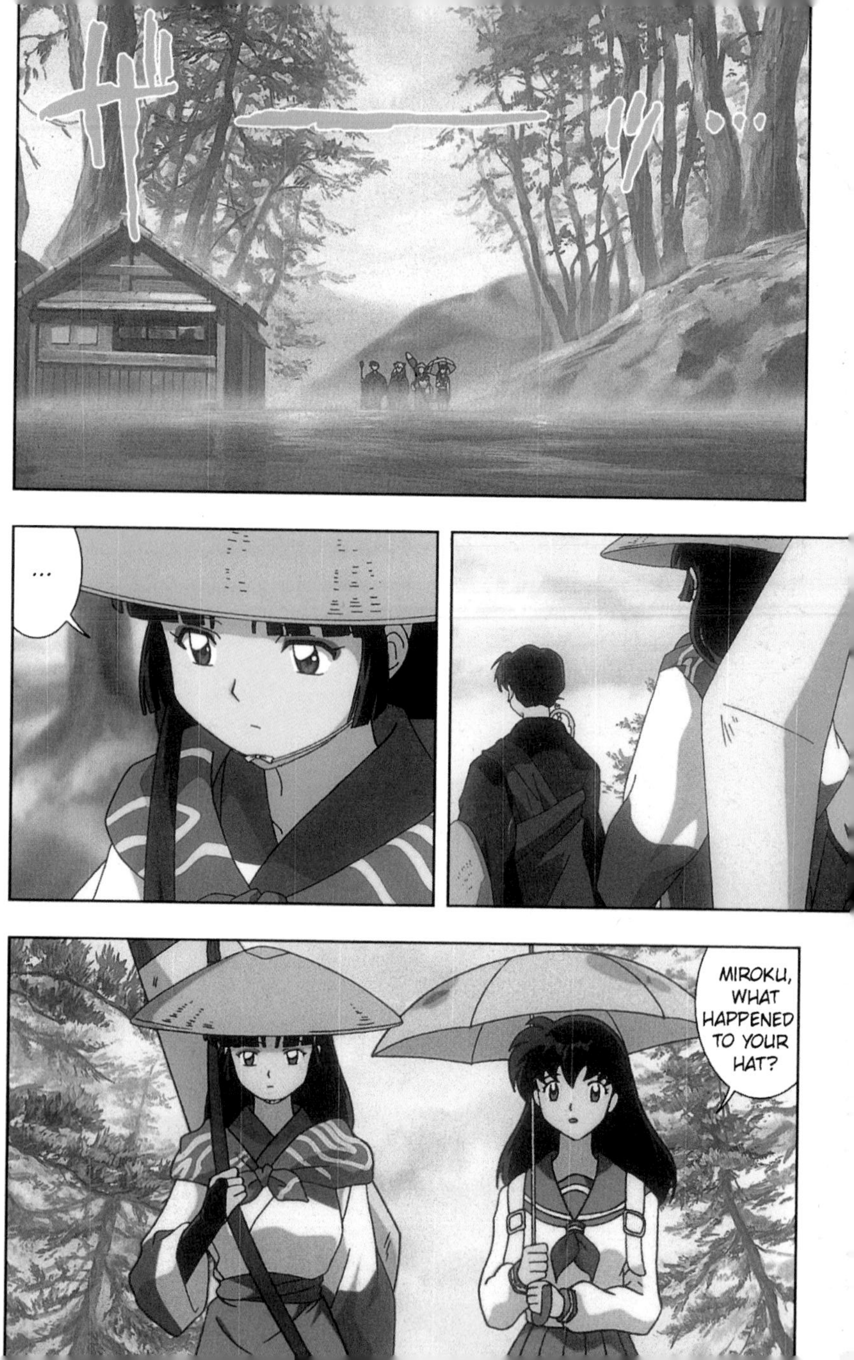
ザーッ...
...
MIROKU, WHAT HAPPENED TO YOUR HAT?

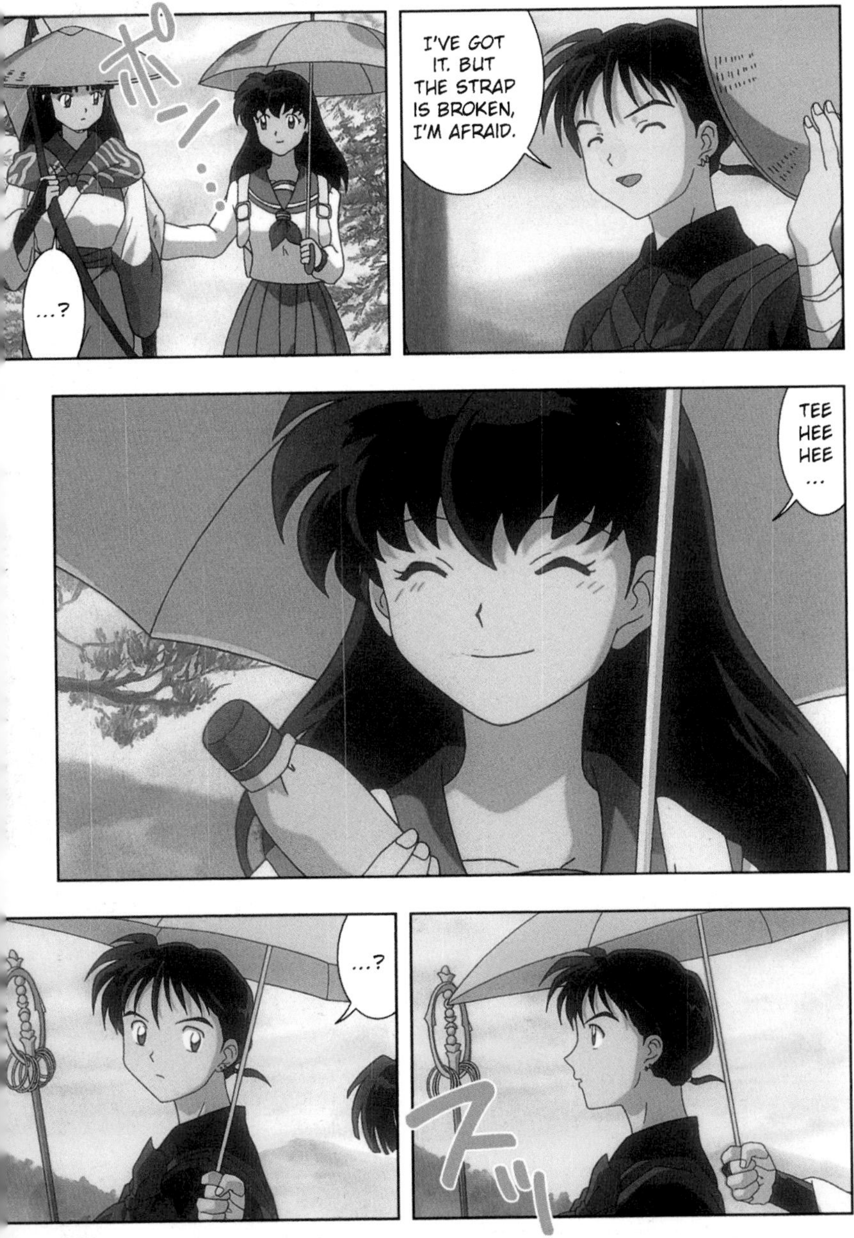
I'VE GOT IT. BUT THE STRAP IS BROKEN, I'M AFRAID.
ポン…
...?
TEE HEE HEE ...
スッ
...?

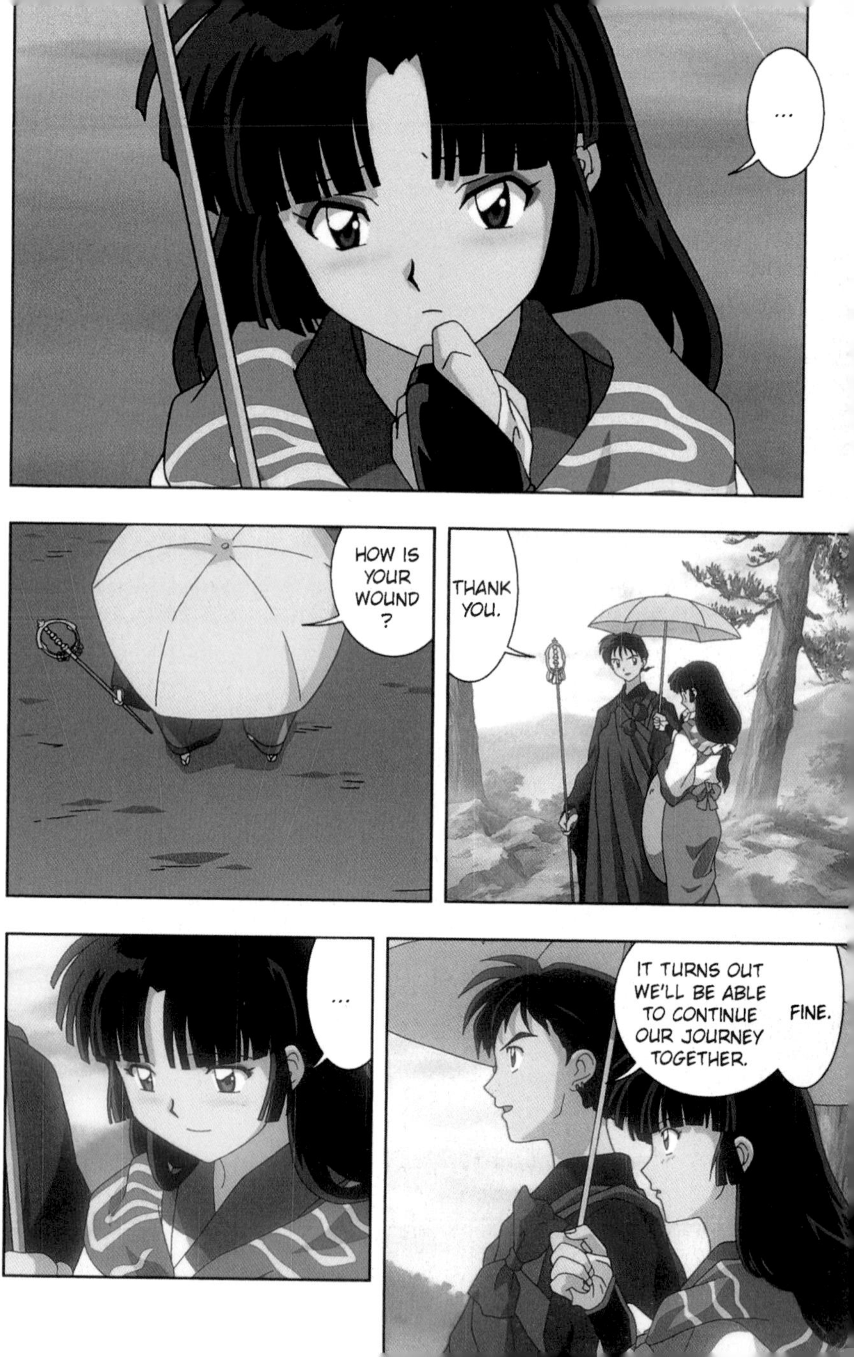
...
THANK YOU.
HOW IS YOUR WOUND?
FINE.
IT TURNS OUT WE'LL BE ABLE TO CONTINUE OUR JOURNEY TOGETHER.
...

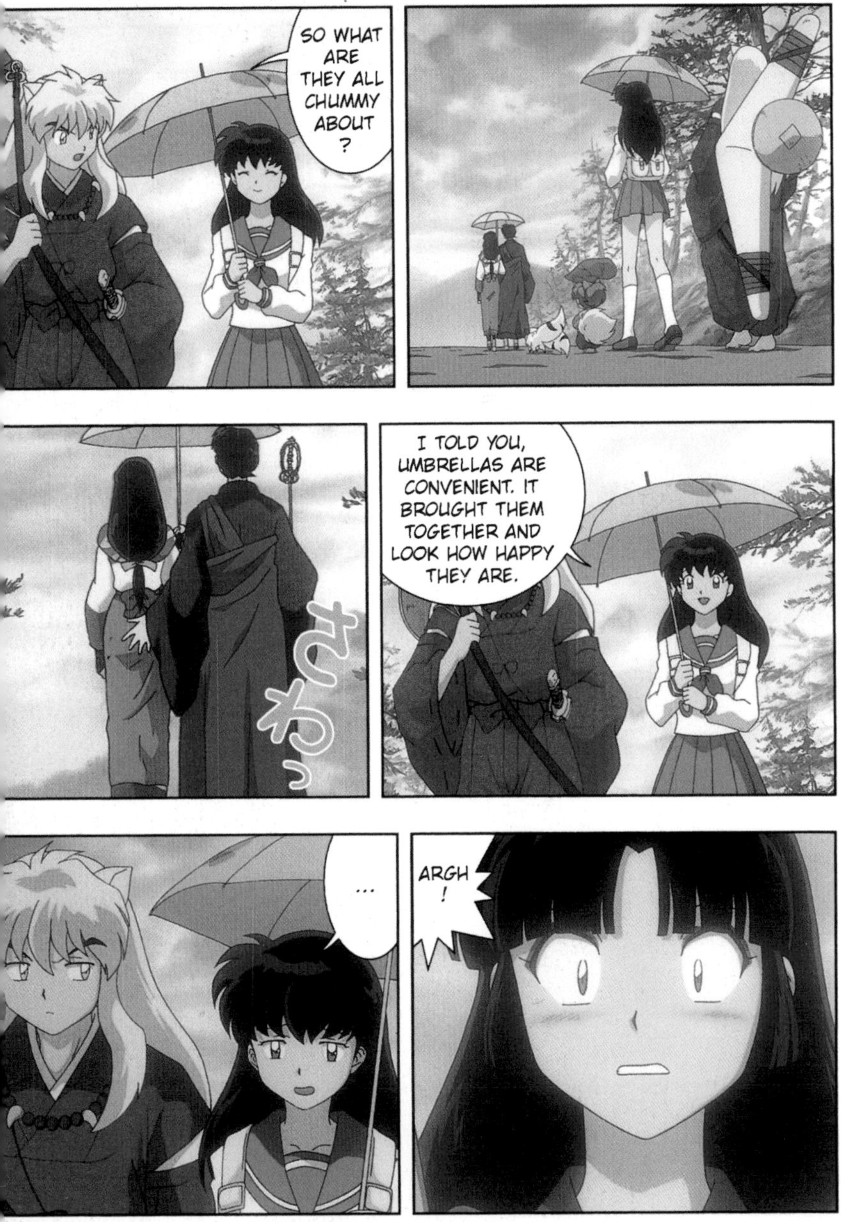
SO WHAT ARE THEY ALL CHUMMY ABOUT?
I TOLD YOU, UMBRELLAS ARE CONVENIENT. IT BROUGHT THEM TOGETHER AND LOOK HOW HAPPY THEY ARE.
さわっ
ARGH!
...

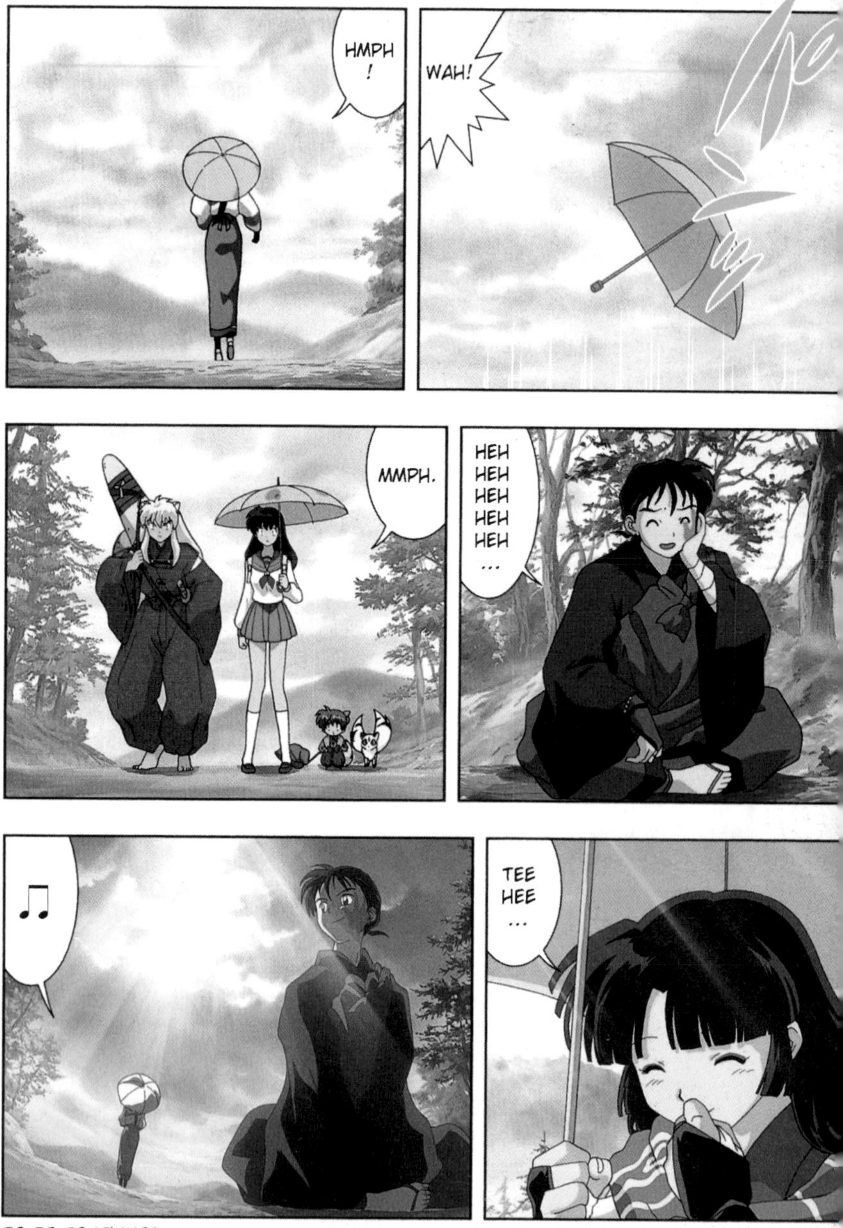
WAH!
HMPH !
HEH HEH HEH HEH HEH ...
MMPH.
TEE HEE ...
♫

TO BE CONTINUED...

Glossary of Sound Effects

Each entry includes: the location, indicated by page number and panel number (so 3.1 means page 3, panel number 1); the phonetic romanization of the original Japanese; and our English "translation"—we offer as close an English equivalent as we can.

18.1   FX: Dohn (explosion of light)
18.4   FX: Toh (Karan lands on roof)
18.5   FX: Za... (a footfall)

19.3   FX: Ta (panther demons withdraw)

20.4   FX: Ka (burst of light)

21.1   FX: Doh (Inuyasha blocks attack with Tetsusaiga)
21.2   FX: Doh (attack propels Inuyasha backward)

22.2   FX: Ga (Sesshomaru steps on Jaken)
22.5   FX: Goh (Hachi flies up)

23.1   FX: Suta (Hachi touches down)
23.3   FX: Pyo—n (sproing)
23.4   FX: Pa—n (Inuyasha slaps his cheek)

28.2   FX: Pyon (hop)
28.3   FX: Ba (jump)

29.1   FX: Goh (whoosh)
29.3   FX: Pon (pop)
29.5   FX: Toh (Inuyasha lands)

32.4   FX: Za (Royakan steps out into the open)

34.4   FX: Goh (whoosh as staff breathes fire)

35.1   FX: Suu... (Toran uses her power)
35.2   FX: Goh (Toran's power whooshes)
35.3   FX: Doh (powers collide)
35.4   FX: Goh (whooshing)
35.5   FX: Shururu... (something flying through air)

36.1   FX: Gin (clang)
36.2   FX: Cha (Toran grasps staff)

Chapter 76
Target: Sesshomaru and Inuyasha

6.2   FX: Dosa (Kagome thrown inside cell)

7.2   FX: Fuu... (Kagome faints)
7.5   FX: Zawa... (rustling)

8.1   FX: Za (wall is sheer in front of Inuyasha)
8.2   FX: Goh (Wind scar whooshes)
8.3   FX: Ka (flash of light)
8.4   FX: Zaaaaa... (barrier gives way)

9.1   FX: Goh (Koga's whirlwind)

11.3   FX: Za (demons land on roofs of village)
11.4   FX: Suta (Karan alights before Inuyasha)

12.1   FX: Zan (Inuyasha strikes with Tetsusaiga)
12.3   FX: Toh (Karan jumps up to roof)
12.4   FX: Bun (Sango throws Hiraikotsu)

13.2   FX: Bon (bonk)
13.3   FX: Doh doh doh
         (Shippo runs with demon in hot pursuit)
13.5   FX: Dohn (blast from Wind Scar)
13.6   FX: Goh (Whoosh)

14.3   FX: Ta ta ta... (panther demons flee)
14.4   FX: Da (Inuyasha pursues fleeing demons)
14.6   FX: Toh (Inuyasha alights)

16.1   FX: Shuuu... (hiss of smoke)

17.2   FX: Hyu (cat demons throw spears)
17.3   FX: Gin (clang)
17.5   FX: Ka (flash of bright light)

36.3 FX: Goh (Karan conjures and throws fireball)
36.4 FX: Ba (Toran attacks)

37.1 FX: Da (Karan leaps)
37.2 FX: Da (Inuyasha leaps)
37.4 FX: Ba (flame fired at Inuyasha)
37.5 FX: Baki (punch)

38.1 FX: Goh (Karan whooshes away)

39.1 FX: Kaa... (fire burns brightly)
39.2 FX: Ka (bright light)
39.4 FX: Goh (whoosh of Shuran's fire attack)

40.1 FX: Bari bari (crackling)
40.2 FX: Bari bari (crackling)
40.3 FX: Bari (crackle)

41.1 FX: Bari (crackle)
41.2 FX: Bari (crackle)
41.3 FX: Ba (Sesshomaru attacks)
41.4 FX: Fuwa... (Toran alights, cloak billowing)

43.4 FX: Ta ta ta... (running)

44.3 FX: Goh... (whoosh of flames)
44.4 FX: Goh (whoosh)

45.1 FX: Ga (flames strike demon)
45.2 FX: Zuba (slash)
45.3 FX: Zan (strike)

47.2 FX: Ba (wild dogs emerge)
47.3 FX: Ta (dogs run off)
47.4 FX: Uro uro (dogs run around, confused)
47.6 FX: Da (Koga leaps off)

48.1 FX: Za za... (sound of Koga leaping)
48.2 FX: Goh (whirlwind engulfs Koga)
48.3 FX: Ba (Koga kicks out)
48.4 FX: Za (Koga flies upward)

49.3 FX: Za (Koga descends back into forest)

50.1 FX: Za za za... (rustling)
50.2 FX: Za (Shunran appears)
50.3 FX: Doga (Koga strikes the ground where Shunran just was)

50.5 FX: Fuwa (petals thrust in air)

51.3 FX: Da (Shunran leaps)
51.4 FX: Zan (Koga slashes at flowers)

52.1 FX: Ji ji... (candle sputtering)
52.2 FX: Dosa (Sango and Miroku land inside the cell)

53.4 FX: Gashan (Shuran slams door)

54.5 FX: Don (Jaken thumps his staff)

55.1 FX: Za (cats appear)
55.2 FX: Da (running)
55.4 FX: Goh (two headed staff breathes fire)
55.5 FX: Da (cat demons dodge)

56.1 FX: Ba (Inuyasha attacks)
56.2 FX: Zuba (slash of claws)
56.4 FX: Toh (Inuyasha touches down)

57.1 FX: Da–(panther demons run off)
57.2 FX: Ta ta ta... (Jaken runs off)

61.4 FX: Zun (Sesshomaru steps on Jaken)

63.2 FX: Da (Inuyasha leaps away)

68.3 FX: Poh... (jewel shards glimmer)

71.1 FX: Kaa... (shining)
71.2 FX: Ba (Shuran casts an attack)
71.3 FX: Da (Koga dodges)
71.4 FX: Ba (Koga lunges)

72.1 FX: Za (rustling)
72.3 FX: Cha (Inuyasha draws sword)

Chapter 77
The Panther Devas and the Two Swords of the Fang

74.1 FX: Gara (Shippo climbing out of rubble)
74.2 FX: Gaba (Shippo standing up)

75.4 FX: Pyon (Myoga leaping)
76.2 FX: Cha (sound of sword)

185.5   FX: Ta (running)

187.1   FX: Goo (Sango powering up)
187.2   FX: Da (running)
187.4   FX: Guo (demon winding up to swing)
187.6   FX: Za (boomerang hitting ground)

188.1   FX: Gin (impact)
188.2   FX: Ta (leaping)
188.3   FX: Baki (kicks)
188.4   FX: Do (monster falls)

189.1   FX: Doka (impact)
189.2   FX: Ga (impact)

190.2   FX: Bun (throwing boomerang)
190.3   FX: Zuba (impact)
190.4   FX: Zuun (monster falls)

191.2   FX: Piku (twitch)

192.1   FX: Doka (impact)
192.2   FX: Garan (boomerang falling)
192.5   FX: To (landing)

194.2   FX: Cha (grabbing)
194.3   FX: Ba (throwing)
194.4   FX: Bishi (impact)

195.1   FX: Shuuu (dissolving)
195.3   FX: Ta (running)

196.1   FX: Gii (door opening)
196.2   FX: Gara (wooden statues rolling out)

199.3   FX: Goo (flames)
199.4   FX: Gooo (flames)

200.1   FX: Zaaa (rain)

202.1   FX: Zaaa (rain)

203.2   FX: Pon (pat on back)
203.4   FX: Su (reaching out)

205.4   FX: Sawa (Miroku grabbing it)

206.1   FX: Pan (Sango slapping Miroku)

Chapter 78
Only You, Sango

146.1   FX: Zaaa (rain)
146.4   FX: Zuun (smashing wall)

147.1   FX: Doga (monster attacking)
147.2   FX: Do (impact)
147.3   FX: Shun (arrows released)
147.4   FX: Baki (impact)

148.2   FX: Zaaa (rain)
148.3   FX: Zaaa (rain)

151.1   FX: Zaaa (rain)

152.2   FX: Za Za Za Za (marching)

154.3   FX: Zushi (money bag falls on table)

155.5   FX: Za (dismounting horse)

157.3   FX: Gyu (holding her hand)

158.4   FX: Zan (demon slayed)
162.3   FX: Jiro (staring)
163.3   FX: Su (standing up)

164.2   FX: Zuru (Sango slipping)
164.4   FX: Pan (smack)
164.5   FX: Gara (opening door)

165.2   FX: Don (bumping into each other)
165.5   FX: Shito shito (quiet rain)

167.2   FX: Riin goon (wedding bells)

172.5   FX: Su (quietly walking away)
173.1   FX: Za (jumping out of bushes)
173.2   FX: Pashi (tapping)

177.2   FX: Su (holding hands)

180.1   FX: Ta (running)

181.3   FX: Su (walking away)

185.1   FX: Zuun (footsteps)

INU YASHA

Read the action from the start with the original manga series

Full color adaptation of the popular TV series

The Art of **INU YASHA**

Art book with cel art, paintings, character profiles and more

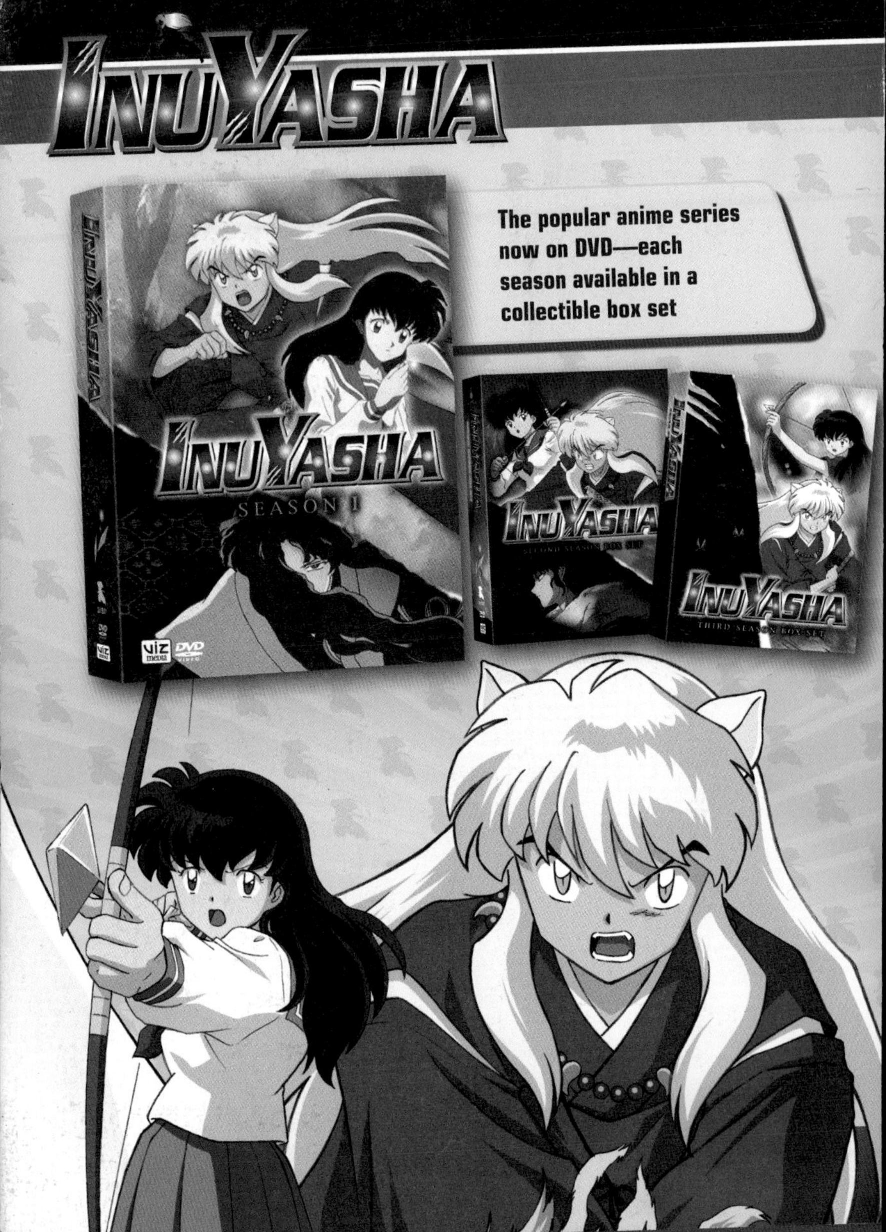
InuYasha
The popular anime series now on DVD—each season available in a collectible box set
InuYasha
SEASON 1
InuYasha
InuYasha
THIRD SEASON BOX SET

LOVE MANGA?
LET US KNOW WHAT YOU THINK!

HELP US MAKE THE MANGA
YOU LOVE BETTER!

The
Necessary
Grace
to
Fall

WINNER

OF THE

FLANNERY

O'CONNOR

AWARD

FOR

SHORT

FICTION

The

Necessary

Grace

to

Fall

Stories by

Gina Ochsner

The University of Georgia Press

Athens and London

Published by the University of Georgia Press

Athens, Georgia 30602

© 2002 by Gina Ochsner

All rights reserved

Designed by Kathi Dailey Morgan

Set in Adobe Garamond by Bookcomp, Inc.

Printed and bound by Maple-Vail

The paper in this book meets the guidelines for
permanence and durability of the Committee on
Production Guidelines for Book Longevity of the
Council on Library Resources.

Printed in the United States of America

06 05 04 03 02 C 5 4 3 2 1

Library of Congress Cataloging-in-Publication Data

Ochsner, Gina, 1970–

The necessary grace to fall : stories /
by Gina Ochsner.

p. cm. — (Winner of the Flannery O'Connor
Award for short fiction)

ISBN 0-8203-2314-4 (alk. paper)

1. United States—Social life and customs—
20th century—Fiction.   I. Title.   II. Series.

PS3615.C48 N43 2002

813'.6—dc21   2001041059

British Library Cataloging-in-Publication Data available

To my family

Contents

The Necessary Grace to Fall   *1*

What Holds Us Fast   *22*

How the Dead Live   *40*

Unfinished Business   *52*

Cartography of a Heart   *73*

Modern Taxidermy   *84*

Then, Returning   *105*

Eulogy for Red   *122*

Sixty-six Degrees North   *137*

The Erlenmeyer Flask   *155*

From the Bering Strait   *170*

Acknowledgments   *181*

The
Necessary
Grace
to
Fall

All summer had been a medley of jumpers and fallers. The previous spring, simple dismemberment, and the winter before that, freakish hurricane-related deaths and injuries—deaths by debris, Leonard, Howard's immediate supervisor and cubicle-mate, called them.

"You're lucky. All I ever seem to get are the old folks," Leonard said, when Howard pointed out that his claims had been following these discrete and eerie patterns. "All natural. Nothing fishy— except that one old gal. One hundred and two years old, survived a fire in the nursing home only to die from a penicillin reaction in the hospital."

"What a shame," Howard said.

"Still. One hundred and two. That's beyond ripe. I'll bet she drank Boost or something."

Howard pushed his glasses up onto a tiny groove on the bridge of his nose. With all the power bars, energy drinks, and vitamins

Leonard consumed, Howard was sure he would push a hundred at least. Before he started at Hope and Life Insurance, Howard had never met anyone as fanatical as Leonard about the maintenance of his own body, not even the gung-ho insurance sales staff on the second and third floors who formed weekend running clubs and circulated back issues of *Runner's World* on the break tables.

Despite his discovery that death was not as random as most people thought, a notion that for some reason gladdened Howard, he still found his job disappointing. When he'd transferred from medical data coding to investigations, Howard had entertained visions of dusting for fingerprints at crime scenes, determining whether or not his deceased policyholder was the victim of a poisoner or a strangler based on the friction patterns, those delicate whorls and swirls a simple piece of adhesive tape could pick up from doorknobs and medicine bottles. He thought at the very least he'd get to look at police reports, maybe even interview the bereaved. He had thought somehow he would be more necessary, able to see things others couldn't, for most problems came from being unable to see, not from not knowing or feeling. And so for these last nine months Howard had been processing claims, waiting for something to catch his eye: a murder disguised as suicide or a manslaughter passed off as a careless accident, large term policies taken out on people whose net worth didn't warrant insuring.

"You're an investigative *assistant*. So, it's not brain surgery. It's not like you have to do any real investigating," Leonard informed him on his first day. "It's pretty ordinary stuff really. Suicides— always the pink forms. We don't pay out unless the policy is at least two years old. We usually get a police report confirming it's a suicide and not, say, a homicide made to look like an accident. If it's one of those . . ." Leonard tapped his pen against a mini-file cabinet nearly hidden under his desk. "We wait for the coroner's report and for the police to clear any kin expected to inherit. Natural and accidental deaths—goldenrod—we pay out. Still, all you got to do is wait for the appropriate reports and file them with the policy. No big deal."

Howard's shoulders slumped and he could feel a space widening inside his rib cage. He had hoped for something more exciting. A little more murder. He wanted to study with practiced suspicion the beneficiaries. He wanted to know if they would glide, vapor-like, walking around as if undressed. He wanted to know how tragedy hung on the face and what he would say when he saw it.

The only excitement he'd found on the job was working with Ritteaur, the coroner's assistant. Occasionally, Howard couldn't read his handwriting and would have to call for clarification. Though he knew it was morbid, he couldn't help being curious about everything that went on in the lab and would pump Ritteaur for all the grisly details of the cases that came across Howard's desk. Sometimes when he was bored or, like today, wanted to dodge Carla, his wife, and her noontime phone calls, he phoned Ritteaur even when he could read his handwriting just fine.

"Ritteaur, it's Howard. I got a question on an older file, Pietrzak."

"Oh, yeah. I remember him. This one you would've *loved.*"

"So was he dismembered before or after death?"

"Both. But mostly after."

"Was the 'before' dismemberment accidental?"

"Sort of. It started out that way. Then the wife got ideas, seized an opportunity, if you know what I mean, and finished him off."

Howard felt his stomach tightening.

"They found most of his body cut into tiny pieces and stuck in a sump. The wife tried to flush him down the toilet, one flush at a time. There's a joke in there somewhere, but I can't find it just yet. Ka-toosh!" Ritteaur laughed, making a flushing noise. "You tell me the human creature isn't one sick animal," Ritteaur continued.

"Yeah. Pretty sick." Howard nodded his head in a mixture of disbelief and horror. He hung up the phone and studied the Pietrzak file. It never failed to amaze him how many husbands and wives, ordinary and sane people who'd sworn to love one another, killed each other. Before he started at the company, Howard had been optimistic about both hope and life, sure that life was good and so were most of the people in it. It never occurred to him that he might have to fear Carla, or she him, someday. And this made him sad, knowing that there were mysteries, little pockets of darkness people kept from each other. He wondered what it was that had set that woman off if it wasn't something small, very very small—that had bugged her for years.

At 12:05, Howard's phone rang and the white button indicating an in-house call began to blink.

"Lunch?" Carla also worked at Hope and Life, fourth floor, in the medical coding department. When they had first married, they always ate their lunches together in the break room. Now Howard made a point of being on the phone or out of the office during the lunch hour. Not out of malice. In fact, there was no particular reason why he wanted to avoid his wife. He just got tired of their regular lunches that over time began to feel forced, wearing on him like a habit that needed breaking. People need space, he reminded himself, though he knew she'd never let him get away with such a flimsy reasoning.

"Not today. I just got back from the coroner's lab and I haven't got much of an appetite left," Howard lied. "You know, all those smells."

"Right," Carla said, drawing out the word the way she did when she wasn't sure whether or not to believe him.

"Another bridge-jumper," Howard said, leaning forward to read the file label on the blue folder Leonard had deposited on his desk that morning. "Johnson, Svea." Howard tapped the edge of the unopened file with his ball-point pen.

"She's dead, right?"

"Very."

"Good. Because if I thought, even for a minute, that you were screwing around, your stuff would be out on the lawn, Howard. You know that. Right?"

"Right," Howard said, wondering if Carla had really wanted to eat lunch with him at all.

⌣

Howard believed in human kindness, felt it was up to him to perform small acts of it whenever he could. But he wasn't kidding himself. He desperately hoped his good intentions would bring back to him some small act of kindness in return, he didn't care how small. Besides, life was too short not to try, he reminded himself. That's why before he was hired at Hope and Life, Howard had volunteered at a suicide hotline where he tried to talk people out of taking those fatal doses, out of pulling the trigger. *I know how you feel,* he had wanted to say. *I'm just like you.*

After a few weeks of doling out modulated and appropriate responses, Howard improvised, telling his callers about his grim high school summers spent chicken picking, about how he had worked at twilight, in that blue light of his grandparents' broken-slatted barn, picking the unsuspecting birds up by the feet where they sat in their own dung and dust. Sometimes, in the kicked-up dust, he thought he could smell their fear as he loaded them in cages on the back of the flatbed truck. That's when he'd hear them start talking, begging for mercy. "*Help,*" they'd squawk, "*Please,*" or worse, "*We'll come baaaaack.*"

Though he hated that job, hated what he had to do, somehow sending those birds to their deaths validated his own life. This was hard to explain, even to himself. But he'd tell his callers anyway, desperate to make a connection. Smelling their fear, knowing their desire to live had worked for him, he'd tell them. Hearing a smaller animal plead, beg for the grace of just one more day, and these insignificant birds with brains the size of a pea. If a chicken could cling to life, then why couldn't he? This was what got him through each shift in the barn, each miserable night spent lying on his bunk with dung-lung, his voice split and cracking, frayed to a hoarse whisper.

There must be something to get you through, he'd urge. *Maybe buy a pet, a goldfish.* Invariably the callers hung up then and Howard would get that feeling, always accompanied by the taste of acid in the back of his throat, that he'd failed again. He had this same feeling about that Svea Johnson woman, for a cursory glance at her stats revealed she was his age, had lived in the same neighborhood he had grown up in. No doubt they'd gone to high school together, and yet he could not remember her.

Howard drummed his fingers on top of the blue file. It unnerved him how the fact of time and location forced a commonality between him and this woman he should have known but didn't. He leaned back in his chair and wondered, had she known him? Had she been one of those dumpy girls hiding behind a stack of books in the library, one of those disappearing girls with a disappearing face so nondescript it blended with anything? Or had she been beautiful, so beautiful Howard had decided she was unattainable and had thus relegated her to the deep pocket of his for-getfulness, for he knew his memory was like that: he could forget anything if he decided there would be no occasion to know it later.

Leonard pushed back in his chair and cracked his knuckles. With his conical buzz-top haircut, even his head looked muscular. As Leonard leaned over his keyboard, Howard noted how minute activities like typing brought into sharp focus the muscles in his forearms. Leonard pushed back in his chair again, this time to rifle through the lower drawers of his desk where he kept a large stash of energy bars. Then he unpeeled the metallic wrapper off a Tiger bar and took a bite.

"Want some?" Leonard offered the rest of the bar to Howard.

Howard shook his head and pointed to the unfinished cinna-mon roll gummed to the corner of his desk.

"Treat your body like a temple, and it'll take care of you," Leonard said, his mouth full of energy bar.

Howard blinked and pushed his glasses back onto the deep groove at the bridge of his nose. He didn't know what to say when people discussed their own bodies. A body was what it was. Then he thought of Svea Johnson's body, falling head over heels perhaps. Or floating for a brief second before plummeting. He wished he could remember her, had some shred of recollection, for it was hard to conjure a faceless body, hard to imagine telling her what he wished he could have said: how unforgiving water really was, that of all the ways to jump off a bridge, none of them were good, this much he'd learned from Ritteaur.

Howard's phone rang. The white button blinked and he sighed before he picked up the receiver.

"Don't be late for dinner tonight, Howard." It was Carla again. "I'm cooking a Martha Stewart recipe." Howard knew that meant she'd spent too much money on hard-to-find ingredients, and would spend too much time trying to make the dish look like it did in the *Martha Stewart Living* magazine. "Presentation is everything," Carla had explained when he asked what difference it made if a salad had radichio or endive in it or not.

"OK," Howard said, sliding the phone into the cradle. He pressed on his sternum. Before working in the coroner's office, Ritteaur had interned for a mortician. Ritteaur had told Howard how corpses, once pumped full of embalming fluid, tended to bloat overnight and it was necessary to push on their torsos and vent the gases through a plastic plug inserted in their abdomens. Howard thumped on his chest with the heel of his palm and wondered if he might not benefit from just such a hatch incision to let bad air out.

Sometimes Howard imagined himself utterly split, a ghost Howard, his consciousness hovering next to the corporeal Howard sitting there now, his fingers gripping the ribbed steering wheel of his blue Skylark. For it seemed clear to him that in all things there were two Howards at work: the Howard who wanted to arrive home in time for dinner so as to please his wife and the Howard who knew even as he promised that he would, he wouldn't. The Howard who knew he shouldn't leave work early, would have no good excuse should Leonard notice his absence, and the Howard who secretly hoped he'd be missed, knew that questions would be asked. How else could he explain it? For here he was, four o'clock, his foot heavy on the gas pedal, driving toward the Laurelhurst neighborhood where both Howards knew he would troll the old streets, the one Howard not sure what it was he thought he'd find over there at 745 Madison—hoping, in fact, it was a vacant lot of thistle and beer bottles, the other Howard knowing it wasn't so, knowing too that neither Howard would rest until he saw the house Svea Johnson had once lived in.

As he drove, the hills in the distance turned smoky under the late afternoon August heat. Howard rubbed his forehead. He should be at work. He should be inputting data, he said aloud even as he turned onto Weidler. He told himself he had no idea why he was doing this, though the other Howard knew this drive had more to do with making reparations, with jostling a faulty memory to reveal something of Svea Johnson. For Howard had either never known her or had forgotten her, forgotten her completely, and it bothered him that this could happen, that the same thing could and would happen to him someday.

You could read a lot about people from the houses they lived in, he reminded himself as he drove past the Laurelhurst park, past the huge iron posts, the remnants of an ancient gate marking the Laurelhurst neighborhood from the Rose district. And then he wondered, could sorrow leave its mark on the brickwork? Would he read the traces of grief in the troubled surface of stucco, in the warped panes' suggestions that theirs had been a family full of secrets and hidden hurts?

Howard nosed the whistling Skylark onto Madison. He circled the block, even numbers on the left, odds on the right. In his squeaking car, idling at five miles per hour, he was as obvious as a headache and he didn't like the oily feel of what he was doing, felt he was trespassing, though in truth he was idling along the very same streets over which he'd once ridden his bicycle hundreds of times as he delivered newspapers in the inky darkness of night. Still, it didn't feel right and he drove away, willing himself not to read the house numbers. He looped past the park three times, drove by the house he had spent his boyhood in, past all the houses along his old paper route. Then, delinquent both in fact and intention, Howard turned toward home, toward Carla and her dinner.

When he pulled into the driveway, he turned off the engine. From his car he could see Carla's shadow at the kitchen window, her dark form moving behind the scrim of the lowered window shade. Howard thought of the Johnsons again, tried to imagine their shapes moving from room to room, and he felt acres and acres of empty space growing inside of him, pushing everything else out of the way. His heart, his lungs—none of it mattered—and he could swear he felt them shrinking to the point where he could see himself reflecting pure sky, the vastness of that inner space.

~

"Where've you been?" Carla met Howard at the door, a spatula in hand. "You missed my Capillini pasta with red caviar. Endive salad and marinated artichoke hearts."

"I got held up." Howard pulled the door closed, felt the bolt slide home under his hand. "I'm sorry," he said, his mouth tasting like he'd swallowed a fistful of change.

"I called at your desk and left a message with Leonard. He said you left early." Carla set the spatula down on the stove and followed Howard to the bathroom where he pulled down his pants. Carla crossed her arms over her chest. "If there's something you need to tell me, you can just tell me. You know that. Right?"

"I'm OK," Howard said, flushing the toilet. "I just feel a little different, that's all. Like there's an itch in my arteries."

Carla went back to the kitchen where Howard heard a whole battery of kitchen noises: savage rips on the roll of tinfoil, garbled choking from the garbage disposal, all the sounds women make in a kitchen when they're angry. After a while Carla came back to the bathroom. Howard hadn't moved except to pull the lid of the toilet down and sit on it. She wanted a scene, he could tell, and here he was, full of guilt and too many character faults to count. For starters, Howard did not have the energy to give his wife what she wanted and rightfully deserved: a real fight, something, anything to prove to themselves they still felt the way people should.

"An itch in your arteries?" Carla rocked back on her heels and studied him. Then she turned on the tap, pulled out her toothbrush, and began scrubbing her teeth so vigorously Howard knew she couldn't really hear him.

"Like how you feel when you hang your head out a car window, how all that wind crowds your throat." *For a moment it scares you, and then it's pure joy,* he wanted to add.

Carla spat, turned off the tap, put the toothbrush away. "You're so late, I already sent Kevin to bed." Kevin was Carla's eight-year-old son from a failed marriage. For an eight-year-old, Howard thought Kevin seemed strangely devoid of life, ghosting the hallways, ducking past Howard when he'd stretch his hand out to rumple his hair. Kevin spent most of his time holed up in his room, fiddling around on his computer, and Howard sincerely hoped he'd do something risky one of these days, get into some trouble, sniff rubber cement at school, smoke a cigarette, anything. Just to be on the safe side, Howard had tried to tell him a little about the birds and the bees a few months back. Kevin had sat cross-legged, looking at him and blinking rapidly. The point is, he'd told Kevin, life and love are ultimately cruel but fair, breaking each and every one of us down to bits, "and disappointment, just get used to it."

"Can I go now?" Kevin had asked, still blinking, and Howard realized then these were things you did not say to an eight-year-old.

Carla pulled her ratty yellow nightgown over her head. "He needs you, Howard. More than you know. Boys need a strong male role-model."

Howard stood and stepped out of his pants. "They need fresh air, too."

Carla sighed, climbed into bed. "Kevin's got that karate test at the Y tomorrow night. 7:30. Don't be late, OK?"

"OK."

She turned her back to Howard and switched off her bedside light. In a matter of minutes, he knew she'd start mumbling data codes. Her favorite: 99803: Venipuncture. He used to think it was cute, her bringing her work home with her. When they both worked in the coding department, they'd spout codes over dinner dates, during commercials, a sort of foreplay and mounting evidence that they shared the same sense of humor: 66701, Bipolar manic depression; 39099, Male pattern baldness. All one of them had to do was pick a person out of a crowd or in a restaurant, point and recite a code, and they'd both bust up laughing. 41000: Liposuction. Now he had to work hard not to smother Carla with the pillow when she began her nightly litanies, and remind himself that once he had thought her funny. But then Howard recalled his own quirks: his wearing the maroon-striped tie every Tuesday and Thursday, wearing the brown paisley every Monday, Wednesday, and Friday. Maybe they were all just forgetting how to live.

Howard spent most of the next morning avoiding the Svea Johnson file. By 10:05, when the exodus for the coffee pots had died to a trickle, he duckwalked his squeaky-castored chair closer to Leonard, who had his fingers laced behind his neck. Leonard grimaced and twisted first to the right and then to the left. Oblique crunches. Leonard did these every morning during their allotted ten-minute coffee break.

"People always overlook their obliques," Leonard explained.

Howard nodded. "I've got this strange feeling," he said, thumping his chest with his knuckles. "Like I'm gulping sky, can't get enough of it. Other times I feel I'm drowning on air. Can a person do that?"

"Fish." Leonard flapped his hands at the side of his neck, indicating imaginary gills. "They do it all the time."

Howard pressed on his sternum again, then untucked his shirt and lifted it to show Leonard his chest. "No, really. I think there's something wrong with me," he said.

Leonard leaned forward in his chair and narrowed his eyes. "No kidding. Your obliques have completely disappeared. If your ribs weren't there, your insides would be sliding all over the place. Too many beers, Buck-o."

"No, that's not it," Howard said, tucking his shirt back into his waistband. "I think it's more serious."

Leonard shrugged. "Nothing more serious than a bad case of underdeveloped obliques."

"Right," Howard said, adopting Carla's habit of drawing the word out as she exhaled.

For over an hour Howard sat at his desk trying to work up the courage to process the Johnson file. But the mere sight of it, of knowing that she was most likely a jumper because it was August, the month of jumping, depressed him. Howard looked at the blue file and felt that space expanding, pushing against his lungs. He laced his fingers behind his neck as he'd seen Leonard do every morning. Maybe his problem could be isolated, squeezed into form by a series of isometrics. Maybe this was why Leonard worked out so much. Howard grunted and leaned to the right, then to the left, repeating the movements until he could feel a tingle in his armpits, the first signal that his deodorant either would or would not fail him. After five minutes, he gave up. He pushed on his rib cage, lightly fingering the spaces between the bones, feeling as spacious inside as before, if not spacier.

Outside, the sky was a cloudless blue, so pure Howard had to look away. He picked up his phone and dialed the coroner's office.

"Ritteaur, it's Howard calling on the Johnson autopsy results." Howard had his fingers crossed. He was hoping against all odds that she had been a faller and not a jumper, feeling that either way, he was responsible for her.

"Come take a look for yourself. We'll get a beer after," Ritteaur said.

Howard grabbed his keys. He knew it was against company policy to drink on lunch hours, but it was a Friday and he was feeling that space again, was hoping Hope and Life would catch on fire, was hoping every office worker would steal staplers and envelopes, hoping every beneficiary got paid in full.

⌣

When Howard pulled open the metallic doors of the coroner's lab, he walked into the sharp smells of formaldehyde and antiseptic, thick in the air and carried as a stinging slap to the nose. On a table lay the body of a woman, a white sheet peeled back to her feet. The yellow laminate toe-tag read *Johnson, Svea*. Even though her skin was bluish and dark circles ringed her eyes, Howard could see that she had been a beautiful woman and he regretted he'd come.

Ritteaur pressed a forefinger into the woman's arm, leaving an indentation. "The body's a glorified sponge," he said, pulling out a skinny measuring wand that looked like a cocktail swizzle stick. He measured the depth of the pitting, then tossed the tiny ruler into a stainless steel sink. "At first I thought it was suicide. The bridge and all. At any rate, she got to the morgue quicker than most of our water-victims do and we had to wait a while to see if any bruising would appear. Anything suspicious—ligatures or marks around the neck or on the arms. Bruises don't always appear on the body right away, especially on submerged flesh. So we let her dry out in the cooler."

"And that's when you found bruises?"

"That's just it. None. Zippo. So I'm thinking suicide. Then I look at her fingernails and I see tiny bits of moss under the nails and two of the nails on her right hand broken off."

"She fell." Howard felt a surge in his chest.

"Or she intended to jump but at the last moment had second thoughts."

Howard closed his eyes, imagining what he would have said if Svea had called in on the hotline, feeling again that maybe he owed her something, should at least be able to locate her in a dim memory of a school assembly, the taking of a photo, but there was nothing.

"So what's the verdict?" Howard swallowed, tasting metal in his molars.

Ritteaur shrugged. "I still got to do the Y-incision, poke around in the stomach, run some blood tests."

"Do you believe in dignity for the dead?" Howard draped the sheet over Svea Johnson's body.

Ritteaur laughed. "Are you kidding? In this business? You think this is bad," Ritteaur poked the dead woman's big toe, "wait until the mortician gets ahold of her."

Ritteaur pulled the sheet back and looked at the woman's face. Her eyes were open, but chilled and empty, the way the eyes of fish look when set out on ice. "She's in pretty good shape, all things considered." Ritteaur forced the eyelids closed with his thumbs. "We had a decapitation in here a month ago. The family wanted an open-casket funeral, if you can believe that. But I'm telling you, those embalmers can work miracles. They trimmed the ragged edges, splinted and sutured the head to the neck, and painted liquid sealer over the stitching. Then they threw a turtleneck and some makeup on the guy, and I swear to God, if I hadn't seen him on my table just a day before, I wouldn't have even suspected."

"No." Howard put his palms on the examining table and leaned on it. "That's not what I meant." He adjusted the sheet to cover Svea Johnson's pitted forearm. "I mean on the paperwork, 'accidental death' sounds more dignified than 'botched suicide,' don't you think?"

"Hey. I'm not going to tell you how to do your job. I just wanted you to see for yourself what we got here. My opinion is it could go either way."

"But your report—"

Ritteaur pulled off his surgical gloves with a loud snap. "It's still incomplete. But judging by what we got so far, I vote for accident."

"OK." Howard patted down his stomach, his hands fluttering. " OK," he said again, backing out of the two-way door, away from the smells of the lab.

"How 'bout that beer?" Ritteaur untied his scrubs, pivoted, and tossed them into a steel clothes hamper at the far end of the lab.

Howard shook his head and waved his hands out in front of him. "Another time." He felt his throat seizing tight, like a drawstring being pulled, and he didn't know if the formaldehyde was getting to him or if he had brushed against a true sorrow for this Svea Johnson, a stranger.

Howard checked his watch. Though Leonard would be back from the gym any minute now and Carla would have called and left messages, Howard could feel that other Howard unpeeling like the silver and felt backing from an old mirror and his heart began to beat faster. He closed his eyes and pinched the bridge of his nose. Before he knew it, he'd eased the Skylark toward the Laurelhurst neighborhood, past the long and low elementary school, one six-year complaint of noise and misery. Howard turned onto Madison Street and sat two doors down from the Johnson house, considering how he'd purposefully forgotten all those years, grade school and junior high. He'd willfully, willingly forgotten the awkwardness of his body, his body a menagerie of flawed parts as he had only been dimly aware then of what he knew now: how the body's mysteries lay not in the parts themselves, nor their shapes and functions, but in the naming of them, and in the particular nomenclature for how those parts could and would fail. And whether the naming came in the form of medical coding or as scribbles from a forensic pathologist, Howard was continually astonished by the subtleties, the lies such language imposed.

As Howard walked down the narrow corridor to his cubicle, he could hear his phone ringing and knew, again, it was Carla.

"Howard. Just a reminder: Kevin. Y. 7 P.M. Green belt karate test." Carla sounded like she was calling out a fast-food order. "Sure. OK," Howard said and slid the receiver in the phone's cradle. He hated these Friday night karate tests. It took forever to get through the hordes of White belts, all of them bad. Yellow and Orange belt tests were a little better; at least when the instructor counted, you could bet half of the students would execute the same move at the same time. With White belts, you could never be sure of anything. And Howard hated the parents, crowding the mats, the metallic flash and pop of bulbs, the edgy whining noise of film rewinding.

Howard leaned back in his chair and palmed his heart, bearing down on his chest with the heel of his hand. He hoped his internal organs would just disappear and he could give himself over to his internal gases and float, balloon-like, up and out of the office.

～～～

On Fridays, beautiful Fridays after everyone else had left early, the hours emptied and a calm filled the office, a liquid quietude welling along the corridors, around cubicles, lapping over the tops of Howard's shoes. Howard loved this quiet startled from the eventual lack of noise: the gradual winding down of the phone's nervous rings around five, the flurry to the elevator and the rubbery sound of its wobbled stop and the door bumping open. The copy machine, switched off, lid open as if cooling itself, made trickling noises like the ink was pooling somewhere. On Fridays after five, Howard felt he could think a little more clearly and he rolled in his chair, dreaming of policies that were never cancelled, claims never rejected, families redeemed by the careful and sympathetic coding a man with Howard's sensibilities could extend. In these moments of calm, the two Howards, his will and his action, neatly fused. This is what he was telling himself anyway, why he would even consider going back out to Madison Street. For this combined and profoundly optimistic Howard, the Howard who believed in doing the right thing, believed he could do right by everyone if only he tried a little harder, found himself once again, before he could fully comprehend the consequences, behind the steering wheel of his temperamental Skylark.

Howard sat in his car, drumming his fingers along the curvature of the wheel grip. He would knock on their door and with confidence, he would apologize for his intrusion. "But it would help if you could tell me a little about your daughter," he'd say, "anything that goes to character or state of mind." He would of course be professional, take notes, politely look at photos. And he'd be careful to give nothing away. They'd never know Ritteaur suspected suicide, never know of Howard's dilemma. He'd ask them, carefully, about high school. Perhaps he'd mention that he might have been their paperboy.

Outside the car, Howard could hear the crickets rubbing out the music of their long legs. The air was cooling and the sun dropped behind a thick grove of oaks at the end of the street. Howard started the engine, kept his foot off the pedal and allowed the car to idle past the Johnson house. Idling at this speed, moving in a straight and true line toward the darkness, he knew that the earth moved as well, turning in the opposite direction, moving entire continents and everything on them, including Howard and his whistling Skylark, turning so gently, so surely not even a dog stirred. Howard braked suddenly. He sensed more than saw motion behind him and glanced in his rearview mirror. He felt his stomach shriveling, for there in the mirror he watched Carla's blue Impala fishtail at the end of Madison and turn the corner.

At 7:30 Howard's desk phone rang. Howard straightened in his chair.

"I saw you." It was Carla calling from the Y.

Howard thought again of the woman of a thousand flushes. He moved his mouth, formed the beginnings of words on his lips. At last he settled, "I know."

"I don't know what's going on with you, Howard." Carla let her breath out in spurts. "But this has got to stop. People count on you."

"I know it." Howard pressed on his sternum, then followed the ridges of each of his ribs with his fingertips. He was feeling expansive again, like if he took a big enough breath of air, he might up and float.

"I forgive you," Carla said at last, but Howard could hear the mercury rising in her voice and knew that though he might in fact be forgiven, his transgression would be remembered on a long long list of grievances. "Whatever you were doing over there, I forgive you. But you had better stop. And you better be here for Kevin's test."

Howard swallowed. "I'll be there," he said.

Howard opened the driver's side door of his car and slid in behind the steering wheel.

He started for the Y, but as he approached the bridge, he slowed and parked in the soft sand shoulder. Overhead, August's moon, round as a month full of fallers and jumpers, glowed against the deepening sky. He walked to the bridge, ran his hand over the rough cement siding. His maroon-striped tie flapped in the wind, slapping his right shoulder. He didn't know where Svea Johnson had jumped or fallen. He knew now that there were five ways to fall off a bridge, according to Ritteaur, but as Ritteaur admitted, he was only an assistant, and there could be many more ways of falling than either of them had ever dreamed of. Howard knew that Svea Johnson had not been drinking, had not taken pills. She had probably stood first behind the spot where she would later sit. Maybe she had even held her arms up, like Howard was doing now, testing the air for flight. Maybe she was just having a bad day, a very bad day here in this extremely vexed land, and, like Howard, was looking for that one gesture, that break in the monotonous tide, the necessary grace to fall.

Howard planted his elbows on the cement and leaned over the railing as if to read the water. If a body is exiled, he thought, it's because it is contained by skin. Is that how she felt? Did she give herself over to the collapsing arms of the air, to all that space within and without, a falling between the ribs and then here between the arms, between fingertips and sky? Was hers an ordinary sadness that brought her to this bridge or a more resonant sorrow lodged behind the breastbone? Did she sit swinging her legs back and forth and then finally say, "Oh, the hell with it," and push herself over? Did she scream as she fell, or plug her nose?

Howard removed his shoes and in his stockinged feet balanced up on the thick cement handrail. Parsing through these borrowed thoughts, he could see now how easy it was. It wasn't so hard to imagine, no, not at all. A murmur of resignation washing over you, the body spinning in a full revolution between hope and despair. Howard felt light, giddy in this feeling of anti-gravity, and for the first time in months, Howard felt like laughing.

"Stop it," he muttered, climbing down from the ledge with caution, much more tentative about this minor action than any other in his whole life. He'd been right all along in feeling like he'd failed people, only they weren't jumpers and fallers, and it amazed him what he'd allowed himself, the lapses, what he hadn't learned yet. And for all of his empty spaces, this is what pulled him back. There was his Tuesday/Thursday God-awful maroon-striped tie, for starters. Kevin's Green-belt test and the knowledge that he should and could probably try a little harder with the boy, try to manufacture some genuine feeling. He could tell Kevin his chicken-picking story. And then, of course, there were all those things he hadn't lived to see: the appearance of new suns, distant limbs of the galaxy, the relief of intolerable urges, and other small kindnesses. This was something he could have told Svea Johnson. Howard slid his shoes on then, still feeling that lightness, but with it a sense of forward motion propelling him to his car.

What

Holds

Us

Fast

From the time she was eight, when she suddenly lost her dog to a disease she'd never heard of but that sounded like a Mexican beer, Claire had been watching and waiting for death. From her great-grandmother, Claire learned that death was a natural process of the body, like breathing, and that it was nothing to fear. From her mother, a healthy woman taken away by an aneurysm, who left without a sound and with a tiny smile playing at the corners of her mouth, Claire discovered that death does not discriminate. From her grandmother Eugenia, who was dying of cancer, she learned that dying hurt. But what people tended to forget, Claire realized one day as she emptied her grandmother's drainage shunt, was that the pain of dying and living were remarkably the same.

"When will the living not hurt so much?" Eugenia asked Claire as she leaned on her granddaughter and half walked, half crawled to the bathtub. And Claire knew that Eugenia could easily substitute dying for living as they were each variations of the same theme. But that was dying. Death was another animal entirely. In death, she supposed, nothing hurt, nothing could hurt you. Of course, she couldn't be sure, but what she didn't know, she filled in with her imagination and all the information she had gathered from all the funerals she'd witnessed and wakes she had helped her best friend, Jeannette, cater.

Claire liked the wakes best because they were usually held in the home of the deceased and she liked studying the photographs these people left behind and hearing the stories told about them. She could eavesdrop with impunity and it was what she heard that continually amazed her. Before taking the catering job, she had no idea the repertoire of grief or the huge and continually expanding range the simple "I'm sorry" could command. "I'm very sorry" transported empathy to another landscape of sorrow entirely, and she could hardly listen to these exchanges without choking up. In her mind she substituted herself for the bereaved widows, sisters, mothers, and in the saddest catering job ever, a new bride. Sometimes, too, she envied the survivors because she could tell that they knew suffering. They were the lucky ones, yes—lucky because, she thought, you had to suffer in all kinds of ways before you could understand anything.

One day Claire read to Eugenia from the newspaper that some high school kids had taken the statue of Ronald McDonald from a local McDonald's and held it for ransom. When the store manager wouldn't pay, they sent pieces of Ronald through the mail: first a gloved hand, then the round nose, and finally a size 20 clown shoe.

"That's just the way some people *will* go and do," Eugenia remarked, fanning herself with the *TV Guide*. Claire understood this well enough. Sometimes after being around Eugenia, around the smells of an old woman shedding her body, Claire would have to get into her old Chevette and just drive, her eyes fixed on the yellow line down the middle of the road. If it were mid-afternoon, she would head for the cemetery, where she knew she could drive by the retirement center and see the old folks out on a patch of crusty lawn in their lawn chairs, waiting for a funeral procession to roll by. At first, seeing them in their straw hats and sun block, watching for the motorcycle cops with their binoculars like they were waiting for a parade, disgusted Claire. But then eventually she found herself slowing down, checking her rearview mirrors, and, finally, parking in the shade of an alley, a willing spectator. In Midland there wasn't much to do and Claire figured that this sort of curiosity was really just testimony to people going mad in the great expanses of dirt, pushed around as they were by the wind, held down by the heat.

Claire turned to the obituaries and read aloud while Eugenia sat propped up against her pillows, her address book open.

"Start with the *A*'s," Eugenia said, and Claire read in alphabetical order while Eugenia crossed out the names she recognized in the address book.

"Arnessen, Mauritz," Claire said while Eugenia ran her fingers along the names in her book as if she were playing Bingo. "Alzheimer's," Eugenia added, crossing the name out with her black Magic Marker.

"Butler, Eula."

"Butler." Eugenia repeated softly. "She was an oil-field woman from way back." Eugenia set the marker down and closed her eyes.

Claire knew Eugenia's oil-field women stories. Most of them went the same, telling about how the women weren't really bad women, just down on their luck. But one story Eugenia liked to tell bothered Claire because she couldn't be sure if it was real or not and because, unlike the other stories, typical stories of despair, this one was about a woman named Lita who almost got away.

At dusk, while the other women put on their lipstick and high heels, so the story went, Lita sewed a silver dollar dress. She told the other women that whoever wore this dress, whoever could walk bearing the weight of the dress, would be the woman who would save them all. *From what?* Some of the women giggled, holding their hands to their mouths, and Lita smiled and said *from ourselves.* But none of the other women could even lift the dress, unfinished as it was, let alone walk in it, and Lita continued to work on the dress unchallenged. Then one summer evening when the light lasted a little longer than usual, Lita put on the dress for the first time. The silver dollars shone like a million little mirrors and they caught and cast the last light of day. The men in the fields ending their shifts whooped and whistled when they saw her shining in her dress, like the Phoenix before it burned out, but Lita didn't hear them. She thought only of the dress, her eyes set on the oil fields and beyond to the widening sky, her feet lifting, stepping evenly through the dust. And then she stumbled. Maybe she caught her feet in the dress or maybe the land just opened under her. At any rate, the dress was so heavy that she couldn't right herself and she lay there in the dust, unable to move.

"Then what?" Claire had asked Eugenia, the first time she'd told the story.

"Nothing. That's it."

"She shouldn't have been there, then. Or she shouldn't have sewn that dress." Claire hated untidy stories. "That's a stupid story."

〜

When Claire read the obituaries to her grandmother, she was struck with the sparse descriptions, impressed by the brevity with which each person could be dispatched in print. But she didn't mind reading them, she explained to Ray, her sometime boyfriend, because of all the newspaper reports and columns, she thought the obituaries were the most accurate.

"If you could write your own obituary, what would you say?" Claire asked Ray one evening as she folded his boxer shorts just the way he liked: two folds, one in half and then half again. Ray sat in front of her computer, typing, and Claire stacked his boxers on top of the printer.

Ray looked up, wrinkled his nose, and adjusted his glasses. "I don't know. I don't like negativity. I'd prefer to imagine what I'd say if I won the Nobel Prize or the Kentucky Derby or something." Ray turned back to the keyboard.

Claire nodded. Sometimes she forgot that Ray was a confirmed optimist, that he actually made Eagle Scout in high school, and that he dreamed of being a motivational speaker, of delivering that one message that would unlock everyone's potential. He belonged to the Toastmasters club and helped lead a Boy Scout troop and even now was probably typing a cheery pump-up speech for his Scouts. Sometimes Claire forgot how good Ray really was, how with him, being positive wasn't an act—he really believed all that stuff he told those boys. But sometimes being positive was really a drag. *No,* she corrected herself, *sometimes Ray was really a drag.*

"Lighten up, Ray," Claire said, dropping a pair of boxers on the keyboard. "It was a hypothermic question."

"Hypothetical."

"Yeah, whatever." Claire sat on her futon and studied the back of Ray's head. What people lost sight of these days, she thought, was how to appreciate death. She enjoyed the rituals of death because she cultivated a studied appreciation of it. She understood the great time and care it took a florist to arrange a display (an hour), how long it took a backhoe to dig out a grave (about thirty to forty minutes), how heavy the average casket was (between three and four hundred pounds), and how a church sanctuary amplified every sound, casting to each shuffle of the feet or cough a somber tone so that sound itself had weight. She wondered, too, if other people saw what she saw when she looked at cemeteries. Rows of tombstones, rows like teeth rolling true to the shape of the land and beautiful because each tombstone was a promise that these people wouldn't be forgotten. Sometimes she even imagined what it must feel like inside the coffin, being lowered slowly into the grave. She imagined it being like sinking in thick mud or shallow water and how she would fill out all the space of the coffin, feel the panels touching, pressing the sides of her arms and legs, and how the fit would be reassuring, comforting to her like a good pair of shoes.

Every now and then Claire wondered why Ray was even with her. Watching him sleep beside her, his chest falling and rising, she wondered what he saw in her. She didn't turn heads; guys didn't try to catch her eye in the bars, not even at 2 A.M. when loneliness and desperation drove people to settle. She suspected that she was Ray's pet project, but that at some point he realized she might be unsalvageable and was just sticking it out because Scouts don't quit. Claire leaned over to her nightstand and opened the lid of her music box. A tinny version of "Greensleeves" played while a tiny magnetic ice skater looped a figure eight. Ray stirred and snored softly. Claire shut the music box and remembered how as a girl she loved watching the ice skaters on TV. She watched the Olympics and crossed her fingers for every skater and held her breath before each of their big jumps. She begged Eugenia for ice-skating lessons or a leotard, she didn't care which, because she couldn't get the image of those skaters out of her mind. The idea that something, anything, much less a skater, could turn and turn, whirl and whirl in a perfect circle, endlessly if you just kept the lid up long enough, the blade straight enough, amazed her, and she could not help wondering if she could twirl like that.

"What are you afraid of?" Ray asked one night. They had gone out for dinner and were walking across the gravel lot back to Ray's truck. He liked to ask people questions like *If you won the two-million-dollar jackpot, what would you do with the money?* Or, *If you could be any animal, what would you be?* Most of the time, she figured people played along, gave him the aim-high response he was looking for, and she wondered how he would handle a straight answer. She sensed, too, that sometimes these questions were his way of picking a fight with her.

"Ask me a different question."

"If you could do or be anything, what would you do?" Ray asked without missing a beat.

I want to do something that matters, just one thing, Claire wanted to say. She bit her lip. "I want to get away from here." She kicked at the gravel and sent a rock skipping over the asphalt. "Have you ever noticed how nobody ever seems to leave Midland? It's like we've all fallen into one of those sinkholes." She kicked with the tip of her shoe again, then looked at the sky. Eugenia had told her that in Texas the sky not only filled up all the spaces but seemed to be growing. And she couldn't argue: just a few years ago a parking lot in Odessa caved in and disappeared. Then there was the big patch of clover beyond the abandoned drive-in theater. There one day, gone the next. The land here literally gives way and the sky just gets bigger. People could blame it on poor drilling practices, but Claire knew better.

Ray opened the driver's side of his truck and climbed in. "You could go anywhere you wanted to, if you really wanted to." He slid over and unlocked her door.

Claire scanned the expanse of open sky. The close heat hazed the sky, muted the blue, and pressed on her chest. She stooped and ran her hands over the gravel, letting her fingers feel for a smooth rock.

"No, I couldn't." She stood and threw a sidewinder and watched the rock sail over the hard-packed dirt. "I'm not like you."

Every morning Claire drove to Eugenia's and helped her with her morning routine: breakfast and medication at seven followed by a bath and shampoo if Eugenia was up to it, obituaries by nine, and then TV until lunch. After lunch, Claire drained the shunt protruding from Eugenia's stomach, helped her to the bathroom, and gave her another round of meds. Eugenia liked to watch the game shows and mysteries. She liked playing along with *The Price Is Right, Family Feud,* and *Wheel of Fortune* because, she told Claire, it was a sure way to keep the mind active and Alzheimer's at bay. But she always watched TV with the volume cranked up. Claire supposed it had more to do with drowning out the sound of the drive-through speaker of the Jack-in-the-Box next door than with hearing problems. On this morning Eugenia finished the obituaries ahead of schedule and was watching a taped episode of *Wheel of Fortune.*

"Does it hurt?" Claire asked.

"A little," Eugenia said, bending her toes to keep the circulation flowing. "Your mother always had beautiful feet." Eugenia pointed her toes.

Claire never knew what to say when Eugenia brought up the subject of her daughter. Claire is not an expert on her mother—in fact, barely knew her, and suspects that no one really knew her.

"Solve, you idiot, solve!" Eugenia screamed at the television. The Wheel of Fortune clacked as the contestant gave it another spin. "For the love of God!" Eugenia wadded up her napkin and threw it at the screen. "Move it, Vanna, move it!" Eugenia looked at Claire. "She doesn't even turn the letters around anymore. She just pushes a button and the box lights up." Claire knew that Eugenia had a decade-long crush on Pat Sajak and had hated Vanna for nearly as long. She couldn't see having the hots for Sajak, but she understood being jealous of Vanna, who seemed a little too perfect, even for TV.

"How much do you think those two Fruit Loops make anyway?" Eugenia turned to Claire.

"Oh, I don't know. Enough. More than me."

Eugenia turned up the volume. Claire knew that Eugenia resented the intrusion of reality.

"You reap what you sow."

"No you don't." Claire looked through the window to the fast-food parking lot. The wind carried the garbled sound of the drive-through girl's voice.

"You should have gone to college. Or married. You wouldn't be so strapped now."

"I'm not poor. I got a credit card." Claire studied the parking lot. She squinted, then rubbed her eyes. For a second she thought she had seen a woman wearing one of the sparkly sequined dresses and ice skates out in the dirt beyond the lot.

"Buy a vowel, dummy!" Eugenia yelled at the TV, then to Claire, "I swear to God, I don't know where they find these people."

⌣

The Mobile Pegasus is the most requested design and Claire wonders sometimes if she is not alone in her entrapment, if others don't see the ice-skater following them, too, don't see her whirling like a dervish out in the dirt. Everywhere she looks now she sees the ice dancer—on parking lots, on movie screens, in the haze of midday heat—and she wishes she could break free, like the Pegasus, just fly right up and out of there. The trick with the Pegasus is making sure the places where the wings join the body are carved high enough up on the horse's back. Otherwise, one wrong cut with the knife, one casual bump from a guest who's had one too many, and the weight of the ice would be enough to break off the wing.

Lately, the mermaid's been giving her the most trouble, though. Getting that glacial smile just right, the even split of the fins and the scales that start at the dip just below the navel. She had to carve the scales perfectly because, she noticed, that was the place where everyone looked first, the place where the fish becomes woman. And she knows, too, if she could only stop and admit it to herself, she is trying to sculpt herself there in the ice, each day a new her, a better her; each fish, each mermaid, swan, was really her, caught there, frozen, holding a perfect and unspoiled pose.

In the catering circles she knew people made jokes about her. They called her Dizzy-on-Ice, or more generously, the Ice Princess. Claire had been the first to use blocks of salt water for her sculptures. Salt water freezes two degrees colder than freshwater and she found that by using it she could maintain the integrity of her sculptures longer. And here in Midland, where everything was dust, wind, and sky, she liked this cold, and these sculptures with their ozone-like smell of salt and Freon seemed to her the only beautiful thing. In Eugenia's oversize freezer, Claire was keeping the only post-convention Pegasus whose wings had not broken, because, she figured, with the thermostat set low enough, it would never lose its shape, would never fade or melt like so many other things she'd seen sink into the mud or just dry up and blow away. Only ice held any real possibilities and with the right tools, an endless array for repairs. Still, she couldn't help noticing that sometimes the cooks or the part-time help that Jeannette hired for weekends would drift away from her when she approached to make small talk or ask for some help with the ice.

She tried not to let it bother her. She would play and replay Ray's little speeches, little reminders about negative feedback and how since it took eleven compliments to undo one insult, she should keep telling herself that she was an expert, no, *the* expert in ice. Claire would close her eyes and hear that internal tape recorder playing and replaying Ray's voice. She would try to quell that sound so she wouldn't screw up the drink orders, but the volume on the tape recorder would keep inching louder and louder, gaining a sort of momentum until his was the only voice she could hear. "You're a winner!" she would hear Ray shouting and see him giving her two thumbs-up as she handed over every Mai Tai for a Margarita and Johnny Walker for Jim Beam.

❧

"We should go into business together," Jeannette said to her the night before the Mobile convention. They had finished all the prep work: set up tables, ironed and put out the linens, and all the miniature quiche were cooling on the racks. Claire mixed a batch of Margaritas and poured them each a glass. "Your sculptures kick butt," Jeannette said, pushing a basket of pretzels toward Claire. "We could brush up on your drink repertoire and let you handle the bar."

Claire blushed and cleared her throat. No one, not even motivational Ray, had ever paid her a compliment like this, taken her seriously like this.

"I'm just not sure I'll be around here much longer." Claire jiggled her drink, listened to the ice cubes tinkling, and imagined herself riding the back of an ice Pegasus, flying over the ribbons of highway that cut the Panhandle. Somehow, though, she knew it would never work. She could just see it now: the horse's wings would crack or something, and she could see herself leaning over her broken-down, melting horse, waiting on Boy Scout Ray to save her. "Yeah, I was thinking about heading north. Alaska, maybe. I want to see those blue ice fields."

Through the smoke of her cigarette, Jeannette looked at Claire as if she wasn't sure she'd just heard a funny joke or not. "C'mon. You know the golden rule. Nobody leaves Midland. At least not alive." Jeannette poked Claire in the ribs.

Later that night Claire lay awake and listened to the wind and the regular patterns of creaks from her roof, and wondered what it was that held her fast. She looked at Ray sleeping beside her. He wasn't that great, she thought. But try as she might, she couldn't imagine dumping him. She knew it would be the other way around. She could hear it now: "I can't live like this, here, with you. You're keeping me from my potential," he would say and inside her head, as Ray sleeps, she mentally packed and unpacked Ray's suitcases for him. His basketball and gym shoes won't cooperate. They don't fit, never did seem to fit anywhere in her tiny apartment. She closed her eyes and imagined Clark Gable holding Vivien Leigh. "Frankly, my dear, I don't give a damn," Claire can see Ray saying, and she watches as Gable/Ray slides his arms out from under Leigh/Claire and drops her flat on her ass.

She heard the dogs barking in the distance across the flat sink of dirt that led to the neighbor's property and imagined flying down the highway again on the back of a giant winged horse. But she suspects that things are the same all over, that she might feel the same no matter where she went, and in that case, she wonders, why bother going? The same stars shine at night, no matter where you are, and it is this tiny thought that gives her the most comfort because she could imagine these stars, same as ever, quietly turning in their beds.

~~~~

"Mobile functions are a bitch," Jeannette said to Claire the next day at work. Claire had finished setting the straight pins in a large block of ice and was about to make the first cuts with the Dremel. "I don't know why I do conventions anyway." Jeannette stabbed an ashtray with her cigarette and exhaled through her nose.

"Yeah," Claire nodded. "Funerals are better," she said and bent over the sculpture. With her apron and gloves on and the Dremel humming in her hand, she liked to imagine that she was some kind of doctor, a brain surgeon even, cutting through the tough crust of bone to save someone's life, cutting down the exterior so that the real person could emerge, whole and pure.

Claire took a step back and surveyed the sculpture. So far she wasn't having the usual troubles with the split or the scales. In fact, she was ahead of schedule and feeling a little risky. That's when she thought of the oil field woman and the silver dollar dress. Claire knitted her eyebrows. It wouldn't take much. Leave the crown on the head and leave the split fins, but carve faint lines to suggest a dress, a dress split high up one side, high enough to show she's a mermaid, high enough to show where the scales become skin, and high enough so that if this fish-woman could walk, she'd clear that oil field. She'd keep the scales oblong at the bottom of the fin, but start rounding them out near the thighs until they became like coins at the navel.

Claire felt her heart beating in her chest. She had no idea why she was so excited about this sculpture. Maybe because she was carving an ending to Eugenia's story that she liked a little better and she wondered if she might be able to squeeze this ice sculpture into Eugenia's freezer. On impulse Claire decided to go all out. *What the hell,* she thought as she unspooled the tiny indoor-outdoor lights they kept behind the bar. She wound the lights around the points of the crown and plugged in the strand as the first guest drifted into the convention room.

Claire took her place behind the bar and sipped on some soda water. It had been a bad morning for Eugenia: two of her friends had died over the weekend and every name in the address book was now crossed out.

"That's that," Eugenia said, dropping the address book into the small trash basket beside her bed.

"I'll bring you back something to cheer you up," Claire had promised after they watched the game shows and Eugenia had taken her round of meds.

"Maybe some hotter-than-hell baby backribs," Claire said, grabbing her keys. But Eugenia had already cranked the volume up and was eyeing Vanna with suspicion.

"Slut," she yelled at the TV, throwing the *TV Guide* at the screen.

Claire reached under the bar and pulled out a bottle of gin. She was pouring a shot into her soda water when she caught the glint of ice blades. Claire stood on her toes and craned her neck. That's when she saw them, the three high school girls standing next to her sculpture, gossiping and laughing and striking poses. Claire lined up wineglasses along the edge of the bar. Juvie Three, she mentally named them and noticed how the other guests, her male coworkers in particular, watched them. They were little, lithe, tiny slips of nothing, probably ice-skaters, all three of them. They even looked like that little gold-medalist Tara Lipinski from Sugarland.

Just then, two of the girls flicked their cigarettes into the tub of ice sitting at the base of the oil field woman while the third girl extinguished hers in the navel. Claire felt herself heating up and she clenched and unclenched her jaw. The girls stood sipping champagne camouflaged in Styrofoam cups, which Claire knew one of the guys on staff had given them. Claire thought about what might happen if no one was looking, what she might do to those girls if she was sure no one was looking. She wondered how it would feel to give each of them a whack on the back of the knees. She picked up an ice scoop from behind the bar and headed for her sculpture.

"Move it out," Claire growled, waving the ice scoop. "And grab those butts."

The girls looked at each other for a few seconds and then giggled. Claire felt her face heating up, but before she could think of anything to say, the girls migrated to the cheese and meat table. Claire looked at the stubs. What would have happened if the woman in the silver dollar dress had made it out of the fields? What would have happened next? She wanted to know. It was just a story, some stupid Texas flatland fairy tale, but would she or anyone else any place else be different somehow if just one story had a happy ending?

"Stupid, stupid, stupid," Claire muttered, once for each stub she picked up and dropped in the ice scoop. The lights in the crown had slid a little and she reached over to adjust them. As she did, she noticed that some of the ice at the base had melted and a puddle of water had collected under the cart. That's when she felt it: a sudden jolt to her entire body. Then darkness broken by a tiny pinhole of light.

"Somebody call 911!" Claire heard Jeannette screaming. She opened her eyes, saw Jeannette hovering and the oil field woman broken to bits.

Claire focused her eyes on the tiny cracks in the ceiling. "No." She shook her head weakly. "Don't call 911. I'm OK." Claire reached for Jeannette's arm and pulled herself off the floor.

"You have to go to the hospital. Lord, Claire, you smell like a piece of burnt toast."

"No ambulances. Just drive me in."

~~~

"What was it like?" Jeannette asked later, after Claire had been released and they were driving back to Claire's Chevette.

Claire closed her eyes and felt the cold metallic door of Jeannette's Trans Am against her palm. "I could taste my fillings in the back of my mouth." Claire rubbed her palm over the metal. "When they admitted me and wheeled me into the examination room . . ." Her voice caught in her throat and splintered to air. She coughed and swallowed. "I felt as if I were seeing myself wheeled down the lighted tunnel and it was a good feeling because for a split second I felt like I finally understood something." She wiped her palm on her thigh. "And then there was the music."

Jeannette ground out her cigarette and downshifted.

"Like heavenly music?"

"Naw. It was more like polka, I think."

They drove for a few minutes and Claire watched the sun caught in the legs of the oil derricks and noted how the oil refineries could slice the sun up, make the sun seem smaller than it was.

"You scared me today." Jeannette lit up again. "When you started to come to, you said something about saving the oil field woman."

Claire scanned the surface of Jeannette's dashboard, the dust, the ash, her collection of dashboard saints. "It's a stupid story. I'll tell you about it later." Claire ran her tongue over her teeth, checking her fillings, and thought of Eugenia's feet, swelling even now probably.

～～

"I'm hot," Eugenia said when Claire let herself in. Eugenia fanned herself with the *TV Guide* and cursed at the remote control. Claire saw tiny beads of perspiration lining Eugenia's upper lip and the top of her nose.

Claire dropped her keys on top of the TV set with a loud clank, then ran her palm over Eugenia's forehead and nodded. "Feels like fever." She had read somewhere that cancer was a heat-producing chemical reaction in the body, and she wondered if that was why, despite the two fans that were always trained on her, Eugenia was always so hot.

The pan of ice water Claire had left for Eugenia's feet had gone tepid.

"Don't move," she whispered and picked up the pan. She went to the kitchen and stood at the sink, filling the oven pan, when she had an idea. She turned off the tap.

"What are you doing?" Eugenia called.

"Nothing." Claire ran down the flight of stairs to the basement freezer and pushed open the lid. There it was: her only perfectly preserved Pegasus. She remembered how the wings and feathers had taken over three hours. Claire propped open the freezer lid and gently lifted the Pegasus up and out and carried it to the sink. She placed it in the roasting pan and dumped ice cubes and salt around the base.

"It's beautiful," Eugenia gasped when Claire brought the sculpture in and set it at her feet. "Did you do this one for the Mobile convention?"

"No. I've been saving it awhile." Claire put towels all around the pan and then started in on Eugenia's feet, rubbing her toes, then moving up and massaging the arches in circles. "There's no point in keeping it in the freezer forever," Claire said, working Eugenia's ankles with her thumb. "This way, we can watch it go together."

"It seems kind of a shame," Eugenia said, studying the careful split in the underside of the hooves and the wide arc of wings.

"No it's not." Claire pulled out nail clippers and cut Eugenia's toenails. She set Eugenia's feet at either side of the sculpture and began painting her toenails. "How do you feel?" Claire looked up and saw Eugenia's mouth slack, her eyes closed. The sculpture was beginning to list a little. Claire flicked the television off. She pulled back the curtain and saw overhead the stars like little chips of ice carrying their own light.

～

That night when she closes her eyes Claire imagines she is in Greenland, at magnetic North where the forces holding her still are at their strongest, pulling her inward with such strength, such ferocity, all she can do is surrender with her arms akimbo, spinning on the blades of her skates, twirling in a circle that closes tighter and tighter. She sees the ice dancer in the distance and gives her the finger, then pulls her arms in close until the whole world is spinning, is one big blur. She thinks, then, that wanting something, just one thing, might be enough to keep the lid up, the blade straight and turning.

How

the

Dead

Live

The Dead Man walks slowly up and down the staircase of his daughter's house. His tread is soundless and he is glad the ordinary creaks of the fifth and seventh steps do not report his presence for he does not wish to disturb his daughter. He walks the stairs hoping for a sliver in his foot, something to startle his awareness. He can't quite remember what his feet used to feel like, should feel like, but now they are heavy and it is with effort that he picks them up and slides them onto the steps.

Another problem: he is always dropping and losing his glasses on the staircase where his son-in-law, Neil, steps on them. The Dead Man depends upon Karen, his daughter, to find his glasses and to unbend the frames. Later, he'll discover his glasses atop the refrigerator, wiped so clean he believes he can see inside her head and read her thoughts.

At night his daughter's and son-in-law's dreams tumble like lint to the low point of their sloping room, under the door's sweep to the top of the stairs where the Dead Man sits and cards Karen's dreams from Neil's. Her dreams are of artichokes and loam, the sad sound of the geese honking, and the smell of clay. Neil's dreams reek of leather, the exhaust of crotch-rocket street bikes and of a woman named Marla. The Dead Man marvels at the colorless quality of Neil's dreams that unspool in shades of gray. The Dead Man calmly sorts their dreams and imagines he is playing a round of poker with the stars, while beside him at the top of the stairs Shura, his daughter's Siberian Husky, snores softly. Looking at the dog, he thinks he would trade everything he has ever had or known for a single night's sleep.

<hr/>

Only Shura senses his presence. Shura follows him to the swing on the back porch where the Dead Man measures slow arcs through the nights, which seem to him to be getting longer and longer. On the porch Shura sleeps at the Dead Man's feet and chases birds in his dreams, running the crows off into a mud-fish sky. The Dead Man has never envied a dog so much as now. He envies all the night animals that curl up like the ends of paper, fold up in darkness and go to sleep in the quiet. He considers the cease-less movement of the sea, wonders if, like him, the sea is jealous and, given a last wish, would want to hold still within its tremu-lous boundaries and slumber.

Some nights, the Dead Man studies the moon and thinks in the calm of darkness is where he would want to sleep, if he *could* sleep. But thinking this way wears on him and he licks his finger and holds it out, testing the pitch of the earth's trembling. In those moments he wonders if there are other walking, breathing dead summoned from trampled memory. He might like to get together a game of poker, bet the pale dreams of his son-in-law against the dreams of someone else's in-law.

The Dead Man counts his shallow breaths and phlegmless

coughs as he swings and smokes Neil's cigarettes, enjoying those cigarettes even more, knowing that dead men shouldn't be able to smoke. A collection of his daughter's memories, the Dead Man is held together by his faulty suspenders and his dentist's bridgework. He knows that mourning can afford a clarity of vision. He suspects that each day in the hour before dawn when most people are dreaming his daughter is fishing through memories of him, panning for the different parts. A camping trip in Minnesota reveals his hands, cracked by wind and water. A Christmas long past yields the handkerchief she gave him, now folded and refolded so many times it is an exercise in geometry. Her fifth birthday brings back the cleft in his chin, and the best, a prewar memory, two legs— count them: one, two. The Dead Man rubs his hands along the muscles in his thighs, marvels at the wonder of them, aware that he had never done this in life.

This piecemeal restoration amazes him for what she remembers and how she remembers, and even more important, what she forgets. Parts of him are missing, little lapses between the bones. His daughter's memory, though good, has skipped over some essential ingredients like water and blood and the dark bodies of his internal organs. He would like to lay his hand on the darkness inside himself, to touch it, to name it, for in between his ribs are endless openings, each rib another vaguely phrased question. Sometimes when the wind picks up, the Dead Man thinks that if he could stretch his arms out wide enough he could be borne by the wind, his hollow bones singing like lyres.

The Dead Man wonders how long his daughter will keep him in her house. He wonders what will happen when she lets go. Will he be caught and carried away by the wind as a balloon accidentally released by a child? Will he be catapulted to the moon? Will he go to hell? Is he in it already? These thoughts tire the Dead Man, reminding him that even in death there is desire and the state of being wearied by desire. He wishes she could hear him, held fast in her house. He wishes he could grab her by the shoulders and give her a hard shake. "Let me go," he'd demand. "Please," he'd say, a word he'd used sparingly all his life. After all, he had his reasons for diving headlong from the ninth floor of the Providence Center Parking Garage and he wishes his daughter could understand this.

For now, the Dead Man spends his days in his daughter's front yard where Neil has collected battered and broken-down VW bugs and buses. He runs his hands lovingly over their rusting shells and bent frames. He is walking in a graveyard of used cars and feels he is on holy ground, and wishes, once again, that he could feel his feet.

The Dead Man had lost a lot of things in life: his hair, his temper, his patience, and a few teeth. In death the catalogue continues: the sense of taste, his voice, and these losses never fail to surprise him; he never figured these sensations could simply vanish like the last of a pen's ink. He can't recall how things should feel against the skin, under the fingers. He can't discern changes in temperature (though when Karen catches Neil in an outrageous lie, he can still hear the mercury drop in her voice). He knows that soon all he'll be left with is weight, with knowing what is light and what is heavy.

Hungry to touch and be touched, a kiss and a stinging slap are one and the same to the Dead Man, who treasures both. Unable to shrug himself free of itches, the Dead Man thinks the flies have returned. He looks at the ants and sees only teeth, at the grass, which yields only blades.

The Dead Man can smell sugar going to grain long before it does. He can smell food going bad in the refrigerator days before it spoils. Owing to the powers of his nose, the Dead Man thinks he is becoming a dog. He is also an expert on shit. In the droppings left like miniature core samples over the yard by the wintering geese, he detects the presence of clover and other grasses. In his son-in-law's shit, which looks and smells like hard-boiled eggs going bad, he smells red meat and knows Neil has been eating meals without his daughter, who does not cook red meat. The Dead Man can smell his son-in-law's infidelities and he hopes Neil is nursing a small colon cancer.

The Dead Man is conscious of his daughter's pregnancy before she is. Her skin smells differently, more metallic, and he feels a kick at the place where his heart used to be, an echo. The Dead Man is also aware that his daughter is unhappy and that her first thought upon discovering her pregnancy will be one of hope. She will pray that a child is just the thing that is missing in her marriage, the thing to make a quick mend. But in his newly acquired prescience and the amazing faculties of his nose, the Dead Man is sure that just the opposite will be true, that Neil is on his way out the door, and that this child, as beautiful as he knows it will be, will only hasten Neil's departure.

The Dead Man waits at the top of the stairs. In the bathroom, his daughter holds a plastic wand in her urine stream. The Dead Man knows it's a boy and wishes he could tell her so, and that it won't matter: her husband will leave anyway, but, like having a baby, it will be a good thing. Still, he is sorry that she will soon learn that being left is its own kind of deadness.

He counts the seconds along with his daughter, waiting for the pink stripes to emerge on the test strip. When the lines appear, Karen opens the bathroom and hunts out Neil, her mouth flattened into a tight grimace and her eyes watering. It is an old and familiar look, one the Dead Man recognizes instantly: Karen is both happy and sad at the same time and will check her elation and fear to match Neil's, will wait on him to decide what will win out, smiles or tears.

Confronted with the litmus strip, Neil is speechless. The Dead Man bites his bottom lip hard enough to have drawn blood had he been alive.

"It's OK, Hon." Neil breathes and blinks. "It's better than OK. It's wonderful." Neil holds Karen's hands in his as if they were two cold, small fish. The nervous blinking gives Neil away. Blink. Blink, blink, blink. The Dead Man hears each damn blink.

～～～

But for the wind shouldering through him, rattling his bones, nothing would make sense. The Dead Man especially likes the rush of wind sweeping up at nightfall. It reminds him of the bending elephant grass from his days on Hill 881 South in Khe Sanh, of being one of the few who survived (minus a leg). The wind reminds him of breathing, tells him that though he is dead, somehow through the regenerative powers of will, or perhaps loneliness, he is still alive. In the wind, the Dead Man thinks he can hear the voices of all those he once loved: his platoon commander Jerry Shiporsky—St. Jerry of the Overbite—picked off while crapping in a latrine. He remembers his wife, Ray Lynn, who left him because she was tired, she said, of nursing a man who couldn't heal. In the wind held aloft by the cold currents of nighttime blasts, the Dead Man hears them calling him, urging him, *Jump*, they say, and the sound filling his ears is beautiful music.

Karen spends most of her time eating and sleeping and dashing to the bathroom where it is a fifty-fifty guessing game: Will she empty her bladder or her stomach? Today it's her stomach, and when she emerges from the bathroom to sit on the edge of her bed the Dead Man considers mopping her brow with his over-folded handkerchief. He shuffles toward her, but stops when he sees her fingering an old picture of him just returned home from the war. He always hated that picture of himself. In it his eyes are hollow, like the sound of laughter in an empty room. In this moment, he feels remorse and almost wishes he hadn't jumped. He remembers how carefully he propped his crutches up against the cement ledge. But if he were honest with himself (and now it's hard not to be anything else) he feels remorse in fractions, two parts regret to one part relief. And he is sorry for this. He knows Karen is angry. But thankfully, not punitive. After all, she's recalled the prewar image of him and lucky dog, he's got both his legs back now. But then the Dead Man sees a strange look settling over Karen's face and she rips the photo, violently and into tiny pieces. Watching this stops him cold, like the shock of ice water, and he has no idea what to do next.

When he was alive, he contemplated all the ways a man might die. Now that he is dead, the Dead Man watches his son-in-law and counts the ways a man might live. He finds Neil contemptible, hates him, in fact, and has enough hate in his empty chest for three men. He despises Neil's stories and his nervous blinks. When Neil tells Karen a lie, the Dead Man can see it in Neil's eyes, which go blinkity, blink, blink.

Neil is a thirty-year younger version of the Dead Man and this revelation comes as a kick in the hollows of the Dead Man's chest.

The discovery should make him more sympathetic toward Neil, but it doesn't. He hates Neil more for it, for what he is doing and will do to Karen. The Dead Man notes the gathering lines around his daughter's mouth and eyes. As he studies her, his remorse solidifies into a single hardened image, the face of his wife. And the Dead Man puts a finger on a true sorrow from his younger years, when, like Neil, he was full of shit.

If he concentrates, the Dead Man can recall the fatal flaws of his personality that haunted him in life. He carries his shame like buttons on the gig line of a shirt. He was an ass, he thinks, in spite of his pain meds. He recalls dead-end arguments with Ray Lynn, arguments she never could have won, for his point in arguing was not to be right or to prove anything, but to deliver sharp, angry words that felt good to shout and that he would forget having said before nightfall.

His son-in-law is careless with his daughter's heart: he no longer opens doors for her, and one evening, when Karen trips over Neil's feet, he does not try to catch her. Seeing this hurts the Dead Man in the hollowed cavity of his chest where his heart was. He considers the pain in his empty chest, astonished at the power the living have over the dead. He thinks he would like to stay here a while longer to take care of his daughter. On the other hand, he notes that all his feeble parlor tricks—all his attempts to spur his daughter to a just anger so that she will say the words that will make Neil go—have failed.

Each night after he is done sorting, the Dead Man places the dusty lumps of Neil's nighttime dreams next to his daughter's hairbrush, hoping she will detect what he can: the red strands of Marla's hair, the smell of gasoline and polished chrome, the scent of quick and easy lies and sure departures. But each morning Karen sweeps the tufts into her palm, flushes them down the toilet, scolds Shura for shedding so much, and walks to the staircase where she will discover again, with renewed amazement, the Dead Man's bent glasses.

Time haunts the Dead Man. He knows that since it takes at least nine months to bring in a life, it will take about nine months for his daughter to finish mourning his. If he has calibrated the clocks correctly, he should go about the same time the baby is born. With only so much space for each person in another's sphere of love and attention, the Dead Man takes delight in knowing that his daughter, despite her unswerving nostalgia, will have to slowly release him.

To help him count the wait, the Dead Man collects clocks, watches, egg timers, bedside alarms—even a sorry metronome belonging to Ray Lynn—depending upon those tiny clicks and ticks to sing out the thousands of seconds of every day. They become ridiculous, melodramatic in their reverberations, measuring Saturdays, which follow Wednesdays and Thursdays and Fridays, each of which are equal to their value. He has never been good with time, he thinks, each tick another small suffering. He remembers the VA hospital, the absence of clocks, but time heavy in the fold of the curtains, drawn and undrawn. The clanking of the food cart, which wasn't a bell, but might just as well have been. The throb of each wound, carrying its own separate heartbeat, and Ray Lynn holding his hand counting aloud: *One, two, three.* In spite of all manner of measuring, he is beginning to think that time occupies only as much space as is felt in the bones. He notes, with an unerring sense that defies those ticking household clocks, how a short time, these months of climbing his daughter's stairs, bear stretch marks lengthening to years, to decades of memories.

Now the Dead Man marks time by the wags of Shura's tail, Neil's snoring, and the buzz of a lawnmower trimming grass in an unseen yard beyond the hedge. He thinks about math, negative numbers in particular, and the infinite march of numbers in two directions at once. The similarities between integers and time is not lost on the Dead Man, who noted just the other day that his good watch was running backward.

The days are lengthening, a ribbon of light stretching a little longer through the afternoon. The Dead Man can't wait for the dark, thinks it is in the cool of the dark when a numbered beauty marks the wind that he can feel thrumming in his bones. As the sky darkens, exposing tiny stars, distant toothaches every last one of them, he thinks again of playing poker, and of the transparent dreams—both his and Neil's—he'd gladly gamble away. Next door, the old ladies are arguing with a game show host, and the sound of friction grates the air, in the clacking of the geese's bills, in the bristled movement of the laurel hedge. With envy he watches the geese beat at the air and take labored flight over the hedge, their hollow bones catching the wind while his bones bear years of weight, a lifetime of gravity.

It's February now, the month of iron, and he feels his daughter's hold on him slipping. Early one evening Karen goes into labor. With each contraction, a little more of the Dead Man fades, as if a fine dust of the photographer's silver has settled over him. As her labor progresses, the empty spaces inside his chest and between his bones expand. By the time Neil stuffs an old gray travel bag with Karen's toiletries, the Dead Man can no longer see his shoes. He imagines he is upping the ante with the constellations. The two old men huddled in the sky have two-of-a-kind and a full house. But the Dead Man doesn't hesitate. He'll bet Neil and meat-eating Marla will marry before the year is out, that Karen will name her boy after her father.

Six hours after Neil and Karen leave for the hospital, a thin rain taps against the rusting hulks of the VW frames in the yard. The Dead Man has never felt so good, but it is a fragile feeling. With each passing minute he feels weaker and makes his way to the back porch. He is disappearing bits at a time, particle by particle, memory by memory. He had heard that 30 percent of ordinary house dust was actually dead skin cells. Now he knows this is true and he can feel himself flaking to dust. And he was right about light and heavy, too—he has no sensation of either. With care he wipes his glasses to better study the changing boundaries of his body.

He can't hear the clocks anymore. The plucks of the rain sound the same to him now as the ticks of Neil's blinks. The geese are still bickering in the backyard, fighting over the sweet spots to roost. They sound like the neighbor ladies quarreling and at first the Dead Man can't tell—is it the geese or the old women he hears? The noise wears him out and suddenly he is tired, as tired as an ocean, and thinks if he could drift to sleep, his sleep would fill a cosmos.

The wind picks up and pins the neighbor ladies' trash against the laurel hedge. The Dead Man lifts what is left of his arms and imagines that wind lifting him into a similar, weightless flight. He feels himself unraveling, one rib at a time, and he has never been so happy to be forgotten. He is glad, too, that Karen is not here, for he would have felt compelled to say goodbye, and he couldn't imagine a task any harder. So many things the Dead Man would have wanted to tell his daughter. So many things he would clarify so that she would not have to know them the way he does. But he knows that even if he still had his voice, she would not hear it, as she has never heard it, preferring instead to own each ache for herself, each wound another scar.

The Dead Man tilts his head back and counts out his last seconds among the stars. *It's here,* he thinks. And with a quick and exquisite pain he pulls a short breath through his nose, feeling the last of his lungs go. He closes his eyes, giving himself over to the settling darkness within and the darkness without, happy at last, and happy that he can know it.

Unfinished
Business

It is a fact that as someone is remembering Ciri, someone else is just as diligently forgetting her. This much Ciri has gathered, having eavesdropped on almost every conversation anyone has had about her. She's dead, but she's not resting peacefully. Far from it. The part of her that was not her battered and blue body hovered at the precinct windows where Ciri could sit on the long bench heater and listen to Deputy Hornacek and Detective Daniel Hauer. For it is in listening and watching that the small clues are given, she wants to tell Rita, the weary dispatcher who doubles as Deputy Hornacek's assistant, typing his reports, filing others, taking messages.

In the pull of her shoulders, the downward sag of her mouth, Rita's not happy and not above hiding it. She's not as necessary as she'd like to be and Ciri would like to say, "Snap out of it," but lately she's short on goodwill. Rita's deliberate misplacing of her file bothers Ciri and from equal parts spite and boredom, Ciri has taken to stealing Rita's chewing gum. Still, there is not enough gum in the world to help her wear down the shapeless hours, and for the last day and a half she finds herself unable to stay away from the state forensic crime lab, the city police department, and Detective Daniel Hauer, who is working her case.

Ciri reaches into the top drawer of Rita's desk for some gum and makes her way back to the heater where Hauer taps a pencil on a pad of paper and stares at the traffic moving below. Rita sneezes when Ciri brushes past her and Hornacek lifts his nose as if picking up on a new scent.

"I could help you." Ciri nudges Detective Hauer's elbow so that his pencil skitters off the edge of the notepad. Detective Daniel Hauer is single and good-looking. Though Ciri was never a flirt, she has a newfound confidence now that she's dead.

"Mary and Joseph," Hauer says, leaning over to retrieve the pencil, which has rolled under the heater. Hornacek makes to put a quarter in a glass jar set out for the Boys and Girls Aid Society on a nearby file cabinet. Anyone who cursed had to put a quarter in the jar and so far Hauer was the leading contributor.

~~~

"What do we got so far?" Hauer flipped open his pocket-size pad as he stood at the threshold of Ciri's door. Two days earlier it had been Angie and Ciri's front door, and because she was so sure Angie would come to her senses, dump Dale, and move back in, Ciri hadn't bothered removing the piece of masking tape that read *A. and C. Nunez*. They'd decided it was safer to make it sound like they were married, like they might even have a whole apartment full of kids, so that no one would ever know theirs was an apartment occupied by two moderately good-looking single women, one in her late twenties, the other a tad older. Ciri's mother had offered to lend her Mr. Twenty Percent, the head-and-shoulders dummy she kept in the passenger seat of her car to scare away any would-be carjackers. But Ciri had declined, feeling safe enough as long as the locks worked and Angie lived with her.

"Not much. Nunez, Ciri. Thirty years old. The landlord says no husband or boyfriend, no kids, no pets. No witnesses." Hornacek pulled out his handkerchief and cleaned his right nostril, then his left, twisting the cloth inside the bulb of his nose. He refolded his handkerchief and opened the lid of his metal tackle box, revealing four tiers of photo film, pencils, powders, brushes of all sizes, tape, Superglue, and chalk. Ciri smiled at Hornacek's meticulous organization of tools, which reminded her of her own poppi who, with similar care, used to fret over his box of fishing tackle and lures.

Then Hornacek uncovered her body and began to examine her skin. Ciri can't watch, though she knows he is touching her with great care, her body like a fossil, a fragile piece of forensic evidence. Instead she turns and follows Hauer through the apartment as he snaps photo after photo. She cocks her head at an angle, imagining how Hauer must see her apartment through his lens: the stack of books on her kitchen counter, the dirty plate and dripping faucet, her mother-of-pearl rosary dangling from the corner of her bathroom mirror, that five-by-seven black and white photo, the only picture Ciri liked of herself. She experiences a strange rush of pleasure when she sees Detective Daniel Hauer stop and study the photo, then drop it along with her opened address book into a brown paper bag.

When someone arrives from the DA's office to remove Ciri's body, Hornacek pulls out his chalks and begins outlining the lay of Ciri's arms and legs. Ciri likes the fact that Hornacek is a little old-fashioned, chalking around her body as detectives do in movies. She wonders if he can read a story in how a body falls, whether a person was dead before the fall or dying as she fell. Ciri remembers a made-for-TV movie about a body found crumpled in the space between a refrigerator and a dishwasher. Later detectives discovered it had been a battered housewife who thought she could hide from her husband and was bludgeoned to death in her hiding place. Ciri wonders then what story her body tells: her chin pointing to the ceiling, her arms spread to her sides as if she were making an imaginary snow angel in the middle of her area rug.

When Hornacek straightens up and blows on his hands, Ciri sees the chalk outline of her body and is stopped cold. A diagram of a ghost, the spare outline is beautiful, and Hornacek is beautiful for having drawn it. It occurs to her as she watches Hornacek bend over the outline and wipe the chalk from his hands that he is saying a prayer. From the practiced stoop in his shoulders, a sure sign of sadness, she knows the prayer is not for her, but for someone like her. Ciri puts her hand on the swell of Hornacek's back. "Carla," she hears him whisper and she knows that when he looks at her outline he will think of his daughter Carla, and when Ciri's name is spoken he will mentally substitute Carla's name for hers. Ciri rests her head on Hornacek's shoulder and hears in his breathing the regret he carries, how looking at his chalk drawing makes him fear for Carla, who has not spoken to him in over five years. *Is she OK?* he is wondering even as Ciri's body is carried away. *What is she doing right now?*

Hauer watched Hornacek rubbing his hands together, watched how he dusted with powder, and he knew that processing a scene was not a chore. There was something holy—no, not holy, but sacred—about a crime scene where they brushed against the last traces of a life gone, the scene becoming all the more important for what it could tell. How, like a prophetic message, it might mean so much more later.

Hornacek, on all fours, his face mere centimeters from the middle of a dark green area rug, lowered his nose and inhaled deeply. Over the years Hauer has noticed that while some people point with their fingers, gesture with their thumbs, Hornacek points with his nose and never misses. "Cat. You can't argue with the smell of a cat." Hornacek pulled a carpet knife from his tackle box and cut a perfect square from the middle of the rug.

"I'll take it to the lab," Hauer said, dropping the square into a brown bag and ducking under the police tape at the front door. He knew Hornacek would be there for hours, scouring the floor in a slow radius, his nose leading the way. Hauer wanted to pull names and phone numbers from the dead girl's address book. He wondered, and then wondered why he wondered, if the dead girl had known a lot of men.

Hauer climbed into the squad car. "Ciri," he said, not noticing that Ciri had slipped in beside him and was checking her reflection in the mirror. "Ciri," he said again, slowly, as if trying out the name.

Always, always, she is snapped back by the sound of her name. This is what keeps her here, she thinks, all this unfinished business: her dripping faucet that Grievy, the landlord, promised to fix and never did; Angie's jade plant by the sink in need of watering; her mother waiting to receive her body. All that had fallen apart, all manner of things undone. *Entropy,* Angie would have said, was driving Ciri crazy. At nights during those long hours bulging with unfilled minutes, Ciri calmed herself by going to the beauty salon behind their apartment where she straightened Angie's, Dixie's, and Neela's work stations. At quitting time the women threw all the different colored and sized rods for the permanents together in a big tub and Ciri liked separating them into their respective piles: the tiny rods for the older women who wanted tight little curls, the medium-sized ones for those after the Botticelli look, and the big fat rollers for waves.

"Entropy is the natural order of things," Angie would remind Ciri as they watched the solutions, fixers and dyes, all shades of blonde, brunette and the fiery colors of red dye swirling down the drain in the middle of the parking lot behind the salon and in front of their kitchen window. "Everything pines for chaos. A dish wants to be broken, a violin string yearns to snap, paint longs to fade."

Ciri always rolled her eyes when Angie talked like this, imagined this was what Dale told Angie every time he broke up with her. Now Ciri thinks Angie may have been onto something as she notes how Hornacek has marked her favorite area rug with a geometric wound.

Ciri slides a little closer to Hauer, who cracks the window.

"I could help you," she whispers and he slaps his arm, as if swatting away a mosquito. "Daniel," she tries again, "Daniel," and this time he claps the side of his head with an open palm as if trying to force water out of his ear.

~

If it is a fact that all these things are true, then it is also a fact that so many others are not.

While she thinks she should have seen her attacker, ought to be able to recall something, she couldn't and can't. What she remembers: the shock registering as a gasp—her last one, in fact. This life wasn't endless. Ciri had neither feared nor embraced death. It was what happened to you when your body was tired of living. But now that death has embraced her, she does not know quite what to think. She has not in death achieved any new wisdom, any insight on how better to live, though this much she knows: a person should not die young, at an age when the body doesn't know anything else but living. And while she had thought that in death a person would be carried to a state beyond feeling, she is surprised to discover that this is not so as she feels things now she thought she wouldn't: an odd tingle every time she sees that five-by-seven picture propped up on Hauer's desk, her heart quickening at the sound of her name, sweat at the armpits, on the palms. There's a buzzing in her fingertips, too, in the beds of her fingernails, a thrum, and if it weren't for the fact that she knew she was thoroughly dead, she'd swear she was still alive.

Still, for all the media hype, ghosting has left her a little disappointed. She assumed she would be sensed as a chill, a change in pressure, or as the sound of sad moaning. A trick, a slight, she thinks, while the rabbit suffers in the hat. Instead only Rita, because of her allergies, and Hornacek, because of his amazing nose, seem to sense her.

"Is that you?" Rita narrows her eyes at Hauer, just returning from Ciri's apartment. Ciri sniffs in the direction of her armpits and brings her wrists to her nose.

"What?" Hauer is studying Ciri's picture and doesn't even look at Rita.

"That smell. God, it's overpowering. What are you wearing?" Again, Ciri brings her hands to her face. She can't smell a thing, only the nonsmell of skin, which carries a scent she can't detect because it is her own smell.

"Nothing." Hauer flips open Ciri's address book.

"It's like Easter lilies or something." Rita's face bunches up and she sneezes three times before Hauer looks up.

"I love you," Ciri whispers, her lips close to Hauer's ear. Hauer's nose twitches a little and he gets up to crack a window. Ciri follows him, sliding one of Rita's quarters next to the glass jar. It thrills her that Hauer thinks about her, but she hopes she is more than a mystery in need of solving. She prays it's more than that, for no one has ever paid as much attention to her as Hauer is doing now and she likes the idea of Detective Hauer going to bed at night, unable to sleep, for thinking of her.

Only in the examiner's lab where the sharp smells of sterilizers assault her nose does Ciri hang back. For when she sees her own body before her, blue like the body of someone else, she cannot maintain the fantasy of living among the living. "I'm dead," she whispers in disbelief and touches the chin of her uncovered face in a moment of courage, noting the blue lips, the postmortem lividity, the bruising under the eyes where the blood has settled, and open wounds where she sustained blunt-force trauma. What a wonderful joke, she thinks, very funny, but laughing without sound is too much like crying and Ciri doesn't like to consider much the fact that she is dead. Nor does she like the look of the scalpels honed so sharp she thinks they could cleave the Ciri that is dead from the part of her that is not, and she stays away from the metal instruments, preferring instead to follow Virgil, the pathologist, around the room. When he stops and bends over Ciri's still body, his eyebrows knit together in a tight V, Ciri comes up behind him, peers around his shoulder. She can hear what he is thinking: *Why her?* A question she'd asked herself many times already. When he continues to stare, crossing his arms as if by concentrating he could get the answer out of her, Ciri shrugs half-heartedly. She'd rather smell his aftershave, a scent Angie would have approved of, and imagine him asking Angie out than consider what he has done and will do very shortly to her body.

A latent bruise on her neck has surfaced in the last hour, a thumbprint-shaped mark, and Virgil unrolls a large sheet of plastic. Ciri can guess what's next: he'll fume her body with Superglue to raise a print. She's seen this before on TV. But Ciri is not thinking about her bruises or those prints. She's thinking instead about Virgil and Angie, wondering how she can get the two of them together, and wondering what to do about her hair. She fingers the dark clumps of her hair, still wet from last night's rain. She wishes now she'd taken Angie up on that color-weave and she hopes, too, that when Detective Hauer thinks of her (she can hardly think his name now without feeling a pull behind her ribs), it is her five-by-seven photo that comes to mind, that picture wedged between the keys of the unused keyboard pushed to the side of his desk.

Hauer hated using interpreters in the room. The lag between what was asked and answered meant endless doors opening and closing, and he could never be sure that Jenni, the interpreter, was conveying the proper sense of urgency. He'd go it alone with the dead girl's mother, but he didn't trust his Spanish and didn't want to risk losing a lead because he couldn't recall the one essential word, his slip passed over as an untranslatable lapse sealed with a shrug and a glassy smile.

Hauer passed the vending machine full of nervous food: pretzels, peanuts, air-crisp chips popular with the drunks and the parents of first-time juvenile offenders. Hauer always kept quarters in his pockets for coffee, which was better brewed from their ancient machine than what Rita made in the main office. He would have bought Sigrid Nunez, the dead girl's mother, a cup of coffee or maybe even a bottle of that pricey bubble water except he was out of quarters again. Even worse, he realized as he seated Mrs. Nunez in the interview room that he had the wrong file in his hand. Hauer left Mrs. Nunez and searched his desk.

"Where's the Nunez file?" Hauer rubbed his forehead and looked at Rita from beneath his hand. Rita, on her way to a coffee break, her hand resting heavily on the shiny stem of the break room door handle, turned.

"Who?"

"Nunez!" Hauer shouted.

"Oh. Right." Rita's hand slid off the handle and slapped the side of her thigh. Ciri, intrigued by Rita's aggressive forgetfulness, followed her to her desk where all of the files neatly hung in her bottom drawer. When Ciri bent her body close to Rita's, pressed her ear to Rita's, she could hear what Rita was thinking: *At least the dead can rest.*

But, of course, Ciri was not resting. Ciri's mother knew this and had already petitioned the DA's office to hurry the forensics team and allow her to give her daughter a decent Christian burial. But Ed, a fiber expert, was not finished yet. Nor was Virgil, who at that very moment was executing a Y-incision down the length of Ciri's torso, a delicate procedure that registered in Ciri as a prolonged tickle.

Back with Ciri's file, Rita brushed Hauer's arm as she handed it over. Ciri knew that any other day Rita would have made it a more deliberate touch. But she could see by the way Rita pressed her fingertips along the sides of her nose that the dusky smell of Ciri, concentrated like a heavy pollen in this tiny conference room, was bringing on a cluster headache. Ciri stood behind Hauer, intending to read her report. But seeing her own name in print, in the past tense, raised the hair on the back of her neck, and she resumed her perch on the radiator near her mother.

"She was my only daughter, a good girl." Mrs. Nunez spoke

quickly, her prayer cards splayed in a tight grip of a saintly flush: St. Jude, St. Anthony, St. Christopher, all Ciri's favorites.

"Any boyfriends?"

Mrs. Nunez gripped the strap of her purse and shook her head.

"Any bad feelings about anyone?" Hauer's last question, but Jenni asked Mrs. Nunez instead if there were bad feelings between her daughter and anyone else. About. Between. Ciri slapped her forehead with an open palm and began conjugating the verbs of being and nonbeing, all the states of rest and restlessness, which only the dead can know.

"Oh no. Not my girl." And here Ciri's mother spread her cards out face down on the table and began to cry quietly into her handkerchief. Ciri turned her gaze to Hauer, who shifted in his chair. His lips were moving, forming the starts of words, and she knew he was rifling through the recommended phrases, looking for a fit and drawing a blank. Finally her mother wiped her nose with the handkerchief and returned it and the prayer cards into her open purse, which she then shut with a loud snap.

"When can I have the body?" Mrs. Nunez asked.

Hauer tapped his pencil and looked at Jenni. "We're waiting to lift a print. Tell her we hope real soon."

It is a fact that when somebody speaks of this, undoubtedly there will be others speaking of that. A waste of time, Ciri could have told him. Talking to her mother would tell Hauer nothing except this kind of thing shouldn't have happened. Perhaps there was a lesson to be learned here. Perhaps she had done something wrong, she thinks when she sees through the open window her mother's Honda Civic parked below and in it Mr. Twenty Percent, the head-and-shoulders dummy her mother had perched on a cardboard box in the passenger seat. From the side and from behind, Mr. Twenty Percent looked real enough, much more than the 20 percent of a person that he was, and only people who had ridden in her mother's car knew the difference.

Perhaps she should have bought her own Mr. Twenty Percent to sit in a chair by the window. Perhaps she should have packed up when Angie left for Dale. Then again, perhaps living with her mother and her mother's safety mannequin, things would have turned out the same, things being the same all over. Ciri pressed her hands against the thick glass of the conference room windows. There was always something, and it seemed that no matter what you did, your decision became you, inseparable from who you were and where you were.

Still. It's odd how her mother asks for her body, careful not to mention her name. It hurts Ciri that she's become unmentionable on her mother's tongue, and she marvels at her mother's unflappable strategy for moving on: the assortment of prayer cards, the stockpile of casseroles in the freezer. Her mother was as rock solid as a twenty-year argument hardened to a single "no."

Ciri pulls her palms from the glass. "I'm here. I'm still here," she says, her voice suspended between languages and carried in the quiet clanks of the venetian blinds. In time, she knew, it would be harder to make contact: already as Virgil processed the fingerprints lifted with the glue fumes, she could feel herself slipping, the outlines of things fuzzing over, blurred by the surrounding light. And with each new procedure that Virgil performs, she feels a little less vital, less substantial.

That evening, when the outside darkness of night falling overtakes the inside gloom of the police department, Ciri heads over to the beauty salon. Inside the close-cropped darkness of the long narrow salon backlit by the pass of red taillights and the sweep of the head-lights from oncoming traffic, she sorts the towels: those used to mop perm solution from those stained from dye jobs. When that's done, she lines up Dixie's combs in order of length and spacing of the teeth and Neela's brushes in order of bristle size. In the space around the empty chairs, in the space where Ciri imagines Dixie's arms held over a customer's head or where Neela bends over a washtub, working wet hair under the nozzle, she can see and hear what they had been thinking about throughout the day.

"Why won't he love me?" she hears in Dixie's sighing, which starts up around three o'clock and continues with greater fre-quency until quitting time at six, leaving a trace residue on the double wide mirror in front of Dixie's station. In the worn metal groove on the pedal of Dixie's chair lift Ciri can read that Dixie still hopes, still believes in the best, and from how clean her brush bris-tles, that Neela likes to think any snarl will untangle if a person just keeps at it. Angels, these women, Ciri decides. Angels with sawed-off wings, murmuring the encouragement to their unhappy cus-tomers that they themselves needed to hear.

After she sweeps hair clippings from around the base of each chrome-stemmed chair into a large pile, Ciri whisks the hair into a small dustpan with a hand broom. She notices that some of the hairs cling to the frayed ends of the plastic bristles, and she taps the broom over the lip of a garbage can, shaking the hair loose. A per-son's life is like this, she thinks, a person like these strands of hair, hard to tell where the beginning, where the end.

Suddenly Ciri hears a tremendous crack inside her chest and she buckles over the back of Angie's chair. She fingers a widening expansion between her ribs and knows that Virgil has snapped open her rib cage. Ciri pulls herself up from the chair, feeling as if she's swallowed the sky, feeling gassy and the closest so far to floating, as she imagined a ghost might, and she heads back to the precinct, back to Detective Daniel Hauer.

~~~~

The second interview, the one with Grievy, the landlord, inspired in Hauer and Hornacek a mutual bad feeling. For a dimwit he seemed unusually adept at misinterpreting their questions. And then there was the reek of cat.

"I thought pets weren't allowed at the apartments," Hornacek said, sneezing into a handkerchief.

"They're not." Grievy smiled. "But I got one 'cause I'm the landlord and who's gonna complain?" Grievy removed the cellophane from a pack of cigarettes, ripping the bottom of the pack and bringing a cigarette to his mouth all in one smooth motion.

"What's this key for?" Hornacek held up his hand to reveal a small gold-colored key.

"Storage." Grievy's smile widened a bit and it occurred to Hauer that he'd seen that frozen sort of smile before, only it was on a man he'd once known who'd been shot in the chest and for a few seconds didn't know it.

"And this one here?"

"Storage. Tenant property, some of it. They pull out, leave their stuff. I gotta store it for a reasonable length of time. Then I can sell it or keep it or whatever. There's a law about it."

"Mind if we look at these storage units?"

"No problem." Grievy's gaze slid to the window.

Grievy is their hottest lead and Hauer wishes again he'd paid more attention at the academy, paid more attention in general to people and their quirks. He knew already that Grievy had a sloppy trail of DUIs and two cases of unlawful entry, both into the apartments of former tenants, and once he'd been caught urinating in a tenant's refrigerator.

"Did you know Ciri Nunez well?"

"Who?"

"Ciri Nunez. The dead girl."

"Nope."

"Ever visit her, stop by her apartment?"

"A couple of times. I was fixing the plumbing under her sink."

Grievy looked at Hornacek, who was cleaning out his nose, and then back at Hauer and shrugged. "Old copper pipe. Fittings all shot. I bought new pipe—plastic—and fittings for her sink yesterday. I was going to install it but the police were already there."

Hauer pretended to take notes on his notepad. Actually he was thinking about those cat hairs, and about the murder weapon, a heavy object, and wondered if he could get someone out to those storage units before Grievy got there. It was a long shot, but if he could get Grievy to stay and smoke a few cigarettes, make stupid conversation, cats vs. dogs, anything, maybe they could get the warrants in time. Hauer knocked on the window and signaled for the chief.

It's her last day, Ciri knows. She's feeling light and floaty again, even though she's sure Virgil has replaced every organ he's removed. She feels as if there is much less of her present and she's noticed it's harder to keep track of all her people and what they are thinking. She is glad to note that her body has been released to a mortuary where the embalmer has done wonders for her complexion. They can't do a color weave like she wanted, but she sees that someone has combed her hair out and arranged it just the way

Angie used to. Ciri remembers Angie's jade plant and a last load of laundry she'd left on spin cycle and she makes her way back to the salon. But she's feeling tired today. All this moving around, following Hauer and eavesdropping everywhere has worn her out, and when she gets there she sits in Neela's chair and slowly turns herself in circles. Though she's tired, she can still see with clarity, a wonderful lack of complication, things she'd never noticed before. In the air above Angie's station, and around Neela's chair, as an aura of all her daytime breathing, a foggy cloud hovering in the air. It's desire and longing linking them all to each other, a compounded regret gritting the mirrors, the stainless steel chairs and washbasins. And she can hear it now too with her relevant ear: *Please appreciate me,* Neela's hands say as they scissor about an elderly woman's head. The woman, desperate for illusion, is receiving a blueberry rinse. *Please tell me I look pretty,* the woman thinks, *a compliment— I'll take anything.* Dixie to her no-name husband who is, without a doubt, a cheater, and Angie to Dale: *Please love me.*

⌣

Hornacek rested the phone against his neck. "It's Virgil. He got a lift on a partial patent and full latent."

Hauer jumped from his chair, resisting the urge to run a victory lap around the station. Their killer was sloppy, God bless him. God bless all the sloppy psychopaths, every last one of them. Thank God for blood, for there's power in blood, this much Hauer remembered from Sunday school, and thank God for prints, and yes, thank Him for all those pesky little cat hairs. We need more of it, blood, hairs, fluid; so many problems result from a lack of them. But not this time, and Hauer visualized himself clicking his heels together in glee as he waltzed down the waxed corridor of the second floor of the police department to the crime lab downstairs.

When Hauer returns, Ciri takes her place on the heater where she swings her feet, letting them kick the heater with soft thuds only she can hear, although she notes with perverse pleasure that Rita is reaching for a bottle of aspirin. Despite the fact that her nose is all a-twitch, Rita is proud of herself, Ciri can tell. For three seconds she is in possession of something Hauer wants.

"Hey." Rita touches Hauer's elbow. "While you were downstairs with Virgil, Hornacek and I ran the partial against the latent and then ran both of those against our fields of known offenders."

"And?" Hauer shifts his weight from one foot to the other. It's the little clues that give everything away, Ciri would like to remind Rita, for Ciri can tell by the way his voice flattens when he talks to her that Rita doesn't have a chance, not if they were the last two humans on the planet.

"We got a match."

"Grievy?"

"Yup." Rita pops her gum and the sound is like a wet slap.

"The little shit," Ciri says, reaching for a quarter from Rita's desk. She's not wholly surprised, the dirty old lech. She'd never really believed him when he said he needed sugar or an egg. Never knew if there was some half-hidden joke she was missing or that he expected her to miss, and she didn't trust people who played around with words like that.

⌣

As she walks past a long line of cars at the cemetery, Ciri is surprised to see Detective Hauer leaning against his unmarked squad car. His arms are crossed in front of his chest and for the first time since she's died, she can't hear what he is thinking.

"I love you," she whispers in his ear. "Listen." She'd like to say so much more, like to point out the convergence of light growing at the horizon, the migration of spirits, the gospels spelled out in the nighttime stars, those pulsing bits of enamel reminding us *we are here, we are here, we know that we know.* Though he can't hear her, can't see what she can, Ciri hesitates. It would be good to stay here with Hauer, to watch him live life, even if it is not with her. But she knows without even bothering to imagine it that some woman will wear him down like a bad habit and Hauer will love her, and if not her, someone just like her. They will marry, they will have kids, and on it will go. Ciri would never be important, never the essential thing, she knows, and this is the sticking point, the spot that rises to a blister.

Someone speaks her name, Father Dismus maybe, and Ciri finds herself pulled beyond will toward a small gathering of people standing around what she knows is her casket. She sees Angie. From the way she is still clutching a tiny spritzer bottle of hair spray attached to her key chain, Ciri knows that it was Angie who had worked on her hair. For some reason she cannot explain, this is what makes her cry. Ciri wishes Angie would have dumped Dale so that they could have been better friends. Ciri could have told her how to relax, how to let her hips do the moving when she danced, how to get down and salsa, woman, forget that ballroom crap.

The embalmer and his two sons, each wearing the appropriate expressions, stand a few paces back, ready to lower the casket when the priest gives them the cue. Never so badly has Ciri wished she could do some haunting: pop open the casket lid and shout "Boo!" for it all still feels like a joke, a silly blunder that hasn't quite worn off. Especially since the Nunezes have been dying at a steady rate of one every two years for as long as Ciri could remember. But they were a large family and the passing of so many elderly aunts and uncles did not seem unjust.

"It was their time," Father Dismus said at each of the masses held in memoriam. "God in his goodness takes us in His time." He says this again now, standing beside her casket, to Ciri's amazement, and she cannot help popping her gum near his good ear, the left one, to which he delivers a substantial slap. Beside Father Dismus, her mother stands, a flutter of prayer cards flying from out of her open purse. Her mother is on fire, enflamed by grief, which, in turn, inspires a fierce and unswerving anger she has never known before and likely, after this, never will. Her mother's anger lays claim to a true and real sorrow and she is sorry to have seen it.

"It doesn't hurt." Ciri wants to comfort her mother any way she can, a cool hand along her cheek, a touch to that startle of white at her forehead. "Don't be afraid." It's true, she wants to reassure her mother, Angie, all of them. Life is beautiful and good. But they had nothing to fear, for so was this, pure and simple, the simplest of things.

Hauer hated funerals. He had been to more than he could count, prepared eulogies for too many friends. He wasn't planning on attending Ciri Nunez's, it was too movie-of-the-week-ish. Only TV detectives attended funerals, hanging back behind a gumline of stones, amidst rain and umbrellas and sleek black sedans lining a gravel drive. But there was something to seeing a casket lowered into the ground, the earth calling back its own. And now that he was here, now that he'd been seen, he couldn't just leave.

Though it was only spring, the sun didn't know it, shining so strong as to make the new leaves on the trees look shiny and wet. Behind the priest in a grove of birch, sad and weepy looking trees, a flock of small dark birds lifted from the branches in a single flash of motion as if will were so simple as to only require the beat of wings. For some reason seeing this comforted Hauer, who had noticed lately the growing rareness of true and beautiful things. Still. He wanted to get back to his cluttered apartment where he could push open all the windows, shake off this cloying smell. He wanted to go home and rest his elbows on the sills of the open windows and drink steadily, drinking with patience through the hours. He would watch the split-tail swifts and listen for a solitary whistle, the cue that held them together, for a sound, any sound that would harden to something that lasts.

Hauer turned. Something hit the hood of a nearby car with a solid thump. A bird, he thought. A bird mistaking the windshield for sky, and Hauer opened the driver's side door, slid his body behind the steering wheel.

The embalmer's sons release the winch and begin to lower Ciri's casket. Her mother grips Angie in a fierce hug, and the two women turn from the open grave. She can go now, if she chooses. She's seen death, has caught a vision of what will happen next and she is not afraid. That thing that had snapped her back as a rubber band, again and again, for a missed detail, the sound of her name, for leaking faucets and other people's peace of mind, was gone. Like that. Gone and she was free now to go. And she's free now, too, of all those great and complicated longings for all that she'd lost and for what she'd never had. This, too, is funny and Ciri tosses her shoes over her shoulder where they land with a loud thunk on Detective Hauer's squad car. She twirls in circles over her casket, blowing kisses and laughing at the sheer absurdity of it all. Relieved and free, free at last.

Winded, Ciri stands on her casket. Eye-level to the grass and the retreating feet of her mother and Angie, Ciri begins a prayer, a laundry list of wishes for the people who had become so important to her. Let it be like this, she breathed, let Dixie and her no-name husband cultivate in each other a true and lasting love. Let there be goodness for Angie, and even Rita. Let Hornacek and Carla be reunited; let them recall from memory's willed dust the lost details of the hours of all the years they'd neglected. Let her mother in Ciri's absence be surprised, no, astonished by joy which overruns her sorrow; let her speak her name. Let there be forgiveness and healing for all of them. Let their combined despair be displaced by wonder in all that they'd missed, the lapses they'd allowed themselves. And God, let Hauer not too quickly forget her.

Cartography

of a

Heart

"A darkness that bleeds indefinitely in
a world like this one who could know
what mends things made of skin?"
—Jody Rambo, "Sublunary"

Because O'Neil's heart had been skipping and had threatened to
give up altogether, the doctors decided to give him a new one.
O'Neil was not a very important man. He had fought in a war, an
unpopular one, and had in fact already nearly died several times.
For these reasons and a few more he would have been hard-pressed
to name, O'Neil was tempted to call off the replacement procedure. But the doctors insisted. After they took a lot of pictures,
measuring with ultrasound to determine the exact size of heart they
were looking for, they discovered that they'd never seen anyone
with a heart like his, a heart of such unusual shape. This discovery
aroused a certain amount of scientific interest in the cardiology
unit, and the doctors wondered if anyone else in the city could also
be carrying such an odd-shaped heart.

How his heart got into such a state, O'Neil couldn't figure. He
had been in love once. It was a good love affair and innocent, con-

fined to the realm of hand-holding and quick stolen kisses. And when he was drafted and sent to Vietnam, O'Neil only allowed himself to think of Marianne, to savor the thought of her at night when the ordinary daytime sounds crossed the boundary into nighttime noise and he could have his thoughts to himself. In this way he stretched the memory of Marianne, rationing her out to fill the nights of an entire tour.

But when he returned home, Marianne was gone—dead, her parents told him, of food poisoning. The sheer stupidity, the terrible irony of her dying instead of him bore down upon O'Neil like the sudden pressure he'd feel just before a nosebleed, only this pressure was in his heart, pushing on the chambers of his heart. That was the first time he had really taken any notice of his heart. But after that, it seemed to pain him on strange occasions for no particular reason: at his kid brother's wedding, after eating summer sausage, at his father's funeral, and once, in a movie theater. At first he was embarrassed, but after a while his discomfort outweighed his shame and finally he made an appointment at the VA hospital.

Later, when he came in to view his X-rays, the cardiologists, Dr. Gatlin and Dr. Moore, told him it was no wonder his heart wasn't cooperating with him. His heart was an anomaly, they said. Anomaly wasn't a word O'Neil cared for much because it hinted at trouble, suggested a huge fuck-up was in the works, or a nightmare that had patiently grown wings and was now waiting to hatch.

But the doctors were right: O'Neil's heart was kidney-shaped and abnormally large, with the muscle itself nearly twice the size of an ordinary man's. The chambers of the heart, however, were unusually small, so small that Dr. Gatlin wondered how O'Neil's heart managed to move his blood around at all. When the doctors showed him this, the darkened images on the film made darker against the white light, O'Neil thought of the ten thousand eggs of his youth, the generous pats of butter on his bread and dollops of cream in his coffee, and silently cursed.

Even worse, O'Neil would need a heart that was very much like his present one as his rib cage, sternum, and interior musculature had over time reshaped themselves to accommodate that strange heart. An ordinary heart would not do, Dr. Moore explained to O'Neil, as he had noted over the years how the whole of the body so often and fatally rebels against its parts. In the meantime, the doctors sent O'Neil home with a panic alert that would ring into ER and told him to rest easy, to wait, to try not to vex or agitate his unusual heart.

Finding a perfectly fitting heart proved to be even harder than the doctors thought it would be. For several months O'Neil waited, trying not to think about the tightness in his chest or about the person who would have to die in order for him to have a new heart. But when the phone rang beside his bed one afternoon he knew before he even picked up the receiver that it was the hospital calling, that someone, the right someone, had at last died.

~~~~

The day of the surgery broke over the flat skyline of the city. O'Neil took a cab to the hospital. It was the dead of summer and already the air had run to humid, though it was still early morning. O'Neil waited in the visitors' lounge and trained his eyes on the ceiling where the overhead fans beat the air. Looking at them made him feel a little off-kilter, a little like slipping out of himself because each of the fans sliced the air at different speeds, and for an instant he felt as if he were back on the airfield, on the tarmac, watching the rotors spin, the slow wind-up dance to the tune of the turbine's whine and drone. He couldn't help looking at fans, ceiling or otherwise, lawnmowers, blenders, helicopters—anything with blades—without feeling a sense of danger and the taste of his fillings in the back of his mouth. He remembered a guy from his unit who dismounted from his chopper, leaving the rotors running. Who knows what he was thinking about—his wife, his kids—or maybe he just remembered something he'd left in the cockpit. But he turned around sharp and walked into the tail rotor, which neatly sliced his face from his head.

O'Neil had never seen a man without a face, and the oddest thing about the incident was that the man, who had a funny name like Emil or Emile but whom everyone called Eddy, went on to survive in spite of himself. O'Neil had gone to visit Eddy out of respect and curiosity, and though it was clear that it pained him, Eddy would talk with O'Neil, telling him about the whirlpool baths the nurses used to remove the scars of the burn patients, the new plastic nose the doctors were designing for him, how it would clip in and attach just under the bones of his forehead. They'd trade gossip about the men in the burn ward, the men in the psych wards, and the women they had loved and wanted to love. This is when Eddy would invariably mention his wife, a woman O'Neil categorically disliked. That she took the kids and left her husband while he was still in the hospital seemed to O'Neil an expired cliché, an expected joke made no less cruel by its anticipation. She couldn't live with a man she couldn't look at, Eddy carefully explained during O'Neil's last visit, moving his mouth slowly so as not to open the healing scab that was his new face. She couldn't live with a face that couldn't be kissed.

Then O'Neil had told Eddy the story of the Emperor who had no skin. Of all the skins offered to him by beautiful princesses wishing to be chosen as his new bride, the Emperor picked the princess who brought the skin of her dog, for he had always wanted a tail to wag. This had made Eddy laugh, a strange sound at the back of his throat, and listening to it made O'Neil's chest go tight and his heart turn leaden. A nurse in crisp whites had come in then, whisking the privacy curtain around the steel semicircular curtain rod and O'Neil had left, his chest hurting. If all a man wanted was to love and be loved, why couldn't he have it? he had wondered as he waited for the elevator.

⌣

The nurse called O'Neil's name and ushered him into pre-op where he exchanged his clothes for a gown that fastened in the front with tiny black Velcro dots. Then he was wheeled to the service elevator and down to the surgery staging area where a different nurse, green face mask and all business, dropped a cc of painkiller into his IV and wheeled him into the operating room. O'Neil, now groggy and feeling not a particle of pain in his chest, considered telling Doctors Gatlin and Moore the story of the Emperor's skin, the story of Eddy's face, and wondered if he would ever hear the story of the owner of the used and unusual heart beating in the ice chest on the gurney next to him.

⌣

Afterward, when the new heart was in place, his chest felt tender and there was a certain amount of pink scar tissue raised at the surgical site, but all in all O'Neil felt good and his chest light. When it was certain his body would not reject the perfectly fitting heart, his thoughts turned again to the Emperor, the unconventional gift of the wild princess, and he wondered what other changes this heart would bring. He had heard rumors from other heart transplant patients—of strange dreams, ghost pains and twitches, reminders of lost parts and donors.

The doctors sent him home with anticoagulants and new

batteries for the panic pager, and every week O'Neil went in to see the doctors and answer their routine questions. For a long while he felt he was disappointing Dr. Gatlin and Dr. Moore.

"Any trouble breathing—shortness of breath?" Dr. Gatlin would ask, the stethoscope to O'Neil's chest.

"No."

"Any tightness or heaviness in your chest or arms?"

"No."

His favorite question: "How is your sex life?"

When Dr. Gatlin got to this one, O'Neil would roll his eyes to the ceiling and shrug.

But then one day, a day in spring when the birds were reclaiming the sky, O'Neil awoke feeling different, different somehow in his heart. He took the bus downtown and sat outside smoking. There was no denying the strange kick in his chest and the blood coursing differently through his veins, and he realized that he had a great and natural desire to love someone with his new heart.

He walked to a corner café that sometimes sold day-old donuts for half price and slid into a booth. And then he saw her: the woman for whom his new heart had been beating all these months. He knew it from the way the gait of her walk behind the counter matched the contractions in his ventricles. O'Neil followed her with his eyes, noted the curve of the back of her neck, the way her rib cage sank into her hips as she held a coffeepot in one hand and read back a phone order to the cook. He sat in the booth and studied her, her light talk and chatter, and tried to think of things he could say, something funny that might make her want to seat him in her section next time he came in.

Then he thought of Eddy again, whom he hadn't visited in a while, and thought how Eddy probably wanted to love someone, too. O'Neil wished that he could close his eyes and pray that God would give Eddy a new face. If he could have a new and perfect heart, then why couldn't Eddy have a new and perfect face? But even as he thought the words, he stopped himself. What was God supposed to do about it? Make a movie star face sprout out of Eddy's head, just like that?

Just then the waitress walked toward his booth, coffeepot in hand. He could tell that she was young, probably too young for him. But he remembered Eddy, thought of the regrets and fear that had held both of them back, and O'Neil decided to do what Eddy could not. And so he smiled, said something half witty, and decided if she showed an ounce of interest to pursue her with the ardor he should have pursued all the other women whom he wanted to love and wished had loved him in return.

In time, O'Neil and the waitress became lovers. Her name was June and she smelled like apples and sometimes like mint. He liked her because with her freckles she reminded him a little of Marianne. She would retell the stories of her day—the customers, their smells, how much they tipped, and with whom the cook was flirting—could tell these stories without pause, her talk an endless flow without a vein. She moved into his apartment, carrying a beat-up red suitcase and a small wire cage with a yellow canary named Petey inside. Petey's chirping filled his tiny kitchen with happy yellow noise, and O'Neil was glad for the combined noise of Petey and June for it kept him from thinking too often of Eddy, or of wondering too much about all those noises his donor had loved and left behind.

The simplicity of it, the ease with which their love fell into a simple rhythm, comforted O'Neil, who was learning to appreciate the occasional anomaly and had noted that too few things in life were simple anymore. Every night, when her shift was over, he would rub June's neck and then her feet, pushing the skin around the ankles and kneading the thick skin of her heels.

"You're an angel," June said to him one night, mid-story while he was rubbing.

"No I'm not. I've done things, some of them bad," O'Neil said, sliding his hand to the back of her neck, the place where her head and neck joined, and laying his head on her chest. He could hear then past her constant chatter, and as he did, listening very carefully to June's heart, he discovered that there was nothing there. He closed his eyes and held his breath, listening again for her heart, and exhaled at last when he heard a steady beat. He kissed her then, his forefinger at her throat checking her pulse, just to be sure.

That night they made love: a nondescript expression for O'Neil punctuated by the realization that even then, even as he was loving her, his heart did not beat any faster. Not with excitement, not with danger or mere lust, not with anything at all. Afterward he sat watching June paint her toenails, sat and smoked one cigarette after another, thinking that maybe because his heart had become so steady this meant he had finally matured and this love he felt for June, though not exciting, was a better kind of a love, his heart a better heart than the one before.

꜌

On an ordinary day that O'Neil had thought would unspool exactly as the day before, he awoke to the sound of Petey squawking and making strange clicking noises. June was at the mirror penciling in her eyebrows. He could tell from the quick deliberate jerks she was making with the pencil that she was mad at him, and he knew a fight was brewing. When June picked a fight, O'Neil would close his eyes and imagine June was Marianne and imagine what he would have said to Marianne. He'd imagine them both throwing their arms up at the same time at some point in the argument and laughing, laughing so hard they'd cry, and crying so hard they'd forget what it was they were fighting about. That was how it was supposed to work, O'Neil had always thought. But then June advanced, one hip jutted in her coffeepot pose, a pose of an older woman unafraid of a fight. O'Neil practiced deep breathing techniques the nurses told him to use when he felt stressed and waited for June to start in.

"You have the paper eyes of a face that can't be read, a heart that can't be touched," June said, tapping the place where his chest hair had grown back with her long eyebrow pencil sharpened to a point.

No, O'Neil wanted to protest, *not an untouchable heart, only a new, unknown heart.* But he knew she was right, that it couldn't work, and the thought was painful, right down to the capillaries.

"I can't live with a man who can't be loved," June said, and O'Neil bit his tongue and counted his breaths, thinking of the Emperor and wondering if any of the beautiful princesses had refused him because of his strange condition and what the Emperor would have said to them if he had been given the chance. That was the problem with tales—they hinted at a truth that wasn't actually there, a truth that was conditional on the belief that the human heart was noble, had great capacity for love, for loving the ugly and unlovable when one look at a guy like Eddy, at a guy like O'Neil even, would show that it just wasn't so. Not in this world.

When O'Neil had counted to twenty, he swallowed. "OK," he said at last, and he meant it. He was OK with it all—with June leaving him and her reasons why. But his heart dropped a notch in his chest, seemed to lurch and tip, and the steady strong rhythm he had enjoyed since the operation faltered and skipped to an uneven one-two punch beat. As she left with her red suitcase with the bad clasps, O'Neil noticed her clothes were leaking out and wondered if her suitcase might be bleeding. He held Petey in his cage out to her and watched her lug her suitcase and the bird down the narrow steps outside their apartment, each bump of the suitcase and squawk from Petey an arrow to his heart, and wished she would at least let him help her. *Is this what he would have had with Marianne?* he wondered. Is this what he had avoided? And for some reason the thought made him very sad, for he would have liked to have known for sure.

All the rest of the day he could feel himself unraveling inside and thought about using the panic alert. He actually thought then, too, that he missed his old heart, that bruised lump of muscle with the hardened arteries, which in all the days of crossing canyons and rivers and entire jungles had never given him this kind of trouble.

O'Neil opened the kitchen window and listened to the angry clicks of June's shoes on the sidewalk below. He could tell by the way her footfalls sounded like sharp slaps that she was mad—mad in her heart, mad that he had hurt her somehow without either of them even noticing it until now. He leaned on the sill to catch a last glimpse of her disappearing around the corner. Outside on the street two lovers sat on the stoop holding hands and exchanging glances. Looking at them made O'Neil's chest hurt and he wanted to shout: *Stop! You are making a big mistake!* But as he watched them, his hand still at the panic button, he noted the care with which the man tucked a long strand of hair behind the woman's ear and realized that he might be witnessing something rare, that this couple might make it, might be two of those movie-of-the-week love story lovers who risk everything to save their love even as the world turns to fire and ash around them, and he couldn't help hating them a little for it.

O'Neil imagined that his heart, now pierced like St. Ambrose's, pierced like an old carnival target, was leaking at the edges. He closed his eyes and considered asking God to do a quick mend when he felt it: a tiny pocket of buoyancy in his chest. He felt a quickening, a bubble lodging in his heart, while outside the kitchen window he could see the flatiron sky hemmed in ten thousand stitches of light.

"So this is it," he said, clutching his chest and sliding against the refrigerator into a sitting position. He thought he'd hear more sound: bombs falling, the whistle of explosives. He worked the panic pager off his belt loop and lobbed it into the kitchen sink. His breath was coming in short gasps now, and in the pauses he thought he could hear the quiet whirring of his heart, that noise the washer makes on spin cycle just before the final click and pause.

Modern
Taxidermy

The trouble started one night when I looked around my flat, looked at it as if I had never seen it before. I realized how sterile, how empty it had become. These days a lot of flats look empty in Warsaw, but somehow, without my even noticing until then, mine seemed especially so. My fig plants had died. I had over-watered them, and they wept for days before they finally expired. So on that night I opened the window and tossed them into the trash bin that sat in the alley. Outside my window, the pigeons roosted on ledges; their cooing sounded like a mother mumbling into her child's neck. I set my teakettle and some cabbage to boil on the stove. I looked at those pigeons, at the way the tall buildings splintered the last light, and at how that light caught the ordinary colors of their feathers and made them glitter like jewels. They were pigeons, I knew, but in that moment of retreating sun they could have been peacocks. Just then, the kettle shrieked and I knew what was missing.

The next day I decided to see Henryk at his pet shop. We'd played chess every Saturday and Sunday night for three years and he'd beaten me almost every time. I thought he won because his philosophical talks rattled me and I couldn't concentrate. The night before, Henryk had told me that for every living Jew in Warsaw there were at least ten ghosts, maybe more. When he talked like this, bad memories—all the stories I'd heard and wished weren't true—crowded my thoughts like too many aunts and uncles at a funeral, and I wished, for just a few days, Henryk weren't Jewish.

I walked to Henryk's along the streets of this new Warsaw, a city transformed by loss. You can see it in the dormers, the bricks, the concrete: pieces of the old buildings reused to construct exact replicas, *Like the phoenix from the ashes,* the tour guides say. But the memories are still lurking inside the stone, and ghosts have settled over the streets and in the cornices of buildings as a fine dust or like soot, and sometimes it hurts to look too closely at this city.

I walked toward the corner bistro where they sometimes sold day-old pastries for half-price and occasionally gave them away for free. It was raining and I kept my head down, my eyes skimming over the cigarette butts and ticket stubs and tiny pieces of paper that littered the sidewalk. The soles of people's shoes looked like wet tongues licking the cement, drinking from the concrete. I saw Spinster Karlova just ahead of me, sitting out in front of her shop and smoking a cigarette in the rain. She normally spat on my shoes whenever I passed by her, and I couldn't help noticing that today, as I approached, she stamped out her cigarette and disappeared into her shop, pulling the door closed with a loud bang. Finally, I reached the bistro and seated myself at a tiny table close to the kitchen.

I was tempted to forget about Spinster Karlova, but I've noticed lately that I don't seem to fit anywhere and that people don't seem to like me much. I planted my elbows on the table, propped up my chin, and thought: when did I become such a loser? It was more than I could figure and disturbing, too, because I couldn't put my finger on it. No major confrontations with the authorities, no involvement with disenfranchised student radicals, no disillusionment with God, no girls, and thus, no girl trouble. As near as I could tell, I'd had a normal existence with normal troubles. Now, when I should have been somebody, something, I was nothing.

From my back pocket I pulled out Henryk's sales flier, unfolded it carefully, ironing out the creases of the paper with my palms. In the photo the birds were caught in mid-flight, their wings outstretched and their tail feathers splayed. Each bird seemed more brightly colored than the next. I thought of the drab yellow walls in my flat, the peeling plaster and dead plants.

I sat at the table for a good half hour, waiting for service. I wanted to order the leek soup that sometimes came with a fish head in it if you were lucky, but the waitress refused to take my order.

"Kasia!" I whistled through my teeth, but she kept talking to the dishwasher and pretended not to hear me. I pulled Henryk's ad closer. I looked at the birds again. I liked the way that with those bright colors they seemed happy, seemed to defy the gravity, the general gray of this city.

"Hello, Mirek." It was Tomic Kamenzind, the bistro owner.

"Hello, Tomic." I moved my elbow over the flier.

"I hate to ask you this." Tomic held his hand over his mouth and chin and seemed to be talking more to his hand than to me. "But, well, you see," Tomic's eyes swept the bistro, "we are rather busy today, and you don't seem to really be needing this table." Tomic tugged at an imaginary hair on his chin.

I nodded and pushed my chair back from the table. Tomic smiled, a smile in the shape of relief, and then he vanished behind the swinging doors for the kitchen. The flier was still there on the table and I folded it back up along the creases and slid it into my back pocket. I knew what I had to do.

I stood underneath the enormous lime tree outside Henryk's shop and paced in front of his windows. I had just quit my understudy job at the theater, and instead of feeling desperate about money I felt bold and a little giddy. Still, I wanted to make the right decision. Through his open door I could hear his swans bickering way in the back, and the warm-throated cooing of the ringed turtledoves in the cages near the front windows. It was the bright flutter of wings behind the glass that finally got me, though, and I stopped pacing, pulled my hands out of my pockets, and finally went into the store.

I found Henryk behind the counter studying the latest chess magazine and moving pieces over his chessboard.

I held out his flier. "I need a bird."

"Of course you do. Nothing is as good as a pet," Henryk said, sliding off his stool. I recalled how each of my plants had died within days of each other and watched Henryk walk to the cage where a cockatiel sat preening her feathers. He opened the cage and the bird hopped onto his thick finger. Then he muttered something to the bird and she flew onto his shoulder. Henryk coughed and wiped at his eyes with his free hand. With all the dust and bird feathers in his shop, he had become a bit asthmatic and his eyes ran at the corners like soft-boiled eggs.

"You let me tell you something about birds." He turned and shook his finger at me. "What most people never know about birds is they're sensitive, like young women, like a baby. They have feelings, Mirek. They can feel as passionately about things as you do."

"Then maybe you should quit lining the cages with political papers," I said.

"I mean it—you should think of this bird as your best friend." Henryk held the bird out to me. I touched its back, ran my finger down its tail feathers. She was pale gray with touches of light yellow, altogether a very muted and pastel bird. I wondered if she would sing sad or happy songs. Either way, I thought, she would fill my flat with her color, with her noises. With her there, it wouldn't be so empty.

Then she flew onto the desk and kicked at some papers. She ducked her head and bobbed up and down for a minute. It seemed an utterly confused and silly gesture, but she looked happy. I nudged her into the palm of my hand and held her to my chest.

"OK. I'll take her."

As we walked home along the narrow streets, I scrolled through a mental list of names for my new bird. I thought of naming her after the woman who lived across the hall from me, but I didn't know her name. I could only imagine that it must be something beautiful so I gave my bird the prettiest name I could think of, Alina. I could feel Alina fluttering and scraping at my scarf and every now and then I'd pull back a corner of the scarf and take a look inside and talk to her.

"I'm not a bad person, really." Alina stopped fluttering at the sound of my voice, and I continued, telling her what I'd tell my friend, telling her everything I would have told Henryk.

"I play the violin and sometimes I can be quite funny. I used to be a tour guide and then an actor and I might have been great, but then I quit. Anyway, I'll read the theater reviews to you and we can listen to the neighbors fighting."

She was a beautiful bird. She did that bobbing gesture again and I had to laugh. Henryk was right. I should have bought her months ago.

We walked by the theater where I had studied. Up on a ladder, a city worker opened the glass tops of the lamps and wiped at the glass. I stopped in front of the theater and peered in through the small window. I wanted the director, Mrs. Jasenska, to come running out and beg me to return, to tell me how desperately I was needed, but I knew no one would really miss me there. I had only been an understudy, and not even very good at that.

My shining moment had happened just the other day when Mrs. Jasenska asked us all to be animals. She believed in epiphanies. She believed that when we had one, our identity anxieties would all be resolved.

"Character, Mirek! Know who you are!" Mrs. Jasenska had prompted. I remembered I'd thought about how moths throw themselves against light bulbs, but I didn't know what to do with my face. So I decided to be a leech. But when I saw the guy imitating a dog, saw the way he rolled and shook and barked, I realized that he was better than me and I was consumed by jealousy. I watched him bounce and wiggle and I hated him, and hated myself for hating him. I inched my body toward him while he sniffed at me and barked. It's hard to explain why I did it, but when he barked at me and pawed at me with his hand, I dove for him and tackled him. His elbows buckled and he crashed to the floor. I remember I'd thought how strange it was that he didn't struggle, and then it had occurred to me that he was waiting for me to get off him. Just as we were walking off the stage he turned to me and said, "You're an amazing leech." All that night and the next morning I thought about what he had said.

The following morning I went to the theater to talk to Mrs. Jasenska. She was sitting in her seat with the tiny light attached to the back of the seat in front of hers. She was drinking coffee and eating a macaroon.

"I'm sorry, Mrs. Jasenska, but this isn't for me."

A piece of the cookie tumbled out of her mouth.

"I don't like myself anymore, not now, not knowing that the animal I best resemble is a parasite. That's not a good feeling." She had finished the macaroon and was sucking on a peppermint. Her breath whistled through the holes and fissures of the candy.

"Well, you were a marvelous leech, Mirek," she said.

"Thank you," I said. I backed up, nodded to her, and walked up the aisle and out the door. As I pulled the door shut, I heard her crunch the peppermint between her teeth. I could not stop thinking about what it meant to be an amazing leech. The metaphoric connections frightened me and it hurt my head to think about it.

I continued to walk home, and when I reached my building I carried Alina up the narrow staircase to my flat. I hurried with the key and almost forgot to look over my shoulder at the flat opposite mine. When she wasn't fighting with her lover, the beautiful neighbor woman across the hall would sometimes leave her door slightly ajar. When I walked up or down the stairs, I could see her moving around her flat, putting her things away or reading a book. She had dark hair that in certain light looked dark red, burnt brick red even. I wanted to tell her that she should shut her door, that you never know what can happen to you in the city, but then, if she did, I would never see her. Just then Alina coughed. At least, I thought maybe it was a cough. I hadn't thought birds could do that.

⌣

"Something's wrong with Alina," I said. Henryk moved his queen's pawn and took my knight. "She won't make any noises." I

stared at the pieces and my eyes blurred. "She won't eat, either."
Henryk studied the board.

"Maybe she's caught a cold," he said.

I moved a piece, then returned it, then picked it up again, then finally left it where it had been all along. As usual, Henryk was beating me badly and I couldn't see the point in continuing. I tipped over my king.

"Let's play another time," I said. Henryk began picking up the pieces and putting them in his case, each in its contoured felt compartment. He folded the board, placed it snug inside the lid of the case, and snapped the case shut.

"All right. Maybe tomorrow," he said.

I put on my coat and walked home, worrying about Alina the whole way. My teeth ached as they always did when I had a bad feeling about something. I could just imagine what Henryk would say: *Premonitions are like bad dreams, the voices of your dead ancestors telling you the stories you don't want to know.* And I knew what I'd find when I opened the door. I could feel it as I was walking up the stairs, with each step, a terrible sense of dread. I unlocked the door and walked over to the window ledge above the sink. Alina was lying flat on the sill and her wings had fallen open a bit as if, finally, after all that bobbing and fluttering, she was truly at rest. I picked her up and put her into the long cardboard box where I kept my watch. I wrapped a handkerchief around her. Then I put the kettle on and sat looking at her in the box.

Some birds live in freezing climates and never die of colds. Large gusts of wind can blow fledglings from their nests and later they are eaten by cats and sometimes dogs, or birds can mistake windowpanes for empty space and fly into the glass, break their wings or necks, but to die of a cold? I pulled the watch box closer to me and studied Alina. Her eyes were still open. I remembered how we

Modern Taxidermy 91

were taught to die on the stage—quietly and with our eyes open. I nudged her with my finger. She felt cold already, and hard, like a small potato.

I went to the drawer and pulled out a fork. I lifted her wing and examined the downy fluff underneath. I went to the sink, washed off a knife, and sat down at the table with Alina. Surely, there must be some evidence of what had killed her, but I wasn't sure how to start. I imagined she was like a dinner quail and that I could quarter her and, using the knife and fork together, cut her into small squares, sawing against the grain of the meat. I positioned my fork and knife over her breast and could see right away that this would never work. She still had all her feathers. I picked her up by her feet and placed her in a pot of water. "Forgive me, Alina," I said, and looked up at the ceiling. I put the lid on the pot and turned the burner on high.

When she had boiled awhile, I looked inside the pot. Her tail feathers had come loose and stuck to the sides of the pot, and there was a thick layer of oil bubbling on the surface of the water. I placed her on the tines of my fork and brought her over to the kitchen table where the light was best. Except for some small feathers and fluff on her belly that hadn't boiled off, she was completely bare, her skin bluish gray. Starting at the base of her neck, I sliced along the swell of her breast until I could peel back the skin. Then I gently pulled at the muscle wall until it, too, was flayed and I could see into Alina's chest. And here was the amazing thing. At first I couldn't believe it. Then I thought, I'm making some kind of mistake. I found my tweezers in the kitchen drawer and pulled at her tiny rib cage until it snapped apart. I couldn't understand it. No matter how hard I looked, I couldn't find her heart.

"Poor Alina," was all I could say. How had this happened to her? Who would ever believe me if I told them my bird was missing her heart? I found a piece of string and tied her rib cage back together. Then I folded her muscles back into place as best as I could and pulled her skin back over her muscles. There was nothing I could do about her feathers.

"Alina, I'm so sorry," I said. I held her in the palm of my hand, and as I opened my door the neighbor woman from across the hall came out with a small bag of trash. She looked at me and smiled, then looked at Alina in my hand. I opened my mouth, I wanted to explain, but the woman had rearranged her face and she was no longer smiling. Her lips were pressed tight, as though they'd been sewn together and smiling now would hurt.

"No. Please—you go ahead," she said, waving in front of her. And so I carried Alina down to the bin, carefully placed her inside, and pulled the metal lid down over her.

I went back inside the building and climbed the stairs to my flat. The neighbor woman's door clicked shut behind me.

～

"I need another bird," I said to Henryk. I had been standing under the lime tree, waiting for him to open the shop, and wondering if my bird had ever really been alive in the first place, if I hadn't just hallucinated the whole thing. When he saw me as he rounded the corner, his chess case under his arm, he looked surprised. "Alina's dead," I told him.

"Who?"

"The bird."

"Do you want me to take care of her?" he asked, holding the door open for me.

"No." I kept my hands in my pockets and walked toward the birdcages. I had resolved to buy another cockatiel, but none of them seemed to me as beautiful as Alina had been. Finally, I settled on a turtledove because, though they cannot sing, they make comforting noises.

"Turtledoves are happiest when kept in pairs," Henryk said to me. "What people don't know about turtledoves is that they are like old married couples; they may bicker quite a lot, but they hate to be separated." I thought about Alina. Would she have gotten better if I had bought her a mate?

"All right. I'll take two."

Henryk brought the second turtledove out in a cage. I brushed their chests with my finger and pressed gently along the swell of their breasts, feeling for their bones and hoping everything was all right in there.

"See that pearl ring around his neck? See how his ring is more vivid than the female's?"

I nodded.

"That's how you tell them apart."

I pulled out my wallet and counted out some bills.

"Look," Henryk said. "I can tell you're upset about Alina. Why don't you take this home with you?" He handed me the cage. In between the wire bars he had wedged a pamphlet, "Your Turtledove and You."

I brought Vera and Vlatig home and hung their cage up by the window. I turned the lights on low and filled their tiny water bottles. I waited for them to warble, but they just sat on the perch and stared at me. I pulled my violin out from the closet and played for them until a dark patch of sweat formed where the violin rested in the crook between my neck and shoulder and my hands ached. I looked at the birds. They were still staring at me. The next-door neighbors began knocking on the wall, so I put my violin away, turned out the lights, and went to bed. But I had a bad feeling, like a bad taste in the back of my mouth, and my teeth hurt. I closed my eyes and listened to the noises on the street.

Across the hall, the neighbor woman was arguing with her lover. I loved the sound of her voice, and I thought it was beautiful, even when she shouted. I could hear her thundering in the apartment, the crashing of glass. I wondered if she was breaking priceless heirlooms, and if so, which ones she was ruining. I closed my eyes and waited for morning to come. I listened for the birds, but they were silent. I pulled back the covers and crept out of bed. The street lamps created strange and shifting patterns over their cage and the bars cast long thin shadows on the wall behind them. I peered into the cage. There they were, at the bottom of the cage, eyes open and completely still.

I carried the cage to the kitchen table and switched on the light. I nudged them with the tweezers. They didn't move. I ran my fingers through my hair and lit a cigarette.

It wasn't hard to open them up. Their feathers were shorter and I didn't bother trying to remove them. I discovered that if I made an incision just above where the wings connected to the torso, I could cut and peel the skin in a fluid motion. The muscles gave me more trouble. I hadn't boiled the birds, so I had to sever each muscle and tendon from the bones before I could pull it back.

It took me over an hour for Vlatig. The smell stopped me cold and I smoked a cigarette to get the scent of him out of my nose and off my fingers before I started in on Vera. When I had exposed both of their rib cages, I stopped for a minute. I hoped I would find everything in there as it should be, but I had that bad taste in my mouth again. I looked at the clock on the wall. It was nearly four. The garbage trucks would be coming around soon.

OK. This is it, I thought as I snapped apart their rib cages. At first, as far as I could tell, they looked normal: they each had their lungs and tiny graying bumps—their stomachs I supposed. But each of them was missing a heart. I wrapped them in newspaper and put them each into a separate shoebox. I took them down to the trash bins and laid them on top of a neighbor's mound of potato peels. Back upstairs, I could hear the neighbors' voices and I wondered what people argued about at four in the morning. I shut my door quietly and went back to bed. Suddenly, I was very tired.

～

"Hi, Henryk," I said the next morning. I stamped my feet. It was the end of April, but still cold out and wet. The sky dumped water and I wondered if all the earthworms might not drown in their beds. My entire body ached, I was smoking another cigarette, and I felt terrible.

Henryk looked at me for a moment, then unlocked the door and pushed it open for me. He pointed to my cigarette. "I thought you quit," he said. "You don't look so good—did the birds keep you up all night?"

"Yes," I said. I walked into the store and hurried past the birds. The vivid colors of the fish interested me, but I wanted something that would pay attention to me and something that needed me. I wanted birds that sang happy songs or could recite jokes, and if I couldn't have a bird, then I wanted a cat or a dog.

In the pen where he ordinarily kept his rabbits, Henryk had a kitten. She was rolling around in the sawdust and straw and mewling. She was a Siamese with blue eyes so brilliant and deep they appeared violet. I took one look at her and thought of my redhaired neighbor.

Henryk pulled out his chessboard and I helped him set up the pieces.

"So tell me, what did you name the turtledoves?"

"Vlatig and Vera."

Henryk opened with a trademark move of a Queen's Gambit. I could see a corner of that chess magazine sticking out of the drawer. I countered.

"You know, I always thought you were the kind of guy who should have pets," he said. "Some people shouldn't have them, you know?" I studied the pieces and wished Henryk would stop talking. "Pets are hard work. Responsibility. Like having a baby. They don't listen to you, and don't always do what you want them to do." He moved another pawn. He was trying to put me on the defensive.

I nodded at the pen with the Siamese in it. "How much do you want for her?"

Henryk looked up at the board and bit his lip. "I don't know, Mirek. Is it such a good idea to have birds and a cat?"

"To tell the truth, Henryk, I didn't want to mention it. You'll think I'm a terrible person, but Vlatig and Vera, they died last night." Henryk stared at me. "It was painless. At least, I think it was painless. I can't explain it. I did everything the pamphlet said to do—I gave them food and water and kept the heater on and opened the window a crack. Maybe I'm just not good with birds," I said at last. My hands shook and I stuffed them into my pockets.

"What makes you think you'll be any better with a cat?" Henryk asked.

"I don't know." My voice sounded very quiet and hollow in my own ears. "I have a good feeling about this," I said. I could see Henryk was really thinking.

"You can't afford a Siamese, Mirek," Henryk said finally. I moved another piece. I looked at the corner of that chess magazine.

"What if we played for her? If I win, I get the cat; if you win, I'll never mention it again." Henryk studied his hands for a long time. He was probably thinking of how I never win.

"All right then," he said.

⌣

Night had fallen. I carried the kitten tucked underneath my scarf. She burrowed in the hollow of my armpit and I could feel the soft pads of her tiny paws on my chest. She smelled like sawdust and some sweet animal smell that I could not name.

"Ester," I said to her. "Your name is Ester because you are the one who is going to make it." I walked quickly through the streets. Damp air had settled in and the flat light from the street lamps illuminated small circles of fog. I caught my reflection in a window. Ester had worked out from underneath my scarf and was looking around. I was smiling and my cheeks were flushed, and my heart skipped a beat because for a moment, looking happy like this, I didn't even recognize myself. I ran up the steps of my apartment building, nodded to my beautiful neighbor coming out of her flat, and closed my door shut behind me. I put Ester in the middle of my bed and banked the blankets and my pillow around her. I ran to the cupboard for a tin of fish.

"Only the best for Ester," I sang out in my stage voice. I rifled through the kitchen drawer, looking for a can opener. The knife and tweezers were there in the sink and I pretended not to notice them. I brought her the fish and offered her a small piece of it. She sniffed at it, then turned her head away and curled into a tight ball. I stroked the softest patches of her fur, on the top of her head and around her tiny ears. I did an impersonation of the landlord, then one of Henryk. Then I imagined I was back in the theater with Mrs. Jasenska and did my best imitation of a kitten. I licked my hands, purred, arched my back. I rolled Ester over with my nose and listened for her heart and for her breathing with my ear on her chest. Her eyes were closed and when I rolled her over, she didn't struggle to right herself. I nudged her tiny legs, her head. She didn't move. I put my ear to her chest. I could hear a faint beating. I studied her, watching for signs of life. She opened one eye and looked at me, and then closed it again. I gathered her up in my arms and held her to my chest and listened to the uneven sound of her breathing.

In the morning, I met Henryk as he was opening his shop. "How's the cat?" He asked. He was having trouble with his key. I pulled a cigarette out of my coat pocket. But my hands trembled so badly, I couldn't light it. I shook my head slowly, let the cigarette fall from my lips. "Stop this," Henryk said. His hand was on my elbow and he gave it a shake. "Stop doing this, Mirek."

"Believe me, I wish I could. I don't even know what it is I'm doing exactly." The door was open now and Henryk stepped through.

"Stop it, Mirek, I mean it," he said to me again and closed the door behind him.

I walked home but I didn't want to go inside my flat. I was experiencing a terrible déjà vu and my stomach hurt. I pushed open the door to my flat and stood there in the doorway for a moment. I could hear nothing. Behind me the neighbor woman's door clicked shut. I stepped forward, pulling my door closed.

"Ester?" I walked toward the kitchen, then turned and looked at the bed. "Ester, are you all right?" I could see her on my bed. She hadn't moved from where I had left her earlier that morning. I sat next to her and looked out the window. It was only 10 A.M., but already my feet hurt, and I was tired.

I didn't even bother examining her. I picked her up and it seemed strange to me how stiff things become when they are dead. Her feet stuck straight out and I couldn't get her legs or paws to bend without forcing them. I had run out of shoeboxes. I dug around in my closets and found an old hatbox. I put her food dish and the toy mouse she had never played with in the box and tied the lid down with a piece of string. I walked to the door. Outside in the hallway I could hear the neighbors screaming at each other and the sound of dishes breaking against the wall. I stepped out into the hallway. The beautiful neighbor woman's lover was storming down the stairs and shouting obscenities at the top of his lungs. I was glad Ester was dead and couldn't hear it. Just then, the neighbor woman opened her door. She had been crying and her lip was cut and bleeding. I held the hatbox with Esther in it. Our eyes met and I looked away.

"I'm sorry," I said. "I didn't mean to stare. It's just that—"

"It's all right," she said. She stood looking at the floor for a moment and then looked up at me. She stepped forward and touched the lid of the box. "What's in the box?" she asked.

"Nothing. Nobody. I mean, it's nothing." Her dog, a snowy longhaired Samoyed, pushed from behind her and nudged the lid from off the box and sniffed at Ester.

"Laika—no!" The woman said, pushing her dog back into the flat, and pulled her door shut. "I'm sorry about that."

"No. It's all right." My voice cracked. And then I started crying. I had never cried like this before in front of strangers, and it was not a good feeling. Not like the fake cries on the stage. She put her hand on my shoulder. And then I looked at her, saw her lip, and felt shame. I set the hatbox on the floor.

"Forgive me," I said, pulling out my handkerchief. "You're hurt."

She took my handkerchief and dabbed at her lip. I could see the bones of her face, how they were like those of a small animal, like the tiny and changing bones of a pigeon.

"You're Mirek Wieja, aren't you?" she asked. I nodded. "I wondered. I like to try and match the names on the mailboxes with the tenants in the building. Yours is one of the few names I hadn't matched up yet." She was still dabbing at her lip. Then she held out her hand to me. "I'm Anya. Would you like some tea?" I looked at her tiny hand and then I looked down at the box.

I wanted to do the right thing, so I told her that she was very very beautiful, but she should stay away from people like me. I was not a good person. I was the sort who was likely to get into trouble, had gotten into trouble. There were things about me that she would never understand. I told her all of this, but I've noticed that with some sorts of women, they never listen. As if no matter what you do or say, especially what you say, they persist in falling in love. As if falling was an unstoppable thing to do, as if love was like gravity.

"I'm sorry," I said, biting my lip. "I'm late for a chess game." I picked up the shoebox and ran down the flight of stairs. I tossed the box into the trash bins and ran back to Henryk's. It wasn't yet lunchtime so I was surprised to find his shop door locked. In the window a sign hung crookedly, as if Henryk had been in a hurry when he taped it:

SHOP, AT THE VERY LEAST, CLOSED

I looked up at the dark clouds about me. The air smelled metallic and heavy and I knew it would rain again soon. I turned on my heels and walked back to the apartment building, back to Anya.

Her door stood ajar. I knocked softly and the door swung open.

I stood there on the threshold and felt the warmer air of her apartment on my face and hands. I could smell the grease frizzling on the stove and the musty smells of Laika, and I felt lonely again because though I was warm I could see how far away she was from me as she stood at the sink, turning on and off the tap. I could see her reflection glancing off the windowpanes above her sink, and she looked like a ghost with huge empty eyes, the sounds of her bustling, the sounds of the city filling her eyes. And I knew I loved her. Yes, it was at that very moment I thought, *These are the thoughts the great tragic heroes of the plays and operas think about their lovers, this is what real love is.* And then I was disgusted with myself because by becoming so aware of this moment, of this feeling, I had somehow ruined it already. I lit a cigarette and took a deep drag. She turned and walked toward me.

"I thought maybe you'd come back," she said, handing me a teacup.

"This city has bad dreams." I told her.

"What?" She walked back to the kitchen and moved around, turning the tap off and on, washing her hands, drying them. She pulled a head of lettuce from the refrigerator and rinsed it under the tap. Watching her do all these things, hearing the noise of her, it all sounded like different shades of sorrow and I imagined even the lettuce would soon wilt with grief.

"You should go away," I said. "Just go away from here. Warsaw is not a good place. Too much has happened here. It's like every step you take you might be standing on someone's grave marker. And the memories." I stopped to grind my cigarette in her ashtray. "They are like ash falling, fallen over everything."

"You're wrong," she said.

"No," I continued. "Even the buildings look sad." She laughed and shook her head and her long hair shook too, her hair that curled in the perfect ringlets that were so fashionable before the occupation. I bet women offered her good money for her hair and just then all I wanted to do was put my hands in it, comb it out with my fingers, examine it lock by lock to see just where the coppery red strands began and ended.

I touched a strand and rolled it between my thumb and index finger.

"Did you know that human hair has amazing tensile strength?" I was making this up and maybe she knew that, because she laughed and blushed a bit. "Oh, yes. In the camps, they shaved off female prisoners' hair and made netting out of it." This part I wasn't making up, but I wished to God I hadn't said it. I cursed myself, my stupidity, for that is the one taboo in this city, the one thing we dare not speak of, the one thing we do not name.

Her kettle whistled and Laika's toenails clicked across the wooden floor. She turned to the stove and I saw that whitest part of her neck. She looked up then and I caught her look in the reflection of the glass, and then it was me I saw in her eyes.

"Why are you so afraid?" she asked. Then she turned to me and laced her fingers around the back of my neck and she kissed me.

~~~

"Mirek," she said. "Mirek—" I could hear my jade plant weeping in the corner. "It doesn't hurt." She closed her eyes slowly, as if even that was a huge effort. I wrung a cold washcloth and placed it on her forehead. In the hallway outside my door, Laika scratched and pleaded softly. I squeezed my eyes shut.

She coughed. The sound of it was like an old key dropping in a lock. I could see the dust gathering on her already, as if sorrow could be some kind of sediment, something like a fine mist, like memory, like every other inexplicable thing that covers the land, covers you so that unless you are looking carefully you hardly notice it at all. And yet, of course, it's there—behind the ticking of the clock, behind the rattling of a latch, every cough in a toilet stall, the hairpins falling without sound on the carpet.

"There are so many things I wish I could tell you," I said to her. She closed her eyes and smiled. "But they don't have words, I couldn't tell you even if I tried." I bent over her and put my head on her chest. Her heart slowed even as I listened. Laika began to whine more insistently then, and outside rain began to fall.

"Tell me," she said.

Then,

Returning

Oh, for the incorruptible body of a saint. Pranas stopped digging and breathed through his mouth. He watched Lukšas, his boss, pick though the ruined cemetery. Pranas tightened the band of the swim goggles Lada had found and given him. Yellow tint. He discovered that wearing them made the horror of finding a body minus an arm or leg a little easier to take. In some cases he was lucky: someone had the incredible foresight to bury their dead in bright dye-fast clothing. If he could match pieces of a skirt here to the rents of the bodice there, a right arm of an unraveled sweater to the left, it might do.

A terrible matching game. He had only these remains and some battered photos to go by. The Russians used to laugh at their river ways, scolding, *How silly. A photo of the dead—as if you'd forget.* Or worse: *As if you'd want to remember.* But sometimes this old practice of mounting photos on the stones came in handy. Like today.

Pranas knelt and examined the battered photos spread out around his feet. Once he'd fully recovered a body and reassembled its parts, he was to locate the appropriate grave and headstone and hope he'd matched all things up correctly. It reminded him of a childhood game he'd played with his sisters, "Memory." He remembered he hadn't been very good at it.

"Are we in hell, Lada?"
"Is it cold?"
"Yes."
"Then yes."

Yes, turnip. Or cabbage. Or whatever happened to be seasonal. *My little Kapusta. The cabbage can breathe.* And here came Lukšas holding a garlic bulb to his nose. Overhead a flint sky that split the light into fractions, the sun retreating in halves and then fourths.

Last night, Pranas had fogged the windowpanes, boiling his fingers and dipping them in candle wax. All this and a sink full of burning books. Philosophy, despite his mother's objections, was eminently practical. Anyone could see how much better Kierkegaard burned than Lada's anatomy texts. Lada spooned a bit of sugar onto a plate: ration-stretching, the next Olympic event.

"We are the champions," Pranas proclaimed, pushing back in his chair, his arms in a victor's pose, his scrawny caved-in chest puffed out. Gone were the days of line-standing in Vilnius when you could earn a few litai by holding places for others as they stood in neighboring lines of equal importance. Lightbulbs or bread? Oranges or socks? It was a guessing game. And now what were the stupid and lazy to do? Thank God for the mishap with those errant bombs.

Yes, too bad they fell on the cemetery, now torn up, bodies willy-nilly, parts thrown here and there. But Pranas, an optimist, approached Lukšas, the Chief Undertaker, all fear and trembling, and miracle of miracles, he was hired straightaway. Mercy.

Lada collected things. Some days buttons. Scraps of newspapers. Other days she collected tourists—Germans and Americans in the main—herded them around, sheltered under a broken-spoked umbrella she'd found on the trolley. After the Russians left, everyone wanted to talk. Lada interpreted all their questions, their impossible versions of history, their guilt and shame. She supposed they all had come around to see what was left of Lithuania, such a small and unimportant country. Parsing through the rubble they mused aloud: *What has become of the beautiful parks with the birches? Why does the river Neris look so dark and strange?*

At night, she went home to Pranas and his chattery bird Svengali. She chewed the ends of her fingers and gnawed candle wax while he burned books smuggled from the library. She recounted stories she'd collected for him during the day, stories with weepy sentimental titles and clichéd characters, stories that ran in circles, the endings cropping up before the beginnings, and middles, which were nowhere in sight.

"Do you remember Voja Luik? I saw her today, shaking on her calcified legs. You remember? She gave singing lessons. In Italian. In German. In summers you'd throw open the windows and we'd listen to the downstairs neighbors' passionate quarrels."

The downstairs neighbors knew how to put up good fights, very entertaining, better than anything Lada had seen in movies and Lada loved to hear the noise of their fury, the crashing of their ruined heirlooms thrown against walls. She loved to hear what would happen next, that and of course Mrs. Luik's students, their voices little birds warbling to flight.

Atanas Lukšas hadn't wanted to hire Pranas and the Russian. They had bad teeth, some of them jagged slivers. But it was hard enough to find anyone willing to work the graves, those beds of superstition and curses. This freakish bomb-letting, for which everyone responsible was terribly ashamed, had spooked away his normal crew of groundskeepers and just this once Lukšas decided to overlook the painful employment histories and dental work of his unlikely recruits. In the old days Lukšas would hand applicants a Rubik Cube at their interview. If they couldn't solve it, they didn't get the job. Simple. But he'd lost his regular crew and misplaced his Rubik Cube, all of which encouraged a strange bloom of compassion. In spite of his better judgment, he liked Pranas and the Russian—whatever his name was. They were hungry and everyone knew hungry wolves hunt harder. Besides, they'd work for as little as two kilos of bread a day.

Pranas breathed over the open kettle of bleach. *Oh, for an unsingeable forearm. For a city of incorruptible flesh. For the saints and their bones bleached to relic and for the smell of roses.* Pranas boiled the ends of his fingers in the kettle and watched the clouds of his breath and the kettle's steam cloud the windowpanes of their kitchen, a tiny room where they smoked and had a hot plate plugged into the wall.

"What do you suppose the devil does with all his free time?" Lada tapped the windowpane with her fingernails. Tap. Tap.

"He burns cabbage and reads." *We all know the devil is mad for books and that is why we offer up our favorites: Nietzsche and Hegel, Kant and Bonhoeffer. All the big daddies.*

Tap. Tap. Tap.

Oh for a game of chess.

"Have you been drinking?" Tap. Tap. Tap.

"Not nearly enough." *Oh, for a cigarette.*

He had given his pack to Lada so she wouldn't have to keep cadging them off the tourists.

That and because he could hardly bear that stench, the smells of the dead and the wet earth on his fingers, carried in the dirt under his fingernails.

～

Pranas leaned into his shovel and grunted. For three days he and the Russian had been digging. All on account of the bombs. Not smart bombs, just your ordinary run-of-the-mill dumb ones, these. And now what to do? Parts of old bodies mixed with parts of even older bodies, new graves formed out of old ones. And then, of course, the tragedy with the three nuns come to pay their respects. A case of very bad timing and of course, if anyone deserved a spot in the city cemetery, certainly they did, those noble sisters, those vanguards of chastity, vessels of sacrifice and potentially incorruptible, though it was much too soon to tell.

It had poured all day, and now, at twilight, the rain stopped and the sky filled with ash. The air turned to soot, which settled over the trees, the streets, the stones, as a second skin.

Lukšas , his boss, materialized from behind a stand of birches, bearing cloves of garlic.

"How about leveling out new ground and digging everyone a new grave? That way freshly dead or not, everyone has a space and we can be sure just what's what." Pranas stood and brushed the mud from the knees of his trousers.

Lukšas pushed a garlic clove into his left nostril and scratched the stubble sprouting from his chin. Overhead a gritty darkness, the sky a wet newspaper no one could read. "No good. Some people paid extra to be buried in a particular spot. Near the chestnut tree. Away from the chestnut tree. Near the Serbs. And everyone wants away from that Vyacheslav the Cossack and his horse. You see?" Lukšas waved the air away from his nose.

Pranas nodded. He could feel his muscles tightening, tiredness settling into his bones like a thick damp fog, turning him into a heavier, more substantial Pranas. At least the dead could rest.

Pranas removed his yellow goggles, spat in each eyepiece, and rubbed them dry with his sleeve, before him the bodies of the dead, each one of them a story needing finishing.

"It's all very upsetting." Lukšas made his way toward the undisturbed grave of the Cossack and his horse.

Pranas put the swim goggles back on. With them on, the whole world turned yellow and viscous. The limbs of lime trees twinned and overhead the first stars swam. Pranas bent and picked up the warped side panel of a coffin. Nearby he could see the faded blue fabric of a suit. Everyone should wear goggles, Pranas decided.

⌣

"Comrade."

Pranas turned and looked over his shoulder. Prohibited by all that is holy from looking the Russian in the eye, Pranas looked to his tobacco-stained fingers.

"Comrade. Let's drink and be friends."

Pranas crossed himself and spat on his shovel. Every devil said that. Pranas narrowed his eyes. The man's face was a mess of furrows and acne. He could be a devil. But there were no nubs for horns. A younger devil than the lines on his face suggested.

"All right. A drink. So long as its cognac."

They walked to the corner bar where you could stand outside and drink from paper cups. Though there were empty seats at the bar, they decided to stand outside on account of the way they

smelled. Around them the sky wavered, equal parts air and mois-
ture, threatening to run again to water.

"A toast."

The Russian cleared his throat, the warm-up, Pranas knew. God.
Russians and their toasts. Pranas tossed back the shot. From inside
the bar, he could hear German tourists, boisterous laughter.

Pranas avoided the Germans. He had no good reason, no good
explanation. He supposed it was on account of his grandfather.
The terrible ones, he'd called them. *They have no souls.* That and
the fact that he had failed German miserably in school. He just
couldn't get his tongue around it. *Nein,* he'd say, or *Nyet* when
they'd ask for directions, careful to make his *no* sound like a *yes.*

"Another." Pranas held up his hand, tapped on the steamy
window.

He'd heard German spoken in such a way it could have been a
song. Soft in the mouth, full in the throat. Anything could be
beautiful if you closed your eyes and refused to look. Anything
beautiful could be ugly with enough examination. Pranas pulled
out his goggles. The sky was all smoke and behind the bar plumes
of ash curled in the air. Soot chalked the city like tarnish on a
daguerreotype, and with his goggles on, the buildings along the
street took on texture like a photo of an old photo. Later he would
look up the word *myopia* in a pocket dictionary Lada had found.
He liked the sound of it. He liked the looks of it.

Lada had visions. Buttonhole visions of night so deep there was no
name for it. A darkness so dark you could poke your eyes out by
stumbling around in it. In that kind of night, the tiniest changes
in the dark could masquerade as a form of light. She was hearing
things now, too. Everywhere she went the sounds of flight followed

her, the rustle of feathers, the beating of strong wings. Inside her chest she felt each beat of those tremendous wings, the left wing despair, the right wing joy, both flapping simultaneously and in equal force.

In the evenings, when the light became a desperate thing, Lada studied Svengali. *Don't keep a bird in a cage; it can't breathe,* Pranas's mother had warned. But a bird knows what it is. And cages, whether right or wrong, well, a bird does not feel sorry for itself. Look at how Svengali sings, the ease with which his tiny chest lifts in song. Lada lit a cigarette and craned her neck toward the bird. When she clucked at Svengali, he unfurled his wings as if to fly. As light as the feathers were on the upper side of the wings, the undersides were dark, and Lada was amazed at the inky depths of that darkness. *Noch, Nacht, Nachtis.* Under his wings, the bird carried night.

~

"I'll tell you an incredible story," Marek, the Russian, said, leaning over the handle of his shovel. It was dawn. Pranas rolled his eyes heavenward. Yes. There were the crescent moons, both of them, creeping through the blurred willow, the sky sour and striated like three-week-old milk. Pranas closed his eyes.

Nobody dies of love anymore, Lada said, the summer before, a lifetime ago. She climbed into the boat, the blockish heels of her shoes overturning river rock in dull thuds. She was Jewish and studied languages at the university and had big plans for a Ph.D. All this made her immensely exotic to Pranas, who had failed at the university and had no plans. She collected things, words mostly, she told him, and he wondered what kind of stories she could tell in her many different languages.

"You'd never know by looking at me, but in my hometown, Kharkhov, I was Ded Moroz three years running."

Pranas overturned a shovel full of rancid earth. He tried to imagine Marek as jolly old Grandfather Frost. His uniform was ripped in several spots and covered in grime and soot. His coat was too big and when he lifted his arms to shield his eyes from the rain, he looked like a big ugly flightless bird. Unsteady in his boots, an altogether unsoldierly looking soldier, Pranas could only guess what being in the Russian army was like for such a man.

Pranas opened his eyes and adjusted the goggles. "Sure." Pranas nodded.

Marek smiled then, a crooked smile, and Pranas could see he was missing most of his teeth on one side. Pranas wondered who had done it—his fellow comrades or the Chechen Mafia making trouble in the border towns.

I'm holding out for small miracles, but I might settle, Lada said, smiling at him.

What? Pranas blinked. A second date, the kind that could have gone either way. Pranas borrowed the rowboat from a friend of a friend and he rowed in circles across the dark water, letting the boat drift where it would. She practiced her Russian on him, fluting the edges of each word, every word a small bird in her mouth, but wrong all the same, he wanted to tell her.

Nichevo. She had said finally. *"It's nothing to us."* They were talking politics and Pranas objected to the uncommon number of Russians left over, dissidents, defectors. Who knew what to call them? But why didn't they go back where they belonged? Lada shrugged when he asked, shifted her weight from off the oarlock, and stretched her arms along the gunnels. All that time the oarlock must have dug into her kidney and still she hadn't said anything except *It's nothing.* Pranas recalled a man he knew shot dead that previous winter for netting a bloated fish among the reeds. As if he wouldn't share. He watched how the steam rose from the body like a last wish. *There are no words for this,* Pranas said then, and said again now with Lada, resolving for the next hour, for the next few days, to forget everything.

When they bottomed out in the reeds, Pranas pretended to lose his balance, fell against her. She laughed, a full-in-the-throat laughter, and he knew how it would go, that he could stop worrying because before she had even gotten into the boat with him in her ridiculous shoes, she had already decided *yes.*

Pranas adjusted his goggles and leaned into the handle of the shovel.

Yes and her fingers spread across his thin chest, pushing against him a little, guiding him. She licked his ears, his eyebrows, his mouth.

"You should have seen the way the children yanked on my beard, crammed my pockets full of sweets."

On her tongue, a torah of love. Pushing himself in her, he bore her weight with his hips, setting the boat to a slow rock, the water doing the work for him.

"It's really something." Marek sweated over the shovel handle.
"What?"
"To be loved like that for a day."
Pranas grunted. After rain, the ground was heavy with clay and wouldn't give.

Yes, she said again.

"I suppose so." Pranas kept digging.

~~~~~~

At night her mouth would be tired of talking, her face tired of working the muscles up down, up down in fascination, in delight, confusion. It was important to make them feel like you were listening, her boss told her. She was an excellent listener, her brows pulled together, lips pursed.

Most of the time Lada liked the tourists, their innocent eyes sweeping the streets, the rivers, the forests, proclaiming it all good, better, even beautiful. And Lada knew some Russian, enough to trade, enough to curse properly. Lithuanian was such a disappointment in that department: *The devil take it* or *Toad!* There were days when you needed the three-story curse words the Russians had mastered, words involving indecent acts and other people's mothers. That could get you somewhere. And you could talk to them. Obsessive chess players, they believed in logic, and you could talk your way out of a trip to the nickel mines, out of a fatal bullet, if you were smart.

"Tell me a love story."

It was night again, a grainy dark that inked their windows. Pranas had come home with apples, an incredible find.

Too bad it's a love story you want. Love stories have ill-mannered heroes and the endings usually turn out badly.

"I have no words left." Lada licked his ear instead, moved her fingers over the features of his face, tracing lines in the dirt on his cheeks, along his brow. Over these last years, what with all the fallout from cracked and failing reactors, and now these bombs, she'd noticed everyone turning to ash, their features sanded over in dust, their faces empty. These days anyone could have the face of an angel or a devil, for they were very hard to tell apart with all this soot. In fact, it was not uncommon at all to see people stop under lampposts, grab each other by the shoulders, and peer intently into each others' faces, looking for the features that would remind them of the man.

___

They were making some progress. Just. At this rate they'd have work for another two weeks. And then what? The national question. Pranas applied his weight and overturned another bone. Someday this would make a good story. A story that had poisoned the country, but whose scent he promised himself he would not remember.

___

"It's nothing to us." Lada remembered saying. It was a second date, maybe the third, a test in a foreign language, the kind you spend translating yourself into the person your date might desire. Behind them the river sang, sang as always and Lada shrugged and nibbled on her thumb. She studied languages, not politics. And now she was a little tired of speaking Russian, though she had nothing against the language. Russians here, Russians there. She honestly didn't care, couldn't remember a time in all her twenty-three years Vilnius hadn't been occupied by some foreign army or another. And Russian was easier on the ear than German.

They'll all leave soon and then we'll wonder how we'll get along without them.

That's like saying if we are thrown into the sea, we'll hold our breaths.

Lada shifted her weight away from the oarlock and pulled Pranas onto her chest. *We're drowned already. That's what I'm saying.*

"What are you saying?" They had seen her lips moving and Lada blushed.

"It's a terrible curse to dream in daylight," she said to Russian-speaking Finns. Sturdy souls, they knew twenty different names for a tragedy and she was glad she didn't have to explain. The sky closed in and she heard the umbrellas push open, the sound like that of the sudden and heavy beat of wings.

~~~

The dead could rest. The cabbage could breathe. That morning Lada discovered a traveler's phrase book abandoned along the bank of the Neris. Lithuanian to Russian. The spine had been broken, the book folded to a page of emergency phrases: *Help!*

Lada waited outside the new kavine for her group. They were American tourists and wanted to drink coffee in this new coffee-house that looked like a laundromat, all shiny and silver inside. Starbucks. A cup of coffee cost as much as a pack of cigarettes. God help you if you wanted milk in it. And on the napkins, clever sayings telling you to live.

The tourists were Lithuanian Americans from the Lithuanian-American Historical Society, to be exact. They'd come around to examine their genealogical roots. Many of them had spent their lives saving to travel here, but they still asked dumb questions. *Why does it rain so much? How soon to the cemetery?* They all wanted to see the resting spots of their great-grandmas and grandpas, and Lada hadn't told them about the bombs.

It's important not to upset the Americans, her boss instructed her. *Don't bother them with the truth, even if they ask for it. Tell them a story, anything.* Besides, she needed their hard currency.

~

Pranas and Marek were stumped. Metatarsals or metacarpals? Tibias or fibias? A terrible guessing game. And what to do with them all? These questions and many more knocked the insides of Pranas's head. Should they dig all new graves for all the bodies, old and new, or attempt to relocate old graves and place the appropriate bodies in them (Pranas's suggestion)? Or should they group all the bones together and let the wild dogs sort them out (Marek's suggestion)?

Pranas adjusted his goggles and wiped the mud from his hands on his trousers. Overhead the light was turning liquid, a river with no bottom. Pranas imagined himself resting in the cool mud of the riverbed, watching the sky through the water and the water flowing over him, all the cigarettes, the newspapers, the clutter of words and people flowing over him and past him, the water carrying everything away. Lodged in the deep, he'd rock gently, moved by the water, held by the mud, the recipe for man. He'd make the place where thoughts came from return to trampled mud where they'd slip to nothing, and disappear altogether, those empty thoughts, those useless objects.

On a nearby headstone gummed down with globs of Juicy Fruit, St. Anthony for lost things, St. Jude for hopeless causes. Lada brought them by earlier for luck and Pranas had kissed the miniature saints as he stuck them to the granite. *For miniature miracles.* Then he had kissed her. *On her tongue, a torah of love.*

Pranas bent and wrestled with another femur. The mud hung in thick clumps to the bone. Pranas stood and wiped his hands, beginning to believe that his life really was as simple as water and mud.

～～

How soon till the cemetery? Lada walked her group along the Neris, on Kalvariju gatve, over the bridge of good proletariat fathers. They'd seen Gediminas' hill, heard the story of the wolf, and now on to the Great Cathedral. Still, they wanted the old cemetery, the cemetery in disarray, and Lada was running out of points of interest, stories to tell. She'd taken them to that Starbucks twice already, explained Gediminas' vision of the iron wolf, how when the wolf howled with its iron jaws, Gediminas knew to build Vilnius, voice of the wolf, here, along the river in this land of unbroken howling.

Lada walked her group to the gates of the old city cemetery. Excavation didn't sound right, and bombs were out of the question. Relandscaping might do.

"At last," a white-haired man breathed. "We're here." He pulled the thick leather strap of his camera over his head and removed the lens cover. Through a cluster of birches, Lada saw a disk of yellow, Pranas's lamp, warming the gold lettering of a nearby headstone. And then from out of the birches came Lukšas, the Chief Undertaker, cursing in Russian and waving his arms.

"Just what I need—an international incident." Lukšas screamed and flapped his arms. Lada turned to her group and coughed politely. "It's an old superstition. A river belief. It's bad luck to take pictures in a cemetery." An outrageous lie. She forgot to ask Pranas if any of the photos remained and if so, if they were still intact, mounted on the headstones. Lada opened her umbrella, tried to cover as much of the gate as possible with her body and the umbrella.

"Get them out of here!" Lukšas, now at the entryway, put his hands on Lada's shoulders, spun her around, and steered her clear of the gate.

"I'm sorry." Lada turned to the group. "He says it's ill-advised."

"But we've come all this way," the man with the camera said.

"He says, actually, the cemetery is closed. All week. For repairs, you see." Lada waved in Pranas's direction, careful to keep their view blocked with her open umbrella.

The kneebone's connected to the thighbone.
The thighbone's connected to the . . .

〰️

"Will you see St. Anne's now? The architecture is really quite lovely." Lada pulled on a strand of hair, shepherded her distraught group away from the gate. She opened and closed her umbrella. The beating of wings. Open and close. Open and close. She'd soar to a land where she could exchange a *vui* for a *tui*. She would beat her wings, one side day, the underside night. She would leave the crush of useless things, the philosophy and candle wax, the impossible questions.

It's not raining. Why are you doing that?

And how beautiful, how deliriously grand she would feel, that burning inside, that internal beating bearing her up on strong wings. A return to air and flight. She would escape the troubled ground, the heavy air to the pure and uncluttered dark where it is always night.

. . . hipbone.

Yes. And she'd spread her knees apart to give him room and the whole time he'd worried about crushing her bones, bruising them at the very least.

They'd made a long line of the bones, largest to smallest. Then came Lukšas, St. Lukšas of the garlic. Pranas pulled his goggles onto his forehead, put his hands on his waist.

"This is all you've done? In three weeks, THIS IS IT?" A garlic clove popped out of Lukšas' nostril with a loud whistle. Pranas could see the blood pumping in a blue vein raised along Lukšas' temple. The truth was they'd simply given up. A story with an unlikely beginning, they dug and dug. A terrible middle, they studied photos, arranged and rearranged, an ending nowhere in sight.

Night had fallen. They were tired. Lada and Pranas sat in their kitchen drinking. Lada liked how, with lights out, night leveled everything. She looked at the dark form of Svengali inside the cage. His wing, for instance, underside or topside, white or black, appeared the same, made equal by the absence of light.

They passed between them the bottle of Stakliškės and she could feel it rotting her teeth even as she swallowed it down in desperate gulps.

"Tell me a story," she whispered, laying her head on Pranas's shoulder. "Anything."

Eulogy for Red

"Hate is unfortunately always much more observant than love, and more observant even than an insufficiency of love."—Josef Skvorecky, from *The Bass Saxophone*

That was the day I awoke and red was gone. At first, I didn't notice it: my flat faces a shadowy inner courtyard where old Vaclav, the manager, keeps the trash bins and the Ukrainian couple next door hang their laundry. It was early in the morning and I climbed out of bed, trying not to wake Madla, and dressed in the dark. But when I reached the street I saw that something was wrong: red was missing, like someone had erased it from a color test patch, had washed it away from the air and the sky and everything under the sky. The glowing of the sunrise pushing up from behind the hills bled in stale shades of slate and cobalt and shale. The trees, which had gone to blood and fire and all the warm colors of fall, now looked frozen as if in the photographer's silver, the leaves pale like old paper money.

I kept walking, shaking my head in disbelief, walking like a tourist whose head wheels in all directions. I watched the traffic creep by and noted how stopping and going at intersections had become a matter of looking for green. The red had drained from the neon signs hanging at the windows of the shops, cafés, and pubs along Spálená Street and Václavské Náměsti, both of which seemed a little dull, even naked, without it. Gone was the red from the bricks, as blood leached from stone, and even the rooftops looked colorless and cold, like the scales of chapped lips. It made me think of looking at the world through the shard of a bottle or a piece of colored glass, or of those cheesy plastic tourist slide viewers, the kind that had only three color slides mounted inside and that over time faded out into the sepia brown colors of the earth and aged photography. I looked up and wondered if Mars, that red planet, had been affected, too, and if I could even pick it out from the nighttime sky with my cheap toy-store telescope. Finally, when my neck started aching, I went to work.

⌁

I work on newspapers and before I start my shift I usually stop in at the basement break room and harass Mack, an apprentice copywriter who thinks he's Willie Nelson or John Denver or something and who wears a big Tombstone belt buckle. We exchange off-color jokes and office gossip and then I hang up my coat, get a cup of coffee, and head for the print floor. But today Mack had his earphones turned way up, and besides the tinny noise coming from his earphones and the ordinary noises of the press dulled by the concrete walls, I could hear nothing strange, nothing unusual, no cries of panic, political harangues, or philosophical musings. Everyone was strangely quiet, as if contemplating a joke that they'd all heard but no one had gotten yet.

I looked at the blue line proofs lying on the break table, expecting a 24-point or maybe even a 36-point headline. But there was nothing about red in the proofs either. I scratched the stubble on my chin. Shouldn't there be a special feature, a quote from somebody important in the scientific community? *How did we come to be here stranded by red into the blues and what should we do about it?* I wondered. From what I could gather, the president hadn't yet made a statement. He had left Prague suddenly for Brno and then Slovakia and I thought, *Maybe he's been too busy to make a statement.* I wondered if we shouldn't make some sort of comment for him. After all, as printers and distributors of news, it wouldn't be too far afield.

I sat on my stool, watching the cylinders spin, the whole time feeling guilty, as if I were participating in a lie, and wondering what I could say about red. I was still shaking my head and chewing the inside of my cheek, sure that I was sleepwalking and that this was just another strange dream. Finally, the bell rang and I got up from my stool, as did the others, and we all filed out to make room for the next shift while the wheels kept rolling.

All the way home from work, I kept looking for signs that I was not alone in this, that others were worried, too. I went past the butcher's shop where they chop off heads for a reasonable price, noted the light gray smears on the butcher's apron, the ashen splatters on the block. I passed my hands over my eyes and blinked. I pinched myself. I cleaned the lenses of my glasses, but only the birds nesting in the trees were willing to acknowledge that something was wrong: I could tell from their loud squawks, shrill cries, and the long throat-rending screeches that they were upset, and I worried for the redpolls and robins.

I walked home, deciding to call in at Loli's, whose flat was on the bottom floor of our apartment building. If anyone had theories about red, it would be old Libuše, or Loli, as she called herself now that her husband had wandered off for good. Her flat opened up to the street where she ran her tiny florist shop. She lived in the room at the back where she grew her more exotic flowers under plastic flaps and beehive-looking contraptions. What she couldn't contain in her sleeping room spilled out into the courtyard: topiaries in stucco pots and flats of herbs, potted geraniums, and hanging baskets of flowers and vines whose names she had told me but I had forgotten.

Loli had the kind of laugh people mistook for a cry and that could stop cold all conversation around her, but I always liked visiting her because she was a little crazy and because her efforts had turned the courtyard into a green oasis of life. It was hard to be depressed or sad around Loli, who saw no good use for such things.

I walked past the Widow Dubček's, stopped in front of Loli's flower stand set up on the street, and noted her latest project: a large privet hedge that was really a series of individual potted bushes lined up to give the appearance of a solid wall of hedge.

Most of her roses were bleached of all color and the freesias looked like they'd turned to stone. She was bent over her lilies and crooning to them the way some people talk to little dogs or kept birds. Then she saw me and started waving her hands around.

"So what do you make of all this?" I asked her, sweeping my arms out wide toward the street and turning, my attempt at an expansive gesture.

"What?" Loli wrinkled her nose and wiped her gritty hands on the sides of her skirt.

"Red. It's vanished, you know."

"Oh. That." Loli turned back to her lilacs. "What's got me worried—I'll tell you what I'm worried about." I sighed, for this was the key turning, the battery charging, and any second now she'd start in again on her theories of invasive organic gardening and how it could save the planet if we'd all give it a try. And then I felt embarrassed that I was embarrassed by her, and ashamed that I was the kind of guy who was impatient with old women.

"I'm thinking of trimming the hedge in back and coaxing out the form of an animal—a fish or bird maybe—because I read just today that every garden should have a joke in it, something amusing that draws the eye and a laugh. Which do you think I should do—a fish or a bird?" Loli asked.

"I don't know," I said, brushing my hand along the biting edges of her meticulous privet hedge. "A bird might be nice," I said and stared down the street, letting my eyes blur in and out of focus, watching the people moving past me coming home from work. It felt good to let my eyes fix on the street, staring without purpose, without thought really. Then I felt Loli's gaze sliding over my face and shoulders. I shook my head, waking myself from my reverie, and saw Loli, a harried look on her face, worried, I knew, for me. I shrugged and walked back down the corridor, past the Widow Dubček's, to the stairs and to my flat. But the whole way I was thinking of the red woman of Ramadan who chases those who try to cheat death, her red eyes burning, and wondering if the red woman was to blame, thinking there must be someone to blame.

That evening, twilight unspooled in unexpected shades of glowering yellows gone to gray, the softer colors of long-burning embers, the colors of lye and ash, and I actually put my hand to my ear, sure a quiet fireless smoke would start thundering and we'd all be done for. I stood outside my flat and watched the sky cool and I remembered a day when I was in primary school, a day just like this one, a day we all stood around staring up at the sky. Except then we were waiting for a total solar eclipse. My father had made pinhole viewers out of shoeboxes for each of us kids. I remember his fervent warnings and of putting the shoebox to my eye and being afraid, terribly afraid that I'd make a mistake, at the critical moment flinch, blink, miss it all, or worse, blind myself by looking at the eclipse with the naked eye.

That night I dreamt that my mother came to me stuck to the flip side of a bottle cap and floating on a red tide along the banks of the Vltava. "Oh, Mother—what's happened to you?" I cried. She unfurled her wings, then folded them up again, for she was a little swan with her old human, mother head stuck on the tiny curving white neck of a swan. She spun her head around in a full circle, snapping open and closing her golden glassy eyes.

"Don't worry so much. This is what happens when you die," she said, nibbling at something bothering her in her feathers. I thought she was an angel and a fish, like both these things and like neither of them at the same time, all at odds there in the red Vltava. She glided soundlessly onto the wide lip of the river's bank, then disappeared into a slurry of fireflies beneath the branches of the willow and lime trees along the river's edge. I settled in my covers a little deeper and could hear faintly as if from very far off, though I knew it was as near as just under my bedroom windowpane, the Widow Dubček hollering at her cat, and I worried for the cat and thought, if I get a chance, I will grow catnip for it in pots and reserve the very best of my trash for that poor cat.

I awoke the next morning with a bad taste in my mouth and lay beside Madla, listening to her heavy breathing and thinking about red. I thought then that we should be very careful with what colors remained, taking great care to remember and preserve them accurately and with reverence. Maybe we'd been careless, had taken red for granted, collectively forgotten red and so it disappeared. Maybe it was still here, even now, but we had all changed and couldn't see it. Entire cities had disappeared, I knew, without a trace from memory and maps alike, simply because people had forgotten to remember them. Then I thought, maybe we are just stunned, like those birds that fly into the windowpanes of buildings, mistaking the glass for sky. We'll rouse ourselves, wake ourselves from this redless dream, and all will be as it was before.

I kicked the covers over onto Madla, pulled on my trousers, and went to the kitchen where I stuck my head out the window. It was a late October morning, and now without red the whole world had gone blue, the hillsides and outlying fields retreating to purple and then a dark that didn't have a name on any color wheel. There was Loli hosing down the courtyard in her hip waders and her husband's fishing hat that jingled with tackle and artificial flies. Then I remembered her comment and wondered if taking red away wasn't the gardener's joke on us.

I pulled my head back in and sat down at the kitchen table with a pencil in hand, determined to do something, and made a list of everything I knew about red:

1. It is a primary color at the lower end of the visible spectrum.

2. Red can vary in hue from a deep dark blood color to a very light rosy pink.

3. It is one of the first and last colors of sunset, one of the longest lingering colors.

4. Red is frequently associated with anger, bad financial moves, and communism.

5. They say there is the tiniest bit of red in every strand of hair on

every head of every person on this planet and that only dead or dying hair doesn't have traces of red.

6. My mother's hair was red and when I was a baby, mine was too, but since has turned brown.

7. When I grow a beard, it is red, except of course now my beard is a grayish white.

I read my list over twice and closed my eyes. I thought if I just concentrated very hard, I could bring red back, even though I knew it was silly to believe anything so big depended upon my efforts. When I opened my eyes and red was still gone, I decided to go looking for it there in the kitchen. I could hear Madla stirring in the bedroom and her old radio, an outdated box that sputtered and struggled behind static like a moth at a screen, buzzed to life. I was on hands and knees, my nose in the refrigerator, sniffing for the scent of red, and I opened a jar of beets that had blanched entirely, then put my ear to the vent, listening for red. All the while the most beautiful jazz rendition of "Stardust" floated in from the bedroom.

"Help!" I cried into the vent. "I can't remember what red looked like!"

"Go back to sleep!" Someone from upstairs yelled back down through the vent.

Madla appeared in the kitchen then and yawned. "It's no big deal, Jindrich. They'll issue new currency, make new recommendations in the house, and there'll be nothing more to it," she said, setting the egg timer and retreating for the toilet, where I heard the shower running and I knew this was the last consideration she was giving it.

Oh, this is silly, I thought. Stupid. Worse than that—clichéd. This is the kind of cheap stunt an art teacher with the ink on her license still wet and a wild look in the eye would propose to her students: *Paint a tomato, a strawberry patch, a broken watermelon, a bleeding heart without using any red,* and rock on her heels, eyebrows arched, a tight triumphant smile stretching across her face. I looked around, sure that a siren would go off, and the joke would be revealed and we'd all have a good laugh at the prank someone had managed to pull. Behind me Madla's egg timer ticked while upstairs the Ukrainian couple were fighting again, and I thought the woman was accusing the man of taking something from her. I sighed and stared at the ceiling, trying to make some sense, read some pattern in the cracks sprawling across the ceiling like bad handwriting.

Madla was still showering. I went to the toilet anyway, reached into the medicine chest for my razor, soaped up, and started shaving with quick even strokes. Then the timer rang and I flinched, nicking myself. But it didn't hurt much and I hardly even noticed the gray spotting of blood. The sun broke open over the hills then—a quiet, yellow, unspectacular affair—and I knew I had better be getting to work.

I let myself out of the flat and went down the stairs. There was Vaclav, the manager, kicking at the weeds growing in the cracks along the courtyard. He was mad for books, especially those of Kierkegaard and Nietzsche. He didn't like me, I knew. He didn't like it that I didn't know philosophy and that Madla stayed over with me sometimes.

"It's not that I'm old-fashioned," he had said, confronting me in the stairwell one day last spring. "But the sneaking around bothers me. Do you have to be so furtive about it?" He had asked and I assured him that I didn't know what he meant and nodded to him to show my respect for his opinions.

"You see!" he cried, pointing a bony finger at me. "There it is again. Furtive!"

But today he hardly looked at me.

"Red's gone," I said to him.

"Yes, I know that, you idiot." He still wasn't looking at me.

"Well, I didn't have anything to do with it. It's not my fault, you know."

"How does anyone know anything?" he asked, finally swinging his gaze up to mine. I wanted to shake him, God I wanted to rattle him when he started talking like that. Instead, I shoved my hands in my pockets and started walking away, faster than the day before, but just as amazed at the sight of people like me moving along, as if nothing had happened, nothing had been lost, and even now as if there was nothing to lose.

⌣

"Hey, Mack," I said, hanging my coat up onto the peg and reaching for the coffee machine. "What's new?"

"Nothing." Mack was fiddling with his cassette player.

"You seem a little out of sorts." I was testing him, trying to see if he would speak to my fear and admit that yes, something was out of sorts, dreadfully out of sorts.

"No. I'm just blind with boredom." Mack finished with the tape player and crumpled his empty paper cup of coffee and tossed it into the trash bin. "See you," he called and pushed through the door, his head down and the music up.

I picked up a test copy from the break table, sure that with a whole twenty-four hours of redlessness, somewhere someone would be up in arms about it, and any minute now our phones would be jangling off the hook, our intercoms abuzz with electricity and life. But just as the day before, everyone was strangely serene and calm about the loss of red, as if it had never really been with us in the first place. And again, today, the newspaper was uncustomarily silent on the issue. I found an obituary for red and a few eulogies, one by an old woman who'd survived Birkenau and had more close-up encounters with the color than most. *"A bright and fiery companion of orange and yellow, survived and missed by many"* her eulogy read, or something like that, describing red by what it was not. I went upstairs and sat there the whole shift, staring glumly at the presses, wishing the bell would ring so that I could go home and think in the quiet and the dark.

"This isn't right," I said to Madla that evening when I got home from work. "What's wrong with everyone?" I poured myself a stiff drink.

"Oh, Jindrich. I wish you'd lighten up," Madla said, wiping her hands on her skirt. She leaned toward me and ran her fingers over the stubble of my beard. "Besides, I think you look very dignified with gray hair."

I tipped my head back, finishing the drink in one swallow.

Outside, the sun was setting again, a distant throb and a cluster of gray, like a malignant cancer fire-star on an X-ray. "Well," I said, dropping my hands at my side, "I guess that's it. Red's really gone." I turned around, slowly unable to believe it, thinking it was some kind of colossal trick that would wear off once we could acknowledge it as such.

"It was never my favorite color," Madla said, snapping open her cigarette case and frowning at the botched sky outside the window. Then she rummaged through her purse and tossed out her tubes of lipstick, each another dull shade of gray. She rested her chin in her hands and kept staring. I thought she was looking at the sky, looking for red maybe, but then I saw she was really watching her own reflection in the window, watching the way her bloodless lips turned white when she puckered to take a drag from the cigarette. She blew a heavy cloud of smoke.

"Oh, it'll come back—don't worry," she said at last, bending her head to check the sky as if red's going was a simple change in the weather.

That night, the TV's glow looked even greener than usual and the figures slurring across the screen had yellow, green, and blue skin tones and I thought: at last, the answer to dull TV programming—I might actually make it through a whole hour of television without feeling sick or depressed now that everyone looked like a Martian.

And I kept watching, still thinking that maybe we'd hear a pop from the TV or crackle from the radio and the culprit would come forward. That's when a public announcement message scrolled across the bottom of the screen. I thought: at last—someone will say something, someone will do something. But it was just a weather warning: the barometer had dropped unexpectedly and a storm was coming.

I went to bed. I lay there studying the dark and tried imagining it as a deep dark red, a dark that could have been red, a red sunk in shadow. Then I gave up. Try as I might, I couldn't remember red. I recalled a trick my uncle, blinded by war, had taught me. If you squeeze your eyes shut, he said, you can see unseen colors by rubbing your knuckles over your eyelids, digging them into the eye sockets. That night I lay there in bed, my jaw clamped and eyes clinched, rubbing my eye sockets for all they were worth. And it worked: I began dreaming of red stars swimming like firebugs over the water, which was also red, that fiery color of passion, the color of the heart and of heat. In fact, everything in my dreams—the dogs, the kestrels, the swifts, the sounds of the trains and of people's voices—was shaded in reds: brick red, maroon, vermilion, blood red, reds of the desert, reds of the tropics, coral reds of the sea, sapphire and magenta.

⌣

Some say the end of the world will come in a blinding flash of light and fire. Others believe the sky wolf will open his great jaws and swallow the sun in a long digestion, leaving the world to ice. But I figure it's going to be slow and drawn out so we can take note of each little change. We'll wake up and all be smaller, paler, shrinking as the sky unravels in bolts of color, only one color will be missing, and then the next day another color will be gone. Then everything and everyone will resemble each other completely with only the slightest variations of gray distinguishing each thing from another. That's when the snow will fall, dropping down quietly, hesitating in the air and on the palm like a small bird scared into flight, drifting and settling into imperceptible mosaics of pure white upon white, until at last the air and the ground under the air goes blank as an empty canvas.

I woke up, afraid I'd overdone it with the eye sockets, but thinking I could dream for days and not come up with anything so perfect. And then I felt a little ashamed. If it's true there are two tongues to every language, a tongue of love and one of hate, maybe what we were seeing here was a message from God in a celestial tongue of love, of grace, only it was incomplete as yet, and we didn't know how to read it. In fact, some of us had yet to even see it or recognize it. Yes, maybe that was the trouble. But the trouble was with us, with me, not with the landscape that had diminished and wicked out to a world of boot-polish blacks and ashen whites and the colors of stubble that outlives the man.

That morning, Madla and I went out to the courtyard to watch the storm roll in. We were looking over the rooftops. And then I thought if this was the end, how I couldn't say or do one thing that really mattered now, and even if I could, I wouldn't know what that one thing I should do or say was. I was in fact the kind of guy who could make his mother a little deader than she already was every time I opened my mouth. And I felt a sorrow then as thick and chalky as an aspirin too long out of the bottle, dissolving on my tongue, leaving a bitter aftertaste that I knew wouldn't go away no matter how much I drank. And I realized that this was the end-of-my-life flash: not seeing my life rewind as if on a cheap movie reel, but seeing myself for what I was. No wonder so many people feared the end.

A wind kicked up, catching a newspaper in full bloom against the courtyard brick. I could hear Loli behind her privet hedge, choking with her strange laugh, and I wondered if she was indeed crying. And then there was Vaclav in the stone corridor singing with cheer: *That's the fucking end, said Amundsen.* I pulled Madla closer and imagined I could hear our blood whistling like old radios, bleating like broken-down clocks.

Overhead, the birds keened and wheeled in tight circles and raised their pitch and I wondered if I should say a little prayer for them, the kestrels, those half-formed angels falling from sky, for the beautiful redpolls and the swifts, all unsettled by the smell of a storm and the sky's pallor.

But instead of being afraid I felt grateful. Yes, for all these things and many many more I was grateful, and to have had them here with Madla whose warm breath even now fogged the face of my watch and who made me think that if I could know just one thing, one tiny thing, know it completely, even if that thing was not her, but only near her, that could be enough. Then I could forget it all: the horror that if I looked inside myself there might not be anything at all to see, the mystery of my mother now happily drifting along in my dreams, and the fact that no matter how hard I tried not to, I had failed her in ways I might never understand.

Above us the sky burned with blues and yellows and greens, the green stripes of the sky matching the green irises of Madla's eyes. I felt my breath catch at the back of my throat, a quickening in my lungs, and I thought *My God, what a sight, this ancient watery landscape of color,* and it seemed to me then the days had never been so beautiful as these, and as this one in particular.

I wrapped my arm around Madla's shoulders and pulled her head to my chest and breathed in the smell of her hair. Madla squeezed my hand. "I love you," she said quickly, like the last thing you whisper as the lights die down and the projector flickers to life.

Sixty-six
Degrees
North

Laika shook the vodka bottle. Frozen solid. She dropped it back into her pack and kept walking. She should have brought Spirt. Rocket fuel, you had to be careful, know when to stop. Vanka's uncle, by all accounts an idiot, drank 300 grams of the stuff one night and went blind. Then again, he was the kind of a guy who'd smash a compass to get to the alcohol inside, he was that smart. But Spirt was good stuff, Vanka had told her. Only you had to remember where you were.

At 50 degrees north, you mixed half Spirt to half water. At 66 degrees, two-thirds Spirt to one-third water. A Siberian barometer. This way, who needed a map? One look at the bottle and you knew how far north, how cold. This was important here in the taiga in dead winter where removing a glove to point a compass spelled sheer madness and a certain loss of fingers. For there was no argu-ing with a cold that stopped clocks, cracked the synthetic soles of boots, splintered windows from panes—a cold that would shatter the moon if only it hung a little closer.

Though today it was a balmy twenty below, warm enough to fool one into smiling, at this latitude it was better not to, she had told a German couple earlier that morning as they waited at the station for the Baikhal bus. Not unless you were carrying bear fat, the only salve for sudden and careless gestures. But there were trade-offs. For its cruelties, there was something beautiful in the cold that froze one's breath so that entire words fell tinkling to the ground, a magical sound, what Siberians called the whisper of stars. An irregular beauty, you never got used to it, but beauty could be like that, a surprise, like the drama sparking from the end of a match on a subzero night. And there was something simple about this cold that divided all things into the categories of frozen and unfrozen, something true and right about this ice, an ever-widening river consuming its own banks. Only what remained mattered, the ice neatly cutting what lived from what didn't. That part was hard to explain to the German woman, who seemed to take the blistering cold personally. But now, with the station behind her, the couple safely trundled off for Lake Baikhal, Laika turned for home.

All the roads here in Om-Yakon ran straight out into the ice fields. More than once Laika had wondered what would happen if she followed one of those roads and kept walking through this land where darkness bled six months of the year, where the constant sameness glazed the eye. But thinking like that ground her down like a worn tooth in an aching gumline. No, it was better to think from day to day, minute to minute, the general stupidity being the same now as before, the same here as anywhere else.

When she talked this way, her Uncle Grisha would pipe up. "God is in the tragedy of lonely space," he'd say, his face tormented by thought. People got like this, philosophical and depressed, living here in this two-thirds land of ice and thaw, people two-thirds frozen, one-third not. And Laika couldn't spend too much time around her uncle, whose words hung in the air as fragments and interruptions, roads deadening to ice fields.

Before, she had carried ice. With Vanka, south through the Urmany, the world's biggest and coldest bog. They had to work fast here, where all the rivers flowed north and froze early. But Laika found, traveling south, traveling north, that she preferred ice to snow, liked how quietly ice grew, making snowfall sound loud by comparison as they carried back the essentials: penicillin, nails, onions, and sometimes sheet music for jazz, and once, boogie-woogie. She liked working on the ice, how ice told a story if you knew how to read the shavings and cracks, how to interpret the different sounds of buckling. And of course there was Vanka. Now that he was gone, she couldn't work the river by herself. And though she was the kind of girl who could enjoy weeks of silences, words were what people paid for and she could make as much interpreting for the occasional tourist as she could transporting goods over the ice.

Laika scraped her boots against the stair landing and let herself into her babushka's apartment. Uncle Grisha, chronically unemployed, sat in a chair, holding his head in his hands, teetering, Laika supposed, on the edge of something profound. And then he started singing, one of those songs not found in books but learned on buses, in cells, translated like a disease, like a pox in the language. The song was a string of phrases that, it turns out, were names: Anya and Vanya, Andryei and Alexei, rhyming verses about Magadan, new torments and old, startling details, so that while they could not fix the story to a particular person, they knew it was true.

Next to him sat Baba, a typical indestructible Russian babushka with her floral print shifts, her prayer cards. Famous for having made it out of the nickel mines, an unheard of feat, she was the town's undisputed mayor because of it. *Try telling her what to do,* the set of her shoulders and face seemed to dare, *go on.*

Laika filled the kettle and set it to boil. They sat without speaking for a few minutes, listening to the plaster chinking fall in chunks to the floor and to the wind whistling through the cracks and spaces. Not a bad sound, if you liked whistling. If it was a particularly strong gust, the wind might blow in two octaves at once as it carried away their words, so that people two doors down could hear parts of their conversations, their arguments and complaints, the punch lines to jokes, secret family recipes. And since she'd moved into Baba's windy apartment, Laika had noticed she'd developed a bad habit of repeating herself.

She reached into her coat pocket and pulled out a yellow paper, a work order from the Yakutsk Intourist office, unfolded it and smoothed it over the edge of the table. "Remember those Americans we took ice-fishing a few years ago? They're coming back," she said to Grisha. "This time they want to go sledding."

Her uncle laughed. "Not the fat ones—the Polar Bear Club?"

The kettle sighed loudly and Laika pushed it off the burner. Every year since 1981 these same Americans went someplace freezing and swam in the ice or went alpine climbing or danced nude in a blizzard to prove to themselves that they could. And fortified by their fat, they usually made out all right, except for minor cases of hypothermia and hangovers. They'd gotten special permission through the consulate to visit Om-Yakon, which was not a closed city. She knew she should forgive them. They couldn't help themselves, all that money and so much time on their hands. Life was a lark and they were curious. How cold does it get at the coldest place in Siberia?

They would want photos. She could imagine them setting up their cameras on tripods, looking for the trick of light that would turn this ramshackle town into a Renaissance scene, or at least a bearable snapshot. Still, she hoped the bureau girls in Yakutsk had reminded them. At this temperature, the film would shatter like glass inside their cameras, and Laika couldn't speak for the lenses either. If they couldn't have photos, they'd want stories—startling details of the cold, how it catches one, something to take home with them. Laika sifted through her limited repertoire, trying to recall the ones that might do. There was the woman who went crazy, thought she was a wolf and bit her husband's neck while he slept. There were alcoholic tales of wild sled rides over the ice fields resulting in mostly minor injuries, and a few major ones. Pretty ordinary stuff, though, and the endings never seemed to work out right.

"I need a good story to tell," Laika said, piling more wood in the stove. Though they had central heat creaking through their apartment, it was never enough.

Grisha had his head in his hands again, and terrified of the quiet, which was like a space in the chinking, Baba cleared her throat.

"I'll give you a story, only don't stop me once I've started. It's bad luck to break a story into parts, and repeating it . . ." Baba shook her head slowly from side to side. "That's like dying twice."

Laika nodded, for the warning was itself a ritual part of the story. What with the way the wind could carry off the hearts of their stories, the best of their ideas and intentions, who knew how they would be recombined, where the spaces in the chinking would lie?

Laika steeped the tea in the strainer as Baba began the story, always the same story, the tale of the boy and girl whose love is so fierce, so unswerving, they will die for it. They slip downriver on a boat, but are so anxious to escape the general stupidity of their village that they forget the important things: nails, penicillin, jazz sheet music. Days later, they are found together, cold and dead.

Baba is telling the story again and Laika hates her a little for it. How like those lovers, when the story starts, it moves in one direction, willed beyond motion. She hates the lovers, too, dismayed by the tragedy, by their utter predictability. How it will happen again and again, for it is bad luck to leave a story unfinished.

Laika studied the work order, which, though flattened, was still creased enough to balance on a central fold and tip back and forth with each draft blowing through the apartment. She could understand why the geologists and archeologists were interested in studying this blinding cold. There were secrets encrusted deep within the permafrost. The ice could tell time as well as any clock if you knew how to read the striations. All this digging might bear witness to centuries of cold, of slow changes, of people long gone. Even now they had the ice-smashers and drills going all day and through the night. They never turned them off, not even to refuel, now that winter had set. But the Polar Bear people? Who could say? Laika had tried to dissuade them from coming. Om-Yakon was not a winter resort and there was very little to see here. *Why not watch the winter weddings and the famous sani races on Lake Baikhal?* she had asked them.

~~~

In the morning Laika waited as a bus pulled alongside the station, a metal rail next to a cement stack of stairs that emerged from a mound of ice. She watched the bus door open, how the carriage of the bus nosed up, bolstered by its shocks, as the Polar Bear Club members, each one larger than the one before, stepped off the bus. Jim, Ted, Leo, Mike: their names were stitched to the outside of their heavy thermal parkas with the emblem of a big white smiling Polar Bear. Laika had forgotten how fat they were, and they seemed to her perhaps even fatter than before, though this time they brought a new member, Patty, a woman Laika did not recognize. Laika couldn't keep from staring at the woman's backside where the woman's butt and back seemed absolutely joined so that no matter from what angle she looked, Laika could not determine the place where one ended and the other began. Laika ushered them to the café inside the station where they could get coffee, cognac, and Siberian sandwiches, thick slabs of lard between two pieces of black bread.

"Wow," Mike, the youngest and skinniest Polar Bear, said, placing his hands against the triple panes, fingers spread, "the coldest place on earth." Outside the windows the wind kicked up, carrying crystals of ice, blurring the low buildings and everything beyond them to white.

"So this is where people got exiled?" Patty, the woman, said, her breath let out slowly though her teeth.

"Here. There," Laika nodded. "Any place there was something to be dug: nickel, diamonds, gold." She nodded toward mountains to the east, buckles just visible through the sheering ice, and began to count how many Russian cities were built on the bones of slaves: Leningrad, Norilsk, Magadan . . .

"A terrible man." Patty clucked her tongue the way you might cluck chickens home, while her eyes remained on Laika's, looking for agreement. Conscious that a woman reading a newspaper had stopped reading to listen, Laika shook her head, felt the words escaping her, and cleared her throat. Even now during Glasnost, everybody knew what you could say and what you couldn't. But here was a story she could tell Patty: Baba as a twenty-year-old carving out nickel at the bottom of a 30-meter shaft drilled through permafrost. Tied to a rope, she worked twelve hours, sometimes fourteen, pulled out only when she met her quota, and sometimes not at all. But there was no lesson to be learned from such a story whose ending, even now, wasn't fully worked out.

"Heroes have bad manners," Laika said at last, sealing the subject with a hazy smile and turning to the men. "I've arranged for dogs with a friend of mine, Ivan. Because of the cold, the rides will have to be quite short. And he says he hasn't enough dogs for everyone to ride at once. We'll have to go two at a time and alternate teams of dogs." Laika tried not to let her gaze slip to the incredible girth of the men's stomachs, to Patty's immense backside. Fed on their own fat through the winter months, they'd never die in the gold mines of Magadan.

Jim, the Polar Bear Club leader, invited her to stay and drink with them, and because just yesterday she'd resolved to spend less time around Uncle Grisha, and because watching Baba die a little each day depressed her, Laika agreed. They drank vodka, then cognac, and she felt herself carried by their high spirits, felt her shoulders relaxing, and even shared a joke, which they didn't get, and then her flask of Spirt.

"It's watered-down rocket fuel, so be careful how you smoke," she laughed.

Mike, who was only half the girth of Jim, winced as he swallowed a mouthful. "This reminds me of the stuff they gave me at the base camp." He took another sip. "When we were climbing Mount Everest and we ran out of oxygen and had to turn back. Fast." Laika could see the muscles in his jaw working, trying, she supposed, to suppress a grin. "That was the same year I lost two toes snowboarding in Antarctica." He laughed and Laika marveled at what things people took pride in—wondered, too, if he thought often about his missing toes. As Mike described the cold, how it made him feel each drop of blood flowing to his foot as pinpricks, and then, at the last, how he felt nothing at all, she was conscious that she was blinking uncontrollably, the scope of that kind of folly beyond her comprehension. Listening to him, knowing that there was some essential thing she did not understand, she felt as if she were becoming a fish, one of those that froze each fall and thawed in summer, a little dumber each year for having been frozen.

"Have you ever done something like that?" Mike asked her then, and Laika felt her stomach seize up. *You couldn't make mistakes like that here,* she wanted to tell him. *Pay attention* was every mother's mantra, the last words on every father's lips. Still, she'd made mistakes. But how could she explain what had happened to Vanka? How utterly stupid it was. A gesture, a careless slip that was now costing him three years of hard labor. For what? He had given her his papers because he wanted her to hold them, to know that he loved her that much. He might as well have chopped off his own head. Without the necessary papers, travel documents, he had no right on the river ice. *You could be anyone,* the police said as they took him away. *Anyone at all.* An unforgiveable crime. But this, too, would be hard to explain to her happy-go-lucky group and so much talk made her teeth ache.

Laika held her glove up to her jawline, feeling entirely like a girl with glass teeth.

"No, I'm sorry. Nothing of interest to tell." She took a generous swallow of alcohol and capped the flask.

~

On the way home, Laika collected the mail and Baba's medicines. Baba was dying as surely as a day on the calendar. She had seen Cuckushka perched in the tree outside their window, Cuckushka who knew the number of days a person had left to live. Laika knew that Baba had stood under the tree as Cuckushka sang, had asked, "How many?" and heard the answer. Now Laika knew Baba didn't want to recover only to linger through season after season. Death was one last necessary chore and she wanted to perform it well, believing that dying was what you gave to the living, and how a person died, that was a gift, too. You could see how easy it was to think this, here where earth and sky traded places, the broken clouds slow-moving ice over the darkness of the night sky.

Laika pushed open the apartment door and stopped to scrape off her boots.

"Those on the threshold always need the biggest push," Baba yelled from her bed by the stove where she drew the sign of the cross in the air in broad invisible strokes. She might have been talking about town politics, or perhaps she was complaining about Grisha, who had failed again to apply for a new work card. Baba had a cold cloth over her eyes and a pile of aspirins on her bedside table. Laika kissed her grandmother on both cheeks and set a long narrow envelope next to Baba's hand.

"You read it," Baba said, pushing the envelope away.

Laika opened it and read the letter printed in bold on the university letterhead.

The geological surveys indicated a large number of anomalies in the ice. In short, they'd discovered that there were bodies out there, ancient ones, and scientists at the state university in Yakutsk wanted to extract them from the permafrost for further study. What did the people of Om-Yakon want to do with the land? they wanted to know.

"Do?" Baba bolted in her bed. "Plant it with roses. The hardiest we can find. An ocean of roses!" Her papery arms swept the air over her bed. "As far as the eye can see, nothing but roses!" She collapsed back onto her pillow and Laika replaced the fallen cloth. She kissed Baba again and went to her own bed where, stretched out in the calm of the dark, she could think. Already she was dreading the morning. She would have to work with Ivan, a terrible drunk whose dogs weren't the nice sort you'd want to pet. And then the

Polar Bears. Laika closed her eyes and imagined how she'd endure their gazes and the sound of her own weary voice. She could hear the couple from the apartment above her fighting, all the ordinary sounds of apartment despair and the woman's violent sobs: *Why won't you talk to me?* And the man's reply: *What?* delivered sharp and short like a slap. *Shhh.* She'd have to remind herself not to shush the Polar Bears. *It's in the silence that you can hear.*

In the morning Ivan showed up with his dogs. He had a heated kennel, which he kept on an oversized sled attached to his car. They met outside the Brazil, a café where you could buy tobacco and tripe and cow heels soup so thick you could skate on it. The drinks were good, too, and to Laika, that's all that really mattered. Inside, the Polar Bears were waiting for her.

"What are they digging out there?" Patty asked, pointing toward the geologists stringing up sight lines over a patch of ice. She could lie: diamonds, musk oxen, a lost inheritance, evidence. Anything at all.

"Bodies, I think." Laika held her gloves up to her nose and mouth, and shrugged. Outside, the dogs were kicking and biting and bothering one another in their harnesses, and Ivan threw an ice chunk at the café door.

"I think Ivan is ready." Laika watched as Leo and Jim, the heaviest Polar Bears, won a coin toss and made their way to the door. "*Bozhe moi,*" Laika mouthed silently, *My God.*

Ivan's dogs were happiest when working, everyone knew that, but today was especially cold and it seemed to her silly to work the dogs hard on a day they didn't have to. But she knew Ivan needed the currency and she sincerely hoped the dogs were sturdier than they looked.

Ivan began to whistle then, setting a pitch that would have raised tundra swans to flight if it weren't so cold. At the headboard, Leo and Jim stood shoulder to shoulder. Ivan shouted at the dogs and they began pulling, their shoulders lowered into their harnesses. The sled moved a bit, then stuck on a crust of ice. Leo hopped to the side of the sled and ran a few meters, giving the sled a push. They went like this, stopping and starting, Leo running alongside, then jumping on the sled, which then jerked to a halt.

"This is torture," Ivan yelled back to Laika. "I don't like this."

For five more minutes the dogs kept struggling against the deadweight of the Polar Bears, but it was too much for them and Laika couldn't bear to watch it. The dogs at the wheels and rear would drop from exhaustion before giving up, she knew. At last, when they'd gone only a few meters farther, Ivan whistled, signaling the dogs to rest. The two dogs at the rear were panting and had to be stopped if they were going to survive. Ivan unbound their hitches while cursing Laika, calling her names she had not heard in years. She turned for the café, holding her gloves to her eyes, reminding herself to ignore the stinging, to imagine that beyond the frozen shroud of their insignificant town, this general stupidity, above them a million kilometers away the stars were bone-dry, every one of them.

Laika entered the café and sat with the remaining Polar Bears. "I'm sorry this didn't work out," she said as Jim and Leo pulled up their chairs. "But Ivan thinks it ill-advised. He says it's not a good day for pulling." Through the windows they watched Ivan, still cursing, load up the dogs and drive off, the tires kicking small lashes of ice.

"We have to do something. After all, we've come all this way. We have to do something," Jim proposed as a toast, and with dismay Laika watched the others raise their shot glasses and drink. She couldn't imagine what they'd think of next.

They continued like this, drinking and thinking of things they might do for an hour at least. Wearied by their talk, Laika took pulls of Spirt and imagined possible stories she could tell, if only they'd let her.

Before long, they were drunk, no denying it. Drinking in this two-thirds land did it every time. The talk had swerved into politics and other vague abstractions and listening to them made her head and jaw hurt. Laika took another swig, felt a burning inside her teeth, and wondered again what she could tell them—stories of the ice, how she and Vanka had to offload entire trainloads of supplies at Irkutsk and float them downriver, navigating during nights deep as a pocket because they had to beat the cribbing ice. How it was nearly impossible to get milk here because what milk there was sat in tankers and spoiled along muddy roadsides for lack of petrol and navigable roads. She had stories, a whole decade of winters full of them, but they were not tales that made good stories, no punch lines except the time Glasha, the banker's wife who considered herself above everyone on account of her flawlessly spoken French, fell headfirst in a latrine.

A harsh scraping of a chair against the floor snapped Laika from her reverie. Before anyone could stop him, Jim had taken off his jacket, his extra-large thermal fleece pullover, the Gortex waders and thermal leggings, and dashed outside. Laika had never seen such a large person move so fast; if she hadn't witnessed it herself, she wouldn't have thought it possible. She ran to the door, feeling by comparison as if paddling through setting ice, moving in slow motion.

"Please!" she shouted to Jim, who hugged himself as he hopped up and down. "It's very ill-advised, what you are doing!" But she could see that he couldn't hear her, the wind having carried off her words.

And then he'd had enough and was barreling past her through the open door, past his fellow Polar Bears standing with their faces pressed to the window, back to the round table where his clothes were. The café owner brought him a shot of cognac and a tiny stuffed parrot and an old button with a saying popular several years back: "Thank God it's Friday!" though, in truth, it was still Thursday. Laika watched as Jim pulled his clothes back on and sat very still, as if he were in a movie theater, watching in muted colors as the action happened to someone else. The Polar Bears congratulated him, slapped their palms against his, and bought him another round of drinks. Laika kept watching for signs of hypothermia: clumsy fingers, stuttering, cherry-red earlobes. But there was nothing.

"I could tell it was cold because my lungs felt heavy. But other than that . . ." Here Jim stopped to look around at all the faces at the table. "I didn't feel a thing."

The Polar Bears were leaving. Siberia had disappointed them, but they wanted Laika to drink with them at the station café. They were headed south to Irkutsk, that place where the sun encouraged snow, a land where a person had a shadow to receive him. When she'd carried ice, it had been their southernmost stop, and she was jealous. Inside the café they were waiting for her: Jim, Ted, Leo, Mike, and Patty all bundled up in layers of fleece and Gortex so that each Polar Bear took up the space of two people, and in Jim's case, maybe even three.

When Patty saw her walking toward their table, she rubbed the sides of her immense thighs with her hands and shivered. "I'm so cold," she said, leaning toward Laika. "I don't know how you can stand it."

"But you're a Polar Bear!" Laika exclaimed before she could stop herself.

Patty leaned back, rested her elbows on the shelf of her hips. "It's not my fault," she explained. "I've got a sluggish thyroid."

Laika detected a hint of something in her voice best left alone, more of that nostalgia. She felt sorry for Patty then, being as fat as she was. Except for her Uncle Grisha, who believed that a woman without a large backside was like a church without a chapel, men as a general rule, she knew, didn't even look at women who got too fat. Laika wished there was something she could say to Patty, something to cheer her up about the cold maybe. How living like this from cold to warmth, seasons of suspended dark to sudden flushes of light, was like a kind of grace. How there was something redemptive about this latitude, for if you endured the press of winter, then you had survived, lucky enough for another summer of aluminum foil at the windows, fleas digging down in the scalp, and another season of stories. Lord, the stories—how they needed them—coaxing shape to the unformed hours, hours upon hours of sameness, when the only changes were a few more or less drops of mercury in view as they waited for the thaw. But this was hard to explain and she was ashamed that she could not interpret this and felt it was a great shortcoming in her. Who was she to determine what a person could or could not understand simply because there were no words for what she wanted to say?

Instead Laika began to tell Patty a story, a warm story made warmer because it might not have been true:

"Once, in spring when we were fooled into believing in the thaw, we had an ice storm. The ice slicked the trees in a thick skin of glass, as if the trees, anticipating spring, grew careless and breathed too much. Some birds—tundra swans, if you can believe—had gotten thrown off their flyway by the winds and trapped by the cold. They just sat there under those trees, surprised by the ice, their wings and feet frozen, their eyes frosted over. They couldn't see a thing. It would have been easy to kill them all. With a little whack, their brittle necks would have snapped. And believe me, tired of dried fish and lard, we all thought of it, too. Instead, we wrapped them in our shirts, held them against our chests, brought them into our apartments where we kept them in our kitchens until the storm had passed."

"At last," Patty sighed. "A happy story. Don't you get tired of hearing about people who go and do the worst thing they can think of?" Patty blinked rapidly, as if she were going to cry, and touched Laika's elbow. Laika didn't finish the story, how it was a good thing those swans got blown off course, how they would have never made it to their wintering grounds, how eating them later was a favor and the best meals most of them had all that winter. Instead Laika shifted her weight in her chair, uncrossed and crossed her legs.

"Let me tell a better one," she said, suddenly emboldened to animate what didn't exist but could under the right conditions, if every *if* were fulfilled. She began the story, that old stupid tale, not caring whether Patty understood or not, whether she even heard it or not, the wind having picked up and taken what it would. Only this time she made some changes: the boy slips though the ice, into the depths below where he waits, frozen, for the girl to find him. But not to worry, she hires the best scientists from Yakutsk with sonars and drills. A happy story. They find him suspended three meters below the ice, conjugating dead verbs in a steady murmur. It's likely that he'll recover, for the heart can withstand the shocking and sustained freeze, decades of freeze, so long as they bring him out slowly and with great care.

When the words ran out, Laika pushed her lips together with such pressure she could feel the outline of her teeth behind her upper lip. She embraced Patty, pressing her lips first on Patty's left cheek, then her right, stamping the story with a kiss that was really for the boy and the girl, ending it this way as though there were no end because the end of a story told in a strange language is like the end of some other story.

Laika heard their bus approaching, the clicking of the tire chains, the loud Hungarian engine wheezing through the chromatic scale with each downshift. At last it pulled into the bay, where the driver made no attempt to hide the fact that he was drinking and not about to open the doors until he was good and ready.

Finally, the bus door squeaked open. The Polar Bears climbed up the steps one by one and carefully squeezed through the tiny aisle, selecting their seats with care so that their weight would be evenly distributed over the chassis. When the men had all boarded, Patty bent for her suitcase.

"I'm sorry," Laika said to Patty, whose thick fingers had turned white from the pressure of gripping the suitcase handle. "I'm sorry things didn't work out."

"Oh," Patty said, blushing a little, "we'll think of something."

Laika watched the bus rumble off into the diminishing one-third light, and turning toward Baba's she uncapped her flask and considered the unlikely bloom of a rose, the flush of her grandmother's cheeks. She could hear Baba now, yelling, the sound of her voice and the noise from the kettle becoming the same and indistinguishable. When the end of time came, it would start here, where with their broken clocks they would be the last to know it. The end would start as it always did, with a general emptiness, the inability of the land and the people on it to give.

But it was OK, Laika decided, if she couldn't give. It was OK, too, if a person couldn't hear or listen, could not understand, though she wished her words could have pointed the Polar Bears as a compass toward some insight, no matter how small. But it was not her fault, nor theirs, that they had come to this place and would leave it no more conscious than when they had first arrived, though she was sorry for Ivan's dogs, sorry that the Polar Bears were disappointed, and sorry for all that she could not tell them about: Baba, who'd asked Cuckushka on the branch how long she'd live and heard the answer carried from tree to tree, and about Vanka, the endless spread of larch from here to Magadan, the unspeakable ice shredding the trees to white.

Is it enough, she wondered, to think these things? To keep walking and be at peace with the land, thinking of hints at substance, of fairy-tale boys slipped under ice, Baba's imaginary crush of roses? In spite of her lacks, was it enough? If not, she breathed in small measures between her gloved fingers, then let it be like this: let there be life below the ice, let them wear it down with a patience that outstrips the imagination, with an unflinching eye let them view their past and accept their future. Let the ice fields yield to the pick and the sonar, and let this half-healed land forgive us, this land of cracks and scars. Let it, too, bear roses.

The
Erlenmeyer
Flask

When she was a lab assistant, it was Eva's job to notice patterns. Her trouble, even then, was that she couldn't stop bringing her work home with her. In everything that she did or saw, she noticed patterns: in the weave of the tablecloth, in the stone of the fireplace, in the measured sweep of the clock's hands, or the way that Norm's turning off the bush radio signaled the quieting down, the tucking in, the drop of night's hasp.

The other day while ironing a shirt, Eva held up the iron and just looked at it, the series of small holes for steam on the iron side, the two pour-spouts at the top of the curved handle, that long hollow of space. She studied the flat of the iron, thinking that by doing so she would find some clue in the pattern of the holes. She recalled how some patterns could be counted on and made sense, like Norm's morning rituals or the even gaps in between all of his front teeth. And then in a small pad that she carried for the very purpose she noted other patterns that, though occurring often enough, too frequently never made sense:

> For every loss, there is a second,
> sometimes more painful loss to follow.

> Occasionally, the second loss may produce or
> inspire a third loss, as loss begets loss.

But after a while, Eva became so adept at noticing patterns, they began to wear on her. While running test after test at the lab—cell blots, titrations, glucose checks, and thyroxin indexes—she would get bored and draw a little smiley face on a memo pad and write: *Be back in five minutes,* or if she was in a bucky mood: *Kiss my ass,* and would go to the can and just sit there thinking. When Barrow Diagnostics fired her, a month ago to the day, she was relieved because she had just written in her notepad that she was running out of patterns to notice at this laboratory, which seemed too small, even for Barrow, Alaska.

When Eva married Norm, she liked him because the river ruled him, and when she was around him she felt the river in her as well. There was something steadying, elemental, and pure in him that reminded her of math, of the mad march of numbers, falling like chips of ice, in clean even increments, falling against each other. "When you turn from the river, then you've forgotten how to live," Norm would say to her. And Eva had to agree. She liked the way that life turned around the sudden drop of winter: the freeze-up when the ice folded in buckles, then the thundering roar of break-up in spring. Sometimes, late at night when she turned off the radio, she thought she could hear it coming, quiet at first like the thrum of the heart's pulse, and then louder, the ice jamming the riverbed and the earth turning and grinding itself down.

For over fifteen years they had lived there in Whitehorse, the lower tundra of mud and mosquitoes. Norm ran a river barge up and down the Yukon, bringing the necessities—refrigerators, fuel,

beer, and sometimes even used pickup trucks and engine heaters—
to people living in towns so small they didn't have roads. Norm
would tie off, throw out some planks, and unload the supplies,
leaving them there right out in the snow.

At first, Eva liked his strange work schedule: on the river from
4 A.M. to nearly midnight during the long light of summer, only
six hours, maybe less as fall approached, until his work tapered off
altogether when the ice came in October. But after a while she
noticed that his schedule became another strangely consistent pattern of inconsistency: home later and later in the fall when the river
let him off earlier and earlier. Sometimes in winter, when the river
had frozen solid, when he should have been home all day, he stayed
away days on end. Eva would wait for him, hold dinner up for him
and wonder where he was, sure that he had grown bored with her,
sure that he was having an affair.

⌣

Now at thirty-nine Eva is willing to admit that she is slowly
cracking up: it's there, she thinks, in the lines around her mouth,
the long straight one across her forehead. Bit by bit, cell by cell,
she is changing. At night she lies in bed, Norm's long form barely
discernible in the dark. She can feel her teeth moving around in
her gums; if she lies perfectly still she can feel them move to the
time of Norm's slow deep breathing. She thinks about snapping on
the bedside lamp and writing in her notebook, but, then again, if
the patterns hold, and she has no reason to believe they won't, she
should have plenty of time to record these small slips.

How and when she began to lose it, she's not sure. She suspects
her body began to betray her, to fail her in all the small ways, sometime after Evan was born. When she stands in front of the mirror
in her old dance leotard that doesn't fit, she suspects it's her son's

fault that she is such a mess. She pinches her stomach, the flesh riding over her hipbones, and eyes the eighth-grade school photo of her son that Norm has insisted they leave out. Eva studies the picture of Evan, that thin hint of a mustache above his upper lip, and she feels her heart drop, for in spite of that fuzz he was still only a child. She sets the picture back on the dresser, turning the image of her son to the wall. She had never thought having the picture out a good idea. Why remind themselves of their loss? Eva recalls her rule of loss and notes that as one loss hastens the next, soon everything begins to look like loss, the sharp smell of it clinging to the curtains, the tablecloth, her hands. With her brows knit together, Eva catches herself in a mid-discovery: she can actually read her loss in the lines on her face, and she reaches for her notebook.

⌣

Small things prey on her, too. Norm's dream in which Eva hears the washing machine in the garage thumping against the pantry wall. An uneven load, and Eva goes to investigate. She pads out to the garage in her floppy green slippers and bathrobe, carrying a huge mound of laundry. In the dream, she pushes open the pantry door with her elbow and dumps the laundry at Norm's feet, where she calmly begins separating the whites from the coloreds. On top of the washer/dryer combo sits Norm's sweetheart, a petite woman—a synchronized swimmer, no less.

"Who swims in Alaska anyway? And synchronized swimming? Come on," Eva remembers teasing Norm once.

"It's a very athletic sport," Norm said in such a way that she knew she'd made a mistake, that she might pay for it later.

And she does, for in the dream Norm and the sync-swimmer go at it, bumping in time to the spin-cycle rhythm of the wash.

"Tell me again about that dream you had—the one with the swimmer," Eva asked Norm one day while she rinsed boiler onions under the tap.

"That wasn't my dream. You dreamed it," he said evenly. Eva turned back to the sink and wondered if he was playing a trick on her.

～

Since she's been fired, Eva has turned her attention up and out, keeping notes on the moon, which has always seemed a strange paradox:

> The moon is the earth's only natural
> satellite, rotating around the earth
> in a fixed and regular cycle. The moon
> may appear to move faster at certain times
> of the night, slower at others, but,
> in fact, the earth's velocity is constant,
> and therefore, so too is the moon's orbital
> velocity.

She thought what a great word *paradox* was, how it was one of the few words that not only rolled in your mouth when you said it, but rolled in the mind, round and luminous like the moon. This blank-faced moon that stared, unblinking, down at her was the same moon that witnessed the sorry events of everyone else's lives as well. Despite the few pounds of rock removed, drives of a golf ball, and big steps of man, the moon changed more than it was changed itself. It was the moon that pulled at the tides, leaving jellyfish stranded like dropped coins and fish gasping, incited dogs to howl, short tempers to ignite and the unborn to leap. But Eva liked looking at the moon, liked even better to think that because she could understand one small thing about the moon there was hope she could understand other small things as well.

> *What one believes to be true about the moon*
> *is completely inconsequential as the moon is*
> *not affected by systems of beliefs and is*
> *wholly incapable of holding a system of belief.*

Of course, Eva had not planned to outlive Evan, and his sudden death complicated a pattern she had taken for granted. In her notebook she made a list of all the women she knew who had not suffered any great tragedy. In another column she kept a running tally of all the women she knew who had lost a child. She put a star next to Stella Travers' name because she had lost both of her children at the same time in a car accident. It bothered Eva that even with her notebook and lists, death was not tidy. The ends did not fold neatly at the edges like a well-made bed, and she knew of no clean crisp numbers she could match to death.

Sometimes she wondered what Evan was feeling that day, there at the last, the dogs howling at the door and Evan locked in their garage with the car running. She wished she could have saved him. Since she didn't, she wished she'd seen him once more before he died. She would have asked him to forgive her for being wrong so many times, for being a flake, for not knowing that he had been planning to do this thing for months.

"Good thing he didn't drown himself in the river," the sheriff said to her the day she found Evan in the garage, "or we'd have never found him." Behind them the dogs barked and pulled at their chains.

"Could you turn off those flashing lights?" Eva asked the sheriff and scraped at the ground with the toe of her boot. Even though the thaw had come, the ground was still hard, too hard for a burial in Whitehorse.

Later, at the funeral home, a woman who'd lost her son, a bush pilot in the Dawson Range, found Eva and gripped her shoulder. It occurred to Eva that now others might be adding her name to private lists of loss, too. "Good thing you have the body," the woman said. "At least you have that."

"Yeah." Eva heard Norm's voice behind her, felt his hand on the small of her back. "Good thing," he said, steering her down the steps of the funeral home and toward their car while she blinked and wondered at the dogged capacity people had for finding good in things immutably bad.

⸺

Now Eva prefers living up here, in the upper tundra, three hundred and thirty miles within the Arctic Circle. When she walks, there's the crunch of her footfalls in the ice, and in high tundra the earth is firmer and she knows that no matter what, with so much ice, her weight will be supported. In the lower tundra, it was different. She used to walk the riverbank with fear and fascination as each step sent the ground quivering and she could never be sure of anything.

A few years back on an Easter Sunday, a woman wandered into the marsh with her three children and reemerged with none. Things like that happened in the flats and no one knew who to blame, or if blame was even necessary. Drilling machines, people, dreams, dogs—they could and had simply disappeared, taken by the mud and pressure, the earth's desire to call back its own. After Evan died, Eva gladly left with Norm for the high country.

"What can I lose?" she said to him, then, and now she still says it, sometimes with clenched teeth when she can't think of anything else to say.

> The moon exerts a gravitational force on
> large bodies of water. However, some bodies
> of water are affected more than others.

When they first moved to Barrow, Eva was determined to make a fresh start. She bought a self-help tape, "How to Rekindle Your Marriage." She wrote Norm little love messages, wifely missives designed to let him know that she was thinking of him, even when she wasn't. She'd write notes like "I love you," and then "One day at a time." But after a while she thought, *Who do I think I'm kidding?* And she took down her inspirational notes, trading them for reminders and instructions that would bring results: *Don't forget to buy dog food.* At first Norm would return the favors, sometimes even drawing pictures. Her favorite: an enormous mosquito humping a turkey and below, a caption: *Alaska—where the mosquitoes are big enough to stand flat-footed and fuck a turkey.* But lately his notes, too, have taken a more practical turn. Today, taped to the oven door, is a piece of paper on which Norm has drawn a finger with a red string around it. Underneath it reads in bold red letters*: Did you turn off the oven today?* The finger looks like a cock, and Eva can't look at Norm's sign without smiling a little.

Remorse slicks like oil that can't be scrubbed off, and she thinks it is highly underrated and more useful than most people know. Losing Evan has taught her this, and she would love to see Norm fall apart a little. She'd like to see some evidence that he is sorry. When she looks at him, she can almost hear the smooth whir of his internal machinery going *tick, tick, tick* like the clink of the oil derricks. She'd like to stop it, to crush that mechanism, the spring inside Norm that has kept him going and going, as if nothing at all had happened.

Eva fingers Norm's sign. How would he feel to be the one to discover a body, her body? she wonders. Eva envisions the tragic accident from all different angles: first the look of shock, then horror as Norm interprets the scene: the smell of gas, the red oven light on. Then Eva: her legs buckled underneath her body, her cheek resting on the oven's wire rack.

Her favorite scene is the knife accident scenario. How would Norm's face look if he came home one night late, much later than he should, on a night in the dead of winter—came home to find she's had a fatal mishap while preparing his favorite dish? The camera zooms in as he registers the fact that she died for him. His face twists with grief, with genuine guilt.

"What are you doing, Eva?" Norm, home early, catches her by surprise. She's sprawled across the kitchen floor, one leg twisted over the other in a death pose.

"Back exercises." Eva scrambles up from the floor and adjusts her shirt. Norm scratches his head, then steps around her to reach into the refrigerator for a beer.

"Are you OK?" he asks, studying her, and she realizes then how hard it must be for Norm to be Norm, how hard it is to be married to her.

"Sure. I'm fine." She nods and takes a swig of his beer. "Really."

But when he looks at her like that, his eyes turning soft, she wants to wrap her arms around him and comfort him. She wants to whisper quiet words from childhood and draw him into the center of herself, into that darkness where all things get lost, where everything gets ground to nothing. But something always pulls on her and she doesn't know why, but that space between them seems the most impossible to close. She remembers a science demonstration of magnets when she was in the third grade. *Why should two metals repel each other?* she had wondered, and she left for her homeroom feeling sick to her stomach, convinced the science teacher had tricked her.

～～～

Part of her problem, Eva thinks one day while washing dishes, is that she doesn't fully yet know who or what she is or what she is becoming. She can only testify to the forces that tug her and the unseen things pressing upon her. She imagines that inside of her is a black dark hole shaped like an Erlenmeyer flask. She frowns and catches her hips on the edge of the drain board. Everything seems to have a hollow sound to it: the hum of the refrigerator, the glow of the TV, the edgy and panicked crackling of the radio. The empty sound of nothing haunts her and she wonders if the emptiness hasn't invaded her as well, if she still has a heart beating in her chest because there's no noise there, nothing moving, and the deepness of that hole frightens her. She opens cupboards, rifles through the boxes of crackers, and eats the dry cocoa powder with a spoon, the jumbo marshmallows and cans of peaches in heavy syrup, eats without tasting, stuffing that space inside of her.

That night when Norm's steady breathing gets on her nerves, Eva creeps into the kitchen. She picks through his packed lunch of all the things he loves: egg salad with pimento on wheat, a dill pickle, Oreo cookies. She eats it all, her hand moving to her mouth in a steady motion. Afterward, she wipes the crumbs from the front of her nightgown and leaves a note in the refrigerator at the spot where Norm's lunch used to be: *You've been Yogi-Beared.*

Other ways my body has betrayed me:
1) Sagging butt
2) General all-over weight gain
3) Hair going gray

And here's another problem: she can't remember things as well as she used to and lately she's been seeing things out on the bay ice: tundra swans that don't belong out there and seem doomed to freeze. She will walk out and test the ice to see if it will hold her. If not, she'll get a long pole and push on the birds, try to rock them out of the ice. They'll soar up and away with two or three heavy beats of their wings, then crane their necks at impossible angles and say things like "Thanks a million," or "You're the best, Eva." She'll turn sharp to see if anyone is standing behind her, if it's all some kind of a prank. But the dogs behind her aren't even moving, are bored by the sight of the ice and have curled up, tucked their noses under their tails and squeezed their eyes shut.

There are the days when she sees children out on the bay ice. Those are the terrifying days because if they falter there's no saving them. And the worst days, when she sees Evan floundering on the ice. She'll see the bright turquoise scarf she made for him five Christmases ago. Movement, a flash of color, and she knows it's him, a beautifully sculpted bird bound by ice and waiting for her.

⌒

Eva is changing again. She's losing weight so steadily that people are taking it personally. Every day Norm asks her if she's angry with him and then one day she realizes that yes, yes she is and she is paying him back for being happy when she isn't, for recovering when she can't.

She would like to feel happy, is certain she would recognize happiness if she felt it. She is not one of those who were born to suffer and who have learned how to like it, or the kind that aren't suffering but wish they were. The grief counselor in Whitehorse had suggested dance lessons—had said it could give her that raison d'etre. But even then, Eva had shaken her head. No. She likes the idea of a martial arts class better. With so many more unaccountable feelings, she's leaking at the edges, can hardly contain them all. She'd like to pay her fifty dollars and kick somebody's ass without guilt. But then, she'll pull back the curtains and catch sight of Evan's bright orange parka on the ice, his blue scarf, and she knows she can never leave this house, could not risk missing him again when he needed her most.

One day Eva stood at the kitchen window and chewed on her fingernails, noting how hunger nibbled at her, got at her in those empty spaces. Hunger was a pain that resembled only itself, she thought, as her stomach tightened like a drawstring pulling close. *Breathing hurts now, too,* she wrote in her notebook. In the distance she saw a bush plane sewing a straight line, a thin white thread across the sky. *Drawstring, even the sky gets hungry.* Then she heard him: "Mom." There's no mistaking Evan's voice, clear as a bell. But it was a pitiful noise and she had never heard Evan sound so sad. Eva dropped the notebook.

"Don't move, honey!" She screamed, pulling on her boots. She ran across the snow and out onto the ice without testing it. When she got to where Evan had been, it was a bird stuck in the ice, wintering where it shouldn't. After checking for footprints, for any signs at all of Evan, Eva abandoned the bird to the ice and walked back to the house. She stood on the porch watching the bird, waiting to see if it would become Evan. But the bird wasn't struggling anymore and she knew it could be too late. She filled a double boiler with cold water and marched back out to the bird, determined this time to save it. Eva poured the water around the bird, working it free, and carried it inside her coat back to the house, leaving the boiler out on the ice. Later, in her notebook, she noted that it takes a desert, an ice desert even, to produce a mirage.

When Norm came home, stamping the cold from his boots into the floorboards, Eva sat and peered out the window, the bird wrapped in Norm's flannel shirt and cradled in her arms.

"That bird's gotta go." Norm nodded at the tundra swan. "Everything it needs is out there." He pointed to the door with his thumb.

Eva felt a slow cold starting at her feet and spreading upward. She knew she should say something. Instead she stared at Norm's face. His nose was like Evan's, but not the mouth. If she closed her eyes and concentrated, she could redraw Norm's features, as with an Etch-A-Sketch, sand over the lines.

Norm sat at the table and pulled a toothpick out of his shirt pocket and clamped it between his front teeth. Eva turned to the windowpane and traced an imaginary box around her reflection, felt the bird rustle its wings. "Sometimes I think I'm forgetting what Evan really looked like."

Norm pulled off one boot and then the other. "We could have another kid. It's not too late."

Eva closed her eyes and swallowed. She could hear the soft machinery of Norm's heart going *whir, whir, whir.* She wondered if she could catch him on the jaw with her fist, knock him clean off the chair, if she swung hard enough. She opened her eyes. "No. No more kids." She leaned in toward the window and studied the ice.

Norm sighed. "I'm just saying we could try if you wanted to." He moved the toothpick from the left side of his mouth to the right. "You're not the only one who suffers, you know." He stood up and switched on the bush radio.

That night, Eva could hear their dogs baying and the clang of their metal tie chains. She stood at the kitchen window. The dark was just light enough and she could see against the endless seam of sky and ice a full moon low and heavy over the frozen bay. She looked at the moon that seemed to her one looming and perfect reflection of ice, a perfect sphere surrounded by the dark water of night sky. If it was true what some people said about the moon, true that the moon reflected secret knowledge, symbolized the unconscious and the making of codes, then, Eva wondered, what had she learned, what code was she solving, what mystery would she crack?

Eva went back to the bedroom and climbed into bed alongside Norm, who was asleep already, his back to her. She pressed her body against his, surprised and relieved that even now, when it was clear they both were changing, had changed, she still fit.

She felt her face relaxing, her jaw unclenching. She took in the smell of Norm's skin, felt a glimmer of calm in knowing that now, when she was feeling so strange, there were some things she could still count on: that there were thirty-two holes on the bottom of her iron, that the weave of the Herringbone comforter was slightly off, that Norm's front teeth had small spaces between them. If the patterns were holding in the morning, Norm would still be there, despite her fears to the contrary.

There is serenity in ritual, Eva decided. With sudden satisfaction she imagined that other women, like her, looked up each night at the violet skies, and like her, counted their dead among the stars and like her, attempted to call the elements to attention, snap them to a rise, making the parts more to the sum. Eva wondered if they, too, thought of that twilight hinterland of clear and hard resolution and if even now they weren't, like her, breathing in time to the rhythm of their refrigerator's hum, hot water heaters, and husbands. Eva felt her lungs emptying of everything, the space inside her collapsing a little. She settled back among the covers, her head finding that groove in the pillow while outside, the moon, a hairless animal, crept toward sleep.

From

the

Bering

Strait

Up here at the top of the country, the half-light gets trapped be-tween double-paned windows. The light freezes and sticks be-tween the glass like a cold sap. The birds, too, have a hard time get-ting around. Sometimes the ice catches them in mid-flight and for days they are stuck crooked in the freezing sky. If they are lucky, a warmer rain will unfix them, and if they are luckier still, none of their bones will snap from the shock of sudden flight, and they will fly south where they belong.

It wasn't always like this. We used to have springs of wet snow and starlings, springs of impossible, violent blue skies. But slowly it became clear as each year passed that winter was stealing days from spring, until eventually the thaw stopped coming altogether. Those were the years the fish froze solid in the water and our chil-dren stopped growing.

I remember the last true spring. The thaw came in the middle of the night, *like the bridegroom for the bride,* my wife Dolores says to anyone who wants to hear the story of the Last Thaw. There we were lying in our bed. The sun had set early, so the sky was black and thick as liver. We heard a groaning like some huge animal was sleeping below the ice and beginning to wake, to claw its way out. Then we heard a terrific crack, like the sound of a bone snapping, only much louder. We lay still in our bed, afraid to breathe because when the breakup happens, for a moment you're not sure if it's the thaw or an earthquake. Then I leapt out of bed, ran to the kitchen, and brought back a bottle of wine and two glasses.

"American Beauty," Dolores said, touching her glass to mine.

"Royal Princess," I said.

This was the game we played, naming prizewinning roses from the rose catalogues. This was how we welcomed spring, planning our gardens, worrying over the beds, mulch, the enriched soil fortified by worm castings.

⌣

When we walk outside, even the hairs in our nostrils freeze stiff and it hurts to breathe. And here's another problem: our words and tears turn to ice on the tips of our tongues or in the corners of our eyes. It's hard to tell them apart, too, because when they chip off and fall they look like little slivers of glass caught on our mustaches, sleeves, and the tips of our shoes. To cope with these problems, we have by unspoken consensus decided to try not to talk or sweat or bleed or cry. We have come to discover that exposing any of our bodily fluids is a very dangerous thing to do. Still, we make mistakes.

Last week, Mushie broke into the pharmacy and helped himself to a packet of codeine tablets and a few cc's of morphine. Then just yesterday he did himself in on antifreeze. It had to have hurt like hell, like swallowing a Cuisinart jammed on high, but maybe, for a minute or two, he felt warm. They say that's what happens when you die, just as you are dying, even as you are freezing to death, for one split euphoric second, you are on fire.

I knew something was wrong when I saw his dogs tangled up in front of the pharmacy. They were baying and howling, trying to push through the front door of the pharmacy, but Mushie had left them hooked up to the sled and the sled was jammed up in the frame of the door. I unharnessed them and they tripped over each other, trying to get to Mushie.

In the puddle of liquid that surrounded him I could see the striations of neon green and cobalt blue. If a peacock feather melted, maybe it would look like this. I smelled the plastic gallon jug of antifreeze. It smelled oily and a little sweet. He had curled himself into a fetal position so I rolled him to his knees, put my hands under his armpits, and dragged him outside to the sled. In this weather, he could have drunk Freon and died quicker. This is not at all how I'd do it, I thought. And yet I couldn't deny that with the way the colors seemed to melt around him he was transformed somehow and that this was beautiful. I strapped him onto the sleigh. I rubbed off a few drips of antifreeze from around his mouth and pushed his eyelids closed with my thumb. I didn't bother harnessing the dogs. They followed the sled for about a mile and then veered off toward their kennels.

When I reached home, I wrote down on one of Dolores's yellow Post-it pads what I saw when I found Mushie. The puddle, the way he was hugging his knees, the way pearly drops of those brilliant colors of the Caribbean—that's what I actually wrote—colors of the Caribbean, pooled out around him like an oil slick. I wrote all this down because I thought it was important to remember, and because, of course, it would be too hard to say.

That night I carved a sculpture for him. I carved him with the flaps of his hat fastened down over his ears, his eyes squinting against the glare of the snow and laced tight against an invisible wind. That is the hard part—capturing motion, suggesting something that's not really there. I used a penknife for the lines in his face and around his eyes. If you keep a small pan of lukewarm water nearby, all you have to do is dip the knife once, lightly tap it against the side of the pan, and then the knife is warm and wet enough to make fluid cuts in the ice.

I worked on Mushie all night and through the next day. His hands were the hardest for me to sculpt. I wanted to show him as he was—one hand gripping reins and another holding a bottle or the whip, but for some reason I couldn't get the fingers right. In the end, I hid his hands in the ruff of his dogs' fur. He is leaning forward on the sleigh, one elbow resting on the headboard, his other hand cradling his favorite dog, the lead, Skete.

I kept the garage door open so the wind could blow in flakes of snow. I sprinkled the dogs' coats with water because I wanted the snow to attach to the guard hairs so their fur would look fuzzy. It had taken me all day to shave long narrow slivers. Getting the fish-hook curl into the ends of the shavings was the hardest part. I used one of Dolores's sewing needles as sort of a curling rod and exhaled slowly so that the ice would warm up slightly, curl, then refreeze. I was done and I let the wind score the ice a bit to give it the weathered look. Dolores came out, that yellow Post-it stuck to her index finger. She hadn't bothered to put her parka on, just her ratty old sweater. She looked at me for a long time. She folded her arms across her chest, bit her lip, and shivered.

"You're jealous. You're jealous he's dead," she said. Her words fell onto the concrete and shattered into jagged pieces.

"What?" I asked, covering my mouth with my hand. "Could you repeat that?" But of course she couldn't. She snapped off the garage lights and stepped into the house. I turned the light back on and kicked the pieces into the old snowdrift outside the garage.

People seem to think this cold must have happened overnight, that one day we just woke up and found ourselves in this mess. But when I look out all around me I'm nearly blinded by the unending gray light and I know, it's coming, it's come, as regular and steady as my breathing. The blank sweep of the ice stretches on, everywhere, ice.

Dolores and I stay up late and we watch the television weather reports. One night they showed a segment about a gardener in Anchorage who coaxed some dwarf roses into bloom. Outside, the ice fell from the sky like old salt.

"The dirty bastard," Dolores said. I wheeled the TV out of the bedroom that very night. So now I watch the TV by myself. The eerie blue-green incandescent glow of the screen is the same strange shade of blue that the snow reflects under the Arctic light. People think snow is white, but if you look carefully in the shadows of the snow, you can see that it is really blue. When I go outside for a smoke, I think of those explosive blue skies of spring, Bering blue.

⌇

The weather bureau sent a team of researchers up here to study the freeze patterns. We all laughed as best we could without freezing our lungs. You may have heard this kind of laugh before. It is a tortured sound, you wouldn't even think a human capable of it, but you'd be surprised. Anyway, they came in with their helicopter mounted with a special engine heater and all of their equipment—thermometers, barometers, dopplers, radars, and small satellite dishes. They even built a greenhouse. We couldn't figure out why. Up here, heaven in a greenhouse, it would be too cold for anything to grow. But they wanted to experiment and they insisted that certain northern hybrids of roses were suited for inclement weather. We all nearly lost it that time. The corners of my wife's eyes froze shut for two days. It was a laughless cry, though. And then she got sick and wouldn't get out of bed. One day, to cheer her up, I brought her pictures of roses.

"I almost forgot what they looked like," she said. She traced the edges of the roses with her finger. I taped pictures of roses all over the walls while she sat propped up in bed, thumbing through the rose mail-order gardening catalogues like Burpees and Jackson and Perkins and watching the gardening channel on cable TV.

"Fertilizer—that's very important," she muttered. I could barely hear her, she was so weak, and I knew what was happening to her— I could almost see it—the gray creeping past her ankles and up her shins. She tapped at a white JFK prize rose with her index finger. "You gotta feed those things—they're like people, you know."

～～～

My wife's mother calls almost every day. She wants to know what the hell is going on up here. I tell her that we are on the edge of a new Ice Age—a new millennium of freeze, that it is coming for her next, does she have enough lightbulbs and toilet paper? The silence on her end of the phone is heavy and then she asks me if I'm still going to AA. I tell her that I quit because it was getting too crowded. She calls because she wanted to talk to Dolores, but talking is dangerous and Dolores is too sick to move.

More than once I'd thought of packing up and leaving. I was out the other day fueling up my Dodge. But before I could even get the gas through the funnel, the gas had frozen solid. That's when I thought to myself that we could really be in trouble up here. And it's not that we don't have heaters or electric blankets, fireplaces, and microwaves. In fact, one of the researchers has a tiny sunlamp. But it's like even with all these things people can only take so much of this blistering cold. The thought that when you wake up that it is out there waiting for you is almost too much.

There's a funeral every other day, it seems, but nobody cries, of course. When our daughter died two months ago, I carved a swan family out of a huge ice block. The mother and father swan are nudging the swanlet into flight. The swanlet looks like it is flying right up out of that stump of ice, flying right out of this place.

"It's like the phoenix," Dolores said, dabbing at her eyes.

"Yesterday it was 80 in Phoenix—don't even *talk* to me about Phoenix," I said, running my fingers along the neck of the baby swan. She'll never melt away in this freeze, and I think that there's something perfect about all this cold.

Mushie found them, our daughter and her three high school friends, on the way back from working out his team. The dogs started whining and pulling against their harnesses. They pulled Mushie toward what he thought were some dumb-shit optimistic ice-fishers. When the dogs saw them, they howled and tangled themselves up in their reins and refused to run. But the girls, they were sitting in a circle, holding hands, listening to Bob Marley. They were frozen still, bluer than blue, Mushie said, and the radio was still playing. Energizer batteries. Sometimes it's the small things that really amaze me. I wrote to the CEO of the Energizer Batteries and told them how impressed I was with their batteries. I explained how my daughter's radio played forty-eight hours straight, no problem, in the middle of an Arctic freeze when everything else froze solid. The president wrote me back on Energizer stationery with that drum-pounding pink rabbit on the top, thanking me for my interest in the product. He wished there were more customers like me.

The weather bureau researchers are packing up and getting ready to leave. They're tired of the cold and they're afraid of what it could do to them. Someone threw an ice rock and shattered a square of the greenhouse and they've interpreted this action as a sign. They're leaving on the Swedish freightliner tomorrow even though they didn't finish collecting all the data. They're leaving in a flurry of equipment and printouts and the knowledge that maybe they've failed here. Still, it wasn't hard to get them to talk, once I gave them a bottle of gin and some long straws.

Two of the researchers thought that the ice caps had expanded and where we all thought we were living on frozen steppe, or permafrost, was actually an ice shelf, like an extension of Greenland. They explained that the cold was working not only above the ground but below it as well, pushing the soil south and replacing it with ice, as far down as you'd care to dig, everywhere ice. There were some other theories: the polar disparity theory, the alien conspiracy theory. But my personal favorite came from the guy who brought the roses in. He attributed the cold to mass hysteria. That's right—we're all hallucinating the freeze.

"Well, then, aren't we all a bunch of crazy losers?" I said. He laughed, a choked sort of laugh, and he forgot to cover his mouth with his scarf or mitten. Later, they had to load him on the freighter with a very real oxygen mask strapped to his face.

I check in on Dolores every hour. Sometimes I read to her. I lean over and put my ear to her mouth to feel her breath because she's so still and turning such a strange shade of gray, I'm not sure she's alive. But today she caught me by surprise. I leaned over and she grabbed my arm, clenched it tight, and pulled me down to her.

"Are the roses in bloom yet?" she asked. I wanted to buy her a whole garden of roses. I wanted to throw ice blocks at the greenhouse. I wanted to rip up those roses in there, grind the stalks up in my mouth, chew them up and spit them out.

"Well, are they?" she asked again. I looked at her lying there, at her purple lips and the tiny pearls of snot frozen on the end of her nose. I looked at her, held up by her pillows, and I lied to her.

"There's a very small, small but sturdy bud on the Jacob's Ladder."

"That's a climbing rose, a trailer."

"Yeah. Maybe a couple of weeks, it'll open, three weeks tops."

Sometimes I hate myself, I really do. She looked at me for a long time. She shouldn't do that—her eyes could freeze—and I was just about to remind her when she shut them at last. She collapsed against her pillows and the entire bed shuddered.

"I'm cold," she said. I put two more blankets on her, turned up the thermostat, and then I went outside.

⌣

I think about what Dolores might be feeling, how it feels to slowly freeze, about how I am feeling. I think about how your heart still beats as it always did, but there is a tightness as if papier-mâché or plaster of Paris has been slathered over your heart and has now solidified. Your heart is fighting like a bird from within the shell, fighting to break free from the weight of the cold. And then your heart, over time, doesn't fight as hard as it did the day before. And so it goes, and so it goes, until one day your heart just stops. Literally stops cold. Like that. And it's true what they say, it's true that when the cold consumes you, it consumes you completely, takes you as if it had been waiting for you your whole life. And when it does, all you can do is feel the weight of it crushing your chest, and you close your eyes then and allow yourself this once to dream of the sun.

Acknowledgments

Some of these stories first appeared in magazines: "What Holds Us Fast" in *In-Tense,* "Cartography of a Heart" in *Columbia: A Journal of Literature and Art,* "Modern Taxidermy" in *Hayden's Ferry Review,* "Then, Returning" in *Chelsea,* "Eulogy for Red" in the *Crab Orchard Review,* and "From the Bering Strait" in *Fish Prize Stories.*

The
Flannery O'Connor
Award
for
Short Fiction

David Walton, *Evening Out*

Leigh Allison Wilson, *From the Bottom Up*

Sandra Thompson, *Close-Ups*

Susan Neville, *The Invention of Flight*

Mary Hood, *How Far She Went*

François Camoin, *Why Men Are Afraid of Women*

Molly Giles, *Rough Translations*

Daniel Curley, *Living with Snakes*

Peter Meinke, *The Piano Tuner*

Tony Ardizzone, *The Evening News*

Salvatore La Puma, *The Boys of Bensonhurst*

Melissa Pritchard, *Spirit Seizures*

Philip F. Deaver, *Silent Retreats*

Gail Galloway Adams, *The Purchase of Order*

Carole L. Glickfeld, *Useful Gifts*

Antonya Nelson, *The Expendables*

Nancy Zafris, *The People I Know*

Debra Monroe, *The Source of Trouble*

Robert H. Abel, *Ghost Traps*

T. M. McNally, *Low Flying Aircraft*

Alfred DePew, *The Melancholy of Departure*

Dennis Hathaway, *The Consequences of Desire*

Rita Ciresi, *Mother Rocket*

Dianne Nelson, *A Brief History of Male Nudes in America*

Christopher McIlroy, *All My Relations*

Alyce Miller, *The Nature of Longing*

Carol Lee Lorenzo, *Nervous Dancer*

C. M. Mayo, *Sky over El Nido*

Wendy Brenner, *Large Animals in Everyday Life*

Paul Rawlins, *No Lie Like Love*

Harvey Grossinger, *The Quarry*

Ha Jin, *Under the Red Flag*

Andy Plattner, *Winter Money*

Frank Soos, *Unified Field Theory*

Mary Clyde, *Survival Rates*

Hester Kaplan, *The Edge of Marriage*

Darrell Spencer, *CAUTION Men in Trees*

Robert Anderson, *Ice Age*

Bill Roorbach, *Big Bend*

Dana Johnson, *Break Any Woman Down*

Gina Ochsner, *The Necessary Grace to Fall*